500 places where you can make a difference

1st Edition

by Andrew Mersmann

with Carrie Havranek
& Kisha Ferguson

John Wiley & Sons Canada, Ltd

Contents

About the Author

Andrew Mersmann has volunteered on service projects ranging from working and living with the homeless on Los Angeles' Skid Row to saving stranded pilot whales in Key West to a humanitarian excursion by horseback in Rajasthan, India. He is a travel writer and Editor in Chief of *Passport Magazine* and has been a restaurant reviewer, entertainment writer, and celebrity profiler. After a long run with non-profit arts organizations in both Los Angeles and New York, he stepped into travel writing via an extraordinary journey to Machu Picchu. He has been a featured speaker, interview guest, or moderator on several travel talks, from the *New York Times Travel Show* and the 92nd Street Y-TriBeCa to *Oprah and Friends* on satellite radio.

About the Consultants

Carrie Havranek is a freelance travel, culture, and food writer who writes the Global Price Index and Smart Deal of the Week columns for Frommers.com. She has written for *Paste*, the *Well Fed* network, *Destination Hyatt*, and *Beverage World*, among other publications. She lives in Easton, Pennsylvania and teaches writing part-time at Lafayette College.

Kisha Ferguson is a lifelong nomad whose world travels eventually made her start *Outpost*, a magazine dedicated to independent travel and world culture. While she was Editor-in-Chief, *Outpost* was awarded Magazine of the Year at the 2003 Canadian National Magazine Awards. Kisha is currently a senior writer and producer at CBC News in Toronto.

Acknowledgments

Thanks, first of all, to you, reader. The fact that you're inclined to even flip through the pages of this book means that you are intrigued by making a difference. Please do. The world is an amazing place—you should go there—and touch it.

To my parents and brother who all taught me, by example, that no one at life's table can be well served unless there is enough for everyone. Thank you to Paul Horne who first sent me traveling for a living, and Robert Adams and Don Tuthill who keep sending me. Liz Welsh first caught my attention about the topic telling me about her umpteenth trip focused on endangered or imperiled animals. I can never express enough gratitude to those with whom I've volunteered, from whom I've learned more, around campfires in Rajasthan or barrel fires in the streets of Los Angeles, than in any classroom.

Tremendous gratitude for my editor, Gene Shannon, who has calmly stood still, with easy humor, pointing the way, trusting I'd eventually see and understand. And to Matthew Scrivens, who did a lot of digging and pointing in the right directions as well.

And finally, Bob Pederson, with whom I'll never get to travel enough, who patiently and perpetually teaches me that choosing NOT to take every impossible and unlikely chance, would be ridiculous. Thank you.

An Invitation to the Reader

In researching this book, we discovered many wonderful places. We're sure you'll find others. Please tell us about them, so we can share the information with your fellow travelers in upcoming editions. If you were disappointed with a recommendation, we'd love to know that, too. Please write to:

Frommer's 500 Places Where You Can Make a Difference, 1st Edition
John Wiley & Sons Canada, Ltd. • 6045 Freemont Blvd. • Mississauga, ON L5R 4J3

Published by:

John Wiley & Sons Canada, Ltd.

6045 Freemont Blvd.
Mississauga, ON L5R 4J3

ISBN: 978-0-470-16061-9

Editor: Gene Shannon
Project Editor: Lindsay Humphreys
Editorial Assistant: Katie Wolsley
Photo Editor: Photo Affairs Inc.
Project Coordinator: Lynsey Stanford
Interior book design: Melissa Auciello-Brogan
Production by Wiley Indianapolis Composition Services

Front cover photo: Green Sea Turtle researcher hydrating a female surprised by very low tide, Rocas Atoll, Brazil
Back cover photo: Reef monitoring in Belize; volunteer provides reading help in Kenya; a volunteer carries a water jug in Tamil Nadu, India; young volunteers build housing through Habitat for Humanity in New Orleans

For reseller information, including discounts and premium sales, please call our sales department: Tel. 416-646-7992. For press review copies, author interviews, or other publicity information, please contact our publicity department: Tel. 416-646-4582; Fax: 416-236-4448.

Wiley also publishes its books in a variety of electronic formats. Some content that appears in print may not be available in electronic formats.

Manufactured in the United States

1 2 3 4 5 RRD 13 12 11 10 09

An Additional Note

Please be advised that travel information is subject to change at any time—and this is especially true of prices. We therefore suggest that you write or call ahead for confirmation when making your travel plans. The authors, editors, and publisher cannot be held responsible for the experiences of readers while traveling. Your safety is important to us, however, so we encourage you to stay alert and be aware of your surrounding. Keep a close eye on cameras, purses, and wallets, all favorite targets of thieves and pickpockets.

A Note about Money & Currency

You'll want to consult your tax adviser to evaluate what expenses are eligible for deductions, but some, if not all the costs of volunteer travel should be tax-deductible. If you add a week of sightseeing, you lessen the amount that you can claim, but it is possible that airfare, accommodations, meals, guide services, local transportation, and more are all tax-deductible if they are expenses incurred in service to a non-profit organization. The organization you book your trip with may also be able to provide you with some information about this. We've tried to identify which trip providers in the book are considered non-profit organizations by adding a 🎗 icon beside their name, but it's always a good idea to confirm this information with the trip provider.

There may also be discounted airfare available for people volunteering on an international project. Check www.volunteer.flyforgood.com.

Prices listed in this guide are denominated in either US dollars or British pounds, based on the currency in which prices were supplied by the trip provider. In instances where the original price of the trip is in a different currency, that price has been converted to US dollars at the exchange rate applicable when this book went to print. Please confirm all prices given in this guide with the trip provider.

Frommer's Icons

We use two feature icons to help you quickly find the information you're looking for. At the end of each review, look for:

ⓘ Where to get more information

🎗 Charitable organization

Frommers.com

Now that you have this guidebook to help you plan a great trip, visit our website at **www.frommers.com** for additional travel information on more than 4,000 destinations. We update features regularly to give you instant access to the most current trip-planning information available. At Frommers.com, you'll find scoops on the best airfares, lodging rates, and car rental bargains. You can even book your travel online through our reliable travel booking partners. Other popular features include:

- Online updates of our most popular guidebooks
- Vacation sweepstakes and contest giveaways
- Newsletters highlighting the hottest travel trends
- Podcasts, interactive maps, and up-to-the-minute events listings
- Opinionated blog entries by Arthur Frommer himself
- Online travel message boards with featured travel discussions

A Letter from the Author

Do you find yourself saying, quietly to yourself, "I want to change the world and I want to be changed"?

Service travel is not a new idea. These kind of trips have been around for a long time: the good work of volunteers in the Peace Corps; students who took a gap year to help paint a monastery while backpacking through Europe; or celebrities who travel to war-ravaged nations to lend a voice and bring awareness. But the easy availability of these trips is somewhat new. We are just learning that almost anyone can escape their day-to-day existence, immerse themselves in another culture, and make a valuable contribution while they're there. There are opportunities for us to be of service in small doses, for the length of time that our vacation allows, rather than make a long-term commitment.

What had been missing was the understanding that this is something I can do. This book aims to be that bridge, to awaken your imagination and point out a few projects that might turn you on to listening to your heart and finding a way to make a real difference in the world.

In the early days of the new century, there were three disastrous events that shifted the paradigm of how we, as a culture, react to misfortune. The attacks of September 11, 2001, the Southeast Asian tsunami in 2004, and Hurricane Katrina in 2005 brought the average person's compassion to the surface and translated it into action in an unprecedented way. There were plenty of other disasters before, during, and after, but these three, compounding the pain, made something click. Religious scholar Karen Armstrong says that compassion makes us "dethrone ourselves from the center of our world and put another there." It has become a time that people look to themselves to try to do something. On September 12, 2001, everyone in the world was an American, and the aid and assistance poured toward New York City and Washington, DC, as never before. When the tsunami struck Thailand and other coastal countries of Southeast Asia, kids gathered change and donated their allowance in unprecedented international outreach. College students sacrificed beer keg handstands and beach bonfires to flock to New Orleans and the Gulf states to clean up and rebuild after Hurricanes Katrina and Rita. People decided, "I will reach out for no better reason than I can." Folks who barely had two nickels to rub together gave one away.

At roughly the same time, the Internet and 24-hour news cycles on cable television expanded our awareness. Suffering and disease and hunger went from being conceptual to actual. With information grew a new and intense desire for authenticity . . . to feel that we are part of the community in which we spend time, and to feel as if travel can give us an experience not everyone gets to have.

A common objection is that there's enough to do at home, that we should work in our own community rather than places far away. Of course, the two are not mutually exclusive—there is also great value in seeing every destination as part of our community. As Dr. Martin Luther King said, "Life's most persistent and urgent question is, 'What are you doing for others?'"

Every time you make an effort, you shift the world—and cause change in bigger ways than you imagined possible.

"We think that we're not happy because of what we're not getting, but really we're not happy because of what we're not giving."

—Marianne Williamson, author and founder of *The Peace Alliance*

1 Animal Welfare

A Lion of Tsavo at the Taita Rukinga Wildlife Conservancy

Surveying Wildlife 1

Research Cross River Gorillas

On the Trail of the Great Apes

Lebialem Highlands, Cameroon

CAMEROON, A COUNTRY THAT'S NESTLED AMONG SIX OTHERS, CONTAINS SHARP JUXTAPOSITIONS that comprise much of Africa: The Sahara and the sea, extreme heat, and more moderate climates. About 200 ethnic groups live in environments ranging from rural tribes to modern cities. It's hard to be bored here.

Your accommodations won't be swanky—two-person tents in rough terrain (no bathrooms), simple foods, and high heat and humidity—but compared to the gorillas and chimpanzees you'll be watching, you'll be living like royalty. The destruction of the apes' habitat is their biggest threat, even greater than the illegal bushmeat trade. The development of wildlands into farms and plantations and the numerous roads for local transport and logging cut the primates' ranges down to an uninhabitable patchwork, endangering both Cross River gorillas and Nigeria-Cameroon chimpanzees.

Locals are now beginning to understand the value of conservation and recognize the apes—once viewed as a nuisance species that raided crops—as an endangered species vital to the region's web of life. Part of the challenge here is educating indigenous tribes and developing a wildlife preserve. The primary focus is to survey and record the habits of the remaining 250 to 300 apes. You'll work with local scientific staff and live among the tribes, meeting with the kings and chiefs, teachers and children who call the African rainforest home.

Your life will be a nomadic one, breaking camp each day to move to the next site (with the help of field guides and porters). You'll cover steep ground, sometimes making for extreme hiking and trekking, as you follow family bands of gorillas and chimps. You'll look for animals and nest sites, signs of feeding and habitat, and you'll photograph and note GPS coordinates. You'll encounter other endangered primates and hundreds of bird species and other wildlife. English is the project language, and you'll receive field training in scientific survey techniques and GPS tracking and mapping.

YOUR NEXT STEP: Global Vision International (✆ **888/653-6028;** www.gviusa.com). This 2-week project, US$1,990, includes meals, tent accommodations (without bathrooms/plumbing), project training and support, and side trips to a wildlife rehabilitation center.

DON'T MISS: More so than many African nations, Cameroon has a high percentage of land devoted to national parks, and wildlife still outnumbers human visitors. **Boubandjidda National Park** covers 544,000 acres (220,150ha) and is Cameroon's largest and most remote park, located along the Chad border. It is home to roaming lions, rare black rhinoceros, and dinosaur fossils.

ⓘ www.ambacam-usa.org

2 Surveying Wildlife

Study Madagascar Fossa

Exploring a Protected African Forest

Mahajanga, Madagascar

If you're looking for a challenge of man versus beast and want a truly different experience, the rare, difficult fossa, which lives in a part of the world known for its indigenous, unusual species, may very well be your match.

The 333,592 acres (135,000ha) of the Ankarafantsika Protected Areas Complex is one of the last and largest tracts of dry deciduous forest on the island of Madagascar. It's ironic that the mysterious fossa, which inhabits the park, has only 7% of its original habitat remaining. The fossa is a species similar to the mongoose, native only to Madagascar, and is in rapid decline. Deforestation and hunting threatens this endangered species and several others in the region. Your team, led by the premier research scientist of fossa, will monitor them, but it won't be easy. Fossa are extremely rare, predominantly nocturnal, and quick.

You'll hike for miles each day, set humane traps for the elusive creatures, use radio-tracking transmitters/receivers to keep tabs on study cases, and measure and record data on captured subjects. Monitoring the habits of this rare species will help in future conservation efforts. Madagascar's iconic lemur will be easier to spot than your target species (the fossa is actually a predator of the lemur), and you'll see plenty of other wildlife throughout the national park in the Island's northwest sector.

You'll be immersed in the forest landscape, with free time to explore from your tented research station and base camp.

Releasing a fossa into a protected area

Precious woods (often poached) and orchids, as well as prehistoric-seeming giant Baobob trees, are the walls of your world for these two weeks.

Camp life between research sojourns is easygoing. Evenings are often spent sharing festivities, music, and meals at the nearby village and neighboring women's cooperative.

YOUR NEXT STEP: Earthwatch (✆ **800/776-0188;** www.earthwatch.org). This 13-day expedition, US$2,550, includes tented research station accommodations, meals prepared by a local cook, and full project support. A US$35 Earthwatch membership is required.

DON'T MISS: To get a sense of local customs on a grand scale, visit the incredibly evocative ruined temples of **Ambohimanga.** It is historically and religiously significant to the people, and was the birthplace of the state. The *Indiana Jones*–like citadel's main gate is an enormous stone disc; 40 men were needed to roll it into position.

ⓘ www.tourisme.gov.mg

Surveying Wildlife

3

Elephant Conservation

Tracking the Giants

Damaraland, Namibia

YOU'RE IN BUSHMAN COUNTRY, SO IF AT THE END OF THE DAY YOU HAVEN'T HAD ENOUGH interaction with African culture, you can see the famous White Lady painting, along with the petrified forest, believed to be millions of years old, and massive, massive rocks waiting to be admired—or climbed.

Thanks to diligent conservation practices, Namibia is one of the only countries in the world where the elephant population is growing. In the northwest open area inland from the Skeleton Coast, desert-adapted animals like black rhino, giraffe, baboon, lion, leopard, cheetah, and black-backed jackal also thrive. Subsistence farmers have also moved into the area in the recent past, however, and competition for scarce water and grazing causes direct conflict between people (and their domesticated herds of cattle, goats, and sheep) and the herds of elephant.

You'll patrol via a 4x4 vehicle and on foot, spending days bush tracking and collecting data from identified herds of desert-roaming elephants. You'll also put in time improving the superstructure around rare water sources with fencing and walls that limit (but don't eliminate) free access by the elephants. You don't need any special training but will quickly gain a skill set that has you comfortable approaching enormous and often dangerous animals on foot, as well as camp craft, scientific recording, navigation, GPS tracking, and compiling identification kits on individual elephants and herd groups.

This is wide-open land without a power grid, so when you sleep under the stars (with mosquito netting) at a different campsite each night, you'll really appreciate the lonesome beauty of the African night sky. Farmers and shepherds are nomads, so cities and even villages of any size are unseen here—your team (including wildlife experts and support staff) will be truly on its own. You'll come home with survival skills and a renewed connection with nature after working to support the re-emergence of the Damaraland elephants.

YOUR NEXT STEP: Twin Work & Volunteer Abroad (© **800/80 483 80;** www.workandvolunteer.com). This 2-week project, US$2,240, includes meals prepared collectively over an open fire, accommodations in tents or under open sky at mobile campsites (with Bushman showers/drop toilets), tracking, training, and full project support. **Global Vision International** (© **888/653 6028;** www.gvi.co.uk) does a similar 2-week Namibian elephant project, US$1,200, including camping and meals, project training and support, as well as project time spent building structures in the community.

DON'T MISS: In the Damaraland region, you'll find **Twyfelfontein,** home to more than 2,500 San (Bushman) prehistoric rock engravings. Their 6,000-year-old secrets are not entirely unlocked, lending—along with the charred nearby landscape of volcanic debris known as Burnt Mountain—an eerie air of mystery to this arid land.

ⓘ www.namibiatourism.com.na

4 Surveying Wildlife

Sea Turtle Conservation

Standing Watch Amid Volcanoes & Rainforests

Chacocente Wildlife Refuge, Nicaragua

SURROUNDED BY MESMERIZING VOLCANIC LANDSCAPES, YOU'LL WORK WITH CONSERVATIONISTS from sun up to sun down to study several species of threatened sea turtles. Later, head north to León, the country's intellectual capital, to explore the rich cultural side of Nicaragua.

Many eco-zones in the Southern Hemisphere have one or two species of sea turtle that come ashore to lay eggs each year, thus beginning one of the most perilous journeys on Earth. Farther north, Nicaragua is home to five species (of seven worldwide), all in the shadow of volcanic landscapes filled with fragile and endangered species. Sea turtles in particular are poached for meat and eggs, making them highly endangered. Basecamp International is partnering with Fauna & Flora, a charity working to conserve threatened ecosystems and species worldwide, for this project at the enormous Chacocente Wildlife Refuge on Nicaragua's Pacific coast.

You'll support the scientific staff by following up on field investigations and doing conservation and restoration programs, flora and fauna management, and data collection. While your focus will be broad and have you studying and recording the diet, nesting, migration, and social patterns of many species, a particular weight is given to sea turtles. You'll have your fair share of days devoted to monkeys, birds, and reptiles as well, but when sea turtles arrive, it's all hands on deck (or on beach).

From the beach you move inland to a stretch of mangroves that give way to wetlands and eventually a lush forest that climbs the sides of the volcano. Each band of habitat has its own cast of plant and animal characters, many of them in trouble.

You'll be thoroughly trained in Spanish language and the rural culture upon arrival to make your work flow smoothly. Training also includes techniques to conduct biodiversity surveys, aid in turtle monitoring and beach patrols (with some time at the hatchery and—if your timing is right—a nighttime release), and compile species inventories of mammals, birds, and butterflies. Awareness-raising work also needs to be done with the local indigenous people, providing environmental education that stresses the rational use of resources and shows the outcome of indiscriminate foraging of wildlife.

You'll be based in a communal tent camp where everyone pitches in to cook over an open fire (and gather firewood), and you'll bathe in a waterfall. This is a multifaceted project, so it's only fitting that your free time be just as diverse. Camp life is mellow, but you'll have opportunities (with a fee for local adventure providers) to horseback ride, take cultural tours, and strap an old snowboard onto your hiking boots and go volcano surfing down the slopes.

YOUR NEXT STEP: Basecamp International (© **866/646-4693**; www.basecampcenters.com). A 4-week project (longer available), US$1,715, includes tent camp accommodations, communally prepared meals, airport transfer, comprehensive project training and materials, a week of culture and language orientation, and 24-hour support.

DON'T MISS: After working hard and roughing it in a completely remote forest zone, you'll likely want a change of scenery. Head north of León to the **Hervideros de San Jacinto,** a lunar-like (or at least boiling-moon-of-Mercury-like) collection of natural sulfuric hot springs and boiling mud baths fed by an underground river and heated by the Telica volcano.

ⓘ www.visitanicaragua.com

Surveying Wildlife 5

Wet & Wild Amazon

Following Pink Dolphins and Giant River Otters

Iquitos, Peru

The Amazon is an amazing place, and Iquitos, as a jungle city, is no exception. This large, isolated tropical center is the jumping-off point for rainforest exploration.

You'll spend a little more than 2 weeks living aboard a riverboat on the mighty Amazon, the world's largest river. This rainforest zone is home to more species of plant and animals than science has been able to count, and some of the most charismatic are unique to the area. The mythology-laden pink dolphin (yes, they are blush-colored) and entertainingly playful giant river otters (who can grow nearly 6 ft./2m long) are some of the most well known, and they are surrounded by monkeys, turtles, fish (including piranha), macaws, and hundreds more.

Your vintage rubber-boom-era riverboat will be a moving home base in the remote Lago Preto and Pacaya Samiria Reserve regions near the headwaters of the Amazon. You'll set out daily via motorized canoe to conduct surveys of the river dolphins (both pink and gray), manatees, otters, fish, caiman, and river turtles. Other times you'll be land-based on a hike to survey macaws, peccaries, tapirs, deer, monkeys, and game birds. This rarely penetrated eco-zone still has a thriving population of wildlife, but your efforts are needed to keep it that way. Farther along the huge chocolate-brown river, hunting, the illegal timber trade, and the exotic pet trade have all helped decimate the wildlife. It is an uphill battle to keep this region pristine and healthy, aided by the study findings of your team.

Your three-level restored riverboat has a bathroom/shower in each cabin, as well as air-conditioning, and when the boat is underway (often at night for repositioning), you'll relax in the library, watch films, or hang out on deck. The hum of the

Surveying along the Amazon River

motors will easily lull you to sleep for a siesta between the morning and dusk research ventures (as well as night surveys for caiman, bats, and other nocturnal species). You'll also meet and socialize with indigenous people from riverside villages you'll stop at along the way.

YOUR NEXT STEP: Earthwatch (✆ **800/776-0188;** www.earthwatch.org). This 16-day expedition, US$4,150, includes meals, project training, and full support. A US$35 Earthwatch membership is required.

DON'T MISS: You'll fly into **Iquitos** to meet the boat, and may want to spend a couple of days before or after the expedition in this completely isolated city (accessible only by air or river) and its mélange of architecture, including an improbable metal-clad building by Gustav Eiffel.

ⓘ www.visitperu.com

6 Surveying Wildlife

Amazon Rainforest Conservation

Living & Learning at a Wildlife Preserve

Madre de Dios, Peru

You'll gain a truly comprehensive view of the Amazon's ecosystem with this program, where you can study the flora, fauna, and birds in the southeastern part of Peru.

The Amazon is the largest river in the world, surrounded by some of the most biodiverse rainforest. This jungle remains remote, and tribal life along the banks of the mighty river and her tributaries has undergone few changes through the years. More bird and insect species can be found here than almost any region in the world, and plant variety is unmatched. Several projects surveying and recording jungle life await you in this verdant playground.

You'll live and work in the thatched-roof conservation center, and you'll get on-the-job training with conservationists. You might spend one day cutting new paths in the jungle, the next doing population studies and surveying salt licks where thousands of macaws roost, and then move on to mammal observation at mud pits used as footprint/track recording sites. There are species here that have never been recorded. You'll be monitoring and recording data on several categories of flora and fauna, ranging from jaguar and puma to tarantulas and tortoises. Some of the land in the 1,500-acre (607-ha) reserve is untouched and some has been cut back for farming in the past; it is from comparative study of the old and new forest that scientists are learning about the effects of humans on biodiversity, and the rainforest's potential for regeneration.

While the days are full, nights are spent relaxing around the center, where you'll sleep in open-walled buildings above the labs and common rooms. A waterfall nearby is a welcome respite (especially since there is no hot water at the center), and the evenings are lit by candlelight because the generator runs only a few hours each day. English is spoken at the center, and local team members will be eager to practice, so getting to use your Spanish skills might be tough (and is not required).

YOUR NEXT STEP: Travellers Worldwide (✆ **+44/1903 502595;** www.travellersworldwide.com). A 2-week project (longer assignments available), £995 includes three communal meals daily, accommodations in the group lodge with shared bath (cold water) in a separate building, full project support and training, and airport transfers to/from Cusco (9–10 hours on a bumpy, unpaved road, then a final river crossing by boat).

DON'T MISS: The city from which you'll arrive and depart is **Cusco,** the Incan "navel of the universe" and home of the gods. The colonial churches, cathedral, and manor houses, as well as Inca Empire historical sites like the fortress **Sacsayhuaman,** can fill an additional several days of exploring before or after your volunteer project.

ⓘ www.visitperu.com

Surveying Wildlife **7**

Mkhuze Game Reserve Project

Tracking Big Game

KwaZulu-Natal, South Africa

PEOPLE PAY THOUSANDS OF DOLLARS FOR A GUIDED SOUTH AFRICA SAFARI VACATION, complete with game drives. But for a fraction of that cost you will contribute labor and get a coveted perspective—really learning about the animals in their habitat.

KwaZulu-Natal, the nation's first UNESCO World Heritage Site, is one of the most famous game regions in all of Africa. Join this project for 3 weeks and you'll be part of an important research team monitoring endangered or threatened species, including cheetah, leopard, white and black rhino, elephant, buffalo, and wild dog.

The Mkhuze Game Reserve is inside KwaZulu Natal, off the beaten tourist track, and the nearly 100,000 acres will be your headquarters and home. You'll find a revered and protected area little changed since 1912, with a wide array of natural habitats, including mountains, savannah, swamps, woodlands, sand forest, and river forest. The work, environment, and target species you'll study—as well as all the other species that thrive here (hippo, crocodile, fish eagles, pelicans, wildebeest, warthog, hyena, and loads of hoofed animals)—make it impossible to be bored. You'll learn to track the target species visually, sometimes using radio telemetry, then photograph and record data about their movements, behaviors, numbers, and more. Each day's work brings the important endangered species research into sharper focus. There may also be the opportunity to up your adrenaline levels even higher and assist in the capture, radio collaring, and reintroduction of various large species.

Each day will be divided between morning and evening work shifts, with a long stretch of afternoon unscheduled for exploration, swimming, and relaxation or napping. You'll be surprised at how well you'll sleep in the thatched-roof staff accommodations, exhausted from your active day in the South African sun, gaining a more intimate understanding and closer access to priority species than any commercial safari can give you—all while helping ensure the survival of these wild animals.

YOUR NEXT STEP: Travellers Worldwide (© **+44/1903 502595;** www.travellersworldwide.com). This 3-week assignment, £1,545, includes housing in lodge staff quarters, communally prepared meals, full project support and training, and airport transfers.

DON'T MISS: After your stay in the heat of Africa's wildlife park zone, a little foray at the beach is just what you'll need. You're close to the town of **St. Lucia** and its beaches, boat excursions, and whale watching. **Sodwana Bay,** one of Southern Africa's best scuba diving sites, is also in the area.

ⓘ www.southafrica.net

8 Surveying Wildlife

Elephant Conservation Project

Protecting Endangered Pachyderms

Matale District, Sri Lanka

YOU'LL BE ABLE TO MAKE A GROUNDBREAKING EFFORT IN THE CENTRAL PART OF THIS SMALL island, helping to alleviate the plight of elephants whose numbers are dwindling. In your spare time, explore one of the island's many spice gardens, which showcase the country's specialties, including vanilla, cinnamon, and cardamom.

You'll join forces with the Sri Lankan Wildlife Conservation Society to catalog and conduct surveys in several elephant roaming zones. Watering holes, grassy plains, and forests are habitat for the endangered pachyderms—less than 3,500 wild elephants remain in Sri Lanka. Your fieldwork will inform sustainable conservation programs and projects intended to resolve conflicts between humans and elephants. As a bonus, you'll also be part of the groundwork to establish the first Trans-Climactic Zone National Park in Sri Lanka.

The threats to the elephants include ivory poaching, loss and fragmentation of habitat, and degradation of living zones from human pollution and development.

A lack of electricity at camp means you'll rough it in your new digs at the field base station. Solar-powered lights beat back the darkness for a little while, but make no mistake, you're in the wilds of this enchanting Asian island. In the morning, you'll hop on a bike or hike to research outposts in order to collect data, interview locals about elephant crop raiding, and assess elephant damage. Your afternoons will be spent relaxing, except on days when you'll be assigned to do an elephant observation run in the jeeps, watching and recording social interactions and ranging patterns. Some nights you'll do nocturnal investigations and surveys, based in a tree hut.

Endangered wild elephants of Sri Lanka

YOUR NEXT STEP: Global Vision International (✆ **888/653-6028**; www.gviusa.com). The 2-week project, US$1,470, includes housing in a basic field station (with shared kitchen and cold water plumbing), meals, project transportation, training, and support.

DON'T MISS: One of the most vibrant export industries of Sri Lanka is tea, so a visit to the iconic town of **Nuwara Eliya** in the heart of the tea zone is a great side trip. It is a study in opposites, as British-style Georgian and Queen Anne homes, with hedgerows and gardens, are side by side tiny homesteader shelters and miles of hillside tea crops in this foggy, serene retreat.

ⓘ www.srilankatourism.org

Surveying Wildlife **9**

Swimming with Sharks (and Rays)

Conservation on the California Coast

Monterey, California, USA

WINE COUNTRY IS JUST BEYOND YOUR DOOR—OR DOCK, AS THE CASE MAY BE—AND THE Pacific Coast Highway makes for some stunning scenic driving. If that isn't enough to entice you, San Francisco should provide plenty to see once your marine work is finished.

The coast of Central California is one of the most beautiful seasides in the world, and Monterey Bay is home to a wide array of ocean animals. Surfers know only too well that sharks are no strangers here. You'll study seven species of sharks and rays on this project: leopard sharks, gray and brown smooth-hound sharks, bat rays, thornback rays, shovelnose guitarfish, and round stingrays. In the mid–20th century, oyster fishermen in nearby Moss Landing, in an ill-founded attempt to eliminate the predators of their bivalve crops, killed off hundreds of sharks and rays—using tools like pitchforks, shotguns, and dynamite. The vagaries of nature, habitat changes, and natural ebb and flow of species was to blame, not predators, so despite the hunt, the oyster population collapsed. In the last several decades the shark and ray populations have been protected. The study of the recovery of these seven populations is an indicator of the general health of the bay.

You'll spend most of the day in a wetsuit, setting nets in the bay and open waters to capture, measure, record, and tag the animals before releasing them back into the water. When you have specimens in the nets, the research team will teach you how to determine species, gender, whether they've been previously tagged, and perhaps fit some with radio transmitters. A tiny fin clipping for DNA typing might be taken (not harming the animal). You'll learn how to input all the data you've collected in the field—broadening the scientific knowledge about why some species are recovering while others are lagging—and perhaps begin to see patterns that will illuminate the reasons why. You'll work part-time from small boats and the remainder from the shoreline and tidal salt marshes.

Pajaro Dunes, a relaxing holiday community of shoreline beach houses and condos, is home for the next 10 days. You'll share a four-bedroom house with the rest of the volunteer team, enjoying evenings by the fireplace, DVD player, and high-speed Internet. The project staff comes in and prepares meals for you, and you'll pack a lunch to eat on the fly between your scientific duties. During free time, enjoy excellent kayaking and hiking right out your back door or head into Monterey to Cannery Row for restaurants, pubs, and galleries or to walk the breezy streets of the city before returning to fall asleep to the sound of the waves hitting the beach.

YOUR NEXT STEP: Earthwatch (© **800/776-0188;** www.earthwatch.org). This 10-day project, US$2,650, includes beach house accommodations, meals prepared by staff, field training, local transportation, and support. A US$35 Earthwatch membership is required.

DON'T MISS: At the northern end of Monterey Bay is the city of **Santa Cruz**, vying for the title of Surf City and secure in its reputation as the most laid-back of beach towns. The beach boardwalk amusement park has one of the nation's oldest wooden roller coasters, the nearby redwood forests are a dreamlike journey among ferns and the towering giants, and the downtown is full of great dining, bookstores, coffee houses, drum circles, street musicians, farmers' markets, and colorful locals.

(i) www.seemonterey.com

10 Surveying Wildlife

Bats, Birds & Small Wildlife

Monitoring & Planning on the Savannah

Swaziland

This small but friendly African country can be a quick stop if you're moving through South Africa to Mozambique, but there's lots worth sticking around for. Check out the Ezulwini and Malkerns Valleys; the former is home to the country's royalty and the latter is worth investigating for handicrafts.

When you think of African wildlife, the big beasts—lions and leopards and elephants—come to mind. But the sharp blade of endangerment cuts in all directions, and smaller species of birds and mammals are equally threatened, often more so, from encroaching human development and degradation of their habitat. Swaziland itself is lesser known than other African nations; still true in many ways to their traditions and uncomplicated lifestyle, the Swazi people's harmony with the environment makes them particularly dedicated to its preservation. You'll work with project experts on monitoring several species: night drives searching for nocturnal hunters; day transect parties where you'll methodically cover a grid pattern to study fauna and search for nests, roosts, and dens of birds and small mammals; searching for evidence of large raptor hunting and the nests of threatened birds; weighing, measuring, and ring-tagging young birds for future study before release; putting up nets and harp traps for study subjects; and monitoring already-tagged subjects with GPS tracking devices. All of this helps to paint an accurate picture of the health of individual species and their interdependence within the ecosystem.

Your work will help create a conservation plan for the region and the locals, who are growing more aware each day of the work that must be done. This is a society with strong ties to the land and traditional ways. You'll be part of a village life that will seem quite unfamiliar: plenty of witch doctors practice in this monarchy; tribal gatherings and feasts are full of dancing and competition between bands of warriors; and if your timing is right, you may be here for the annual "reed dance" festival in August or September or the Inewala ceremony in late December or early January. (Keep in mind that the project has needs throughout the year.)

Base camp is in rustic cottages or small tents within the national park. There is no electricity, but you won't miss it as you quickly settle into a simple rhythm during your 4 weeks on the project. In your free time, you may want to take advantage of tour options nearby, including whitewater rafting, mountain biking, and horseback riding, but the wildlife access right outside of camp is spectacular enough to keep you exploring and discovering new things every day.

YOUR NEXT STEP: The Society for Environmental Exploration (**Frontier)** (✆ **+44/ 20 7613 2422;** www.frontier.ac.uk). This 4-week project, £1,695, includes camp accommodations (basic cottage or tent), three meals daily, airport transfers, local orientation and project training, and 24-hour support.

DON'T MISS: After all that fresh air and outdoor living, get down to the root of Swaziland with a **cave excursion.** Speleological trips into the mountainside are half-day adventures, with several hours spent underground in the caverns and winding narrow passageways inside the Mdzimba Mountains. Isn't that the whole reason you got so familiar with bats on the project?

ⓘ www.welcometoswaziland.com

11 Surveying Wildlife

Wildlife Conservation Adventure

A PhD in Big Game

Kilombero Valley, Tanzania

The large animals are what will bring you here for work, but this second-largest wetland in East Africa is also known as an important bird area, its habitat crucial to the conservation of global bird populations.

In partnership with the University of Dar es Salaam, this project is all about the big animals: elephant, leopard, lion, hippo, and buffalo. This wide savannah on the Kilombero floodplains is home to a web of wildlife and tribal village outposts. The once-plentiful mammal populations in this region are currently in decline (in part because human populations are on the increase). You'll be surveying and monitoring these shrinking communities, learning bush-tracking techniques, and condensing all the data you record into usable reports that will help to bring attention and awareness to the international scientific and conservation communities about the pending crisis. Habitat and conservation plans are dependent upon this research, and the effort to find a delicate, symbiotic, and balanced relationship between man and beast is finally being prioritized.

The end result of your fieldwork will be wildlife pattern mapping and species distribution, recording levels of habitat disturbance, and creating survey reports on species large and small. Larger predators follow the patterns of their food sources, so some of your work will be setting up bucket and canopy-net traps for the study of smaller mammals, frogs, bats, and insects. For the big fellas, you'll set up camera traps, sand pits for tracks, and

Studying a spider in Tanzania

your own visual sightings. This work will be by day and by night, with afternoon downtime for rest—just like the animals on the savannah.

Camp life among your fellow volunteers, research professionals, game trackers, and wildlife guards is easy and simple. The campfire provides the main gathering spot, a waterfall plunges into your swimming hole for exercise and bathing, and card games and chess tournaments provide the wild nightlife. A few songs, a few games, some time being hypnotized by glowing embers and millions of stars, and you'll drift off to bed. On the nights when local tribes invite you to a feast or festival, it will be exhausting after so much quiet repose.

YOUR NEXT STEP: The Society for Environmental Exploration (Frontier) (✆ **+44/ 20 7613 2422;** www.frontier.ac.uk). This 3-week project, £1,095, includes remote African bush camping in a large, communal *banda* (bungalow) and sleeping on raised bamboo platforms, two meals daily, in-country ground transport, local orientation and project training, and 24-hour support.

DON'T MISS: The name Tanzania comes from the combination of *Tanganyika* and *Zanzibar*, so a jaunt to **Zanzibar,** the spice island, and scuba diving amid the shipwrecks and large coral reef off the eastern coast, is a great way to wash off the dust of the savannah.

ⓘ www.tanzaniatouristboard.com

Rescue & Protection 12

River Dolphin Study

Dolphin Research, Houseboat Living

Mamirauá, Brazil

Dolphins that live in a river? Just another example of the diversity and unexpected mysteries to be found in the mighty Amazon River. Studying these amazing creatures is one part of a larger effort to ensure sustainability of both the ecosystem and tourism.

Your base is a floating house tethered to fallen trees in the flooded Amazon forest of Brazil. From here you'll aid the tireless efforts of the Mamirauá Institute for Sustainable Development. A small skiff will motor your team along rarely accessed tributaries and black water lakes, in search of the Amazon's rare pink dolphins. The legendary dolphins are believed to have the power to transform into beautiful young men who come into villages and charm away the loveliest girls. They are a protected species from hunting, but that doesn't put an end to the degradation of the river habitat they call home. Gill nets, construction, mercury-laden gold mines, and small inlet dams threaten their survival a little more each day.

This reserve area is a bountiful wildlife region overflowing with flora and fauna, much of it unique to this location. Research on the dolphins (both pink and gray) includes tracking new births and calf development (you haven't seen cute until you've seen a baby pink dolphin frolicking in glassy water). The growth cycle of young and adult dolphins is also monitored, as is group movement and interactive behavior. This research work is depended upon by dolphin projects around the world, contributing to the health and protection of many species.

You'll venture out with alternating morning or afternoon teams each day for a full 5 to 7 hours of field study and tracking on the water. Your off-duty hours will

Searching for pink dolphins

likely be spent resting, as the heat and hard work can drain you. Life on the floating house is simple but comfortable, with hammocks or beds, solar power, and basic bathroom and kitchen facilities. The quiet of the area (aside from the usual sunrise and dusk din of birds and insects waking and growing more active) is like a lullaby, and while you can spend free time hiking or paddling the calm waters, chances are you'll swing in a hammock and cat nap.

YOUR NEXT STEP: Global Vision International (✆ **888/653-6028;** www.gviusa.com). This 2-week project, US$2,690, includes accommodations in the floating base station, shared meals, scientific and field training, project transportation, and support from the field team.

DON'T MISS: After being immersed among the trees, get above the canopy with an **Amazon Air Tour.** Board a Cessna hydroplane that takes off right from the water's surface, then gives you an aerial view of the flooded forest, Meeting of the Waters, and **Manaus** city. www.amazonastravel.com.br

ⓘ www.turismo.gov.br

13 Rescue & Protection

Giant Panda Conservation

Nurturing the Bears in a Mountain Forest

Ya'an City, China

OTHER THAN ITS FAMOUS BEAR RESIDENTS, THIS MOUNTAINOUS AREA IS KNOWN AS THE starting point of the Sichuan-Tibet stretch of the historic Tea-Horse Road. The city is one of the places where tea culture got its start; don't miss a trip to its markets to purchase some of the amazing blends available here.

In 2003, in an effort to help the giant panda (one of the planet's most endangered species and a symbol of goodwill for the Chinese nation), the Befengxia Panda Base opened as part of the world's largest giant panda migration. In 2008, a devastating earthquake struck the Sichuan Province of China and did extensive damage to a sister panda base in Wolong, making Befengxia China's most important panda protection program. Befengxia's natural landscape is beautiful, with waterfalls, forest, rolling rivers, and expansive grounds covering almost 15,000 acres (6,070ha). Whenever possible, after training in this wild but protected zone, feral pandas are returned to free-range environments.

Six kinds of bamboo grow here, and more than 80% of the habitat is covered in vegetation, so it is panda paradise. More than 20 spots in the broadleaf-shaded grounds have been set aside for panda-related activities—including dedicated grazing grounds, "kindergartens" for young pandas, and a panda hospital/nursery/research institute—and you rotate from one to the next.

During your time in this mountain getaway where you'll live in a hostel within the base habitat, you'll be trained in the care of pandas and might be asked to do a range of tasks, from cleaning enclosures, preparing their vegetarian diet, gathering and recording behavioral data, and the part you'll talk about most when you get home: interacting with the adult and baby pandas.

YOUR NEXT STEP: WLS International (✆ **+44/870 479 5145;** www.gapyearinasia.com). One- or two-week assignments, US$795 to US$1,150, include basic hostel accommodations at the project site, breakfasts (other meals on your own), airport transfers, local transportation, and a volunteering fee paid for direct support of the project.

DON'T MISS: The 230-ft.-high (70-m) **Leshan Giant Buddha** was carved from the side of a mountain to calm the turbulent waters. He sits facing Mount Emei, with visitors gathering at his feet, clearly understanding the local saying "The mountain is a Buddha and the Buddha is a mountain."

ⓘ www.cnto.org

Rescue & Protection **14**

Animal Rescue & Care Program

Touring, Aid & Yoga in India's Pink City

Jaipur, India

Jaipur is India's first city to benefit from some careful urban planning, protected by high walls and bisected by straight, wide avenues. In your time off from working with animals, you'll want to explore the city, shopping for brassware, rugs, linens, and other crafts.

Life can be tough for the economically disadvantaged in and around Jaipur, and the ever-growing population faces daily troubles with hunger and disease. Unfortunately, families that once had space and food for pets are frequently forced by circumstance to turn these animals out to fend for themselves. Add to this already unhappy equation a lack of affordable access to spay-neuter programs and you have a burgeoning population of street animals suffering neglect, disease, and mistreatment. You'll contribute by helping treat sick animals, vaccinating the healthy, and working to sterilize strays to curtail the unhealthy population expansion.

Your efforts won't be restricted to veterinary pursuits, as very valuable project time will be spent helping place animals in happy homes and working on community awareness. When out in the "field" (Jaipur's streets), you'll be based in an animal ambulance from which you'll help professionals identify and transport animals in need back to the shelter.

Knowing that this project can be emotionally harrowing, project organizers work hard to find a balance. There is daily yoga instruction, frequent cooking classes, and several guided trips in and around the beautiful palaces and Haveli mansions of Jaipur, the "pink city." English is the primary language on the project, and many of the residents will converse easily (and want to practice), as English is taught in Jaipur schools.

YOUR NEXT STEP: Center for Cultural Interchange (© **312/944-2544;** www.cci-exchange.com). The 2-week program, US$1,590, includes housing in the dormlike base camp, where you'll share a room with other volunteers and meals prepared by a local cook. Training, project support, side trips and city orientation tours, and airport transfers are included.

DON'T MISS: It'll seem a little touristy, but the royal elephant ride up the switchback trail to Jaipur's historic **Amber Fort** is undeniably Rajasthan in mood. The white-marble and red-sandstone fort overlooks the pink city of Jaipur and beautiful Maotha Lake.

ⓘ www.rajasthantourism.gov.in

15 Rescue & Protection

Lions of Tsavo

Safari Tent Camping & Research in the Wild

Nairobi, Kenya

IN ORDER TO UNDERSTAND ANIMALS YOU NEED TO IMMERSE YOURSELF IN THEIR PATTERNS AND rhythms. This unique opportunity in a preserved wildlife habitat gives you the chance to track, tame, feed, and otherwise try to learn more about what threatens these lions.

They look a little different than in *The Lion King*, but the maneless lions of Tsavo are no less magnificent, and they make clear why the common nickname King of the Jungle is entirely apt. Within the almost 170,000-acre Taita Rukinga Wildlife Conservancy, these regal beasts rule at the top of the food chain. Lions can be tough to spot, but your expert team of trackers will lead from jeeps three times a day, then you'll nap in the afternoons, just like the lions. When a pride or individual lion is located, you'll scan for prey, whip out your camera and video recorder to help identify individuals (using whisker patterns), and record their behavior. Other local species rarely seen on traditional safaris include civets and aardwolves.

The zone you'll traverse is part of Kenya's largest wildlife sanctuary, nearly 5 million acres (2 million ha). Lions here kill a large number of livestock each year, so local farmers hunt them to save their herds. Simultaneously, naturally wild habitat is being converted to cropland or burned for the charcoal trade, crowding the lions into ever smaller corridors, where their behavior and social patterns are compromised. Your study and contribution to this project helps the understanding of the needs of this lineage of lion, and will help conservation efforts to try to find the best way for lions and humans to coexist peacefully.

Home base is a comfortable tented research camp mid-wilderness. There is electricity, flush toilets, and hot water, so it's relatively luxurious here, affording you the opportunity to really settle in for your

Tracking a lion in Kenya

2-week assignment. Spend evenings over long meals learning the history and folklore of the English-speaking (and eager to practice) staff before heading off to bed and falling asleep to the sounds of the wild. A lion's roar outside camp will be bone chilling, but it's really the one sound you'll want most to hear.

YOUR NEXT STEP: Earthwatch (✆ **800/776-0188;** www.earthwatch.org). This 13-day assignment, US$3,150, includes safari tent accommodations, meals prepared by staff, field training, local transportation, and support. A US$35 Earthwatch membership is required.

DON'T MISS: Before you head *Out of Africa*, head to the house of that book's author, now kept in the same condition as when she lived there. The **Karen Blixen Museum** house and gardens, overlooking the Ngong Hills, display a blend of original furnishings and props from the Oscar-winning 1985 film that was shot here.

ⓘ www.magicalkenya.com

Rescue & Protection **16**

Biodiversity & Colobus Monkeys

Living in a Swahili Village in the Coastal Forest

Shimoni, Kenya

PEOPLE FLY HALFWAY AROUND THE WORLD TO EXPERIENCE KENYA'S GREAT DIVING AND FISHING opportunities. This small fishing village is your base, but it's not a run-of-the-mill destination—unusual coastal caves, which once served as hiding spots for Arab explorers, run along the coast and into the forest.

Facing the highest rate of species extinction due to habitat loss, the East African coastal forest is one of 11 "hyperhot" conservation priorities on the planet. The populations of black and white Anghon Colobus monkeys here are some of the most important animals in Kenya for study, and they are critically endangered. Training in biodiversity hotspot information gathering will be provided as you track and record the movements and behavior of the Colobus. The rare Zani elephant shrew and certain endangered butterflies will also be part of your focus.

You'll be living in a traditional Swahili village, completely immersed in the culture and considered a member of the community. The idyllic Indian Ocean coastline might lull you into forgetting how vital the work is, but the project leaders will keep you passionate—and busy. You'll be up before the sun for dawn bird surveys, early-day primate tracking, afternoon habitat surveys, and evening game searches. But it isn't all exhausting—your job may be to lie on your back for an hour to observe the play of a band of Colobus in the trees overhead.

You'll get free time to snorkel in and around Kenya's best coral reefs in this protected marine area. Your home is a shared tent that has access to the Shimoni Reef Lodge for electricity, kitchen, and shared bath, but after a few days, you'll truly see no reason to have a roof over your head.

YOUR NEXT STEP: Global Vision International (✆ **888/653-6028;** www.gviusa.com). This 2-week project, US$1,290, includes basic accommodations in shared tents with lodge access, communal meals prepared on a rotating basis, project transportation, training, and support.

DON'T MISS: Although it's a dark chapter of history, it's important to remember it. The **Shimoni "Slave" Caves,** said to hold slaves before shipment to Arabia, are quite close to the lodge. The caves are believed to travel underground for 3 miles (5km). Iron shackles can still be seen on the walls, and well-preserved wooden crates, used to transport slaves, are still found here. Archeological findings show that these coral caverns have been inhabited for several centuries.

ⓘ www.magicalkenya.com

Rescue & Protection

A Month of Hippos

Nomadic Camping & Conservation

Senga Bay, Malawi

LAKE MALAWI IS SO LARGE ITS SURFACE AREA OCCUPIES SPACE IN THREE COUNTRIES, MAKING it the third-largest lake in Africa. Its shores continuously attract travelers who want to enjoy the natural beauty, warm tropical waters, and protected habitat in its national park.

When you think of the most dangerous animals in Africa, lions, leopards, or some of the other big cats come to mind. In reality, however, the ones you have to be most careful of are the buffalo and hippos. Three tons of floating, grazing laziness, hippos can move awfully quickly when they want to.

In Malawi, hippos are highly threatened by the human population, and they need your help. You'll spend days aboard a research boat, traversing giant Lake Malawi and following the southern shore, observing and recording the behavior and movement of the hippos. You'll plot locations and movement by GPS, as well as gather secondhand stories of hippo encounters from local fishermen (translators provided).

Some off-lake days you'll visit local communities to promote hippo conservation and to help develop eco-campsites that better protect and respect the indigenous pods of hippos. Since these giant animals are relatively indiscriminate in their nocturnal feasting, they tend to destroy crops on local farmland. In retaliation, farmers shoot hippos, also indiscriminately. The human-animal conflict has reached crisis levels for the hippo population—their numbers have plummeted to only 10% of where they were 20 years ago.

Your month of hippo time will be pretty rugged. You'll bring your own tent and sleeping bag and set up in a new shore camp each day. While you are out on the boat, support staff transports your tent and luggage to the next campsite so it will be waiting for you when you come ashore. Simple food is prepared for you. Some nights you'll stay in small rural villages and meet and celebrate with local tribes.

YOUR NEXT STEP: The Society for Environmental Exploration (Frontier) (✆ **+44/ 20 7613 2422;** www.frontier.ac.uk). This 1-month project, £1,495, includes staying in satellite campsites in new shore locales or small villages each night, sleeping in your own tent, and enjoying hearty communal meals prepared for you. Training and project support, ground transfers, local orientation, and 24-hour support are also included.

DON'T MISS: At the southern end of enormous Lake Malawi is the world's first freshwater national park. Deep, clear water and mountainous backdrops, hundreds of fish species, and an ecosystem as important to evolutionary species study as the Galapagos make snorkeling in **Lake Malawi National Park** a rare treat.

ⓘ www.malawi-tourism-association.org.mw

Rescue & Protection **18**

Wildlife of the Mongolian Steppe

Hiking & Cultural Immersion

Ulaanbaatar, Mongolia

Mongolia receives very few visitors in comparison to its neighbors to the east and west, but that very unspoiled nature makes for an authentic experience, albeit one of extremes—the open expanse of the Gobi Desert, the huge snow-capped mountains, and, yes, the Internet cafes in its capital city.

Space doesn't get much more wide open than on the Mongolian Steppe. Your view is uninterrupted for miles as you look across the vast, and sometimes unforgiving, landscape of the Ikh Nart Nature Reserve. You'll observe and record the behavior and migration patterns of a broad range of grassland animals, including Argali sheep, Siberian ibex, mountain goats, hedgehogs, Pallas's cats, Corsac foxes, and vultures. Vegetation is sparse and desertlike, so spotting the animals will be easier than you think. You'll take the occasionally strenuous hike over rocky outcrops to get to study points.

You'll be living steppe-style in a traditional Mongolian *ger* (yurt) with your volunteer colleagues, and you'll have plenty of free time to explore this wilderness and satiate even the deepest craving of wanderlust. Your work will add to the general conservation knowledge about these threatened species in this unique ecological zone. As every undeveloped habitat in the world is shrinking with human expansion, this research will help guide protection measures before the situation reaches a crisis level. Sharing the steppe with you are wolves, ibex, gazelles, wild asses, eagles, hawks, and multiple rodent species burrowing underground.

An extra benefit to this trip is the cultural immersion in the Mongolian community. On the steppe, horses are the main form of transportation and tent life in the ger is surprisingly comfortable and, in a sense, timeless. Small social groups enjoy meals together and stories and songs by the fire without modern and technological distractions. You'll sleep well as the wind buffets the woolen walls of your home after a hard day's journey.

YOUR NEXT STEP: Earthwatch (© **800/776-0188;** www.earthwatch.org). This 2-week excursion, US$2,950, includes cozy accommodations in a shared ger house, cook-prepared meals, project training, and research supervision. A US$35 Earthwatch membership is required.

DON'T MISS: As an incremental step toward returning to your cerebral life after the profoundly uncomplicated and physical life of this project, stop in Ulaanbaatar at the **International Intellectual Museum** to peruse its collection of puzzles and mental challenges to get your synapses firing again. http://museum.pixel.mn

ⓘ www.mongoliatourism.gov.mn

19 Rescue & Protection

Cheetah Conservation

Farm Living in Namibia's Largest Safari Park

Windhoek, Namibia

NAMIBIA'S CENTRALLY LOCATED CAPITAL CITY HAS GERMAN ROOTS AND IS THE STARTING place for most safari-going travelers. You'll find a vast expanse of desert, a long coastline dotted with dunes, and an extensive national park system, chockablock with native, endangered, and otherwise important species.

Few animals capture our imaginations like the big cats, and the sleek, streamlined racer that leaves them all in the dust is the cheetah. These lanky felines are the fastest land animals on Earth, but they can't outrun the manmade threat to their survival. Conflict with humans has the biggest impact on wild cheetahs, as farm livestock make an easy meal for these superb hunters. Diminishment of habitat and shrinking gene pools also make the cheetah's life difficult. The largest population of cheetahs on Earth is in Namibia, but their numbers continue to decrease.

Your work at the headquarters of the Cheetah Conservation Fund will include wildlife surveying, feeding and caring for captive cheetahs, and entering all your information into a database. Sometimes wild cheetahs are rescued and humanely captured, and you'll be asked to help collect biomedical samples to assess the animal's health and get it released back to the wild as soon as is practical. Your study data on behavior and ecology is part of a large effort to protect the species and strengthen protection laws. The care of resident cheetahs at the project is also an important component of the attempts to turn the statistics around.

Home is a huge working farm, Eland's Joy, where you'll bunk in a two-person, solar-powered bungalow. The farm is also home to kudus, hartebeest, oryx, duiker,

A cheetah in the vast Namibian desert

steenbok, warthogs, jackals, leopards, brown hyenas, numerous bird species, and an array of smaller animals. In your free time, you'll make a day trip to Etosha National Park for a broader safari experience. Etosha is the largest park in Namibia and chock full of elephants, zebras, lions, rhinos, giraffes, and wild cheetahs. You'll speak English, Namibia's national language, on the project but hear plenty of Afrikaans and German.

YOUR NEXT STEP: Earthwatch (✆ **800/ 776-0188;** www.earthwatch.org). This 15-day project, US$4,050, includes shared bungalow accommodations, group meals prepared by a staff cook, project and survey training, and full project support. A US$35 Earthwatch membership is required.

DON'T MISS: When you think of Namibia, you likely picture the dune-rippled desert and rough Skeleton Coast, but take the time to visit the expansive **Fish River Canyon,** the world's largest earth fissure after the Grand Canyon.

ⓘ www.namibiatourism.com.na

20 Rescue & Protection

Stray Animal Care

A Tropical Shelter

Vieques, Puerto Rico

This island, about 11km (7 miles) east of Puerto Rico, served as a U.S. military training base for more than 50 years. These days it's gaining attention as a relatively unexplored tourism destination, although more and more travelers come to enjoy its sandy beaches and laid-back atmosphere.

Hundreds of stray dogs, called *sato* in Puerto Rico, start as pets (or the offspring of pets) that are discarded by their owners. As strays, they run in packs, scavenging for survival. This small shelter on the island of Vieques—once a military zone and now an under-the-radar tropical vacation haven off the big island of Puerto Rico—takes in and rehabilitates as many street sato as it can handle. Extra hands for the care of these loving but unloved animals are always needed.

You'll clean kennels and feed dogs in the shelter, and work in a mobile clinic alongside local veterinarians. Spay and neuter programs attempt to decrease the number of unwanted animals. More endearing work is also part of every day, like the often joyous task of helping the animals socialize with one another and humans. The tumbling play of puppies with a new lease on life (and a newfound reserve of energy with an appropriate diet) is hard to resist. Even

One of Puerto Rico's many stray puppies

more rewarding is when one of these terrific companions is placed in a loving home.

The shelter also owns a nearby home where volunteers can stay for weeks, months, and sometimes indefinitely. If tropical splendor on the lovely island seems like it will be just too luxurious and relaxing, you can volunteer to transport some of the Puerto Rican dogs to Vermont, where they stay and get strong in a sister shelter before being adopted.

YOUR NEXT STEP: Explorations in Travel (✆ **802/257-0152;** www.exploretravel.com). Volunteers choose the length of stay, with a minimum of 1 week, and pay a US$975 placement fee. Included is housing in the project home near the shelter, but the rest of your expenses are your responsibility, including food and local transportation.

DON'T MISS: You're only 30 minutes from San Juan and all the nightlife you could ever need, but the most fascinating nightlife you'll experience may be a night kayak in Vieques's **Bioluminescent Bay.** The paddles seem to stir stars as the water around glows vivid green whenever it is disturbed. Slip in and swim a while to really feel transported to outer space.

ⓘ www.gotopuertorico.com

Rescue & Protection **21**

Animal Welfare

Caring for Pets that Need Care

Cape Town, South Africa

CAPE TOWN IS RENOWNED AS A LIVELY, BEAUTIFUL, CULTURE-FILLED CITY. WHEN YOUR WORK caring for the animals is done, explore the town, visit its famous wineries, or take in gorgeous views of the region's sloping mountains and rugged coastline.

You may guess that your veterinary support volunteer assignment in Cape Town will have you cuddling puppies and a few kittens all day long—and you would be right. But you'll also work with donkeys, geese, parrots, pigs, and any other animal that gets domesticated in a large city. This project provides welfare veterinary service to pet owners who can't afford a private vet service and supports animal welfare officers who tirelessly work to vaccinate, care for, and provide sterilization for animals from poorer communities. The project has been a great success and is growing, trying desperately to keep up with demand.

You'll split your time between the recently opened permanent clinics in Cape Town and the mobile clinics in townships and neighborhoods that provide both general and occasional emergency services for animals. Except in serious cases of abuse, animals are treated, nursed to health, and returned to their owners. Because of your work, families are able to keep their beloved pets even if they've had a change in financial circumstances (the cause of most animal abandonment in any city). You'll be fully trained for your tasks and fully introduced to life in this beautiful city by the sea. You may also pitch in with marketing and community relations, helping impart the wisdom of spaying and neutering pets. English is taught in all Cape Town schools, so communication is effortless.

You'll live with a local host family in one of the trendiest neighborhoods of Cape Town, so during downtime you'll find plenty of distraction. Days off can be spent sightseeing and taking activity tours in and around the city.

YOUR NEXT STEP: Twin Work & Volunteer Abroad (✆ **800/80 483 80;** www.workandvolunteer.com). This 2-week project, US$1,289, includes hosted room and board (morning and evening meals) with a family in the city, project training, and support.

DON'T MISS: The long and difficult history of **Robben Island** is nothing to be proud of—it was a place of banishment and prison for hundreds of years and is now a UNESCO World Heritage Site. The most famous incarcerated prisoner was Nelson Mandela, exiled with other political prisoners during the terrible reign of apartheid.

ⓘ www.southafrica.net

22 **Rescue & Protection**

Rehabilitating Rescued Horses

Working & Riding Along the Eastern Cape

Chintsa, South Africa

Saddled up and ready to ride, you'll gain a new perspective on your surroundings—the "wild coast" of the eastern cape of South Africa—and the needy horses that you help return to optimal health.

For the past decade, the Dickerson family has been working with the Wild Coast African SPCA on the troubling but rewarding task of rescuing and rehabilitating abused and neglected horses. They created the New Hampshire Rehab Centre to nurture

Rehabilitating a rescued Chintsa horse

equines back to health and vitality. Chintsa horses generate both tourism revenue and income for the rehab program via trail-riding opportunities with the rescued horses.

You'll be actively involved in the rehabilitation of horses, both on the ground and in the saddle. You'll prepare feed and special diet meals for recovering horses, groom, assist with veterinary examinations, muck stalls and water horses, and help with exercising and training. You needn't start as an expert at horsemanship, but by the end you'll feel like one, with plenty of time for trail rides and ring work. A 2-day trail excursion is included. You'll stay in a lagoon-side cottage near the shore of the Indian Ocean, and your free time will be packed with exploration and wandering the Eastern Cape's magnificence. The crashing waves, seen from the saddle, will be an indelible memory, as will the effect your warmth has upon these strong yet improbably fragile animals.

YOUR NEXT STEP: Aviva (✆ **+27/21 557 4312;** www.aviva-sa.com). This 2-week project, US$1,205, will fly by when you get into the routine of cottage life on the lagoon, prepared meals, and the hard work you've been well trained to do. Also included are airport transfers, in-country transportation, and trail ride time.

DON'T MISS: The Eastern Cape is home to the Xhosa people and birthplace of Nelson Mandela, and also host to some gnarly waves. Surfing is extraordinary at **Jeffrey's Bay,** where people call the famous "supertubes" the world's best waves.

ⓘ www.southafrica.net

Rescue & Protection **23**

Black Rhino Research

Catch & Release

Hluhluwe-Umfolozi Reserve, South Africa

YOU CAN BECOME AN INTEGRAL PART OF SOMETHING SPECIAL BY HELPING INTERNATIONAL nonprofit organizations learn more about this troubled species. Camping out on the grounds of Africa's oldest park, you'll have a front-row seat to see Big Five game—including the black rhinoceros.

The black rhinoceros is a critically endangered species, and 10% of the small remaining population is found on this 237,000-acre (95,910-ha) wildlife reserve. All of Africa's Big Five also call Hluhluwe home, so your time spent here will be adrenaline-packed, to say the least. You'll help researchers ascertain how individual rhinos respond and recover from capture-and-release operations and how the herd units cope with the change in their population. A deeper understanding of these processes will inform and determine policy for species management throughout the animals' wild habitat.

The Rhino Research Programme is working with the World Wildlife Fund to reintroduce the species to other reserves in the region. Being involved with such a threatened species can feel like being at the center of an emergency, as any decision that affects this herd population also affects a large proportion of the animals left in the world. It remains a challenge of public relations as well, since the relatively abundant white rhino is seen on practically every safari jeep trip for tourists, so visitors don't recognize the very real threat to "rhinos."

In addition to the wild animals you'll study, you'll help with the care of captive rhinos being prepared for relocation. These animals are strengthened with a special diet and conditioning to improve their chances in the wild. You'll bushwalk during the days and stake out watering holes at night for the best sightings. Your downtime will be quiet around camp, except when you are contributing to cooking and cleaning chores.

YOUR NEXT STEP: Enkosini Eco Experience (✆ **+27/82 442 6773,** or **206/604-2664;** www.enkosiniecoexperience.com). This 2-week program, US$1,395, includes farm house, hut, or tent accommodations (varies by nomadic site location), meals, orientation tour, telemetry and other training, and living expenses in the field.

DON'T MISS: The field site is near the world-famous surfing beaches of South Africa's eastern coast. The **Dolphin Coast** is a relaxed holiday destination with water sports and beach time beckoning you.

ⓘ www.southafrica.net

24 **Rescue & Protection**

Elephant Orphanage

Bathing & Bottle-feeding Baby Elephants

Pinnawela, Sri Lanka

SITUATED NEAR BUDDHIST MONASTERIES AND A LAKE IN THIS ISLAND NATION'S HILL COUNTRY, this elephant orphanage is a popular attraction located about halfway between the capital, Colombo, and ancient royal city of Kandy. You'll play a hands-on role in supporting the mental and physical health of these large animals.

You'll assist *mahouts* (elephant handlers) at an elephant sanctuary and orphanage in 25 acres (10ha) of lush forest. This is hands-on elephant work: you'll bathe the gentle giants twice daily in the river—a process they love—clean and maintain enclosures, perform maintenance repairs as needed, and the giggle-inducing part of the job is working with the babies. These little trumpeters are nearly helpless and depend on you for bathing, bottle feeding, and mental stimulation and play. Mostly they depend on you for love and affection, as they've been lost or abandoned by their mothers.

This sanctuary has been caring for elephants for decades but still operates at a severe deficit of resources and is perpetually in need of helping hands. With the guidance of the mahouts, you will have great latitude to devise your own games and activities to challenge your young charges, who, if bored, tend to get a little too mischievous and find trouble. A recent breeding program has broadened the scope of volunteer work.

You'll live with a host family nearby, but the location is relatively remote, so free time will be spent exploring the immediate vicinity, hiking, and enjoying the peace and quiet (aside from the occasional blaring of an elephant trunk). While you'll be able to get by with English, you'll appreciate the language and cultural teaching that goes along with this project. But you'll find the most rewarding communication is non-verbal and frequently takes the form of a trunkful of river water aimed right at you.

YOUR NEXT STEP: Institute for Field Research Expeditions 🎗 (✆ **800/675-2504;** www.ifrevolunteers.org). This 2-week project, US$645, includes host family accommodations, meals, trip insurance, airport transfer and in-country transportation, language and cultural teaching, and full project support.

DON'T MISS: The largest, best preserved cave temple in Sri Lanka is **Dambulla.** Dating from1 b.c., it was known as the Golden Temple. A tremendous collection of 153 sacred Buddha statues are found in this underground cavern, as well as other idols, surrounded by more than 22,000 sq. ft. (2,044 sq. m) of murals.

ⓘ www.srilankatourism.org

Rescue & Protection **25**

Orangutan Health

Monitoring the Health of Apes

Sumatra, Indonesia

PACK YOUR HIKING BOOTS AND WATERPROOF CLOTHING. THE WILD, RUGGED ISLAND OF Sumatra—home to the coffee bean of the same name—invites adventurous travelers to experience its volcanoes, untamed landscape, vibrant tribal cultures, and to scuba dive in its waters.

We know apes are our closest relatives in the animal kingdom, but some of their behaviors are startling, making them seem much more closely related than we thought. The origin of the word *orangutan* is Malaysian and means "forest person." On this project, you'll know why. These red-haired primates in the Sumatran jungle

Orangutans of Sumatra treat their illnesses with specific plants

self-medicate with specific doses of plants to treat illnesses such as an upset stomach and to combat parasites. No wonder they are being studied!

This project is the first of its kind, investigating ecological conditions and overall fluctuations in orangutan vitality and how the animals keep themselves healthy. Based in one of the largest national parks of Indonesia, you'll be surrounded by tropical rainforest, mangroves, and giant mountains. You may be trekking for lengthy stretches to locate the bands of animals for observation and data collection. Your days will be full with organizing samples, preparing equipment, assisting the field scientists, nest counting, and actual study once you locate the orangutans. The orangs' neighbors (with whom you'll probably become acquainted) include the Sumatran elephant, giant flying squirrel, and the dancing lemur. You'll enter your gathered data into the computer system each evening.

You'll be roughing it in tents, with pit toilets, no hot water, but lovely environs in verdant rice fields. For a portion of your 2-week trip you'll be staying overnight in the jungle, while other evenings will have you at the permanent base station camp. Your free time is limited, as is the range of things to do, save for exploring this wild zone and experiencing this ancient rainforest habitat like few people ever will.

YOUR NEXT STEP: Global Vision International (✆ **888/653-6028;** www.gviusa.com). This 2-week trip, US$1,280, includes basic tent accommodations and camp meals, project orientation, scientific training techniques, and species background.

DON'T MISS: Proposed as one of the New Seven Wonders of the World, Sumatra's **Lake Toba** is the largest volcanic lake in the world. The steep mountains ringing the lake are picturesque, as is Samosir Island, in the middle of the lake, with small villages and plenty of water-based recreation options.

ⓘ www.sumateratourism.com

26 Rescue & Protection

Langur Project

Building Sustainable Eco-Tourism

Khao Sam Roi Yot, Thailand

A FEW HOURS FROM BUSTLING, CROWDED BANGKOK IS ANOTHER WORLD ENTIRELY—"THE mountain of three hundred peaks" is home to a national marine park that boasts caves, steep limestone mountains, short hikes with scenic views of the water, and animals that need assistance.

Though reminiscent of small monkeys, the dusky langur (or spectacled langur) is a slightly different species. It is only found in three zones of Southeast Asia, and its forest habitat is shrinking every day. Deforestation is encroaching on their treetop homes, and hunting for meat and sale in export markets is hurling them toward extinction. The Dusky Langur Conservation and Community Centre, with your volunteer help, is working to educate locals in the small fishing village of this region about the positive effect conservation and wildlife tourism can have upon their struggling economy while simultaneously preserving natural habitats.

You'll be observing and recording the langurs' behavior in their natural forest habitat, occasionally leaving food and water for the undernourished populations that can no longer roam large-enough feeding areas to support their numbers. Gaining a clear picture of the habits and behaviors of the langur will aid in the formation of a conservation and protection strategy. The shared goal of creating eco-tourism possibilities for the village of only 250 residents will benefit both wildlife and local human communities. The centre has worked hard at introducing eco-sustaining practices to the shoreside village, as well as rehabilitating and then releasing langurs back into the wild. One side effect of the hunting is the large number of orphaned baby langurs that must be cared for and raised until they can become self-sufficient.

You'll live in air-conditioned beachfront bungalows, and meals are taken at local restaurants (included in the trip price) that specialize in wonderfully spicy, fresh-caught seafood. Your work is on a regular daytime schedule, so evenings and weekends are free to explore the region's natural caves, beautiful beaches, local temples, and the Huai-Yang waterfall, a popular tour spot.

YOUR NEXT STEP: Go Differently Ltd. (© **+44/1799 521950;** www.godifferently.com). This 2-week project, £640, includes air-conditioned beach bungalow accommodations, all meals (in local restaurants), English-speaking assistance, and project orientation/support.

DON'T MISS: For a little post-assignment R&R, head straight to the seaside village of **Hua Hin.** This beach community is ground zero for some of the best spas and spa traditions in the world—you owe it to yourself to get at least one amazing Thai massage (or book a few days of spa vacation after all your hard work).

ⓘ www.tourismthailand.org

Rescue & Protection **27**

Chimpanzee Sanctuary

Land of the Chimps

Ngamba Island, Uganda

PERHAPS MORE THAN ANY OTHER PERSON, JANE GOODALL IS SYNONYMOUS WITH CHIMP studies, and on Ngamba Island you'll see the fruits of her labor—and learn that much is yet to be done. With Lake Victoria and its many islands (including the relaxing Ssese) as the setting for your work, there's plenty to do in your downtime.

Africa's wealth of what biologists call "charismatic megafauna" (wildlife that endears the public to conservation and species' survival) means there are many opportunities to work with injured or orphaned animals that are familiar from the toy store and animated films. Chimpanzees are astounding in their similarity to humans, and caring for them can be a lot like babysitting. The Ngamba Island sanctuary is supported by the Jane Goodall Institute and offers 1- and 2-week "long stay visits" where volunteers work on habitat improvement, field observation, and work with the local nomadic communities as well as directly with chimpanzee populations in the wild and at the sanctuary.

The program is designed to immerse you in the life of the chimpanzees, to help you understand their plight in the African wild, and to put you to work directly aiding in their rehabilitation and care as well as encourage your advocacy for the species. Some of the time you'll clean cages and prepare food, repair and maintain enclosures and other facilities of the sanctuary, and some hours will inevitably be spent crunching data, typing chimp diaries, and maybe even selling items in the project's gift shop. But then there will be the time spent in the nursery with the babies, and the sublime daily forest walks. You'll walk for an early-morning hour with a juvenile band of chimps through their forest habitat, and you'll be unable to stifle your laughter as they climb all over you, play bite, grab your hair or glasses, and then quietly stride by your side, holding your hand.

You'll be living in the Wild Frontiers tented camp on the island, enjoying meals prepared for you by project staff and relishing having plenty of downtime to nap, dream, chimp watch, hike, and explore (there is incredible bird-watching here). At dusk every evening, 50,000 fruit bats fly overhead, blackening the sky on the way out for their nightly forage.

YOUR NEXT STEP: Chimpanzee Sanctuary and Wildlife Conservation Trust (✆ **+256/41 4320662;** www.ngambaisland.org). Prices for 2-week programs vary by season: low season (Mar–Jun and Oct–Nov) US$2,250; high season (Aug–Sep and Dec–Feb) US$3,250. Tented camp accommodations and all meals provided, as well as park entrance fees and transportation to/from the island.

DON'T MISS: Most tourists visiting Uganda are on the trail of primates (both the chimpanzees and the mountain gorillas bring people from far and wide), so as a change of pace, pump up your adrenaline on a white-water rafting trip on newly established class IV and V rapids on the **Nile River.**

ⓘ www.visituganda.com

28 **Rescue & Protection**

Diamondback Terrapin Conservation

Helping Turtles in Coastal Salt Marsh

Barnegat Bay, New Jersey, USA

Residents from New Jersey, New York, and Pennsylvania frequent crowded Long Beach Island during summertime, but the northernmost tip of this 30km (18-mile) stretch is a special, unspoiled place: it's near a state park and home to colorful turtles whose shells look like intricately laid mosaic tiles.

Barnegat Bay is one of the nation's most extensive salt marshes, and the estuary is home to terrapins, small turtles with beautifully ornate shell designs. The terrapins have begun to move on in search of alternate regions in which to live—unchecked human development has left them no alternative. A broad spectrum of birds and fish are also being affected by human encroachment in this delicate ecosystem. The roaming range of the terrapins was once from Massachusetts to Texas, but coastal pollution and beach erosion has cleaved their habitat into piecemeal scraps.

From a research boat, you'll monitor the nests of these turtles—the only US native turtles found in brackish waters—and also humanely capture, tag, and track them. You'll measure pernicious sound pollution levels and record environmental and ecological data. Project teams (depending on the timing of your trip) also mark and tag hatchlings and determine hatching success.

The 9-day excursion includes lots of hard work balanced by free time, in which you'll want to take advantage of the wonderful kayaking and canoeing, lighthouse visits (Old Barney, one of the country's most photographed, is a short distance away), and the natural splendor of the 180 acres (73ha) of still-undeveloped coastal habitat. Your base will be the Lighthouse Center for Natural Resource Education, where you'll have an air-conditioned double room, shared bathrooms, dining room (all meals are prepared and served by a local chef), a computer lab, and laundry facilities.

YOUR NEXT STEP: Earthwatch (© **800/776-0188;** www.earthwatch.org). This 9-day assignment, US$1,950, includes housing in the comfortable research center, all meals prepared by a local chef, research training, and project supervision and support. A US$35 Earthwatch membership is required.

DON'T MISS: With all the natural estuary splendor of Barnegat Bay, there's no reason to stray far for relaxation after your project ends. A great choice is a **sailing charter** on the bay from Cedar Creek Marina—take a personalized sunset cruise or rent a boat if you have the skills to be a skipper.

ⓘ www.oceancountygov.com

Rescue & Protection 29

Teton Songbirds

Halting Species Decline in the Grand Tetons

Jackson Hole, Wyoming, USA

Budding bird lovers, listen up: the songbirds of Wyoming need your help. Heed their call and soak up the stunning, sharp splendor of the Grand Teton National Park, part of the Rocky Mountain range and the setting of many films.

You've heard of the canary in the coal mine, an early warning of poisonous gases that could eventually kill miners. The decline of migratory and resident songbird populations in Wyoming might signify the same thing. Researchers are studying the remaining birds and their habitats to try to understand and, ideally, halt their decline. The work is being done in the postcard-perfect Grand Teton area, surrounded by three majestic mountain ranges that are home to scores of American species. To lose a vital element of the ecosystem will have effects that ripple throughout the local ecology.

You'll develop a keen eye as you hunt for nests and help to relocate color-banded tagged birds. The seasonal tracking of these study birds paints a picture we need to understand about migratory patterns, choice of home, and breeding success. You may help set up mist-net traps, band the birds for release, and complete subsequent environment surveys of vegetation and nests. It remains a frustrating mystery as to why, for the past 30 years, the chickadees, sapsuckers, grosbeaks, thrushes, warblers, woodpeckers, and vireos have been disappearing—your help might be the key to the puzzle.

You'll return home in the evenings to your comfortable residence lodges on campus at one of two Teton Science Schools. Both are beautiful facilities and close enough to town to burn off any excess energy in local pubs and restaurants (though your meals are provided on campus). Spend downtime exploring the mountains, hoping to spot some of the resident bison, wolves, bears, raptors, and trumpeter swans.

Watching songbirds in Grand Teton National Park

YOUR NEXT STEP: Earthwatch (✆ **800/ 776-0188;** www.earthwatch.org). This 9-day program, US$2,150, includes housing in campus lodge or cabin facilities, all meals, research training and instruction, and project support. A US$35 Earthwatch membership is required.

DON'T MISS: You're already based in one of America's most stunning natural areas, the Grand Tetons, so take time to explore it on a breathtakingly scenic **horseback mountain excursion.** Many trail ride providers operate out of Jackson Hole and the surrounding communities, any of whom can match you to a good horse no matter your level of riding experience and expertise.

ⓘ www.wyomingtourism.org

30 Rescue & Protection

Saving the Crocodiles

Catching Crocs at Night

Lusaka, Zambia

PEOPLE TRAVEL HERE FOR THE FAMOUS WATERFALLS, THE WALKING SAFARIS, THE BIRDS, THE lakes, the wildlife—but check out the capital's friendly people and the abundant crafts for sale at its busy markets to gain the full range of an African experience.

If you're naturally a night owl, why not make your way to the mighty Zambezi River and spend your nights catching crocodiles from a boat? Your high-powered

Nile crocodiles of Zambia

spotlight beam will flash along the banks and water level, looking for the telltale red pinpricks of a croc's eyes reflecting the light back at you. You'll ease up on them, barely coasting so as not to startle them, and eventually measure and tag them. Grab a cat nap, and then in the morning, track tagged crocodiles with radio tracking devices or visit local schools and communities to educate the locals about the importance of the crocodile.

About 70% of Zambia's flowing water makes its way into the Zambezi, the fourth largest river in Africa. This is the habitat for the Nile crocodile and a vast number of mammals, birds, amphibians, fish, and reptiles. Most of them fear the croc, which can grow to nearly 20 ft. (6m) long. The impact of hide hunting, egg harvesting, and the capture of wild animals for illegal breeding farms has severely compromised the Nile crocodile population. The research data gathered on your project will help establish conservation practices and successful species management.

You'll stay in a well-shaded campground area overlooking the river. The volunteer team pitches in and helps with cooking and cleaning, and camp life is relaxed and easy. Since the lion's share of the work is done at night for the nocturnal crocodiles, daytime is spent sleeping and getting to know your fellow volunteers. There's plenty of distraction as you watch elephants and hippos splash, grazing animals eat their way across the plains, and the occasional drama of the bush that makes high-definition wildlife television pale in comparison.

YOUR NEXT STEP: Earthwatch (© **800/776-0188;** www.earthwatch.org). The 2-week project, US$3,050, includes camp accommodations, campfire-cooked meals, croc research and interaction technique training, and project support. A US$35 Earthwatch membership is required.

DON'T MISS: You're not going to go all the way to Zambia and skip its most famous sight, **Victoria Falls.** Tribes originally called the awesome falls "the smoke that thunders," and thunder it does as more than half a million cu. m (18 million cu. ft.) of water per minute plummet over the edge during flood season.

ⓘ www.zambiatourism.com

31 Animal Habitats

Coastal Ecology

Mapping Bahamian Beaches

Long Island and Great Exuma, Bahamas

Lend a hand in studying the erratic, ebbing shorelines of the Bahamas, whether replacing native vegetation or using technology to map the coast. Your work will preserve the ecosystem and record the effects of both man and devastating natural events, helping to ensure that the area's natural beauty remains intact.

Thirty towns and major communities in the Bahamian archipelago of islands take advantage of ideal locations near the islands' shores. Those locations are only ideal as long as that shoreline stays constant, but it doesn't. Your work will include mapping and plotting the shape of the shore via GPS and satellite maps, transplanting native plants, and occasionally constructing artificial reefs to maintain the integrity of the shoreline and keep it from eroding and vanishing. Like many ecological efforts around the world, this battle is a race against time. Reversing the harm done to the environment and beginning repairs will be a slow march toward progress, but not every habitat can wait.

Development and tourism in the Bahamas has led to a greater appreciation of its beauty (and some wonderful vacations), but the price paid by the islands themselves has been dear. Caves, wetlands, marshes, rocky coasts, hardwood forest, farmland, mangrove stands, and sandy beaches are all part of the Bahamas, and the interdependence of these eco-zones is just now being studied. Your work, beyond the observation and data collection that will fill your days, may also include reforestation of coastal regions with native plant

Undertaking sampling on the shoreline of the Bahamas

10 Beaches Where Wildlife Comes First

Doing something great for the planet and having a beach vacation needn't be mutually exclusive. Work or play, you'll spend your time at the glorious junction of sand and sea, in service to some magnificent creatures.

A crocodile hatchling in Turneffe Atoll, Belize

32 Turneffe Atoll, Belize (Crocodiles) The American crocodile is endangered throughout North and South America, but in Belize it's still thriving after nearly 200 million years. You'll monitor this threatened species, collecting data on reproductive success/egg counts, nesting habits, hatchling behavior, measurement and identification of individual animals, and lots more hands-on tasks. Morning and night excursions provide the best encounters, so your days are relaxed, with project training interspersed with swimming and snorkeling. ***The Oceanic Society*** *(© **800/326-7491**; www.oceanicsociety.org). An 8-day excursion is US$1,975.*

33 Nicoya Peninsula, Costa Rica (Sea Turtles) You'll surf (or learn to), live on the beach, swim, and work researching three species of sea turtles and preparing hatcheries. Some of the work is in the middle of the night, so daytimes are sometimes spent relaxing, in surf lessons (provided at partner surf school), and exerting yourself with a siesta. It's not all play, and the work is important, as before these conservation efforts were put into place, poachers took almost 95% of unprotected sea turtles and eggs. ***i-to-i*** *(© **800/985-4852**; www.i-to-i.com). A 2-week project is US$1,345.*

34 Accra, Ghana (Shore Birds) You'll work alongside the scientist team leaders in the Important Bird Areas on Accra's shoreline, monitoring flocks, nest zones, and flight/behavior patterns. You'll also aid the community education programs of the Save the Seashore Birds Project and Wildlife Clubs that help raise awareness and appreciation of the many bird species, notably several rare types of terns, found in this region. ***Ikando*** *(© **+233/21 222 726**; www.ikando.org). A 2-week project is US$913.*

35 Zakynthos, Greece (Loggerhead Turtles) Eighty percent of the world's Mediterranean loggerhead turtles nest around this Ionian island, and the ever-expanding tourist industry has directly led to their decline. You'll do your Greek island vacation the responsible way by aiding the conservation of the species, patrolling beaches, educating tourists, rescuing injured animals, and working to clean up their beach habitat areas. You'll also pitch in at the Sea Turtle and Wildlife Information Centre. ***Global Vision International*** *(© **888/653-6028**; www.gviusa.com). A 2-week project is US$1,700.*

36 Shimoni, Kenya (Dolphins and Whales) This small archipelago of islands near the border with Tanzania is a magnet for cetaceans. You'll spend time in and on the water amid whale sharks and manta rays and observe and record data on dolphins and humpback whales. Inland, you'll survey Colobus monkeys, as well as promote anti-poaching campaigns and community outreach projects with local villagers. ***Global Vision International*** *(© **888/653-6028**; www.gviusa.com). A 5-week intensive program is US$3,150.*

Bottlenose dolphins in Shimoni, Kenya

37 Michoacan, Mexico (Sea Turtles) Volunteering with the local university and villagers, you'll work with Negra and Golfina sea turtles: collecting eggs, reburying them in the protected sands of Turtle Camp, attending to the needs of hatchling turtles, and collecting statistical information. When the time comes, you'll transport baby turtles back into the sea. Your downtime will be relaxing in coco-palm-constructed shelters on the practically virgin beach. ***Canadian Alliance for Development Initiatives and Projects*** *(© **604/628-7400**; www.cadip.org) A 2-week trip is US$265, with another US$265 paid directly to the project upon arrival.*

38 Ranong Province, Thailand (Sea Turtles) This project's biosphere reserve protects the mangrove forests that lend viability to the struggling turtle population. Project workers also care for macaques and gibbons in the neighboring rescue center when not monitoring turtle nests, identifying flipper tracks, and tagging and recording adults and nests. ***Center for Cultural Interchange*** *(© **312/944-2544**; www.cci-exchange.com). The 3-week program is US$1,650.*

39 Mahe, Seychelles (Coral Reef Species) Scuba skills will come in handy as you make twice-daily dives around this reef in the Indian Ocean, collecting research data on coral and fish species, whale sharks, turtles, octopus, and lobster species. The data helps paint the picture of the reef ecosystem's health and is used by the Seychelles government for marine wildlife management policies. ***Global Vision International*** *(© **888/653-6028**; www.gviusa.com). The 35-day trip is US$3,370.*

40 Aberdeenshire, Scotland (Whales and Dolphins) The northeast coast whales and dolphins are threatened with becoming as difficult to spot as the Loch Ness Monster. The Cetacean Research and Rescue Unit will take you out in inflatable boats to spot them, record their behavior and location, and make note of pod behaviors. When back on shore, you can pair the research with other gathered data to create thorough field reports. You may also help with the rescue of stranded marine animals. ***Earthwatch*** *(© **800/776-0188**; www.earthwatch.org). An 11-day project is US$2,450. A US$35 Earthwatch membership is required.*

41 St. George Island, Alaska, USA (Fur Seals) The Prilobof Islands in the Bering Sea (known as the Galapagos of the North) are home to a high density of marine and land animals, including the northern fur seal, whose numbers and viability are monitored by this project's scientist-led team. You'll carry out observations from a rookery and take notes on the size of the herd, genders, ages, and behaviors. The terrain is rugged but beautiful. ***Earthwatch*** *(© **800/776-0188**; www.earthwatch.org). A 10-day excursion is US$3,250. A US$35 Earthwatch membership is required.*

species. Some of the ecological damage is due to natural forces (such as Hurricane Ike in 2008), and much is due to man. It is hard, exhausting work, but the result can have an immediate impact on soil retention, an invigorated tidal zone life and habitat, and other benefits for the shore plants and animals above and below the tide line.

You'll be based in shared apartments or dormitory-style housing, where food is provided (you'll prep your own breakfast and lunch, while dinners are made for you), and there are plenty of distractions during your free time. Wander the settlements and explore the island or take to the waves—snorkeling, boat trips among the many islands (some uninhabited), or just crashing on the beach can all be on your itinerary. You'll close your eyes and rest with a particular satisfaction as you listen to waves lap the shore, knowing that you're part of the reason that shore is there.

YOUR NEXT STEP: Earthwatch (© **800/776-0188;** www.earthwatch.org). This 11-day project, US$2,350, covers shared accommodations in apartments or dormitories, meals, research training, and project supervision and support. A US$35 Earthwatch membership is required.

DON'T MISS: It's been around for less than a decade, but the **National Art Gallery of the Bahamas,** in an 1860s-era Nassau villa, has an important collection of art from Bahamian artists as well as some unexpected ex-pats. You probably wouldn't predict you'd have to come to the islands to see originals by Winslow Homer. www.nagb.org.bs

(i) www.bahamas.com

Animal Habitats **42**

Rehabilitation of Abused Animals

Nursing Wildlife Back to Health

Villa Tunari, Bolivia

THE ACCOMMODATIONS ARE SPARTAN BUT SUFFICIENT AND THE DIFFICULT WORK OF WITNESSING what happens to neglected or abused animals may move you to tears. Once your important work here is done, travel to sunny Cochabamba or the country's largest city, Santa Cruz de la Sierra, for some R&R: Villa Tunari is about halfway between the two.

At this pair of neighboring wildlife refuges, you may spend 2 weeks assigned to one particular animal that needs your care and attention or perhaps work with many animals and species every day. There are monkeys, birds, and reptiles here, along with a few larger animals like wild cats. Dozens of animals are brought to the refuge every week. Parque Ambue has more varied work, but Parque Machia has better living facilities (electricity, hot showers, and so on) and included meals, so you'll decide which is best suited to your goals and interests. Although rewarding, this volunteer opportunity can be emotionally challenging. You'll see the results of animal cruelty, abuse, and environmental damage. To counter these forces is the purpose of the refuge.

The project is eager for volunteers, and many people choose to drop in. The park's philosophy toward animals extends to human volunteers: none are turned away. Since there are permanent volunteer translators, you needn't be fluent in Spanish, but of course it helps. Your work time, from 7:30am to 6:00pm, will be varied in its demands and the ebb and flow of duties, with new challenges every day (if not every hour). Feeding, playing, cleaning, and lots of hands-on care is the order of the day for your charges. Longer-term volunteers with additional training even get the opportunity to walk wild cats for exercise along jungle paths.

Life is simple at these two parks, with shared room accommodations in cabins or tents. Meals are provided at one park, and must be purchased in town at the other. Basic kitchen facilities allow for self-catering, and local restaurants are very inexpensive (US$4–US$5 per dinner, less for breakfast and lunch). The parks are also open to the public during the day, so you'll have the chance to share your incredible experiences.

YOUR NEXT STEP: Comunidad Inti Wara Yassi (no phones in park, e-mail: intiwarayassi@gmail.com; www.intiwara yassi.org). This 2-week excursion, US$145-$200], includes simple accommodations and meals (only at one of the camps, the other is self-catering), training, and care education. Your independent spirit and ability to get along without lots of supervision is a definite plus here.

DON'T MISS: It is practically a requirement when visiting Bolivia to be sure to go to **Lake Titikaka** and the shore town of Copacabana, a former Inca ceremonial site with astrological observation ruins and temples. The Copacabana Virgin statue is now a pilgrimage stop for hundreds of believers every August 5.

(i) www.visitbolivia.org

Animal Habitats

Crocodile Conservation Center

A Month of Reptile Research

Chennai, India

You'll be a master-of-all-trades—snake and croc wrangler, English translator, safari guide, and general good company to those you encounter. In your spare time, visit Chennai's temples and churches, a testament to the city's diversity.

In the 1980s, 8 acres (3ha) of coastal land south of Chennai (formerly known as Madras) was set aside as a trust for the study and conservation of India's three types of crocodile: the mugger, the gharial, and the saltwater. Beginning with just 30 adult crocs, the center has bred more than 5,000 crocs over 30 years, and today it houses more than 2,400 crocodiles representing 14 species, as well as a dozen endangered species of turtle and tortoise. Several other reptiles and amphibians elicit squeals of delight, such as monitor lizards, pythons, iguanas, and King Cobras. This humble spot of land along the world's longest stretch of beach is now India's most important center for reptile/amphibian conservation, study, and education.

If scaly things are your passion, you'll have plenty of contact as you feed and water animals, clean and maintain enclosures, help the scientific staff collect data, help support the education camp working with local children, act as an English-speaking visitor guide, lead day and night safaris, and facilitate and supervise visitor handling of non-dangerous pythons and baby crocodiles.

It is a month-long assignment, so you'll really get to know the distinct personalities of many of the animals in your care and certainly gain an appreciation for a herpetologist's expertise in the field of crocodilian studies. That's like a major in crocodiles with a minor in snakes and lizards. You'll live simply at the center's facilities, with two meals provided daily and easy access to the big-city life of Chennai (India's fourth largest city).

YOUR NEXT STEP: Twin Work & Volunteer Abroad (✆ **800/80 483 80;** www.workandvolunteer.com). This 1-month project, US$1,495, includes group accommodations on-site, two meals daily, training, and full project support.

DON'T MISS: Since you're in the spirit of volunteering and helping where help is needed, it could be fascinating to see the progress at **Marina Beach.** More than 8 miles (13km) long, it is the world's longest beach and was slammed hard by the December 26, 2004, tsunami. Horrific death and destruction struck that day, but the community continues to work hard and has made real progress toward revitalizing the area.

ⓘ www.tamilnadutourism.org

Animal Habitats **44**

Wildlife Rehabilitation Center

South African Safe Haven

Hoedspruit, South Africa

BEASTS LARGE AND SMALL FIND RESPITE AND REHABILITATION AT THIS SANCTUARY FOR threatened, injured, and otherwise needy species. For those who want to take their education a step further—and relax a bit—arrange for an excursion to nearby Kruger National Park, the largest game reserve in the country.

It's tough being a wild animal in Africa. There's that pesky food chain, upon which you can never really be high enough; there's the hot, dry weather; and there's often a big lack of fresh drinking water. Add humans meddling with your home; food, water, and freedom of movement, and the odds aren't exactly in your favor. The Moholoholo Wildlife Rehabilitation Centre tries to provide respite and a safe haven for the endangered species of South Africa. Some have been abandoned, others orphaned, more poisoned, and many injured by natural or man-made dangers. Sick and injured wildlife is brought to the center from far and wide to be rehabilitated and, in the best-case scenario, reintroduced to the wild. Animals that can't be returned to their natural habitat become ambassador animals for the center that help educate schoolchildren and visitors. Moholoholo also runs a terrifically successful breeding program for threatened species.

You'll spend cherished hours hand-rearing orphaned cheetahs or warthogs, caring for and feeding resident ambassador animals, aiding the medical care of injured and recovering animals, and helping in the capture of injured wild animals and, if you're timing is right, the release of rehabilitated animals. You'll keep the more mundane aspects of a wild animal habitat in top shape and contribute to food preparation, cleaning, the repair of habitats and enclosures, and some office work.

Home is in dormitory-style shared rooms with hot showers, a communal lounge, and kitchen facilities. Your meals are provided at the sister business, a safari lodge attended by tourists, where you'll dine with staff. You're out in the bush, quite near Kruger Park, so much of your free time will likely be spent on non-work game drives and relaxing at camp—you'll need your strength for the animals.

YOUR NEXT STEP: Enkosini Eco Experience (USA: ✆ **206/604-2664;** www.enkosiniecoexperience.com). Your time at Moholoholo can be as brief as 1 week, US$995, but you'll probably want to stay longer.

The fee includes all meals, housing at the center's volunteer facilities, field training in animal care and husbandry, extra activities (safari game drives, for example), and transport from Hoedspruit to the center.

DON'T MISS: Just 10 miles (16km) from Hoedspruit is a small regional airport where you can take to the skies on a wonderful **microlight flight** over the game reserves. See the bird's-eye view of the animals and ecology in which you've been immersed, from what amounts to little more than a bicycle with wings and a small motor.

ⓘ www.southafrica.com

45 **Animal Habitats**

Baboon Sanctuary

Protecting Primates

Phalaborwa, South Africa

YOUR IMPORTANT PROTECTION WORK TAKES PLACE AMID A TOURIST'S PLAYGROUND. DRIVE through the Drakensberg Mountains on the popular Panorama Route, and linger over the spectacular views that give this self-drive its name. Close to the project site is Kruger National Park, which includes 16 eco-zones; here you'll see wildlife that runs the gamut of South Africa's animal kingdom.

The Baboon Sanctuary doesn't discriminate. No matter what kind of animal you are—mammal, raptor, reptile, or bird—you can find nurturing care here. The eponymous mascot animal, however, is the Chacma baboon, and more than 400 of them live here, most of them orphans receiving long-term or lifetime care. Baboons, while classified as "threatened," receive no protection under South African law, and are regularly shot or poisoned by farmers, captured for the pet trade, killed and dissected for traditional spiritual and medicinal purposes, and/or fall victim to human obstacles like road accidents and power lines. Former laboratory animals also are given refuge here after occasional releases and confiscations.

The goal is to rehabilitate and release as many animals back into the wild as possible, and sometimes full troops of baboons can be returned to open territory. (As habitat is compromised, however, these opportunities become more rare every day.) There is also a resident troop of about 60 wild baboons that lives just outside the sanctuary, filling the trees along the river at night and interacting with the residents, both human and primate. You'll assist in daily operations at the sanctuary, as well as helping in the rehabilitation program. The days are full and exhausting as you move from one enclosure to the next, each holding a troop of up to 18 baboons. You might start the day at the baby baboon crèche changing diapers, bottle feeding, and playing with youngsters, fill water containers and feed trays after lunch, and be on behavioral observation duty all afternoon. However your day is divided, you will have plenty of primate time.

You are in a remote locale far from the next small town but can head in on food runs if you need a dose of civilization. Rustic cabin and tent accommodations are home to the volunteer team (and your morning wake-up call will probably be young baboons scampering across the roof), and everyone pitches in to clean and cook mostly vegetarian meals. The sanctuary borders a malarial zone, so be sure to check with your doctor about inoculations before your trip.

YOUR NEXT STEP: Enkosini Eco Experience (✆ **206/604-2664;** www.enkosiniecoexperience.com). The Baboon Sanctuary needs volunteers to make a 4-week commitment, US$1,695, which includes rustic housing in cabins, tents, or converted containers, communal meals, intensive training, project support, and a guarantee of constantly changing duties.

DON'T MISS: After a month in the rough with a bunch of apes, you may feel the need for some of the finer things, like a few days in South Africa's terrific wine country. **Stellenbosch** is the country's leading wine area, a shady, quiet country town full of vintner's estates, a young vibe with the local university, elegant tasting rooms, and quite a few dining options from upscale to simple street food. www.tourismstellenbosch.co.za

ⓘ www.southafrica.com/limpopo/phalaborwa

Animal Habitats 46

Wild Horse Sanctuary

Living Free in the Black Hills

Hot Springs, South Dakota, USA

THIS PART OF AMERICA BRIMS WITH ICONOGRAPHY—IMAGINE OLD WEST COWBOYS, OR soaking your weary bones in the hot springs for which this southern Black Hills Town is named. Mount Rushmore and the Freedom Trail are nearby, too. But this wildness—specifically the horses—is also threatened.

Every year the US government rounds up wild horses and puts them up for adoption. Herds have grown so large, and available grazing land and open territory has become so small, that the land can no longer sustain all the animals that call it home. The capture-and-adopt mission is a noble effort, born of right ideals, but the program's effectiveness has decreased each year. Fewer individuals and ranches are interested in adopting wild mustangs, and animals go unadopted and uncared for, meaning that many eventually have to be put down. Rancher Dayton Hyde saw hundreds of formerly wild mustangs languishing in government feedlots and dedicated himself to creating a wild horse sanctuary in South Dakota.

More than 400 horses now run free across 11,000 acres (4,452ha) of canyons and riverbanks in the Black Hills. The sanctuary is run entirely by volunteers, many coming for a week or two, some never leaving. What you will do on this project will depend somewhat upon the season you visit, but rest assured you'll be busy. Some of the horses are "special needs" and need to be fed, watered, and cared for more attentively than their wild brethren. At certain times of year, horses must be moved from one pasture zone to another to allow grass to regrow for the next season. Other odd jobs you might perform or help with include giving tours of the sanctuary, mending fences, even working in the gift shop.

There is a cabin for rent overlooking the river to call home (book early) and RV hookups if your home is mobile. There is no cost for volunteers, and your meals and entertainment off-project will be up to you. Stay as long as you like, and then stay longer—the horses need you.

YOUR NEXT STEP: Black Hills Wild Horse Sanctuary (✆ **800/252-6652;** www.wildmustangs.com). No cost to volunteers, except burning lots of calories working hard. A cabin is available for rent (US$150 a night), and meals and other costs are your responsibility. Full training in horse care and other project specifics is provided.

Wild mares in the Black Hills of South Dakota

DON'T MISS: Nearby, you'll find the **Mammoth Site of Hot Springs, South Dakota,** the world's largest mammoth research facility and site of ongoing paleontological digs and an interactive museum. Some 26,000 years ago, a sinkhole caved in, and wandering mammals came to drink from the bubbling springs but were unable to get out of the sinkhole. An inordinately large number of fossilized remains are still being uncovered in this treasure trove of natural history. www.mammothsite.com

(i) www.hotsprings-sd.com

47 Animal Habitats

Western Wildlife Trails

Animal Corridors Along the Continental Divide

Salt Lake City, Utah, USA

In Red Butte Canyon, wildlife need safe routes to find food and survive, and humans keep interrupting their pathways. If you're a trailblazing person who loves hiking, tracking, and keeping close eyes on your surroundings, this trip may be just the challenge you're looking for.

You'll hike deer trails in rugged mountains, occasionally tearing your eyes from the magnificent scenery to look at the GPS tracking device you carry to map game trails and kill sites, notate wildlife census information, count tracks, and survey vegetation. You'll also prepare carnivore scent and track stations, and capture it all on film with remote cameras you'll monitor. You'll be on your feet and covering hilly ground for 5 to 6 hours a day, so bring moleskin for blisters.

Some of your trails are the same ones used by Lewis and Clark a couple of centuries ago, and your goal is to help design effective wildlife corridors along the western edge of the Continental Divide. The open region has been fragmented, and populations of wildlife get more and more isolated all the time, which seriously reduces their health. A corridor linking free-range areas can work if the animals will use it to get from one zone to another regularly or seasonally. The research on this project helps to understand travel and behavior patterns, which will be the basis for corridor creation through these mountains.

You'll bunk in a university guesthouse with shared accommodations, your hearty breakfast is in the field, and you'll have easy access to student dining areas for dinners (included). A parallel project occurs in Pierce Creek, Idaho, where lodging is in cabins and meals are prepared together and shared.

YOUR NEXT STEP: Earthwatch (© **800/776-0188;** www.earthwatch.org). This 8-day project, US$1,950, includes research technique training, project support, housing in shared university facilities (or cabins for the Idaho project), and meals. A US$35 Earthwatch membership is required.

DON'T MISS: You have to be relatively fit to hike the 1,065 vertical ft. (325m) to the entry of the astounding caverns of the **Timpanogos Cave National Monument,** a system of caves and tunnels high in the Wasatch Mountains. Occasional evening programs (both underground and above ground at dusk) offer spectacular views of the American Fork Canyon. www.nps.gov/tica

(i) www.slctravel.com

2 Working with Children

Students running through the streets of Udaipur

Orphanages 48

Direct Care Projects

Orphan Care in the Land of Che Guevara

Unquillo, Argentina

IF YOU'RE THE KIND OF PERSON WHO REVERES NATURE BUT LIKES PROXIMITY TO CITIES—AND all the art galleries, colonial architecture, restaurants, and nightlife they offer—Unquillo, with its verdant mountainsides in plain view, situates you well, close to Argentina's second-largest city.

The majority of children (from infants to 10-year-olds) you'll be serving in this project have been orphaned or abandoned in and around Córdoba, Argentina's second largest city, and are now residents of small group homes and orphanages in Unquillo, about 20km outside the city. You'll also have the opportunity to work with children with physical or developmental disabilities who just need someone to spend time with and pay attention to them or help with physical therapy and other tasks. Even with the best-intentioned (but overworked) staff meeting the physical needs of the kids, food, shelter, and medical attention do not a childhood make. Volunteers bridge a deep gap between sustenance and success.

You will have almost as varied a day as you would as a parent, from helping with mealtimes and playtime, to entertaining with games, song, dance, or quiet-time reading, to getting a group to nap, and helping older children with homework when they return from their school day. You might take a group of kids on a day trip, plan a talent show, or work with a team of little ones to plant window boxes before reorganizing the toy shelf in the group room. Design new activities to engage one or a handful of children and you are a hero. You're a hero anyway, with just the smallest gestures, from someone taking the time to brush hair or fingerpaint or play a game of checkers to teaching how to draw or to bake banana bread. At the care homes for children with special needs, some may be older than at the orphanages, but the same craving for personal attention and connection will drive you and fill your days.

When you come to the end of long and exhausting days, you'll return to your host family to enjoy traditional homemade meals and the support of a familial-type bond with people who go out of their way to nurture you while in Unquillo. Days off will fly by with so much to do and see in the area. You're quite close to metropolitan Córdoba for urban exploration, or head away from the city into magnificent countryside for hiking and trekking to Pan de Azucar mountain and other national parks and lakes.

YOUR NEXT STEP: Projects Abroad (✆ **888/839 3535;** www.projects-abroad.org). They'd be delighted if you'd stay longer, but 2 weeks, US$2,345, includes accommodations with a host family, all meals, training and support, and comprehensive medical and travel insurance. While you can get along without it, some conversational Spanish will be a big help for interacting with the children and care-home staff.

DON'T MISS: Elevating Che Guevara to a cultural icon is controversial for many, but there is no denying that the home where he grew up is an attraction for many visitors. The **House of Ernesto Che Guevara** in Alta Gracia is chock-a-block with his personal effects, writings, photos, and exhibits about the life and death of this famous Argentinean.

ⓘ www.turismo.gov.ar

49 Orphanages

Orphan Group Home

Parenting in Bulgaria

Plovdiv, Bulgaria

ANCIENT CIVILIZATION BUFFS, TAKE NOTE: PLOVDIV IS BULGARIA'S SECOND-LARGEST CITY, called the "city of the seven hills" because of its mountainous location on the two banks of the Maritsa River. But it's also one of Europe's oldest settlements, predating Athens and Constantinople, replete with unspoiled ruins and cobblestone streets.

A group home with 140 young members, ages 5 to 15, uses international volunteer forces to supplement the care and attention resident children receive. Most kids are socially disadvantaged and some may have learning disabilities. Living in a group home—sharing meals, playtime, and sleeping quarters with other kids—is seen as an important aspect of adapting to life in mainstream society, as is having the influence of adult staff and volunteers. Run more along the lines of a boarding school than an orphanage, these are youngsters who, like all of us, crave attention and an outlet for their energy.

This program is set up as a work camp for volunteer participants between the ages of 18 and 35. Your time with the kids at Rodopski Pansion will be intense because you'll live and work under the same roof. It's a bit like being a cruise director, as you'll be asked to organize games, sporting events, gardening, workshops, walks in the city, and field trips to museums and other civic sites. You may also lead teams as you take on domestic and simple maintenance tasks at the home. While some staff members are bilingual, past volunteers have found that without a lick of Bulgarian language, communication still flows, and some of the time the youngsters will enjoy practicing English as a supplement to their school language studies. Your creativity and breadth of ideas will be tested as the students quickly master new games and songs: teach urban dance or the jitterbug, choral singing or still-life drawing, carpentry or painting—there is an insatiable appetite for new experiences. Sharing photos and stories from your home is often quite fascinating for kids who have, to this point, not made it very far from this stand-in for home. Older children will benefit from some life-skills coaching as they prepare to move out on their own—everything from setting up mock job interviews to reading road maps contributes to independent success.

You'll live at the orphanage boarding house in a wing separate from the children and enjoy meals prepared by the on-site kitchen staff. It is a complete immersion into the world of this Bulgarian care home, where you'll spend so many of your waking and sleeping hours. Exploring the city and nightlife are great ways for the volunteer team to blow off steam.

YOUR NEXT STEP: Canadian Alliance for Development Initiatives and Projects (✆ **604/628-7400;** www.cadip.org) The 2-week project, US$277, includes accommodations on-site, meals, and project training and support. You'll get yourself to the project site for the first day of work camp. Designed for participants ages 18 to 35.

DON'T MISS: In the heart of capital city, Sofia, you'll find her most admired piece of architecture, the **St. Alexander Nevski Memorial Church,** a copper and golden dome-topped Byzantine beauty outside and in. The jaw-dropping interior is resplendent with Italian marble, Brazilian onyx, African alabaster, frescoes, and woodcarvings by the best Bulgarian and Russian artists. The crypt is home to a large collection of icons and murals from the country's many monasteries.

ⓘ www.bulgariatravel.org

Orphanages **50**

Farm Orphanage

Rural Living at the Thai Border

Koh Kong, Cambodia

CLOSE TO TOURISM SPOTS IN THAILAND AND PHNOM PENH, KOH KONG IS A QUIET PLACE that might appeal to someone wanting to raise a family. For children who've lost their parents, this project provides the idyllic farm life that those who brought them into the world may have wanted to give them. That's where volunteers like you come in.

So many children who grow up without parents or a family home are in large urban orphanages and group homes; while these institutions may care very well for the children's practical needs, much of the exploration and adventure of childhood gets lost. This rural Cambodian area near the Thai border is where you'll find a terrific little orphanage farm project, where kids have a home and assembled family among the necessary discipline and wonderful exuberance of farm life. Cattle, pigs, and ducks also live here, so the heartwarming—and eventually heartbreaking—work of raising and nurturing animals is part of everyday life for children here, balanced with schoolwork and social interactions with their fellow residents.

You'll focus on the kids (of course, if you'd like to milk cows, slop pigs, and collect eggs, surely nobody will stop you) and their enrichment. Teach them new games and sports, converse in English so their language skills can grow outside the pressure of the classroom, lead groups in painting, drawing, or clay workshops, and teach some games with cards, dominoes, checkers, and more. Even simple instructions and new skills on which to focus are incredibly helpful: playing Hangman in English requires plenty of bilingual knowledge and learning tic-tac-toe takes strategizing and problem-solving skills. (Then move on to chess!)

You'll be living at the farm/orphanage, staying in rooms with your fellow volunteers, and taking meals that the staff prepares with the team and children. Even when you aren't "on duty," you're part of the farm community and will share quiet moments as well as chaos with the group. For getaway days off, the surrounding area is naturally stunning, with beautiful valleys, beaches, and crashing waterfalls. As a border town with Thailand, Koh Kong offers plenty of shops, restaurants, and some nightlife if you need a little "adult time."

YOUR NEXT STEP: Take Me to Volunteer Travel (✆ 65/6220-1198; www.takemetovolunteertravel.com). Volunteer posts at the farm/orphanage can be as brief as 3 days or as long as 1 month. 3 nights: US$440; 1 week: US$470; 2 weeks: US$550. Fees cover lodging and meals at the farm, airport transfers, project training and support, and a donation to the orphanage.

DON'T MISS: At the slow-paced village of **Kratie** on the banks of the Mekong River, you can meet some of the most honored residents—freshwater dolphins. French

Sharing a meal at a Cambodian farm orphanage

architecture that survived the ravages of war sits side by side with Khmer buildings, and the very rare Irrawaddy dolphins (perhaps as few as 15 remain) swim the river just north of town. Choose from a couple sedate little resorts along the river to enjoy a lazy day or three.

ⓘ www.tourismcambodia.com

51 Orphanages

Rural Children's Home

Orphan Entrepreneurs

Hebei, China

IN THE NORTH OF CHINA, OUTSIDE OF BEIJING, YOU'LL FIND THE LARGE RURAL AREA OF HEBEI, famous for its delicate porcelain. Sandwiched between Beijing and Tianjin, the province boasts the easternmost end (and less visited portion) of the Great Wall. This is your backdrop for a project that will appeal to people dedicated to lending a hand to children just when they need it.

The orphanage project here—with a portion of its residents being students with disabilities—is an amalgam of interests. In order to bring more income into the orphanage and disabled care facility, they've opened a bakery that employs residents of both. Volunteers work with the children on everything from language studies and other school lessons to finessing business plans to increase the support from the bakery. The kids are quite effective entrepreneurs and have launched a home delivery service for baked goods.

Your work as a supportive volunteer will engage you on several levels, from child-focused play and mentoring to repairing wheelchairs and other rehabilitative apparatus, to strapping on an apron and baking. The bread that you and the now gainfully employed residents bake will be sold and delivered (hop on that bike and pedal) to funnel income into a fund for more wheelchairs and orthopedic equipment. You may also go off-site to some foster homes that are partnered with the orphanage to help with simple maintenance and repairs, perhaps painting a newly placed foster child's bedroom or assisting a skilled electrician or plumber who will make repairs to structures to assure the children who have arrived in new homes have the best environment possible.

You'll be staying at the orphanage along with the resident children, and dining there as well. Day in and day out, your influence and passion will bring a breath of fresh air. The volunteer teams are eagerly anticipated, since every visiting worker has stories and even personalities that seem exotic when your horizons don't extend beyond Hebei. Hearing about your life and basking in the care and attention you bring helps to impart not just skills and hands-on help but hope as well.

YOUR NEXT STEP: Take Me to Volunteer Travel (✆ **65/6220-1198;** www.takemetovolunteertravel.com). The duration of your stay is negotiable, but a general 2-week period, US$780, includes food and lodging on-site, airport transfers, project support and guidance, and a donation that will extend the reach of your work with the children.

DON'T MISS: In nearby Beijing, take a side trip to visit the **Lama Temple,** built in 1694, one of the largest and most important Tibetan Buddhist monasteries in the world. Originally the residence of the royal court, the temple is intricately ornamented and a treasury of Buddhist art. The names of rooms alone are inspirational: the Hall of Harmony and Peace, the Hall of Everlasting Protection, the Hall of the Wheel of the Law, and the Pavilion of Ten Thousand Happinesses.

ⓘ www.cnto.org

Orphanages **52**

Orphanage Outreach

Jack of All Trades

Monte Cristi, Dominican Republic

IN RECENT YEARS, THE DOMINICAN REPUBLIC HAS EMERGED AS THE NEXT GREAT CARIBBEAN destination. From the mountains to the coastline, you can hike, golf, swim, snorkel, or just relax on the beach. But Monte Cristi, on the northwestern tip of the country and home to a national park, is off the beaten path for most travelers, so you can enjoy its splendor in relative quiet.

There's no reason to become a grumpy Miss Hannigan when working at this Dominican orphanage, but you will be worked hard as a Jack- or Jill-of-all-trades as you become indispensable around the facilities for a week or two. This orphanage houses about 40 boys and girls, and they have opened a new learning center with computer labs and an English institute to help the kids in their studies. In addition to a dedicated staff that is like a surrogate family for these kids, international volunteers pitch in to help, exposing the children to diverse stories, languages, cultures, and love.

You'll live at the orphanage facilities, so there's no time wasted commuting—you are up and active from breakfast onward.

After helping out in the kitchen and dining room, perhaps the morning is spent cleaning and working with the littlest residents who don't head off to school. Games, songs, short lessons, storytelling, puzzles—plenty of activities will make the early hours fly by until lunch. Another round of meal preparation and serving/cleaning and then it's more hours to fill until the older kids return from school. Maybe some gardening work outdoors or light repair work, then more creative ways to fill the younger kids' day. When the school-age kids return, you can tutor and help with homework, create English conversation groups for language practice, and help with the children's chores—there's always more to do. Dinner, more quality time with individual children or small groups, and everybody is ready for bed early; the next day starts soon.

Accommodations are summer-camp-like, in ramadas (traditional sun shelters) with permanent floors and roofs but tarpaulin walls to allow maximum air circulation. The town of Monte Cristi in the north is small and quiet, with industry, the salt flats, and fishing providing the roots of the modest economy. After bounteous meals prepared by the local chef at the orphanage, a walk through the sleepy town is a great way to explore and find some evening quiet time. For an excursion on your day off, there's a beautiful national park beach nearby.

YOUR NEXT STEP: **Orphanage Outreach** (✆ **602/375-2900;** www.orphanage-outreach.org). Your tenure on this project can be from a week to several months. 1 week: US$800; 2 weeks: US$1,200. Fees include accommodations in group camp structures (modern bathrooms and showers, but no hot water), meals prepared by a local cook, project training, and in-country transportation. Project staff is on-site with you and always available for support.

DON'T MISS. See some Jurassic-era sights at the **Amber Museum** in Puerto Plata. It contains a large collection of the world's preserved insects, plants, and small animals that were trapped in the golden goo that solidified with the decades. The amber-trapped mosquito of the movie *Jurassic Park* is here, and it's the least of the now precious sepia glimpses into the past.

ⓘ www.godominicanrepublic.com

53 Orphanages

Child Care Work

Lending a Hand in Addis Ababa

Addis Ababa, Ethiopia

THOSE OLD ENOUGH TO REMEMBER THE LIVE AID CONCERTS PROBABLY FIRST LEARNED ABOUT Ethiopia as an African country stricken with poverty and famine. The situation has improved, but much work remains for those with a generous spirit, a way with children, and a genuine interest in improving the plight of children in Africa's fourth-largest city.

In decades past, Ethiopian children were iconic images of starvation and suffering to people around the world, with images of their distended bellies and exposed ribs broadcast on newscasts around the globe. Famine and conflict remain serious issues, but the added scourge of HIV/AIDS combined with widespread poverty has left far too many children orphaned and trying to make a life on their own. Childhood, as we know it, is a luxury these youngsters don't have, as they become adults by necessity

Working with children in Addis Ababa

before their age is in double digits. Even those in homes face incredible odds against improving their lot—more than 75% of Ethiopians live on less than the equivalent of US$1 a day. This project works with several children's facilities throughout the nation's capital, supporting overworked and underpaid staff to bring consistency and stability into the lives of these children.

Your work with these astoundingly resilient kids will be at several locales, from orphanages to day-care centers, kindergartens, and group care homes. In addition to hands-on work with children of many ages (changing diapers, feeding, joining in playtime, and supporting studies and homework), you may also be asked to take a group on an outing in the city, to a field for sports or other games, or just come out to share a picnic meal in the fresh air. Depending on the timing of your stay, you'll participate in one of several annual fundraising events, crucial to the project's survival. Informal English lessons encourage the children to use their new language skills, which is also an important element of your contribution.

Your time away from the children's facilities is spent with a volunteer host family. Your meals are taken care of, and the large city of Addis Ababa has lots to see and experience. Go slowly at first, since the city is at such a high elevation that you'll find yourself winded and exhausted after very little effort.

YOUR NEXT STEP: Projects Abroad (✆ **888/839-3535;** www.projects-abroad.org). A 2-week project, US$2,395, includes meals and lodging with a host family, project training, local transportation, local staff support, and comprehensive medical and travel insurance.

DON'T MISS: On this stretch of the mighty **Nile River,** there is plenty of excitement and drama. Called *Tis Isat* locally, the Blue Nile Falls is 1,312 ft. (400m) of raging water plummeting into a chasm 150 ft. (46m) deep. The impact creates mist that produces an almost perpetual rainbow, and you can hike all around the headwaters and pools, as well as cross the river via papyrus boat.

ⓘ www.tourismethiopia.org

54 Orphanages

Orphanage Assistance

Helping Kids & Community in Rural Ghana

Accra, Ghana

Volunteers with a sense of humor, an optimistic spirit, and boundless energy will have much to offer children who have very little—physically and psychologically—in the poor areas of Ghana. When you can spare the time to nourish yourself, take a breather and relax on the beaches or explore Accra, the country's capital.

The rural areas outside Accra can be a tough place to grow up. Food and water can be scarce at times, unemployment is high, incomes are low (very often below the established international poverty level of US$2 a day), and HIV has taken an enormous toll on communities. Children, from infants to young adults, are abandoned or orphaned, some having lost their parents to AIDS, some of whom are very sick themselves. This project works with small orphanages and group homes to find powerful and caring ways to add some measure of quality to the lives of these vulnerable kids. In addition to direct work with orphaned children, the organization dedicates its efforts to several other community enrichment programs, from education and clean water systems to environmental protection and microfinance loans to start small businesses.

Your volunteer work with orphans outside Ghana's capital will be very child-centric. You'll care for them, nurture them, play games, teach simple skills as well as art, music, and sports, occasionally take groups out on jaunts to new places, and sometimes provide simple nursing attention to some dealing with HIV or other diseases. Your most important goal each morning is to make smiles bloom on faces, create laughter that comes from the belly, and help form amazing memories to push out the preponderance of bad ones. It can be emotionally taxing as you open your heart to kids facing such odds, and you can be certain that, unfair as it is, no matter how old you are, you will likely outlive plenty of them. But you will make each day better beyond measure than it would have been were you not there.

You'll live in town with fellow volunteers, perhaps with a host family or in a shared apartment for larger groups. All meals are locally sourced and prepared for you, and your evenings are free. Days off and downtime will likely be spent in and around the village you'll call home, and often motivated volunteers will opt to spend even more time with the kids, developing more enrichment activities and learning, or just gathering a group to get a change of scenery outside their normal sphere of activity. You'll be given basic language instruction for local dialects, and there is quite a bit of English (and French) spoken, so communication may be choppy but will flow, like your affection, before you know it.

YOUR NEXT STEP: Volunteers for Amelioration of Rural Areas (✆; **233/20-9425179** www.varas.org) in partnership with **Volunteer Abroad** (✆ **720/570-1702;** www.volunteerabroad.com). A 2-week project, US$570, covers accommodations in group housing or host family placement, three meals daily, local support, cultural and language orientation, and airport pickup.

DON'T MISS: One of the most relaxing areas of Ghana is at the shore, so take a day trip to or spend a few days at the Cape Coast. The main attraction here is the beach, but you can see from most vantage points the infamous Cape Coast Castle.

This UNESCO World Heritage Site is now a museum, but the former Portuguese colonial fort was the center of the slave trade, and the harrowing dungeons will be hard to forget. It brings a whole new resonance to the beach when you remember that this stretch of sand was the last African soil thousands and thousands of Africans would ever touch.

ⓘ www.touringghana.com

Orphanages **55**

Street Children Orphanage Program

Offering Protection From Drugs & Gangs

La Ceiba & Copan Ruinas, Honduras

ALTHOUGH YOUR WORK WILL TAKE PLACE IN COASTAL LOCATIONS CLOSE TO FANTASTIC ADVENTURE travel opportunities—whitewater rafting, for example—you may not need such a challenge after spending time with teenagers who sorely need attention, guidance, and some instruction in the vagaries of English slang.

In both of these Honduran cities, a population of teenagers and pre-teens have become ensnared in the worlds of drug abuse and gang membership. Many are orphans, left to fend for themselves in the streets; some were abandoned, and some have run away. The common thread that unites them is their difficult street life. This program works directly with these kids, who've been rescued by child-care organizations and placed in loving group homes. The children receive education, medical help when needed, and stability in an environment that puts their needs first—for some, it is the first time in their lives that they have been a priority.

You'll have quite an array of duties, from teaching basic English and playing games, teaching song and dance, and art projects to pitching in around the kitchen to prepare nutritious meals or maybe doing the seemingly endless loads of laundry. Your time with individual kids or small groups will engender incredible connections, as the youths tend to open up and express their true feelings to non-judgmental visitors more than staff on duty. Your ability to create trust and openness is the key to helping many of these kids deal with the anger and hurt with which their circumstances have saddled them.

You'll stay in one of these Honduran towns with a host family, who will prepare your meals and give you a feeling of connectedness to the community in which you are immersed. Some Spanish will be helpful but definitely not required, as all your contacts for the project are bilingual. To exorcise the energy of the work that may be weighing on you, days off can be spent releasing your stress at some of the best beaches around, with magnificent snorkeling and diving in one of the world's largest bio-preserves. Then it's back to the kids, who will challenge you and work your last nerve even as they work their way, indelibly, into your heart.

YOUR NEXT STEP: Global Crossroad (✆ **972/252-4191;** www.globalcrossroad.com). A 2-week project, US$1,145, includes local support and training for the project, lodging with a host family that will also prepare and provide all your meals, airport pickup, and comprehensive insurance coverage.

DON'T MISS: Quite near La Ceiba is the **Rio Cangrejal,** a river with fantastic class III and IV rapids for some invigorating white-water rafting. It is considered one of the best rafting rivers in Latin America, and hiking to the put-in spots past milder waters affords many opportunities to leap off of towering boulders into the waters below. (You can be confident of the depth when you see plenty of others living out their own dream leaps.)

ⓘ www.honduras.com

56 Orphanages

Orphanage Service

Bridging the Gap in India

Bangalore, Delhi, Dharamsala, Kolkata, India

THE FILM *SLUMDOG MILLIONNAIRE* HAS BROUGHT THE PLIGHT OF CHILDREN IN LARGE INDIAN cities to the rest of the Western world. You can make an appreciable difference in these locations but also have time to explore the dazzling, confusing, ancient, beautiful world of India while you're at it.

It isn't easy growing up parentless, and when you're in a large, crowded city and surrounded by economic hardship, it can be even more difficult to dream of a life beyond your current circumstances. A large number of poor and disadvantaged children are placed in urban orphanages throughout India, one of the more populous nations on Earth, and the challenge of meeting all their needs sometimes seems unachievable. Government programs fall short, so several non-government organizations bridge the gap with private orphanages and group shelter homes. This project works with these smaller facilities to try to bring as much quality into the lives of the children as possible. They are hopeful environments, but make no mistake, it takes tremendous effort to keep that hope alive and thriving.

Children from one of many orphanages in urban India

Your volunteer work will cast you in many roles. From surrogate parent to teacher to entertainer to confidante, wherever there is a gap, you're the one to fill it. You'll supply both practical skills and affectionate attention. Teach English, read books, coach arts and crafts projects, lead indoor and outdoor games, organize educational tours, teach personal hygiene, and encourage cooperative play. You may also work with teams of kids cleaning, mentoring with homework and monitoring their academic progress, preparing a special meal with a group of youngsters, and teaching others how to set and clear the table. Ask them to teach you a game or song or stories, and watch them come alive when an adult really wants to listen to what they have to say. To respect and welcome their contribution and really learn from them is huge—it's what we all want, to be heard and understood.

Local community organizations place volunteers at orphanages year-round, and if you prefer one city location over another, there is need in each program. Housing is in shared apartments or homes in residential neighborhoods. Occasionally (or at your request) volunteers may be placed with a host family. Meals of local cuisine are prepared for you, and the distinct differences in the regional cooking styles of these cities guarantees a culinary treat. Each city has lots to explore on your days off, from museums and parks to markets and shopping districts, all of which will seem tremendously foreign when you arrive and become as comfortable as the corner store back home as you immerse yourself in urban India.

YOUR NEXT STEP: Volunteering India (✆ **+91/124 4307993;** www.volunteering india.com). You can dedicate yourself to the kids for as little as 1 week, US$450, or up to 3 months, US$1,595. Fees cover lodging in a shared apartment with other international volunteers (or host family placement), airport transfers, cultural orientation (including greetings, customs, and basic Hindi-language teaching), English-to-Hindi language books, project training, and 24-hour local support.

DON'T MISS: When most of us imagine India, we think of heat, desert, perhaps the brown waters of the Ganges River, but India is an enormous nation with a huge variability in climate and ecological zones. For a taste of cold, snowy India, head north to the Himalayas and the state of **Ladakh.** Go to Leh Town and tour the numerous Buddhist monasteries as well as the nine-story palace in the former royal capital of the Old Kingdom—it is believed to be the inspiration for the Potala in Lhasa Tibet, perhaps the most famous Buddhist construct in the world.

ⓘ www.incredibleindia.org

Orphanages **57**

Children of the Rising Sun

Tutoring & Touring in East Africa

Watamu, Kenya

THE LOW-KEY WHITE SANDY BEACHES OF WATAMU ATTRACT VISITORS WHO ARE INTERESTED IN quiet experiences and the protected Marine National Park, teeming with sea life, including coral and sea turtles. Visitors are also close to the ancient Gede ruins of an Arab city.

Here in small rural villages on the shores of the Indian Ocean, children who are orphaned or abandoned have little chance to fend for themselves. The Children of the Rising Sun support home is where dozens of kids have found refuge and solace and a family of devoted staff and visiting volunteers who are united in guaranteeing the children's success. Several acres of land were donated by a hotelier, and dormitories and support facilities occupy part of the plot, while a fruit and vegetable farm fills the rest of the acreage, providing nutritious food for the residents. In addition to helping care for and nurture the kids, volunteers diligently help create a vocational training center and a woodworking shop.

You'll play and work with the kids, tutoring them in school lessons and homework, chatting in English for conversational practice, commandeering troops of helpers to clean and assist in the kitchen and make improvements to the facilities. Sewing, art projects, songs, and more make time pass quickly. The majority of your volunteer hours are focused on morning efforts, and afternoons are at leisure. The trip is balanced with work and excursion time, exploring the land and sea in the area with guided trips and cultural immersion programs.

A beachside hotel is home base, and while modest, there is a swimming pool, air-conditioning, and Western-style meals. You are adjacent to an enormous marine park teeming with sea life, as well as the ancient Gede Ruins of an Arab city. This vacation has built-in guided trips to these sights and more, such as a weekend foray to a local island that only uses donkeys for transportation, snorkeling, dolphin-watching boat trips, beach time, a mangrove forest to scout, and a weekend visit to the Masai Mara for an adrenaline-pumping game-spotting safari.

YOUR NEXT STEP: Eco-Resorts (✆ 866/326-7376; www.eco-resorts.com). This 13-day project, US$2,500-$3,600 depending on number of volunteers on the project, includes all accommodations (hotel and safari camp), meals, cultural programs, transfers, diver/guides, park fees, and multiple excursions.

DON'T MISS: Just outside Nairobi, you'll find the AFEW (African Fund for Endangered Wildlife) **Giraffe Centre,** where the endangered Rothschild giraffe is protected and nurtured. Make the considerable climb to the elevated feeding platform to come nose to nose with them and feed them their favorite thorny acacia branches. The colonial manor house at the centre gets plenty of these long-necked visitors, who stick their heads in the windows to see what you're up to.

ⓘ www.tourism.go.ke

58 Orphanages

Orphanage Support

Helping Out In Big-City Mongolia

Ulaanbaatar, Mongolia

How many people do you know that can say they've been to Mongolia? The journey to this extreme place will find you meeting children in extreme circumstances, where the smallest help—reading a child a story or feeding a baby—can make a big difference.

In the best of circumstances, kids in Mongolial face plenty of challenges from environmental, cultural, and economic pressures. The precarious balance of family life can be toppled far too easily with a small shift of circumstances. High levels of unemployment, and poor wages for those who can find work, mean many live below the poverty line, making for a disproportionate number of abandoned Mongolian children. In the capital city of Ulaanbaatar, it's a rare block that isn't populated by

Lending a hand in a Mongolian orphanage

homeless children (many of whom in the bitter winter weather move underground into sewers and heating vents). Children who find placement in orphanages are spared the street life, but these institutions are filled to bursting and understaffed, so that meeting the most basic needs of survival for their charges is often an accomplishment. Volunteers from around the world endeavor to pour a little love and individual attention into a minimalist system of sustenance.

You'll be posted in a children's home or orphanage to help relieve the pressure on staff and contribute time and effort to the kids who live there. Twenty orphanages and care centers are served by this far-reaching project, from infant programs to large capacity facilities that help all ages (with up to 120 residents). Your schedule and activities will depend upon the age range of the children you'll serve. If in the infant program, you'll spend most of your time on direct care of babies up to age 3, some of whom need an unusual amount of care because they are facing disabilities as well as abandonment. Older kids will need help with homework, lessons in English (care center staff will be eager to practice their English skills as well), practical help with everything from hygiene and getting dressed to job hunting, and plenty of love. Providing one-on-one attention, even if it's just a lullaby or story, is the greatest gift you can give.

A host family will introduce you to the cultural traditions that make Mongolia such a fascinating destination. Meals are provided and are a mix of local cuisine and several staples you'll recognize. Free time in Ulaanbaatar can be as vivacious or as relaxed as you'd like, with options across the spectrum from upscale dining to simple walks through residential neighborhoods or quality time with your fellow volunteers or host family.

YOUR NEXT STEP: Projects Abroad (✆ **888/839-3535;** www.projects-abroad.org). A 2-week trip, US$1,795, includes lodging with a host family, meals, project training and backup, and full insurance coverage.

DON'T MISS: For a very specific and rare cultural experience, make your way to the

Chandman district of Hovd Aimag Province to hear a **khuumii performance.** Khuumii is "diaphonic singing," where performers are able to make two distinct sounds come out at once, usually a low, rumbling throat singing with a higher tonal melody. It is an art that takes years to learn and is a tradition revered but rarely practiced by newcomers, as the skills are so difficult to learn.

ⓘ www.mongoliatourism.gov.mn

59 Orphanages

Work With Nepalese Orphans

Video Night in Kathmandu

Kathmandu, Nepal

AN ENCOUNTER WITH THE BUSY, CROWDED, MULTICULTURAL CITY OF KATHMANDU WILL stimulate the senses, but you'll also find quiet beauty in the capital's temples, architecture, and nearby World Heritage Sites.

Nepal is a tremendously gentle nation with an advanced spiritual sensibility. In addition to a challenging terrain in the Himalayas, Nepal has been through several years of political instability and crippling poverty. Kathmandu is a hubbub of noises and colors, tiny crooked streets, and bustling outdoor markets full of not only goods but gossip and laughter. In spite of all this good humor, too many children have been orphaned by war and violence or abandoned by parents who couldn't afford to feed their families. This program works with eight orphanages to add more quality to the daily life of the kids. In addition to Kathmandu, some of the facilities (and offices for the project) are in Chitwan and Pokhara.

You'll assist overworked staff by pitching in at mealtimes and with some cleaning around the orphanage. Simple English conversation is one of the most celebrated things about volunteers, as youngsters and staff alike look for any opportunity to practice English. You may teach some English lessons to small classes of children, or care for younger kids who are not yet of school age. In the afternoons, when school attendees have returned, teach some songs or poetry or art projects. Did the boys finish their homework before they went outside to play soccer? Can you get the three girls in the corner to share, in English, what's so funny and making them giggle all day? You may need to help little ones get dressed, brush their teeth, and get their shoes on the correct feet. Maybe a group is ready to be taken to the park or a museum—you'll be a perfect chaperone. You can certainly take some relaxation time, but there won't be a shortage of things to do with and for the kids.

As part of a cultural and language immersion program, you'll spend a few days placed with a host family. Through there eyes you'll experience firsthand what Nepalese life is like. The rest of the time your lodging is in a hostel in the center of town, with easy access to shops, restaurants, and other businesses just outside the door. All meals are included, and you'll find Nepalese cooking quite similar to Indian food. The busy city center and those winding roads and alleyways will fill your free time with amazing discoveries. Just taking a break for tea at a little table outside a cafe and watching the world go by will provide some of the most spectacular people-watching you've ever enjoyed.

YOUR NEXT STEP: Institute for Field Research Expeditions (© **800/675-2504;** www.ifrevolunteers.org). A 2-week program, US$745, includes accommodations (both host family and hostel), meals, cultural and language program, project training and 24-hour support, travel insurance, and in-country travel. Also: Kathmandu orphanage program with **i-to-i** (toll free: **800/985-4852;** www.i-to-i.com). A 2-week project, US$1,090, includes guesthouse accommodations, breakfasts and dinners, airport pickup, in-country orientation, and 24-hour support.

DON'T MISS: It can be hard to get a sense of the culture of Nepal since it's so diverse. Kathmandu, especially, is multiethnic, multicultural, multireligious, and multilingual. An interesting insight into this world can be found at the **National Ethnographic Museum,** with a permanent exhibition of 11 different ethnic communities (Thakali, Sherpa, Tamang, Gurung, Rai, Limbu, Chepang, Jyapu of Newar group, Magar, Sunwar, and Tharu) and their traditional homes, clothing styles, music, art, architecture, way of life, and more.

ⓘ www.welcomenepal.com

Orphanages **60**

Children's Programming & Care

Help Kids in the Shadow of the Andes

Cusco, Peru

FOR THOSE WHO WANT TO VISIT THE RENOWNED MACHU PICCHU AND LEAVE A TANGIBLE impact on the people they meet, this program pairs you with children in Cusco—helping them with homework or conversational English to improve their odds for a better financial future.

More than one million international tourists travel to and through Cusco every year, many of them on the way to Machu Picchu. But of all the millions of tourist dollars spent in this beautiful, colonial, high-altitude town, very few actually filter down to the locals. More than 50% of the families in Peru live in poverty. Kids are hit hard by a lack of education, nutrition, and job prospects, and this multifaceted project aims to level the playing field, giving kids a way out of the spiral of poverty.

You'll spend some of your time in orphanages, one for boys and one for girls, serving more than 70 local children. You'll assist staff in activities, playtime, supporting the children's English-language studies, and some minor improvement work around the facilities like painting, decorating, and gardening. Other volunteer hours are spent at the community library, helping kids with homework, teaching word games and chess, reading with them, and assisting library staff with other projects that may come up. Never fear boredom, as you'll also spend some of your time at the free education program, supporting English-language studies with conversation groups and prescribed lessons with the teachers. You'll also have the opportunity to share any vocational skills you may have, teaching kids computers, cooking, weaving, ceramics, painting, and more. So many

Children at the community library in Cusco, Peru

youngsters in Cusco place all their hope in begging or selling postcards on the streets to tourists; some may have saved and purchased an inexpensive shoe shine kit but have few other chances. Those in this program are guaranteed a better chance than polishing sneakers.

Even with this multipronged approach to serving Cusco's kids, your schedule has lots of free time to explore the Incan ruins and sacred sites all around Cusco, as well as the museums and cathedral, with its large art collection, in town. You'll stay at a hotel, and meals are provided. There is access to restaurants and bars for any taste, from edgy fusion cuisine or elegant candlelit dinners to small stands with homemade street food to scenester bars and *chicha* houses (serving the fermented corn beer).

YOUR NEXT STEP. Globalteer (✆ **+44/ 0777 150 2816;** www.globalteer.org). 1 week: £640, 2 weeks: £720. Fees cover hotel accommodations, meals, airport pickup, a donation to the project, local orientation, and project training and support.

DON'T MISS: On the border of Peru and Bolivia, take a trip to **Lake Titicaca** and the lovely, small, shoreside town of Puno. Up in the Andes Mountains, sacred, glacier-fed Titicaca is the highest navigable lake in the world at an altitude of 12,500 feet (3810m), and the floating villages, the Uros islands, are entire floating communities based on rafts made of tortora reeds.

ⓘ www.peru.info

Orphanages **61**

Orphanage Assistance

Mentoring, Culture, Beach Time

Tacloban City, Philippines

TAKE THE TIME TO CONTEMPLATE THE INFLUENCE YOU'VE HAD VOLUNTEERING WITH DISPLACED children during a walk on the country's longest bridge, the San Juanico Bridge. You can also contemplate where else you want to visit in this country of more than 7,000 islands.

Children without family structure in the Philippines find shelter and solace in orphanages and group homes that give them care and compassion. These homes focus on empowering the children to discover a productive way out of poverty and exploitation; however, while the best intentions back up the focus on the youngsters, there is often a chasm of reality between ideals and what is possible with limited staff and budget. This program puts volunteers like you into the orphanages to work with kids and staff for several hours a day, while also respecting the element of "vacation" and providing cultural programs and tours to round out your understanding of the local culture.

Your job is to be coach, teacher, parent, friend. You'll help with the children's daily routine, from personal care to dressing to helping get food into each hungry mouth at mealtimes. You'll also be an incredible help for lessons, mentoring and tutoring with English-language studies and other schoolwork. Come with some ideas of games you can teach, practical or creative skills you can impart, and sports you can teach and coach. Health education, kitchen skills, and gardening can be explored, and the one-on-one or small group teaching is the kind of personal attention that makes a meaningful difference in the children's lives.

Filipino food is fantastic, and you'll enjoy morning and evening meals that are prepared for you in the home you'll share with your host family. You'll find Filipino hospitality to be incredibly generous, and absorbing the culture and family dynamics will enrich your travel memories. Your work time each day won't be more than about 5 hours, so you'll surely make your way to the beach, explore town, go to the bustling markets and wharf, and visit nearby villages up the coast. Some excursions are built into the trip so you can see sights of importance to the culture and pride of the nation.

YOUR NEXT STEP: World Endeavors (✆ **866/802-9678;** www.worldendeavors.com). While longer commitments are certainly encouraged, 2 weeks, US$1,237, includes stay with host family, two meals daily, airport transfers, in-country travel, tours and excursions, project training, and support.

DON'T MISS: The most recognizable Filipino name for most of the rest of the world is Imelda Marcos. The **Santo Nino Shrine and Heritage Center** is a luxurious palatial residence built to her specifications while her husband was in power. It includes 13 opulent bedrooms—not one of which has ever been slept in by Marcos or any of the family or friends she intended to host there. There are phenomenal works of art and antiques filling every inch of what has become a captivating, if frustrating, attraction for visitors to see the unconscionable excess.

ⓘ www.tourism.gov.ph

62 Orphanages

HIV Orphanage

Helping the Children of AIDS Victims

Chiang Mai, Thailand

You'll need energy, creativity, and ideas to keep up with the children here as you take in Chiang Mai's beautiful natural landscape and temples, trek through the mountains, and learn about the unique hillside tribes that have settled here.

This orphanage amid the rice paddies of Northern Thailand serves parentless children who are living with HIV. Dozens of kids who have lost their parents, many to AIDS, have found a new home in this Christian-based project (which notes that volunteers are not expected to be of any particular faith and there is no element of proselytizing in the project). Don't assume that because these youngsters are fighting a life-threatening illness that they are sedate or sickly. The orphanage walls vibrate with the energy from its residents. There is full-time international and Thai staff, and they can always use more helping hands.

Volunteers organize sports activities, create new games and challenges (both physical and intellectual), teach and play music, converse in and teach English, and run arts programs. Any enrichment activities will find a valued place here. In addition to elevating the quality of life and recreation at the orphanage, you'll be able to connect in a meaningful way with individual kids, with plenty of attention and hugs. Even now, decades after the discovery of AIDS, some people still don't understand the syndrome and falsely believe that you can catch it from casual contact—and there's still a stigma attached to it here. Your physical comfort with these amazing kids goes a long way toward bolstering confidence—and confidence is healthy.

Your lodging is in a single or shared apartment with other volunteers, and you are responsible for your own meals. Plenty of low-cost eateries are near both the orphanage and the apartment. An orientation course will get you comfortable with some basic language (although English is the language at the orphanage, some Thai words will help you navigate the city in your free time), introduce the culture and history, and provide a thorough city tour. Being in Chiang Mai is a fascinating prospect, whether you're working or not. It's a truly beautiful region with plenty to see and discover, from hundreds of temples to exquisite crafts and markets to natural distractions. Organizers can also point you toward recommended optional activities, including Thai cooking classes, Thai massage courses, and jungle treks.

YOUR NEXT STEP: Volunteer Visions Thailand (✆ **330/871-4511;** www.volunteervisions.org). The 2-week project, US$695, includes apartment accommodations, training, local orientation, language, and city tours, airport transfer, and project training and support. Meals aren't included, but many inexpensive vendors and restaurants are nearby.

DON'T MISS: Kao Yai National Park is a beautiful region with rivers, jungle, expansive grassland, forest, and mountains. Nature hikes cross from one amazing ecosystem to the next, in the tracks of elephants and other wildlife. Nature puts on a breathtaking show every night at dusk when a million bats stream out of a mountain cave near the edge of the park, painting the twilight sky black as the gracefully undulating flying mammals head out over the corn fields to forage for insects.

ⓘ www.tourismthailand.org

10 Ways to Give Schools the Tools for Learning

It is fairly simple to donate money or vouchers for school supplies to children or entire villages that would not otherwise have them, but to deliver them in person into the hands of wide-eyed youngsters is a remarkable experience.

63 Guatemala City (and Rural Villages), Guatemala The Rainbow World Fund is a lesbian, gay, bisexual, transgender outreach program that each year sends a mission to Guatemala to distribute school supplies and medical items donated to the organization. Volunteers travel with two American Catholic sisters to schools, churches, and orphanages to bring them art supplies, writing instruments, paper, and more. Programs exploring spirituality and traditional healing are included. ***Rainbow World Fund*** *(© **415/431-1485**; www.rainbowfund.org). The 10-day trip is US$1,500.*

Delivering supplies to children in Copan Ruinas, Honduras

64 Copan Ruinas, Honduras Several times a year Paramedics for Children organizes school supply missions, and anyone can join these weeklong whirlwind tours to Honduran cities and villages. Built-in adventure excursions include horseback riding, nature walks, visiting ruins, and so on, and volunteers spend each night at the comfortable project hacienda. ***Paramedics for Children*** *(© **704/763-2585**; www.paramedicsforchildren.com). The 1-week fee is US$1,200 and includes a US$500 donation.*

65 Ahmedabad, India Relief Workers International (RWI) serves rural India with a focus on medical camps and school supplies for children. The RWI team provides deworming medication to every child in the schools and then distributes important educational materials. ***Relief Workers International*** *(© **413/329-5876**; www.reliefworkersinternational.com). The 12-day humanitarian trips are US$5,950.*

66 Khumbu, Nepal The trek to base camp on Mount Everest is one of those bucket list items. While you're acclimating, stopping for tea with villagers, partaking of ceremonies, and making your way up to the Khumbu ice fall, you'll stop to deliver school supplies, medical supplies, and clothing to rural villages through which you'll pass. ***World Wide Trekking*** *(© **801/230-9089**; www.wwtrek.com). This 19-day trekking excursion is US$3,500.*

67 Baltimore, Maryland, USA When you visit Baltimore, you can adopt a student and provide the school supplies, and perhaps clothing/school uniforms, he or she needs. The Fund for Social Welfare matches volunteers with financially disadvantaged families. You can do a "direct adoption" and deliver the specific items needed to families, or be anonymous and have the program deliver supplies. ***Baltimore County Department of Social Services*** *(© **410/853-3024**; www.baltimorecountymd.gov).*

68 Statewide, Connecticut, USA Read to Grow volunteers can give time to literacy and provide books to children who don't have them. Time is spent unpacking and sorting donated books or delivering them to a school. A hospital program delivers books to pediatric waiting rooms and care programs. Volunteers can also visit families of newborns at the hospital and discuss the importance of reading to children from day one. ***Read to Grow*** *(© **203/488-6800**; www.readtogrow.org).*

69 Nationwide, USA and Canada First Book gets reading materials into the hands of underprivileged children all across the United States and Canada. It is the signature charity of the US Coast Guard and uses guard warehouses and project support to move materials around the two nations. As a volunteer, you can help assemble book orders at warehouse facilities, help children-in-need charities that come to pick up books, and help with field deliveries to local organizations. ***First Book National Book Bank*** *(© **866/READNOW**; www.firstbook.org).*

70 Hoi An, Vietnam This volunteer expedition includes tutoring, refurbishing school buildings, upgrading classroom spaces, and reading to and interacting in English with children during school breaks and after-school programs. You'll distribute coloring books, crayons, and other supplies, and also distribute teaching texts to school staff. You'll also set up simple library systems and instruct locals on how to best organize, catalog, and maintain the portable libraries. ***GlobeAware*** *(© **877/588-4562**; www.globeaware.org). One week is US$1,390.*

71 International Port Cities Yacht Aid facilitates volunteer delivery of school supplies by boat captains, crews, owners, and guests on yachts that are headed to coastal towns for their own travels. The founder of the organization found such a willingness on the part of locals to help every time he came ashore that he wanted to find a way to give back. Yachters have no trouble putting a few boxes of pencils and books into the hold before setting sail and unloading to waiting schools when they arrive in port. Partnerships are everywhere from Bali to Belize, the Galapagos to Alaska. ***Yacht Aid Global*** *(www.yachtaidglobal.org).*

Children with new educational material provided by Yacht Aid

72 International This global project endeavors to get computers and computer knowledge to youth in 2,500 schools, libraries, and orphanages in 65 developing countries. Volunteers gather and then ship donated computers to small, local partner organizations. Volunteers are needed near your home to get machines ready to ship, and in the recipient countries. If you have tech skills and computer repair experience, you can be extraordinarily useful internationally, but non-computer savvy volunteers also make the project work. ***World Computer Exchange*** *(www.worldcomputerexchange.org).*

Orphanages 73

Children's H.O.P.E.

Showing Kids What They Can Do

Nationwide, USA

IT'S NOT JUST KIDS IN THE DEVELOPING WORLD THAT NEED PLENTY OF HELP. CONSIDER THE opportunity to serve in homes in many American cities with much to offer visitors. You can volunteer amid: the nonstop nature of New York; along the shores of Lake Michigan, and the skyscrapers in Chicago; the fun-loving vibe of New Orleans; and in the shadow of the renowned St. Louis Gateway Arch.

The Boys Hope Girls Hope organization has facilities in several US cities (and some in South America as well), where children from broken homes or no homes are raised in an environment of hope and promise in residential, non-institutional homes. These kids have extremely high expectations placed on them and are expected to be academic scholars and pillars of the community. They are challenged in school, on playing fields, intellectually, socially, and spiritually, to be the very best they can be. In addition to the home environment and academic rigor, these children are supported through college. While the program is residential, parents or guardians retain custody of their children and support their elevated goals while the kids live away from them.

Reading to students in the Boys Hope Girls Hope program

Volunteers like you are essential in providing these young scholars with what the program calls H.O.P.E.—Homes, Opportunities, Parenting, Education. In addition to powerful positive role models, volunteers bring a supportive air of respect to the youngsters. You can serve as a mentor or tutor to help with homework and preparation for each day's lessons; you can be an events coordinator or chaperone, taking smaller groups of kids on special enrichment field trips; you can introduce your own special skills in arts, computers, sports, or other projects that will challenge and reward these hardworking kids; and you can also help out administratively, keeping the home projects going strong and assuring the best possible service for the resident children.

There aren't organized trips with travel or stay arrangements for Boys Hope Girls Hope projects, but with homes in St. Louis, New Orleans, New York, Chicago, Cincinnati, Detroit, Cleveland, Phoenix, Baton Rouge, Southern California, and Denver, many of the most popular travel destination cities in America provide you with an opportunity to volunteer and dedicate some of your vacation time to these extraordinary people.

YOUR NEXT STEP: Boys Hope Girls Hope (national office ✆ **877/878-HOPE;** www.boyshopegirlshope.org). No organized travel arrangements for visiting volunteers, nor specific durations of volunteer options. When you know your travel plans will bring you to a BHGH city, get in touch with the local home to see how best to help support their goals.

DON'T MISS: From Bourbon Street to Wall Street, the Golden Gate Bridge to Mile High Stadium, you'll find too much to fill your days before, during, and after your volunteer time with BHGH in every city where they are found.

ⓘ www.usatourist.com

At-Risk Youth & Street Kids

Children's Community

It Takes a Village

Santa Cruz, Bolivia

BE PREPARED TO PUT YOUR TALENTS, INTERESTS, AND SKILLS TO GOOD USE ASSISTING CHILDREN in Santa Cruz. Within just a few hours of the city's recently restored central plaza, it's possible to visit Incan ruins, Jesuit missions, and a national park.

The urban center of Santa Cruz has an extraordinarily aspirational program dedicated to getting kids off the streets and into a caring shelter where food, clothing, medical care, and school are all available. More than 400 children are in the program, living in a de facto "village" where they study, play, and are cared for in ways that seem quite foreign to so many that had found themselves cast out. Volunteers and tireless staff provide a bottomless well of love and support to foster genuine confidence and self-respect among the young residents. Kids range from infants to 18 years old, and facilities in the village include a day nursery, school, single mothers' institution, house for teenage girls, house for teenage boys, a bakery business, carpentry workshop and studio, and a sewing business. Residents are taught everything from taking care of their environment and home to marketable skills that generate income for the programs as well as prepare them for taking their rightful place in society when they leave the program.

Volunteers (who need to have some Spanish-language skills—classes are available on-site if you need to brush up) work in nearly every aspect of operations, depending on their skills and interests. Are you great with infants and toddlers? Spend your days at the nursery, tending to the littlest ones. Have the patience of a teacher/saint? English-language and other classes always need more adults to help keep studies efficient, as well as new and interesting. Can you teach sports? Art? Music? Carpentry? Maintenance and gardening? Cooking? Sewing? Computer skills? Can you show young parents, many of them children themselves, how to care for their babies? Maybe you'll need to just accompany a child to the doctor or dentist and hold their hand to allay their fears. All of your time and efforts can be put to great use at the village. Your schedule will be mostly weekdays, but weekends are the opportunity to go with kids off-site on special trips and excursions, so jumping in to assist with those is a great opportunity as well.

When your day is done at the village, home is with a local family who will provide a private room and your morning and evening meals (you'll enjoy lunches at the children's village). Your Spanish will come in handy at home as well, as you learn so much about the customs, culture, and urban life in Santa Cruz. If you aren't going on field trips over the weekends, the big city provides plenty of opportunities to check out shops, marketplaces, dining and drinking spots, museums, street performances and cultural activities, and more, for a truly Bolivian vacation.

YOUR NEXT STEP: Twin Work & Volunteer Abroad (✆ **800/80 483 80;** www.workandvolunteer.com). A 2-week project, US$582, includes host-family lodging, meals, project training, and support. Spanish lessons can be made available within the structure of your trip.

DON'T MISS: To relax and fall into blissful, lazy days, visit the colonial city of **Sucre,** known as the "white city" for its dazzling bleached architecture. This UNESCO World Heritage Site. noted for its beautiful buildings, is arranged on a grid, making it delightfully easy to explore tiny streets and shady dappled squares.

ⓘ www.visitbolivia.org

At-Risk Youth & Street Kids **75**

Keeping Kids In School

Protecting Cambodia's Pearls

Phnom Penh, Cambodia

SPEND AS LITTLE—OR AS MUCH—TIME AS YOU WISH GETTING TO KNOW THE CHILDREN WHO could use your help with English, schoolwork, and everything in between. And take the time to explore the city itself, known as "The Pearl of Asia" in the 1920s.

Phnom Penh is the wealthiest city in Cambodia and the country's capital. Known in the 1920s as the Pearl of Asia, the city has since fallen on hard times, especially during the Vietnam War and occupation by the Khmer Rouge. Families have had a particularly tough time recovering, and often kids end up fending for themselves. This English teaching program, which you can undertake from 3 days to 365 days, focuses on children from the poorest slum areas and on families struggling to stay together. Many of the area's most vulnerable children and teens are specifically targeted by the human trafficking trade and are forced into prostitution or sometimes sold into adoption houses. Your work in the classroom and after-school programs is a direct infusion of enthusiasm and novelty that historically has kept kids engaged and interested in school. It's not just the presence of a stranger in school, but a stranger who is, seemingly inexplicably, committed to the quality of their lives.

You may be asked to accompany classes on weekly excursions, teach skills like art and cooking, introduce them to concepts of saving and spending and other small business skills, and any other area that inspires both you and a room full of children. Depending on the season in which you visit, the project and volunteers also create student fun fairs at targeted neighborhoods to get children and entire families involved and emotionally invested in the schools.

You'll live in a hotel but spend your days and eat meals with the teaching staff and other volunteers at the main school, which also serves as a residential orphanage for the kids that don't go home to a family at night. Free time in the evenings and weekends can be spent with alternative teaching projects, if you are so inspired, or exploring the city, a major tourist center in Cambodia, with amazing *wat* temple structures and other religious and royal examples of Khmer and French-flavored architecture.

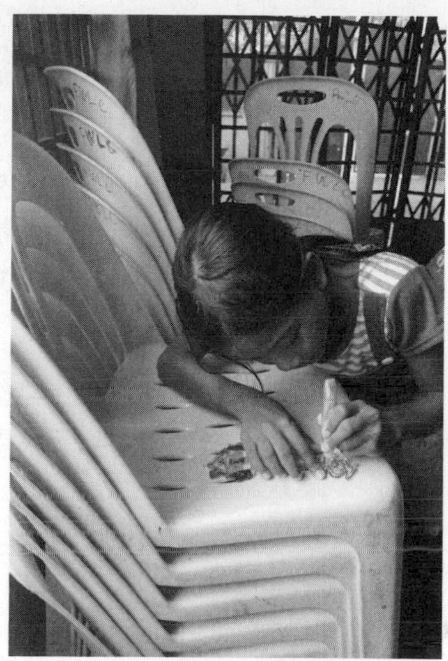
A young girl works on a glass painting activity in Phnom Penh.

YOUR NEXT STEP: Take Me to Volunteer Travel (✆ **65/6220-1198;** www.takemetovolunteertravel.com). Three-day programs, US$580, or the more common 2 weeks, US$935, cover housing in a small, basic hotel near the school project site, meals that are prepared for you and served at the school, airport meetings and transfers in both directions, as well as an operational donation to the orphanage.

DON'T MISS: The city was named for the pagoda-style temple on a hill called **Wat Phnom.** It is still a very active religious pilgrimage spot, with a stream of the faithful heading to the shrines, vendors, and fortune tellers on the hill. The large stupa at the temple complex contains the remains of 15th-century ruler King Ponhea Yat, who moved the Khmer capital from Angkor to Phnom Penh.

ⓘ www.tourismcambodia.com

At-Risk Youth & Street Kids

76

Street Programs

Bringing Classrooms to the Desert

Udaipur, India

INDIA'S "CITY OF SUNRISE," WITH FOUR SURROUNDING LAKES AND PRESERVED HINDU architecture, is often thought of as the most romantic city in the country. It will be your jumping-off point as you bring much-needed education to the children of nearby tribal communities.

In spite of being one of the most rapidly progressing economies in the world, India's many rural areas are far behind the curve. Northwestern India, in the stunning desert region of Rajasthan, has a plethora of isolated tribal communities that live in harsh conditions and extreme poverty. Hand in hand with some of the most pressing economic woes is a high level of illiteracy and poor access to health care. In the tiny villages and towns surrounding Udaipur (and indeed all through this arid region), legions of children have no access to school—and many have no access to homes, family, or shelter. In larger communities they would be considered street children, but in many of these locales, streets are dusty dirt roads used by camel carts and sacred cows but rarely motorized vehicles. In the land of the maharajas and some of the most noble forts and palace structures, many Rajasthani children play in the sand, eat little more than onions and millet, and, if they are lucky, work full-time herding goats.

You'll work alongside full-time volunteers determined to bring scholastic parity and opportunity to the kids of this region. Classrooms—often without electricity, windows, desks, chairs, or supplies—are a gathering place out of the sun for teachers to give predominantly oral lessons about history, math, reading, writing, and the rest of a basic curriculum. Attendance can be spotty since children may be needed for harvest or quite simply be unmotivated to attend the overcrowded, underfunded schools. You'll help relieve some of the classroom burden by teaching groups of kids English, basic math, and other subjects. As part of the project you'll receive lessons in basic Hindi and cultural workshops to help you better understand and be understood. In the afternoons and evenings, informal lessons are taught to street children and those who may have been working during the day—no matter how young. You'll also work in care centers, participating in health campaigns and being a child advocate in many difficult arenas.

You'll share a residence with other volunteers in a rural area, and all meals are prepared for you. While there is plenty to be done with the project day and evening, the trip is organized to give you a well-rounded Indian immersion experience, with cultural classes (yoga, cooking, dance), Hindi-language lessons, and field trips to the Monsoon Palace on Pichola Lake and the Taj Mahal in Agra, as well as opportunities to explore more of Rajasthan. (Udaipur, Jaipur, and Jodhpur are popular travel destinations in Rajasthan, all with beautiful sights and truly warm hospitality). Besides the added value of these structured programs, you'll have plenty of relaxation time. Your experiences will open up a new and authentic world to you.

YOUR NEXT STEP: Global Vision International (✆ **888/653-6028;** www.gviusa.com). A 2-week project, US$1,590, covers shared project house accommodations, all meals of local Indian cuisine, project training, extensive cultural orientation (including Hindi lessons, yoga, cooking, and so

School children in the desert region of Udaipur

on), plus team excursions to major cultural sites.

DON'T MISS: Formerly known as the Maharaja of Jaipur Museum, the **Maharaja Sawai Man Singh II Museum** takes up part of the pink and white regal complex of the City Palace, alongside the royal Moon Palace family residence. Personal collections from the royal family as well as an armory, audience meeting halls, welcome palace, and courtyards are all intricately decorated and filled with antiques.

ⓘ www.incredibleindia.org

77 At-Risk Youth & Street Kids

Street Children Project

Helping Kids Find a Home in North Africa

Rabat and Salé, Morocco

Morocco's French influence often gives it a European feel, but the vast deserts and plentiful camel traffic will remind you you're in Africa. These twin cities of Rabat and Salé are home to Hassan Tower and the Mausoleum of Mohammed V, but you're also not far from the modern-leaning Casablanca and the bazaars of Fez.

Morocco's street children are not just a few little ragamuffins cheekily offering to give you guided tours or sell you trinkets—though that may be the extent of the experience most tourists have. More than 10,000 children live and work in the streets of Morocco, and most have nowhere else to go. This volunteer project works in tandem with the Street Children Project of Morocco to reintegrate children who face difficult, seemingly insurmountable, circumstances. Much of the outreach is in the district of Sidi Bernoussi's bus stations, harbors, and town centers, the de facto gathering places of the makeshift society of street youth. Through direct assistance and creative socio-recreational workshops (such as art and drama), kids are engaged, challenged, and, most importantly, acknowledged, which can be the first step toward seeking available assistance for food, shelter, medical attention, and community.

You'll work in teams with other volunteers, social workers, educators, psychologists, artists, and students to set up places for vulnerable children to drop in and to develop programs that go out to meet them in their street environment. Your duties will include teaching English, mentoring, and tutoring (some of the kids remain enrolled in schools but have no home to return to in the evenings), organizing sport and art workshops, and being available to talk with (and genuinely listen to) children one on one (most have some English from time spent in school, even if they have dropped out) and help guide them toward the services and resources that many don't know are available to them.

You can choose to live with a host family or in shared accommodations in a hostel. All meals are provided, and you'll be completely ensconced in Moroccan culture and life. While time on the streets reaching out to kids can be emotionally challenging and quite draining, your free time in Rabat and Solé will renew and refresh your spirit (so you can return rejuvenated to serving the kids). You'll find great restaurants, bustling marketplaces, busy waterfront areas, and lavish museums and architecture, so the stories you bring home won't be exclusively about kids in hard times but also the enriching cultural experience you enjoyed.

YOUR NEXT STEP: Global Crossroad (✆ **972/252-4191;** www.globalcrossroad.com). A 2-week project, US$999, includes accommodations at a hostel or with a host family, three meals daily, project training, support, and supervision, airport pickup, and full insurance coverage.

DON'T MISS: Avoid the cheesy tourist versions and seek out the authentic-feeling experience of **camel trekking** in Morocco's Atlas Mountains or in the Sahara Desert. Choose an overnight excursion, sleep in tents or under the stars, and truly live the fantasy.

ⓘ www.visitmorocco.com

At-Risk Youth & Street Kids

78

Talibé Center

Taking It to the Streets

St. Louis, Senegal

ST. LOUIS IS WEST AFRICA'S FIRST FRENCH SETTLEMENT, AND ITS HISTORIC CENTER SITS perched on an island near the mouth of the Senegal river. Bird lovers will be enticed by Djoudj National Park, located an hour away and home to more than three million of the feathered creatures.

Among West African nations, Senegal is a model of political stability and peace, yet unemployment and economic distress has led to a large exodus of emigrants to Europe and farther abroad in search of work and income. Often, this means one or both parents leaving the family home and country with the hopes of sending for children later. The departure of work-aged adults and additional burdens like HIV/AIDS have left a disproportionate number of Senegalese youth on the streets, where

Working with homeless Senegalese youth (known as Talibés)

they become known locally as *Talibés* (students of the world). This outreach program works with street kids in care centers, school facilities, and a drop-in center, taking programming to the streets to encourage street kids to come to the center for a nutritious meal and activities. Too many kids are left with no recourse but begging for food and change.

You'll need at least some basic French for this volunteer opportunity, as this town north of Dakar is more French than most of the rest of the nation. Mornings are spent in local schools, helping lessen the burden on overtaxed teachers often trying to teach 40 to 50 students in a crowded classroom. You may split off with a smaller group of students to focus on specific activities teaching numbers, basic vocabulary *en Français* and in English, or perhaps with arts and sports activities. Your afternoons are spent at the Talibé drop-in center for street children helping out the staff, serving free meals to the kids who attend programs, and assisting the kids with tasks they often don't have the luxury of getting to outside—like brushing their teeth or washing their clothes or themselves. Additional activities, like games and crafts and music, are great ways to keep children engaged and provide an alternative to wasting away on the streets (where drugs and sexual abuse are often inevitable).

A host household will be your home base, providing you with a quiet and welcoming place to stay and eat all your meals. Talibé staff members are caring and extraordinarily grateful for the help of volunteers, not to mention a great resource for how best to spend your downtime in St. Louis or exploring farther afield.

YOUR NEXT STEP: Projects Abroad (© **888/839-3535;** www.projects-abroad.org). A 2-week project, US$2,345, includes housing with a host family, three meals daily, project training and support of local staff, airport pickup, and comprehensive medical and travel insurance.

DON'T MISS: You'll be rubbing your eyes, certain you're not seeing correctly. It's not your vision, it's the salt. Senegal's pink lake, or **Retba,** is a mysterious rose-hued lake. The water is pink, and because of very high salinity, everything floats. Aside from messing with your mind about all the properties you thought you understood about water, there is also another visual oddity, with white mountains of harvested salt all along the shores. It is a photographer's dream.

ⓘ www.senegal-tourism.com

At-Risk Youth & Street Kids

79

Youth-at-Risk Project

Working (and Living) With Community Leaders

Cape Town, South Africa

The dramatic juxtaposition of beaches and mountains makes for a stunning backdrop to cosmopolitan Cape Town, the third-largest city in South Africa. It's not surprising that such a beautiful spot is known for its vibrant arts and culture too.

The streets of Cape Town run the gamut from leafy lanes lined with mansions to rough-and-tumble bad neighborhoods where you don't want to be after dark. The latter category makes for a terrible childhood, and kids who are forced to grow up too soon often find themselves mired in a world of drugs and crime. This project works to interrupt the negative cycle and get children into the school routine, provide support, and find the way, different for every child, to help them break out of the circumstances of the streets. Many kids have been physically or sexually abused, abandoned, orphaned, or have run away. The most important work of the project is instilling self-worth and pride in kids that deserve the best but just don't know it yet.

You'll teach English and help with homework in language and other subjects (most of the kids are ages 13–18), teach and supervise sports challenges, art activities, and music programs, help kids with their garden projects (where they are learning to nurture growth), support staff in the kitchen to get meals served to kids who have no consistent access to nutritious meals, and perhaps pitch in with a paintbrush to help with some maintenance and upkeep projects. The project also runs life skills courses, performing arts, and career development classes with which you can help. Some of the kids will respond openly and gratefully, and some, through no fault of their own, are remote and difficult to reach. Some of the most important skills they learn on the streets are how to protect themselves, both physically and emotionally, and that can result in some pretty thick walls and a genuine reticence and lack of trust. Your patience and ability to still give your energy and assistance demonstrates that the equations of the streets, where a high price must be paid for everything, doesn't always apply. Sometimes, people are just willing to give and take nothing in return. It is a huge lesson (for all of us).

You'll stay with a host family. The host households are those of community leaders, committed to supporting the project goals and volunteers who do the work. Three meals a day are provided, as well as the rare experience of becoming a family member and experiencing the culture from the inside. You'll work a busy 40 hours a week, just like at home, but your free time and weekends can be spent exploring the amazing city. Food, cultural celebrations, music, crafts, museums, and natural beauty (stunning beaches and waterfront as well as majestic mountains to hike) are all on offer in Cape Town.

YOUR NEXT STEP: Institute for Field Research Expeditions (© **800/675-2504;** www.ifrevolunteers.org). A 2-week project, US$1,099, includes lodging with a host family, all meals, airport pickup, in-country transportation, project training and support, and travel insurance.

DON'T MISS: Just wipe that idea about penguins in frozen climes right out of your head. The adorable (and loud) **penguin colony** that crowds Boulders Beach on the Cape Peninsula is enjoying the same tepid water and warm sunshine as you. Right around the eponymous boulders that create this protected cove is a small public beach. Lay out your towel, and chances are good that a penguin will waddle up and sit on it with you before the hot sun goes down.

ⓘ www.cape-town.org

80 At-Risk Youth & Street Kids

Animal-Assisted Therapy

Life Lessons on the Farm

Brewster, New York, USA

Little more than an hour away from Manhattan, the pace of affluent Putnam County could not be more different than the urban chaos of the metropolis. It's a great place to give specialized attention to kids who can benefit from a little extra assistance and time away from their troubles.

In Putnam County, New York, the recognized worldwide leader in animal-assisted therapy has a farm school facility that is a slice of heaven. Green Chimneys operates a residential treatment program and special education school that teaches children with emotional, behavioral, social, and learning challenges to care about themselves and others while caring for animals. The 200-acre (81ha) farm has nearly 200 students, half of whom live on-site. In addition to charging youngsters with the care and feeding of horses, cows, goats, and dogs, students tend to the horticultural programs. The philosophy, borne out every day, is that when given responsibility for life and caring for nature, students discover new levels of dignity, responsibility, and respect for all living things. Volunteers are essential in keeping dozens of programs viable.

You can spend the time you have to give assisting in any number of ways, from helping with therapeutic horseback riding programs, library aid, language enrichment sessions with individual students or small groups, before- and after-school activity and care programs for non-resident students, helping augment the daily care of more than 350 animals, helping administratively, or even pitching in with food services at mealtime.

There are no travel, lodging, or meal arrangements for visiting volunteers, but the farm school is close to (and serves students from) New York City, the Hudson Valley, Westchester County, and Western Connecticut, so it won't be difficult to get to it regularly while visiting any of these vacation areas.

YOUR NEXT STEP: Green Chimneys (✆ **845/279-2995**; www.greenchimneys.org). Arrange your own travel, lodging, and meals in New York or Connecticut and contact the organization to jump in to work at the farm school. Training for certain departments or programs is provided. Some programs require volunteers to be at least 18 years old.

DON'T MISS: Get your literary/historical fix as you follow the hoofbeats of Ichabod Crane in the actual villages of **Sleepy Hollow** and **Tarrytown,** the settings of Washington Irving's *The Legend of Sleepy Hollow*. You may not run into any headless horsemen, but you'll find steepled churches, adorable colonial homes, and Sunnyside, Irving's own home, each looking picture-book perfect.

ⓘ www.iloveny.com

At-Risk Youth & Street Kids **81**

Support Sioux Youth

Boredom-Busting in South Dakota

Pine Ridge Reservation, South Dakota, USA

SIX DAYS ON A NATIVE AMERICAN RESERVATION WILL FLY BY WHEN SPLIT BETWEEN KEEPING Sioux children intellectually engaged and exploring the prairies of the country's national parks and other landmarks. In fact, you may want to stay longer to explore.

This quick trip combines creating activity camps for Native American kids at risk with sightseeing and cultural exploration in the Badlands. Two on-reservation Boys and Girls Clubs give kids a safe haven, free of drugs and alcohol, jealousy, and violence that can be all too present in their lives. Activities that entertain and intellectually challenge youth and teens have proven an effective antidote to boredom, which can sometimes lead to mischief or more troubling pursuits. Having the opportunity to explore social connections in a non-judgmental atmosphere can do wonders for self-esteem and also build lifelong friendships.

Your 6-day excursion in South Dakota includes a full day exploring Mount Rushmore and the Crazy Horse Memorial before getting to the reservation. The work is a day at each Boys and Girls Club creating day camps. You'll lead and assist in a variety of one-hour workshops and clinics in sports (basketball, volleyball, soccer, relay, track and field, and more) and arts and crafts projects. You'll also be immersed in the culture with learning exchange programs, including native music, dance, and history as well as a powwow, sweat lodge, and sleeping in a tepee. You may also be asked to assist with some small administrative tasks or minor work around the clubs, but the majority of your attention is entirely focused on the kids.

Accommodations for the group are different depending on your location, from staying overnight in a traditional tepee to a hotel in Rapid City. Meals are provided (except for lunch on sightseeing days, when the group will stop at restaurants), and you'll also gain important knowledge about the culture and history of the Sioux Indians and the Pine Ridge Reservation. Your non-work time is scheduled with cultural activities and touring monuments and the nearly lunar landscape of the enormous Badlands National Park, with its buttes, pinnacles, and spires rising from the stone.

YOUR NEXT STEP: Ambassadors for Children (✆ **317/536-0250;** www.ambassadorsforchildren.org). This 6-day project, US$875–US$1,220 depending on how many volunteers share accommodations, includes lodging in hotels as well as nights in a traditional tepee, most meals, cultural orientation program and events, sightseeing excursions, park entrance fees, educational materials, and all ground transportation.

DON'T MISS: Uncover a part of American history at the **Minuteman Missile National Historic Site,** where the Air Force buried top-secret weapons that were never launched under the prairie. Two of 150 missile silos and launch control facilities have been preserved for visitors to explore the Cold War chapter of history ranging from the Cuban Missile Crisis to the signing of the arms reduction treaty by Presidents George Bush Sr. and Mikhail Gorbachev.

ⓘ www.travelsd.com

82 Safe Spaces to Play

Reconstruction of Amazon Schools

Constructing Classrooms in the Jungle

Macas, Ecuador

With just a little money and some hard work, you can help rebuild schools that are ravaged by the elements in the Amazon. With a bit of time on your own, you can see the river yourself, or explore the city.

While the difficulty of life in the Amazon rainforest means that very young children have to contribute to their family's survival—often necessitating them being pulled out of school for rice harvest or other hard work—the schools are there and the classrooms are ready. Since families have different needs (and how many children they have can affect whether kids can go to school), class attendance can be quite sporadic and the cast of characters changes almost daily. The school programs in small villages tend to be run by a single teacher with very limited supplies. Homes in the region are thatched-roof structures, often on stilts (since the Amazon and tributaries rise and fall so dramatically each season), and nature takes a toll on all buildings, including schools. Many schools just don't get maintained, so roofs leak, timber rots or is bug-eaten, and the perpetual humidity makes for a prime mold-growing environment. This project is rebuilding schools throughout the mostly impoverished region, supplying lumber, nails, screws, and sheets of zinc to cover roofs for the first time.

You'll work alongside community members to see the project through, from purchasing tools and materials to doing the labor—roofing, painting, shoring up structures, replacing rotted wood, fixing desks and chairs, and repairing bathroom facilities. The work can be strenuous but not overly technical. Most schools don't have glass windows or particularly precise carpentry needs, and the work, all done by hand without electrical tools, will be a significant improvement over current classroom conditions. You'll be trained on construction skills if you don't come to the project already comfortable as Bob the Builder.

You'll share a volunteer house near the city, with shared rooms and bathrooms. Bring your own sleeping bag and towels, and since it's at least a month you'll be spending here, you'll likely want to bring comfort items (extra blanket, comfy pillow,

Reconstructing a school in Ecuador

and so on) if you're not used to living in rustic conditions. You'll also need intermediate Spanish skills, as the people in the various communities served speak only Spanish or Quechua. In your free time you'll want to join the rest of the group exploring the rainforest and visiting indigenous Shuar river towns, along with amazing waterfalls and mirror lakes where there is more wildlife to spot than you'll experience almost anywhere else on Earth.

YOUR NEXT STEP: Ecuador Volunteer (© **+593-2-2557749;** www.ecuadorvolunteer.org). There is a 1-month minimum commitment on this project, but it is free to volunteers, save a US$150 materials charge that will fund the purchase of building materials and tools. Your accommodations in the volunteer house and all meals are covered in exchange for your work. A project representative will meet you at the Quito airport to transfer you to the home base near Macas.

DON'T MISS: It's a memorable experience to be outdoors, up to your chin in steaming water while the air temperature is frigid. At 10,000 ft. (3048m), high in the Andean Cordillera at the entrance to the Amazonian jungle, you can soak and relax in several hot springs and pools at the **Papallacta Thermal Center and Spa.** If you dare, the course of relaxation proscribed by locals is to plunge yourself into the freezing mountain river in between dips in the healing hot waters.

(i) www.ecuadortouristboard.com

83 Safe Spaces to Play

Mayan Schools Project

Rural Renovations

Sansirisay and Llanos de Morales, Guatemala

These two villages, about an hour and a half from Guatemala City, need extra hands to paint a school, tend to sports fields, and improve residents' quality of life. The several hundred people who live here cannot always count on having running water, electricity, and plumbing.

In Guatemala, a definite chasm exists between the descendants of the Mayan Indians, who make up at least half of the population (but earn only a fraction of the national income), and the non-Indians. Most of the small rural communities center around agriculture and the coffee trade, and in these villages, more than half of the primary-aged children don't attend school. Education is a difficult luxury for families that struggle each day to eat and get the work done in the fields and town. Malnutrition, disease, and lack of drinking water plague these central highland communities. This organization works directly with a local, community-founded organization to be sure each project undertaken is what the villages need and want. The primary schools have been built but need improvements and renovations to be both safe and inspiring places to learn. Each of these two villages has a primary school and a pre-school that need volunteer attention and labor.

The schools will be renovated and painted, both inside and out. The effort required is not monumental, but the community is so taxed by the work requirements of everyday subsistence that this care hasn't been prioritized—it would be a difficult decision to let crops rot in the field in order to paint and repair the schoolhouse. There will also be outdoor work, improving soccer fields, and other recreational activities during and after school. You can also pitch in on a project constructing a new water pump that will benefit every member of the community. Your work will be hard, but you'll be lauded by the local communities for taking on tasks they recognize as important but have thus far only hoped to accomplish.

You'll be completely immersed in a Guatemalan village, where you'll live with a family (while some homes have electricity and plumbing, you can't count on this, so be prepared to do without) and eat meals with a community group of volunteers and villagers. A local woman spends much of her day preparing food for the project members over an open fire. Free time tends to inspire team members to set out together and explore the region, from archaeological sites and museums to incredible hikes through natural splendor.

YOUR NEXT STEP: Global Citizens Network 🎗 (✆ **800/644-9292;** www.globalcitizens.org). A 2-week project, US$1,575, includes lodging with a host family, all meals, hotel accommodations for the first night in Guatemala City, airport pickup and in-country transportation, and full training and support.

DON'T MISS: You'll want to make your way to **Tikal,** an ancient Mayan city in the north. At one time it was the largest Mayan city in the world, and only 30% of it has been unearthed from impenetrable overgrowth. Pyramids, temples, and residences can be explored amid the verdant jungle and its haunting monkey howls and bird songs.

ⓘ www.visitguatemala.com

Safe Spaces to Play 84

Restore Schools & Playgrounds

Sprucing Up Neglected Learning Institutions

Pune, India

MOST PEOPLE THINK OF MUMBAI OR DELHI WHEN PICTURING INDIA. BUT PUNE, INDIA'S eighth-largest city, is equally dynamic—home to universities, technology company outposts, and Iyengar yoga. You'll be able to channel that energy as you contribute your handyman skills to improving schools that are suffering from years of neglect.

Pune is a hotbed of higher education in India, home to the Film and Television Institute of India, the Armed Forces Medical College, the National Defense Academy, and the Symbiosis Educational Society. So it's surprising that primary, middle, and high schools (often combined in one school) would be neglected, but that is too often the case. It has been decades since the schools targeted by this work camp project have had any updating or even a coat of paint. Most classrooms don't have blackboards, and desks and chairs might be better used as firewood in many cases. The surrounding grounds often inspire depression more than imagination. Many of the playgrounds have never had slides, swings, or monkey bars, so installing a jungle gym and parallel bars can make a world of difference.

You'll provide manual labor, from repairing furniture to decorating and painting classrooms and building exteriors. While you're outside, pitch in to erect a swing set or slide so kids have somewhere to play. Any teacher can tell you that if students don't burn off some of their youthful energy before and between classes, it's impossible to keep order among students in the classroom. Whether you're a handyman or novice, your hard work and willingness to jump in on any task is all you'll need to be a valuable member of the team.

The work camp team stays together in modest guesthouse accommodations. You'll share a room with other volunteers and the group also shares communal meals. Pune is a relatively easygoing city not far from Mumbai but is light-years away from the chaos of that enormous city. You'll pass the time talking with locals and your fellow volunteers, and fill your weekends exploring the city's museums, restaurants, shops, and marketplaces.

YOUR NEXT STEP: Canadian Alliance for Development Initiatives and Projects (© **604/628-7400;** www.cadip.org) A 2-week trip, US$265, includes communally prepared team meals and accommodations in shared guesthouse accommodations and full project support. You'll travel to the site on your own from the Mumbai International Airport, and upon arrival, an additional US$154 is paid directly to the project hosts.

DON'T MISS: If you have some extra days before leaving India, consider traveling through part of the country by luxury train. Several lavish train experiences still impart the rococo adornment of the days of the maharajas. The **Deccan Odyssey** travels through the mystical land of Maharashtra, where for several days of sojourning you'll pass through thick jungles, home to tigers, on your way to the laid-back beaches of Goa.

ⓘ www.incredibleindia.org

85 Safe Spaces to Play

Building Rural Schools

Construction, Camping & Culture

Fort Dauphin, Madagascar

The land of vanilla—that flavor so prized in cooking and baking—is a beautiful island far off the southeastern coast of Africa: more than three-quarters of the flora and fauna that lives here cannot be found anywhere else. Your project's base is Fort Dauphin, close to many beautiful beaches.

The rural areas around coastal Fort Dauphin are, in many cases, without schools or recreational options for kids. This project, in partnership with and at the request of the community, is adding new two-room school buildings to island communities. Most of these villages have lacked access to formal education or the required facilities, so creating the space for learning will allow teachers to assemble classes and help youngsters break the generations-old cycle of poverty. The Malagasy government has committed to training and recruiting educators once the infrastructure is in place. The national goal is to construct 3,000 classrooms by 2012. Currently, children may have to walk more than 10 miles (16km) to get to a school, with no guarantee there will be space for them when they arrive.

You'll work with the volunteer team to build a two-room school from the ground up. A technical specialist oversees the project, so you'll be trained and supervised in every area of construction you try. Every aspect of construction is undertaken, from setting stone floors to installing the tin roofs and the steps in between—which also includes bathroom/sanitation facilities (the first-ever for many

Building a school in rural Madagascar

of these kids) and a potable water system. You'll also furnish the school by building chairs and tables, blackboards and shelves, making the approximately 20 ft. x 40 ft. (6m x 12m) two-room building ready for kids and teachers to move in. The schools built thus far have completely transformed the character of the villages in which they're located.

Camping out in the beautiful and remote natural areas here will be quite a retreat from what you're used to at home. You'll be completely immersed in Malagasy culture, from the spicy foods you'll enjoy to the local people with whom you'll work, play, and relax. There is an organized excursion to a nature reserve famous for lemurs, as well as day trips to rural markets and into the city. You're likely to enjoy an entourage of children following your every move, as you'll achieve celebrity status in the villages. More than 2,000 children from the area have already been given a new opportunity for learning from the project, and thousands more are waiting for you.

YOUR NEXT STEP: Global Vision International (✆ **888/653-6028;** www.gviusa.com). A 2-week project, US$1,190, includes campsite accommodations, all meals, project training and supervision, and full organizational support.

DON'T MISS: Malagasy culture is inextricably tied to its ancestors. The most important decisions made by individuals, families, and even businesses and government are done so only after consulting the dead. Get a peek into the life and reverence for ancestors at the **Antananarivo Museum of Art and Archaeology.**

ⓘ www.tourisme.gov.mg

Safe Spaces to Play **86**

Student-Designed School

Laying the Foundation in the Peruvian Andes

Pamashto, Peru

BUILT AND DESIGNED FOR STUDENTS, BY STUDENTS, AND WITH ASSISTANCE FROM AN ONGOING cadre of volunteers who want to immerse themselves in a rural way of life in Peru, the school you'll work on is crucial, and so is its constant upkeep.

At the junction of the Andean foothills and Amazon rainforest, you'll find the small city of Tarapoto in the northeast of Peru. Continue about an hour along dirt roads and you'll eventually end up in Pamashto, a small town perched in the hills, and home to Quechua and Lamista people working the fertile land to make their living. This project, in partnership with a local grassroots organization, has already built a school here that was designed by the students—who better to decide what is needed to make learning comfortable? The next steps are to build a dining room (that the entire community can use for gatherings) and kitchen facilities and make much-needed improvements to the outdoor play area.

You'll work on several construction tasks, including laying the foundation and building the floors, walls, and roof. The sponsoring organization specializes in small-scale development projects, so there is ample training to get you comfortable swinging a hammer and lending your brute (or not-so-brute) strength as the new expansion goes up.

When you first arrive in Tarapoto, you and your volunteer colleagues will stay in a family-owned lodge. Then you'll move into a host family home, where you will be welcomed like a long-lost relative returning to the fold. While the team is split up among many host family homes, meals are a great time for everyone to gather and enjoy the local specialties prepared for you by a village cook. In the past, volunteers have banded together in their free time, heading out to explore the area, meeting most of the villagers, and perhaps river rafting and swimming in the nearby Mayo River.

YOUR NEXT STEP: Global Citizens Network (✆ **800/644-9292;** www.globalcitizens.org). This 2½-week project, US$1,725, includes in-country lodging (combination of guesthouse and family homestay), all meals, in-country travel including airport pickup, training and materials, a project donation to the local charity, and emergency insurance coverage.

DON'T MISS: For a unique insight on the Inca Empire, as well as other lost civilizations of Peru, visit Lima's **Gold of Peru Museum** and the **Arms of the World Museum.** Both are outstanding and enormous private collections of the same man. The gold museum has five halls overflowing with some of the most important gilded treasures of the Inca, Nazca, Lambayeque, Chimú, Mochica, Frias, Huari, and Vicus cultures. Amazingly detailed work on headdresses, drinking vessels, chest plates, arm bands, and countless other items only begins to hint at the richness of the region before colonization. The arms museum showcases more than 20,000 pieces of weaponry from around the world.

ⓘ www.peru.info

Safe Spaces to Play

Building Playgrounds

A Place to Play for Every Child

Nationwide, USA

WITH HELPING HANDS SUCH AS YOURS, CHILDREN ACROSS AMERICA CAN HAVE GREAT PLACES to play no matter where they live—and because this nonprofit has a national, widespread outreach, you can choose carefully and volunteer in a place that will give you your own playtime too.

With the ultimate goal of having a safe, great place to play within walking distance of every child in America, KaBOOM has fanned out across the United States to install slides, jungle gyms, climbing walls, sandboxes, swings, rope domes, seesaws, and spring-mounted riding animals in as many locations as possible. Land is donated and partnerships formed in communities, soil and other environmental factors are tested, projects are publicized, and build days are organized as great block parties or festivals where dedicated volunteers come together to convert open space and unused lots into amazing play spaces that will rock many kids' worlds. KaBOOM was started because of a story of two kids who died while playing in an abandoned car—something that could have been avoided if they had a safe space to play.

You can work on any number of projects in nearly every state. When you make travel plans, consult the build project search engine to find what projects are in the area where you can help. It takes a lot of hands to raise a twisty slide. KaBOOM projects also include skate parks, sports fields, and ice rinks all across the country. Depending on the project and your interests and skills, the actual work you do will vary. Help is also always needed for spreading the word, preparing and serving food for work crews, painting murals, building benches, constructing shade structures, and so much more than just playing around.

There aren't formal trip arrangements for KaBOOM play space build projects, and you can dedicate your time and effort to programs when you're away from home or in your own community.

YOUR NEXT STEP: KaBOOM (✆ **202/ 659-0215;** www.kaboom.org). KaBoom doesn't sponsor structured trips, so you can lend a hand on build projects wherever you may wander—KaBoom projects are in nearly every state.

ⓘ www.discoveramerica.com

3 Sharing Your Knowledge: Teaching Vacations

An English teacher with her students in Delhi, India

English as a Second Language 88

Open Doors to Employment

Become a Citizen of the "Capital of Happiness"

Salvador, Brazil

TEACHING ENGLISH TO ADULTS AND YOUTH WILL HARDLY SEEM LIKE WORK IN BRAZIL'S "CAPITAL of happiness," where the pace of life is easy, the African culture is plentiful, and the beaches stretch for miles along the warm Pacific coast.

Not every volunteer vacation program can claim that it works with small, local non-government organizations, where the need is most critical; but this English teaching program does so diligently. Teaming with locally run programs, it uses donated funds to teach English to the children of Salvador, and some adults as well. You'll practice general English conversation skills and writing with one or several students at a time. Sometimes you may also assist teachers in general classroom activities, playtime, and arts and crafts projects. You can also put your skills to work with after-school groups of at-risk children and teens.

Adult classes are focused on empowering locals to prepare for work in the tourism industry, so you'll gain a deep understanding of Brazilian life as you translate history and tour highlights. You don't need classroom experience to help with pronunciation, work on alphabet drills, teach vocabulary, and engage in conversation. English is no cakewalk to learn, and plenty of practice and repetition is needed to become fluent.

Salvador, the capital of the state of Bahia, is known as "Brazil's capital of happiness." The population is easygoing, and locals spend much of their time outdoors—dining, dancing, partying—in the shadow of some of the nation's most beautiful architecture. The 1990s saw a renaissance in the downtown district, and this area, the *Pelourinho*, is now the beating heart of the city, just a short distance from miles of Pacific beaches and nearby tropical islands.

Your home base is in a generally safe residential neighborhood where you'll share an 11-bedroom/10-bathroom house with other volunteers and staff. Plenty of rooms, two lounges, and an outdoor garden make it a nice place to come home to after a long day's work. Brazilian cuisine is prepared for you, and the neighborhood has plenty of cafes and dining options if you'd like to eat out.

YOUR NEXT STEP: Cross-Cultural Solutions 🎗 (✆ **800/380-4777;** www.crossculturalsolutions.org). A 2-week assignment starts at US$2,664 ("peak" season, from May to mid-Aug, US$2,864) and includes lodging in the group project house, with on-site offices and support, meals, country and project orientation, local transportation, airport transfers, and additional cultural excursions on weekends.

DON'T MISS: Arembepe, 1 hour away from Salvador, is commonly known as the Hippie Village. This bohemian beach town drew the counterculture in the 1970s, from Janis Joplin to Roman Polanski, who found the tropical palms and ocean tidepools the perfect place to drop out for a while.

ⓘ www.turismo.gov.br

89 English as a Second Language

Countryside Teaching

Last Glimpse of a Disappearing Way of Life

X'ian, China

CHINA IS ANCIENT, YES, BUT ONLY X'IAN CAN BOAST BEING AN ANCIENT CAPITAL TO 13 dynasties and the start of the Silk Road. It still serves as an important hub, most recently in the economic invigoration of the country's interior, making your role as an English instructor something of a cultural ambassador.

Like most volunteer English-language programs, this is less about teaching the rules of grammar and more about improving conversational skills. Teaching English here, in the public schools in the Chinese countryside, is a cultural experience you'll not soon forget. While China is undergoing a mass migration to large urban areas, the small rural villages are losing both their population base and skilled professionals. Qualified, motivated teachers have moved to big cities, leaving a vacuum in English training among farming families and the less well-off. Your general knowledge of English will enable you to teach your students how to express themselves in a comfortable and nuanced way, going well beyond the Dick-and-Jane drills of textbooks to chats about weather, history, health, happiness, travel, and so much more.

English education has become a national priority in China, but only private schools can afford native-speaking instructors. You'll spend 30 to 40 hours at work per week, a full-time commitment to the kids in the village where you'll live. A host family (usually also quite keen to practice their English with you around the dinner table) will introduce you to neighbors and friends, so you'll quickly feel part of the community. Classroom time will be shared with teachers, who may use your energy and skills in supplemental activities like arts and crafts and outdoor sports. After a morning of classroom lessons, you'll engage in small group or one-on-one conversations, which will increase your students' confidence and lead to eye-opening interchanges for you as well.

Your free time in the village will be spent with new friends and neighbors, enjoying long chats and relaxing at family gatherings. Out in the countryside there won't be many restaurants or pubs to distract you, but the relationships you build will create memories that last much longer than a Tsingtao beer or the sounds of coins dropping into a jukebox.

YOUR NEXT STEP: Institute for Field Research Expeditions (✆ **800/675-2504;** www.ifrevolunteers.org). You'll decide how many weeks to spend teaching English. There is a US$799 fee that covers placement administration, airport transfers, and project support. No matter the length of your stay, the village school places such a priority on your work that it covers homestay accommodations and three meals daily at its expense, with no additional weekly or monthly fees.

DON'T MISS: It's an amazing sight when you first lay eyes on the famous **Terracotta Warriors.** Looking down at this life-size army—created in 211 to 206 B.C.—it's hard to imagine they were buried in a farmer's field until the 1970s.

ⓘ http://en.xian-tourism.com

English as a Second Language

Teen English Workshops

Living in the Shadow of a Volcano

Antigua, Guatemala

HOME TO COFFEE PLANTATIONS, THREE VOLCANOES, BAROQUE ARCHITECTURE, AND MANY colonial ruins, Antigua—also referred to as La Antigua—is a UNESCO World Heritage Site worth exploring. Given these attributes, it's not surprising that Antigua is also home to many Spanish-language immersion schools.

There are long-term programs teaching English to Guatemalan children, but the organizers have recognized the added benefit of bringing short-term volunteers into the program to help out. It's important, of course, for the students to practice their English lessons as rigorously as possible, but there's added value in having them converse with native English speakers like you and introducing them to many different accents and regional dialects. Having additional volunteers allows full-time English teachers to break kids into smaller groups for much more personal attention in a dynamic workshop setting. Children make the biggest strides in their learning when they're working with volunteers who challenge them in new ways and with varied stimuli.

You'll be working with small groups of teenagers who are as eager to practice English conversation skills as to learn about your life, music, and culture. You'll be teamed with long-term volunteers and work side by side with trained English teachers. You'll get lots of quality time with both individual students and groups of five or six. You may also go on field trips, where you'll be asked to chaperone groups of teens.

At the end of the day, you'll come home to a host family in the charming Spanish colonial town of Antigua, giving you a chance to really get to know the Guatemalan culture. Meals are prepared for you at home, and lunches during the week are provided at the school. While Spanish is not absolutely necessary, some comfort with the language will stand you in good stead when you're away from school. One-on-one Spanish tutoring during the afternoons is also available if you'd like to build your own skills. A few excursions include a trip to a yoga facility for training and a guided journey up the Pacaya volcano.

YOUR NEXT STEP: Global Vision International (✆ **888/653-6028;** www.gviusa.com). Two weeks teaching English in a small village outside Antigua, US$850 (longer or shorter volunteer assignments available), includes host family accommodations, all meals, project training and support, local transportation, and some weekend excursions.

DON'T MISS: You can gain insights into Antiguan society on a visit to **La Azatea Cultural Center.** Sights include a coffee museum set in a former coffee mill, a Mayan music museum, a costume and village life museum, a traditional Guatemalan restaurant and cafe, an equestrian center, and a working coffee plantation.

ⓘ www.visitguatemala.com

91 English as a Second Language

Hungarian Classroom Support

An Eastern European Education

Hódmezõvásárhely, Hungary

Many people don't think there are still places in Europe where English-language instruction assistance is needed. With this program you can serve as both an informal cultural attaché and teacher's aide in a city named for three separate villages that joined together in the 15th century.

If, by the end of your 2 weeks as a language volunteer, you can pronounce the name of this town, you will deserve a medal. And if your students have gained half that much skill in English, you will be a great success. Your job is to support teachers in the classroom, helping with student work and lesson plans. What you bring to the table are natural skills in pronunciation and casual usage, which are often beyond the teachers or the outdated textbooks available to them. The mayor of the village has led this effort, understanding that, in a global society, it is hugely beneficial for students to improve their proficiency in English.

While teaching, you'll speak to the class about their work and, more importantly, about personal issues close to your heart. You might chat about sports, or food, and discuss how you spend your day at home. Using your imagination, you can teach students letter writing, perform a play together; organize a debate about subjects in the news, vote on political issues, write shopping lists, and so on. Each volunteer offers students a different teaching style and increases their facility with spoken English.

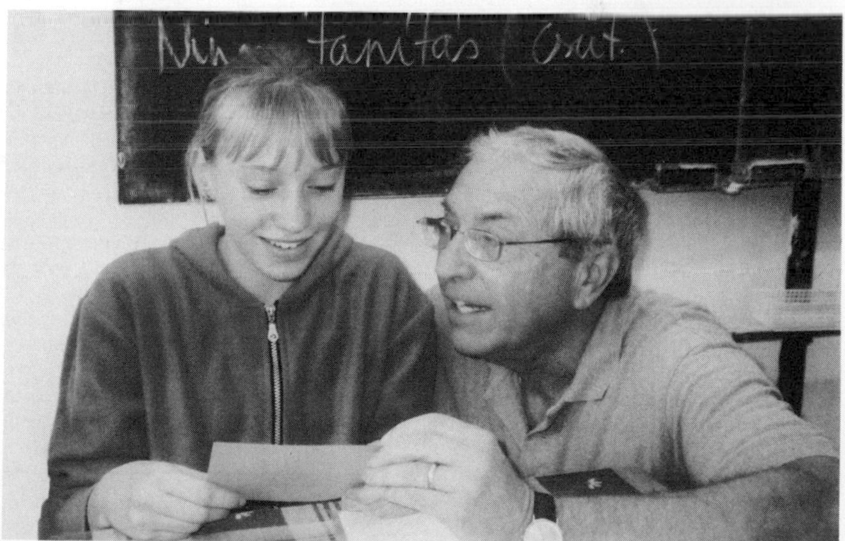

An English language volunteer helping a student in Hódmezõvásárhely

You'll be staying at a hotel in town, in a double room. It's a short walk to an Internet cafe, grocery store, bank, shops, and your assigned school. Locally prepared meals are provided, so expect great filling food, complete with laughter and gregarious conversation with fellow volunteers and locals. The town is small and friendly, and in just 2 weeks you'll be recognized when you walk about, enjoying intimate country village life.

YOUR NEXT STEP: Global Volunteers (✆ **651/407-6100;** www.globalvolunteers.org). A 2-week project, US$2,695, includes hotel accommodations and meals, project support, and orientation in the town of placement.

DON'T MISS: Budapest is a must-see city, with stunning architecture, a vibrant culture, and active nightlife. When in Budapest, make like the Hungarians and enjoy soaking in the public baths. The most famous bathhouse is the **Gellert Bath and Hotel**, built in 1918 and restored to its original splendor. Soaking in the curative waters in gorgeous art nouveau surroundings is a sublimely relaxing retreat.

ⓘ www.hungarytourism.hu

English as a Second Language **92**

Children's Language Program

Calm Amid the Chaos of Urban Delhi

Delhi, India

YOU CAN BRING ENGLISH TO LIFE IN DELHI, HOME TO MILLIONS AND THE SECOND-LARGEST CITY in India. A microcosm of contemporary India, with its stark juxtapositions of rich and poor, old and new, Delhi is a fascinating, ever-modernizing metropolis. Your efforts will help children understand the language and put it into practice, preparing them for their future in that big city and beyond.

English is taught in most of India's public schools, but the experience is often limited to learning vocabulary lists and diagramming sentences. As a volunteer in elementary schools or orphanages, you can help teachers bring the language to life. What is the name of what you're wearing? The color of your hair?

No experience is required, simply the desire to speak and gently correct pronunciation or word use in lively conversations. You'll play games, sing, give cooking lessons, play charades, give names to the sights and sounds around you. Some who may be struggling will benefit greatly from your one-on-one help. Classes may take place in a public school, orphanage, or children's shelter; you may also choose to work on English skills with a local women's group in the afternoons and evenings as an additional service to the community.

You and other volunteers will live in a residential project house with kitchen facilities. You'll have easy access to the project site (you may each be working at different locations or within different classrooms in the same school), though you may need to use public buses—a daunting experience at first. Breakfast and dinner are provided at the project house; you're responsible for your own lunch. Once your duties are done, you're free to explore one of the most vibrant, bustling cities of the world.

YOUR NEXT STEP: Volunteering India (✆ **91124/4307993;** www.volunteeringindia.com). 1 week: US$450; 2 weeks:

A volunteer and her students in Delhi, India

US$575. Fee covers group housing, two meals daily, airport transfers, cultural and local orientation, basic language lessons, and 24-hour project support.

DON'T MISS: If you return home from Delhi without seeing the **Taj Mahal,** your friends and family may send you right back. The city of Agra is a few hours' drive from Delhi but worth the chaotic trip. The experience is even more unforgettable if you spend a night in Agra and wake to see the Taj at dawn. This glowing white marble mausoleum, built by Shah Jahan as a memorial for his favorite wife Mumtaz Mahal, is one of history's most profoundly romantic expressions.

ⓘ www.incredibleindia.org

93 **English as a Second Language**

Island Education

Live Life at Island Speed

Wasini Island, Kenya

CONSIDER YOUR WORK IN THIS REMOTE, SWAHILI-SPEAKING ISLAND OFF THE COAST OF KENYA as playing a part in boosting the global economy—Kenya's government has made learning English a priority, one way to increase its tourism profile. Wasini Island has a lot to offer: bird-watching, safari, and other maritime activities are all possible.

This volunteer teaching opportunity offers adventure outside the classroom and genuine satisfaction within. You needn't be a certified teacher, and completing this program can get you introductory certification in TEFL (Teach English as a Foreign Language). The island, off Kenya's coast, is Swahili-speaking, but the Kenyan government has made English education a priority to help develop the region's tourism infrastructure. Volunteering to teach English to the next generation will help the national parks and marine conservation programs here to achieve an international status commensurate with their ecological wealth. The children of Wisini Island know the importance of English as a global language and are eager to learn. Local teachers do what they can with donated textbooks, but your reinforcement of pronunciation and conversational nuance makes all the difference.

You'll work in the classroom with full-time teachers, with your conversational abilities serving as your most valuable asset. Expect to ask and answer questions about your home, discuss your favorite foods and sports, and describe the weather back home. The give-and-take of conversation and question-and-answer sessions is tremendously important. After lunch, perhaps you'll work on writing poetry together, teach traditional or pop songs, or take everyone outside to learn a game—the more rules to be explained and digested, the better. Later in the day, you'll walk to the orphanage and spend some time reading stories in English, teaching more songs and dances, and answering questions about the world as you know it. Teaching a simple game like Hangman or creating word search puzzles is a satisfying challenge.

You'll live in a community of volunteers, sharing meals, planning sessions, and orientation activities. Shared accommodations are modest, with sporadic electricity; expect to bathe in the ocean nearby or take a bucket bath near the river. The island is renowned for dolphins, whales, whale sharks, and manta rays, so a snorkel and mask might as well be permanently affixed to your head. You'll be completely absorbed into the island's communal life, stopping in next door for a cold drink with locals, joining large community gatherings for celebrations and storytelling, as well as interacting with an enthusiastic corps of volunteers (you'll share the base with volunteers working on marine conservation programs, so there'll be no shortage of things to talk about). Hike through the mangroves and coastal forest or sit on the beach and watch

Smiling for the camera in Wasini Island, Kenya

the stars come out over this vast, exotic, protected wildlife park area.

YOUR NEXT STEP: Global Vision International (✆ **888/653-6028;** www.gviusa.com). A 2-week project, US$1,190, includes shared accommodations, all meals, project training (and TEFL certification if desired), community orientation, and full project support and supervision.

DON'T MISS: From space it must look like a piece of rare jade, nestled on a beach of white sand. In the far north of Kenya is **Lake Turkana,** the largest desert lake in the world. The coast of this massive inland sea is longer than the entire coast of the country. The water is ethereally turquoise, sitting amid miles of arid desert and lava. Some of the earliest dated fossils have been found at Lake Turkana, which is known as "the cradle of mankind"—and crocodile-kind. It has the largest crocodile population on Earth, so watch your toes.

ⓘ www.magicalkenya.com

94 English as a Second Language

University Language Program

Teaching Young Eager Professionals

Dolores Hidalgo and Querétaro, Mexico

HISTORY BUFFS MAY REMEMBER THAT DOLORES HIDALGO AND QUERÉTARO ARE TWO PLACES that played pivotal roles in Mexico's independence. Nowadays, the former attracts travelers to its pottery and ice cream, and the latter, a larger city, is full of colonial architecture. Your work with university students is in one of these two inspiring environments.

You'll do more than identify colors and shapes in this English-language program. The teacher's syllabus is just the stepping-off point for conversations that often continue long after the classes are over. For 4 hours a day, you'll be in conversation with individuals or small groups of English speakers practicing their skills. Some are business students, others are studying international relations and politics or are literature majors or individuals seeking to master the niceties of the language. Teaching experience is not required. It's the professor's job to teach written skills and grammar; you're brought in to facilitate conversation. General lesson plans are to get the ball rolling, but the conversation is far more important than the content. The more creative you can get—the more you can simulate a normal conversation—the better. Late afternoons are often spent in planning meetings with salaried teachers and volunteers.

The project is based in universities in two cities. Both offer three filling meals and comfortable, basic, double-occupancy rooms in a traditional Mexican hotel in easy walking distance of classes. Free time is built into your schedule to explore your host community, each of which is rich in history, with plazas perfect for people-watching, as well as restaurants, museums, theaters, and bustling open-air markets.

YOUR NEXT STEP: Global Volunteers (✆ **651/407-6100;** www.globalvolunteers.org). A 2-week assignment, US$2,495, includes project training and support, hotel accommodations, and meals.

DON'T MISS: Oaxaca, one of the best-loved, traditional towns in central Mexico, is rich with character and charm. The city's main square, the **Zocalo,** has been the heart of the town since the early 1500s. Seek out the Cathedral of Oaxaca and the former Government Palace. Ancient laurel trees provide dappled shade for listening to live concerts and dining al fresco at the plaza's restaurants and cafes.

ⓘ www.visitmexico.com

English as a Second Language 95

English Outreach Programs for Dropouts

Keeping Learning Part of Village Life

Tacloban, Philippines

ONCE YOU'RE OUTSIDE THE CLASSROOM, TACLOBAN IS A FIRST-CLASS URBAN CENTER, LOCATED on Cancabato Bay between the islands of Leyte and Samar. It's close to universities, shopping, tourism, government, and commerce for the entire Eastern Visayas. But it's also located in close proximity to beaches and world-class diving and, anecdotally speaking, the home of Imelda Marcos, famous for her extensive shoe collection.

This project has two goals. The first is to teach conversational English to children in a rural village. Since Filipino schools begin English-language instruction in first grade, children learn to read early in life, but conversation with native speakers is badly needed. The other goal is to lend a hand to struggling teens and to adults who left the public education program for any number of reasons but who are now motivated to reapply themselves to study. Classes for teens and adults are less formalized, since the community cannot afford to pay full-time teachers for them, but the students are usually eager to challenge themselves and improve their fluency in a language that is seen as a necessary skill for success.

You'll be immersed in this rural community, engaging the elementary schoolchildren in language arts classes and helping out the classroom teachers through the day with other tasks as needed, from yard duty patrol during recess to reading stories during study hall. The rest of your working hours will be spent teaching teens and adults in the town of Tacloban. Your position as a role model, as much as your input into English-language lessons, is tremendously valuable in reigniting a passion for learning.

You'll be living with a Filipino host family, eating home-cooked meals twice daily. You're on your own for lunch at the school or in the village, usually with fellow volunteers and the classroom teachers. Free time is yours to team up with other volunteers or experience town life on your own—only your personal sense of adventure limits what you can do, from sharing meals or drinks with new friends to taking weekend day trips to other parts of the region.

YOUR NEXT STEP: Global Crossroad (✆ **972/252-4191;** www.globalcrossroad.com). A 2-week assignment, US$1,064, includes host family lodging, two meals daily, airport transfers, comprehensive insurance coverage, 24-hour project support, and training.

DON'T MISS: Near Palawan you'll find the **Puerto Princesa Subterranean River National Park,** an otherworldly underground river with green waters that wind beneath the mountain for 5 miles (8km) through a dreamlike network of limestone caves before opening again to sea and sky. A boat tour though the cave system is mystical, as are the surroundings in a protected rainforest.

ⓘ www.tourism.gov.ph

96 English as a Second Language

Language Camp

A Manor House in the Country

Siedlce, Poland

SITUATED ABOUT 2 HOURS EAST OF WARSAW, THE CITY OF SIEDLCE PROVIDES A PASTORAL setting for teaching adults and children in a number of traditional and atypical educational environments.

In some of the small towns in the Polish countryside, volunteers arrive season after season at the Institute of Social Services to continue the tradition of teaching English as a second language to the region's children, as well as to unemployed adults who attend classes (since English is now a requisite skill for many jobs). The undulating hills and country farms form a beautiful backdrop for the converted country manor house, where the organization takes up part time residency in summer. Students and volunteers both reside here. Conversation is the order of the day, and the most important skill you'll need is the gift of gab.

Your teaching time, about 4 hours a day, will focus on a small group of students. Additional time is spent planning teaching strategies with the full-time classroom teachers. Depending on the time of year, you may teach at the manor, or you may commute to neighboring village elementary and middle schools. In addition to giving classroom instruction and leading group discussions, you may accompany the students on field trips or initiate games and activities. You'll also help individuals or small groups tackling their homework after class, and bring energy to rehearsals for class performances (in English) for parents and others in the village.

Your work with adults, while still focused on discussion and oral language skills, requires an entirely different level of conversation, as most are highly motivated entrepreneurs and teachers, all aching to be fluent in English as soon as possible.

You're not far from Warsaw, which makes a terrific weekend diversion; and on weekday evenings you can explore the surrounding woods and valleys and enjoy rural life with the community. You'll get to know your small band of pupils quite well, and are likely to spend casual free time with them, pursuing everything from horseback riding to tennis. Rooms at the manor house are shared, and some of the project schools also have shared cottage accommodations. All meals are provided, and volunteers tend to join forces to conquer the kitchen chores.

YOUR NEXT STEP: Volunteer in Poland via **Global Volunteers** (✆ **800/487-1074;** www.volunteerinpoland.org). A 2-week project, US$2,495, includes housing in mountain chalet cabins or the manor house, meals, and full training and cultural orientation.

DON'T MISS: Malbork, the largest medieval castle in Europe, was the seat of the Grand Master of the Teutonic Order and is exactly the kind of place where you'd expect to see dragons and damsels in distress, with its defensive towers, high-walled gates, and giant reinforced doors. Outdoor concerts have replaced swordplay, along with light shows and other alfresco entertainments.

ⓘ www.polandtour.org

English as a Second Language

97

Short-Term Teaching

Thai Culture, Beach Life

Ao Luk, Thailand

You might not know this warm tropical paradise, with superior snorkeling, fishing, and diving opportunities, that tempts those who want to teach English. Ao Luk is not far from the resort center of Phuket, which you probably have heard of, and boasts the same beauty that made the popular Phuket so famous.

The beach communities of southern Thailand have recently undergone an explosion in popularity for tourists, and this rapidly changing environment has brought a renewed focus on preserving the local culture. The language of tourism in Thailand, as in many places, is English. Thai teachers and students alike look forward to the time when volunteers come to share English conversation skills with them and give them the chance to practice and improve their conversation skills with native speakers. Students of all ages, both in the classroom and out in the community, actively seek opportunities to start a dialogue with English-speaking volunteers and frequently check in—"Did I say that correctly?"—while chatting.

Teachers in Ao Luk communities have limited resources and many demands on their classroom time, so your volunteer efforts will go a long way toward improving the learning experience for students, who benefit from personalized attention and smaller study groups. During one-on-one tutoring sessions after class, you can help students with homework and study skills. Later, you can work with community leaders to develop English-language tourism materials, brochures, training manuals, or websites.

You have a choice of living at the base camp in dormitory-style housing shared with fellow volunteers or living with a host family in a traditional Thai household. Meals are provided in both scenarios, with base-camp groups cooking and cleaning as a team. Your free time will likely be spent immersing yourself in village life. Thai-language instruction and Thai cooking classes are also offered. The beach is a powerful draw to visitors, so if you're like most volunteers on this project, you'll enjoy leaving long trails of footprints in the white sands, splashing in the warm waters, hiking into the lush green mountains, or exploring a nearby system of caves.

YOUR NEXT STEP: Global Vision International (✆ **888/653-6028;** www.gviusa.com). A 2-week project, US$990, covers housing in either base-camp dorms or with a host family, meals, cultural orientation, project training, and 24-hour support.

DON'T MISS: The cinematic beauty of the **Phi Phi Islands** off the coast of Phuket can't be denied—no wonder it was featured in the movie *The Beach* and draws intrepid travelers looking to escape into the tropics. Recuperate from travel woes on the sugar-sand beaches and gaze up at the steep cliffs and rock formations that make this island so memorable.

ⓘ www.tourismthailand.org

98 English as a Second Language

Hill Tribe Education

A Lifeline to the Outside World

Chiang Rai, Thailand

The surroundings in this northernmost province are replete with Buddhist shrines, villages, ruins, and a path slightly less traveled path than the one to Chiang Mai. But the challenges that await instructors in Chiang Rai are not necessarily things the average traveler always sees—they're tied to the difficulties that face many of the people in this mountainous part of Thailand.

Many of the hill tribes of Northern Thailand are very poor, with the incidence of unemployment, drug addiction, illiteracy, and extreme poverty much higher than in neighboring Thai towns. The hill tribes still speak languages and hold beliefs that are distinct from elsewhere in the country. When this hill tribe project was launched with local children, only 5 families (of 200) were found to be free of addiction to drugs. A "clean sweep program" was instigated to have entire villages kick drug habits simultaneously, offering one another unprecedented support in the struggle. The kids of these families, some with addictions they inherited from birth, struggle to make a fresh start. Barely half of the hill tribe children of school age are actually enrolled, and far fewer will see their education through to graduation. Children become an important part of the village workforce at a very young age, supporting their families; and too often there are cases of human trafficking in women and children.

Your volunteer work in these small villages outside Chiang Rai will be nearly as challenging as it is rewarding. Much of the time you'll be teaching English, a language embraced by the community as a necessary stepping stone toward success in the world outside their own. You may also spend mornings painting a classroom and fixing up a communal eating area, then helping to create materials to promote human rights or fight drug trafficking. Staff members may also be eager to improve their English skills, so you may have a parent-and-teacher group to work with in the afternoons. Your English skills will also supplement the work of building and improving the project website, creating fundraising materials, and developing HIV educational materials.

Life in the small villages will be straightforward. You'll stay in dormitory accommodations and pitch in with group cooking and cleaning tasks. You'll spend downtime on trekking excursions, learning Thai cooking, and shopping with villagers at a bustling open-air market. The weather is often hot and sticky, so you're likely to spend free time simply lying still and relaxing with your adopted community. The tribes make use of working, domesticated elephants and will insist that you ride along one day.

YOUR NEXT STEP: Mirror Art Foundation 🎗 (✆ **+66/53 737 412;** www.mirrorartgroup.org). A 2-week stay, US$286, includes group housing in shared dormitory accommodations, shared weekday meals (weekends you're on your own at inexpensive restaurants), elephant rides, trekking fees in national parks, training, airport pickup, and cultural orientation and support.

DON'T MISS: The royal villa of the Princess Mother of the King of Thailand, north of Chiang Rai, is a great site to visit. The **Doi Tung Royal Villa** and its **Mae Fa Luang Garden** are a wild pastiche of styles—the villa is part traditional Thai, part Swiss chalet, and the nearly 10,000 acres (4,047ha) of flowering botanical gardens are an awesome sight, especially in the winter when the blooms are at their most lush.

ⓘ www.tourismthailand.org

10 Places to Learn a Language While You Teach One

These programs give you real, tangible skills to bring home as you learn the local languages in classrooms or through private lessons in exchange for sharing your English skills with the people the programs serve. It is language quid pro quo, and perhaps the most effective form of cultural immersion.

99 **Cochabamba, Bolivia** Four weeks in Bolivia, where the Andes meet the Amazon, will be pretty memorable even if the only thing you bring home is memories of the friends you made and the useful work you did as a volunteer teacher. Bringing home a more advanced grasp of the Spanish language will be icing on the cake. ***The Society for Environmental Exploration (Frontier)*** *(© **+44/20 7613 2422**; www.frontier.ac.uk). The 1-month program is £1,050.*

100 **Maceio, Brazil** While teaching the children of this community English-language skills that increase their confidence and competitiveness for higher education opportunities, volunteer language teachers gain Portuguese language skills as well as the tangible and intangible benefits of cultural interchange. Children participate in the school program for free—a huge asset where school attendance is based upon affordability. ***Volunteer Maceio*** *(e-mail: sergius_al@yahoo.com; www.volunteermaceio.org). There is no cost, with accommodations provided rent-free in an apartment within the school building.*

101 **Wuhu, China** Mandarin may be incredibly difficult to learn, but English is no cakewalk either. Try explaining "I before E except after C" or the spelling of the "A" sound in "neighbor" and "weigh." If you can do this, maybe you ought to be teaching English in Wuhu as a volunteer. And if you care to learn Mandarin as well, sign up for an equal number of hours of Chinese language instruction. ***Aston Language Centre*** *(© **+86/553-3834699**; www.astonedu.com). Programs run at least 6 weeks. This exchange is cost-free. Single-entry Chinese visa required, US$100.*

New friends at The Mélida Anaya Montes English school in El Salvador

102 **San Salvador, El Salvador** The Mélida Anaya Montes English School depends upon volunteer teachers to impart English-language skills and a socially conscious sensibility. Professional Spanish classes are also offered. During the day, you'll teach English to children and adults interspersed with classes in which you're the student, learning Spanish. ***Center for Exchange and Solidarity*** *(© **503/2226-5362**; www.cis-elsalvador.org). A 5-week session costs only a US$100 enrollment fee.*

103 **Accra, Ghana** In exchange for your contribution teaching English, you'll learn not just one, but two tongues, as Ghana has more than one indigenous language. You'll be exchanging life experience as much as syntax and tenses while living for 1 month in a local community. Your work week will be spent teaching

English while learning Twi and Ewe and gaining an understanding of local life and culture. ***The Society for Environmental Exploration (Frontier)*** *(© **+44/20 7613 2422**; www.frontier.ac.uk). A 4-week assignment costs US$1,315.*

104 La Ceiba, Honduras You'll be helping to set up a Honduran school devoted to reaching out to poor and underprivileged youth. For 4 weeks you'll be teaching English in exchange for Spanish-language training—mornings you give; in the afternoons, you receive. Opportunities exist to earn a Teach English as a Foreign Language (TEFL) certificate. Your free time can easily be filled with scuba diving, horseback riding, beach time, and rainforest hikes. ***The Society for Environmental Exploration (Frontier)*** *(© **+44/20 7613 2422**; www.frontier.ac.uk). The 4-week program is £895.*

105 Delhi or Bangalore, India Working and conversing with a fluent English speaker is a rare opportunity for young pupils in India. You'll create additional extracurricular activities to support their studies and give them more engaging ways to practice their language skills. You'll have to be sure to carve out some time for yourself to practice the Hindi you'll be learning at the same time. ***Volunteering in India*** *(© **+91/124-4307993**; www.volunteeringindia.com). 1 week: US$450; 2 weeks: US$575 (longer arrangements possible and encouraged).*

A volunteer in India sharing a craft with his young student

106 Chisinau, Moldova The poor, landlocked, former Soviet country of Moldova has two official languages: Moldovan and Russian. Skilled teachers have been lured away from public schools in favor of higher paying language academies, leaving a vacuum for ordinary children. More than diagramming sentences and preventing participles from dangling, you'll be questioned tirelessly about life in your home country, giving kids new language skills while you work on your Russian. ***Projects Abroad*** *(USA: © **888/839-3535**. CAN: 877/921-9666; www.projects-abroad.org). A 1-month placement is US$2,245.*

107 Chimbote, Peru You can teach one pupil or a class full of international and immigrant students working on their English grammar, reading, writing, and conversational skills. At the small Mi Segundo Hogar school, you'll be teaching both children and adults in two or three classes daily. You'll also learn Spanish through a few hours of instruction each week. ***Peru 109*** *(© **888/737-8109**; www.peru109.org). A 2-week program is US$850.*

108 Odessa, Ukraine At the Odessa Language Study Center's seaside summer language camp, you can volunteer to teach English and in return get 4 hours of daily instruction in Russian. The program uses formalized European curriculum guidelines for classes, then balances the pedagogy with a hefty dose of fun. ***Odessa Language Study Center*** *(© **+380/482-345058**; http://studyrus.com/terms.html) Room, board, and Russian-language instruction at no cost; program length at your discretion.*

English as a Second Language 

Tutor Children of New Immigrants

Bring Language to the Land of 10,000 Lakes

Austin and Worthington, Minnesota, USA

You can immerse yourself in a microcosm of contemporary immigration issues and help children of new immigrants learn the language that will help gain them entry to American culture as part of this program. Located in the southern part of Minnesota, you'll share your knowledge in a relaxed lakeside setting.

While politicians argue about immigration until they're blue in the face, America continues to absorb and assimilate new cultural influences. In Midwestern communities, established families join with new arrivals from Mexico, Guatemala, Russia, Sudan, Vietnam, Somalia, Cambodia, Bosnia, Laos, Ethiopia, Eritrea, and other countries, stamping their own diverse identities on the heartland. The turn of the century was a boom time in the growth of both Austin and Worthington, Minnesota, and learning English-language skills is eagerly, almost frantically, pursued in an effort to assimilate as quickly as possible into the North Star State.

As we all know, language skills come most easily to the young, so while English may not be spoken in newly established homes, the children are learning as much and as quickly as they can (and bringing their new knowledge home with them). Conversational English is the most important, and often missing, link in the public school curriculum. Memorization and textbook reading don't lend themselves to comfortable dialogue and easy interaction between neighbors, so you'll play a pivotal role in leading discussion groups with kids, giving them the confidence they need to communicate in a new language. Classroom teachers are too often overwhelmed

Tutoring children of new immigrants in Minnesota

by the sheer number of students in crowded classrooms, so in addition to leading students in oral exercises, you'll also be offering a pair of hands for other classroom activities such as art and sports. Supplemental after-school activities, with study hall and tutoring sessions, will round out your days with these multicultural kids.

Home base for the Austin project is dormitory-style, with fellow volunteers. Worthington project members stay in shared cabins on a lake. Meals are taken with your associates. There's ample free time in the evening and weekends to explore the region, enjoying rural America and the neighborly qualities of small-town life.

YOUR NEXT STEP: Global Volunteers (✆ **651/407-6100;** www.globalvolunteers.org). One week in either of these Minnesota towns, US$995, covers the cost of accommodations in dormitories or shared cabins, all meals, airport pickup, and full training and support.

DON'T MISS: To be truly immersed in Americana, when in Austin (or the vicinity), go whole hog and visit the **SPAM Museum.** This tribute to potted meat is 16,500 sq. ft. (1,533 sq. m) of tongue-in-cheek honor and praise for a "culinary masterpiece" (tongues and cheeks being two major components of a tin of SPAM).

ⓘ www.exploreminesota.com

---

110 English as a Second Language

English for Disadvantaged Children

Good Morning, Vietnam

Ho Chi Minh City, Vietnam

The largest city in Vietnam is relatively young, founded in the 18th century, and for many Americans carries an association with the Vietnam War. But it also bears a reputation as a busy, eclectic commercial hub that is yours to explore, with the Vietnam History Museum, the popular Ben Thanh Market, and the Saigon Opera House.

A family can be defined in many ways, and only one of them is based on biology. The children in this teaching project are no longer able to live with their families for one reason or another: some were orphaned, abandoned, or abused. The shelters where they now live are passionately committed to creating a new family community for them, offering stability and renewed trust. One of the top teaching goals for all age levels is learning English as a second language, Native speakers like you bring the language to life, supplementing blackboard and books with dynamic, real-life conversation.

You'll work weekday mornings with elementary schoolchildren in a classroom setting. The full-time teachers in the classrooms are usually too outnumbered and challenged to provide much one-on-one instruction. You'll take small groups of kids to other rooms and establish conversation groups, working to correct pronunciation and develop a facility with dialogue. You'll also work in tandem with the teacher on other classroom efforts, such as playing games, singing songs, and drawing. Extracurricular activities can take place spontaneously, as kids flock to their foreign visitors after lessons. Having some fun ideas up your sleeve never hurts.

Project life is easy, with evenings and weekends free to explore Ho Chi Minh City (formerly Saigon) and other areas of the country. The staff is happy to arrange excursions and day trips for you. You'll live in a project dormitory or with your fellow volunteers in a group guesthouse. Food is provided, but the group prepares it together for communal meals. You may also opt to eat at a small restaurant near the project base or with a host family. Ho Chi Minh is a big city with lots to discover, so you'll find much to see and do there.

YOUR NEXT STEP: Global Crossroad (✆ **972/252-4191;** www.globalcrossroad.com). A 2-week project, US$1,264, includes housing in a project guesthouse or dormitory with shared rooms, meals, comprehensive insurance; airport transfers, project training, and in-country support.

DON'T MISS: Downtown **Ho Chi Minh City** on a Sunday night is like a scene from the movie *American Graffiti.* The slow cruising up and down the streets (called ***di choi***) is done on scooters and motorbikes instead of hotrods, but the sensibility is the same—young people, older folks, and entire families slowly maneuvering through traffic or walking the streets on Sunday nights. When you get tired, grab a table at a colorful outdoor cafe or bar for front-row people-watching.

ⓘ www.vietnamtourism.com

Arts, Crafts & Business **111**

Circus Arts & Theatre Design

Livin' La Vida Rio

Rio de Janeiro, Brazil

The birthplace of bossa nova and "The Girl from Ipanema." The beaches. The statue of Christ on Corcovado. The devil-may-care, fun-loving attitude. And the drinks laced with the sugar-cane-based spirit cachaça. Setting aside the intriguing volunteer opportunities, why wouldn't you want to go to Rio?

An exciting and unconventional project has been steadily growing in Rio, teaching troubled and at-risk youth how to express themselves in a variety of creative ways. Volunteers from around the world gather here and inspire one another to channel their energy in positive, imaginative ways. Young people from lower-income neighborhoods also learn the practical skills they need to enter the competitive, professional world of the circus. The program has a workshop and teaching space that are shared with other community organizations. It also has a tent—a big circus tent.

The focus here is on circus arts, as well as set design and the construction of sets for theater and the film industry. Teens learn set construction—including carpentry, painting, and rigging—with professional crews who serve Rio's stage and movie business. The circus classes are as varied as the volunteers, who, like you, bring a new burst of energy every time they join the group.

Your own passion will dictate how you best commit yourself to inspiring the kids of this project. You can lend a supportive hand to the group if you're not an expert or you can take charge if you have a skill to impart. Direct a play, lead a dance class, teach a new style of graffiti art, create puppetry shows, document your work with video—everything is possible. You might also work with a film crew, shooting a creative screenplay, or instruct a group in sound design, lighting, computer animation, or even how to be a DJ. If you have the will and the talent, you can design and create outlandish costumes, work on vocal performance skills, turn sports skills into performance, lead a group in swordplay, stage a combat, even teach fire-eating. The goal is to be available for anything these kids can dream up and to help them bring ideas and passions to life. It's an outrageously effective channel for energy and inspiration, and you'll come away wondering why every town doesn't have the same programs.

You won't want to leave the creative space of the tent, but when you do, home will be a shared apartment or flat, where meals are shared with fellow volunteers. Some basic Portuguese will go a long way toward making communication fluid with the kids, even though English is spoken on the project, so get those language tapes now. Historically, volunteers have found their free time absorbed by last-minute rehearsals, trying to get a coat of paint onto the doors of a set, working out the beat of a song, and choreographing curtain calls. Time is irrelevant when you are swirling in this kind of energy, but of course just outside the tent is the city of Rio de Janeiro, with all its rival energy and frenetic flow. You may find sleep is extraneous.

YOUR NEXT STEP: Volunteer Abroad (✆ **720/570-1702;** www.volunteerabroad.com. 2 weeks: US$499; 1 month: US$988; in conjunction with the Center of Socio Cultural Activities and Circus. The fee covers the shared accommodations in project housing, shared meals, airport transfers, full project training and support (especially if you're developing new skills previously unexplored—highly recommended), and help in finding a Portuguese-language class (at extra cost).

DON'T MISS: The beautiful white Oscar Niemeyer–designed spaceship across the bay from Rio is actually the **MAC** (Museu de Arte Contemporânea, Niterói), the contemporary art museum, with brilliant views back toward the city. Like New York's Guggenheim, the graceful round structure is as beautiful as the vivid art collections gracing its walls.

ⓘ www.riodejaneiro-turismo.com.br/en

Arts, Crafts & Business

Khmer Cultural Projects

The Traveling Teacher

Several locations, Cambodia

A BURGEONING TOURISM DESTINATION, CAMBODIA OFFERS FAR MORE THAN THE AWE-INSPIRING ruins of Angkor Wat—boat trips up the Mekong River, the vibrant city of Phnom Penh, and a healthy dash of unpredictability. After your month spent here you'll understand why it's become so popular so quickly.

This project is part volunteer work and part cultural immersion, as you visit several of the best-known cities of Cambodia as well as off-the-beaten-path villages and towns. It's a month-long commitment but a nice blend of work and exploration.

In the first part of your journey, you'll explore major points of interest (Phnom Penh, the Killing Fields, National Museum, and so on). In the second part, you'll live in a traditional village and immerse yourself in Khmer culture. Through your interactions, you'll be introduced to the local language and cuisine, native rituals, dance, song, the art of puppet making, and more. After absorbing so much of the culture, you'll have the chance to give back, teaching conversational English, arts and crafts, and other skills. You needn't be an accomplished artist or teacher to make a powerful contribution. On your working days, you'll be in schools, talking and playing with small groups of students. Later in the day you'll repeat some of the same tasks at the orphanage.

Immersed in Khmer culture and the Cambodian way of life

Coming home in the evenings to your host family is an uplifting, warm experience (and a guarantee of good eating). Families are carefully chosen for their interest in making deep, personal connections with visitors from other cultures and learning about their lives firsthand. The program is well structured, so your days off are filled with excursions. There are few questions about Khmer life, history, and culture that you won't be able to answer by the time you return home after such full immersion.

YOUR NEXT STEP: Projects Abroad (✆ **888/839-3535;** www.projects-abroad.org). A 2-week project, US$2,545, includes host family lodging, meals, touring costs and guides, project training and cultural orientation, enrichment classes, comprehensive travel and medical insurance, and 24-hour support.

DON'T MISS: The floor of Phnom Penh's **Silver Pagoda,** also known as the Temple of the Emerald Buddha, is covered with more than 5,000 silver tiles. It is home not only to the headliners—a large golden Buddha and a beloved crystal emerald Buddha—but also several other treasures, making the Silver Pagoda a glittering ode to the steadfastness of the culture—and one of the only surviving Cambodian temples that wasn't damaged by the Khmer Rouge regime.

ⓘ www.tourismcambodia.com

113 Arts, Crafts & Business

Preserving Ghanaian Art & Culture

The Art Scene in Africa

Accra, Ghana

If you are curious about African culture and history and you have some artistic gifts, then put your skills to the test in Accra. But should an escape from the arts and pace of the city be in order, there are a handful of excellent beaches not far away.

You don't need to be a patron of the arts or even have clay or oil paint under your fingernails to join this project—but a passion and excitement about art will serve you well, as will some experience in the business of selling, promoting, and preserving art. The mission of this organization is to capture, record, and promote Ghana's history and cultural traditions for future generations. They collect and display indigenous artworks and promote programs that get every generation, especially today's youth, interested in their heritage. Volunteers work directly with highly respected Ghanaian artists and curators at ArtHaus in a creative workshop environment for painters, sculptors, printmakers, photographers, and other artistic types.

You'll be placed where your personal skills can be of the most help to the project, in fields from graphic design to film editing, text editing to cataloguing. If you've done fundraising before, you'll be in great demand. You'll be a superstar if you have web design experience—but sometimes you'll also need to pitch in and help set up exhibits or plan events. You'll also rub elbows with the Accra art world and be asked to attend cultural events and gallery openings, gaining an insider's view of the city and its creative movers and shakers. Before you finish your stint and head home, you'll document what you've worked on thus far, where progress is needed, as your own progress so the next volunteers can pick up where you left off.

Daily life will swirl around the scene at ArtHaus, on the outskirts of Accra, but when it's time to cap the paints and go home for the night, you'll head back to the project group house that you share with other volunteers in the town's center. A short walk gets you to shops, restaurants, pubs, and Internet cafes. Your free time is—what free time? You're schmoozing with the art crowd, remember? Enjoy!

YOUR NEXT STEP: Ikando (✆ **+233/ 21 222 726;** www.ikando.org). This is a 4-week minimum assignment, though you can plan on working here much longer if you're a budding artist. The US$1,239 fee covers accommodations at the project group house; local orientation and project training; airport transfers; 24-hour support; and a project donation to the ArtHaus and host organization.

DON'T MISS: There are 10 **Abosomfie Fetish Shrines** around the city of Asante, still revered and used by traditionalists in the region. These sacred buildings are the home of particular deities and gods who ceremonially inhabit the bodies of holy men, who in turn act as conduits, passing on the wisdom of the elders. The sacred rites are fascinating to watch and are refreshingly off-the-beaten path of most tourists.

ⓘ www.touringghana.com

Arts, Crafts & Business

114

Art as Rehabilitation

Building a Bridge Back to Society

Delhi, India

ART BECOMES A WAY TO HELP NAVIGATE LIFE FOR THE YOUNG PEOPLE YOU'LL WORK WITH inside the classroom. Outside the classroom, rejuvenate your creativity and get inspired by a world of colors, noises, tastes, and smells among the millions in the city of Delhi.

Young people addicted to drugs, many living on the street, seek out this project for a creative outlet and a way back into productive habits. Parallel programs work with other special needs of children, teens, and adults. Working with individuals or small groups, you'll conceive and teach craft projects and help run workshops in music, sewing and embroidery, woodworking, candle making, computer animation, and any other creative skill you bring to the table. You'll be doing de facto counseling, giving participants an opportunity for intensive focus and free expression. You'll also initiate casual conversation so participants can discuss the issues they're confronting in a non-threatening, non-clinical environment.

You'll be sharing your time and talent with marginalized individuals in a wide array of ways, encouraging self-expression through art, leading discussion groups in English, and orchestrating creative games and dance. There will be times when you'll lead the group and times when you'll be supporting the staff and other volunteers. You may move from a public meeting space to a school to an orphanage through the day, as the program serves several populations in Delhi.

The work is bound to be exhausting, requiring razor-sharp focus and patience, so you'll heave a sigh of relief each night after a satisfying job well done. You can relax and let your hair down in a shared hostel or in a private home, should you opt to live with a host family. In either scenario, three Indian meals are provided daily, and in the evenings or other free time, you can dive into the swirling, colorful chaos of Delhi, with endless opportunities for exploration and iconic Indian experiences.

YOUR NEXT STEP: Global Crossroad (✆ **972/252-4191;** www.globalcrossroad.com). US$1,011 covers 2 weeks' shared hostel or host family accommodations, meals, project training, airport pickup, 24-hour project support, and comprehensive travel and medical insurance.

DON'T MISS: Visit the lovely, quiet retreat in the wide-open courtyard of **Raj Gat,** where Mahatma Gandhi was cremated. You'll find an eternal flame burning above an unadorned black granite marker. It is a profound place of simplicity, conducive to meditation and giving thanks.

ⓘ www.incredibleindia.org

115 Arts, Crafts & Business

Arts & Crafts Projects

Learn Ceramic Traditions & Culture

Guadalajara, Mexico

Here you can learn the finer points of Mexican pottery and traditional culture, while at the same time increase your facility with Spanish. The cultural element goes beyond firing a kiln, as Guadalajara is the birthplace of mariachi music, the Mexican hat dance, and perhaps its biggest alcoholic export, tequila.

The Guadalajaran districts of Tlaquepaque and Tonala are prized for the beautiful ceramics that are traditionally produced here. Many local craftspeople work in various forms, but it is the ceramic tiles, vessels, and housewares that attract shoppers and tourists and bring stability to the local economy. There are many pottery workshops in the area, and volunteers are trained to become ceramicists, working in a family-owned studio. The products you help create are sold in local markets or exported, providing the neighborhood with steady income. The workshops began by producing handmade ceramic tiles, but over the years they branched out to make commercial wall plaques, jugs, and even sinks and basins, all glazed and decorated in traditional styles.

Decorating ceramic pottery in Mexico

You'll be involved in every step of the production process during your time here. You'll assist in the art of making molds for the clay and learn the recipe for mixing the clay to get the perfect consistency for casting. The patience (and forearm strength) needed to push the clay evenly into the molds to get the cleanest design is a learned skill. Painting comes next. You'll need perseverance to keep at it through the day, but you'll learn traditional patterns and designs and be able to imbue them with your own creative flair. Once you've decorated the work, you'll be taught the glazing process. The completed work goes into the kiln for firing, and then it's time to start on the next batch.

It's satisfying to work hard, with tangible results, but you'll be pleased the workday is brief. You'll wrap up the day in time for a late lunch with your host family. Some conversational Spanish will be important for both ceramic training and life in your new home, where you'll be served three meals daily and have a private room. Your free time can be spent visiting the many other artisans and workshop spaces in Guadalajara, a region famous for its craftwork. Art galleries, museums both contemporary and historical, arts and crafts markets, and beautiful public art in plazas and churches are all waiting to be explored.

YOUR NEXT STEP: Projects Abroad (✆ **888/839-3535;** www.projects-abroad.org). A 2-week apprenticeship, US$2,395, includes lodging with a host family, three meals daily, training in the workshop, comprehensive insurance, and 24-hour support.

DON'T MISS: To celebrate your accomplishments, take the **Tequila Train** from Guadalajara and enjoy the desert scenery en route to Tequila and Jalisco. Once there, visit several distilleries for tastings, learn the differences between tequila, mezcal, and pulque, and discern the subtle variations in flavor and smokiness. It isn't all harsh like the bargain-brand liquid fire you may remember from your party days.

ⓘ www.visitmexico.com

Arts, Crafts & Business **116**

Teaching Art, Drama & Computer Skills

Living among the Zulus

eMakhosini Village, South Africa

YOU'LL FULLY IMMERSE YOURSELF IN AN ENTIRELY DIFFERENT WAY OF LIFE IN SOUTH AFRICA when living in this remote village, teaching arts and crafts to children and helping them retain and preserve ties to their culture.

In the heart of the Zulu Kingdom, you can teach English-language skills and other arts to the children of eMakhosini, the king's village. Though the title is lofty, many of the families in this rural village are seriously impoverished, and the population of about 6,000 residents depends on only one primary school to educate its youth (a second, smaller school is being shuttered). Tradition trumps modernity here in a community governed by tribal elders within a stone's throw of the sacred burial spots of the original Zulu kings and the birthplace of famous King Shaka. The South African government has determined that a tourism infrastructure is the only way to make this community economically stable, but in order to do this the next generation has a lot of work on its hands, including learning English and placing a renewed focus on preserving and nurturing tribal history and arts.

Your volunteer work will be varied, and all of it in English (your students' first language may be Zulu or Afrikaans). Computers have recently been acquired for the school (not enough—so if you have a used one to donate, it will be welcome), and there is a computer teacher, but anything from basic Windows to navigating the Internet needs to be learned. In "life orientation" programs, you'll work with some 20 students—about one-third of the class—learning and performing songs, dances, and plays. You'll want to assist classroom teachers with formal lessons, but improvisation and new performance ideas are always welcome. Finding creative ways to blend contemporary performance with traditional culture, perhaps reinterpreting and dramatizing legends or adding a new beat to historic songs and dances, gives these young people a renewed interest in their Zulu lineage and develops in them a sense of responsibility for the preservation of their culture.

Home base is in a farmhouse in the neighboring Heritage Park, with several bedrooms and shared baths, living room, and kitchen. Meals are included. You can team up with other volunteers to cook at the farmhouse or hang out in small cafes and snackbars in the park—a destination for wild game observation. Free time is usually spent around the village with new friends, absorbing the tribal culture and way of life. Game viewing is a prize activity on weekends.

YOUR NEXT STEP: Travellers Worldwide (UK: **+44/1903 502595;** www.travellers worldwide.com). A 2-week project, £795, includes communal housing, shared meals, airport transfers, project training, and full support.

DON'T MISS: The concept of flight figures prominently in some Zulu legends, so why not get a bird's-eye view of the Zulu Kingdom where you've been working so hard? Flight schools and charter businesses give you the chance to try **paragliding** or take a **helicopter flight** over the region. Seeing herds of buffalo or rhino from above is an amazing experience. The helicopter may startle them into magnificent group movement, while paragliding transforms you into an almost silent observer.

ⓘ www.southafrica.net

Arts, Crafts & Business

Teaching Computer Skills

Helping the Survivors of the Tsunami

Wadduwa, Sri Lanka

For those who have a fascination with Buddhism, Asian culture, and tropical beaches, but who want to go somewhere off the beaten path, this small tropical island fits the bill. It also provides volunteers with some very real opportunities to put computer skills—from basic to advanced—to work.

While the Boxing Day tsunami that devastated so many coastal regions in Southeast Asia was years ago, the effects to the Sri Lankan communities can still be seen. Tourism, a major source of income, became undependable in the years following the tragedy, so new coping techniques and businesses needed to be explored. Computer literacy has become incredibly important in advancing the community's goals, as well as in assuring some stability for individuals and families. Children and adults look for guidance in mastering both basic and more advanced computer skills,

Students working in a computer lab in Sri Lanka

including code writing and programming. It isn't required that you be a computer genius or expert, but if you have advanced skills, you'll definitely get to put them to use.

Your volunteer time will be spent with students in informal computer lab rooms, helping them tackle the basics of Word or Excel and learn how to maintain databases and project plan files. Even making use of the mouse or track pad are skills that must be introduced, since so many students are starting from scratch. One of the most valuable tasks you can teach is how to create and update a résumé, as most of the adults who come to this project are using newfound computer skills to increase their employability. Children and adults sometimes commute for miles for computer training. There is a set syllabus to get all students to a level of computer literacy, and additional tutoring and coaching on your part is a great asset. Some English is taught, but this project also has a translator to help reach every student, regardless of language ability.

Life in this tiny coastal village is easygoing, and you'll be living with a host family. The computer lab rooms are in a central project house within walking distance. You'll find that you'll while away the evenings and weekends, enjoying the beach and the camaraderie in the village. Your host family will serve as your social committee, so you can expect to visit several local homes for meals and conversation.

YOUR NEXT STEP: Projects Abroad (✆ **888/839-3535;** www.projects-abroad.org). A short-term (2-week) placement is US$1,795, but sticking around and teaching for longer is always welcome and a great benefit to returning students. The fee covers host family accommodations and meals, full insurance, project training and support, and translation services.

DON'T MISS: The largest museum in Sri Lanka, the **National Museum, Colombo,** was also the nation's first, established in 1877. It has national treasures from across the island, including the beloved Puppetry and Children's Museum and an enormous collection of ancient palm-leaf manuscripts written in several languages. More than 12 million books and publications line the library shelves.

ⓘ www.srilankatourism.org

118 Arts, Crafts & Business

Artistic Outreach Programs

Inspiring the Vulnerable in Northern Thailand

Chiang Mai, Thailand

The Northern Thai city of Chiang Mai has a fascinating mix of cultural influences, with traditional Thai, Burmese, and hill tribe people coming together in this balmy tropical region. Volunteers can add their own human and creative touch while helping others in the community to express themselves.

This project provides arts training and outreach programs to several populations and humanitarian groups in Chiang Mai, from sex workers and oppressed women to orphans, HIV/AIDS patients, and refugees from across the border with Burma. You'll work directly with the art director, running creativity workshops and setting up community exhibits of the student work. Through your efforts, individuals are encouraged to find a voice for change through creative self-expression in the visual, performance, and experimental arts.

The mission of the Canvas Art Program is to "promote expression and cultivate the creativity that lies inside each individual. We use art to create an atmosphere of inclusion and belonging where often there is none. Art is used as a catalyst for releasing and challenging personal and societal stresses whilst encouraging cultural changes and awareness." Sometimes your role is as coach, sometimes as appreciative audience, sometimes as gentle constructive critic. Depending on your skills and interests, you may lead or assist a dance class, develop an acting curriculum that adapts to students of different ages, write brochure and grant proposals, or develop your own teaching unit based on

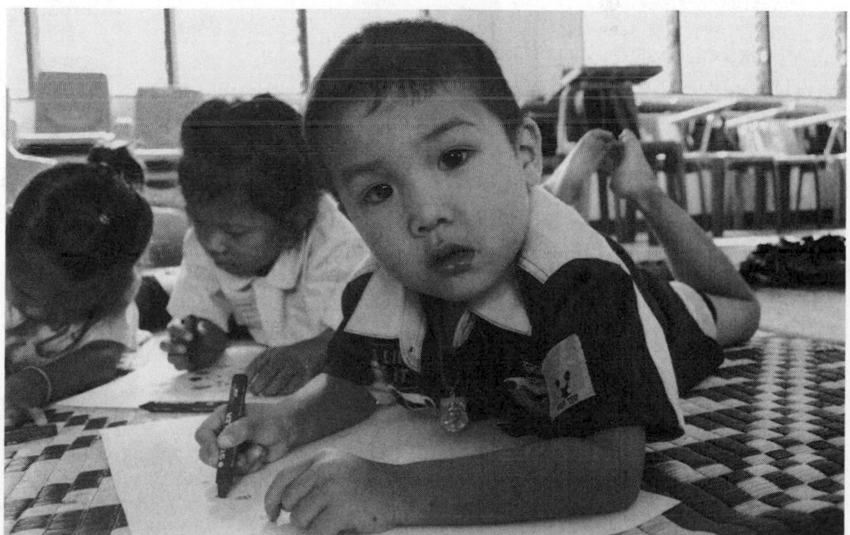

Young artists in Chiang Mai, Thailand

your passion or expertise. Your work simply needs to inspire people and get them up and out of their chairs (and out of their self-limiting behaviors and beliefs).

In the center of the old city, the project has a group house that is your home away from home as well as the base of operations. A live-in cook provides three Thai meals daily. The work doesn't fit into a tidy package, so sometimes you'll have free time in the day, sometimes at night; perhaps you'll work hardest on the weekends. Chiang Mai is a tremendously popular destination for international tourists, and you'll know it like the back of your paint-splattered hand by the time you say good-bye.

YOUR NEXT STEP: Cultural Canvas Thailand (✆ **850/316-8470;** www.culturalcanvas.com). This 3-week project, US$1,399, includes lodging at the project's group house, Thai meals, project training, in-country cultural orientation, and comprehensive insurance.

DON'T MISS: It is nearly impossible not to whistle the marching song from the 1957 award-winning film *The Bridge on the River Kwai* when you're making your way across the **bridge on the River Kwai.** It's not the largest bridge or the most scenic, but it's a big part of the history of central Thailand and a big part of classic American movie history.

ⓘ www.tourismthailand.org

Arts, Crafts & Business **119**

Art History as Business

Crafting Culture

Kpalim'E, Togo

TOGO IS TRYING TO BOOST TOURISM AND PRESERVE ITS INDIGENOUS ART FORMS. VOLUNTEERS who opt for this small West African country will learn how to tell a story through textiles and preserve the country's important stories. When you need a break, there is excellent hiking through nearby mountains.

The long and proud tradition of Togolese textile arts is virtually unknown to those locals not directly involved in the business of creating or selling the works. Batik prints, indigo cloth, Kente dye-stamped Adinkra cloth, embroidery, and lace are all hallmarks of the fabric arts sought out by discerning international buyers. With financial limitations upon public institutions, arts are not taught in schools (where it often feels like a boon to have books), so the cultural significance and storytelling subtlety of cloth art is being lost as a new generation comes up unaware of this ancestral lineage. Several small, local nongovernment organizations have sprouted up to help nurture the textile arts and other local craft specialties back to health, making them a viable source of income as tourism increases. As tourism grows, so does the demand for authentic, locally produced art.

As a volunteer, you'll participate in the creation of crafts and also in the art of selling them. Working with students from the village, you'll learn the art of fabric printing and batik, carving ornaments and bracelets, and beading. All the materials to create the handiworks are locally sourced, supporting local initiatives. The products you make under the mentorship of the teachers will be sold at market, and funds will cycle back into the outreach program. The flip side of the project is in establishing a commercial infrastructure for local marketplaces, and even exploring the possibilities of overseas or Internet commerce, imparting your small business expertise (if that's your skill set) and potentially doing some web-building.

You'll be staying with a host family in Togo, sharing meals and long conversation with your new family, and others in the village who gather to share good times in the evenings and on weekends. You'll have plenty of downtime on days off to explore the surrounding region and learn even more from neighboring villages and long hikes through the wilderness.

YOUR NEXT STEP: Global Crossroad (✆ **972/252-4191;** www.globalcrossroad.com). A 2-week project, US$1,011, includes: host family lodging and meals, comprehensive insurance coverage, airport pickup, project support, and skills training from master craftspeople.

DON'T MISS: Make a stop in the village of **Togoville**, from which the nation takes its name. The most famous structures in town are the Roman Catholic Cathedral, a shrine to the Virgin Mary, and many, many traditional voodoo shrines.

ⓘ www.togo-tourisme.com

120 Arts, Crafts & Business

Navajo Nation Arts Education

Learn to Live Like a Native American

Tuba City, Arizona, USA

Step into a completely different pace of life and learn something about North America's past and present by learning (and living) traditional Navajo practices. The barren beauty of the Southwest will beckon when you have time to explore.

The largest reservation in the United States is home to the Navajo Nation, covering territory in Arizona, New Mexico, and Utah. The Navajo revere their cultural heritage and tribal traditions, but pressures from a modern, fast-paced world tend to diminish their ancestral knowledge with each successive generation. This program emphasizes creating active arts programs for youth to explore traditional styles and forms of expression. Despite the best efforts of elders, young people quite naturally are drawn to computers and television and pop music, often at the expense of traditional arts. It's a challenge today to find the proper balance between past and present, and the boarding school in Tuba City has found creative ways to strike that balance, with support from volunteers like you.

In addition to mentoring Native American children and helping them with their school work, you'll participate in a schoolwide arts program that combines traditional arts and crafts techniques with modern sensibilities. You'll continue and expand this work, creating opportunities for creative expression and guiding Navajo youth as they find ways to reconcile traditional arts and crafts techniques and their own current influences and priorities. You can also help to organize library exhibits and plays, or set up computer lab programs. You can even work in teams with students and community members to build traditional hogans (sacred ceremonial huts). While Tuba City residents face general economic hardship, the partnership of students, parents, community, and school officials has created a vibrant

Taking a break near Tuba City, home to the Navajo Nation

learning environment that celebrates the individuality of each student as well as honoring the spirit of the tribe.

You'll be living communally with the volunteer group in a traditional Navajo hogan with separate bathroom and shower facilities. Meals are provided, with lunches at the school cafeteria and dinners that vary night to night, sometimes prepared by the team, sometimes by locals, and sometimes at Tuba City restaurants or diners. Your free time will be filled with fantastic forays into the immediate surroundings, as well as with visits to the Grand Canyon, Navajo Monument, and Monument Valley—all fantastic side trips. You'll also enjoy cultural evenings of traditional song and presentations on Navajo life.

YOUR NEXT STEP: Amizade (✆ **304/ 293-6049;** www.amizade.org). 1 week: US$965; 2 weeks: US$1,930. Fees cover group lodging in traditional hogan sleeping quarters, meals, and full project training. Participants must arrange their own transportation to Tuba City.

DON'T MISS: After seeing the Grand Canyon and other nearby natural wonders, get in touch with a different side of the spirituality of Arizona and spend some time in **Sedona.** The red-rock area is believed to be host to several Earth energy vortices that are said to aid in healing, psychic awareness, even communication with beings from other planets or dimensions. A vortex tour takes you through beautiful, peaceful countryside, whether you're looking to communicate with others or just yourself.

ⓘ www.arizonaguide.com

121 Arts, Crafts & Business

Arts Leadership

Teach in the Shadow of Victoria Falls

Livingstone, Zambia

One of the seven wonders of the world, the large, impressive Victoria Falls won't be far from your hostel door. Nor will elephant gazing, or ample opportunities for excellent fishing. Welcome to Livingstone, where arts education is suffering but tourism is thriving—here's where volunteers can make an appreciable difference.

Livingstone is a colonial village with a tremendous draw for tourists, since it's the town nearest to the famous Victoria Falls, but locals who aren't employed at resorts and other tourism support businesses are faced with difficult financial challenges. The poverty level in town, despite appearances to the contrary, is quite high, and schools in the area are barely getting by. Arts education is seen as a luxury when only a few qualified teachers can be hired. Occasionally an adult from the community or a motivated visitor will launch a drama or dance program, or inspire groups of students to paint or draw, but those opportunities are few and far between. Volunteers visiting for short-term visits inject new vitality into arts programs and give children opportunities at artistic exploration and expression that would not otherwise be available to them. Former drama programs, for example, focused on such subjects as AIDS education, bullying, and peer pressure, giving not only the participants, but also audiences, a new forum for discussion and education.

You'll be working as an adjunct instructor, supporting the classroom teachers in their often-overworked day and working at several poorly funded private schools. In addition to teaching the arts (everything from painting to drama and music), you may be asked to take half the class in the morning and lead English discussion groups or referee a soccer match during outdoor breaks. As the children attempt and then master new creative skills, confidence blossoms. You'll see evidence of that as time goes on: conversations grow more animated, individuals share and show off the fruits of their labor, and in drama and dance programs, some of the most tentative performers during rehearsal come out and shine before an audience of their peers and parents. You may have to scramble to create costumes from the most unlikely materials, or find scraps of wood to create a set, but from the most ragtag resources comes the most inspired art.

You'll be sharing a room with other volunteers at a hostel in the center of town. Accommodations are basic but quite comfortable, and there is even a swimming pool on-site as well as an Internet cafe. Food is not provided, but local stores have plenty of staple items you can prepare in the hostel's kitchen, and there are many inexpensive dining options in town. Your evening and weekend free time can be the busiest time of all, as there's so much to do and see in this region. The mighty Zambezi River and Victoria Falls are deservedly known as Wonders of the World, and the opportunities for game tracking, hiking, canoeing (watch out for the hippos and crocs), and other natural adventures are almost endless. There are well-established adventure excursion companies in town, if you'd like to try microlight flying or bungee jumping.

YOUR NEXT STEP: Travellers Worldwide (UK: ✆ **+44/01903 502595;** www.travellersworldwide.com). This 2-week project, £645, includes shared accommodations at a hostel, full project training and support, and airport transfers. Meals are your responsibility.

DON'T MISS: Doctor Livingstone, I presume? While in his eponymous town, take an afternoon to see the museum containing a large collection of one of the most famous explorer's personal items and correspondence. In addition to David Livingstone's personal effects, there are several displays of cultural significance and a representative array of gorgeous indigenous arts.

ⓘ www.zambiatourism.com

Libraries & Learning Centers **122**

Converting Classroom Space

Building Beijing

Beijing, China

MENTAL AND PHYSICAL STRENGTH MAY BE REQUIRED TO LITERALLY CREATE THE SPACE NECESSARY to educate the expanding and migrating population of China. These changes far outpace the country's ability to maintain its infrastructure in a way that ensures all children learn what is required in order to succeed.

China is changing more rapidly than just about any nation on the planet, and that can sometimes lead to growing pains. As the economies of China's major cities have boomed, they have been flooded with people from the countryside seeking an easier, better life. Beijing has seen an influx of millions of new residents, which the current infrastructure can't support. Officially, citizens must obtain permission from the government to relocate from their registered region or else they forfeit all social services like health care and public education. The result? More than 150 million migrant people are marginalized and don't officially "exist" in the cities. An entire generation of youth is falling through the cracks, without much hope for prosperity or even stability. This volunteer project will take you to the one and only non-profit middle school for migrant children in all of Beijing—a school that can't begin to handle the burden of students who would enroll if they could. The school has been put in a former factory building, but the space remains quite raw in many areas. Volunteers work tirelessly to build classroom spaces so students can be taught in an environment more conducive to learning.

Your building skills will be called upon, whether you are handy with a hammer or can paint or even help with cleaning. Each time a group of volunteers finishes a project and creates a new classroom, a new conversion begins. Even school furniture is built from scratch, so you may be helping furnish rooms or improve bathroom facilities or outfit a kitchen space or offices. For a change of pace, you can also help teach and tutor children working on English-language skills, since classes are being conducted all around you. Project goals and needs shift as tasks are completed, so you may be asked to perform a wide variety of tasks to improve the school.

You'll stay at a small hotel in Beijing's 5th Ring, quite near the school, so you can walk to work each morning. Meals are provided and shared with the group at local restaurants. Evenings and weekends are great times to explore this enormous city and nearby sights, including the

Forbidden City, the Great Wall of China, and the Summer Imperial Palace. You can set off on your own or as part of an organized excursion.

YOUR NEXT STEP: GlobeAware (✆ **877/588-4562;** www.globeaware.org). The 1-week project, US$1,380, includes hotel housing, meals at local dining establishments, cultural excursions, transportation to the base hotel, and full training and support.

DON'T MISS: The most photographed section of the **Great Wall of China** is at Badaling. This Ming Dynasty section of the wall is like a great spine that runs along the mountain ridges. Beacon towers rise above the massive undulating wall at the highest point of the pass from Beijing to the north. This UNESCO World Heritage Site is one of the most scenic spots in China.

ⓘ http://english.visitingbeijing.com.cn

123 Libraries & Learning Centers

Libraries & Exploration Center

Reading in Paradise

Avarua, Cook Islands

THE SOUTH PACIFIC IS WELL KNOWN FOR BALI, TAHITI, AND FIJI, BUT MANY DON'T LIKELY KNOW about the quiet, remote beauty that the Cook Islands offer. Don't worry about packing reading material. On the largest Cook Island, Raratonga, volunteers with interests in reading can help with the needs of libraries and their infrastructure and collections.

In the coastal Cook Island towns, restoration projects have improved community infrastructure, but some of these communal spaces are beginning to show the wear and tear of time and use. More than one library is in need of a major internal overhaul, with updates required to shelving systems and reference materials. Donated books and periodicals are waiting to be catalogued and integrated into the stacks. A world-famous whale exhibit and children's learning stations need tender, loving care. A reading program at the senior activity center needs readers, as does a children's reading program designed to make the Maori youth more conversant in English.

You will bounce from one program to the next, some physical, some cerebral. Several libraries need painting and cleaning. Reshelving is delayed because shelves need repair or the collections have simply outgrown them. Archived documents need a storage system that protects them. You'll find an appreciative audience when you read stories to the children in the library or school reading programs. When their energy level gets too high, then the mamas and the papas (respectful terms for village seniors) are always pleased to have you come talk, read, play cards, or lead activities with them. Then it's back to work, sprucing up a local museum exhibit, say, or throwing yourself into other socially invaluable activities.

When you put down the hammer and books, you'll retire to a beachside hotel, with its double-occupancy rooms, kitchenettes, TV, even a swimming pool amid landscaped gardens. Locally prepared meals are part of the package. After such a bounty of fresh produce, you'll never look at the fruits at your home supermarket the same way again. Free time is mellow, spent relaxing with new neighbors and fellow volunteers. You'll also enjoy beach days and exploratory forays into the island's interior or farther along the beautiful shore.

YOUR NEXT STEP: Global Volunteers (✆ **651/407-6100;** www.globalvolunteers.org). A 2-week project, US$2,595, includes shared beach hotel accommodations, meals, project orientation and training, and 24-hour support.

DON'T MISS: The sawtooth skyline of **Raratonga,** the best known of the Cook Islands, gives you a hint of the many adventures available to you beneath its jagged peaks, in its deep rift valleys, and along its treasured tropical beaches. After plenty of wild exploration, come into town, dodge the countless chickens roaming freely in the streets, and visit the main marketplace on Saturday for informal singing competitions to see who has the best pipes on the island.

ⓘ www.cookislands.com

Libraries & Learning Centers **124**

Rehabilitating an Education Center

Helping the Kids of Cape Town

Cape Town, South Africa

SOUTH AFRICA EMBODIES THE EXTREMES OF THE CONTINENT'S OFFERINGS—SUBTROPICAL coastlines, vineyards, deserts, safaris, indigenous peoples, cosmopolitan cities, and a heady mix of races and cultures. Beyond what most travelers see, though, it's home to poverty and illness. Consequently, it's a place where your sheer dedication and physical energy can invigorate others.

Think of it as your own episode of *Extreme Nursery School Makeover* and you're Ty Pennington, bringing boundless enthusiasm to the task of transforming the lives of the children of a Cape Town township. Township life is particularly grueling, with too many people living in single rooms with cardboard walls and tin roofs, hundreds sharing one hand water pump, and no central electricity, plumbing, or trash disposal. The townships are outside the city and some of them have areas where modest apartment blocks have been built, and cinderblock homes and buildings are occasionally converted to rustic schools. During your 2-week tenure here, you'll work to convert a dilapidated nursery school into a new learning center for the community.

Scrub brushes, paint brushes, mops, and brooms will all feel quite familiar in your hands by the end of the run. Walls will be sanded and prepped, holes will be patched, and floors will be repaired. You'll find that the young people who benefit from all your hard work will be particularly enthusiastic. Your energy can't flag when theirs is so abundant. Spend breaktime, lunchtime, and after-work hours playing games, reading stories, and singing songs with the kids—they can be remarkable teachers in their own right and will teach you their own songs and dances. Schools are usually the focal points of township life, and amid all the difficult conditions, many of the children are dressed in school uniforms and focused on studying.

You will either live with the team at the very comfortable volunteer project house or in a Cape Town hostel in shared quarters. Three meals are provided daily. Your time is divided into work days and cultural exploration days, so you'll have opportunities to explore some of the city of Cape Town, much of which is truly magnificent, from the plateau of picturesque Table Mountain down to the beautiful beaches along the shore. You'll have team-building

A nursery school in Cape Town

exercises and adventure activities, so by the end of your assignment, you'll be bonded with your fellow volunteers more closely than you thought possible.

YOUR NEXT STEP: i-to-i (toll free: **800/985-4852;** www.i-to-i.com). A 2-week project, US$1,995, includes shared accommodations at the project base center or in a city hostel, three meals daily, country orientation and sightseeing, adventure excursions with the group, project training and support, and transfers to/from the airport.

DON'T MISS: Just up into the foothills, outside Cape Town, you'll come to **Stellenbosch,** the leading wine region of South Africa (and probably the continent) and home to several picturesque estates. The wine route takes you along a well-marked trail, and wineries have terrific tasting rooms. Raise a glass and toast a job well done.

ⓘ www.sputhafrica.net

125

Building a School

Marley & You

Petersfield, Jamaica

HONEYMOONERS KNOW THE BEACHES, MUSIC LOVERS KNOW ITS MOST FAMOUS SON, BOB Marley, and java enthusiasts revere Jamaica Blue Mountain coffee. The real story of Jamaica these days is in community building, with its rapidly growing emphasis on agricultural sustainability fostering a sense of culinary nationalism among its residents. Be a part of that pride by lending your muscle power to build a school and a community.

Well away from the all-inclusive beach resorts, playing Bob Marley on continuous loop, is the real Jamaica. The former sugar plantation town of Petersfield is undergoing a community renaissance as they move away from subsistence farming and toward a sustainable eco-model that incorporates tourism and local empowerment. Local organizations of motivated leaders are improving village infrastructure and bridging the gap where government programs fall short. This particular project involves you in the building of a primary grade school in the neighboring community of Galloway. You'll also sharpen your community organizing skills working alongside locals.

While the actual school facility is being built by volunteers, innovative teaching programs are being launched so that children can hit the ground running as soon as the doors are opened. Your skills will contribute to both sides of this effort. Interior and exterior construction work will benefit from your skills in carpentry, painting, electrical, and plumbing work (don't worry, you'll learn the skills or become a fabulous assistant). You'll spend mornings working on the construction project, then after a long lunch you'll enjoy some free time or double up on your efforts by helping the burgeoning videography programs, organizing a youth empowerment camp, or visiting some of the marginalized kids in hospitals and hospice programs.

You'll stay with a host family and share meals at the family table when you're not dining communally with the volunteer group. Evening cultural programs and lecturers will immerse you in Jamaican life, teaching you about the island's communities and the stunning natural environment. With your new friends you'll explore the interior and the beaches where tourists rarely wander. A visit to the waterfalls and caves that only locals can show you is like entering another world, and can swallow an entire afternoon.

YOUR NEXT STEP: Amizade (© **304/293-6049;** www.amizade.org). This 2-week project, US$1,591, includes accommodations with a host family, meals at the host home or with the volunteer group, and training and support.

DON'T MISS: Just as in the United Kingdom, the town of **Bath** in Jamaica was named for the curative mineral springs found here. Locals enjoy the healing waters of underground springs, both scalding hot and crystal clear and cool. The island's medical community endorsed the curative powers of these waters as far back as the 18th century.

ⓘ www.visitjamaica.com

Establish Libraries & Children's Centers

Bringing Hope to the Himalayas

Multiple rural villages, Nepal

HOME TO THE SKY-HIGH HIMALAYAS, NEPAL IS AN INEXPENSIVE DESTINATION THAT ATTRACTS hikers, trekkers, and nature lovers. But the country needs help, and volunteers can ensure that its children are educated, literate, and familiar with English.

A little paint, a little plaster, and voila, there's a school. Well, it may not be as simple as that, but it's also not as difficult as you might imagine to bring a learning institution into being (or up to snuff) that serves an entire Nepalese community. Rurally based children attend several schools in the region, but come together at a community library and children's resource centers. Some of the centers are quite modest, with only two or three rooms (the hope is to one day have one for every village), but the space is still cherished as a learning environment and gathering place for village youth before and after school. In addition to creating, maintaining, and improving the centers, volunteers help children practice their English and give tutoring in other studies.

You'll often be working in tandem with villagers as you learn traditional construction methods and build new resource spaces or add on to existing centers. Planned improvement projects include painting, adding indoor restrooms, installing plumbing for drinking water, laying carpet, and decorating the spaces to make them cheerful. Each center has different needs, and your project organizers will determine where your efforts can be best put to use, and what each day's tasks will be. As the centers become self-sufficient, operations are taken over by village residents, so the project helps create employment for locals as well.

You'll be living with a host family, quite often in the home of one of the school's teachers or the principal, so your efforts on behalf of the village children are doubly appreciated. When you first fly into Kathmandu, you'll be given a cultural orientation course as well as basic language instruction to make your transition seamless (though you may find lots of gesturing and charades will come in quite handy). Meals are an amalgam of Western and local cuisines provided by the host family, though sometimes the volunteer group will all dine together. The hospitality of the community where you are stationed will fill your time and your heart. Each village has its own wonderful corners to explore, which will occupy the time on your days off.

YOUR NEXT STEP: INFO Nepal (✆ **977/01-4700210;** www.infonepal.org). A 2-week project, US$258, includes lodging with a host family, meals, cultural programming and sightseeing tours, and project support. The bus ride from Kathmandu to your host village is an additional cost, but bus tickets are quite inexpensive and the project staff will get you on the bus and meet you at the other end. The entire learning and resource center project is funded by volunteer fees and donations, and part of the fees go toward salaries for local staff of established children's centers.

DON'T MISS: If you're a duffer, playing a round on the world's highest golf courses earns you bragging rights and a round of drinks back at the clubhouse when you get home. The greens of Kathmandu and Pokhara offer some great holes, and scenic views of the Himalayas. **Til Ganga course** and the **Gokarna Golf course** are located in Kathmandu. In Pokhara, you can find **Fulbari Resort Golf** and the **Himalayan Golf Course.**

ⓘ www.welcomenepal.com

4 Scientific Research

Moai statues in Rapa Nui (Easter Island)

127 Archaeology

Studying Easter Island

Adding Pieces to the Puzzle

Rapa Nui, Chile

Some trips can only be described as extraordinary: like flying to a remote UNESCO World Heritage Site far off the coast of Chile and helping decode the archeological mysteries of Easter Island. Your help on the puzzle that has vexed scientists for decades will be used to look for answers to today's modern problems.

Easter Island (now called Rapa Nui) has fascinated scientists, culture vultures, even UFO theorists, for as long as we've been aware of the mysterious *moai* statues for which the remote island has become famous. On the northern and western coasts of Rapa Nui, pockets of undiscovered cultural clues wait to be unearthed. You'll search for prehistoric dwellings, earth ovens, evidence of farming and livestock, and more while trying to piece together the puzzle of the area's original inhabitants. It won't be difficult to get in the mood, as much of the island is host to cave paintings and petroglyphs, ceremonial centers, caves, and, of course, those enormous guardian statues.

Searching for clues in Rapa Nui

You'll be adding to the empirical knowledge of the island, much of which is still shrouded in mystery. The Rapa Nui people underwent a huge, devastating change in the 17th century, and your work can lead to answering some of the remaining questions. Carbon dating samples will give a timeline; freshly excavated places of work and worship will add to the cultural understanding. The team of volunteers and guiding scientists are, like you, hungry for knowledge, and this project, with its plentiful and dramatic discoveries, satisfies that need. The formerly thriving flora of the island is mostly gone, replaced by sparse, arid growth on the slopes of three volcanoes—your research can help scientists learn why and how it was so devastatingly deforested.

As such an isolated microcosm, Rapa Nui often serves as a global model for the study of environmental degradation and cultural collapse. The current citizenry of Hanga Roa, the island's only town, are of predominantly Chilean and Polynesian descent, and most speak Spanish, so your language skills will help with fluid communication, but Spanish is not required for the trip. You'll stay, as a team, in a small family-run hotel in town, and meals will be prepared by a house cook, leaving you even more time to explore—all under the watchful eyes of the moai.

YOUR NEXT STEP: Earthwatch (✆ **800/776-0188;** www.earthwatch.org). The 2-week trip, US$3,850, includes meals, residential hotel accommodations, and full project support. A US$35 Earthwatch membership is required.

DON'T MISS: Your stay on Easter Island will be a time of discovery, beyond the volunteer tasks, and it is easier here to get away from it all than most places on Earth. Rapa Nui is considered the world's largest open-air museum, with more than 400 moai, ruins, and temples, so you'll enjoy lots of walking and wandering. Experience the openness of an island without copious vegetation blocking the views by taking a **horseback ride** on the beach and volcanic hillsides.

ⓘ www.visit-chile.org

Archaeology 128

Roman Town Excavation

Life Before Reading

Reading, England

BY DAY YOU'LL BE BUSY WORKING ON A ROMAN SITE THAT HAS BEEN EXCAVATED RELATIVELY recently. When your time at the site is complete you can explore other nearby Roman influences, such as the town of Bath, as well as pagan influences such as Stonehenge.

The discovery of a Roman town in Reading, England, has made for many seasons of interesting and enlightening archaeological digs. Unearthing this village dating to the late Iron Age and early Roman era has yielded plenty of information about daily life in the town found near modern-day Silchester. This was the administrative capital the Romans established in southern Britain, and each year's digs focus on one of many *insulae* (city blocks). The insulae were Roman-occupied from the 1st century b.c. through the demise of the town when they abandoned it in the 5th or 6th century a.d. One of the main questions posed by the project is: What was life like in this village before, during, and after Roman occupation?

Working with the experts and student staff of the local university's Department of Archaeology, you'll spend 1 week (or more if you wish) in what the Romans called Calleva Atrebatum. The insulae were first excavated in 1893 as part of a 20-year project by the Society of Antiquaries of London, and teams have been adding to the field of knowledge since. Several notable attractions have been unearthed, including an ampitheater, a forum basilica, and both residential and public buildings. You may be digging, cleaning, and gathering artifacts, sorting through ceramic and slate roof tiles and floor mosaic pieces, photographing and recording the location of tableware and pottery, counting the numbers of wine barrels, or any number of other tasks as daily life is recreated like a life-size jigsaw puzzle.

You'll be camping out on-site, in your own tent, and sharing meals prepared for and by the whole team. Porta-potty bathrooms and solar showers are packed up at the end of each season, as is all evidence of recent residents, leaving the site pristine when it's not being worked. Your downtime will often be spent at camp in the general camaraderie of dig life, and on weekends many will choose to go to the more modern local town and pub to let off a bit of steam.

YOUR NEXT STEP: University of Reading (✆ **+44/118 378 6255;** www.silchester.reading.ac.uk). Each week on-site, £250, includes campsite life, 6 days of meals, excavation technique training and field school, and project support. You'll get yourself to Reading, and bring your own tent and sleeping bag, pad, pillow, and other gear for your comfort.

DON'T MISS: Reading is located between Oxford and London along the banks of the Thames River. Next to the town's famous Abbey ruins and Forbury Gardens is **Reading Prison,** once home to famous inmate Oscar Wilde, who wrote *The Ballad of Reading Gaol* during his internment here.

ⓘ www.visitbritain.com

129 Archaeology

Transylvanian Archaeology

Hunting Vlad the Impaler

Deva, Romania

TRANSYLVANIA, IN TODAY'S CENTRAL ROMANIA, CAN BE TRANSLATED INTO LATIN AS "THE LAND beyond the forest." In this project, you can explore the medieval ruins of Vlad the Impaler that have inspired literature, vampire tales, and horror movies.

Working with Romania's Museum of History, you'll explore archaeological sites in the Carpathian Mountains that have yielded new information about Vlad the Impaler (whose story inspired Bram Stoker's Dracula). You'll work alongside experts in the field to uncover clues about medieval life and more distant eras, and be part of a trained volunteer team that specializes in archaeological digs or in reconstruction of ceramic pieces and other finds. Volunteers also spend time in the museum helping with translations and designing tourist information materials. Project sites are located throughout the mountainous region.

Your days on-site will be in the field, in museums, or both. You'll be trained in excavation techniques and will get hands-on time unearthing...well...earth, with the hope of finding a treasure or two. You'll excavate, clean, and catalog pottery, tools, and other artifacts. You'll also identify and uncover ancient graves (you may want to carry a wooden stake or garlic with you), recover bones and grave artifacts, compile reports on fortified Saxon churches, and study gardens and other dig sites, notably a summer palace. At the museum you'll reconstruct and label, catalog, and photograph found items, write up reports of the fieldwork, and create proposals for new dig sites that will go to national and international donors.

Your accommodations will vary depending on the sites being excavated at the time of your volunteer stint. The main base in Deva, a city of 80,000 people, has a project guesthouse for volunteers. If your project base is farther afield, you could be camping in tents, staying in a hostel, or with a host family. All meals are provided, and the diet is heavy on meats and bounteous fresh vegetables in warm months. Weekends are usually spent in Brasov, a large mountain city where you'll find plenty of culture, dining, bars, and exploration options.

YOUR NEXT STEP: Projects Abroad 🎗 (✆ **888/839-3535;** www.volunteer-archaeology-romania.org). A 2-week project, US$2,445, includes accommodations in a guest house, family home, hostel, campsite, or combination, three meals daily, airport transfers, project training, and 24-hour support.

DON'T MISS: The main gateway for the country is the capital city, Bucharest. While much of the city's original architecture has been lost, a fascinating stop is the **Palace of the People.** Built by the tyrant-president Nicolae Ceau escu, it's the second largest administrative building in the world after the Pentagon. It took 20,000 workers and 700 architects to build the 12 stories, 1,100 rooms, gargantuan lobby, and four underground levels. Rooms are larger than football fields and festooned with crystal chandeliers, antiques, priceless artworks, stained glass, regal carpets, mosaics, and the kind of excess that runs quite contrary to the philosophies of the communist regime that built the place.

ⓘ www.romaniatourism.com

Archaeology 130

Solomon's Royal Store City

Uncovering the Iron Age at the Oasis of Peace

Tel Gezer, Israel

THERE'S AN ENDLESS AMOUNT TO SEE IN ISRAEL—THE TEMPLE ON THE MOUNT, THE DEAD Sea, and the Wailing Wall, for starters—but you can also dig some of the most historic dirt on earth in this ancient holy land and add another piece to a biblical puzzle.

Just a 20-minute drive outside Tel Aviv, on the western flank of the foothills overlooking Israel's coastal plain, is the Tel Gezer Archaeological Project. This *tel* (mound site dig) is actually comprised of two mounds and the saddle of earth between them. The mound, known as Gezer, is mentioned in ancient sources, including the Hebrew Bible, which refers to it as one of the royal store cities of Solomon. In the 2nd millennium b.c. it was a fortified Canaanite stronghold known for its 10 standing megaliths. One thousand years later it was conquered by the Egyptians and given as a dowry gift to King Solomon. The study area is about 30 acres (12ha).

The accumulated knowledge at Tel Gezer shows successive occupations of the city over extended periods of time. You'll be investigating the regional boundaries between Judah and Philistia during the Iron Age. You and your fellow volunteers, along with project staff and experts, will excavate a large swath of the hillside and uncover layers that are well delineated and specific to the Iron Age. Within these stratified layers, the historical evidence uncovered will answer many questions about this ancient city. Your smaller focus will be on finding clues to the relationships among ancient palaces, fortification walls and defensive structures, and domestic structures—giving a peek into the relationships between people who resided in each social stratum. Previous Iron Age artifacts have been found here, so the goal is to flesh out the fullest understanding possible of what life must have been like in Gezer as its ruler, a noble, a peasant, or a slave.

While working for 2 weeks at the site, you'll come home at the end of the day to the Oasis of Peace guesthouse, part of a unique community with Jews and Arabs living together. The hotel grounds have air-conditioned suites scattered throughout, all walking distance from the dig, and the public rooms of the hotel are used for evening lectures about the history of the region as well as processing, labeling, sorting, photographing, and logging discovered items. You'll share meals that are prepared by hotel staff with the rest of the team, and drop into a deep sleep from another exhausted day in the field.

The Tel Gezer Archaeological Project

YOUR NEXT STEP: Tel Gezer Excavation (✆ **817/923-1921 x4455;** www.gezerproject.org). A 2-week project, US$1,825, includes hotel/guesthouse accommodations near the site, prepared meals, project training, and support.

DON'T MISS: You're so close to Israel's main cities of **Tel Aviv** and **Jerusalem,** you'll want to see both. When you're in Tel Aviv, don't forget to head to the south side of the city's coast, to **Old Jaffa,** one of the oldest port cities in the world with bustling markets and cobbled alleyways, as well as a vibrant renaissance with new hospitality businesses, gourmet restaurants, and cultural venues popping up every day.

ⓘ www.goisrael.com

131 Archaeology

Restore a Medieval Village

Restoration Along the Mediterranean Coast

Liguria, Italy

IF YOU'RE INSPIRED BY OLD VILLAGES, ROLLING HILLS, WOODLANDS, OLIVES, VINEYARDS, AND the chance to preserve a medieval way of life for generations to come, then say *ciao* to wherever you are and come to the coast of Italy, ready to work.

The drooping silver shimmer of olive trees, wispy mimosa plants catching the breeze, the sound of gravel crunching underfoot as you round an old stone wall into a sunny courtyard—these are impressions, unchanged for hundreds of years, of Val

Bevera, a small valley that is home to Torri Superiore, a medieval Italian village. Change is underway here, some of it positive and some more pernicious. The region's Cultural Association is restoring and transforming this hamlet into an ecological village and cultural research center—with your help.

Maintenance and repairs need to be done on old homes and larger, former storage buildings, to ready them for a new life hosting courses and field study classes in biological agriculture, ceramics, shiatsu, and the starting point for a number of trekking excursions. You'll be spending days under the Mediterranean sun clearing paths and installing environmentally sensitive signage and culturally sensitive improvements that blend with the historic essence of the structures. English is spoken throughout the project site, and you'll rest your head each night in lovely guesthouse accommodations.

This boomerang-shaped stretch of Mediterranean coast is home to beautiful stretches of undeveloped beach and hillsides for long, contemplative walks in between work sessions. Of course, the wine that will accompany lunches and dinners will make 2 weeks of intense effort feel truly vacationlike.

YOUR NEXT STEP: Canadian Alliance for Development Initiatives and Projects (✆ **604/628-7400;** www.cadip.org) A 2-week project, US$265, includes communally prepared team meals and accommodations at a guesthouse and full project support, but you must travel to the site on your own. The nearest airports are Nice or Genoa.

DON'T MISS: Genoa, the main seat of Liguria, was the European Capital of Culture in 2004, and remains an enchanting destination for a day or weeks. One of the most famous Ligurian sites is the **Castle of the Stone;** many legends surround it, like the belief that the devil built the bridge to the site in one night in exchange for the soul of the first passerby (don't worry, others have already visited).

ⓘ www.turismoinliguria.it

Archaeology **132**

Preserving Ancient Roman Heritage

Plentiful Finds in Tuscany

Pisa, Italy

BEYOND THE FAMOUS LEANING TOWER, PISA'S IMPORTANT MARITIME ROLE MEANS THE CITY is rich in Roman history waiting to be unearthed. Once your 2-week project is complete, it will be difficult to resist exploring nearby Florence, Siena, and the rest of gorgeous Tuscany.

The bucolic landscape of the Tuscan coast holds some intriguing secrets. Work and stay in protected parklands and medieval villages as you help a scientific team excavate a Roman maritime settlement, Poggio del Molino. You'll survey land and landmarks, collect organic samples, and gather and document pottery shards, metal fragments, coins, and other artifacts. This area was a longtime center for ironworking and trade, so the finds are plentiful, making it one of the most important archaeological sites in Italy.

Since the site is so prolific, treasure hunters regularly pilfer from it and threaten to destroy knowledge of the past before it can be preserved. The stunning nature of the region means developers pose another threat, so the dig project is

Excavating Roman artifacts in Pisa, Italy

particularly urgent and highly focused. Your 2-week stay will be intensive, but the team will feel like family as you share meals (and prepare them), live in quiet village apartments, and if you have good timing, enjoy the festivals and cultural celebrations that mark the seasons, harvest, religious and historical holidays, and more. There's almost always a reason for festivity in Tuscany.

It is meticulous work among the building foundations and long-lost tile mosaic floors, but the curving coastline and warm Mediterranean breezes provide plenty of distraction at breaktime. You would want to vacation here anyway, and playing a part in its preservation will make the memories much more vivid.

YOUR NEXT STEP: Earthwatch (✆: **800/776-0188;** www.earthwatch.org). The 13-day project, US$2,950, includes group-prepared meals, apartment accommodations, and full project support. A US$35 Earthwatch membership is required.

DON'T MISS: While you'll be staying in a tiny rural village, the nearby city of **Pisa** is rightfully famous and well trod. Wait until afternoons, when the tour buses have roared away, and wander the city to discover its true beauty. The **Leaning Tower of Pisa** is one of those landmarks everyone longs to check off their list. www.torre.duomo.pisa.it

ⓘ www.pisaturismo.it

133 Archaeology

Diet & Drink

Unlocking Ancient Ways at UNESCO World Heritage Site

Pompeii, Italy

An appetite for both food and knowledge will serve you well as you piece together life in Pompeii just before its place in Italy's history was changed forever. This UNESCO World Heritage Site is partially buried, and you'll work to determine what its inhabitants were eating and drinking just before the city was cloaked in ash thousands of years ago.

Few archaeological discoveries fire the imagination like the lost city of Pompeii. The eruption of Mount Vesuvius in a.d. 79 completely buried the city (near present-day Naples) in ash, not to be seen again until its rediscovery nearly 1,700 years later. Plaster (or resin) casts of people and animals trapped and caught in their last moments of agony are indelibly haunting, exhibited throughout the region as painful symbols of human struggle against the elements. With such a moment in time frozen for scientific study, Pompeii is an archaeological laboratory yielding more information than most sites in the world. This project focuses specifically on daily life, and learning the diet and drinking habits of Pompeii's citizens prior to the day of the eruption.

Your work will include non-invasive inspection of wherever food and drink was consumed, stored, and prepared. You'll explore, document, photograph, draw floor plans, and sketch well over 1,000 structures in the rediscovered city, and the data gathered by you and your team will become part of the comprehensive Food and Drink Coda. The daily life of historical Pompeii has been examined from many different perspectives, but studying the patterns of how every citizen obtained, consumed, and shared food and drink will be one of the most intimate and personal views gleaned from a lost society.

You'll work up a powerful hunger and thirst of your own, and be grateful for your comfortable digs at a family-owned hotel. Air-conditioning, swimming pool, and private (two-person) rooms are a pleasant 10-minute walk from the work site. You'll already be completely immersed in the village life, and the present-day city of Pompeii is filled with distractions, from historic homes to surrounding small trattorias and tavernas for some contemporary cuisine.

YOUR NEXT STEP: Pompeii Food and Drink 🎗 (✆ **301/262-1141;** www.pompeii-food-and-drink.org). A 2-week project, US$3,000, includes accommodations at a small hotel, meals, excavation and recording training, and project support.

DON'T MISS: Get the full picture of the Pompeian tragedy by hiking to the top of **Mount Vesuvius.** This volcano has unleashed its wrath many times throughout recorded history, and still emits an almost constant plume of smoke. You can drive up to the juncture in lava flows, then trek the mostly easy hiking path amid cinders and lapilli. Your view from the summit will be amazing, looking out to the Bay of Naples and the Gulf of Gaeta, then turn toward the crater and its steam jets and desolate, lunarlike jagged walls.

ⓘ www.pompeiturismo.it

Archaeology **134**

Fossil Excavation

Desert Dig in Popular Expat Town

San Miguel de Allende, Mexico

MANY VISITORS CONSIDER PERMANENTLY RELOCATING TO SAN MIGUEL DE ALLENDE AFTER spending time exploring its cobblestone streets, mix of baroque and neoclassical architecture, and enticing Mexican crafts. This city in Central Mexico has also played an important role in the country's history and is full of excavation opportunities.

San Miguel de Allende has a disproportionately large number of English-speaking expats, and the charm of the town has become quite the "find" for baby boomers looking to retire where their money can stretch farther than at home. The cultural flavor of the 16th-century colonial village remains vibrant, the food is amazing, the hospitality gracious—but the natural record of history that remains locked in the rocky soil and hillsides is in danger of being lost forever. The area's popularity

Digging for fossils in San Miguel de Allende

has brought rapid growth and development, and unfortunately, much of the land available for development in the San Miguel basin is rife with fossilized evidence of small and large vertebrates.

You'll excavate specimens as old as 5 million years, and plaster-jacket them for safe transport. You'll photograph, sketch, and write a record of your discoveries with the team, led by a leading scientist in the field. Your days will be dusty, spent digging in dried arroyos and desert canyons, so you'll find simple joy in a hot shower, a swim in the pool, and collapsing into your soft bed at your shared hotel accommodations, and you'll especially grow to cherish the hearty cuisine.

When you tire of troglodytes and trilobites, wandering amid the city's restaurants and art galleries will bring back your modern sensibilities, or find a happy medium by exploring San Miguel's beautiful colonial churches and museums.

YOUR NEXT STEP: Earthwatch (✆: **800/776-0188;** www.earthwatch.org). A 1-week project, US$1,550, includes meals prepared by a staff member with your help, hotel accommodations, and full project support. A US$35 Earthwatch membership is required.

DON'T MISS: Since you're going to be in a digging mood, extend the experience and go to San Miguel's **Guanajuato Mummy Museum,** where the mummified remains of more than 100 ancestors from this village, many who were unceremoniously exhumed in the early 20th century when their families stopped paying grave taxes, are displayed.

ⓘ www.visitmexico.com

Archaeology 135

Archaeological Research Week

Education & Excavation in Navajo Country

Crow Canyon, Colorado, USA

THE AMERICAN SOUTHWEST IS RIFE WITH NATIVE AMERICAN ARTIFACTS, AND CROW Canyon— whose ancestral inhabitants were the Pueblos—is a living laboratory with a dense concentration of archeological sites. You'll gain a deeper appreciation for present-day life here by encountering, for example, the tools used by this land's ancestors.

This full-immersion program into the historic Southwest teaches volunteers (both adults and teens) excavation and field research techniques. Your new skills will be put to use unearthing information and artifacts from the area's dig sites, inhabited hundreds of years ago by Pueblo Indians (Anasazi).

Your excavation training is done on-site at Goodman Point in the Hovenweep National Monument, and there's some hiking required to get to the work zone. Back in the lab, you'll wash and catalog items of interest that date back from more than 700 years ago. You'll be taught the overarching history of the region and ancestral traditions, tour facilities and collections not yet introduced to the public, go on guided excursions to Mesa Verde National Park and the Sand Canyon Pueblo excavation site, and enjoy evening guest lectures about the current research work on the archaeology of the Southwest. You'll enter this field week a novice and leave with dirt under your fingernails and a real understanding of the research work being done to answer questions about the past. Many alumni of the research weeks return year after year.

The learning campus is 170 acres (69ha), and accommodations are shared Navajo-style log cabins (hogans) with a separate restroom/shower structure (bring your own bedding and towels). All meals are included, including vegetarian options and a full salad bar. While there are learning programs some nights, other nights are usually spent with your new volunteer colleagues, whiling away the evenings in the rocking chairs on the deck. You can also take a hike through the woods, watch mountain sunsets, and try to spot some of the abundant wildlife that calls this beautiful area home.

YOUR NEXT STEP: Crow Canyon Archaeology Center (✆ **800/422-8975;** www.crowcanyon.org). A 1-week trip, US$1,400 (less for returning alumni), includes extensive field training and learning programs, shared hogan accommodations (you provide linens), three meals daily, and guided excursions.

DON'T MISS: One of the most exciting adventures in this beautiful state is a river-rafting trip down the **Colorado River** or the **Arkansas River.** You can shoot rapids in sections of the country's finest white water, where sheer canyon walls suddenly fall away to wider vistas with quaking Aspen trees and forested hillsides. Sections of these two rivers are appropriate for every level of expertise, from adrenaline-pumping insanity to a lazy float on glassy calm waters.

ⓘ www.colorado.com

136 Archaeology

Roman Ruins

Bringing Up History in Wine Country

Porto, Portugal

PORTUGAL DOESN'T GET AS MANY TOURISTS AS MUCH OF THE REST OF THE MEDITERRANEAN does, and that's a shame—or a blessing, depending on your perspective. With vineyards to visit, fresh seafood to savor, and beaches to enjoy, there's no shortage of things to keep you stimulated once the hard work of caring for old Roman ruins is finished for the day.

The bracing but comforting scent of eucalyptus still fills the hillsides as it did in 138 b.c. when Decimus Junius Brutus founded the Iron Age village whose remains were used as the foundation for the Roman city of Talabriga. Not far from Porto in Portugal's rolling, hilly North Country, Talabriga is the site of excavations in one of the more idyllic spots you'll ever dig, a part of wine country more beautiful than postcards can convey. Working hard alongside grad students and professional archaeologists, you'll be thankful for the breezes on this coastal mountaintop. The view makes it easy to see why it was chosen as a strategic military outpost—whoever controlled this location controlled the river traffic, as well as anyone crossing the land.

The volunteer work is quite structured, with 4½ hours of excavation work every morning followed by a hearty lunch, then 2½ hours of lab work as you classify and study the accumulated finds. You'll get what amounts to intensive instruction in excavation technique and history, as well as lectures on Roman archaeology. What you learn will come into crisp focus on the included cultural/historical excursion. It's nice to occasionally get your focus out of the dirt.

It's an easy 10-minute walk to the site each morning from the cozy hostel where you'll stay. Evenings are free, and while coaching and instruction are in English, you may want to brush up on your Portuguese after a day on-site so it will be easier to navigate the small host town's bars, restaurants, museums, and shops. The beach is only a 10-minute drive away, so your day off can be spent splashing in the Atlantic and enjoying some of the startlingly fresh seafood for which the Porto region is famous.

YOUR NEXT STEP: Ecomuseum of the Cape of Cavalleria (✆ **+351/34 971-35-9999;** www.ecomuseodecavalleria.com). A 10-day project, US$900, includes hostel accommodations, three meals daily plus snacks in the field, local transportation, an intensive learning course, cultural excursion, accident insurance, and project support.

DON'T MISS: You can't miss the undulating hillsides covered in grape vines, so make a point of taking a day (or several) to go wine tasting in the **Douro** region, named for the easy-flowing Douro River. Wineries and tasting rooms abound, boasting several local vintages and the famous Vinho Verde that brings international oenephiles here year after year.

ⓘ www.visitportugal.com

Archaeology **137**

Episcopal Palaces

Mansions & Moats

Aberdeenshire, Scotland

Churches have often played pivotal roles in developing communities and educating people. In rural Scotland, volunteers donate their time to temporarily become experts in the lives of medieval bishops by studying their palaces.

It's a good thing the crocodiles have moved on, since you'll be spending this volunteer vacation in the moat of a medieval summer palace. Fetternear was the palace of the Episcopal bishops of Aberdeen, most notably Bishop Cheyne, who resided here when Scotland was invaded by Edward I. After Edward sacked the palace and trudged away, it was rebuilt in the 1330s, then, many years later, enclosed by a wooden palisade and the moat. After 1560 and the Reformation, the palace passed to the Leslies of Balquhain, who turned it into a mansion residence. The University of Wales, Lampeter, is conducting simultaneous investigations of the former structures and uses of the property while comparing them to the current buildings. The old kitchen was recently discovered, and the newest dig site is the unique moat.

Medieval bishops were responsible for the building of cathedrals, churches, halls, and castles, so their private residences reflect much other medieval architecture. The Scottish Episcopal Palaces Project (SEPP) is in the process of exploring these lofty manors and palaces across the country to better understand the development of bishops' palaces throughout Scotland. Your excavation work will be meticulous so as not to disturb current use (and users) of the building. You'll uncover evidence of building techniques, irrigation (how did they fill the moat, anyway?), and probable human remains.

It is a bit of a contrast as you explore a grand palace, then retire at the end of the hard day's work to a tent at an on-site campground. Facilities are rustic at best, but since this volunteer dig doesn't cost a shilling, you'll be satisfied in knowing you're trading expenditure of calories for insight into the church and royals of Scotland.

YOUR NEXT STEP: Department of Archaeology & Anthropology, University of Wales (✆ **+44/1570 424994;** www.lamp.ac.uk/archanth/staff/dransart/fetternear.htm). You'll spend 1 week camping out in the shadow of the stately summer palace, and with no participation fee, you'll fend for yourself for meals and local transport, so a rental car is a wise choice. The town of Aberdeenshire is 20 miles (32km) away with all the dining, drinking, shopping, and people-watching you could want.

DON'T MISS: Since you've already been mucking in the moat and expecting to find dragon's teeth or bones, why not make your way to **Loch Ness** and go on a monster hunt? Any of Scotland's lakes (lochs) provide a picturesque getaway after a week's worth of hard work.

ⓘ www.visitscotland.com

138 Archaeology

Cliff Dwellings

Native History in the Backcountry

Gila, New Mexico, USA

THERE ISN'T MUCH NEARBY TO ENTERTAIN YOU IN YOUR OFF HOURS IN THIS REMOTE DESERT IN southwestern New Mexico, but perhaps that's the whole point: you can fully immerse yourself in helping to preserve a vital part of Native American history.

Have you ever been hiking in the wilderness when something on the ground catches your eye? You bend down, wipe away the dirt, and your heart skips a beat as you wiggle and pull free an arrowhead or a shard of broken, painted pottery. Your discovery may have been the tip of the iceberg of a previously unknown archaeological site of interest. Despite good intentions, collecting artifacts can erase the chance for archaeologists to learn the secrets and history of a site, so preservation of national heritage through careful methodical study is of paramount importance. In the Gila National Forest, America's first designated wilderness area and one of its most remote parks, the Gila Cliff Dwelling National Monument requires both careful stewardship and study. These were homes of American Indians of the 13th century, and so far, 46 rooms have been discovered at the cliff site of this community.

You'll work with field archaeologists to stabilize, survey, and document this historic site. It's pretty rugged country, so hiking to and from the site takes some effort, but the majesty of the site first thing in the morning or at sunset makes it all

The site of Native cliff dwellings in Gila, New Mexico

worth it. The Mimbres Mogollon tribe from about 550 a.d. to 1350 a.d. occupied the homes. Their ceramics and designs in paint were remarkably advanced compared to other communities of a similar era. You'll be trained and become quite adept with digital photo recording, GPS coordinating, and artifact record reports as you explore the site while simultaneously preserving its integrity. Stone tools, grinding stones, rock art, and pot shards are all part of your field of effort as you team up with the US Forest Service.

The best thing about a national forest, especially in the company of the Sierra Club, is the camping. The group is car camping, so you'll have easy access to all the comforts you bring from home as well as a mobile home kitchen and showers a short walk away. Days are full and start early, but when the afternoon's efforts are complete, you'll have plenty of time to relax in camp or hike and explore before dinner, and it's not far to the hot springs—a welcome relief from strenuous hiking each day.

YOUR NEXT STEP: Sierra Club (✆ **415/977-5522;** www.sierraclub.org). A 1-week project, US$645, includes campground fees in the national forest with kitchen trailer, portable toilets, and shower house nearby, all meals (everyone pitches in cooking and cleaning), field technique training and tools, on-site transportation, and full project support.

DON'T MISS: Winter, spring, summer, fall, the views from the **Sandia Peak** ski area are unmatched. Hop on the world's longest tramway for an 11,000-sq.-mile (28,490-sq.-km) panoramic view as you glide over desert, canyons, and lush forests on the way to the top of the 10,378-foot-high (3,163-m)peak.

ⓘ www.newmexico.org

Archaeology 139

Passport in Time

Preservation in Beautiful Forest Sites

Various locations, USA

PART-TIME DINOSAUR DIGGER. PART-TIME ARCHEOLOGICAL EXCAVATOR. PART-TIME FOREST ranger. Part-time camper. These are just some of the hats you might wear at the location of your choosing in the United States when you're part of a team that's put together to preserve the country's past.

You'll be hanging out with the rangers on this volunteer program with the USDA Forest Service. The Passport in Time programs in national forests across the United States match volunteers with professional archaeologists and historians to work on everything from surveying to stabilizing cliff dwellings, rock-art restoration and oral-history-gathering to analysis of artifacts. Every year new programs and priorities are introduced throughout the forest regions from coast to coast and border to border. You'll be trained in the field by experts to quickly get you up to speed with whatever skills you'll need for a particular project, from excavating a 10,000-year-old village in Minnesota to cleaning vandalized rock art in Colorado to digging at the location of a Chinese mining camp in Idaho. Participants find the perfect project by searching through dozens of available options by date, location, or summary of the work required. You could sign up to work at the bottom of a pit doing paleontology or at the top of search towers doing survey work or facility repairs.

The accommodations at each site can vary from tent camping setups where you'll be responsible for your own food to hotels or RV hookups. Some have a camp cook who rustles up grub (sometimes for a small charge), and for others you'll hit the town greasy spoon or fine dining establishments. Projects are almost all less than 2 weeks in duration, with many being 1 week or less. Some require a commitment for the entire project, and for others you can sign up for fewer days. The website and application information for each project location includes full details for that particular work site.

YOUR NEXT STEP: USDA Forest Service Passport in Time (✆ **800/281-9176;** www.passportintime.com). There is no participation fee for Passport in Time volunteers, but you'll provide your own transportation to the work site. Other variables depend upon the project, including type of accommodations available and meals. All projects include field training from the experts in the archaeology and research division of the National Forestry Service.

DON'T MISS: There are USDA Forest sites in nearly every state, and each year different locales need volunteer teams. Many of them are adjacent to or actually host to famous landmarks and tourist sites you'll want to visit, such as California's extensive Los Padres National Forest that includes wilderness lands around stunning Big Sur all the way down to Santa Barbara...or visit the nation's oldest winery near the Las Cruces National Forest in New Mexico.

ⓘ www.discoveramerica.com.

140 Archaeology

Bone Picking in a Mammoth Graveyard

Work With Top Scientist, Relax in Hot Springs

Rapid City, South Dakota, USA

Travel back in time to an Ice Age right in the Black Hills National Forest area in South Dakota. Its full of American landmarks, and the remains of some of the largest creatures to ever walk the Earth.

Working side by side with one of the leading scientists on Pleistocene extinctions, you'll unearth bone fragments and other evidence of mammoths and other life forms from the era. Pieces of this 26,000-year-old puzzle await in a region famous for its paleontology—and its thermal hot springs, the perfect antidote to a hard day's digging in the dirt.

It is surreal to be sitting in the putty-colored clay with your fine-bristled paintbrush, flicking away the grains of sand and dust from an enormous femur, or delicately stepping between the bones of a huge ribcage on your way to the skeleton of a baby Columbian mammoth. This is the world's largest natural deposit of these elephantine ancestors, and the site is also host to remains from camels, llamas, and the first-discovered north-central plains fossils of wolf and short-faced bear. More than 100,000 people visit this famous site annually, restricted to the boardwalks and viewing platforms, while you are in the depths of the former watering hole, getting that eons-old grime under your fingernails.

Your downtime in the Black Hills of South Dakota will be a truly Western vacation. You can while away the evenings gambling at rustic Wild West casinos, eating cherry pie, and watching as the blazing sunsets give over to star-filled nights. The excursion team stays together, taking over a nearby motel, so the camaraderie built during lazy evenings will last well past the flight home.

YOUR NEXT STEP: Earthwatch (© **800/ 776-0188;** www.earthwatch.org). A 15-day program, US$2,950, includes family-style meals prepared by a local cook, motel accommodations, and full project support. A US$35 Earthwatch membership is required.

DON'T MISS: You're in the heart of American landmark territory, so do the complete circuit of the immediate vicinity, and see **Mount Rushmore National Monument** (www.nps.gov/moru), **Crazy Horse Memorial** (www.crazyhorse.org), **Wind Cave National Park** (www.nps.gov/wica), and **Jewel Cave National Park** (www.nps.gov/jeca).

ⓘ www.blackhillstouristinfo.com

South Dakota's famous mammoth site

Marine Life **141**

Assist With Coral Reef Research

Do Good While You Dive

Blackbird Caye, Belize

A TRIP TO BELIZE TO HELP SCIENTISTS STUDY CORAL REEFS HARDLY SEEMS LIKE WORK AT ALL when you're staying in private beachfront accommodations and you wake up to the sound of surf. But that very beauty is threatened, which is why your help is needed for conservation efforts.

The waters around Belize are home to the world's second largest barrier reef (the Great Barrier Reef in Australia being the largest). Long a magnet for divers, waterborne explorers and recreational divers alike have noticed an alarming decline in the reef's vitality for several years. It doesn't take a science degree to know the ecosystem is hurting. It takes the efforts of individuals like you to turn this disastrous trend around, and committing yourself to the science of ecological repair is pulling more than your own weight.

Belize businesses are developing its coastline and offshore cayes, so conservation and project stewardship are extremely important in responding to the natural needs of the environment that brings so much tourism (and economic vigor) to the country. You'll assist with a monitoring program to help detect stress to the ecosystem and evaluate the general health of this living waterworld. You'll collect eco-data on the reef and sea-grass habitats, observing from the water and on boats the fish and sea-life populations, structure, and health. You don't need dive certification or experience to participate, but you'll need to love getting wet and be comfortable swimming and snorkeling. Keeping track of the reef residents is a census that will have lasting effects on conservation and environmental protection decisions in the future.

After all that snorkeling and swimming in the warm waters of the stunning reef area within the atoll, you'll stay in beachfront cabanas with private baths. Use your relaxation time to practice some conversational Spanish—you won't be required to know that language but will feel more comfortable if you can improve your skills.

YOUR NEXT STEP: The Oceanic Society (✆ **800/326-7491;** www.oceanicsociety.org). The 8-day project, $1,975, includes beachfront cabana accommodations, meals, project training, and support.

DON'T MISS: Mayan history is an important facet of Belize's history, and **Altun Ha,** the most extensively excavated Maya site in Belize, is a must-see. This major ceremonial center consists of two main plazas with 13 significant temple and residential structures. The "Jade Head," the largest jade carving yet discovered, was found here.

Collecting eco-data on coral reefs in Belize

ⓘ www.travelbelize.org

142 Marine Life

Humpback Whale Research

Data Collection in "Brazilian Polynesia"

Praia do Forte, Brazil

A FISHING VILLAGE THAT'S RECENTLY BEEN TRANSFORMED INTO A DEVELOPED TOURISM destination is your base for whale-watching on the coast of Brazil. When you're finished watching the show these grand mammals put on, it will be hard to resist the siren call of the white-sand beaches nearby.

The science of whale communication over great distances provides plenty of mystery and even more harmonious satisfaction. Settle in and whale watch for a couple of weeks on the beautiful beaches of what has become known as Brazilian Polynesia. Sometimes from the sea, sometimes from the shore, you'll collect and collate behavioral data from your observations, conduct bio-acoustic monitoring, and

A breaching humpback whale off the coast of nearby Salvador, Brazil

photograph individuals to add to the identification library (they are identified by patterns on their tail flukes). You'll also put all that research into a usable format at the base station. This endangered species is well known as a showoff, so the jumps and twists and slapping fins and tails will keep you enthralled.

This coastal area of Brazil is a prime mating and calving zone for the humpbacks, so it's an ideal research station to help form conservation strategy for these majestic mammals. You'll quickly become an expert and use your knowledge to teach in nearby fishing village communities about the importance of conservation and saving the whales. The interaction, in English, but also in Portuguese if you know it, stands you in good stead among your new neighbors. One of the most rewarding elements is going on watch with the Coastal Patrol, a youth group of dedicated environmentalists aged 12 to 16.

You'll be bunking in the dormitory-style hostel in town, with plenty of free time to explore the village, snorkel in crystal-clear water, or laze away the afternoons on the sugary sand of some of the best beach frontage in South America. You'll come home with a wicked tan to accompany your new expertise and invigorated passion for conservation of the seas.

YOUR NEXT STEP: Global Vision International (© **888/653-6028;** www.gviusa.com). A 2-week project, US$1,800, includes accommodations at village hostel, research training, local transportation, and 24-hour project support. The hostel has a kitchen where you provide your own meals (except included breakfasts), or you can dine out in inexpensive local establishments.

DON'T MISS: The reef at Praia do Forte extends from shore out 150 feet (46m) in some places. At low tide, pools created by the receding water make warm natural **spa pools.** About 6 to 12 in. (15–30cm) of naturally solar-heated water makes the perfect restorative lounging spa—especially when *barracas* come along to serve you a caipirinha in a floating tray.

ⓘ www.turismo.gov.br

143 Marine Life

Track Humpback Whales

Study & Snorkelling

Osa Peninsula, Costa Rica

It's difficult to imagine a better way to get close to these kings of the sea then by working with the researchers who study them. In your time off you'll be perfectly positioned to explore the rainforests and national parks of this largely unspoiled, southern part of Costa Rica.

As the temperament and temperature of the oceans fluctuate, all life within must adapt and make changes. The larger the species, the more ingrained the habits, so this fascinating research project in Costa Rica is uncovering new information all the time. Humpback whales make seasonal migrations following warm water currents, and were formerly thought to use three primary wintering areas: Mexico, Hawaii, and Japan. Recent research has indicated Costa Rica is becoming a new (or newly discovered) wintering zone as well.

On this intensive study trip, you'll help researchers observe and collect information on the whales' preference and usage of what seems to be fresh habitat, affiliation patterns within herds and family groups, and whether the same or different animals return each year to Costa Rican waters. Identification of individuals, and watching as their families grow and interact, is a primary focus. Your camera will be busy as you photograph the splashing, spouting athleticism of these whales, especially the playful calves that stay by their mothers' side for a year or more. You'll also sport big headphones as you drop a microphone in the water to record the haunting and ethereal whale songs.

When you're not out to sea on the research vessels, your home will be a very comfortable seaside lodge. The nearby Corcovado National Park begs exploring, and they'll have to drag you out of the water if you love snorkeling, as it is spectacular here. The project's ultimate goal is to support the efforts underway to designate this area of Costa Rica as an official marine sanctuary.

YOUR NEXT STEP: The Oceanic Society (✆ **800/326-7491,** whale watching hotline: **415/474-3385;** www.oceanicsociety.org). The 8-day excursion, $2,490, includes beachfront lodge accommodations, meals, and project training and support.

DON'T MISS: Some of the most adrenaline-inducing adventure sports originated in Costa Rica, so tap into the spirit and do a **canopy tour** in the treetops of the rainforest. Fly via zipline or stroll on suspended bridges and walkways at a height normally experienced only by monkeys and birds. You might even book a few nights in a tree house.

ⓘ www.visitcostarica.com

Marine Life 144

Dolphin & Whale Research

Live on a Sailboat in the Mediterranean

Liguria, Italy

THIS IS NOT YOUR USUAL MEDITERRANEAN CRUISE: INSTEAD OF BELLYING UP TO THE BUFFET, you'll study the varied marine life of the sea, with some free time to explore your ports of call.

Living on a sailboat slicing through the crystalline blue waters off Italy's coast is the perfect place to work while on vacation. The Pelagos Cetacean Sanctuary in the western Mediterranean is charged with the protection of a variety of marine mammals that live in the protected region between Italy and France. This project, ongoing for nearly 2 decades, has increased awareness of the need for conservation and protection of marine mammals. The unequaled Mediterranean biodiversity of this area is being affected by human influence on water quality and food sources, so Monaco, France, and Italy have combined forces for the protection of the ocean habitat. This project provides the scientific basis for protection measures taken by the sanctuary.

You'll help in research of Bottlenose, striped, and Risso's dolphins, as well as pilot, large-fin, and sperm whales. You'll be a jack-of-all-trades in field research as you are trained then eventually move seamlessly among photo-identification, distance sampling, remote tracking, acoustic recording for songs, and behavioral sampling. You needn't be an expert sailor, but by the time you return home you'll have plenty of hands-on experience skippering (or at least crewing) your mobile field station/home. Some time will also be spent on the computer, entering data and analyzing recordings from the hydrophone. Weather can affect the daily tasks, but plan on full days of research and tracking while on the move between harbors—and what harbors they are! These are the waters off the Cote d'Azur, Tuscany, and Northern Sardinia—not just the cream of the crop of places to see in the region, but also particularly rich in cetacean populations (it seems fantastic food is indigenous in Italy's waters, as well as on land).

Home is a 68-ft. (21m) sailboat that houses 16 team members with en suite bathrooms in the five cabins. Some evenings you will be in port in one of the amazing harbor cities, so diversion is readily available, but you should also be prepared for a few overnights at sea—which, with the local food and drink, should not be too hard to take.

YOUR NEXT STEP: Global Vision International (✆ **888/653-6028;** www.gviusa.com). The 1-week project runs US$1,117 to US$1,270, depending on the season. The fees cover all training, project support, and room and board on the boat. Additional weeks are available (and popular).

DON'T MISS: One of the three nations cooperating with the cetacean protection efforts of the sanctuary is **Monaco,** which is a great place to kick up your heels dancing, gambling, imbibing, and celebrating the high life after your work, or put your heels on a chaise longue at the beach and just let time drift away. www.visitmonaco.com

ⓘ www.italiantourism.com

145 Marine Life

Dolphin Study

Counting Pods in the Greek Isles

Fiskardo, Greece

Fiskardo is unique in that it remains largely undisturbed after the famous 1953 earthquake that damaged many of the old buildings elsewhere on the island of Kelafonia. Its charm and quiet ambiance is a great place to unwind after a thrilling day tracking dolphins and working to protect their habitat.

Make sure you've got those little elastic seasickness bands around your wrists as you'll spend plenty of time on this trip aboard the *Neptune* observation boat among the Ionian Islands. You'll be counting and recounting to get accurate population figures for the cetacean species in these waters. The dolphins of Greece seem to return to the same region annually, and their movements and behaviors are plotted out on maps as the science team attempts to uncover the patterns and influences on their migration. Of course, in an area as idyllic as the Ionian Islands, people are eager to spend as much time as possible enjoying the regal splendor—and with them come their recreational boats and Jet Skis and litter. All of these are direct threats to the ocean life in the area, and the health of the dolphin pods is beginning to show the effects.

In addition to seaborne observation and tracking, you'll do coastal watches as well as interview local boaters about dolphin encounters. Your data gets entered into the records at the environmental museum where the project is tracked. Some of your time will be spent on dolphin advocacy and education in the museum and bustling harbor area.

This is a mountainous island dotted with small Grecian villages separated by rocky coves and shady tracts of forest. Your little corner of the island is a rustic camp where you'll sleep in a communal caravan or shared tents with shared showers/restroom and a small kitchen/communal building. But if you're awake, you'll be exploring. The hiking is splendid and every turn brings new postcard-perfect vistas, so charge the camera battery each night—you won't want to miss any of it. You'll also snap plenty of shots for posterity so you can remember the villagers with whom you become chummy—project participants have historically spent plenty of time in the village pubs.

YOUR NEXT STEP: Twin Work & Volunteer Abroad (© **800/80 483 80;** www.workandvolunteer.com). A 2-week project, US$738, includes rustic camp life, project training, and backup support. You are responsible for buying and preparing your own food and incidentals.

DON'T MISS: Rare is the land that has a deeper vein of history than Greece, and of course one of the most famous archeological sites is the **Acropolis** of Athens. The main sanctuary on the giant rocky hill, the Parthenon, is dedicated to Athena and is perhaps the most iconic ancient structure of the civilized world.

ⓘ www.gnto.gr

Marine Life 146

Marine Ecosystem Study

Underwater Photography in Paradise

Gau Island, Fiji

Are you a budding Jacques Cousteau? A love of diving and a talent for photography will be an asset for this assignment. Chances are that, after you adapt to the slower rhythms of the island, it won't feel like work.

Four weeks in Fiji—sounds like a dream come true. It is a region of natural beauty, traditions, and a way of life that has remained in many ways unchanged for generations. The thing that has changed, much to the planet's dismay, is the recent imbalance of the delicate marine ecosystem. Working with a team from the University of the South Pacific, this trip is all about getting a picture of the world under the sea—both literally, via photography, and figuratively, by adding to researchers' understanding of the habitat. This information is needed to implement protections that will hopefully interrupt the downward spiral and save several species. More than 1,200 different kinds of fish and marine mammals swim these Pacific waters around the Fijian archipelago, and you'll be studying them on scuba and boat excursions.

You'll dive daily to map the intricate coral reef system, assessing the algae and bleaching damage. For a change of scene you'll also dive among the mangrove stands and sea-grass beds. Move along grid-like transect patterns to observe the swimming community and their behaviors, general vigor, and interactions. This

Photographers on a diving trip in Fiji

study is multidirectional, trying to figure out the effects of global warming, pollution, fishing, feeding, and population of individual species, even of the souvenir market's seashells and coral. All of it takes its toll on the health of Fiji's waters. By the end of this project, you'll be an expert at marine identification.

It won't take long to adapt to Fiji time, where everything gets done at its own pace. Wake up mornings in traditional, communal *burres* (huts) on the beach, have some fresh fruit and maybe a swim in the surf, hop on board the Frontier vessel to go to the day's dive sight. You'll spend the day in and out of the water, collecting, recording, and entering data. The boat is back at the camp before the sun sets. You'll have some camp chores like collecting firewood or rinsing dive equipment, and then a hearty meal cooked over an open fire, perhaps a festival or feast shared with locals, and then drift away from the dying embers to sleep to the sound of waves lapping the shore. Ready to sign up for a year instead of a month?

YOUR NEXT STEP: The Society for Environmental Exploration (Frontier) (✆ **+44/20 7613 2422;** www.frontier.ac.uk). The 4-week project, £1,134, includes burre camp living, communally prepared campfire meals and cleanup, PADI dive training if you need it or want to move up to the next level of certification, camp diving equipment and tanks (bring your own mask, fins, wetsuit, and personal dive gear), in-country ground transport, local orientation and project training, and 24-hour support.

DON'T MISS: After all your time focused on the ocean, turn your attention inland while visiting the Fijian Islands. The northern Island **Vanua Levu** is the island where the TV series *Survivor* was shot, and its *Jurassic Park*-like interior is an amazing jungle.

ⓘ www.fijime.com

147 Marine Life

Improving Coral Health

Learn to Scuba Dive While Protecting Reefs

Andavadoaka, Madagascar

This island is teeming with species not found elsewhere in the world, and marine life, specifically coral, is no exception. It takes an environment that's relatively unspoiled to support it, perfectly suited for those who enjoy a simple lifestyle while they explore.

On the most westerly point of the world's fourth largest island, Madagascar, lies a research station that is a few flutterkicks away from the fourth largest coral reef in the world, Grand Récif de Tuléar. A constant buzz of work is being carried out by volunteers from around the world, as well as Malagasy scientists and international marine experts, all united to protect and save the delicate reef system here in the Indian Ocean. The small fishing village of Andavadoaka is on a lagoon, buffered from the ocean by small islets and coral reefs, all of which, under the right circumstances, support a huge, diverse community of fish and sea mammals that depend on the thriving beds of coral for sustenance and protection. The coral is waning, bleached by global temperature changes, and dying out from elements toxic to the coral. This fertile area is largely unexplored and undiscovered, disappearing faster than it can be charted.

You'll map and chart unrecorded coral reefs while studying their biodiversity and assessing threats to their vitality. You'll undergo intensive scientific training, both lab-based and while snorkeling and on diving excursions. If you aren't yet PADI certified for scuba, you can attain that certification and training while working here—and don't worry, more than half the volunteers who participate every year have never dived before. The first 2 weeks will focus on getting you up to speed with diving skill and confidence (or certifying experienced divers to the next level) and teaching you the scientific background and tactics needed to carry out experiments. Expect to dive and/or snorkel every day, collecting water and sediment samples and photographing and mapping the undulating oceanic floor. You'll identify and describe many species that call these once-pristine reefs home. Without a previous point of reference, the reefs will still appear stunning and vibrant to you, and the team's ultimate goal is to make sure they decline no further and can actually begin a slow and natural recovery.

It's four to a hut in the self-contained wooden eco-cabins that overlook the sugar-white beaches and cerulean lagoon. Your free time will likely be spent in and around camp exploring, recreational snorkeling and swimming, and relaxing. Camp is somewhat remote, so there won't be bustling nightlife out the front door—unless you count the animals frolicking nearby.

YOUR NEXT STEP: Blue Ventures (✆ **+44/20 3176 0548;** www.blueventures.org). Prices for this 3-week excursion vary (most stay 6 weeks or longer), depending on your dive experience. (The more experienced you are, the less expensive the trip.) Advanced Open Water certified: £1,400. Open Water certified: £1,500. No dive certification: £1,600. Non-diving volunteers: £700. Included for all is shared beach cabin accommodations, all meals and snacks, certification dive training, scientific training for field techniques, airport transfers, logistical support, and a 24-hour medic on-site.

DON'T MISS: On Ile Ste Marie, or Nosy Boraha, a narrow tropical island off Madagascar's east coast, the nearly 1,000-acre (405ha) **Forest of Ikalalao** is the only surviving remnant of the original primary forest that once blanketed the nation. The forest is remarkable for its wildly varied orchid species and you are almost certain to spot that poster-child of the island: the lemur. Three lemur species are found here: the mouse lemur, Microcebus, and the larger fat-tailed dwarf lemur.

ⓘ www.madagascar-tourisme.com

Marine Life 148

Watching Whale Sharks

Follow and Photograph the Gentle Giants

Inhambane, Mozambique

Mozambique's beaches are gaining a lot of attention, and Inhambane—which bears the influence of the Portuguese, who established an outpost here more than 500 years ago—is close to several areas that surfers love. But it's also a special area because it's home to dwindling numbers of whale sharks.

When a silent, gray behemoth the size of a bus (up to 40 ft./12m long) swims up behind you in the ocean, you might have cause to jump. When you know it's a shark, you might jump a little higher. When you know it's a whale shark, however, you'll simply turn around and gaze in awe at the graceful beauty of this enormous, peaceful, aquatic vegetarian. No bloody scenes from *Jaws* here (unless you are algae or tiny fish and plankton), the intriguing whale sharks are indeed gentle giants who are, sadly, facing survival challenges they may not meet without your help. The Indian Ocean off Mozambique's pristine shores is attractive waters for whale sharks, and a pretty great location for your vacation.

You'll spend your working time monitoring and recording whale shark numbers and behavior, feeding reports to the scientists and policy makers who will make decisions for preservation and protection. The same symptoms of a sick sea that result in coral bleaching and dying reefs are affecting the whale sharks, as well as fishing nets, sound pollution, and habitat destruction. You'll snorkel among them, amazed at how such a large animal can barely disturb the water around you, photographing them for your own memories as well as for use in specific animal identification. You'll also spend some project time in general reef conservation work, monitoring life and food patterns, as well as the local loggerhead turtles. Additionally, you can train on this project with a dive master to obtain your PADI scuba diving certification or expand your current dive skills and certification level.

The whale shark conservation project base moves with the migration of the sharks, so depending on the time of year (or even week) you schedule your trip, you'll be based on a different beach. Accommodations will be comfortable beach huts just steps from the water, and meals in camp will be prepared by local cooks, featuring specialties of Mozambique cuisine that boasts spicy European and African influences. Evenings are easygoing, with plenty of relaxing, gazing into the sea, and getting to know your fellow teammates. In your free time, book with a small local company and cruise the waters in a traditional *dhow*, an Arab sailing vessel.

YOUR NEXT STEP: The Society for Environmental Exploration (Frontier) (✆ +44/ 20 7613 2422; www.frontier.ac.uk). This program runs a minimum of 4 weeks, £1,135, and may be somewhat nomadic if the whale sharks are on the move. Regardless of whether you're in one spot the entire month or in several, you'll be based in beach huts and have all meals provided as well as airport transfers, full training and project support, and PADI dive training if desired.

DON'T MISS: After living the life aquatic, go terrestrial and visit one of a dozen national parks and reserves for a fantastic **safari.** The Big Five are all found in abundance in Mozambique's wild lands, as well as numerous other species.

ⓘ www.turismomocambique.co.mz

149 Marine Life

Marine Big Five Research & Education

Come Face-to-Face With Great White Sharks

Gansbaai, South Africa

For anyone who really loves marine life and wants a one-of-a-kind chance to see mammals not easily found in other waters, a trip to South Africa is your answer. If you can drag yourself away from the beach, nearby Cape Town has some one-of-a-kind sights of its own.

If it swims or floats and is endemic to Southern Africa, you'll encounter it, study it, observe it, and practically become it on this excursion. The Marine Big Five are sharks, whales, dolphins, seals, and penguins, and they're all your subjects. The leader of this particular pack is the great white shark, and most of your time will be spent seeking them out and recording their behavior. You may share the research vessel with tourists at certain times of year, and you'll be trained to help answer their questions as adrenaline runs higher and higher when you approach Shark Alley. On some occasions, you'll go down in a shark cage for up close (and incredibly exciting) observation.

Some of your time will be spent on Dyer Island, home and breeding ground for jackass penguins, Cape cormorants, and gannets. Just across the way is Geyser Rock, home to 20,000 Cape fur seals—and thus a prime feeding territory for great whites. Migrating whales and dolphins also pass through this marine hot zone seasonally. You'll go out a few times each day aboard one of two ships, *Shark Fever* and the *Whale Whisperer* to collect data and record behavior patterns of the interaction among all these species. The waters can be rough and the action frenzied if sharks are feeding, which sends all the other animals into an agitated state. During such chaos, it can be hard to record dorsal fin patterns, sex and size, and movement of individually recognized animals, but you'll get better with practice. On the whale boat, things are calmer, and you'll track whales and dolphins via GPS to compare seasonal data to years past.

You'll be based in a shared home near the beautiful white sand beaches and walking distance from the Shark House, which serves as offices for the project and tour boat meeting spot. Plan on being busy even when you're on shore, as boats need to get washed down and maintained, wetsuits and other equipment organized and cleaned, and more. You will have plenty of time off to enjoy the beach and quaint fishing villages along the shore, and enjoy some of the best and freshest seafood you're likely to ever have.

YOUR NEXT STEP: Travellers Worldwide (UK: **+44/1903 502595;** www.travellersworldwide.com). The 2-week project, £745, includes accommodations in the project group house with shared room/shared bath, full project support as well as city and project orientation, lectures and scientific training, and airport transfers. Food is not included, but there are several inexpensive stores and restaurants within walking distance and a kitchen at the house.

DON'T MISS: Nearby **Cape Town** is a beautiful city and worthwhile vacation destination unto itself. One of the most iconic sites in the city is **Table Mountain,** so take the aerial tramway to the top of this flattened plateau for stunning views all around. www.tablemountain.net

ⓘ www.southafrica.net

150 Marine Life

Explore Reef Dynamite Damage

Traditional Living, World-Class Diving

Mafia Island, Tanzania

IT'S THE FISHERMEN WHO ARE PACKING THE EXPLOSIVES ON THIS UNDERDEVELOPED ISLAND OFF the coast of Eastern Africa. Accommodations will be beachside camps that qualify as roughing it, but adventurous types will want to dive right into this experience of helping marine experts study the damage caused by explosive and its effects.

Fishing for your livelihood is difficult at the best of times, but for individual fishermen in Tanzania, the large-scale arrival of commercial companies has crowded individuals out of the waters both literally and figuratively. In a desperate attempt to keep up with the cutthroat business climate, some locals have turned to the productive (from the perspective of quantity of catch) but enormously destructive practice of dynamite fishing. You'll sail out on a traditional dhow to get to the day's dive site—a memorable experience in and of itself—before you enter the lush underwater coral forest.

You'll work alongside the scientific staff on dives to observe and record the healthy coral growth, fish populations and behaviors, sea turtle numbers, and inter-tidal creatures. You'll also explore the shoreside mangrove root systems that are home to spiny seahorses and several tiny

Exploring Tanzania's waters for dynamite damage

marine species. Visual census reports, algae assessment, and visual/photographic recording of dynamite damage is all in your job description. Some of your time will be spent bringing the collected data up to date and combining it with other records, but most of the time, you are wet. Get your dive certification or increase your experience while on this assignment that is authorized to certify divers for open water and several advanced diving degrees. You'll want to take advantage of the world-class diving. The huge body of information gathered by you and your fellow volunteers will form the groundwork for local conservation laws and movements.

Life will be rustic in your remote beach camp, which was constructed from indigenous materials by local craftsmen. The *bandas* (huts) are woven from palm fronds and sealed with mud. Stationed in a clearing in a coconut grove, the camp blends in with the surroundings, and low impact is the name of the game. Locals have enjoyed challenging visiting volunteers to impromptu soccer matches and beach volleyball. You'll eat meals prepared for you over an open fire, and count on a bucket bath when you want to rinse off the day's saltwater coating. You might feel like you're sprouting gills when you choose to spend your free time snorkeling and swimming some more, but it's hard to resist the crystal-clear, warm waters of the sea right outside your door.

YOUR NEXT STEP: The Society for Environmental Exploration (Frontier) (✆ **+44/ 20 7613 2422;** www.frontier.ac.uk). The 3-week project, £1,495, includes airport pickup and ferry transfers, local orientation and project training, dive certification, diving equipment, two meals daily, and beach camp accommodations.

DON'T MISS: You've been under the surface, now get high above sea level to the crater of an active volcano. Overlooking Lake Natron and the bushland of Kenya to the north, **Ol Donyo Lengai,** meaning "the home of God" in Masaai, is a still undiscovered-by-tourists climb. The volcano erupts sporadically, sending small streams of gray lava down the crater rim and spitting hot ash high into the air. It's a tough climb to the summit, but stay overnight so you can watch the sunrise over the Rift Valley and it will all have been worth it.

ⓘ www.tanzaniatouristboard.com

Marine Life **151**

Wild Dolphin Research

Cetacean Research on Your Vacation

Oahu, Hawaii, USA

SHOULD YOU FIND YOURSELF PLANNING TO VISIT THE BEAUTIFUL 50TH STATE AND WANT TO take a charter boat to view dolphins or swim with them, this volunteer opportunity provides a wonderful alternative. Volunteers are needed for this informal program to help scientists learn more about dolphin behavior, habits, and habitats.

There are no shortage of opportunities to get involved with the research and conservation of the wild dolphins around Oahu await you. You can choose from boat- and land-based field work to helping in the organization's office, and how much you give is up to you and your schedule. There is no fixed program for volunteers, but all year there is a consistent need for volunteers who are ready, willing, and able to go out on commercial dolphin watching trips (when space allows), to do field observation (photographing dorsal fin patterns for identification), record environmental data and weather conditions, notate sighting locations by GPS and longitude/latitude coordinates, and more. On shore, the need and opportunities are even greater. Your keen eyes are needed to scan video footage for individual animal ID and single and group dolphin behaviors (there are hundreds of hours of underwater film to process). Data is also collected and compiled from other whale-watching and dolphin-watching vessels in an effort to expand conservation programs statewide.

Shore spotting is hugely important to the project, and can be done anywhere, so it's ideal if you want to volunteer only for an afternoon or a weekend while vacationing. The Waianae Coast provides the best sightings and is an important baseline measurement spot for the database. You may also be asked to assist with nature camps that focus on getting youth and special interest groups active in dolphin conservation. No matter how you spend your volunteer hours, the contribution to the wild dolphins is critically important and cannot be done without a volunteer force.

The volunteer program is not formalized, so you'll arrange your own room and board as well as transportation to project offices or in-field sites, and give of your time as generously as your vacation schedule allows.

YOUR NEXT STEP: The Wild Dolphin Foundation (© **808/306-3968;** www.wilddolphin.org). When you know your vacation plans in Oahu, contact the volunteer coordinator to find the times and tasks that will best make use of your energy and enthusiasm. No program charge for volunteers.

DON'T MISS: Oahu is considered the art and cultural center of the Hawaiian Islands, with a plethora of fine art venues throughout the island. Do a museum crawl and explore the world-class visiting and permanent exhibits at the **Honolulu Academy of Arts,** the island flavored fine art at the **Hawaii State Art Museum,** and the modern works of international artists both indoors and out at **The Contemporary Museum.**

ⓘ www.visit-oahu.com

152 Museums, Zoos & Aquariums

Children's Art & Science Museum

Days at the Museum

Cordoba, Argentina

THE SECOND-LARGEST CITY IN ARGENTINA CAN BECOME YOUR HOME FOR SIX WEEKS OF guiding children through an interactive museum, working on your Spanish, and visiting the preserved Jesuit Block, which contains the oldest university in South America.

If you enjoy watching children's eyes light up with discovery, think about volunteering at this Argentinean museum (you'll need an intermediate level of Spanish). Exhibits through the halls focus on earth science, health and bodies, the solar system, and biology/animal science. It's a hands-on experience as kids make their way through wildly colorful and diverse exhibits, stopping at stations to play, climb, paint and draw, act out scenes, and more. Volunteers like you lead groups of young people through structured and playfully unstructured activities and creative games. Great

10 Ways to Help Find the Next Source of Energy

Coal and petroleum, long the fuel forces behind most of the world's power grids, are finite resources and their end, while not upon us, is foreseeable. The great race is on to find the next best energy-providing technology—and there are many places around the world where you can be a part of its discovery and practical application.

153 Cochabamba, Bolivia In this rural village, not quite 20% of families have access to electricity, and this project is working to develop solar options that will cover 98% of households' needs. You'll be dedicated to the whole span of the project, from planning and design assistance to site preparations, educating locals, helping assess environmental impact, and installation. Basic Spanish skills are necessary. ***The Society for Environmental Exploration (Frontier)*** *(✆* ***+44/20 7613 2422****; www.frontier.ac.uk). A 4-week trip is £1,095.*

Taking a break in Cochabamba, Bolivia

154 Shahpur-Jat, India Serious thought is going into India's solar, bio-gas plants, and energy from waste infrastructure. This urban village within Delhi serves as a test case, and this early stage work for volunteers is predominantly in education and advocacy, helping ignite a desire and passion for energy exploration in the community. ***Responsenet*** *(✆* ***+91/11/0981 087 27 48****; www.responsenet.org). Volunteers can commit from 1 week to 1 year, and there is no charge (engineering and water specialists are especially encouraged).*

155 Kashiwa, Japan Japan is at the forefront of environmental awareness and green innovations, and the city of Kashiwa has been developing biofuel as a significant alternative to petroleum. Your work at the biofuel factory (running in conjunction with an eco-friendly soap factory) will be in a supervisory role alongside disabled workers employed by the program. Some basic Japanese-language ability is required, but additional language instruction classes are offered. ***United Planet*** *(✆* ***800/292-2316****; www.unitedplanet.org). A 2-week trip is US$2,345.*

156 Sainte Luce, Madagascar You'll implement an inventive way to conserve Madagascar's forests while providing a sustainable cooking and heating source. You'll be training locals in how to use "improved stoves" that need less firewood and function more efficiently than campfires or fire pits. You'll see the stove projects from start to finish, leaving an immediately usable and sustainable legacy. ***Global Vision International*** *(✆* ***888/653-6028****; www.gviusa.com). A 2-week project is US$1,590.*

157 Kathmandu, Nepal Your first 2 days will be a solar installation workshop, followed by travel to remote communities to put your new skills to work. A guide and translator/technician will supervise and coach your work. For the installation, you'll stay with a host family as you install the new solar energy system into their home.

The program immerses you in the local culture and explores Buddhist lifestyles and environmental sustainability. ***Himalayan Light Foundation*** *(© **+977/4425 393**; www.hlf.org.np). Volunteers travel to project sites on their own. Costs at US$998 per week.*

158 Sabana Grande, Nicaragua Your time in this sustainable community is intertwined with a weeklong Solar Culture course. You'll build a solar oven with the local women's group, you'll make your own solar-roasted coffee at an organic farm, learn the technology of solar dryers, take a solar cooking class, and help with installation of photovoltaic clean energy systems in private homes. ***Grupo Fenix*** *(© **505/915-5722**; www.grupofenix.org). A 1-week project is US$700.*

159 Negros Island, Philippines This is a working tour through several locales featuring water and renewable energy projects in the central Philippines. In addition to helping plant fruit trees and vegetable gardens, you'll work on the supervised installation of biogas digesters. Other project time will be spent exploring and improving potable water delivery systems, alternative renewable energy ideas, and income-generating farm projects for rural families. ***Green Empowerment*** *(© **503/284-5774**; www.greenempowerment.org). A 9-day program is US$1,700.*

160 Ibiza, Spain You may think of Ibiza as a 24-hour party town, but a particularly lovely verdant quadrant is home to a model ecological center, La Casita Verde. The working farm is wind- and solar-powered, recycles all water, and is a center for ecological research. You'll live at the rustic farm and work on the installation and maintenance of the alternative energy grid, promoting green awareness to visitors and helping with permaculture farming. ***Center for Cultural Interchange*** *(© **312/944-2544**; www.cciexchange.com). A 3-day stay is US$1,170, longer visits are available.*

Spreading ecological awareness at Ibiza, Spain

161 Callaway, Minnesota, USA This project works with local universities to transform the way energy is used among indigenous Americans, including implementing wind energy projects. Your work, alongside tribal workers, will consist of hands-on creation of expanded wind turbines and infrastructure, from laying cable to wiring homes to public education to reduce tribal energy consumption. ***White Earth Land Recovery Project*** *(© **218/983-3834**; www.nativeharvest.com). No participation fee; stay as long as you want.*

162 Leicester, North Carolina, USA This program is dedicated to developing earth-friendly farm systems and educating the public. You'll focus on sustainable design and building, including site selection for optimum energy use, on-site water collection, passive solar design, passive solar greenhouse construction, wood-fired water heat, innovative natural cooling, installing micro-hydropower system, graywater recycling, and composting toilets. ***Long Branch Environmental Education Center*** *(© **828/683-3662**; www.longbrancheec.org). Length of stay is negotiable; no volunteer fee.*

emphasis is placed on kids interacting with one another and their environment. In a world that tells kids "Don't Touch" in every language, this is a chance to truly explore with childlike wonder.

You'll learn all of the art and science projects the museum has created for kids to get the very most out of their experience. Your input with additional ideas and activities is wholeheartedly encouraged, so come armed with workshops and games. Your work with small groups of excited children in new (and like all new experiences, perhaps daunting for some) environments helps teach the joy of learning and immersive exploration. If you have prior experience with education or counseling, your input will be highly prized (though no experience is required—just enthusiasm).

You'll stay with a host family while in Cordoba, and your evenings are wide open to explore the colonial city. Spend a sunset at the highest point in the city, beautiful Sarmineto Park. With its trails and rose garden, it's the lungs of the city. Bounteous food is everywhere, though the host family will serve you meals twice a day (except on Sundays, when meals won't be served in your host home). While volunteers who can commit a minimum of 6 weeks are preferred, shorter stints—2 weeks—can be arranged.

YOUR NEXT STEP: Center for Cultural Interchange (✆ **312/944-2544;** www.cci-exchange.com). The 2-week project, US$1,150, includes host family accommodations, two meals daily (except Sundays), local city orientation, project training, and support. You'll get yourself to Cordoba for the beginning of your volunteer assignment.

DON'T MISS: Considered one of the most beautiful natural features on the planet, **Iguazu Falls** is in fact a collection of thundering waterfalls, about 275 of them reaching a height of 200 ft. (60m). It is possible to stand in one spot and be almost entirely surrounded by an array of falling water.

ⓘ ww.turismo.gov.ar

Museums, Zoos & Aquariums **163**

Wildlife Rehabilitation Park

Care for Aussie Animals Next Door to the City

Perth, Australia

Get swept up in the laid-back, fun-loving way of life Down Under in Western Australia. After taking care of animals all day, take care of yourself by visiting vineyards, kayaking, bicycling, or swimming in the warm waters.

Practically everyone at one point during their youth declared they wanted to be a zookeeper. Of course we had no idea how hard the work actually was—we all just wanted to pet big animals. On this wildlife rehabilitation assignment in Perth, you'll get to experience a wide array of tasks, some completely inglorious and others quite sublime. You'll work with an all-volunteer organization, taking care of sick and injured animals from across the diverse Australian wildlife spectrum. More than 80% of Australia's flora and fauna is native only to Australia, so conservation and protection of species takes on an urgent tone. The wildlife park is adjacent to a wetlands education center, which expands the available natural habitats, making the release of rehabilitated animals back into the wilderness much easier on the volunteer team *and* on the animal. More than 3,000 animals are brought to the center each year.

You can expect to work with kangaroos, pelicans, and giant seabirds, which have been blown off course and become too exhausted to continue their migration. The universal goal is to rehabilitate and treat animals to get them reintegrated into the wild as soon as possible. Some animals, due to the nature of their injuries, cannot be safely reintroduced, so they become educational mascots of the center or, often, foster parents for young, injured animals. In addition to caring for individual animals, you'll also prepare food for them, clean and maintain enclosures, do environmental surveying, compile medical and behavioral records, assist with animal captures, and help with the many visitors and school groups who visit the park as an outdoor education center.

When you're away from the park, you'll be based in Perth's Central Business District (CBD), so you're conveniently located near all the comforts (and welcome distractions) of the city. Home is a centrally located lodge with private rooms and shared bath and kitchen facilities, plus pool table, arcade machines, cable TV, and free CBD transportation. Walk to the city's famous Swan River or take a free shuttle to other parks to get back outside—practically an Aussie mandate, even on your day off.

YOUR NEXT STEP: Travellers Worldwide (UK: **+44/1903 502595;** www.travellersworldwide.com). A 2-week assignment, £945, includes lodge-style accommodations in the city's center with meals included, project training and support, airport transfers and city orientation tours, and an indigenous heritage tour in Kings Park.

DON'T MISS: One of the more famous areas of Perth is **Fremantle** (referred to locally as Freo), which is the city's busy port and quite rich in history. Most days, and especially on weekends, you will find markets, live street entertainment, and plenty of alfresco cafes.

ⓘ www.perthtouristcentre.com.au

Museums, Zoos & Aquariums

Han Yangling Museum

Ancient Art & Culture

X'ian, China

Soak up the history, culture, and traditions of China by working in this museum. The town where it's located has played an important role in the development of this ancient country, going all the way back to the Tang Dynasty.

So much of the ultimate China travel experience is exploring the history of a country that reveres ancestry and tradition. China could dominate the world markets of the next century, and it has built much of its strength based on 5,000 years of history lessons, starting with the X'ia. Immerse yourself in the past by volunteering in the underground exhibition halls of the Han Yangling Museum, located beneath the mausoleum in the tomb of Jung Di, the fourth emperor of the Han Dynasty. Art and culture have spanned an incredible array of influences and styles, from emperors through the Opium Wars to the Cultural Revolution during Mao's time in office. Even through the periods of tumultuous unrest when intellectuals and artists were persecuted, great works of cultural significance were stowed away for the future—many of which are now in the Han Yangling, some still undisplayed.

Inside the Han Yangling Museum

You'll be an English liaison to tour guides, helping them with their English as well as guiding tour groups of your own and directing English-speaking guests. This museum, cousin to the one showcasing the famous Terracotta Warriors, is less known but much more up to date, having opened at the end of the 20th century. In addition to interacting with the public, you'll also consult on the translations and grammar of published materials, and if you're web-savvy, the museum is always improving the English pages of their website. Knowledge of tourism or Chinese history can be very helpful but is not required for this assignment.

Traveling to and from your host family house to the museum—and to other museums, restaurants, shopping, and pedestrian areas—is all easily accessible via pedal power. Bicycles are incredibly popular throughout China, and the ringing of bells on handlebars is a chorus that will follow you through the streets. X'ian, the capital of ancient China, is a popular city for visitors, and offers unsurpassed people-watching.

YOUR NEXT STEP: i-to-i (© **800/985-4852;** www.i-to-i.com). The 2-week project, US$1,990, includes three local specialty meals daily, dormitory accommodations at the group project house, full project support as well as city and project orientation, and airport transfers.

DON'T MISS: The **X'ian City Wall,** built during the Ming Dynasty, is the best-preserved ancient city wall in China and also the largest and most complete military facility in the world. It is a powerful symbol of strength and an enormous collection of gates, drawbridges (there's a moat), watchtowers, and weapons of defense.

ⓘ www.cnto.or

Acclaimed Private Zoo

Volunteer Zookeeping

Santa Cruz, Bolivia

THE EASTERN PART OF BOLIVIA PROVIDES AMPLE OPPORTUNITY, BEYOND THE VOLUNTEER project, to observe indigenous species, whether it's the museum of natural history, the amazing sand dunes at Lomas de Arena de El Palmar, or bird watching in Amboró National Park.

Thirty years ago Bolivia's Santa Cruz Zoo was opened to the public without government support or funding, and it's now one of the leading zoos in South America. Not wanting to be a showplace of exploited animals, this facility is entirely based on the tenets of species preservation and education. The work they do in studying and researching conservation and life expectancy has lead to the revival of several individual animals and whole species lines native to Bolivia and beyond. It's an amazing lineage of accomplishment, considering the zoo's humble start, and it still relies upon volunteers and private donors to maintain the excellence of its service to the animals.

Your days are spent as a zookeeper, primarily caring for the animals and their environments—perhaps helping with veterinary work before taking care of a few maintenance tasks on zoo grounds. There may be cages and enclosures to clean before preparing food and feeding animals. Don't forget the informational signs on the cage fronts that need replacing, and the brochures that need folding and filling in the racks. Tomorrow starts again at 7am, so if you don't get the front flowerbed weeded this afternoon, you can start with that—good thing most of your days end by noon. It's a lot to cram into a morning, but then you are free to help out in areas that truly interest you or to pursue other volunteer projects in Santa Cruz.

Your home is with a host family a short distance from the zoo in a safe neighborhood. You'll have a key to the house and can come and go at leisure, but you'll want to be there for the home-cooked meals. Meals are a great time to practice your Spanish—it's not required, but you'll be picking it up in spite of yourself. You'll enjoy days off wandering the colonial-style streets of this still-quaint city that is chock-a-block with cathedrals and churches, museums, small parks and playgrounds, and bubbling lagoons. Just outside of town are great pre-Incan ruins, Jesuit missions, and pristine forests just waiting for you and a picnic basket to while away an afternoon.

YOUR NEXT STEP: uVolunteer Bolivia (© **971/252-1334;** www.uvolunteer.org). The 2-week project, US$695, includes homestay with three home-cooked meals daily, airport pickup, city orientation in Santa Cruz, project coordination, training, and support.

DON'T MISS: If you have a taste for politics and controversy, take the **Che Guevara Trail** from Santa Cruz through the southeast lowlands of Bolivia to La Higuera and visit the guerilla encampment where the counter-culture icon was captured by the CIA and died.

ⓘ www.visitbolivia.org

Northern Studies Centre

Polar Bears for Free

Churchill, Manitoba, Canada

CHURCHILL CALLS ITSELF THE POLAR BEAR CAPITAL OF THE WORLD, AND WITH A HUMAN population of about 1,000 people in this northern town, it's easy to joke that there may be more bears here than people. Nevertheless, it's a lot of work tracking their health and habitat.

Bears, bears, bears. It's not often that people have the opportunity to see polar bears in the wild, but at the Churchill Northern Studies Centre and museum, it's an *ursa-palooza*. In the coldest times of year, this is a snow and ice zone that seems entirely forbidding to humans, which is when the adrenaline-loving folks—like you—pack the parka and head north toward the Arctic. Frogs freeze solid, birds lay eggs that won't thaw for months—and you can choose the deep freeze yourself if you'd like to build and sleep in an igloo or *quinzhee*. Dog sleds and the northern lights are your treat in exchange for some hard work at the centre. This active research facility is open to the public and school groups who come for the bears and other learning adventures in the sub-Arctic zone at the edge of a boreal forest. Different seasons bring folks up to the centre for different natural attractions: the aurora borealis, beluga whale migration, wildflowers and birding, and wildlife photography.

You might be taking snow samples with the research staff or peeling potatoes in the kitchen. Volunteers are needed for every level of work that keeps the center running, from maintenance to administrative support. The center teaches courses on 5-day cycles for youth and adults in birding, arctic wildlife, winter survival, beluga whales, northern lights astronomy, and the local celebrities: polar bears. You'll get the benefit of these learning experiences and lectures without paying for classes or room and board. You may be painting a stairwell or working in the gift shop as a way to sing for your supper, but living with and interacting with the research staff is an energizing and intellectually stimulating opportunity. You could also be washing dishes or participating in bird counts, planting trees, or almost anything else waiting for able hands like yours.

You'll live at the center with the research staff and long-term students in dormitory-style bunkrooms with shared bathrooms. Hot and hearty meals are prepared for you, and there is Internet access. The catch is that on your free time, due to the presence of your neighbors—the polar bears—you can't necessarily just set off on your own for a hike whenever the mood strikes. You can do plenty of exploring inside the center with science labs, a lounge, library, and herbarium among the environmental displays. There are bikes for your use during bear-free times, or you can hang out and shoot pool or watch movies in the lounge.

YOUR NEXT STEP: Churchill Northern Studies Centre (✆ **204/675-2307;** www.churchillscience.ca). Two weeks is the minimum the center hopes volunteers will commit to, and there is no program fee for volunteering. Rustic dormitory accommodations and prepared hearty meals are provided in exchange for 6 hours of daily work in and around the centre. Transportation is your own responsibility, and the centre is remote, so it can take some mastery of flight and bus schedules if your timing is limited. There is a US$12.50 membership fee when you arrive, which will also get you a subscription to the annual newsletter.

DON'T MISS: After roughing it in the great white north, you may crave some urbanity. On your way home, head to **Winnipeg** for a good dose of arts and culture, including lauded performances by Canada's Royal Winnipeg Ballet or the nine different music, art, performance, and culture groups based at the Centre Culturel Franco-Manitobain (CCFM).

ⓘ www.travelmanitoba.com

167 Museums, Zoos & Aquariums

Planetarium Volunteers

Under African Skies

Accra, Ghana

LOVE THE STARS, PLANETS, AND THE MOON? A GHANIAN PLANETARIUM NEEDS HELP TO ensure that things run smoothly and children are inspired to reach for the stars. You'll have plenty of time to make yourself at home in Accra, the dynamic capital of the country

Sometimes all it takes is a vision to make a shift in the world. Faced with what felt to him like an inexcusable lack of interactive educational science centers in Africa, Dr. Jacob Ashong got busy instead of getting discouraged. Mixing his scientific expertise with an abundance of moxie and an ability to make people around him agree with his vision proved the appropriate recipe to get a new planetarium in

Teaching at Ghana's planetarium

Ghana—the nation's first such learning center.

Getting to opening day of the Ghana Science Project was an uphill battle, but the effort hardly ends there. That's where you come in. Volunteers are perpetually needed for a month or many months to run planetarium shows, teach astronomy to school groups, coordinate management tasks behind the scenes, and pitch in with all the small tasks that need doing to get the stars projected onto the ceiling and get kids excited about the universe around them. Technical expertise isn't required (but is warmly welcomed if you've got it), but your enthusiasm is. It won't be difficult to renew your passion when the lights go out and tiny mouths drop open, *ooohhs* and *aaahhs* filling the domed room each time the show begins.

You'll live at the comfortable project house near the center of town, close to the science center. You'll have easy neighborhood access to shops, Internet cafes, bars, and a range of restaurants. You're responsible for your own meals, but several inexpensive options are a short walk away, and the fully supplied kitchen makes the supermarket an easy option. Since this is a longer-term placement than many, you'll truly have the chance to immerse yourself in Ghanian society and the Accra pace of life.

YOUR NEXT STEP: Ikando (© **+233/21 222 726;** www.ikando.org). A 4-week project, US$966, includes housing at the Ikando project house with full kitchen, a donation to the host organization, in-country orientation to life in Ghana, airport transfers, and 24-hour project support on this English-language assignment. Meals are your responsibility.

DON'T MISS: Lake Volta is the world's largest man-made body of water, a reservoir of well over 3,000 sq. miles (7,770 sq. km). It is a recreation region and weekend vacation spot sought out by locals and other Ghanaians alike.

ⓘ www.touringghana.com

Museums, Zoos & Aquariums **168**

Railway Museum

Trains, Tracks & Parties

Portmadoc, Wales

THIS RAILWAY IN NORTH WALES STARTS IN A HARBOR TOWN AND SNAKES THROUGH MOUNTAINS in a national park. It requires perpetual upkeep to keep people moving and keep its designation as the world's oldest independent railway.

Did you grow up with an engineer's cap and overalls? While other kids were wailing like police sirens were you steadfastly *choo-chooing*? More *Little Engine that Could* than *Speed Racer*? The Ffestiniog Railway in North Wales is a great volunteer option for train aficionados from around the world. It is a museum with active working trains that brings history to life. Volunteers come to this town in Wales for a day, a week, or longer to help out around the grounds, sell tickets, refurbish carriages, and more. While the need for volunteers is highest during the peak summer season, the museum is delighted to have volunteer help throughout the year. The Ffestiniog is the oldest independent railway in the world, and more than 5,000 members and volunteers keep the railway society chugging along.

Work needs vary throughout the year, but you could help in any number of ways.

Sell tickets for those going for a ride, work with refreshment services on the trains themselves, do track maintenance, help varnish a 100-year-old engine, or do some landscaping around the museum grounds. You'll be trained to help out in the area that appeals to you most, from security to learning how to fire the engines. You could decide to mix it up and sell souvenirs one day and work maintaining and testing signals on the line the next. Gardening, painting, computer skills, they all come in handy for different job descriptions you could pursue. The length of your volunteer commitment is up to you, so you could spend a season or an afternoon fulfilling those train fantasies in a more tangible way than spending hours in the garage trying to make trees from scraps of lichen for the model train set.

While the train museum doesn't provide accommodations, the railroad does have Railway Hostel accommodations next-door where volunteers bunk for only US$6.60 a night. The hostel has kitchens for self-catering. They'll also make recommendations for other alternative housing all around the area as well as resto-pubs or other dining suggestions, or you can camp out with tent space provided on-site. In your free time, enjoy the celebrations and parties regularly thrown for volunteers, from running an evening disco train to fancy dress parties onboard the line.

YOUR NEXT STEP: Ffestiniog Railway Society (✆ **01766/516-035;** www.ffestiniogvolunteer.org.uk). There is no charge for volunteering and the amount of time you give to the railroad and museum is entirely up to you. Stay at the railway's hostel, campgrounds, or small hotels in the village. Meals and local transportation are your responsibility, while all project training is provided.

DON'T MISS: After working so diligently on terrestrial track transportation, chill out while afloat as you take a **canal boating holiday.** Floating along the network of waterways, you can absorb the beautiful scenery and villages at a relaxing pace. The most popular canals for waterborne holidays are Monmouthshire & Brecon and Llangollen. Eighteenth-century narrowboats keep tradition alive, and their retrofit modern conveniences allow you to drift at peace and in comfort. www.waterscape.com

ⓘ www.visitwales.com

Museums, Zoos & Aquariums

Zoo Assistant

Big Animals, Big Reward

Kuala Lumpur, Malaysia

If working in a zoo isn't exciting enough, the capital city of Kuala Lumpur is teeming with Chinese, Malay, and Indian influences that gives it a fascinating mix of cuisine, culture, architecture, and languages.

Feed the big cats, introduce children to the great apes, scrub the elephants with a push broom, relocate the giant snakes while their cages are cleaned—it's all in a day's work for the zookeeping staff. The Kuala Lumpur area zoos (either Zoo Negara or Taiping Zoo, in suburb villages of Kuala Lumpur) place special emphasis on their breeding program, especially for endangered species. Some of the animals are predominantly unique to the country (Malaysian sun bears, several reptiles) and have particularly tough challenges for survival. Life at the zoo isn't just seals balancing balls on their noses, it's

Working at a zoo in Kuala Lumpur

long days of hard work with as many different needs and requirements as there are animals. No two are alike, so you'll be learning a huge amount about species behavior and diet for orangutans, rhinos, camels, giraffes—you name it. The special emphasis on protecting threatened species makes this assignment particularly rewarding.

Working with the zookeeper you'll attend to the animals 5 days a week. You may take a break from feeding and maintenance to work as a zoo guide for children or lend a hand if the veterinary team needs to catch an animal for treatment. Most of your time, however, will be spent feeding animals, helping build new exhibits and habitat enclosures, improving signage around the zoo, cleaning and maintaining cages and tanks, and ensuring that the zoo environment is ideal for the animals and the guests. You'll also learn endless amounts about animal behavior—why the lions pace even after feeding time, what sets the orangutans off into a screaming chorus, whether the rough play of the tigers is actually playful or aggressive.

Two Kuala Lumpur area zoos make use of volunteers, and team accommodations are on the grounds of the zoo (a three-bedroom house) or in the village nearest the second zoo (a two-story residence). Malay cuisine is served for all of your meals, daytimes at the zoo, evenings at the project house, or you can opt to try nearby restaurants that are refreshingly inexpensive. Weekends are the perfect time to get out and explore more of the country or take a day trip to some of Malaysia's most famous sights. Both zoos are an easy distance to Penang, Singapore, and Kuala Lumpur proper.

YOUR NEXT STEP: Real Gap Experience (✆ **866/939-9088;** www.realgap.com). This 1-month assignment, US$2,189, includes project residence housing, meals, airport transfers, project training and village/city orientation, and 24-hour project support.

DON'T MISS: A small journey north from the Kuala Lumpur region brings you to

Langkawi, a cluster of 99 islands with prized beaches, magnificent lush vegetation, and a mystical history of legends and fables that make the pastoral farm and paddy lands seem provincial until you ride the ultra-modern cable car to the peak of Mount Mat Cincang for an eagle's-eye view of the entire archipelago.

ⓘ www.tourism.gov.my

170 Museums, Zoos & Aquariums

Noah's Ark Wildlife Centre

Animal Care in Stunning African Landscape

Gobabis, Namibia

The cattle that graze in the grassy savanna here have earned this eastern part of Namibia the nickname "little Texas." But it's more than just cattle that need attention—the whole kingdom needs balancing out. That's where volunteers can join the ark.

Namibia is not on many vacationers' must-see radar, but the stunning desert and coastal landscapes—as well as enormous expanses of uninterrupted wilderness—make it a prime locale for those of us who are wild about animals. However, subsistence farmers here see crop raiding and livestock hunting by wild animals as a threat to their own survival. Consequently, many animals are shot, poisoned, and trapped to eliminate the problem. This wildlife center is working to educate local farmers and provide positive solutions to the conflict of man versus animal while also giving sanctuary to orphaned, abused, neglected, and injured animals. This family-run (and volunteer-assisted) refuge is home to lions, leopards, cheetahs, wild dogs, meerkat, baboons, and many antelope species. The center's staff has become well-respected among the local bushman population, and together they are working to develop mutual goals that positively impact the animal population.

You'll feed animals (including bottle-feeding babies); hand rear and care for orphaned infants; clean and maintain enclosures; spend your night duty acting as a surrogate parent (for instance, you might take a baby baboon to bed with you—but remember, there are also plenty of snakes and other reptiles at the reserve, as well as insects and other animals that need just as much care and attention); repair and erect new fencing around the grounds; assist in the clinic for injured animals; and assist field guides for the daily tours when visitors come to the center. The refuge has a commitment never to turn an animal away, so the health of these animals can vary widely. Every week, new occupants arrive. At certain times of year, the center runs a Wild Dog Project that requires volunteer help to identify individual wild dogs (a very rare and disappearing species in Africa), observe and record family patterns, and make note of their eating habits. The center has established an international standard for wildlife rehabilitation and reintroduction.

Life at the sanctuary will be comfortable in raised wooden four-person cabins clustered into a volunteer village. Two sides of each cabin are open to the wondrous views of the surrounding land, and separate bathroom/shower facilities are shared. Your meals are prepared for you and taken with the team (though you'll whip up your own breakfasts in the group kitchen). Your free time is relaxing—there's even a swimming pool on-site. When schedules allow (and schedules that frequently involve emergencies or unexpected arrivals are never predictable), the volunteers are taken on cultural excursions to explore nearby villages and the surrounding lands. There is also a very strong but informal cultural exchange element to this project, as the center makes it a policy to employ members of the community for as many jobs as possible.

YOUR NEXT STEP: Enkosini Eco Experience (✆ **206/604-2664;** www.enkosiniecoexperience.com). A 2-week assignment, US$1,295, includes team accommodations in the "volunteer village" of raised sleeping cabins, all meals (you may pitch in making lunchtime sandwiches), extra activities and excursions, airport transfers, project training, and a donation to the Noah's Ark wildlife center.

DON'T MISS: It is one of the most dramatic and austere landscapes you'll ever lay eyes upon. Namibia's **Skeleton Coast** is a desert expanse with the jarring feature of shipwrecked vessels, from the distant past through the present, strewn about the sand. The ships that ran aground on this notorious stretch of barren land are now well back from the visible waterline and many are partially or even completely buried in golden red sand. Individual masts occasionally stick up like stripped stems from a giant's picked-over flower garden. Make sure your camera batteries are well charged as the sun changes the colors and shadows throughout the day for truly amazing photography.

ⓘ www.namibiatourism.com.na

Museums, Zoos & Aquariums

171

Aquarium Volunteer

Under the Sea, North of 60

Seward, Alaska, USA

Alaska can truly feel like another world, with its fjords, sky-high mountains, dogsleds, laid-back pace, and endless trails for man or beast. Seward can easily serve as the start of your own journey into the wild once you're finished with the demands of aquatic life.

Seward is at the gateway to the Kenai Fjords National Park, a land of rustic grandeur with the horizon-defining Mount Marathon rising above. But mountains and fjords are a world away when you're inside the aquatic center, which transports you beneath the waves, immersing you in the sea life and naturalistic settings of the Alaskan marine ecosystem. In addition to public observational facilities, the center features a research program and rehabilitation programs for sick and injured marine animals. Education programs are also a strong element of the outreach programs, teaching young and old about the wonders of marine science.

You'll work directly with animals in the aviary, marine mammal, and aquarium facilities; assist visiting research teams; provide interpretive learning to complement the exhibits; teach and prepare curriculum for the education program; or consult with the public relations and marketing team and do data entry. Your expertise in all things aquatic will grow exponentially, regardless of how much you know when you begin. The Alaska SeaLife Center has an extensive volunteer program for seasonal (summer) and off-season volunteers in several areas of animal husbandry and support services, education, interpretation, and more.

Seward life is easygoing and spent among extraordinarily hard-working people. You'll come home nights and weekends to dormlike accommodations at the project house, within walking distance of the center. The harbor is bustling, and downtown is filled with art galleries, outdoor adventure companies, and plenty of dining options serving the most amazing fish and hearty cuisine. You'll have to remind yourself you're working as you drift into daydreams while gazing at some of America's most awesome natural settings.

YOUR NEXT STEP: Alaska SeaLife Center (© **907/224-6307;** www.alaskasealife.org). The animal husbandry volunteer program—with sea lions, other marine mammals, an aviary, and more—requires a season-long commitment. There is no fee for volunteers, and no accommodations or other travel arrangements provided by the center. Intensive hands-on training provides for an authentic experience of working in a rescue and education program at one of the world's leading facilities for marine life.

DON'T MISS: Take advantage of one of the many **flightseeing tours** offered in and around Seward, where you'll get an aerial view of the nearby rugged coastline, craggy peaks, and rolling valleys. Small charter planes, helicopters, or hydroplanes all get you up and over Seward and its stunning surrounding land.

ⓘ www.sewardak.org

5 Healing the Environment

Examining the Puerto Rican rainforest

172 Conservation Work

Environmental Protection

Planting in the Land of Oz

Nationwide, Australia

TRAVELING DOWN UNDER—WITNESSING THE VARIED, NATURAL BEAUTY OF THE GREGARIOUS, laid back country firsthand—will inspire you to get your hands dirty to protect it. With many locations in the country to choose from, you can even use it as a way to decide where to travel next, with a new group of friends waiting at each project site.

From the Sydney suburbs to Uluru, from the Great Barrier Reef to Perth, the Conservation Volunteer Australia program assembles teams of international volunteers to go out a week at a time and work on bringing back Earth's eco-balance. Each week (or two), the program places you in a new location, so your timing will establish where in Australia you'll work. Tasmanian projects are also part of the schedule. Groups of 6 to 10 individuals work from 8am to 4pm pulling weeds and invasive plants, tree planting and seed collecting, building fencing and trail markers, surveying flora and fauna, and conducting environmental auditing. The tasks vary depending on the nature preserve or parkland engaged for the week, but it's guaranteed you'll work hard in the great outdoors.

When you arrive, your team leader will brief you and provide any specific training necessary for the workload (identifying particular plant species, using mapping and data collection technology, and so on). You'll also be briefed on the conservation goals for the project and the lay of the land. On some projects you'll be based in the same spot each day, others will have you leading a nomadic life, camping in a new spot each day. Most of your time will be spent in predominantly rural settings, so you should expect to be away from big cities once you begin. The projects are scheduled for 5 days a week with 2 off days. Many participants join for a few weeks, moving to the next locale in the following weeks.

Your accommodations are as variable as the projects themselves. Housing may be in tents (provided, but you'll bring your own sleeping bag/pad), hostels, sheep shearer's shacks, farms, bunkhouses, or caravans. Food is provided on-site, and the team often pitches in cooperatively with meal preparation and cleanup. The season can also affect the type of work necessary in a location. Perhaps springtime in Geelong is focused on eradicating weeds and invasive species from a stretch of nature preserve, and a week in autumn in the same preserve might prioritize planting and protective fencing. Your flexibility is paramount, and just jumping in is the most important required skill. It's an ideal opportunity to see parts of Australia that aren't on the tourist track.

YOUR NEXT STEP: Twin Work & Volunteer Abroad (✆ **800/80 483 80;** www.workandvolunteer.com). A 1-week stay, US$582,includes all meals, accommodations (type varies with project), and project training. You'll get yourself to the team meeting spot on the first day of volunteer work.

DON'T MISS: Your assignment can be anywhere in Australia or Tasmania, so you'll be seeing and experiencing the nature and unique environment of the region where you are posted. It is likely that you'll fly, from North America or Western Europe, into Sydney, so consider booking a few days here before or after your volunteer work. A hugely popular activity that gives a unique view of the city and water is the **Sydney Harbour Bridge Climb,** walking and climbing your way through the steel structure to the top of the central arch of the bridge, 134m (440 ft.) above the bay.

ⓘ www.australia.com

Conservation Work 173

Tropical Forest Conservation

Mapping the Jungle

Botum Sakor National Park, Cambodia

FOR MOST WESTERNERS, THE DENSE, TROPICAL JUNGLES OF CAMBODIA HAVE ONLY BEEN encountered through films or documentaries. Even when you're there, it's thick and remote, with all the challenges one might imagine, and this national park that you'll be working in is no exception.

The nearly impenetrable jungles of Cambodia are home to some of the planet's most endangered species: tiger, sun bear, gibbon, and leopard. Much of Botum Sakor National Park remains uncharted and, in many sections, impassable, as the foliage grows too dense for travel, even with a machete. On this 3-week project, you'll record botanic and soil findings and animals spotted. You may even discover species new to science and certainly unique to this ecosystem. This work requires a good level of fitness, as you'll be trekking over rugged terrain and for long hours each day in pursuit of the scientific support for conservation planning in the Khmer empire. The region is not entirely uninhabited, and you'll visit many small villages where you'll interview (with an interpreter) locals to assess how reliant the communities are upon the forest resources and the ways they interact with the flora and fauna for everything from shelter and food to medicine and recreation.

You'll be fully trained in field research techniques as you gather plant samples, look for and record animal tracks, take environmental readings from various types of equipment, and photograph and sketch specific plants and animals. These crucial surveys will be used to formulate sensitive policies that protect endangered species and habitat. With the cultural immersion in visited villages, you'll also aid in engaging Khmer communities with the priorities of conservation and sensible protection.

Even getting to the base camp for this project is an arduous adventure, requiring bus, car, and, in some seasons, boat. The remote camp consists of a communal longhouse surrounded by tents and forest huts. It's all temporary, and when broken down will leave no permanent scar on the forest environment—a philosophy that carries over to daily life on-site as well. You'll share campfire meals and sleeping quarters with fellow volunteers, clean up in a stream or via bucket bath, and if the work takes you away from base to an overnight satellite camp, string up your own hammock in which you'll slumber under the canopy. Free time can be spent exploring (if you've not lost your taste for hiking from the day's work) or relaxing in camp. The team leaders try to establish at least one community celebration with local villagers where you'll share a feast, dancing, and song, making it a real forest holiday.

YOUR NEXT STEP: Frontier-Cambodia (✆ **+44/20 7613 2422;** www.frontier.ac.uk). A 3-week program, US$1,593/£1,095, includes rustic shared housing in communal

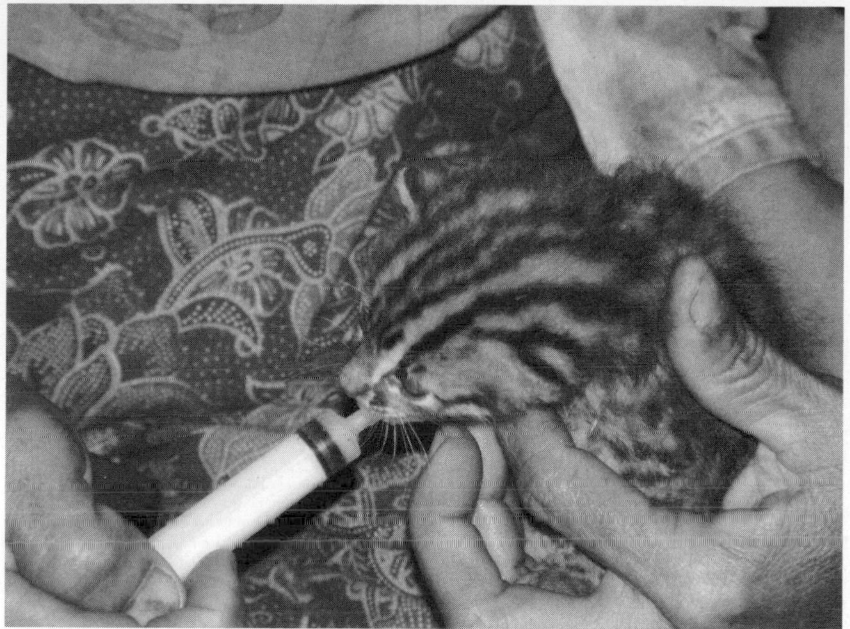

Feeding a baby fishing cat from Botum Sakor National Park

camp, group meals prepared over an open fire (the entire team pitches in cooking and cleaning), field research training, interpreters, airport transfers, and 24-hour project support and backup.

DON'T MISS: It is a difficult chapter in Cambodia's history, but not to be forgotten. You can visit the memorial erected on the site of the **Killing Fields** of Choeing Ek, where the Khmer Rouge murdered more than 17,000 people. Thousands of the victims' skulls are arranged in a harrowing display and a reminder of human brutality. It is a worthwhile pilgrimage to pay your respects.

ⓘ www.mot.gov.kh

174 Conservation Work

Conservation Holidays

Immerse Yourself in the Canadian Backcountry

(Various) British Columbia, Canada

The many wonders of British Columbia beckon to the traveler like Christmas morning: should you take in the majestic mountains at Whistler, the world-class restaurants in Vancouver, or the trapped-in-time towns of the Gulf Islands? There are no bad choices. The wilds of the province are blessed with abundant wildlife and jaw-dropping scenery wherever you decide to visit.

With a tireless dedication to improving the natural world of British Columbia, The Land Conservancy fills the calendar with opportunities to work hard on environmental issues in many locations across the province. You could be weeding out invasive blackberries and thistles in the Ballenas-Winchelsea Archipelago or establish perimeter fencing around new nature preserve land acquisitions on the Horsefly River. Harvest vegetables and transplant specimen plants at a farm on Vancouver Island or do debris cleanup as part of the "Great Canadian Shoreline Cleanup." If you have a green thumb, or just a good strong thumb that is at home in sturdy work gloves, there are outdoor conservation opportunities for you.

Different trips are of different durations, but most range from a weekend to a full week. Your efforts with sustainable forestry projects or wetlands protection will immerse you in some of the most beautiful, wild parts of the Canadian countryside. You might be camping under the stars, tucked in to eco-friendly green cottages, relaxing at farmhouse digs, or popping in for a day's work and going back to your home or hotel. Harvest apples or garlic, refresh and rebuild irrigation channels, repair and replenish beehives—it's all in the line of conservation duty in BC.

Your time won't be completely monopolized by shovel and hoe work. Most projects have built-in exploration breaks, and longer holidays have scheduled trips to wineries, swimming holes, or farmers' markets and more. Meals are included and prepared and served family-style with staff and volunteers working together in the kitchen.

YOUR NEXT STEP: The Land Conservancy (TLC) (✆ **888/738-0533;** www1.conservancy.bc.ca). Trips range from 2 to 7 days, US$133 to US$210, with a US$20 to US$40discount for TLC members. The cost covers accommodations (some camping options will ask you to bring your own tent) and meals during the assignment. Work tools are provided. You'll get yourself to the meeting point for the launch of your project.

DON'T MISS: Explore the wild side of BC with several modes of transportation. Take the **Zodiac, Dine, and Fly** tour where you'll be water bound for two hours in an inflatable speedcraft watching for whales and other marine life; enjoy a dinner (al fresco of weather permits) at the Boathouse in breathtaking Horseshoe Bay; then soar back to downtown Vancouver by floatplane.

ⓘ www.hellobc.com

Conservation Work **175**

Eco-Tourism Exploration

Build Tourism Prospects on Tropical Island

Moheli, Comoros Islands

SCATTERED LIKE CONFETTI IN THE INDIAN OCEAN, THE REMOTE, UNTOUCHED COMOROS Islands are truly a blip on the radar of most travelers. In addition to lazy island life, the islands are replete with a cultural mix of Arab, Persian, African, and Portuguese influences.

Although Madagascar gets lots of attention, it's on little sister Moheli where the tropical floral scent of the ylang-ylang flower mingles with the dusky fragrance of cloves to create an intoxicating perfumed air. The incredible natural riches of the sleepy island in the Mozambique Channel are often overlooked by locals. This project is partnering with the local Comoros Islanders to create the first ecotourism programs that embrace this tropical paradise's biodiversity, with a respect for the land and sea that can be the key to a new livelihood. Islanders face extraordinarily high levels of poverty and unemployment, but ecotours can create jobs and stability for more locals than any other employment opportunity. It is a society where donkeys are the primary transportation, so developing an infrastructure in harmony with the land and that welcomes international visitors will be an enormous economic boost.

The Comoros residents make use of the scientific findings of this project to establish guiding principles for tourism. You'll undertake a variety of jobs, from helping rangers patrol and collect data on the nesting beaches of endangered sea turtles, and identifying and developing underwater snorkel trails that protect coral and other marine life, to signposting terrestrial nature trails and working with artisans who create useful products from palm fronds. You'll also work with school educators (English is learned by many students and is the language of the program) to raise environmental awareness among the upcoming generations.

When not snorkeling and exploring (all in the name of hard work), your base will be either a shared palm-leaf bungalow or homestay accommodations. Comorian cuisine will be provided three times daily, with plenty of local fish and spicy sauces. In your downtime, you can hire an inexpensive boat to take you to neighboring islands for more exploration in almost untouched wilderness or snorkel the crystal clear waters. Local children have been known to challenge and embarrass volunteers in friendly soccer matches—so you may have to go swing in the hammock for a bit after your defeat by nine-year-olds.

YOUR NEXT STEP: Frontier (© +44/20 7613 2422; www.frontier.ac.uk). A 3-week project, £1,195, includes beach bungalow or host family accommodations, all meals, project training and support, and inter-island transportation to the project base from the main airport on Grande Comore.

DON'T MISS: You're already in unspoiled tropical heaven, so stick around after the work is done. It is believed that the tales of Sinbad the Sailor were based on sailing exploration through these islands, and Captain Kidd also trolled these waters, so get in the swing of things on a traditional Omani wooden dhow, and catch the breezes through the channels, gliding over the Indian Ocean as has been done for ages.

ⓘ www-personal.ksu.edu/~omar/Comoros

176 Conservation Work

Rainforest Conservation

Supporting Park Staff

Barra Honda National Park, Costa Rica

Subterranean environments appeal to the inner child in all of us—they're part fort, part hideaway, and ripe for exploration. And the caves in Costa Rica, a country whose beauty and diversity are well-documented, need a few good spelunkers.

Much of the ecotour movement can be traced to Costa Rica. The country was the "must-see" hot spot at the same time green consciousness came to the forefront. Folks have been screaming down ziplines and teetering on forest canopy suspended walkways here long before the trends caught on elsewhere. More than one-quarter of Costa

Descending into a cave in Barra Honda National Park

Rican land is devoted to conservation—more than any other country in the world. Barra Honda is 2,266ha (5,600 acres) of forest, and beneath it lies another frontier—a tangled network of underground caves and caverns, only a small number of which have been mapped and explored. While the Costa Rican government places a high priority on eco-preservation, funding for the national parks still doesn't provide nearly enough full-time staff. Volunteers like you help bridge the gap in keeping the pristine lands protected and preserved for future generations.

You'll spend some time spelunking in those caves, collecting data, and above ground performing wildlife inventories, observational recordings of flora and fauna, and checking and collecting data from fixed sensor cameras. An extensive network of trails also needs maintaining, and you may pitch in with environmental education programs that heighten awareness of conservation goals in neighboring communities.

You'll be placed with a host family in one of those neighboring communities. Your Spanish skills will come in handy in the home stay, but on the work project English will be spoken. Meals are all included, and evenings and weekends you might while away the hours visiting with new neighbors, exploring the park and checking out capuchin monkeys, howler monkeys, peccaries, coatis, birds, reptiles, and small predator felines, or heading farther afield to explore more of Costa Rica.

YOUR NEXT STEP: Projects Abroad (✆ **888/839-3535;** www.projects-abroad.org). A 2-week project, US$2,795, includes home stay accommodations with three meals daily, project training and support, and medical insurance coverage.

DON'T MISS: After the still air of underground caverns, feel the wind in your hair at Costa Rica's **Lake Arenal,** one of the world's best windsurfing spots. In the shadow of a volcanic peak, the lake provides year-round recreational activities, from water sports to horseback riding and mountain biking.

ⓘ www.visitcostarica.com

177 Conservation Work

Biodiversity Education

Stay in Rainforest Eco-Lodge

Sarapiquí County, Costa Rica

YOU DON'T HAVE TO TRAVEL ALL THE WAY TO THE AMAZON TO IMMERSE YOURSELF IN THE beauty—and unique challenges—of living in a rainforest. This Costa Rica experience is inexpensive, and your input will create a significant difference.

A private eco-reserve, the Tirimbina Rainforest Center is devoted to environmental education programs for the children of Costa Rica and abroad (from elementary school through college), and recognizes that only by getting the next generation excited about taking stewardship can we protect the world's biodiversity. In addition to providing outdoor education opportunities to youth, the center hosts international science research teams whose projects benefit the rainforest. The refuge is more than 320ha (800 acres) of pristine rainforest, and public usage is limited to only one-third of the available land, leaving the remaining area as wild and undisturbed as possible. Thousands of students experience the conservation curriculum of the center's eco-education programs each year, coming away with amazing experiences and a new appreciation for the rainforest.

You and your volunteer colleagues will have dual missions. You'll assist scientific research teams in their important work in the rainforest, and you'll work to facilitate the environmental education and outreach programs. You may partner with a local educator to translate printed materials and signage into English or collect field data with researchers studying indigenous butterflies or birds. Sometimes your duties may be as pedestrian as helping control a large group of over-excited schoolchildren as they explore the environment on guided bird walks, reptile hikes, or the "chocolate tour." The education programs are targeted to different ages, and all are participatory and hands-on, so having enough volunteers to facilitate them is important to the experience.

Life at the center is simple, and you'll be rooming in the Tirimbina Lodge, tucked away into gardens and supplied with Wi-Fi, air-conditioning, private bathrooms, and phones. If you'd like to rough it a bit more, opt for staying at the Field Station, with dormitory accommodations and shared bathrooms and common areas. The field station houses the kitchen and dining room for both facilities. Meals are on your own or you may choose to team up with fellow volunteers and shop in neighboring villages for groceries, but the center doesn't provide food for volunteers. The duration of your stay is up to you, and free time will usually be spent relaxing in the reserve, exploring, enjoying the camaraderie of fellow volunteers, or visiting one of the three nearby communities.

YOUR NEXT STEP: Tirimbina Rainforest Center (✆ **506/2761-1579;** www.tirimbina.org). Volunteers reserve placements at one of two housing facilities for as long as desired. The cost is a flat fee of US$10 a day. Meals are not included, but you'll have free access to kitchen facilities. All training and supervision for the project are included when you arrive (getting to the reserve on your own).

DON'T MISS: After living in the wilds and focusing on many wild children, you might appreciate the contrast of mellow relaxation found at the **Tabacón Hot Springs.** The Tabacón River feeds these natural geothermal pools, and there's even a heated waterfall that'll do wonders for tense shoulders. A world-class resort can be found here if you need some pool and spa time.

ⓘ www.visitcostarica.com

Conservation Work 178

Measuring Farming Techniques

Promoting Agritourism in Bordeaux

Bordeaux, France

THE NAME OF BORDEAUX IS EMBLAZONED ON SOME OF THE WORLD'S BEST BOTTLES OF WINE and shipped around the world. There are churches, cathedrals, and cruises on the Garonne River, and did we mention that there's really good wine?

It seems perfectly reasonable to passionate oenophiles that more than three-quarters of the growable land in France's Bordeaux region is planted with wine grapes, but it's not the most farsighted plan for the land. Called a "monoculture," when one crop takes over the majority of the land, it can lead to a decline in biodiversity throughout the neighboring and interacting growth zones. A relatively new philosophy of diversification in agritourism is beginning to take hold, and growers and winemakers are looking at new ways to ensure the incredible grape region remains healthy for generations to come. More kinds of plants attract a more varied range of insects, both beneficial and harmful to the crops, so studies are being done to enhance wildlife in the vineyards and find ways to naturally regulate vine pests. In many wine-growing regions, rose bushes are planted at the ends of the rows of vines—this helps to eradicate some kinds of grape-attacking insects.

New techniques in farming have been introduced, but it's only with accurate

Setting an insect trap in a French vineyard

monitoring that they can assess whether specific tactics are effective. You'll work with a team of research scientists to measure the biodiversity of the viticulture and assess the project's success thus far. You'll also help test new methods, and gather and compile data to report to farmers and vintners about current methods and what the next step might be. You don't need viticultural expertise, as you'll be trained and guided through the necessary tasks, but it doesn't hurt if you love the end product.

When immersed in wine, it seems only right that you be housed in chalet cabins alongside a babbling brook in the shadow of an old mill house. There are several of these bungalows clustered here at Domaine du Moulin des Sandaux, and some even boast a swimming pool where you can float and look out across the rolling hills that tumble down to the Dordogne River. A cook prepares your French meals.

YOUR NEXT STEP: Earthwatch (© **800/776-0188**; www.earthwatch.org). A 5-day stay, US$2,950, includes chalet accommodations, homemade French cuisine, scientific training and guidance, and project support. A US$35 Earthwatch membership is required.

DON'T MISS: Fine wine and fine music rightly go hand in hand, so when in Bordeaux, try to catch a performance at the **Grand-Théâtre.** Completed in 1780, this is an imposing neoclassical building imbued with all the grandeur due you'd expect from an opera house in France—and it is easily one of the best and most elaborate buildings in Bordeaux.

ⓘ www.bordeaux-tourisme.com

Conservation Work

Wetland Protection

Traditional Agriculture in Bavaria

Bavaria, Germany

EXPERIENCE THE BAVARIAN LANDSCAPE WITH YOUR HANDS AS YOU TOIL BY DAY TO PROTECT this habitat. Munich, with its beer-loving culture, is not far away, as are some of the region's famous castles: Neuschwanstein, Linderhof, and Hohenschwangau.

Lake Ammersee is tucked away in a less-traveled nook of Bavaria, with rolling hillsides cut by swift, clear rivers. More than 3 decades ago, the area was designated a *Ramsar* site, or "wetlands of national importance." The lake and surrounding meadowlands are significant for the migrating waterfowl that roost each year in the reeds of small islands and islets. The lake environment requires a lot of maintenance, including an annual effort to maximize the area's viability as a bird habitat. Several local conservation groups lend support to make sure the waterfowl will return the following year.

Your work will be multifocused. Timeless techniques of hay threshing with pitchforks and rakes will give your shoulders a workout, and spending the next day on bog restoration won't be much of a break. Seasonal demands vary, but there is likely to be work on creating new, smaller ponds, and some overall meadow management. Removal of invasive species that can choke out indigenous plants is a never-ending task, and as soon as one stretch of wetland is ship-shape it will be time to move around the lake's gorgeous perimeter to the next. By the end of your stay, you'll know Lake Ammersee like the back of your blistered hand.

Work days usually end at 4pm, so you'll have plenty of time to relax and reenergize. You'll be bunking in a converted clubhouse, formerly a gymnastics club from the 19th century. There's a brand-new kitchen and several improved bedrooms, so you'll be quite comfortable on the lakeshore—diving in the crisp water is a perfect way to round out the day. The host organization also organizes a field trip to neighboring castles and mountain areas for your days off, or you can join the many recreational sailors, windsurfers, cyclists, and hikers who all relish spending time at the lake.

YOUR NEXT STEP: British Trust for Conservation Volunteers (✆ **+44/1302 388 883;** www2.btcv.org.uk). This 2-week project, US$571/£395, includes dormitory-style accommodations and project training and support. There are also day-off excursions arranged and included in the price, but you'll be responsible for your own meals and transportation (towns are nearby, and Munich is quite accessible). English is spoken on the project, but a little conversational German never hurts.

DON'T MISS: Munich's **Nymphenburg Palace** and its 81ha (200-acre) park and botanical gardens are a must-see. Amazing ceiling frescoes and rococo decor accent every inch, from dining rooms to regally done-up stables for the royal horses (now housing one of the world's finest collections of carriages and coaches).

ⓘ www.germany-tourism.de

Conservation Work **180**

National Park Service

Exclusive Access to a Honduran Cloud Forest

La Tigra, Honduras

YOU CAN MAKE A TREMENDOUS DIFFERENCE BY LENDING YOUR TIME TO TAKE CARE OF THIS extensive national park, which is in dire need of helping hands and thoughtful volunteers to tend to the earth and keep things growing.

Only two park rangers manage this national park's 27,519ha (68,000 acres), with a dripping, ethereal cloud forest and more than 700 species of birds. The Honduran economy has provided challenges for the La Tigra park system, so conservation efforts have been put on the back burner. It is considered one of the world's richest natural habitats, and to keep it that way only 70 people are allowed in each day, so it's remarkably peaceful and the sense of isolation is profound. It's an otherworldly exploration zone as tree trunks drip with epiphytes (rootless air plants, like orchids, ferns, and other bromeliads) and dewy moisture is shaken loose by jaguars, ant eaters, ocelots, and other endangered animals making their way through the thick underbrush.

You'll clear and recut trails and work tirelessly on reforestation in zones where the 87 communities that live in the national park cut down burnable vegetation for fuel. New plantings take quickly and grow in the fertile land, so saplings can re-establish a grove within a few years; as the larger trees take root, indigenous underbrush follows, creating freshly usable habitat for the many endangered animals that need shelter and food. The program is massive and entirely dependent on volunteers to get as many native plants and trees into the ground as possible, while the government is simultaneously providing sustainable firewood and charcoal for local families to use as a replacement for the forest's trees.

You'll be living with your fellow volunteers in dormitory-style accommodations within the park. Honduran fare is prepared for breakfast and dinner, and you'll provide your own lunch. Though the housing is comfortable, life in the park is fairly close to nature, so in your free time you can get to know the forest or maybe rally a few of your teammates to explore some of the easily accessible abandoned mines peppered throughout the parkland. There will be lots of hanging out in hammocks when the sun goes down, though you'll likely be invited once or twice by local community members to join them in village gatherings and for large shared meals.

Park staff at La Tigra

YOUR NEXT STEP: i-to-i (✆ **800/985-4852;** www.i-to-i.com). A 1- week project, US$965, covers dorm lodging, twice daily meals, airport pickup (but not return after the project, so you'll arrange your own transfer back), project training, use of equipment, in-country orientation, and 24-hour support.

DON'T MISS: Roatan Island, 48km (30 miles) off the Honduran coast, is one of the top destinations in the world for underwater exploring, offering plentiful opportunities to dive and explore and multiple outfitters to get you trained, certified, or just casually equipped.

ⓘ www.honduras.com

181 Conservation Work

Glacier Study and Conservation

Working and Living on the Ice

Skaftafell National Park and Modrudalur, Iceland

THIS SMALL, ROBUST ISLAND WAS GREEN BEFORE GREEN WAS CONSIDERED COOL. SPARSELY populated—its capital, Reykjavik, has fewer than a quarter of a million residents—Iceland is rich with natural resources, from geothermal waters and hulking glaciers to volcanoes and geysers.

Science can unravel many mysteries, but experts need real-world study to gather hard evidence. Mother Nature, however, doesn't always offer up her secrets freely. Icebergs and glaciers are notoriously difficult to study due to harsh conditions and the difficulty in making observations below the water's surface. When a volcanic eruption struck the Icelandic ice cap in 1996, tons of sediment and ice were washed away. What was uncovered can teach us a great deal about global warming, glacial migration, and floods, and how the frozen landscape responds to events like earthquakes and eruptions.

You'll be very busy during this project, using data collection techniques you'll learn on-site to gather as much evidence

Studying a glacier in Iceland

as possible during a short time. You'll work on two field sites as you gather samples of sediment and glacial ice, photograph and document the size and shape of deposits, and use GPS, ground-penetrating radar, and electronic distance measurers to help scientists understand how enormous ice moves, and how global warming affects that natural process. On the glacier, the world of ice reveals startling visual stimulus, and even back at camp, Iceland's strange, lunar-like landscape is jarring and mysterious but not forbidding.

You'll stay in a series of huts in one of the nation's most popular natural areas. There are accessible restrooms and hot showers; meals, prepared in field conditions, are provided. In your free time you can explore the gorgeous landscape—the nearly treeless terrain makes it difficult to get lost, so long as the weather is good. The view stretches across kilometers of black volcanic rock and high cliffs that look like billowing fabric. Camp life, shared with some of the world's leading earth scientists, promises some memorable conversations.

YOUR NEXT STEP: Earthwatch (✆ **800/776-0188**; www.earthwatch.org). This 8-day expedition, US$2,450, includes meals and research station accommodations in huts, research technique training, and full project support. A US$35 Earthwatch membership is required.

DON'T MISS: Iceland's number-one attraction is the famous geothermally heated pools at the **Blue Lagoon** outside of Reykjavik. The steamy waters ease sore muscles; smear some white silica mud on your face, lean back against black lava rock, and enjoy the dream-like scene. www.bluelagoon.com

ⓘ www.visiticeland.com

Conservation Work **182**

Sustainable Agriculture

Work With Locals, Live in Hacienda

Chalcatzingo, Mexico

IT'S SO OBVIOUS THAT IT SOUNDS LIKE A CLICHÉ: WATER IS CRUCIAL TO ANY COMMUNITY'S survival. With it, you have trade and commerce, food, biodiversity, and transportation. Volunteers can do their part to develop the sustainable practices in this water-deprived village in Central Mexico.

The arid village of Chalcatzingo, Mexico

This "venerated place of sacred water," as the name Chalcatzingo means in the ancient Nauthl language, has become a place where water is scarce. Mexico City, about 2 hours away, built a dam to redirect Chalcatzingo's water for urban use, and this humble agricultural village has suffered ever since. Subsistence farming has faltered as the crops have been choked out. The community has splintered as a result, with families moving to the city for work, leaving a decimated community. This volunteer program works to reinvigorate the village with conservation projects, including irrigation, recycling, and ranching.

You'll work with locals to implement sustainable development. The recycling program reduces waste dumped nearby; the town's sheep-breeding project needs corrals built; local sanitation is improved by installing compost latrines; or you can pitch in with the preservation of ancient ruins.

You and your teammates will stay in a traditional hacienda, dining on tasty local cuisine alongside the residents you've been working with. While there is an enormous amount of work to be done, leisure time is still built into your itinerary. Hang out swapping stories with community members, spend an afternoon in a cooking class (included in the fees), take a language lesson, or spend an afternoon exploring the famous Olmec Empire ruins.

YOUR NEXT STEP: GlobeAware (✆ **877-588-4562;** www.globeaware.org). A 1-week project, US$1,180, includes project housing and meals, project training and support, cultural excursions, and cooking and language classes. You'll be met at the local bus station and transferred to the project base.

DON'T MISS: While Mexico City is part of the problem for this village, there is still much worth seeing in this enormous metropolis. Get to the very source of the Aztec Empire when you visit **Templo Mayar,** a carved stone disc that is the focus of Aztec cosmology. More than 6,000 other artifacts have been recovered from the Templo Mayar site.

ⓘ www.visitmexico.com

Conservation Work **183**

Grassroots Environmental Work

Teach & Live in Rural Village

Chitwan, Nepal

Nepal is famous among backpackers and trekkers for the Kathmandu Valley and the Himalayas, but animals, especially Bengal tigers and single-horned Indian rhinos, are also part of Chitwan's national park. Your work here will help preserve the environment while you learn Nepalese culture.

With Nepal's rapid growth in the past decade, the lumber industry has boomed and the demand for trees has outpaced the natural resources. With the loss of trees around Chitwan, several thousand hectares of soil have eroded and disappeared. This remains one of the most fertile areas of Nepal, but agriculture is being seriously affected by the uncontrolled loss of topsoil and flat land sliding down hillsides. While a large component of the program is teaching local youth ecological and conservation principles and priorities, it also aims to repair some of the damage done.

You'll spend lots of time outside taking small steps that will, in time, have a huge impact. Seeds are collected and planted in nursery spaces, while seedlings are planted to begin the process of reforestation. Invasive species of vines and weeds are cut back and eradicated so forest growth can accelerate. You'll also help botanical experts and researchers in their study of endangered plants.

Upon arrival you'll receive a thorough introduction and orientation to Nepalese culture and society—including language study, traditional foods, and an explanation of the local social systems (such as the caste system and religious beliefs), lifestyles, and customs in family homes. You'll be staying with a host family, who will provide lunch and dinner daily (Nepalese breakfast is usually just tea and maybe a piece of bread). Your free time in this rural hilltop village will likely be spent exploring, meeting new friends and neighbors, and learning more about the natural environment. You can also venture into the neighboring Chitwan National Park for elephant-back safaris, canoeing, and nearly limitless bird-watching.

YOUR NEXT STEP: Twin Work & Volunteer Abroad (✆ **800/80 483 80;** www.workandvolunteer.com). A 2-week program, US$873, includes home stay and twice-daily meals, Nepalese language instruction, project training and support, and cultural immersion.

DON'T MISS: If you'd like to meditate in any of the temples of **Lumbini,** the birthplace of Lord Buddha, you'll have to be patient. This highly revered, sacred place is one of the most popular spiritual pilgrimage spots on Earth and a UNESCO World Heritage Site.

ⓘ www.welcomenepal.com

184 Conservation Work

Environmental Resources

Maintain Island Paradise for Free

St. John, US Virgin Islands

This opportunity in St. John truly reflects the words *volunteer* and *vacation*—by day you'll be working hard to meet the goals of the research station, but when you're done you'll find yourself in a remote tropical playground with enviable choices on how to spend your time.

The Virgin Islands Environmental Resources Station (VIERS) hosts hardworking volunteers, research scientists, school groups, historians, community groups, and divers. The volunteers, however, are the only ones who stay after the sun goes down. Marine and terrestrial natural resources are studied and explored here, and as a facility of the University of the Virgin Islands, environmental research is the primary focus.

Your work won't be glamorous. You might be weeding, improving trails, cleaning up around the center, painting the facilities, doing light carpentry work, or helping in the kitchen or shop. There are water-based and land-based learning centers, ideal for exploration and hands-on study of the tropics, as well as conferences and workshops. You might help set up meeting support items (tables, chairs, equipment, and so on) or even work to update the recycling programs and other green elements of the field station's operations. Guided trail hikes, mangrove walks, shore exploration trips, and flora and fauna identification excursions all need volunteer support to make sure they run smoothly, from guiding foot traffic to copying literature and reshelving written and video library materials. You could even be asked to lifeguard or give swimming lessons (if that's your forté).

This is an opportunity to trade work for board, placing yourself in a remote environment far away from the busy beach bars and tourists in other parts of the Virgin Islands. There are small wooden cabins shared by volunteers, and three meals served daily in the dining facilities. You'll have plenty of free time to hike to a mountaintop or snorkel in the cerulean waters of the Caribbean. You can join in on one of many organized eco-education and research projects, or study on your own. Hiking trails date from the 1600s and meander past sugar mills and rum distilleries. Check off a great number of birds and mammals from your lifetime wildlife observation checklist. You'll realize that 4 hours a day of labor is a small price for this rich experience.

YOUR NEXT STEP: Virgin Islands Environmental Research Station (✆ **888/647-2501;** www.islands.org/viers). The duration of your stay is up to you. As long as you commit to a minimum of 4 hours per day of volunteer work, you will be given accommodations in shared beach cabins, three meals daily, and all necessary training for specific projects. Transportation is not provided, so you'll get yourself to the field station. Laundry facilities and limited Internet access are also provided.

DON'T MISS: St. John is the smallest of the US Virgin Islands, so you'll want to island hop to **St. Croix** and **St. Thomas** to explore some of the varied and colorful historic places of worship. Churches and temple structures have some of the most impressive architecture on the islands, and joining a service can sometimes be an eye-opening celebration.

ⓘ www.usvitourism.vi

Conservation Work 185

Island Conservation

Hollywood Heritage

Catalina Island, California, USA

CAN YOU IMAGINE A PLACE IN CALIFORNIA THAT DOESN'T HAVE ENOUGH TRAFFIC TO WARRANT a stop light? Believe it or not, isolated Catalina Island—even with all its fishing, swimming, scuba diving, spas, and fancy hotels—is that place, as more than three-quarters of the island is protected from development.

Santa Catalina Island is only 35km (22 miles) from Southern California's coast, and the mostly undeveloped island has small pockets of heavy tourism along the coastline (Avalon), a couple of grand hotels from a bygone era, and lots of open space with nobody around for miles. There are broad valleys inland, isolated rocky coves, and 610m-high (2,000-ft.) peaks, one of which is topped by a tiny airport. Most visitors arrive via the ferry system. The island's ecosystem is out of balance, particularly after a fire in 2007 caused extensive damage, and this project is trying to conserve its natural beauty.

Getting to the work area will require some hiking, and once there you'll remove invasive species of plants, monitor and report on seedling growth, remove fences, and dig post holes for new fencing. There might be a beach cleanup day during your visit, trail improvement work, or a full day at the native plants nursery. If it involves environmental improvement on the island, it is within the purview of this project.

Removing fences in Catalina Island, California

There are two project options available. A 6-day engagement includes 4 days of work in the island's interior, some of it strenuous, and volunteer group camping at a remote campsite in raised platform tents (which boast breathtaking views). There are hot showers, flush toilets, and a fully equipped outdoor kitchen where local volunteers prepare team meals for you, or meals are sent to camp by local restaurants in Avalon.

The second option is a bit cushier. You'll only have 2 workdays, interspersed with an eco-Jeep tour, walking tour, guided hikes, visitor access to the botanical gardens, museums, lunch on full work days, and accommodations at a vacation rental cottage or condo. Your other meals are up to you, as you'll be staying in Avalon, where everything is within walking distance.

YOUR NEXT STEP: Catalina Island Conservancy (✆ **310/510-2595,** ext. 112; www.catalinaconservancy.org). A 6-day stay is two-tiered. Camping and extended work is US$180 and includes all meals, tools and training, and shared tent camp accommodations with restroom and shower facilities. Vacation rental stay with 2 moderate days of work is US$288 and includes vacation home, tickets to local attractions, some day excursion tours, project guidance and training, and lunches only on work days.

DON'T MISS: It's a small island where buffalo still roam, but the seashell motif of the **Catalina Casino** is straight out of a black and white film—there's no gambling in this round scalloped hall, but there is a grand ballroom and cinema with Tiffany chandeliers and rose-hued decor. Blend past and present and catch a first-run movie in the historic Avalon Theater in the lower level of the casino amid beautifully restored Art Deco murals.

ⓘ www.catalinachamber.com

186 Conservation Work

Urban and Rural Conservation Study

Studying the Urban Jungle

New York, New York, USA

It's the Big Apple, the city that never sleeps. It has world-class museums, stellar restaurants, melting-pot status, and an important place in American history. You can take all this in for yourself once you've finished exploring the city's "wild" side.

Considering that Manhattan is the most densely populated region in North America, it may seem surprising that the wildlife populations are equally dense and diverse throughout the city. More than 250 bird species have been recorded in New York's five boroughs, and it's not unusual to see local news stories of black bears, deer, foxes, and coyotes in suburban neighborhoods. The metropolitan area clocks in at 8.2 million people, making it a perfect field laboratory for studying how humans affect urban wildlife and what conditions each need to survive and thrive side by side.

Within a range of 160km (100 miles) of the Big Apple, you'll traipse from one research site to the next with the volunteer team and track animals, record data captured on camera traps, identify and quantify birds, mammals, reptiles, and amphibians, and record plant species and eco-system health in relation to seasonal change. From the city parks (with hearty hardwood trees and managed shrubs and

A coyote spotted in New York

grasses) to rural park plots within uninterrupted forest, you'll help researchers compare and contrast the bands of habitat that radiate out from the island of Manhattan.

It's a stone's throw from the city, but worlds away in experience; Rye, New York, is where you'll retire each evening, to an historic farmhouse with modernized facilities or you may camp out on the lawns. A staff cook will prepare and serve all your meals, unless you choose to partake of some of New York's brilliant culinary scene. You can distract yourself in New York City every night if you'd like, making your way back to the project farmhouse just as the birds you study begin their morning song.

YOUR NEXT STEP: Earthwatch (© **800/776-0188**; www.earthwatch.org). A 9-day stay, US$1,750, includes farmhouse accommodations, meals, project transportation to diverse research sites, filed training, and full project support. A US$35 Earthwatch membership is required.

DON'T MISS: It may seem a cliché, but you'll have to see a show on **Broadway**. From the splashy musicals that never seem to age to big-name stars in dramatic turns or cutting-edge experimental performances, the Broadway theater scene defines the entire stage tradition of America and is an enormous part of the nation's cultural profile. Have a fantastic dinner, a few drinks, see a show, then pop into a restaurant row eatery after the curtain comes down and you're practically guaranteed to see the performers who were on stage moments before seated at the next table.

ⓘ www.iloveny.com

Conservation Work 187

Herbarium Plant Research

Work Alongside Scientists at the Smithsonian

Washington DC, USA

AMERICA'S CAPITAL CITY IS ONCE AGAIN A POPULAR PLACE FOR TOURISTS. DURING YOUR downtime, explore the monuments and tour the White House. Stroll through the extensive, free museum system, proud in the knowledge that you're helping to improve one of its important collections.

Plants cataloged at the United States Herbarium

You'll get behind the Smithsonian's velvet ropes to help the United States Herbarium catalog two centuries' worth of precious plant specimens from around the world. Herbs and plants grown for food, clothing, medicine, spiritual use, construction materials, and more are all sampled and stored, and this project team of scientists is researching the historical knowledge about plant use. Many of the specimens are linked to native cultures and their traditions, and part of the focus is looking for links to modern usage. Plant lore is rapidly disappearing among native peoples as tribal groups break up and oral traditions are lost. Cataloging and organizing the enormous database of plant use will help to preserve some of what is fading away.

You'll augment the more than 900,000 entries in the Herbarium database, locate and extract target specimens, examine cuttings and other plant samples, enter your data into the computers, and process digital photography to fill in the visual catalogue. There are more than 5 million plants in the herbaria and 124 million specimens and objects in the museum collection, so it will require diligence and careful attention to detail. The inner workings of the National Museum of Natural History and the other Smithsonian museums are a large part of the intrigue and interest of this project, and your access is unprecedented for the general public.

You'll find your own hotel or housing arrangements in Washington, DC, as well as enjoy dining where you choose (lunches are included in the project fee, as are the first and last dinners). DC has so much history and so many notable sights to explore that you'll need a few extra days before or after your assignment to really get a handle on the nation's capital.

YOUR NEXT STEP: Earthwatch (© **800/776-0188**; www.earthwatch.org). A 5-day project, US$650, includes intensive project training, support, and lunches in the Smithsonian cafeteria as well as the welcome and farewell dinners with the team.

You will arrange your own accommodations, all other meals, and transportation to the museum. A US$35 Earthwatch membership is required.

DON'T MISS: Since you're already in a behind-the-scenes frame of mind, keep the theme going with a visit to the **International Spy Museum.** This is the first and only US public museum solely dedicated to espionage and features the largest collection of international spy-related artifacts ever placed on public display. Plenty of interactive exhibits can supply an entire day of covert exploration. www.spymuseum.org

ⓘ www.washington.org

Tree Planting **188**

Plant Indigenous Trees

Helping Habitat in West Africa

Shisong, Cameroon

YOU'LL NEED TO BE HARDY FOR THIS TRIP, WHICH REQUIRES A CONSIDERABLE AMOUNT OF manual labor to keep the area's water supply clean. Afterwards, you can relax and drive along the Ring Road, just north of where you'll be stationed in Northwest Cameroon, as it winds through some of the country's most striking scenery, particularly green grasses, volcanic mountains, and rice paddies.

In a remote area of West Africa are the English-speaking Bamenda Highlands, a rolling grassland region with large stands of eucalyptus. Plantations of these giant trees have been transplanted here in an attempt at economic growth, but the result has also caused much harm. The trees drain enormous amounts of water from the already parched soil, thus depriving villages of reliable water sources. The indigenous forests have been burned and cut down, so soil erosion is muddying the few water catchments that are still a good source of drinking water. The runoff during the rainy season further floods and pollutes available water stores. The natural solution is planting new native trees around the catchments, as they will establish healthy root systems that counteract erosion and have a stabilizing influence on the surrounding soil and smaller plants.

You'll plant new saplings, working in tandem with locals: some of these tree species support bees (there is a burgeoning beekeeping venture) and some have medicinal properties—and all will help the potable water supply. If you tire of digging holes, the local organization runs other conservation programs, including breeding cane rats, installing beehives, and porcupine rearing. You may have to trek long distances in the heat to get to work sites, not to mention digging and planting all day long, so you need to be fit. But the results are tangible right away: less mud in the water supply, meaning a healthier village.

Your home is a modest but comfortable hotel with a popular bar for burning off extra energy. Many locals as well as expats and international visitors congregate here regularly, so the storytelling and camaraderie will make the nights fly by. Your meals are prepared locally, and there are a few free-time activities built into the schedule, including a field trip to volcanic Mount Oku, a regional palace, art museum, and the marketplace in Kumbo town.

YOUR NEXT STEP: British Trust for Conservation Volunteers 🎗 (**✆ +44/1302 388 883;** www2.btcv.org.uk). This 15-day project, US$934/£570, includes hotel accommodations, meals, project equipment and training, cultural excursions, and volunteer support.

DON'T MISS: Seek out the lowland gorillas in **Lobeke National Park,** part of the larger Congo Basin. The remote park supports high densities of large mammals besides the gorillas, including elephants, chimpanzees, bongos, and other forest species. You can even spend the night in a special watchtower to wake to the sounds of the forest.

ⓘ www.ambacam-usa.org

189 Tree Planting

Rebuilding Indigenous Forest

Plant Trees, Learn Spanish

Quetzaltenango, Guatemala

There are plenty of diversions once you're done helping to rebuild Guatemala's forests: hot springs, volcanoes, and hiking opportunities are all nearby, and you can also improve your Spanish, have a good restaurant meal, and enjoy the nightlife.

Each year for the past 20 years, the Guatemalan government has set aside acreage for reforestation, which sets a laudable example for other nations—but the trees don't plant themselves. The project's goal is to install 200,000 indigenous species each year, including alder, cypress, pine, and eucalyptus. You'll be toiling in the sunshine and, ideally, the dappled shade of local hillsides and groves.

Some of your time will be spent at the nursery collecting seeds, preparing soil, and transplanting seedlings to the forest. The specifics of the work will depend on the season in which you volunteer (seed collecting in the winter, transplanting in the fall, for example). Seedlings are cared for quite delicately, with careful irrigation and fertilization for 5 years. After that, the young trees are viable without special attention. Other times you'll be in the newly naturalized tracts of forest working on pest control, weed abatement, and general maintenance projects, all of which give the young trees the best shot at thriving.

Project life will be a terrific immersion in Latin American culture. You'll be stationed with a host family in town (Quetzaltenango, also known as *Xela,* is Guatemala's second-largest city), with whom you'll also share meals. The project provides free Spanish language lessons for 2 hours a day, so you'll leave with a higher level of proficiency and comfort in conversation. There will be more than ample distraction in the city for your free time, as you explore cultural venues, wonderful local music, restaurants, bars, and shopping venues.

YOUR NEXT STEP: Global Crossroad (✆ **866/387-7816;** www.globalcrossroad.com). A 1-week project, US$975, covers host family accommodations and meals, airport greeting and transportation to the project site, Spanish language instruction, support and guidance before and during the trip, and comprehensive insurance coverage.

DON'T MISS: Guatemala is the largest country in Central America, but still accessible enough to get around quite easily and see a lot. Guatemalans are particularly proud of the ancient Mayan temple sites that make up a large part of their cultural heritage. **Tikal** and **El Mirador** are among the greatest pre-Columbian cities built anywhere in the Americas. Both of these sites are unforgettable destinations with stately tiered pyramids and supplemental stone structures, and both are located in the quiet and lush northern Petén region.

ⓘ www.visitguatemala.com

Tree Planting 190

Community Nursery

Support Youth, Visit Kenyan Villages

Kisumu, Kenya

KENYA ATTRACTS MANY VISITORS WHO WANT TO GO ON SAFARI AND WITNESS THE WILDEBEEST migration in the Masai Mara National Reserve, but there are many other reasons it boasts the slogan "Magical Kenya." With a variety of beaches, lakes, deserts, mountains, and forests, along with vibrant cities and villages, there are so many seemingly opposite experiences it's hard to believe they exist in one place.

The local impact of the slash-and-burn charcoal business and overfishing of the rivers has exacerbated a recent spate of unusually dry seasons in this region. This project, started by the children of the village of Kisumu, established a plantation to replace trees lost from development and incautious use of the land. It has now grown large enough to warrant international volunteer help to restore greener lands, cleaner air, increased beauty, and shade to this region.

Working with local community members, you'll be planting trees along the banks of the River Yalla, Lake Victoria, and other bodies of water. Volunteers will also improve trails, undertake weeding and pruning, install new fencing at the nursery, as well as raised seed beds and erosion prevention measures. You can help promote the program's good works by assisting in the schools that are introducing tree clubs and environmental clubs into the curricula and after-school activities.

International volunteers stay together in a work campsite with spacious and comfortable safari-style tents, all meals prepared, and local transportation provided. English is the main language on the project, but Swahili is spoken in most local households, and part of your non-work time is scheduled for home visits, where you will learn local cooking and traditional songs, dances, and storytelling.

YOUR NEXT STEP: Malaika Ecotourism (✆ **+254/20 2157732;** www.malaikaecotourism.com). Two weeks, US$230, includes volunteer camp tent accommodations, meals, in-country transportation, project training and cultural briefing, project support before and during the volunteer assignment, and cultural excursions led by locals.

DON'T MISS: One of Kenya's great unknown treasures is the site of the **Gedi ruins,** a lost city uncovered in the depths of the Arabuko-Sokoke Forest. Despite extensive study and research, nobody is sure what happened to the town of Gedi and its people when it was suddenly deserted in the 17th century. No signs of war or plague explain why 2,500 people abandoned the large forest city. The ruins include many houses, mansions, mosques, and elaborate tombs and cemeteries.

ⓘ www.magicalkenya.com

191 Tree Planting

Forests & Flowers

Preserving Paradise

Calacalí, Ecuador

IT CAN BE EASY TO FORGET THAT EVEN THE MOST REMOTE OF LOCATIONS CAN BE REACHED BY human civilization, often with negative effects. In Calacali you will be protecting some of nature's most delicate offerings from the intrusions of human progress, while enjoying the privilege of working in some extraordinarily beautiful surroundings.

A few miles up the road from Calacalî, along the Pacific coast of Ecuador, you'll find a wide spot in the overgrown road and the entrance to the El Pahuma Orchid Reserve. The Reserve is 650 hectares (1,500 acres) of a lush, humid, green universe filled with entire constellations of flowers. Bromeliads, orchids, ferns, and other "air plants" thrive here, and birds flock in huge numbers. A network of trails, both easy and rigorous, give you access to pockets of nature where you could believe yours are the first human footprints to ever sink in the mud. With all of this abundance, it is hard to reconcile the fact that many of these hundreds of botanical species are in danger.

The reserve's need for volunteers is critical as roads and other man-made objects chip away at the natural setting, with bulldozers and 4-wheel drive trucks crushing delicate flora beneath wheels and chainsaws that clear everything in their path. You will work as an orchid rescue worker, rushing to transplant the delicate flowers from harm's way in the targeted construction plots of land and relocating them to the reserve. Not far away a new educational garden is being planned at a nature center, so you'll dirty your green thumbs planting, labeling, and caring for native trees and plants as you create a mini eco-zone. Outside of the reserve, reforestation projects will have you collecting seeds, creating irrigation systems, planting trees at the nursery, and helping local schools create their own nurseries and gardens. It is hard work in stunning, but rugged, surroundings, and you'll come home with new gardening knowledge, including the medicinal uses for plants.

You'll be sharing accommodations with your fellow volunteers in research station lodging. There is a large nature center and even a restaurant on the grounds of the reserve, and three daily meals are included in the project fee. Workdays are arduous and last 6-8 hours, but in your free time you are in the middle of paradise, and will enjoy exploring the cloud forest, hiking to waterfalls, surfing or enjoying the beach, relaxing in a swinging hammock, or practicing your Spanish (not required for the project, but helpful). Visiting local Andean villages or heading into Quito (only an hour away) is a nice day's diversion.

YOUR NEXT STEP: Ceiba Foundation for Tropical Conservation (✆ **608/ 230-5550;** www.ceiba.org). A 1-week project, US$105, covers forest lodge accommodations, all meals, project support and backup. You'll be met at the airport, but take a public bus to the project site. Longer project stays are encouraged and charged by the day or month.

DON'T MISS: Where the headwaters of several rivers, including the Santiago River, meet the sea, **La Tolita Island** is a fascinating blend of archeological discoveries and a current traditional village. The island is home to one of Ecuadorian history's most important ceremonial sites where gold and gems were offered to the spirit world and to honor the island's high chief. You can explore grave sites and archaeological digs (though visitor numbers are carefully controlled) and see recovered gold, silver, and even platinum works that scholars laud as remarkably advanced for the era.

ⓘ www.ecuador.us

Tree Planting 192

Rainforest Enrichment

Hiking & Cutting-Edge Preservation

Patillas, Puerto Rico

KNOWN AS LA ESMERALDA DEL SUR—OR EMERALD OF THE SOUTH—THANKS TO ITS VERDANT mountains, Patillas is surrounded by sugar-cane fields and orange groves. But it's also home to an important rainforest, and volunteers will see firsthand how critically their help is needed and how immediately they can make a difference.

Rainforests are chopped down much faster than nature can replenish them, so we lose enormous amounts of acreage every day. The experts working on this project in Puerto Rico's rainforest have hit upon a bold effort that has been carefully monitored for the past 20 years and seems to be providing great results for revitalizing the ecosystem. Three-meter wide (10-ft.) channels are cut through the rainforest, making a grid of uninterrupted blocks of growth. These cut paths mimic the effects of naturally fallen, large canopy trees that routinely crisscross the area. In

Measuring a tree in Puerto Rico's rainforest

these rifts, seedling trees are planted so they can be harvested years later for hardwood and medicinal trees. The project meets the needs of locals, who would normally cut growth indiscriminately, while keeping the forest growing strong.

Your help on this sustainability project will mostly be through manual labor. You'll hike out in the morning through breathtaking rainforest along riverbanks and up steep hillsides to get to the work site. You might spend the day measuring and recording tree size, setting up new plots for insertion growing, tagging and identifying vine species, and sometimes doing native animal species counts. Night expeditions will locate and count Coqui frogs, the tuneful chirping symbol of Puerto Rico. You'll know them by their song—a lullaby for you each night in your tent.

The tents where you and the team stay are raised on permanent covered platforms with an adjacent shower/restroom block. Kitchen staff will expertly prepare (with your help) your meals, and the team dines together in the dining tent. The immediate vicinity begs exploration in your free time. Bathe in rivers, hike to find glassy pools, and enjoy some arranged activities, from cooking class and beach excursions to visits to Old San Juan and salsa dance instruction.

YOUR NEXT STEP: Earthwatch (© **800/776-0188**; www.earthwatch.org). A 10-day stay, US$1,750, includes accommodations in the project structural tents, meals prepared by local cooks, project training and support, and cultural immersion program with excursions. A US$35 Earthwatch membership is required.

DON'T MISS: You can get a break from all that sun by going underground at the **Río Camuy Cave Park.** This 108ha (268-acre) reserve is the site of 1-million-year-old caverns accessed by gentle trails that descend 60m (200 ft.) through fern grottoes. The high-ceilinged caverns are part of the third-largest cave system in the world and home to a unique species of blind fish that has never been exposed to sunlight.

ⓘ www.gotopuertorico.com

193 Tree Planting

Reforestation Nursery Project

Dig Deep

Moshi, Tanzania

Replant, reforest, rebuild: These three words describe your work in Moshi. But lucky for you, it's a town situated at the base of majestic Mount Kilimanjaro, the highest peak in Africa, and it's also a center for coffee growing, so that means there's plenty to do in your spare time.

Deforestation is a global issue, but the dramatic effects of clear-cutting are most immediately noticed in regions where there were a dearth of trees to begin with. While this part of Tanzania is no desert, the loss of older growth mature trees, mostly to satisfy the demand for fuel, is already having far-reaching consequences. Erosion is fouling water tables, and the lack of shade is causing smaller species of underbrush to change—some dying out, some taking over and choking out more delicate growth. The government has recognized that this process is accelerating and is encouraging institutions private and public, as well as all individuals, to take necessary measures to salvage and conserve the scarce land and water resources.

You'll roll up your sleeves and get digging with a community group that has opened a nursery. This cooperative business deals specifically in native tree species, and as a volunteer you'll prepare nursery beds, sow seeds, weed, trim, and prune, and thin some of the species that are being nurtured here. You may also go into the field and plant saplings, collect seeds, replant trees to more viable locations, eliminate or treat diseased trees, and do inventory studies on past plantings to assess the success of the project. It's hard work with instantly appreciable results.

A host family will provide three meals daily (a lunch to take with you to the work site) and a private room and comfortable bed for you each night. English is spoken on-site, and you'll get some rudimentary language instruction as well to make interacting in the village a bit more comfortable. In your downtime, you'll bask in the warm glow of community; having spent the day working side by side with locals and living in the village, volunteers are almost always invited to special community celebrations or simply for conversation over a mug of tea.

YOUR NEXT STEP: Institute for Field Research Expeditions (✆ **800/675-2504;** www.ifrevolunteers.org). A 2-week project, US$753 plus US$349 application fee (covers program promotion and overhead for the organization), includes host family accommodations, all meals, cultural immersion and language instruction, project support, and airport transfers.

DON'T MISS: While safaris looking for the Big Five dominate most Tanzanian travel itineraries, take a different kind of walk on the wild side at the **Meserani Snake Park** near Arosha. Run by local Maasai warriors who also serve as guides, you can get up close and personal with some of the most dangerous snakes in the world, including the Black and Green Mamba, Egyptian Cobra, Puff Adders, and many more, and then take a camel-back safari to a local Maasai village. www.meseranisnakepark.com

ⓘ www.tanzaniatouristboard.com

Tree Planting **194**

Working With Native Plants

Yard Work in the Garden of the Gods

Kaua'i, Hawaii, USA

FOR A FRACTION OF THE COST OF A HAWAIIAN VACATION, VOLUNTEERS CAN IMMERSE themselves in the green, tropical landscape of Kaua'i—and *immerse* is the word here, as it's a wet, humid spot whose flora and fauna need some human intervention in order to thrive.

Four hundred hectares (1,000 acres) on Kaua'i's Eden-like north shore comprise the lush, peaceful Limahuli National Garden and Preserve. This part of the "garden island" is accessed by one main road, passing waterfalls as if they were lampposts, with the Pacific occasionally peeking in through the passenger-side window. The amazing collection of tropical plant species is well above the crashing sea waves, but not all the way up to the peak of Mount Wai'lea'lea, the wettest spot on Earth. Limahuli is a research garden and includes not only indigenous species, but also an opportunity to study many plant species brought to the island by Polynesian settlers, including taro, one of Hawaii's most well-known crops.

Working with garden staff, you'll plant native plants, cut back and clear overgrown areas, and remove non-native invaders. You might also spend some time

Tending to the native plants of Kaua'i, Hawaii

toiling in the nursery, which can include watering and fertilizing, moving plants and containers, or just cleaning up. It's tough work in humid conditions, but such lushness can only be found in humid areas, and you're achingly close to some of the most beautiful beaches in the world.

Aside from rain—and the north shore gets more than its share—the weather is perfect. Even warm afternoon rains are a small price to pay for time camping out in paradise. You'll sleep in the tent you bring along. (Bring other camping gear too, for your own comfort. Kitchen and commissary equipment is provided.) There are available restrooms and a kitchen in case you want to whip up a snack, but meals are provided. Plenty of free time is built in for relaxing island-style. You are quite close to Ke'e Beach, so a stroll there for a swim or snorkel is great even during lunch hour. The Na Pali Coast trailheads are also just around the bend if you'd like to do some serious hiking on your days off. Or you can head back south to Hanalei for some good eating and plenty of the laid-back island vibe.

YOUR NEXT STEP: Wilderness Volunteers (✆ **928/556-0038;** www.wildernessvolunteers.org). A 1-week project, US$259, covers campsite access, all meals, and project instruction. You'll get yourself to Kaua'i's north shore for the start of the project.

DON'T MISS: To see an alternate side of the island's ecosystem, try going **tubing** in the decommissioned sugar-cane plantation irrigation channels. You'll float along these man-made streams cut through vast plains of greenery, occasionally dipping into the darkness of tunnels, all the while reclining in a giant truck tire innertube. If that's too slow for you, fly overhead with one of the many **ziplining** tour companies.

ⓘ www.kauai-hawaii.com

Greening & Cleaning

Shade-Grown Coffee Project

Field Research in an Eco-Adventure Paradise

San Luis, Costa Rica

COSTA RICA'S WATERFALLS AND BEACHES ARE A MICROCOSM OF WHAT'S BELOVED ABOUT THE Caribbean, and the country's conscientious ecotourism policies stand out. People flock to the country's national parks, especially for bird-watching. Take it a step further and learn how birds—and the bees—are important to the country's coffee trade.

There are few cash crops more important to the world economy than coffee. More than 100 million people in developing countries (to say nothing of Seattle) make their living from the bean. Shade-grown coffee has become a buzzword, and natural-growth forest coffee benefits flora and fauna in ways plantation-grown beans can't. The ripple effect extends to the insect community with better pollination, as well as animals and birds that maintain natural seed spreading. Field research is being done to quantify the benefits of shade-grown Costa Rican coffee, and the study will inform the process of official certification of the more desirable bean crop. The farms that are part of this study are members of a small grower's co-op that was generated for dedicated farmers to develop growing methods in harmony with nature.

Surveying a Costa Rican coffee bean crop

You'll visit coffee-growing areas and conduct bird and bee surveys, as well as notating coffee fruit and flower growth. Depending on the time of year, you may do very specific pruning in experimental plots to ascertain growth patterns or prepare research cuttings for lab study. The shade comes from a lush canopy of fig, ceibo, and guanacaste (the national tree of Costa Rica) trees between fences strung from sapling to sapling. The cloud forest reserve of Monteverde is a very refreshing place to toil.

The research station you'll return to each night is a converted dairy farm nestled into the woods. Shared cabins or bunkhouse accommodations are comfy and busy, as a roster of international volunteers and researchers move through on their own missions. A cook's team preps native cuisine, including locally grown papaya, bananas, plantains, mango, coconut, and nuts, and there is a computer lab on premises if you just can't bear being unplugged (but try anyway). On days off, you are neighbor to one of the country's most popular eco-adventure areas, affording you chances to try ziplining, horseback riding, and canopy walks.

YOUR NEXT STEP: Earthwatch (© **800/776-0188**; www.earthwatch.org). A 15-day project, US$2,950, includes cabin or bunkhouse lodging, locally cooked meals, project training, and support. A US$35 Earthwatch membership is required.

DON'T MISS: Whitewater rafting gets the adrenaline pumping, and one of the most exciting runs in Central America is the Class V sections of the **Reventazón River.** Unfortunately, the river is in danger of being dammed in the near future for harnessing hydroelectric power. There are also less energetic sections of the waterway, with Class III whitewater separated by slow floats so you can watch the world go by while spotting monkeys, sloths, and hundreds of species of birds.

ⓘ www.visitcostarica.com

196 Greening & Cleaning

Beach Cleanup

Touring Darwin's Labratory

Galapagos Islands, Ecuador

Although it's named for the majestic, enormous turtles who inhabit these Islands, the Galapagos draws curious nature lovers who know that the Islands are a truly unique ecosystem with many rare and unusual creatures—such as 750,000 species of seabirds, and 22 species of reptiles.

The Galapagos Archipelago is considered one of the most precious bioregions on Earth, and since the time of Darwin it has inspired fascination and awe in the scientific community and among audacious world travelers. In recent years it has become much easier for people to get there—and with such unprecedented access comes impact. There are limits being put in place to rein in the effects of unchecked tourism before they become too great, but a good amount of damage has already been done. This environmental cleanup project helps protect the ecosystem by working with local fisherman to rid the islands' rocky shores of man-made debris and waste. The human footprint threatens the habitat of several significant species in the Galapagos that are exclusive to this region, to the point that the very survival of those species is threatened.

Swimming alongside giant tortoises in the Galapagos Islands

The trip is an introduction to Ecuador with volunteer work mixed in, so you'll have days to explore the mainland before dropping in by small plane to the Galapagos. Swim with sea lions and walk past giant tortoises on the way to meet the squad of fishermen who will be clearing trash with you. Many of the beaches and coastal zones where you'll work are inaccessible to tourists, so you'll see parts of these islands few others have. Plastic water bottles and food wrappers still drift to these remote locales, home to blue-footed boobies or statue-like iguanas.

Life is pretty cushy on this trip, and throughout the Ecuadorian tour you'll stay at three- and four-star hotels or lodges and dine out at restaurants with the group. The small local hotel on the island even has a swimming pool and Jacuzzi, so you can soak away the aches you earn from bending and stooping all day. The tour itinerary is well filled, so free time will be at a premium, during which most of the team will likely walk the quiet beaches and swim in the sea, contemplating the questions of evolution and how we can positively affect the next generation of people and animals.

YOUR NEXT STEP: Hands Up Holidays (✆ **201/984-5372;** www.handsupholidays.com). This 15-day project, US$3,182, includes hotel accommodations, restaurant meals with the group, guide services at every location, and tickets and passage on local transportation and tour activities. It is a real door-to-door vacation excursion, so all your needs are met.

DON'T MISS: Are you a climber? In Ecuador you can go from sea level to above 6096m (20,000 ft.) in elevation, and the **Avenue of Volcanoes** has more than 30 volcanic peaks, one of the world's greatest concentrations. Rock or ice, novice or expert, if you ever wanted to climb, this is the place to strap in and work your way up the rock.

ⓘ www.ecuadortouristboard.com

197 Greening & Cleaning

Restore Inner Island Environment

Reggae & Renewal

Rock Spring, Jamaica

Not far from the popular sandy beaches and nightlife of Montego Bay and Ocho Rios, you can go spelunking in caves that many visitors don't even know about. And just to the east of Rock Spring, get lost in a verdant ferngully or explore the famed Blue Mountains coffee-growing region.

The Jamaica that exists beyond the confines of the all-inclusive resorts is different from what most tourists see in many ways. The island's interior is "Cockpit Country," the last wilderness area on the island, home to many unique species and unusual topography. Uniform limestone hillocks look from above like giant bubble wrap, and below is a complex network of caves and natural springs. While the area is too remote to attract many residents, the few settlers have shown little regard for stewardship of the land, resulting in damage to the abundant limestone.

In conjunction with a local nonprofit community organization, this project will work to instill sustainable development practices in Cockpit Country as well as try to clean up some of the damage already done. Locals have begun developing an ecotourism program that is sensitive to the environment, recognizing the stunning natural setting as their greatest asset. They are using forest resources in a sustainable

Visiting a local school in Rock Spring, Jamaica

and renewable way that also provides a measure of desperately needed economic stability. To further their goals, you'll be dedicated to cleaning up local rivers, caves, and sinkholes so the natural setting can be once again as near to pristine as possible. You'll help mark and improve trails, construct soap residue filtering stations for washing, shore up eroding hillside sections, and share eco-awareness programs in local schools.

Living with a host family, you'll come to know and love Jamaican hospitality. You'll be served traditional meals, and often the team will gather with all the host families for group meals and celebrations. With awareness that hard work in remote areas can cause some burnout in volunteers, plenty of free time has been built into the schedule so you can relax and explore the village community or open nature areas. There are also cultural activities built into the trip, including cave explorations, a cooking class, and patois language introduction to help you really immerse yourself in Jamaican life.

YOUR NEXT STEP: GlobeAware (✆ **877-588-4562;** www.globeaware.org). A 1-week project, US$1,180, includes host family accommodations, cultural exchange and learning programs and tours, all meals, project support, and project transportation. You'll get yourself to the main project meeting spot for the first day of the assignment.

DON'T MISS: You should definitely spend some time in Kingston, and while in the capital, get yourself to **Spanish Town.** In 1534 it was the capital of the island under the Spanish. It's since undergone several name changes under Spanish and British rule and is one of the oldest continuously occupied spots in the Western hemisphere.

ⓘ www.visitjamaica.com

Greening & Cleaning 198

Reforestation Projects

Restoring the Land of the Incas

Cusco, Peru

THOUSANDS OF PEOPLE COME TO CUSCO AS A GATEWAY TO THE HALLOWED SITE MACHU Picchu. But many of them also leave a negative impact on the environment. Here's where you come in: volunteers can blaze a new trail or plant a tree, in the name of sustainability.

In the indigenous Quechua belief system, Cusco is known as "the navel of the universe," meaning that it's at the center of all things. The Andes Mountains that surround the city are a pure expression of rugged splendor but unfortunately aren't untouched by man's waste. One way to contribute to the vitality of this high-elevation mountain region is to spend your vacation volunteering in a reforestation and conservation project. While toiling in the spectacular mountainsides and valleys is an amazing experience, there are also opportunities to be engaged in the vegetable garden and orchard programs of a local orphanage or the community orchid farm.

You'll help clean up and do improvement work on a network of trails in the municipal forest, as well as some nursery work preparing young tree plantings for naturalization on the hillsides. You might also be called upon to help produce and present environmental education programs in local schools and communities, giving the village residents a sense of ownership and personal investment in the health of the forests. Some of the national parklands have been well used but not as well maintained, so there is garbage cleanup, returning the "navel" to its pure state.

Life in the smaller villages outside the rapidly expanding city of Cusco is quiet, and you'll be living with a welcoming host family. Your Spanish skills can be rudimentary, but a little will go a long way in the household. (English is spoken during the project work. Spanish lessons are available for volunteers.) Peruvian cuisine will be prepared for you at meal times (a lunch will be packed for fieldwork), and you will enjoy exploring the small villages or Cusco proper during evenings and weekends. Cusco is a colonial jewel well known throughout the world as the gateway city for the Sacred Valley and Machu Picchu, so you'll find plenty to keep you busy.

YOUR NEXT STEP: Institute for Field Research Expeditions (© **800/675 2504;** www.ifrevolunteers.org). A 2-week stint, US$795, includes lodging with a local host family, meals, travel insurance, airport transfer, in-country transportation, and project training and support are all covered. A US$349 IFRE administrative/application fee is required.

DON'T MISS: One of the most intriguing mysteries in Peru are the enormous desert land drawings, or geoglyphs, known as the **Nazca Lines.** They are designs in the ground where the top layer of red soil and stone has been cleared to form enormous designs in the desert that can only be seen in their entirety from airplanes that fly over. The giant monkey, hummingbird, and geometric figures are amazing from a bird's-eye view—but they have fed many theories of UFO visitations and supernatural powers because of when they were created: perhaps as long ago as 200 b.c. (i) www.peru.info

199 Greening & Cleaning

Cleaning a Historic Attraction

Live in a Rural Heritage Home

Trsic, Serbia

Classified as an ethnovillage by the Serbian Tourism Organization, Trsic has plenty of history and culture to preserve. Beyond, though, lies a country many tourists have yet to explore—the energetic capital Belgrade, the monasteries of the south, and mountains that are playgrounds for hikers in the summer and skiers in winter.

Trsic is the birthplace of Vuk Karadzic, who is credited with reforming the Serbian language, and the town gets plenty of tourism from both Serb and foreign visitors. The significant pedestrian and vehicle traffic, however, has taken a toll on the pastoral setting, leaving behind trash and a run-down infrastructure. New energy is going into cleaning up the site and making the visitor experience on par with the importance of the place. In addition to sprucing up the village, the project is also working to impart an improved eco-sensibility in locals.

You'll be in the woods picking up garbage, clearing overgrown vegetation and weeding, and marking and upgrading paths leading from Vuk's famous home to the 14th-century monastery in town. Swing a hammer and build benches along the paths or picnic tables in the peaceful forest clearings. You'll be working alongside local Serbian volunteers who are particularly dedicated to cultural improvement projects, and many of them are also passionate about language and its study (although the project language is English), so it will be quite a cultural melting pot.

The cottage-style homes you'll be living in are just like the historical home so many people come to visit. The team will prepare meals communally, and they tend to accept the regular invitations that are extended to local villager's homes or big, filling meals. Historical education workshops and excursions are part of the project, so you'll really be immersed in the culture and significance of Vuk and the movement he inspired. You'll also visit local museums and the village school for a special event created as a thank-you for international volunteers.

YOUR NEXT STEP: Service Civil International (✆ **434/336 3545;** www.sci-ivs.org). A 2-week stay, US$235, includes local accommodations in an historic home, project support, local excursions and workshops, and a 1-year Service Civil International membership. Meals are extra, and team volunteers cook communally. You will also be responsible for getting yourself to the project.

DON'T MISS: Keep the theme of your trip going by visiting another cultural center beloved by Serbs. The **Tesla Museum** commemorates Nikolas Tesla, one of Serbia's most famous sons for his pioneering work in physics, wireless technology, and electrical engineering. His face is on the country's currency.

ⓘ www.serbia.travel

Greening & Cleaning 200

Island Cleanup

Be an Eco-Advocate, Enjoy World-Class Diving

Koh Tao, Thailand

THAILAND GAINS A LOT OF ATTENTION FOR ITS BEACHES IN AREAS SUCH AS PHUKET. BUT KOH Tao, or "turtle island," in the Gulf of Thailand, really transports the visitor. With welcoming currents, it's a paradise for scuba diving and snorkeling.

The adventure travel magazines have begun to tout the wonders of the tiny Thai island Koh Tao, so you'll want to experience this formerly undiscovered gem before its popularity explodes. The Secret Garden conservation project is working proactively to stave off the tarnishing of the island's ecology before it's too late. Labor is hard to come by, so volunteers bridge the gap to keep the kilometers of sugar sand beaches and the beautiful jungle interior as green as possible. The project is also very active in advocating for responsible environmental practices in the community and runs youth education programs in the schools.

Educating current and future generations to be true stewards of the land and take the environmental bull by the horns is a huge undertaking. In addition to being an eco-ambassador (English is taught in many classrooms, so you'll be working directly with children as well as with translators), you'll also be wedging dirt under your nails at the project's nursery and on the beaches. Each week the local community organization has beach cleanup days, and you'll also help with environmental research activities and surveys.

World-class diving and snorkeling will beckon in your free time, and when you get home you'll have bragging rights over other adventurers who have likely not reached this remote and pristine island. Home is a guesthouse in town where you'll share rooms with other volunteers and be on your own for meals—local dining options are inexpensive and seafood options are amazingly fresh (and usually spicy). Evenings and other free time will be spent relaxing in the beach town or on the shore itself, with plenty of water-based recreation companies available if you've still got energy to burn.

YOUR NEXT STEP: STA Travel (**© 800/ 781-4040;** www.statravel.com). A 2-week project, US$1,265, includes shared guest-house accommodations a 15-minute walk from the project, training, airport pickup, and full 24-hour support. You are responsible for all meals.

DON'T MISS: Wat Tham Suwankhuha, Phang Nga (the cave of the heavenly grotto) is a huge cave graced by a 15m-long (50-ft.-) golden statue of reclining Buddha. The Buddha is kept company in this stalactite-filled underground haven by countless monkeys and swooping bats. It is a dramatic visit to the underground world in a truly majestic, stark setting.

ⓘ www.tourismthailand.org

201 Greening & Cleaning

Nature Preserve Maintenance

Care for Grounds, Live in Secluded Lodge

Albany, New York, USA

FROM THE CAPITAL OF THE EMPIRE STATE, YOU'VE GOT ACCESS TO SO MUCH: THERMAL waters in Saratoga Springs, the Catskills and its ample hiking and outdoor recreation possibilities, or, farther west, the wineries of the Finger Lakes.

Amid the serene lakelands of upstate New York, the Edmund Niles Huyck Preserve is home base to a number of ecological researchers. The preserve was established in the 1800s and enlarged in the 1960s to cover more than 810ha (2,000 acres) of hardwood forest dotted with crystal-clear pools of water and picturesque streams. It serves as an animal sanctuary for bobcats, otters, black bears, and many varieties of birds. The research station in this area of tremendous woodland diversity is one of the first in the United States, opened in 1938. It's a popular and peaceful oasis of calm that is well used and well loved, and it shows the signs of wear and tear each season, requiring ongoing maintenance.

You'll be working with the preserve's staff to clear and upgrade the extensive trail system, rerouting some trails that need extensive work to combat erosion, marking new trails with signage, restoring older bridges and building new ones over babbling brooks and wetlands, and performing some light building maintenance. While land use is particularly sensitive here, your efforts will help to protect the preserve's fragile ecosystem, maintaining the ideal field research conditions.

You will stay at a secluded lodge overlooking Lincoln Pond, tucked among the trees and boasting a comfortable kitchen, dining room, living room, and shared bedrooms, plus a porch with a heart-swelling view of the pond. Think loons on the lake, fireflies abuzz, and thrumming cicadas in the trees. Hike to the waterfall, kayak or canoe, take a dip in the pond or lake, or fish the streams in your free time. If you get restless, an historic town is close by with restaurants, a coffee house, and a pub.

YOUR NEXT STEP: British Trust for Conservation Volunteers (**© +44/ 1302 388 883;** www2.btcv.org.uk). This 12-day project, US$752/£456, includes lodge accommodations. You'll cook for

10 Places to Connect the World: Trail Building

The shortest distance between two points may be a straight line, but in trail building the most important thing may be creating the opportunity for an afternoon meander through sun-dappled woods or picking your way carefully along a rocky coastline. Crews made up of volunteers make sure the way is clear, accessible, and free of discarded beer cans and snack bar wrappers. Volunteers are people who enjoy the outdoors, like being with others, and work as a team to make a connection.

202 Bella Bella, British Columbia, Canada The mouth of the Koeye River is home to the First Nations people of the Heiltsuk tribe and the Great Grizzly Bear. Volunteers, working with tribal youth, are forging a trail network throughout the area. You'll landscape, clear overgrowth, move rocks and sand, and place signage along the new network, as well as planting medicine gardens—all part of a 1,000-year restoration plan in a formerly logged region. ***Canadian Alliance for Development Initiatives and Projects*** *(© **604/628-7400**; www.cadip.org). A 2-week project is US$265.*

One of the many sea lions of the Galapagos Islands

203 Galapagos Islands, Ecuador The Galapagos Archipelago has captivated travelers since Darwin landed there in *The Beagle*. The rough natural state of the delicate ecosystem is one of the greatest draws, along with myriad species of wildlife found nowhere else; but to see the Blue-Footed Boobies and Giant Tortoises, you need to hike to some remote outposts. Volunteers like you do the work of trail maintenance. ***i-to-i*** *(© **800/985-4852**; www.i-to-i.com). A 2-week project is US$1,490.*

The rolling hills of Tinos Island

204 Tinos, Cyclades, Greece The small municipalities of Tinos Island are connected by an extended network of footpaths. These modest trails are mapped but mostly unmarked and well trod by locals and visiting trekkers rambling through the scenic vistas and shady crags. Volunteers spend days cleaning, posting signage, and opening up and renewing ancient trails, as much of the island is inaccessible by vehicle. ***Canadian Alliance for Development Initiatives and Projects*** *(© **604/628-7400**; www.cadip.org). A 2-week project is US$265; upon arrival, an additional US$38 is paid directly to the project hosts.*

205 Baikal, Russia The Great Baikal Trail in Siberia rings and radiates out from pristine Baikal Lake, and international volunteers build connecting trails, small bridges, and campsites to increase access while remaining sensitive to the ecology of the region. Crews tend to be from many countries, all united in building a sustainable trail system, walking the same ground as Genghis Khan. ***Great Baikal Trail*** *(© **+7/908-6470-744**; www.greatbaikaltrail.org). A 2-week project is US$336.*

206 Appalachian Trail, USA The Appalachian Trail is one that everyone has heard of. Originally built by volunteers, that proud tradition continues as volunteers maintain it, donating more than 196,000 work hours every year. Some trail-work opportunities are trail-wide, while others are regional along this ribbon pathway that extends from Maine to Georgia. ***Appalachian National Scenic Trail*** *(© **304/535-6331**; www.appalachiantrail.org): No formalized package trips.*

207 Colorado, USA Maintained annually by volunteers, the Colorado Trail winds its way 800km (500 miles) from Denver to Durango, through often grueling sections of rough trail in the heart of the Rockies. You'll camp out with a team and leader and improve the trail as you hike. ***The Colorado Trail Foundation*** *(© **303/384-3729**; www.coloradotrail.org). One week is US$50; one weekend is US$25.*

Maintaining the Colorado Trail

208 Bangor, Maine, USA Working to clear the trails of the Moosehorn Wildlife Refuge will involve axes, bow saws, crosscut saws, pruners, clippers, and more. The US Fish and Wildlife Service will train you; this dense spruce, fir, and hardwood forest needs lots of TLC every year, as you help maintain access to the stunning rugged coastline and inland areas. ***American Hiking Society (AHS)*** *(© **301/565-6704**; www.americanhiking.org). One week is US$245 for AHS members, US$275 for non-members.*

209 New Jersey/New York, USA Collaborate with park rangers to devise new signage. Cut back brush and level ground to keep footpaths accessible and pristine. Work on trail surveys to create new trail design reference manuals. These are some of the jobs filled by volunteers working on the 2,655km (1,650 miles) of hiking trails in the Trail Conference. Add rock stairs, remove blown-down trees, build bridges, or do anything else needed to improve the hiking experience. ***New York New Jersey Trail Conference*** *(© **201/512-9348**; www.nynjtc.org). No travel arranged by project.*

210 USA—Nationwide The American Hiking Society has more than 70 trail improvement projects across 30 states, and volunteers, in teams of 6 to 15, backpack and day hike into areas that need trail rehabilitation and land stewardship. ***American Hiking Society (AHS)*** *(© **301/565-6704**; www.americanhiking.org). One week is US$245 for AHS members, US$275 for non-members.*

211 Charlotte Amalia, St. Thomas, US Virgin Islands The surroundings are pretty gorgeous as you work to rehabilitate trails and ruins on the Caribbean island of St. Thomas. Erosion has begun to destroy areas of this system used for nature tours, so the work will be leveling trails, correcting for drainage, and constructing stream crossings. ***Friends of Virgin Islands National Park*** *(© **340/779-4940**; www.friendsvinp.org): No fees, duration flexible; food and lodging arranged but not included.*

yourself or with your volunteer colleagues, or head to local diners, as meals are not included. You'll also get yourself to the project meeting point, the local train station.

DON'T MISS: Since you'll be just outside Albany, go for a tour of the New York State Capitol building. The elegant 19th-century edifice is a beautiful work of granite architecture, with a melting pot of styles on the exterior and interior high-vaulted Moorish ceilings and lavish carved staircases.

ⓘ www.albany.org

Farm & Ranch 212

Farm & Guesthouse Work

Organic Farming on The Rock

Pouch Cove, Newfoundland, Canada

ATLANTIC CANADA'S COASTLINES ARE ROCKY, COVE-FILLED, AND DOTTED WITH LIGHTHOUSES. In this northeastern province (known as "The Rock" to locals), you can see whales, icebergs, and puffins. The pace of life slows down considerably here, making it a great place to unwind as you work.

Willing Workers on Organic Farms (WWOOFers) have made this a favorite volunteer stop for years; it doubles as a summertime guest house and a holistic retreat during the slow season. You may spot whales or icebergs just off shore in early summer, and on shore you'll find blueberry stands on your walk into the woods or along the rocky cliffs to the fishing village, just 30 minutes north of St. John's. The farm has goats and chickens as well as a work-in-progress that will become a healing center (with some volunteer help).

Your tasks during any given day will vary depending on the season. If you're working during the B&B high season, you'll help out around the facility with guests and their needs. The goats and chickens need tending year-round, and there will definitely be daily chores around the farm.

The Points East Guesthouse and Retreat Center is a cozy place filled with art and literature inspired by the region, and while your agreement is to work for your lodging, the hosts' philosophy is that this should serve as a retreat even for diligent volunteers. Meals are served upon request or you can enjoy some of the fresh daily catch in the village. The accommodations are very comfortable, and a porch and garden will beckon to you, particularly as the sun rises, since you'll see it before almost anyone else—this being as far east as you can go in North America.

YOUR NEXT STEP: WWOOF Canada (✆ **250/354-4417;** www.wwoof.ca). The length of your stay is up to you and your hosts, and arrangements can be made for meals. Transportation is your own responsibility, and while there is no formal training, you will work in tandem with your hosts to accomplish what they need done each day.

DON'T MISS: The Rooms looms over the city of St. John's in a colorful homage to the traditional fishing "rooms" that used to dot the Newfoundland coastline. Inside, however, it's a slick cultural oasis that combines galleries and museums to tell the story of the province's natural and human history.

ⓘ www.newfoundlandlabrador.com

213 Farm & Ranch

Organic Farm

WWOOF for Free

Rose Valley, Prince Edward Island, Canada

IT'S THE LAND OF ANNE OF GREEN GABLES, AND THE CAREFULLY MAINTAINED LANDSCAPE looks like it's been torn from a postcard. Volunteers often make repeat appearances here to tend to that healthy soil on organic farms, enjoying the fruits—and veggies—of their labor. You can also relax on walking trails and in the little towns that dot this storied island.

Prince Edward Island is a landscape painter's dream, with rolling green hills giving way to the deep red soil and cliffside views of the crashing ocean below. The lobster traps on farmhouse and cottage lawns that ring the coastal region contrast with the strong bohemian vibe and terrific arts community of the tiny capital of Charlottetown. Only a few roads cut through and around the island, so it is all quite accessible. Where three streams converge on a 121ha (300-acre) plot of partially wooded land is the site of this project's organic farm, run with the assistance of volunteer Willing Workers on Organic Farms, or WWOOFers.

Wake up with the sun and get cracking on your chores, which might include planting or harvesting some of the 60ha (150 acres) of farmed land that grow certified organic fruits, vegetables, and grains. The produce is sold to local restaurants on the island, and in addition to the market garden there is also a greenhouse. The veggies are planted, weeded, and harvested manually (that means you), and field crops are cultivated mechanically (with your assistance). The wooded half of the property is sustainably harvested for firewood and lumber, so your efforts could be called for there as well among the beautiful sugar maples, oaks, and spruce trees.

Your home, for as long as you arrange, is a two-story farmhouse with multiple bedrooms, big kitchen, laundry room, and shared public spaces. You'll prepare your own meals or team up with other volunteers to share kitchen detail unless you opt to enjoy some of the fruits of your labor in the town restaurants. It's early to bed and early to rise for farm work, but there are ample opportunities for hitting a pub in town to blow off some steam, as well as regional museums and cultural attractions to explore before, during, and after you've thoroughly explored the natural wonders of Prince Edward Island.

YOUR NEXT STEP: WWOOF Canada (✆ **250/354-4417**; www.wwoof.ca). The length of your stay is up to you and your hosts, and arrangements can be made for meals. Transportation is your own responsibility, and while there is no formal training, you will work in tandem with your hosts to accomplish what they need done each day.

DON'T MISS: Prince Edward Island is famous for mussels, but doing your own **clam digging** is much more fun. At low tide with a shovel and bucket you can walk the sandbar and find a meal's worth of soft shell, quahaug, razor, and bar clams. Look for the holes in the sand and circle patterns that are the markers of a clam below, dig around a little with your toes, and soon enough, dinner is on. (Make sure you catch the clams that fit within size and weight limitations for sustainable harvest).

ⓘ www.tourismpei.com

Farm & Ranch 214

Orphanage Farm

Sowing Soil & Dreams

Banteay Meanchey, Cambodia

VOLUNTEERS WHO HAVE A WAY WITH CHILDREN AND A KEEN INTEREST IN AGRICULTURAL WORK can make a tremendous difference with this project, which situates you in the northwestern part of Cambodia, at a crossroads close to the Thai border.

Here at the border of Cambodia and Thailand, many travelers pass through the town of Banteay Meanchey. The orphanage, besides being a home for parentless and abandoned children, operates farming and livestock ventures that serve local businesses serving the tourist trade (such as local markets and restaurants). Involving the entire community has been the key to the orphanage's success so far.

Your work on this project will be eclectic: cleaning and feeding at the fish farm; helping care for the farm's piglets; planting, weeding, and picking in the vegetable gardens; or the tough work of toiling in the rice fields. All of it is work that needs to be done to keep the facility operating. There are also teaching opportunities in the orphanage, and some light construction and maintenance work: building a new classroom, constructing a small footbridge, repairing and setting up new fencing around parts of the acreage, and some painting and repair work. Several of the kids who live at the orphanage will be your helpers (or enthusiastic supervisors).

You'll stay at the orphanage, sleeping in dormitory-style rooms and sharing meals with locals, the resident children, and other volunteers. You'll be truly immersed in the world of the orphanage, where most of the staff and volunteer coordinators speak English and the children are all learning, so expect endless questions about your life in language practice conversations. Free time is child-focused as well, and if you've got a playful spirit, you'll quickly have an entourage that follows you everywhere (and if you've got a playful spirit of another kind, a town nearby is famous for its casinos).

YOUR NEXT STEP: Take Me To Volunteer Travel (✆ **+65/6220 1198;** www.takemetovolunteertravel.com). While you can book longer or shorter volunteer trips here, a 2-week project is surprisingly inexpensive. US$550 covers accommodations in the group rooms of the orphanage, meals on-site, airport transfers, and a donation to the orphanage.

DON'T MISS: Take a river cruise along the **Tonle Sap** from Phnom Penh to Siem Reap. It's a great way to laze through Cambodia's wetlands and visit floating villages. Tonle Sap is both a river system and a huge freshwater lake that is now a protected UNESCO biosphere. It is a fascinating body of water and one of the only rivers in the world where the water flow changes direction twice a year, flooding and then partially emptying the lake.

ⓘ www.tourismcambodia.com

215 Farm & Ranch

Organic Farm & Retreat Home

Harvest Time in Provence

Trets en Provence, France

THERE ARE FEW DESTINATIONS THAT FEEL MORE LIKE A VACATION GETAWAY THAN PROVENCE. The fields of lavender, sunflowers bowing on their stalks, cicadas buzzing in the trees as swallows dart in the sky. It is wine and history and good food all wrapped up in a pastoral countryside package.

In the small town of Trets en Provence, a local association has purchased a property that is becoming a social and organic farm, providing food for the body and succor for the soul—it is a "place of relief" for suffering young people and adults. Just as van Gogh came to the area for an escape from the problems of his life, others continue to find solace in these gently rolling hills and vineyard. The farm has been developed mostly with the effort of association members who have a stake in the farm's success and have developed it from the beginning. Volunteers assist in helping it thrive.

The volunteer work here is agricultural, including the planting and harvesting of vegetables and all the secondary tasks involved (weeding, fertilizing, watering, and so on), installing fenced areas for the farm animals and maintaining existing fencing, and some basic maintenance tasks around the buildings as needed. You'll also have plenty of time to interact with the young people who live here, perhaps leading group activities and games. You may also play host to visitors who come to learn about the organic farming process.

You'll stay in a shared room in the main house on this 4ha (10-acre) property. All the facilities of a large working farmhouse are shared, and there is Internet service. Team members all pitch in in the kitchen for meals. Evenings around the farm are quiet and relaxing, or if you head into the modest medieval town of Trets, there is a swimming pool, movie theater, and library to explore, as well as small restaurants. Wednesday is a farmers' market day that brings folks into town from kilometers around. A nearby ranch raises horses if you'd like to ride, and some of the most famous Provence cities (such as Aix en Provence and Marseille) are less than 30 minutes away.

YOUR NEXT STEP: Canadian Alliance for Development Initiatives and Projects 🎗 (✆ **604/628-7400;** www.cadip.org) An 18-day project, US$285, includes communally prepared team meals and accommodations at the project farmhouse, as well as full project support. You must travel to the site on your own.

DON'T MISS: Provence has many facets, and each town is more picturesque than the last. Certainly a must-visit on your itinerary should be the old bullfighting center, **Arles,** with its unmatched town square and tiny, shoulder-wide cobblestone lanes. Also drive the short way to the Mediterranean Coast through the **Camargue** and keep an eye out for the giant flocks of flamingos in the salt flats, as well as the white horses for which the beach area is famous.

ⓘ www.visitprovence.com

Farm & Ranch 216

Model Farm

Promote Sustainable Ecology in Rural India

Tamil Nadu, India

IN ORDER TO IMPROVE THE SOIL, YOU MUST WORK WITH IT AND UNDERSTAND ITS NEEDS AND limitations. But to ensure that these practices continue, you must teach others what has to be done. Volunteers run this model farm, located in the verdant, southernmost state of the country, and sharing the knowledge gleaned from the project with locals is as important as the produce.

For many years, most subsistence farmers in Southern India have cut down trees for fuel and cooking fires and disposed of waste anywhere downwind and out of sight. As the modern world has encroached on these rural areas, plastic bags, bottles, and other non-organic waste (including chemical pesticides and other toxins) have become widespread, and the ability to farm large tracts of land has been compromised by debris. In response to these non-sustainable farming practices, this volunteer project has established a model farm that teaches new agricultural techniques that are better in tune with the land and will improve the farmers' long-term financial prospects.

You'll work in both educational outreach and in a hands-on role on the farm to promote sustainable farming and conservation techniques. Volunteers are 100 percent responsible for running and maintaining the demonstration farm. Villagers come to learn specific new techniques applicable to their circumstances and location. After working with a farmer at

Working at the sustainable model farm in Tamil Nadu

the demonstration project, volunteers then go to the farmer's land to help implement the new ideas. You'll be involved in developing compost fertilizer from farm waste and using earthworms (this clean compost is then taken to market and sold to support the farm projects). As part of a medicinal botany project, you'll help cultivate indigenous plants that have significant curative properties. New plant species are being grown in this nursery all the time as more is learned about how to grow beneficial species. You'll also learn about producing plant medicines on-site that are then distributed throughout the local communities.

Life on the project is easygoing aside from the physical labor, and your time with a host family will be a true opportunity for understanding the rural culture. Some English is spoken, so you'll get along fine while you pick up words and phrases in local dialects. Meals are provided by the host family, and there is a long lunch break in the heat of the day when you'll return to the host home before getting back to work later in the afternoon. Events are sometimes organized among the volunteers to foster team spirit, and weekends are yours to explore the region.

YOUR NEXT STEP: **Projects Abroad** (✆ **888/839-3535;** www.projects-abroad.org). A 2-week project, US$1,995, includes host family lodging, all meals, full insurance coverage, project support and training, and orientation upon arrival.

DON'T MISS: In the Tamil Nadu region, you'll find the temple of **Vaitheeswaran Koil** ("Lord Doctor" in the Tamil language). This Siva temple is dedicated to Vaidyanatheeswarar, the healer of all diseases, and his consort, Thaiyalnayaki. It is believed that a bath in the holy waters of the Siddhamirtham tank within the temple complex will cure all diseases. Nadi Jothidam, an astrology method based on your thumbprint, is a popular traditional skill here.

ⓘ www.tamilnadutourism.org

Farm & Ranch

Sustainable Agriculture & Food Security

Teach Farming in the Shadow of Kilimanjaro

Arusha, Tanzania

THE HIGHEST POINT IN AFRICA, MOUNT KILIMANJARO, RISES STARKLY OUT OF THE LANDSCAPE, a constant reminder of why people come through the gateway of Arusha. There's much that tourism dollars can't do, however, so volunteers can learn how to farm the land using sustainable methods and then share that knowledge with those who need it.

Many of Tanzania's rural farming regions have come close to exhausting the fertility of their land, and crops are suffering. Pesticides and chemical fertilizers have artificially bolstered short-term crop production but done incredible harm to the land's long-term growing potential. Fields are falling fallow and producing diminishing results year to year. This volunteer project aims to educate local farmers about ecologically sustainable methods to increase yield while caring for the land at the same time. The project advocates BIA (Biointensive Agriculture), which is a specialized technique using double-dug planting beds, local crops, organic composting, crop diversification, meticulous planting of symbiotic plant species, and water harvesting. The methods are also more affordable than chemical-based farming.

Educating farmers in Tanzania about sustainable practices

You'll learn the BIA techniques in easy terms that you'll then pass on and teach to the Tanzanian community. You'll work side by side with local farmers to implement new systems of small-scale sustainable farming. You'll also work the demonstration plots to keep them viable and provide follow-up support to farms in the area that have already been trained and adopted the new methods. Parallel to the agriculture project is the HIV/AIDS prevention focus of the program, educating HIV-affected families about this high-yield farming possibility and how that will increase the availability of better nutrition for immunity building. You may also pitch in and help with the distribution of small, portable "sack" gardens for families coping with HIV disease.

Your home base will be either at a local hostel in Arusha or immersed in a family home stay. All meals are provided, and you'll also have an intensive program of culture and language training. Your free time in the evenings and days off will be spent getting to know the village members more thoroughly, enjoying the community camaraderie. There are also day trips arranged for exploring the area, as well as the chance to spot wild animals on day safaris.

YOUR NEXT STEP: Global Service Corps (✆ **415/788-3666,** ext. 128; www.globalservicecorps.org). The 2-week program, US$1,170, includes accommodations with a host family or in a local hostel, all meals, airport pickup, project transportation, training and support, language and culture immersion program, day trips, and safari excursion.

DON'T MISS: One of the most famous landmarks of Tanzania is the **Ngorongoro Crater,** the world's largest unbroken, unflooded volcanic caldera. This giant sunken zone with a complete rim was formed more than 2 million years ago, and it teems with wildlife, including enormous migrating herds of zebra and wildebeest as well as the world's densest population of lions. The crater is 610m (2,001 ft.) deep, and its grassland floor covers more than 260 sq. m (100 sq. miles).

ⓘ www.tanzaniatouristboard.com

218 Farm & Ranch

Ranch Volunteer

I Wanna Be a Cowboy

Cody, Wyoming, USA

GEYSERS, GRIZZLY BEARS, THE WILD WEST, AND YELLOWSTONE NATIONAL PARK: THESE ARE THE images immediately associated with this sparsely populated state. Volunteers can indulge their inner cowboys (and cowgirls) here and become an integral part of a working ranch.

Volunteering on this working cattle ranch will be in some respects the pinnacle of the American Dream, bonding with your horse, seeing the wide open country from the saddle, running cattle, riding fences, ranch-style grub at chow time. You're very close to Yellowstone National Park, so the scenic quality just doesn't get any better. The ranch also hosts visitors, but don't expect a dude ranch experience. Even if you've never ridden before, you have a good chance of becoming an expert when you're done, and you will have worked awful hard.

You'll be paired with a horse appropriate to your riding experience, from novice to rodeo star, and thoroughly taught all the basics so you're completely at ease and safe while riding. The horse will get to know you as you get to know it, and you'll soon discover you're in harmony for long hours on the range. You'll be trail riding,

Working on a ranch in Cody, Wyoming

horse wrangling, cattle gathering, branding, and even participating in large cattle drives as you move the herds. There are plenty of on-the-ground chores to be done as well, from general cleaning up to tacking and untacking your horse and caring for the gear. Weekly activities will require your helpful hands, including veterinarian visits and vaccination days, inspecting and replacing/repairing fences that get damaged by nature and local wildlife, clinics, and riding alongside visiting groups of children and adults.

You'll be bunking up in shared two-person or four-person simple cabins on the property, and the group takes meals together at a central dining/kitchen building. There are showers and laundry facilities to wash off the day's dirt. You can opt out of a half-day or a full-day's work (cattle and horses don't take weekends off, so the ranch is in full swing 7 days a week) to relax and recuperate (with that much saddle time, you'll discover leg and rear end muscles you never knew you had) or explore the surrounding region. If you've rented a car (not required) you can head to Yellowstone for a picnic, the Grand Tetons National Park, Jackson Hole for dining and nightlife, or nearby Thermopolis for a regenerative soak in the world's largest hot springs.

YOUR NEXT STEP: Real Gap Experience (✆ **866/939-9088;** www.realgap.com). A 3-week stay, US$2,799, includes cabin lodging, all meals, detailed horseback instruction and coaching plus full project orientation, all western tack and your level-appropriate horse, and 24-hour project support.

DON'T MISS: Since you're in a Western state of mind, head to **Cheyenne** and the Wyoming State Museum, dedicated to the history and culture of the Rocky Mountain West. Discover why Wyoming is known as the "Equality State" and how local women were the first in America to vote, serve on juries, and hold public office.

ⓘ www.wyomingtourism.org

6 Building Better Communities

An Armenian mason restoring stonework in Gyumr

Building a Community Center

Relax at the Beach in Your Downtime

Salvador, Brazil

THERE ARE MANY REASONS BRAZIL IS ONE OF THE MOST POPULAR COUNTRIES IN SOUTH America: the longest beaches, the biggest rainforest, and arguably the best weather—if you favor sunny and warm. Salvador—with its colonial core, lively music scene and African and indigenous influences—encapsulates the Brazilian spirit.

In this small village just outside of Salvador, the 500 residents have decided that a community center is their highest priority. They face plenty of other issues—from poverty and unemployment to a lack of sewage and water treatment—but a central meeting place will allow them to better address other issues facing them. One of the center's most important uses will be as a place for local artisans to market and sell their crafts—a major source of income for many families. Empowering artists will preserve the local traditions and heritage and work toward a collective sales project that is projected to guarantee income for 200 people and train future generations of craftspeople.

The space will be built from the ground up, so over the course of a week you could be framing, cladding, roofing, walling, finishing, painting, and anything else to get the space ready for village use. When you put your hammer down, additional parallel projects include teaching first aid, basic computer lessons, basic English, or gardening. A community garden is taking shape, and the village concocts a weekly "Big Soup" to help feed the lowest income families. The amount of work completed by previous volunteers will determine the focus of your work (once the community center is done, work rehabilitating the school or building a secondary school will be a great contribution to the village).

Home will be a small inn nearby (with functioning plumbing and intermittent electricity, unlike several residences). The volunteer group prepares fresh, healthy local meals communally. In your free time, explore the incredible environment with hikes on the beach, surfing, and local Salvadoran celebrations. You'll have chances to learn local cooking techniques, woodcarving, capoeira dance moves, and making the village delicacy—ice cream with local fruit.

YOUR NEXT STEP: Globe Aware (© **877/588-4562;** www.globeaware.org). A 1-week assignment, US$1,350, covers small inn accommodations, all meals, cultural programs and fun learning experiences, construction training and supervision, and full project support.

DON'T MISS: After spending your time in the rustic conditions of this small village, for contrast, visit **Brasilia,** the ultra-modern city that looks like the set of a sci-fi movie. Great curvy public buildings designed in the 1950s by Oscar Niemeyer and Lucio Costa make this capital city as mod and space age as the Shanghai skyline.

ⓘ www.turismo.gov.br

220 Construction & Manual Labor

Upgrade Community Facilities

Help Out in Remote Andean Town

Tumbatu, Ecuador

A STRONG BODY AND MIND, AS WELL AS A WILLINGNESS TO ENDURE RUGGED CONDITIONS, WILL be an asset in this isolated, mountainous part of Ecuador. Residents in Tumbatu are looking for help with a wide range of community improvement projects.

In the northernmost sector of Ecuador, the province of Carchi is home to Afro-Ecuadorian communities who maintain a strong connection to traditions that set them apart from much of the rest of the nation. Marginalized from the bulk of Ecuador, this community has been economically challenged for generations. The villagers have partnered with this service organization to accomplish several community improvement projects. Volunteers work side by side with locals on irrigation systems, creating cement benches in a public area, building a laundry facility, and general maintenance and refurbishing of several community buildings. Past projects have met with great success, broadening the scope of future projects to be undertaken.

You'll build forms and mix and pour concrete, work on grading the soil surrounding the new permanent structures, help install framing and walls for brand-new buildings, and likely complete enough of the task so that you'll be painting before you head home. This is a high-altitude location, so you'll get tired more quickly than you might be used to. Be sure your fitness level is appropriate to take on some strenuous work. You can be a novice at construction, just not an unhealthy novice.

The group meets up in Quito, where you'll have a morning to explore the capital's markets and museums before traveling by bus to Tumbatu. When you get to the village, you'll meet your host family, with whom you'll stay in relatively rustic dwellings (don't count on indoor plumbing or showers). Local cooks prepare the team's meals, and you can take turns helping with cleanup. The group's free time is an opportunity for community bonding with your new family and neighbors, and nearby towns offer some enticing opportunities for a weekend day, as do nearby hikes to waterfalls and natural hot springs. Artisans from this region are famous for textile work, so you may want to scout around for something to bring home.

YOUR NEXT STEP: Global Citizens Network (✆ **800/644-9292;** www.globalcitizens.org). A 10-day project, US$1,600, includes home stay lodging, meals, in-country travel, insurance, training and support, and a donation to the local community projects.

DON'T MISS: The city of **Banos** is called Piece of Heaven and has a harmonious mix of entertainment, nightlife, and spirituality. The sedate region appeals to New Age seekers and traditional healers, sybarites who find the plentiful spas and natural thermal springs too inviting to pass up, and adventure sports fans (who enjoy kayaking, mountain biking, rafting, and hiking). Everyone walks the Route of the Falls, where every forest turn yields a new view of one of the 60 beautiful waterfalls.

ⓘ www.ecuador.us

Construction & Manual Labor

Restoration of Medieval Village

Two Weeks in Provence

Saint Victor la Coste, France

You'll step back in time in this medieval village, learning an old, dying skill—stone masonry. And because it will be summer and you'll be in the Côtes du Rhône wine region, close to Avignon, there are some very appealing opportunities for well-deserved relaxation and touring when your restoration work is done.

In the rolling hills of Provence, tiny medieval villages dot the horizon in every direction. Many original structures have begun to fall down, so stucco or cinder-block homes are built up alongside the original buildings. This project is dedicated to restoring the grand stone structures, using traditional medieval building materials and methods and giving international volunteers the time of their lives while doing it. Stone masonry, stone cutting, tiling, paving, and dry stone walling are all going to be added to your construction vocabulary as you help restore the harmony of the homes and larger buildings, allowing the simplicity of stone walls to re-instill that Provençal sense of magic in the hills. This project serves the community being rebuilt while providing an intensive learning experience, as traditional stone mason technique is applied to local materials.

Your project will vary depending on which buildings are underway when you arrive, but it's all based on stonework. You'll clear rubble from collapsed walls, tile roofs, lay floor tile (more stone), construct arches and vaults, and plaster the interior of rooms. Work is hard but satisfying as your technique, alien at first when being taught by local craftsmen, becomes more refined and you watch daily evidence of your efforts bear fruit as a wall is completed, a roof trimmed, a door hung, and a family having a homecoming. Restoration is also being done on rampart walls, village paths, and a medieval castle.

You'll be caught up in the swirl of past and present as you'll live in some of the restored stone houses of the village in double rooms. The houses are set amid courtyards and patios, shaded by trees, and connected by cobblestone streets. The intent in restoring the heritage of these towns is to make them timeless, and you'll soon drop into the languorous pace of Provençal life. Meals are prepared by the staff chef and served communally with the team. In your free time (after massaging your weary muscles), you can explore the countryside and neighboring villages. An excursion with the group is scheduled to tour the region and its lively markets and Roman ruins.

YOUR NEXT STEP: La Sabranenque (✆ **+33/466 500 505;** www.sabranenque.com). A 2-week project, US$750, includes rustic home accommodations, all meals, training and supervision, project support, and a local excursion.

DON'T MISS: Head to the beach and the gypsy meeting spot **Les Saintes Maries de la Mer** in the Camargue Parc Naturel. You'll get there through sprawling plains with salt ponds, flamingos, and pastures with white bulls and white horses. If you time your visit right, you'll see the running of the bulls through the main boulevard with the Mediterranean lapping the shore just below.

ⓘ www.provencetourism.com

Community Construction Projects

Transforming Through Tools

Keea, Ghana

FOR THOSE WHO WANT LOCAL PEOPLE INVOLVED IN THEIR COMMUNITIES ARE BUILT, TAKE heed: The construction projects in Keea are dictated in order of priority by those who live here. And when the weekend rolls around, you'll be centrally located to reach any corner of this West African country.

Construction Projects Ghana, in a joint effort with a local community organization, undertakes building and restoration work in the ongoing development of the Keea region. Several projects are underway at any given time, from building schools to renovating public buildings to installing an expanded solar/electric energy grid system. Qualified builders, architects, civil engineers, and complete novices work side by side with local community members, each given a task appropriate to their skills to increase the viability of the town. Creating safe spaces for learning and community building are the highest priority, and helping individuals and families repair and maintain their homes is also an element of the work. Bringing electrical power into the town's homes has had a transformative effect on residents, and that work continues as solar energy sources are added to the system to foster environmental responsibility and renewable resources.

Your days start early—you want most of the hard labor to be completed before the brutal sun gets high in the sky. By the end of your project, you'll be comfortable with hand tools and building techniques, even if you can't currently hang a calendar on the wall. You'll be given specific work projects each day, from painting or plastering to framing, roofing, and electrical work.

As the heat of the day makes intense work illogical, hammers and nails are set aside and planning and resupplying efforts are undertaken before you head out to nap, explore, and spend time with new friends in the afternoons and evenings. The workweek leaves weekends open to explore the Ghanaian countryside and neighboring villages. The team stays together in a shared project house close to the building sites. The group house is basic but has electricity, running water (an eventual goal for every home in Keea), and a staff member who cooks and cleans for the volunteer group. Your English-speaking Keea project leader was born here, knows everyone in the community, and is a great resource for suggestions for free-time hikes and exploratory excursions.

YOUR NEXT STEP: Twin Work & Volunteer Abroad (✆ **800/80 483 80;** www.workandvolunteer.com). A 2-week project, US$816, includes shared group accommodations in a project house, meals, training, and full local support from on-site staff.

DON'T MISS: A particularly important cultural and political icon for Ghanaians is Dr. William Edward Burghardt Du Bois, and the Accra **Du Bois Memorial Center for Pan-Africa Culture** has a research library and manuscript collection as well as the grave of this famous African-American scholar. It is a humble home preserved and dedicated to the life of this international champion of black emancipation.

ⓘ www.touringghana.com

Construction & Manual Labor

Community Medical Center

Build Health Care Facility Near Lake Victoria

Odienya, Kenya

ACCESS TO RELIABLE AND SAFE MEDICAL CARE IS A UNIVERSAL NEED, AND THIS PROJECT IN Kenya needs volunteers with caring hearts, open minds, and good physical conditioning. At the end of your stay, this is one of the best countries in Africa for going on safari.

The Luo are the third-largest tribe in Kenya and predominantly farm and raise livestock for sustenance in this southwestern region. Villagers hope to have a health center, so this project will work with locals to make that happen. Once completed, the brick health center will serve an area with 10,000 people and will be adjacent to a school for AIDS orphans. The eventual goal includes a main treatment building, maternity ward, male and female wards, staff residences, and support structures. It's a multiphase plan that will be rolled out over time—but the most important thing is to get started right away so medical services can come to Odienya.

After your first night in Nairobi, it is several hours' drive through some rugged terrain to get to the project site. Once situated in Odienya, it's time to get to work. The buildings are brick, so the repetitive work of bricklaying will fill your days. Other tasks will depend on the progress of previous teams of volunteers. You may be working on interior spaces, painting, roofing, flooring, hanging doors and windows, or working on plumbing or electrical systems, or serving as an assistant to more experienced construction workers. The tools are provided; you just bring your energy to the equation.

The volunteer team stays together in one or two local group homes near the health center. While your commute is easy, the accommodations are basic—don't expect to always have running water or electricity. You'll pitch in as sous chef or on cleaning detail, but a local cook will do the lion's share of the cooking. Past volunteer teams have found free time a great bonding experience as they head out together to explore. Lake Victoria is not far, and several nearby villages are worth some weekend surveying. Your first and last nights in Nairobi will be at a hotel.

YOUR NEXT STEP: Global Citizens Network 🎗 (✆ **800/644-9292;** www.globalcitizens.org). A 3-week project, US$2,425, includes shared lodging in a community house (hotel in Nairobi), meals, training, local support, and in-country transportation.

DON'T MISS: So many of our images of wild Kenya are of giant migrating herds and big cats—but the wild waters of **Watamu National Park,** a beautiful Kenyan beach, are off limits for fishing, so the exotic fish populations thrive here. The coral reef is in good shape, unlike so many around the world, and the hypnotic big whale sharks come to visit on a regular basis.

ⓘ www.tourism.go.ke

Construction & Manual Labor

Building Schools & Community Spaces

Step Across the Border

Tijuana, Mexico

LIFE IN THIS BORDER TOWN HAS A COMPLICATED AND SOMETIMES TROUBLED HISTORY, BUT ITS proximity to San Diego makes it an easy place to get to. During downtime volunteers flock to the Tijuana River Valley Park in California, home to 340 bird species.

This community improvement program is structured differently than most. Volunteers pay a fee for meals, accommodation, learning programs, and so on, and they also raise funds through donations to purchase building supplies for the project. The community's end result is not only help with the labor on a building project but also the materials, so a school or a community center springs up without taxing the already cash-strapped village. Located at the US/Mexico border, each year more than 600 volunteers participate to the direct benefit of thousands of Mexican children. The building projects are tackled together with community members: they include building new schools and community centers or enhancing programs for existing community buildings.

You and your fellow volunteers (several groups do this project together, making it a great choice if you'd like to go with a team of family or friends, but individuals also are very involved) will be busy building all day. The construction tasks are easily learned, and you'll be trained for whatever element of work you're assigned. The program runs as a "service-learning" program, so in addition to erecting new structures, your interaction with the locals working with you will begin to open your eyes to the culture and complexities of life at the border. Presentations and cultural activities will also expand this understanding. Spanish-speaking ability is helpful, but it's not required for this to be a well-rounded learning experience.

The volunteer team lives together at the project house in Tijuana, and traditional Mexican meals are prepared for the group by local cooks. Participants are met at the border in San Diego (where you can leave your car) or at the airport and taken to the project home base. When the work day is done, a full schedule of lectures and cultural activities presented by university professors and local experts awaits, addressing issues such as immigration, the environment, public health, poverty, human rights, history, and politics. Excursions to tour the border facilities, the Tijuana cultural center, and other local sites of interest are also scheduled. The participation time can be a long weekend or up to 1 week to truly have an immersion experience.

YOUR NEXT STEP: Los Niños International (✆ **267/419-8318;** www.losninosintl.org). An extended weekend, US$270, or a 1-week project, US$450, includes shared group housing, three meals daily, lectures and cultural activities, transportation from the border or San Diego airport to the project base, and full training and support. In addition, the volunteer team is responsible as a group to raise US$500 per week for building supplies to perpetuate the projects, so your required portion of that will depend on the number of volunteers signed up at the same time.

DON'T MISS: After your time in Tijuana, head west and down the coast of Baja to **Rosarito Beach,** a mellow little beach town just a short distance away. Don't leave without trying several restaurant or cafe versions of fish tacos. You can even be "King of the World" at Fox Studios Baja, originally built for James Cameron's *Titanic*, which hosts the world's largest filming water tanks.

ⓘ www.seetijuana.com

Construction & Manual Labor

Tibetan Community Improvement

Aiding Exiles

Jampaling, Nepal

WAKE TO THE SOUND OF CHANTING. VISIT BUDDHIST MONUMENTS. BREATHE DEEPLY. GAPE at Mount Everest. You're in sacred but also well-traversed territory here, as these mountains are a haven for trekkers who come from around the world.

In the shadow of the Annapurna Mountains, four villages became settlement spots for faithful Tibetans who followed the Dalai Lama after he was driven from Tibet by the Chinese in 1959. While their spiritual leader found a new home in India, these followers made their way to the warm countryside of Pokhara. Each of these villages has about 1,000 people and modest community structures, including a school, health clinic, monastery, seniors home, and carpet factory. Volunteers have worked in partnership with the village communities to ascertain priorities for development, and then worked to bring those plans to fruition. The focus is now on roof repair for several buildings, building a public bathhouse, renovating an irrigation canal, refurbishing a drainage system, creating a recycling center, and building a vocational training center.

Countless and varied job duties will keep you busy. One day may be all about working on water projects, with refurbishing drainage and irrigation, clearing existing canals and ditches, and repairing or laying new plumbing. The next day might be all about framing: putting up walls for a community bathing facility or a workroom for training new tailors or a large studio space for furniture building. Next day, you may find yourself on the roof as you tear away tile and tar paper from leaky areas to replace them in time for the next rainy season. Some of the business plans need some finessing as well, so perhaps it's time for a brainstorming session with villagers about how best to undertake a new venture like recycling or other job training to fill the gap left by the plummeting carpet business (most members of the community speak English).

It takes a while to get to Pokhara, so the first and last days of the trip are in Kathmandu. You'll stay with the volunteer team in a group project house, where you'll share meals prepared by a local cook. Downtime will be spent bonding with the team and the community and likely banding together to take a side trip to go rafting in the rivers of the mountain range, sailing on Phewa Lake, and exploring the other regional villages, temples, and museums.

YOUR NEXT STEP: Global Citizens Network 🎗 (✆ **800/644-9292;** www.globalcitizens.org). A 3-week project, US$2,500, includes project house shared accommodations, meals prepared by a cook, training and project support, medical and evacuation insurance, in-country transportation, and a donation to the local community project.

DON'T MISS: You're better able to serve others when you take care of yourself, so try some yoga in the Himalayan Kingdom. The **Patanjali Yoga Centre** is one of the most respected centers anywhere for pure Ashtanga yoga. You can take classes, then return to a hotel in Kathmandu or stay in residence at the facility for a few days at only about US$10 a day for meditation, yoga, philosophy, diet, and holistic health, as well as trekking in the stunning surroundings.

ⓘ www.welcomenepal.com

226 Construction & Manual Labor

Transforming a Former Military Base

Giving Birth to Hope

Bethlehem, Palestine

A PLACE KNOWN ALMOST AS MUCH FOR ITS POLITICAL AND RELIGIOUS TURMOIL AS FOR BEING the birthplace of Jesus Christ is trying to turn over a new leaf. Visitors come from all over the world to help improve the quality of life through community construction projects.

The Israeli army vacated Eish Al-Ghurab military base, so the municipality has taken the opportunity to create a centralized service area here for the community. Construction is underway to create a kindergarten classroom, a parking facility, youth houses, gardens, and a hospital/medical center. Volunteers help the citizens of Bethlehem in completing these and other construction projects, turning this formerly forbidden zone into an area of hope. Coming from around the world, representing many languages, cultures, and spiritual traditions, an International volunteer team gathers to show their commitment to the improvement of living conditions for all people.

Your mornings are spent on construction sites working side by side with Palestinians to make this a viable cultural hub for Bethlehem. You'll be assigned a new project each day, turning spaces into school rooms and youth residences, and also creating a medical center/hospital building. You'll also put your green thumb to work, clearing open space for vegetable and herb gardens, and planting and weeding the garden spaces that are already growing. You may also spend a day painting or cleaning existing and recently completed buildings.

You'll stay with the team in a project house or apartment on-site. Meals are shared with the team, and everybody pitches in for preparation and cleanup. Afternoon and evenings will be spent in cultural programs showing you Palestinian culture and the context of life during occupation. You'll visit refugee camps in Bethlehem, aid associations, lectures, workshops with politicians and educators, and meet plenty of locals who will share their stories of living through the crisis in the Middle East. Excursions to West Bank cities such as Ramallah and Hebron are scheduled.

YOUR NEXT STEP: Canadian Alliance for Development Initiatives and Projects (✆ **604/628-7400**; www.cadip.org) A 2-week project, US$265, includes shared group housing, meals, project training, and a thorough experiential learning program of cultural activities and excursions. An additional US$189 donation is paid directly to the non-profit host organization when you arrive in Bethlehem.

DON'T MISS: The oldest inhabited city on Earth, with ruins dating back 10,000 years, is **Jericho,** the "city of palms." Palm trees flourish here because of the abundance of water from nearby fresh springs. Being close to the Dead Sea and the Jordan River, the city is more than 396m (1,300 ft.) below sea level and warm in every season (perfect for hiking and touring).

ⓘ www.visit-palestine.com

Construction & Manual Labor

Masonry at Eco Center

Sweat & Stone

Kücükkuyu, Turkey

IN TURKEY, EROSION IS TAKING ITS TOLL ON SOME OF THE COUNTRY'S BEST AGRICULTURAL LAND. Toiling in the hot sun to rebuild olive groves is hard work, but the crop is so important here that it's home to Turkey's only olive oil museum.

The organization leading this project has already completed an education/ecological center here in the Kaz Mountains. The next step for development is to shore up the surrounding olive orchards and fields, where erosion has begun washing away the rich topsoil from the steep hillsides. Volunteers will be tutored by a stone master in the techniques of masonry and building dry stone walls. The terraces being built to "tier" the fields will stop the washing away of nutrient-rich soil and improve the viability of the land, helping improve not only the eco center but the economic status of the village as a whole.

The work (usually for five to six hours a day) will be hard as you shape and stack stone to create walls. The walls serve as land tiers, so there's a fair amount of digging and cutting into the hillside to be done. You'll grade and level the land, clear large rocks, plant or re-plant displaced trees or crops, and construct the walls themselves. The view down to the Aegean Sea is gorgeous, and the new eco center is a great base of operations for the project. The villagers are on the whole dependent on agriculture and livestock, so improving the yield of even one field zone betters the situation for the entire community as well as directly supporting the education goals of the center.

Living conditions are rustic. You'll be camping in provided tents or sleeping on the floor at the center, so bring your sleeping bag. Vegetarian meals are provided, but the volunteer group members will cook and clean up. Evenings are free, and 1 day off is built into each week of work. Together the volunteer corps can decide how best to spend the free day: excursions to local villages or the nearest city, trekking excursions or visits to the seashore, or simply relaxing and recharging for the big week ahead. Your group will often be invited to celebrations in the village (expect to dance—a lot) and to share meals in the homes of those who are hosting you in the community.

YOUR NEXT STEP: Service Civil International (✆ **434/336-3545;** www.sci-ivs.org). A 3-week project, US$235, includes camping accommodations in provided tents or on the floor of the ecological center, meals shared and prepared by the volunteer group, skills training in construction and farming, project support, insurance, and free-time excursions. An additional US$38 donation is paid directly to the host organization upon arrival.

DON'T MISS: You'll think you've arrived on the moon when you visit **Cappadocia,** an astounding landscape of towering chimney rocks and vast fields of bleached volcanic rock perforated like Swiss cheese. Homes, churches, and monasteries are dug into the soft stone and entire settlements lived (and still live) in remarkable and often elegant caves.

ⓘ www.tourismturkey.org

Resurrect a Coal-Mining Town

Preserve National Historic Landmark District

Virginia City, Montana, USA

THERE ARE DOZENS OF OLD MINING TOWNS ACROSS THE UNITED STATES, BUT FEW CAN BOAST a national historic landmark designation—even if it needs some significant refurbishment. Your efforts will help rebuild this Southwestern Montana town, which was once part of the gold rush that led to the settlement of the Western United States.

This Rocky Mountain mining town is looking up thanks to volunteers working year after year to restore and rebuild the late-1800s architecture. There was gold in those hills, and that meant it became *the* place to find fortune. Now the gold is mostly gone, and there are only about 150 citizens of Virginia City remaining. Many homes in the region are in disrepair, and this organization is refurbishing them one by one to help beef up the preservation of this National Historic Landmark district. Brick, log, lumber, slate, shingle—you'll have your chance to work with all of them.

A typical project house has been ignored for decades, and while from the front it looks like a run-down but sound building, it has no roof. The first step is to restore the roof pitch, reroof, and shore up the entire structure for future work. You'll learn historical preservation techniques, including how to stabilize a structure, use period tools and materials, and undertake general restoration. You'll spend a week working outside all day in Montana, where temperatures can vary wildly from day to night, so be prepared for any weather.

The Susan Marr House in Virginia City, one of many buildings in need of repair

This project does not include lodging, meals, or transportation, so you'll make your own arrangements for a place to stay and dining plans in Virginia City. It's a 5-day program, so the weekend is yours to explore, relax, or go home with the satisfaction of a job well done.

YOUR NEXT STEP: Heritage Conservation Network (✆ **303/444-0128;** www.heritageconservation.net). A 5-day project, US$650, covers workshop materials, instruction in historical restoration and construction, and insurance. You will arrange your own travel, accommodations, and meals.

DON'T MISS: It is a chapter of American history that few predicted. In Custer's Last Stand during the Battle of Little Bighorn, the Lakota, Cheyenne, and Arapaho warriors defeated the Seventh Cavalry in what the US military assumed would be an easy victory for them. The **Little Bighorn Battlefield National Monument** is a national park in commemoration of this significant fight. It took too many decades, but there will now be memorials to both the cavalry lost *and* the Native American lives lost on this ground.

ⓘ www.visitmt.com

Construction & Manual Labor **229**

Rebuild & Restore

Nurturing a National Park

Yellowstone, Montana, USA

THEY DON'T CALL IT BIG SKY COUNTRY FOR NOTHING. YOU MAY FEEL SMALL COMPARED TO the powerful landscape and amazing array of wildlife that you can encounter in Yellowstone National Park, but your efforts to rehabilitate the area will make a big difference.

In one of the world's most awe-inspiring tracts of land, Yellowstone National Park and the Gallatin National Forest, volunteers and park services personnel work together to restore historic buildings and improve open areas for the benefit of the indigenous animals. In the backcountry, while remote and mostly untraveled, expansion has driven animal populations into the few remaining open regions of public land in numbers that threaten their vitality. The project's 1,214ha (3,000-acre) ranchland is home to grizzly bears and is a migration corridor for elk. In addition to wildlife, there are historic buildings on this land that need to be rebuilt and preserved. Over the 80 years since these ranch and cabin buildings were first erected, neglect and nature have been cruel. Fields are strewn with rusted farm implements and rolls of wire fencing that need to be removed to make it a safe habitat for grazing animals, and the main ranch and backcountry cabins need dramatic improvement, as do public campground facilities.

You'll work long hard days, mostly outdoors, in this regal country as you restore residential cabins, rebuild horse stables, shore up a water turbine cabin, rebuild a bunkhouse, and do land improvement projects for sectors of the ranchlands. You might be up to wildly different tasks on different days, from rebuilding a porch or replacing a roof to installing fencing and doing grounds maintenance at campsites.

Preserving a historical log building in Yellowstone, Montana

Interpretive signs will need installing, trails will need improving, and sheds will need rebuilding. If it's falling down, you and your fellow teammates will put it back up.

Lodging is dormitory style in a group house, and meals are prepared and shared together. There are some historical presentations and guided hikes with a naturalist or ranger, but for the most part during your free time you'll want to roam—it's just you and Big Sky Country.

YOUR NEXT STEP: Amizade (© **304/ 293-6049**; www.amizade.org). A 2-week project, US$1,326, includes shared lodging, meals, training and on-site staff support, cultural activities and guide, and a donation to the project partners.

DON'T MISS: You've already been in beautiful backcountry woods and meadowlands, so why not add one of the most pristine lakes to your checklist and spend some time in **Glacier National Park.** More than 1,127km (700 miles) of hiking trails surround this mirror-surfaced rugged terrain that looks like the gods shattered a mirror (there are more than 130 named lakes in the park).

ⓘ www.visitmt.com

Construction & Manual Labor 

Renovate Homes

Work Hand-in-Hand with Local Young People

Fayette County, West Virginia, USA

SERIOUS HIKERS COME FROM AROUND THE WORLD TO TRAVEL THE MORE THAN 3,200KM (2,000 miles) of the Appalachian Trail. You'll develop a strong attachment to the trail, and its many mountain peaks, as you work nearby training West Virginian youth in home construction work.

Appalachia is a beautiful region of West Virginia that has not enjoyed the same economic growth as most of the rest of the country—much of the area is a federal empowerment zone because of high levels of poverty and poor job prospects. You'll build relationships along with homes, as you work with and mentor young people from the community. You may be learning construction techniques alongside the young participants, but it's the role modeling and coaching you'll do without even trying that is the real benefit. The project at hand is repairing and rebuilding four coal company houses so that they become viable residences for low-income families.

Your tasks are two-fold. You're doing some light demolition to get back to the good bones of these four houses, cleaning up, and then rebuilding and fortifying the structures, modernizing where possible. Everything from structural work, roofing, and recladding the exterior to paint and plaster, wiring, and installing appliances will need to be done. The most important part is that as you are learning, so are the teens by your side, and while it may be a weeklong service vacation for you, for these young folks, these are life skills and a new vocation. Together you'll tackle the work at hand, but you'll also tackle life issues and concerns as you talk and share while you build. Your presence, even without a formalized program, is mentoring, and is a service greater for the kids than for the houses.

You'll be bunking with other volunteers in dormitory-style shared housing in Beards Fork, West Virginia. Local cooks prepare hearty American fare for the dinners, while you're responsible for breakfast and lunch. The Appalachians are waiting for you to explore in your downtime, as you hike, river romp (tubing), and just enjoy the beautiful nature.

YOUR NEXT STEP: Global Volunteers (✆ **651/407-6100;** www.globalvolunteers.org). A 1-week project, US$995, includes shared dormitory accommodations, one meal daily, project training and support, and airport pickup.

DON'T MISS: You'll shake your head and rub your eyes as you get to the end of a winding Appalachian road and arrive at the **Palace of Gold.** The Indian architecture, complete with domes and stained glass, was built by devotees of Swami Srila Prabhupada, the founder of the International Society for Krishna Consciousness. The marble, teak, precious carvings, inlaid stones, and gilded decor, along with the lush rose garden, stand in mind-boggling contrast to the wild rural Appalachian country.

ⓘ www.wvtourism.com

Build Medical Clinic & Teaching Center

Free Laughs

Pocahontas County, West Virginia, USA

Were you voted class clown? Are you quick with a clever comeback? Unafraid to make a fool of yourself in front of other people? This volunteer project personifies play and work, geared toward levity and laughter, which can often be the best medicine.

The work done by Dr. Patch Adams was changing the world long before (and since) the movie about him was made. Finding ways to heal illness and mitigate pain through laughter and joy completely shakes the medical belief system to its core. All around the world, the Gesundheit! Institute has traveled near and far, opening free hospitals or providing free field medicine, often with red noses, funny clothes, and slapstick silliness that makes everyone feel better. On a 128ha (317-acre) farm in West Virginia, a retreat center and model hospital/clinic is waiting to be created—with your help. Waterfalls, a pond, hardwood trees, and open spaces assure the hospital is set in an ideal environment for health.

To be in a proper Gesundheit! frame of mind, you'll have to take play as seriously as you do work. Much has already been done, with the building of a workshop space, a volunteer dwelling, a staff house, support structures, some landscaping, and more—but a hospital is a gigantic project. No matter what the workload is for the day, you can bet that it'll be done unconventionally and with a level of irreverence and humor that most work in the world could use. The group will get ridiculous together, and get a lot done as well. In addition to construction projects, everyone rotates on cooking and cleaning detail, carrying water, chopping wood, and all the rest of the tasks to keep a group laughing and productive. There's carpentry, woodworking, painting, organic gardening, fencing, transplanting, grounds maintenance, invasive plant removal, and the most important task each of you will take on—clowning.

Your work for 35 hours a week is in exchange for room and board. Volunteers sleep in shared accommodations, and all meals are prepared by the group. Meals tend to be in costume and have a theme, and you may spend free time enjoying cosmic bowling, juggling, and doing the amazing work of visiting local hospitals, nursing homes, and the pregnant women's prison to spread some cheer.

YOUR NEXT STEP: Patch Adams Gesundheit! Institute (✆ **217/278-3933;** www.patchadams.org). Your work is the only charge for room and board for this project (though a financial donation never hurts). Group lodging, shared meals, and lots of fun and support will make the time fly.

DON'T MISS: If you're no stranger to spas, go to the source. Not just the source where natural springs bubble up from the rocks in **Berkeley Springs State Park,** but *the* source, as in this was the first West Virginia spa to open to the public in 1756. There's even the outdoor limestone bathtub where George Washington soaked away his aches and cares.

ⓘ www.wvtourism.com

Clean Water Projects

Potable Water for Villages

Let It Flow

Yaounde, Cameroon

THE WORK WILL BE RIGOROUS, BUT THE PAYOFF FOR THOSE WHO YOU HELP IN CAMEROON IS huge, where access to clean potable water is critically important. While you work you'll learn just what it's like to live in a rural African village.

The organization running the project has many outreach programs, with an intensive focus on improving the lives of the poverty stricken and disadvantaged. Sustainable development, education, health care, malaria prevention, HIV/AIDS education, women's oppression issues, child labor troubles, political awakening, vocational training, and computer training are all issues addressed by this powerhouse local organization. Since all life is dependent on water, the clean water programs are at the very foundation of all their other life-enhancing programs.

Being a volunteer with a focus on water issues is a two-level project. Physical work needs to be done on the drinking water infrastructure, and education needs to be provided concerning hygiene, conservation, health, and community awareness about water issues. The communities of the region still lack a consistent source of potable water. Bio-sand filtering systems have been introduced on a limited basis,

A volunteer on a potable water project visiting students in Cameroon

resulting in better health and nutrition for the community. Local technicians have been trained, and the materials are available—all that's needed is your able hands and energy to work with the locals and fellow volunteers. The work involves digging, moving wheelbarrows and piping; all of it will be taught, and all of it will make more families better able to thrive. Thirty filters have been built for these communities thus far and many more are needed. The good news is that this program helps all the other health and welfare projects have a better chance of success.

You will live with an English-speaking host family (Cameroon is bilingual, English and French) with one or more other volunteers. You'll learn about local culture and traditions, food and cooking techniques, and a bit of the local language as you also help the family members practice their English. You'll likely be sleeping on the floor and will provide your own sleeping bag and mosquito net. Don't count on electricity—several homes have power, but several others do not. Two meals daily are provided by your host family, and in some placements you may want to try a few modest restaurants. Your free time will likely be spent recharging for the next day, and enjoying the camaraderie of the village community and your fellow volunteers, with whom you may want to visit neighboring villages.

YOUR NEXT STEP: Life & Water Development Group—Cameroon (✆ **+ 237/ 77 71 62 88**; www.lwdgc-africa.org). A minimum 2-week commitment is required, but you can stay longer if you'd like. Costs are minimal: US$60 a week for host family accommodations and US$50 a week for food. Training, supervision, and local staff support are provided, as are airport transfers and project transportation.

DON'T MISS: It's easy to get off the grid in Cameroon's **Dja Faunal Reserve.** One of the continent's largest protected rainforests, 90 percent of the nearly impenetrable wild acreage remains undisturbed. The reserve is for all practical purposes a giant green island almost completely encircled by the Dja River and her tributaries. There is incredible biodiversity here, and five threatened mammal species (of 107 identified species) call this protected reserve home.

ⓘ www.cameroon-tourism.com

233 Clean Water Projects

Rehabilitate Water Resources

Keeping It Fresh

Bedrichov, Czech Republic

You'll be based in the northernmost tip of the Czech Republic, but centrally located within easy reach of the best of Eastern Europe—you'll be 2 hours from Prague, the city of spires, and a day trip away from Germany and southern Poland too.

The last decades of the 20th century were not kind to the water table in the Eastern Bloc countries. The mining and processing of coal, the region's major fuel source, led to acid rain, which damaged more than two-thirds of the mountain headwaters, killed forests, and decimated the freshwater fish population. The planet is adept at healing herself, so things are slowly getting better. The leading scientists for this project have helped develop the Czech Republic's management plans for mountain watersheds, and their work continues with volunteers like you. Together you can work to rehabilitate the mountain ecosystem to protect and begin to heal the water resources. The mountains, while still reeling from ecological damage, remain a stunning environment in which to work. They are not strip-mined or clear-cut—this is still a dense forest of Norway spruce, beech, and silver fir.

With the guidance of the researchers, you'll be trained to collect water samples from streams, lakes, and other sources, measure temperature, pH levels, conductivity, and oxygen amounts. Fish and other aquatic organisms have been reintroduced, so you'll be catching and testing them to determine their health, and as you hike through the woods you'll evaluate tree health, collect soil and plant samples, and record erosion measurements. You'll also learn lab techniques, run tests, and compile your data for reporting. You don't need to be a science expert, but by the time you go home you'll certainly know your way around an environmental sciences lab.

How about a 200-year-old mountain farmhouse in an historic village to call home for a while? You'll return each night to TV, laundry, an Internet connection, a sauna, and comfy double rooms. Everyone enjoys an easy breakfast, packs a lunch for the field, and after washing up from the workday heads to a neighboring restaurant for traditional Czech cuisine. In your unscheduled time, this is a hiker's paradise, so you can work up a sweat on the hills, tackle the same terrain on a mountain bike, or visit neighboring castles, museums, and picturesque villages.

YOUR NEXT STEP: Earthwatch (✆ 800/776-0188; www.earthwatch.org). This 15-day excursion, US$2,750, includes accommodations with shared rooms, meals, project transportation, field and lab training, and full project support. A US$35 Earthwatch membership is required.

DON'T MISS: Are you a fan of modernist architecture? Most people think of the beautiful Gothic architecture of Prague, where every surface of public buildings seems decorated like a wedding cake. For some clean lines, in Brno, the **Villa Tugendhat** is the first monument of modern architecture in the country and only the fourth worldwide that received a UNESCO designation. Built as a residence for a textile magnate, this glass-fronted Mies van der Rohe villa was placed on a grassy hilltop in 1928. Steel framing, floor-to-ceiling glass walls, chrome pillars, and furnished by the architect, it is a beautiful example of international modernism.

ⓘ www.czechtourism.com

Clean Water Projects

Restoring Clean Water

Bouncing Back From Disaster

Port-de-Paix, Haiti

HAITI, A POOR AND OFTEN POLITICALLY TROUBLED COUNTRY, ISN'T OFTEN ON THE MUST-SEE list for people who like the Caribbean. But there is much to see, from the lively capital of Port-au-Prince to the Citadelle, a mountaintop fortress to the north, and some very good tropical beaches. As a volunteer, you can explore at your leisure, but you may be most moved by your work helping to reverse the damage of Hurricane Jeanne on the country's clean water infrastructure.

In 2004, the devastating Hurricane Jeanne washed away homes, brought mud hillsides crashing down, and ravaged entire communities in already struggling Haiti. Perhaps the poorest country in the Northern Hemisphere, Haiti's infrastructure was taxed beyond its capacity to feed and care for its people even before the natural disaster struck. Now, even more starvation and critical health issues are wiping out a generation. This clean drinking water program will supply 97,000 people with water for life. Airline Ambassadors was originally a service outreach program developed with the United Nations, in which airline employees could use free mileage to contribute their time to projects around the world. Now available to all volunteers, the Haiti programs are categorized at the highest level of priority.

You'll work at clearing debris from canals and water tanks, as well as rebuilding and repairing homes, delivering medication, and teaching gardening and hygiene programs for more efficient use of water resources. Resource management has been poor in this country, so water has been largely ignored, resulting in preventable diseases and death. In addition to cleaning and repairing water availability and delivery resources (pumps, holding tanks, wells, and pipes), you'll deliver bottled emergency water to the village, along with other aid items like food, clothing, newborn kits, baby formula, and more.

You'll stay in a local residence or with a host family, and share a modest room with two to four volunteers. Food, a scarcity in a largely starving nation, is brought in by the team (along with as much donated food as a chartered flight can hold) and prepared communally by the team. This is an emergency response project, so there isn't a lot of free time for sightseeing or side trips, though you'll have rewarding cultural experiences and lessons on politics and history from local English-speaking guides and experts.

YOUR NEXT STEP: Airline Ambassadors (✆ **866/ANGEL-86;** www.airlineamb.org). The participant fee, US$1,000, covers 1 week's shared accommodation, meals, in-country transportation, guide, training, and support. A US$50 annual fee is required to become a member of Airline Ambassadors and be eligible for their service trips.

DON'T MISS: At the top of a mountain in Northern Haiti is the **Citadelle,** a castle fortress built by Henri Christophe to fend off a predicted attack by the French, who he was convinced would try to recapture the island. It is the largest fortress in the Western Hemisphere, built at great cost (both financially and in human life), intended to house and protect 5,000 people for up to a year. It has never been used for its intended purpose.

ⓘ www.haititourisme.com

235 Clean Water Projects

World Water Corps

Providing the Tools to Succeed

International

THIS PROGRAM TAKES ITS CHARGE OF BRINGING CLEAN WATER TO POOR COUNTRIES SERIOUSLY. Volunteers can visit needy countries around the developing world, training local communities on how to protect and preserve their clean water facilities in the long-term.

Water for People (WFP) runs international programs to provide safe drinking water, sanitation, and hygiene education for people in developing countries. Volunteers go on short-term assignments to train and supervise local communities and guide clean water programs for local stewardship. Bolivia, Guatemala, Honduras,

Malawi, and India all have WFP programs. By 2011 so will Nicaragua, Ecuador, the Dominican Republic, Rwanda, and Uganda.

After training on-site at your country of choice, you'll provide technical support and guidance for burgeoning clean water efforts. You'll do monitoring of building progress, evaluations of project reach and additional needs, mapping, photography of projects and components, metering, and other targeted assignments. Business planning, private sector development, and partner mentoring is also needed. A main component of the project for sustainable water is community involvement, so volunteers will serve as trained technical support to build skills within the community rather than do construction. At least some members of the volunteer team will need to be fluent in the native language, so your multilingual talents can come in handy (though several team members are likely to speak only English, so you're not excluded if you don't have fluency). Some of the project sites can require some pretty rigorous hiking to remote areas, so your match for a particular location may depend on your fitness. The organization matches volunteers to appropriate program locations, taking your preferences into consideration.

Lodging is booked for you, and the volunteer team is housed together and will share most meals. Accommodations vary by locale but can be quite rustic.

YOUR NEXT STEP: Water for People (✆ **303/734-3490;** www.waterforpeople.org). International projects are 2 weeks and there is no fee for volunteers. You are responsible for your own travel to the main city nearest the project and fees for lodging and meals. Insurance, training, and local support and transportation are provided for you.

Rebuilding after Disaster **236**

City Center Recovery & Conservation

Post-Earthquake Reconstruction

Gyumri, Armenia

GYUMRI'S HISTORIC DISTRICT BOASTS MORE THAN A THOUSAND 18TH- AND 19TH-CENTURY buildings, and the Armenian city is one of the world's oldest civilizations. With its proximity to so many other empires, its people have long fought off invaders, making the fight to retain a sense of heritage all the more important.

More than 2 decades after the devastating earthquake that rocked Armenia in 1988, pockets of the nation have yet to fully recover. Additional disruptions at the end of the last century—including the fall of the Soviet Union, Armenia's declaration of independence, and war with Azerbaijan—have made getting back to "normal" a true challenge. Since the war ended in 1994, much of the country has rallied, but Gyumri is still behind the curve. Reconstruction of the city center was at a standstill because temporary housing for 10,000 displaced families filled local thoroughfares and parks. Since temporary housing has finally allowed the majority of those families to relocate nearby, work in the central region can begin. In partnership with a local historic preservation organization, you'll work with architects and volunteers to preserve and rebuild historic buildings as an alternative to demolition.

You'll repair masonry on damaged structures, such as restoring the museum that houses historical and cultural monuments. Local masons will be working with

Earthquake damage in Gyumri, Armenia

you, as well as Armenian students of history and design. The museum building work is vital to protect archives from additional damage from exposure to the elements. You'll be trained in modern masonry and construction methods, as well as historically accurate methods, to preserve the character of historic buildings, many of them in an elegant Belle Epoque style. The important stone and masonry work will allow further structural work with lumber and other materials to be built upon the strong foundations you are establishing.

You'll retire each night to a small local hotel in Gyumri. Breakfasts and lunches are part of the program, and you are free to dine in the evenings at the restaurant of your choice. Field trips to nearby cultural and historical sites are scheduled, and you'll probably choose to spend the rest of your free time with your new friends exploring the city. It's a fascinating amalgam of beautiful architecture and the short-term structures put up in a hurry in response to the disaster. The community has found interesting ways to blend the old and fleeting new.

YOUR NEXT STEP: Heritage Conservation Network (✆ **303/444-0128;** www.heritageconservation.net). This 13-day trip, US$1,770, includes hotel lodging, two meals daily, English-language translation and support, airport transfers, local transportation, insurance, tools and materials, and cultural fieldtrips.

DON'T MISS: The entrances to the homes look like hobbit houses in the mountain village of **Khndzoresk**. There are spectacular views, but the homes themselves are the fascinating draw here—carved from the hollows of the stone cliffs. The residents have created a multilevel, nearly vertical village hewn from the mountain. There are even cave churches, hermitages, and horse stables.

ⓘ www.armeniainfo.am

Rebuilding after Disaster

Earthquake Relief & Recovery

Restoring Homes & Schools

Kemudo Village, Indonesia

THE ISLAND OF JAVA IS AT THE CENTER OF INDONESIA AND HOME TO 120 MILLION PEOPLE. You'll find spectacular national parks, beaches, and volcanoes, including Gunung Bromo and its neighbor Gunung Semeru, and the country's highest peak. Natural disasters have caused extensive damage here, and the scale of rebuilding required can be intimidating.

In May 2006, an earthquake hit the Klaten regency in Indonesia, and 85 percent of the homes and other buildings collapsed while most that remained standing suffered serious damage. International volunteers have been working with locals on relief efforts ever since, ranging from emergency medical, food, and water initiatives to rebuilding efforts. The area's remoteness has meant that progress is slow but steady. Now that the emergency has passed, the main work is recovering and rebuilding homes, community buildings, and infrastructure. Volunteers from many agencies are tackling the vast field of destruction daily with hammers, nails, and nearly limitless energy.

Your work is in construction, but your biggest challenges may be emotional. Kids and families are getting by, but not thriving in the way every child deserves. The construction work is basic and may include roofing, reframing, reconstructing collapsed structures, painting, and finishing work. The local school is of particular focus, and there will be times at the school when you can lay aside the paintbrush and work with the kids, teaching some English, leading some fun activities or games, and giving instruction in hygiene and the importance of good nutrition.

You'll stay in the home of a local English-speaking family (likely sleeping on the floor), from whom you'll learn much about Javanese culture and Indonesia in general. Meals are provided, and some group cultural excursions to neighboring villages and events are scheduled. Free time is an excellent opportunity to truly get to know the community. You cannot help but be inspired by their stories of overcoming the adversity of a natural disaster and doing the hard work of moving forward.

YOUR NEXT STEP: Canadian Alliance for Development Initiatives and Projects 🎗 (✆ **604/628-7400;** www.cadip.org). A 2-week project, US$265, includes hosted private home accommodations and meals, project training, cultural orientation and excursions, and full support. An additional US$167 is paid directly to the local support organization upon arrival.

DON'T MISS: The stunning **Borobodur Temple** was the spiritual center of Buddhism in Java before disappearing from the culture and essentially being lost until rediscovery in the 18th century. The hilltop is adorned with this massive lava-stone pyramid that is six stepped stories high. The whole complex is in the form of a lotus flower adorned with 92 Buddha statues and 1,460 carved scenes from his life.

ⓘ www.indonesia-tourism.com

238 Rebuilding after Disaster

Tsunami Recovery

Helping Tourism Flourish

Kosgoda, Sri Lanka

Turtles come ashore on the beaches to lay their eggs. The ancient therapeutic practice of Ayurveda is alive and well. And while tourism is recovering after the devastating tsunami of 2004, there is still much to do, including mentoring children to benefit from tourism by improving their conversational English skills.

The southern coast of Sri Lanka was nearly wiped off the map in the 2004 tsunami, and while most homes and structures have been rebuilt, the cultural recovery still benefits from the infusion of international volunteer efforts. Every project organized by this organization is planned in partnership with the local community so their priorities are served; right now, much of the focus is on children. Volunteers teach English and other subjects, as well as undertake maintenance and construction work, beach cleanup, and endangered species rescue.

You'll be in the company of plenty of children as you teach English conversation to help the kids take advantage of the opportunities a recovering tourism industry provides. For that reason, you'll also teach English to adults in the community. Additional time with kids is spent on entertainment, games, sports, competitions, and support for schoolwork with tutoring and mentoring. Volunteers also help teach life skills, from nutrition to commerce. You can also help burgeoning local businesses with planning and advice, including computer skills training and business model

Tsunami relief volunteers in Sri Lanka

development. You may need to step off the teaching track to help rescue sea turtles or clear debris that makes part of the beach unsafe.

You'll share a group volunteer house in the village. Breakfasts and dinners are provided, but lunches are your responsibility—try out local restaurants or pack some fruit and bread. Your free time in the evenings and weekends will likely be spent the same way the villagers pass their free time, in the neighborhood among friends. Beach time and hikes in the region are always available to get a broader view of Sri Lankan life and the still-beautiful, recovering, coastal zone.

YOUR NEXT STEP: **i-to-i** (toll free: **800/985-4852**; www.i-to-i.com). A 2-week project, US$1,545, includes the cost of homestay accommodations, two meals daily, project training and support, airport pickup, and in-country orientation program.

DON'T MISS: You've spent your work time on the tsunami-ravaged coast, so if you can add a few days, head inland to the less affected central mountain zonesof Sri Lanka. There are rock climbing and trekking opportunities in lush jungles, and a fun way to trek and spot wildlife is on an **elephant safari.** Riding the gentle giants will connect you to the natural world in a profound way.

ⓘ www.srilankatourism.org

Rebuilding after Disaster **239**

Tsunami Orphanage

Touring & Toil

Khao Lak Province, Thailand

IMAGINE THE BEST OF BOTH WORLDS, A BALANCE OF EXPERIENCES: A COMPREHENSIVE TRIP through the important sights and experiences of Thailand, followed by volunteer time taking care of children whose lives have been forever altered by Mother Nature's destructive forces.

While the Andaman Sea coast of Thailand has recovered remarkably since the 2004 tsunami, many children lost their families in that tragedy and are now supported at an orphanage in the beach community of Khao Lak.

You'll spend three days of this nine-day excursion working at the orphanage. Your tasks will be varied, from washing and dressing little ones, preparing meals and feeding, childcare, some cleaning, and education and recreation opportunities. Teach some English, lead a song or dance, set up a soccer competition, or oversee arts and crafts activities. Most of the need is to free up some of the time of the overworked permanent staff so they can attend to more needy cases or the administrative work required to keep the operation running. You'll need to be flexibile—one minute you may be asked to read a story to a sleepy six-year-old or you could be called to clean up spilled paint the next.

Before and after your stint as a volunteer, you'll have a high-end touring vacation through Bangkok and its temples and palaces, the ancient capital of Ayuthaya, a luxury jungle camp, a riverboat cruise, elephant rides, beach relaxation, and even Thai cooking classes.

The accommodations throughout this tour are luxurious, from five-star hotels to boutique resorts and even luxury tents in the jungle. Many meals are included, but you'll also have ample opportunity to dine out and choose your own restaurant for

A boat washed ashore in Khao Lak Province, Thailand

some lunches and dinners. Plenty of relaxation time is built into the schedule as you travel from Bangkok to the south near Phuket, seeing much of the lower half of the country.

YOUR NEXT STEP: Hands Up Holidays (✆ **201/984-5372;** www.handsupholidays.com). This 9-day tour, US$3,400, includes luxury accommodations at five-star hotels and luxury tented camps, all internal transportation including flights, river boats, tour bus, and so on, some meals as per itinerary, guided tours, and activities. Also **North by Northeast** (✆ **+66/2-611-1988;** www.north-by-north-east.com). Three-day service trips to the tsunami region of Andaman Sea (often as an add-on to other trips), US$283, includes home stay with a local family, meals, insurance, local transportation, an English-speaking guide, and project time with teaching, mangrove reforestation, beach cleanup, Nipa Palm roof weaving, women's business collective help, or working at wildlife rescue center.

DON'T MISS: Since this trip is relatively comprehensive in the more heavily traveled central and southern areas, you'll want to get a taste of the north. Plan a visit to **Chiang Rai,** the quieter sister city of Chiang Mai, with beautiful temples, the royal villa home to the mother of the King of Thailand, and proud handicraft traditions displayed in the marketplaces and museums.

ⓘ www.tourismthailand.org

Rebuilding after Disaster 240

Hurricane Relief

House Party

New Orleans, Louisiana, USA

WITH ITS ENDURING MUSIC, AWARD-WINNING RESTAURANTS, CHARMING FRENCH QUARTER, lively spirit, and creative people, New Orleans worked hard to quickly turn the lights back on and open for business after recovering from Hurricane Katrina. There's still much work to be done, but there are plenty of rewards in a city that truly knows how to let loose.

Hurricane Katrina struck the Gulf Coast in 2005 with such a fury that the region has yet to fully recover. It did greater damage to other parts of the coast, but New Orleans suffered intensely with the breaching of the levees and the flooding of Lake Pontchartrain, bringing one of America's most graceful cities to her knees. While the famous French Quarter, Garden District, and River Walk have for the most part recovered, entire districts will never be the same. The entire incident exposed extraordinary governmental dysfunction but perhaps also inspired a remarkable spirit of assistance in the many people ready to help the Big Easy recover and rebuild.

Habitat for Humanity has one of the highest profiles of any volunteer organization, and its tireless volunteer efforts in and around New Orleans after Hurricane Katrina brought it a new international prominence. It builds homes from the ground up in Orleans, Jefferson, and St. Bernard parishes. You don't need construction experience, since you'll be taught all the necessary skills on-site. While hundreds of houses have already been built, hundreds more in all stages of construction need to be completed so New Orleans residents can finally come home.

Common Ground Relief is rebuilding the Lower Ninth Ward, in addition to its

Rebuilding a house in New Orleans

important advocacy work, soil and environmental testing, and programs to address hunger, unemployment, and addiction issues. Rebuilding Together New Orleans uses volunteer teams to rebuild homes for low-income and elderly residents. Many other grassroots organizations are rebuilding homes, replanting trees, and working to bring the Crescent City back to her former glory. If you are coming to New Orleans, there is a volunteer opportunity for you.

YOUR NEXT STEP: Each of these, and plenty of other non-profit organizations, allows you to volunteer for as long as you wish (check project need when registering) and charge no fees to participate in rebuilding. **Common Ground Relief** (✆ **504/304-9097;** www.commongroundrelief.org). A volunteer group house can host some volunteers for a suggested donation of US$10 a day. Meals not provided. **Habitat for Humanity—New Orleans** (✆ **504/861-2077;** www.habitat-nola.org). Does not provide accommodations or meals. **Rebuilding Together New Orleans** (Preservation Resource Center) (✆ **504/636-3076;** www.prcno.org). Does not provide accommodations or meals.

DON'T MISS: New Orleans is all about music and food, so do a self-designed **culinary tour** to try King's Cake, Muffaletta sandwiches, po' boys, beignets, gumbo, jambalaya, and other Cajun and Creole specialties. Quaff your thirst with local drink specialties like a Sazerac cocktail while listening to live jazz in the French Quarter, and you are a local for the day.

ⓘ www.neworleanscvb.com

241 **Working with the Homeless**

Homeless Shelter

Help Out in Hip Capital

Buenos Aires, Argentina

THIS HOT, COSMOPOLITAN CAPITAL CITY IS CHOCKABLOCK WITH ART MUSEUMS, THEATER, remarkable architecture, cafes, and restaurants that increasingly showcase the country's best culinary offerings. And, of course, there's that famous dance: the tango.

Man does not live by bread alone, and the homeless population of this South American capital needs more than a warm meal to make it through the toughest times. In the Recoleta neighborhood, Mom's Kitchen provides a warm lunch every day for about 80 homeless *Porteños* (residents of Buenos Aires). In addition to the welcome meals, extensive support programs include counseling for emotional and spiritual strength, legal assistance and advice, and some basic skills and vocational workshops to open up new avenues of education and employability. A large portion of the homeless population is neither destitute nor vagrant, but just one or two paychecks removed from what had once been a happy home—and they have an incredible desire to live independently again. Mom's Kitchen tries to help them do just that, with the help of plenty of volunteers.

You'll be cook and teacher, sympathetic ear and staunch advocate, as well as helping the staff prepare and distribute freshly made meals. You may also help with organizing, publicizing, and leading new workshops on everything from job interviewing skills to personal safety. (Intermediate Spanish skills are needed for this project.) Project staff will also train you for community outreach and advocacy programs to help educate the general public about

10 Hotel & Volunteer Packages

More and more hotels and resorts, including some of the top high-end chains, make volunteering a simple prospect with special volunteer packages for guests. Often there are extra perks (spa discounts, free meals, transportation, and so on) and room discounts to reward you for the work you do to better your hotel's community.

242 **Winnipeg, Manitoba, Canada, and Bermuda—Fairmont Hotels & Resorts** The Winnipeg Fairmont has teamed with Habitat for Humanity to offer a Home Sweet Home package with overnight accommodations, daily breakfast, transportation to and from the home-building site, and a post-work amenity kit. At Bermuda's Fairmont Southampton, guests can assist in tree-planting projects for the Bermuda cedar. Kids and adults can help at the property's nursery and on the hotel grounds. ***Fairmont Hotels & Resorts*** *(© **800/257-7544**; www.fairmont.com).*

243 **Colorado, USA—Rock Resorts** All five of the Colorado Rock Resorts properties have a Give & Getaway package, where you spend a half-day working to restore and improve the White River National Forest trails. Program participants receive a discount on their room rate, as well as a hydrating backpack, work gloves, and soothing spa hand cream. Every guest, whether participating in volunteer projects or not, can have a portion of their room fee donated to the National Forest Foundation. ***Rock Resorts*** *(© **888/FOR-ROCK**; www.rockresorts.com).*

244 **Marco Island, Florida, and New Orleans, Louisiana, USA—Marriott Hotels** At Marriott's Marco Island Resort or Doral Golf Resort and Spa, guests can work at the local YMCA on facilities and landscaping or do a morning of beach cleanup at the Biscayne Nature Center; participants receive discounts at the spa plus complimentary breakfast. Each Marriott in New Orleans has a Big Easy Spirit to Serve program, where a Care Concierge helps you volunteer with rebuilding work. A portion of your room rate is donated to Habitat for Humanity. ***Marriott International*** *(© **888/236-2427**; www.marriott.com).*

245 **Miami, Florida, USA—Mandarin Oriental** The Mandarin Oriental can set up an Everglades adventure in an environmental project at the World Heritage Site. You'll participate in tree planting, recycling projects, and invasive plant species removal. The work is in the morning and your afternoons are spent with a park ranger in a naturalism program. ***Mandarin Oriental, Miami*** *(© **305/913-8383**; www.mandarinoriental.com).*

Poipu Beach in Kaua'i, Hawaii

246 **Kaua'i, Hawaii, USA—Sheraton Kaua'i Resort** Book the Malama Kaua'i green getaway package and you can participate in a beach cleanup with Save Kaua'i, join the "vacation and volunteer" program at the National Tropical Botanical Garden, or volunteer with the Kaua'i Monk Seal Watch program. ***Sheraton Kaua'i Resort*** *(© **866/716-8140**; www.sheraton-kauai.com).*

247 Portland, Oregon, USA—Heathman Hotel This boutique hotel in Portland has partnered with the Forest Park Conservancy so guests can work on trail conservancy for a half-day doing cleanup, removing invasive species, and possibly some park maintenance during volunteer work parties. The program also provides a guided discovery hike program. ***The Heathman Hotel*** *(© **800/551-0011**; www.heathmanhotel.com).*

248 Philadelphia, Pennsylvania, USA—AKA Rittenhouse Square The luxury extended-stay property offers guests the chance to provide meals for people coping with life-threatening illness and assist with housing and food for Philadelphia's homeless. You'll help in the kitchen preparing meals and packing them for home delivery. You can also pitch in to tutor for Women of Change, a women's safe haven shelter. AKA will also make a financial contribution to the projects on behalf of every guest who volunteers. ***AKA Rittenhouse Square*** *(© **215/825-7000**; www.stayaka.com).*

Kitchen volunteers at AKA Rittenhouse Square

249 Kiawah Island, South Carolina, USA—Kiawah Island Gold Resort The Ronald McDonald House in Charleston provides temporary lodging for seriously ill children and their families. Guests can bake goodies at the house kitchen, host a game in the house dining room, read a story, sing, or provide other entertainment. You can also pick up items on the house wish list, or make a donation to "share a night" of hospitality for a family (US$48 sponsors one family for one night at the house). ***Kiawah Island Golf Resort*** *(© **843/768-2121**; www.kiawahresort.com).*

250 Grenada, West Indies—Paradise Bay Beach Resort At this rustic eco-resort, a 3-week voluntour package combines relaxation and adventure time with weekday work with local farmers rebuilding after the destruction of Hurricane Ivan. In addition to 5 days a week of clearing, crop work, and farm restoration, you'll also have beach trips, catamaran rides, snorkeling, horseback trips, island tours, local festival Fridays, cooking classes, massage, guided hikes, and more. ***Paradise Bay Beach Resort & Spa*** *(© **473/405-8888**; www.paradisebayresort.net).*

251 International—The Ritz-Carlton Each Ritz-Carlton hotel has its own Give Back Getaway program that gives patrons the chance to serve the local community in a half-day service project. The Ritz-Carlton New Orleans teams you with Habitat for Humanity on home-building projects or with Operation Sudden Impact to replant thousands of trees lost in Hurricane Katrina. The two Miami properties offer the Monument Island Flagler Memorial restoration or helping with the horses and the clients of a therapeutic equestrian center. Programs in other hotels run the gamut from animal rescue to environmental work to children's charities and historic preservation. ***The Ritz-Carlton*** *(headquarters © **301/547-4700**; www.ritzcarlton.com).*

Volunteering at a homeless shelter in Buenos Aires

homelessness, show that there is no shame in needing help, and also reach out to those who are living on the streets to make sure they know help is available.

You'll be welcomed into the home of a local family, where you'll receive warmth, security, friendship, and two meals daily. Upon arrival, you'll have an in-depth city orientation so you'll know your way around Recoleta as well as the public transportation, neighborhoods, culture, and customs of Argentina. Intensive Spanish-language classes are available at additional cost prior to the start of the program. During your free time you can find out what makes Buenos Aires one of the world's most exciting destinations.

YOUR NEXT STEP: Center for Cultural Interchange (✆ **312/944-2544;** www.cci-exchange.com). A 3-week project, US$1,290, includes host family accommodations, two meals daily (except Sundays), project training, and local staff support.

DON'T MISS: If you're an oenophile, make your way to Argentina's wine and food capital, **Mendoza.** Besides some exceptional wines, you'll find some phenomenal food and the area's other famous product, olive oil.

ⓘ www.turismo.gov.ar

252 Working with the Homeless

Homeless Youth Shelters

Serving in South America

Lima, Peru

With eight million people calling the capital their home, Lima can be a crowded, chaotic experience. Beyond its museums and increasing recognition for its diverse restaurant scene, it provides access to the Amazon jungle, the Andes Mountains, and beaches just south of the city.

These two program houses in Lima are designed for street youth aged 12 to 22. Lima is a huge city, and in many neighborhoods life can be pretty hard. Many of the young men and women who live here are runaways, orphans, or fleeing abuse, and the program house has provided nutritional and emotional sustenance, some job training, and educational support. You'll have the chance to work with the residents at both shelters.

Meal preparation and cleanup is a big part of your work with these young people, and while the residents each have duties and chores, your help makes it all run more smoothly. You can also help with English homework and tutoring. Supplemental activities drummed up by the volunteer team have historically been very popular, from talent shows to sports competitions, especially if they involve new skills that are easily learned. You'll want to have some comfort speaking Spanish (there is Spanish-language instruction provided before or during your placement for 2 hours on weekday afternoons). The residents also learn vocational skills as a stepping stone toward future employment, and you can pitch in with that work as well.

You'll stay with a host family, who'll provide morning and evening meals. Lunches are easy to find at any number of restaurants in the trendy Miraflores district (where the houses are located). Your first few days will be spent learning about Lima with cultural orientation and excursions to local tourist sites. You'll find there's never enough free time to explore Lima as much as you'd like.

YOUR NEXT STEP: Twin Work & Volunteer Abroad (✆ **800/80 483 80;** www.workandvolunteer.com). This 4-week project, US$750, includes host family accommodations, two meals daily, orientation program, language classes, project training, airport transfers, and support.

DON'T MISS: Ever seen a condor? Chances are very good that you'll see several of these magnificent birds if you visit the deep canyons near **Arequipa.** When you return to the "White City," bask in the glow from the white volcanic stone used to construct and decorate temples, convents, villas, and palaces in the UNESCO World Heritage Site city center.

ⓘ www.go2peru.com

Homeless Support Programs

Show You Love New York

New York, New York, USA

THERE'S ALWAYS A LOT OF "NEW" IN NEW YORK CITY: TWO NEW BASEBALL STADIUMS, A NEW West Side park situated on old elevated train tracks, and hotels and restaurants that pop up seemingly every day. It's easy to forget an old problem—homelessness—that continues to show a new face.

The majority of New York's homeless have found themselves on the street after job loss, home foreclosure, or other difficulties, and quite often entire families become unable to find shelter. New York's Coalition for the Homeless is a multitiered organization reaching out to street and shelter adults and children. There are several volunteer programs in which you can work to assist this important project.

The Grand Central Food Program needs volunteers every evening, 365 days a year, to serve hot nutritious meals from their mobile soup kitchen. You'll also distribute donated clothing and blankets and answer questions from the general public on homelessness issues.

Camp Homeward Bound is a summer camp north of the city that serves hundreds of New York's shelter kids. The camp needs volunteers to help get ready for the arrival of campers in May and June.

The Bound for Success program uses volunteer tutors and instructors for after-school activities and to help with homework for shelter kids.

You could be a mock interviewer or mentor for homeless women trying to re-enter the workforce via the First Step training program, or even work behind the scenes on the annual special events to raise important funds for the organization.

There are no travel programs or arranged accommodations for volunteers with this organization, but when your travel plans have you in New York City, be in touch to volunteer your time and be matched to an opportunity that best suits your skills and abilities.

YOUR NEXT STEP: Coalition for the Homeless 🎗 (✆ **212/776-2000;** www.coalitionforthehomeless.org). Give as much time and energy as you can when in New York City. You'll make your own arrangements for travel, lodging, and food, and let the organization know how much time you have to give.

DON'T MISS: It's not a visit to New York City without a trip to **Central Park.** The Olmstead and Vaux–designed greenspace is as diverse as the city, attracting everyone from ice skaters to joggers, mounted police to in-line skaters in the grand dame of parks.

ⓘ www.nycgo.com

Feeding the Hungry & Homeless

A Capital Idea

Washington DC, USA

AMONG THE MONUMENTS, MEMORIALS, AND MUSEUMS, THERE'S MUCH TO SEE AND DO THAT costs very little in the nation's capital. That frugal frame of mind suits your task of feeding children who don't get enough of what they need to eat.

It's difficult to understand how five million children in the United States go to bed hungry each night when there is, in fact, enough wasted food to feed every hungry adult and child in the nation. Nutritious fruits, vegetables, bread, proteins, and even prepared foods are discarded every day by the ton, often because it's just easier than passing it on. Many businesses, cafeterias, and restaurants could make better use of leftover edible food, and this project works with several DC organizations charged with feeding and extending care to the homeless. You'll have the opportunity during your 2 weeks to serve with several organizations.

You'll make dozens and dozens of sandwiches each morning as part of the Street Outreach program to serve lunches to those who need them. Another day you'll help staff provide shelter and food, along with services like counseling, housing placement, addiction treatment, and job skills training. You'll also attend workshops

Preparing meals for the homeless in Washington

on social justice and the many issues surrounding homelessness and hunger in America.

While volunteering in DC, you'll stay at a local hostel, and meals during workday assignment time are provided. The hostel has a kitchen, so you can shop and prepare your own meals at other times or go out to experience the capital's vibrant culinary scene. A scheduled city orientation tour as well as cultural speakers will help illuminate the social issues that contribute to homelessness. The city has a nearly limitless number of cultural attractions and museums, so don't worry about filling your free time.

YOUR NEXT STEP: Amizade (✆ **304/ 293-6049;** www.amizade.org). A 2-week project, US$1,326, includes shared hostel accommodations (bring your own bedding and linens), workday meals, project training, in-city transportation (metro passes), local orientation and cultural presentations, and local staff support.

DON'T MISS: The beating heart of Washington, DC, is the **National Mall,** and surrounding it you'll find some of America's best-known sites and institutions. In a short walk, you can hit all the biggies: the United States Capitol, Washington Monument, Lincoln Memorial, Franklin Delano Roosevelt Memorial, World War II Memorial, Korean War Veterans Memorial, and the Vietnam Veterans Memorial. Also bordering the park are the National Museums of Natural History, the American Indian, Air and Space, African Art, and American History; the national galleries; botanic and sculpture gardens; Freer and Sackler galleries; and the Smithsonian Institute.

ⓘ www.washington.org

7 *Share the Health*

Providing medical care in Ahmedabad, India

HIV/AIDS Education 255

HIV/AIDS Prevention Program

Debunking Myths & Stigmas

Buea, Cameroon

SITTING ON THE EASTERN SLOPES OF MOUNT CAMEROON, THIS UNIVERSITY TOWN AND CAPITAL of the Southwest Province of Cameroon is characterized by its colonial-era buildings and laid-back atmosphere. The warm climate, proximity to the beach, and hospitable people make Buea and Southwest Cameroon an exceptional place to live and volunteer.

An HIV diagnosis in the developing world has much different consequences than what is now expected in much of North American and Europe. The cost of drug cocktails and treatments for T-cells is prohibitive in much of the world, including Cameroon. While the country is politically and socially stable, many of its people still rely on subsistence farming for survival, and unemployment is high. Children are particularly vulnerable to HIV/AIDS, since those with infected mothers often have the disease passed to them *in utero*. This project in Buea and the surrounding rural communities tries to bridge the knowledge gap about AIDS transmission and treatment and to support those who are already living with HIV.

You'll be involved in English-speaking outreach programs in the villages, providing culturally sensitive AIDS awareness and education programs. You'll be fully trained to teach about methods of safer sex, the facts and fictions of transmission, and how to debunk the myths and stigmas concerning the disease and those who have it. You'll visit schools, churches, community centers, and clinics, encouraging HIV testing and the benefits of knowing your health status. You can save lives by disproving erroneous information and fear about the disease and replacing them with the correct facts about how to be safe.

Buea is an excellent place to experience the diversity of African cultures—while English and French are two of the main languages spoken, there are more than 200 ethnic languages heard around Cameroon, making it a true melting pot. Your free time will be spent getting to know locals, how they spend their days, and what traditions they honor. The most vivid cultural exploration will be right in the home you'll share with a host family. You can't count on electricity or flush toilets, but you can expect phenomenal hospitality and the amazing three meals a day the hosts will provide. And you can count on it being very difficult to say goodbye.

YOUR NEXT STEP: A Broader View Volunteers Corp (© **866/423-3258;** www.abroaderview.org). A 1-week project, US$795, includes accommodations with a host family, all meals, airport transfers, project coordination and support, and full training. A portion of the fee goes to the local outreach organization.

DON'T MISS: The **Palace of the Sultan** in Foumban is a cross between a Mediterranean villa, a Moorish castle, and a medieval château. It houses the Sultan's Museum and its lavish collection of royal gowns, decor, jewelry, weaponry, musical instruments, masks, and elaborately decorated and beaded thrones.

ⓘ www.ambacam-usa.org

256 HIV/AIDS Education

HIV/AIDS Education & Care

Preparing Adolescents

Akatsi, Ghana

This small town located on the Atlantic Coast might not have a lot to offer visitors in the way of amenities, but its proximity to the ocean and amazing bird-watching opportunities make up for it. It's also worth a visit to check out the world-famous Xavi eco-tourism project, while Ada Foah, the city's seaside, is a popular relaxation destination.

Despite the incredible advances in medical knowledge about HIV, education about treatment and the spread of the disease is still not reaching everyone. In countries where the medical and public education systems are less advanced, the plague continues to take a horrific toll. In Ghana, hundreds of people, many of them children, die every year from AIDS. This volunteer opportunity is working with local organizations in nearby Accra on the issues of adolescent reproductive health and HIV/AIDS education. English-speaking teams promote behavioral change and health awareness in schools, after-school programs, and on-site at medical clinics.

You'll be trained in everything you need to know about AIDS before you begin facilitating group discussions about HIV prevention and sexual health. During an average day, you may work with different populations and visit several sites, from community meetings and working with patients at prenatal clinics to classrooms and assemblies. It's important to consider your comfort with human sexuality and drug use, since you'll be encouraging responsible sexuality and protection measures to teenagers who may ask a lot of questions. Some care for HIV-infected children will also be involved, making them aware of, and perhaps involved in, peer education programs at hospitals and in their communities so that the work can continue after you've gone home.

You'll live with a host family, who'll feed you three Ghanaian meals daily. A thorough orientation and language instruction program will make it easier for you to get by in the city during your downtime. You'll also learn Ghanaian cooking techniques in kitchen classes, so you'll leave with recipes and a belly full of fufu, banku, and yam (local specialties). Accra is a large city, easy to reach from your small town base, with plenty of local shops, marketplaces, and cultural institutions to explore, as well as places where you and your fellow volunteers can hang out with new friends and share a drink or a meal.

YOUR NEXT STEP: Institute for Field Research Expeditions (✆ **800/675-2504;** www.ifrevolunteers.org). A 2-week placement, US$642, includes host family accommodations, three meals daily, in-country transportation, airport welcome, comprehensive insurance, 24-hour support, and thorough project training.

DON'T MISS: It is locally believed that God built the **Larabanga Mosque,** the oldest mosque in Ghana. The striking mud building has pyramidal towers with wooden posts sticking out like antennae at every angle. It is home to one of the seven original Koran texts from Mecca and stands on a particularly holy spot. It has been lauded by UNSECO as a World Heritage Site, but is also one of the most endangered sites in the world because the mud erodes and must be restored every year.

ⓘ www.touringghana.com

HIV/AIDS Education **257**

HIV Outreach

Changing Attitudes & Opening Eyes

Delhi, India

THE SECOND-BIGGEST METROPOLIS IN INDIA (AND SIXTH LARGEST IN THE WORLD), DELHI CAN be a relentless onslaught of audio and visual overload to a first-time visitor. Somehow the city's rapid development manages to strike a balance between the ancient and the modern. Disparate cultures and religions co-exist in a city with a uniquely cosmopolitan vibe, which manages to maintain an intimacy despite its more than 17 million residents.

India's enormous population runs the gamut from some of the richest families in the world to people living in abject poverty. With the caste system still observed in some places, certain people are barred from access to medical care or even food based solely upon their social strata. Even where caste is not the issue, there are huge pockets of uneducated poor in both rural and urban areas. Without basic education or reading ability, an understanding of disease transmission, even when information can be found, eludes thousands in Delhi. As a result, AIDS is misunderstood and ferociously stigmatized, so that those with HIV are often banished from their homes or neighborhoods and cast out from society. Volunteers with this project work with local organizations to increase awareness of the disease, how it is caught, how it is (and isn't) spread, and how to appropriately care for those fighting the syndrome and opportunistic infections.

You're an educator and a counselor—or you'll be soon after undergoing training in this program. Your main goal is to change attitudes and open eyes and hearts, which will ultimately change behaviors. The program is in English, and you'll work to demystify HIV disease and work with those

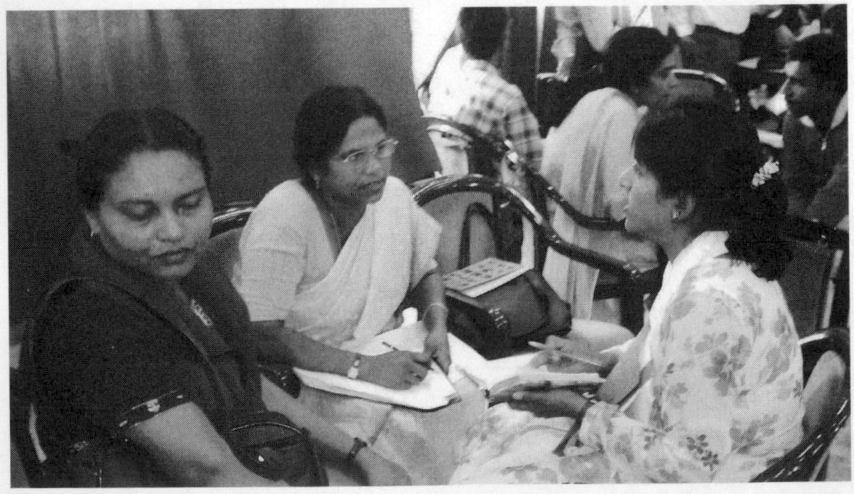

Educating women in India about HIV

infected. At privately run clinics and shelters (for those who have nowhere else to turn because of their illness), you'll provide comfort for patients as well as perhaps running a skills development program. This is not a hospice, and the intention is for patients to be checked out of the program. Many will leave with new job skills like woodworking, candle making, or tailoring, so there is a starting place and an opportunity to earn a living when they are once again healthy enough to work.

You'll live with a host family who will provide three Indian meals daily. When you're not disseminating information in schools and community centers or working in the shelters, your free time can be quickly absorbed by the chaotic energy that infuses Delhi. Both Old and New Delhi have endless places to see and experiences to have.

YOUR NEXT STEP: Institute for Field Research Expeditions (✆ **800/675-2504;** www.ifrevolunteers.org). A 2-week project, US$635, includes accommodations with a local family, three meals daily, full insurance coverage, in-country transportation, and full project training and volunteer support by local staff. An additional US$349 IFRE application fee is required.

DON'T MISS: The once lavish city of **Fatehpur Sikri,** outside Agra, lets you move from one wildly specific architectural style to the next. Emperor Akbar came here in search of the renowned Sufi mystic, Sheikh Salim Chishti, to ask for the blessing of a son. He built this magnificent village of red sandstone and white marble, every inch of which has been lovingly carved, in honor of that son and the saint who blessed him. Much of the city no longer exists, but the inner citadel is immaculately preserved. Its walls, palaces, baths, royal mint, courts, and gardens are still splendid.

ⓘ www.incredibleindia.org

258 HIV/AIDS Education

AIDS Project

Village Clinic Support

Mombasa, Kenya

Home to some of the best beaches in Africa, and surrounded by nature reserves and game parks, Mombassa has a great depth of history and stronger sense of community than exists in the capital, Nairobi. Volunteering here is a chance to live in one of the most ethnically diverse cities in Africa, where Asian and Arab influences mix easily with Kenyan culture, food, and language.

There is no specific medical training or skill required for this volunteer opportunity in the village medical clinics, but you will be assisting local doctors. HIV/AIDS is one of many threats to community health that overwhelm the modest capabilities of the small rural clinics and medical outposts outside Mombasa. A debilitating lack of staff and resources prevents many locals from getting adequate medical care. Clinics can be a single room shared with other programs at a community center or a purpose-built facility that could host many more doctors and nurses if they were available. The harried staff must triage patients like an emergency room, prioritizing people based on the extremity of their need, so secondary programs like HIV education, nutrition counseling, and hygiene are often pushed aside for expedience. Much more could be done for the communities with more sets of able hands.

AIDS education program volunteers in Mombasa, Kenya

Your work will vary based on your skills. Many of your fellow volunteers may have some medical knowledge, but it is not required. You may be working on HIV/AIDS education with locals (in English and perhaps with a translator as required), presenting information materials as a counterpoint to the misunderstandings and fear that cloak the disease. You may also provide some basic counseling on diet and nutrition or teach younger children about personal care and hygiene. Perhaps a quiet afternoon filing and updating records will allow you to be off your feet for a spell before heading to the next clinic to help with a feeding program or visiting with worried patients and their families.

You'll be staying with a host family close to the project site so you can walk or get there with a short commute. Local food is prepared for you three times daily, and many volunteers find that spare moments are nicely spent relaxing and getting to know their colleagues and community members after what can be stressful and exhausting days. Of course, Mombasa has plenty of culture, shops, and museums to explore when you want a change of pace.

YOUR NEXT STEP: Institute for Field Research Expeditions (© **800/675-2504;** www.ifrevolunteers.org). A 2-week project, US$553, includes host family accommodations, meals, project training, airport pickup, in-country transportation, travel insurance, and local support. An additional US$349 IFRE application fee is required.

DON'T MISS: If you need souvenirs, a great place to go and feel good about shopping is the **Bombolulu Workshops for the Handicapped** in Mombasa. Since 1969, this has grown into the country's largest rehabilitation program, supporting 160 crafstpeople with disabilities. The workers have formed their own savings and loan cooperative and medical aid program. Tribal crafts are represented from across Kenya, including Bukusu, Maasai, Giriama, Orma, Mijikenda, and Luo. Traditional Swahili workshops offer bone and other jewelry, tailoring and traditional textiles, woodcarving products, masks, leather goods, and more.

ⓘ www.tourism.go.ke

259 HIV/AIDS Education

Education & Prevention

Teaching the Basics

Arusha, Tanzania

LOCATED ON THE EDGE OF THE GREAT RIFT VALLEY, THE TOWN OF ARUSHA IS KNOWN AS THE safari hub of Northern Tanzania and a popular staging point for tourists making the trip to nearby Serengeti National Park, the Ngorongoro Conservation Area, and most notably Mount Kilimanjaro. The city's modern feel, combined with a frontier-town atmosphere, is amplified by year-round music and cultural festivals.

Africa has been hit harder by the AIDS crisis than most other areas, and the epidemic is tearing down the foundations of not only families and the medical world, but agriculture, tourism, and daily life for every citizen. Eight percent of Tanzania's population, adults and children alike, is infected (and only about 30 percent of the population has been tested for the HIV virus, so numbers could be even higher). With these hundreds of thousands lost to disease—many of them dying or too sick to work—crops go untended, jobs are lost, and families go unfed. This education and prevention program works with volunteers who go into urban and rural communities to offer week-long training sessions in HIV/AIDS prevention. They also cover opportunistic infections (since AIDS itself doesn't kill anyone but leaves them vulnerable to other diseases like pneumonia), life skills, the stigma of diagnosis, and healthy living and nutrition counseling.

Your work here will be in the trenches of education, teaching locals about the importance of testing and knowing their HIV status to protect themselves and their loved ones, as well as explaining the medical realities of the syndrome and its consequences. It will take different approaches

Educating villagers in Arusha, Tanzania about AIDS and HIV

with different groups of adults and children (the program works through secondary schools as well) to get your message across clearly and effectively. AIDS can be prevented, and those who do have HIV or AIDS deserve respect, support, and love from the people in their family, community, and society at large—that is your message. Depending on when you are in Tanzania with the program, there are also youth day camps focused on HIV education with which you can help.

You'll be living in a homestay situation with a host family (if you prefer to stay in a hostel, arrangements can be made, but most volunteers see the benefit of cultural immersion that comes from living with locals), and all your meals are provided. An orientation will include introductory language and cultural training, a safari day trip, and a local tour to get your bearings.

YOUR NEXT STEP: Global Service Corps (✆ **415/788-3666, ext. 128;** www.globalservicecorps.org). A 2-week stay, US$1,170, homestay (or hostel) accommodations, all meals, project training, local orientation and cultural introduction, airport pickup, and in-country transportation.

DON'T MISS: Sure, an African safari in a Jeep is a must-do experience—but how about from a boat? Safari river boats take you past sleeping crocodiles and hippos sunning themselves in half-submerged herds. A **boat safari** is thus far only allowed in the Selous Game Reserve, which includes the Rufigi River, Great Ruaha River, and plenty of lakes where you'll see outrageous amounts of birds and water-species.

ⓘ www.tanzaniatouristboard.com

HIV/AIDS Education **260**

MSM Education

Busting Cultural Taboos

Chiang Mai, Thailand

IT MIGHT NOT BE AS URBAN AND COSMOPOLITAN AS BANGKOK, BUT CHIANG MAI HAS ALL THE same problems when it comes to HIV and AIDS. Traditional restaurants and lodgings are slowly giving way to McDonald's and Holiday Inns, in order to satisfy the growing numbers of foreign visitors looking for sun and fun. Others use Chiang Mai as a launching point for treks to visit with and study Thailand's Hill Tribes.

The cultural taboos that surround HIV and AIDS in most societies mean that people with the disease feel they have to hide their condition, taking energy away from taking care of their health. This organization works with the MSM population of Chiang Mai. MSM stands for "Men who have Sex with Men" and covers three categories specific to Thai culture: men who self-identify as gay or bisexual; male sex workers who often identify as heterosexual although they are active with male clients; and male-to-female transgender. While we learned years ago that AIDS is not a gay disease, unprotected sex between men can still be one of the highest risk categories for contracting HIV. Education and outreach to this target population should help to increase safer sex practices and lower HIV transmission. The program also has English education programs for sex workers, condom distribution programs, school outreach with HIV education, materials to help decrease the stigma attached to HIV, and direct one-on-one counseling.

You'll be involved in all aspects of the organization, from helping with presentations in schools (in English, sometimes with a translator), answering questions on phone and email counseling hotlines, distributing condoms in places where men meet to have sex, conducting workshops with sex workers about protection and the importance of testing, leading nutrition and health lectures for HIV-positive men, and more. Your days and some nights will be busy reaching out to so many different populations. You'll of course be thoroughly trained in the latest HIV/AIDS information before heading out to the field paired with supervising staff members.

The three weeks you'll spend on this project will fly by as you discuss what you face each day with your volunteer colleagues at the shared project house in the old city center. An in-house cook prepares three Thai meals daily, and local staff is available 24 hours a day for everything from shopping or drinking recommendations to troubleshooting. Chiang Mai is considered a cultural capital of Asia, so with so much to do and see, your free time will never seem enough.

YOUR NEXT STEP: Cultural Canvas Thailand (✆ **850/316-8470;** www.culturalcanvas.com). A 3-week program, US$1,399, includes shared project house accommodations, all meals, airport transfers, in-country orientation, insurance, full project training and support, and 24-hour assistance.

DON'T MISS: Live out your fantasies of getting away from it all on a simple raft meandering down a river. In **Chiangdao,** near Chiang Mai, you can spend a full day with an elephant-back safari in the morning, a lavish lunch, then a float on what is little more than bamboo poles lashed together to form a platform. A professional guide will steer the raft along the fast-moving river so you can relax and watch the forest go by.

ⓘ www.tourismthailand.org

261 People with Special Needs

Day Camp for Children with Autism

Help Provide a Classic Summer Experience

Courtenay, British Columbia, Canada

SURROUNDED BY SOME OF THE COUNTRY'S FINEST FARMLAND AND MOUNTAINOUS LANDSCAPES, you'll soon see why Courtenay is an ideal location for a children's camp. Kilometers of sandy shore are ideal for relaxing on, while the rugged mountain wilderness of nearby Strathcona Provincial Park is a must-see. The oldest provincial park in B.C. has dozens of biking and hiking trails in summer—and some of the province's best skiing in winter.

Autism Spectrum Disorder (ASD) kids are high functioning but can have a hard time with social interaction and communication. This volunteer opportunity partners with a local child development association, as well as parents and family members, to offer a social and recreational day camp experience for kids ages 10 to 15. Volunteers are thoroughly trained for a week before meeting the kids so you'll know how to handle these very specific circumstances when you work with individuals or small groups.

Your work each day will be quite focused and sometimes intense as you pair up with an individual camper partner (or sometimes with several) and provide a 2-week recreational day camp experience. Together you'll take on several activities. Perhaps a group will work together in the kitchen to prepare lunch and find ways to cooperate and communicate with one another and with you. Take a few kids on a walking excursion in the neighborhood, farther out into the countryside dotted with lakes and farms, or maybe to the beach. You'll be both camp counselor and group leader with very specifically proscribed tasks and activities that encourage interaction and communication.

Your home base will be a shared group house in Courtenay with other volunteers, and all your meals are provided. The town of 20,000 has a great cultural district with theaters, art galleries, museums, restaurants, and pubs, so you can find plenty to do during downtime. You and your colleagues may also want to explore the region's natural splendor and hike amid the forests and rivers for which this area is famed.

YOUR NEXT STEP: Canadian Alliance for Development Initiatives and Projects (✆ **604/628-7400;** www.cadip.org) A 3-week program (1 week of training and 2 weeks of camp), US$290, includes shared group housing, meals, training, materials, and project support. You are responsible for getting yourself to Courtenay.

DON'T MISS: After working intensely with the campers on trust and cooperation, work out any trust issues of your own with an adrenaline rush as you walk the **Capilano Suspension Bridge.** Built in 1889, this swinging bridge is more than 137m (450 ft.) above the Capilano River. Cross over to the Treetops Adventure Park and make your way across more bridges connecting majestic Douglas fir trees as you traverse the Vancouver Island rainforest.

ⓘ www.vancouverisland.travel

People with Special Needs 262

Work with Autistic Children

Education & Support for Families

Beijing, China

THE CULTURAL, POLITICAL, AND ECONOMIC HEART OF CHINA, BEIJING IS WITHOUT A DOUBT one of the most magnificent cities in the world. Since the Olympics, ancient landmarks now sit alongside modern splendor. Beijing is a city to been seen and experienced—tour hidden neighborhoods by bike, have lunch at Wutasi Temple, or dance the night away in the Sanlintun entertainment district.

Awareness of the issues surrounding autism has grown in leaps and bounds in the Western media, but many other parts of the world have only begun to understand this complex disorder. This project in Beijing is based at the first non-governmental organization in China to serve autistic children. Kids with this developmental disorder, which impairs sensory input, are often extraordinarily withdrawn and unable to communicate or learn the way other children do. It takes tireless patience and effort to work with autistic kids, but those who try can find life-changing breakthroughs and satisfaction that tempers the expected frustration of the work.

You will spend intensive time with individual children and their families on this project. You will be fully trained in the special skills and understanding required of you (no prior experience is necessary), and the most vital job skill is compassion and care. Support for families that may not understand the condition well is also important—just letting them share their frustrations and help them learn to manage expectations is a valuable contribution. There is much to learn about this disorder, and the medical community discovers more every day. Working with kids can include simple games, puzzles, and early language recognition. There is bilingual staff on-site, so English is all you need—and the desire to provide loving attention.

You'll have your own room at a local hostel with a self-catering dining room. You'll be responsible for your own meals but are close to many grocery stores and inexpensive restaurants. In addition to thorough project training, you are also given a city orientation; in your free time, Beijing is one of the world's more vibrant cities, with an inexhaustible supply of diversions.

YOUR NEXT STEP: WLS International (✆ **+44/870 479 5145;** www.gapyearinasia.com). A 1-week, £485, or 2-week, £702, assignment includes basic hostel accommodations near the project site, airport transfers, thorough project training and 24-hour backup, city orientation program, and a volunteering fee paid for direct support of the project.

DON'T MISS: After the focused, careful work of this volunteer experience, go to the other extreme and visit **Shanghai,** perhaps the world's most futuristic city with its sci-fi skyline, intense crowds and culture, and amazing food and sights.

ⓘ http://english.visitbeijing.com.cn

263 People with Special Needs

Children & Young Adults with Disabilities

Powering Independence

Beijing, China

Millions of people from around the world come to Beijing to experience the Forbidden City, walk the Great Wall, or stand in Tiananmen Square. Living and volunteering here will not only allow you to experience one of the truly great cities of the world, but will also give you a chance to interact with Beijingers in a more intimate way than tourists who are just passing through.

This program takes on two projects at once. One aspect is helping a community-based charity that serves those with mental disabilities; the other is working with the program's participants to create viable business models to support and extend the same programs. The community-based charities you'll be working with are pioneers in Chinese programming for autistic and mentally challenged individuals. With the latter group, volunteers work to help foster participants' sense of independence through skills training, field trips to local community sites, and a breakthrough program where participants run tourist pedi-cab tours through the old streets of Beijing. The pedal tours help pay for and support the rest of the programs. Craft items created by participants are also sold to fund programming.

You'll teach English, help supervise and assist in craft workshops, help organize welcome programs and presentations for visitors, assist in personal care for participants who may need it, and help out administratively. Gift cards, calendars, and small woven or woodworking craft items are created in workshops in which you can help, and in between arts and crafts, there are classes for exploring music, dance, sports, and drama, all of them supported and facilitated by volunteers like you. The self-worth gained, as well as wages for craft and tour-leading work, makes an enormous difference to these individuals and their families.

You'll have a room to yourself in a Beijing student housing complex, but food isn't provided. (Of course, you'll never have time to work your way through the fantastic and affordable food options, as Beijing has something for every palate.) You'll be assigned a local host to answer your questions and provide support. Upon arrival you'll also have a city and project orientation to help you feel comfortable navigating both the culture and the physical streets of Beijing on work days and on your free time.

YOUR NEXT STEP: Take Me To Volunteer Travel (✆ **+65 6220 1198;** www.takemetovolunteertravel.com). A 1-week project, US$775, or 2-week project, US$950, includes dormitory-style accommodations, full project training as well as city tour and orientation, airport transfers, and 24-hour support.

DON'T MISS: Beijing's **Capital Museum** is a gargantuan cultural hot spot. Seven stories of exhibition space are chock-full of displays reflecting the city's history, architecture, folk customs, and arts. Most of the cultural relics were unearthed from the Beijing region, creating a long look back into the past of the ancient capital.

ⓘ http://english.visitbeijing.com.cn

People with Special Needs 264

School for Mentally Challenged

Specialized Care in Rural Africa

Asakore Mampong, Ghana

YOU WILL HAVE YOUR FILL OF REWARDING WORK IN A BEAUTIFUL ENVIRONMENT WORKING WITH mentally challenged children in the town of Asakore Mampong. Located outside the city of Kumasi, next to the Atlantic Coast, this small town is dotted with cocoa farms and has all the hallmarks and atmosphere of rural African life.

Asakore Mampong has created a special school for children facing mental challenges. One hundred and fifty students between the ages of 8 and 20 are given a better chance for success here after they were floundering from lack of personal attention in the larger public schools. Kids are transferred here for the school's more nuanced teaching methods, personal attention, and much lower student-to-teacher ratio. In this new, specifically catered environment, students are learning to excel.

Working in partnership with the 22-member school staff, you'll teach small groups of students English through discussion groups and one-on-one dialogue. Math is also on your plate, as you work with individuals or a few students at a time. You'll have great fun during game time as you pursue new activities—some physical, some cerebral—that encourage cooperation, sharing, and socializing. Come armed with some ideas of your own—would you enjoy teaching rhythmic music or singing groups? How about dance or soccer? All of it is put to great use in creating new learning opportunities and challenges with plenty of room for expression.

You'll stay with a host family, who will support you in your work and provide meals (twice daily on weekdays, three daily meals on weekends) as you learn the cultural specifics of village life by being immersed in their home. The first 6 days of your stay are spent in cultural orientation programs in the capital city of Accra, so by

Working with mentally challenged children in Ghana

the time you get to Asakore Mampong, you'll have genuine insight into Ghanaian life—only to be solidified by living and working in the village.

YOUR NEXT STEP: Center for Cultural Interchange (✆ **312/944-2544;** www.cci-exchange.com). A 4-week program, US$1,530, includes 6 days of cultural orientation in Accra, host family accommodations, all meals, and full project training and support.

DON'T MISS: For an incredible look at life under difficult circumstances and ingenious ways to thrive, visit the **Village on Stilts of Nzulezu.** The name Nzulezo means "surface of the water," which is where life here takes place. Built just above the waters of Lake Tadane, the village homes, schools, and community spaces are all on platforms that extend out of the water. You take a canoe to the village, which welcomes visitors every day except holy Thursdays. If your timing is lucky, you may see a birth ceremony—every child is baptized in the lake to protect them from drowning.

ⓘ www.touringghana.com

People with Special Needs 265

Helping Disabled Kids Be Self-Sufficient

Boosting Quality of Life

Cape Town, South Africa

OFTEN DESCRIBED AS ONE OF THE MOST BEAUTIFUL CITIES ON EARTH, CAPE TOWN IS AN IDEAL place to combine a love of the outdoors with social work. Scenic Table Mountain and the wild areas surrounding it are something rarely found so close to a major metropolis.

This special project home in the Western Cape is a center for excellence in treating profoundly disabled (intellectually or physically) children and young adults. There are about 90 residents receiving comprehensive care and a precedent-setting system of "stimulated care" that inspires dramatic improvement in functionality. The team of devoted nurses, physiotherapists, occupational therapists, and medical doctors runs the program designed to increase communication, cognition, physical adaptation and fitness, and socialization. Each young person's treatment is specific to their needs and how they can surmount their next hurdle, whatever that may be. Thoroughly trained international volunteers support the staff in all aspects of the program, giving even more care and individual attention to every resident.

You'll assist in daily quality-of-life programs. Stimulus in physical, social, emotional, communicative, cognitive, and sensory arenas is achieved through specific prescribed exercises and activities in one-to-one sessions. You may assist with physical therapy, helping balance an individual as they learn to walk with crutches, or you may help feed children or lead singing or painting work. Perhaps you'll be asked to arrange and accompany the children on an outing, lend a hand in the kitchen, or assist in fundraising activities. Few aspects of the therapeutic work can't be improved by your willing and able hands and energy. Past volunteers have also initiated their own projects, like scrapbooks and a specially decorated "dream room." You may also help facilitate support groups for parents.

Living with a Cape Town host family gives you a resident's point of view. The host family provides your breakfast and evening meals, and lunches are at the center. You can also stay at a shared project house near the city center if you'd rather fend for yourself (dinners still provided). Cape Town, of course, has some of the world's best beaches, beautiful surrounding areas, a bustling waterfront, and nightlife that rivals most big cities.

YOUR NEXT STEP: Twin Work & Volunteer Abroad (✆ **800/80 483 80;** www.workandvolunteer.com). A 2-week project, US$1,259, includes host family (or shared group house) accommodations, two meals daily, intensive training for the project as well as city and cultural orientation, airport pickup, and full project support and backup.

DON'T MISS: One of the more profound places to visit while in Cape Town is **Robben Island,** the prison where Nelson Mandela and many others were held in captivity. Apartheid's political prisoners, rebel princes from abroad, convicts from the Cape, defiant tribal chiefs—they were all banished to the island at some point in its 300-year history. In 1996, the site was declared a National Museum and in 2006 a UNESCO World Heritage Site, a reminder of a difficult chapter in the nation's history and the price paid for the creation of a free democracy.

ⓘ www.cape-town.org

Assist with Disabled Children

Helping Kids in Famous Beach Town

Phuket, Thailand

EIGHT HUNDRED KILOMETERS (500 MILES) AND A CENTURY AWAY FROM BANGKOK, PHUKET'S idyllic beaches and crystal waters have made it the location of choice for many Hollywood movies. Myriad islands off the coast means there's no end to one's exploring. This beach town hosts an international coterie of travelers here to dance the night away on Patpong Beach, or devour some of the country's best food in Phuket Town.

Living in one of the world's most breathtaking tropical countries may sound like the good life to many of us, but for children with physical or mental challenges, it's a constant struggle. The Special School in Phuket provides home and comfort for disabled children ages 6 to 21. Two hundred and seventy kids live at this school, tended by a staff that teaches and nurtures them to adulthood. Volunteers help bridge the gap between the best intentions of the staff and the reality of insufficient time to dedicate to each and every student. The school also provides life skills and occupational training programs to help prepare its students for life outside the comfort of the facility.

Your days will be filled with quiet joy and raucous laughter as you play with kids, teach new games to challenge them, and create new avenues of stimulation. You'll assist teachers as they discuss life skills and give basic lessons. You can work with different categories of resident children, or move among them all, including the autistic, hearing impaired, and mentally impaired. You can help train kids on working in the bakery, creating marketable crafts, and other vocational training. Your weekends are free, but many choose to join the students on field trips and exploratory excursions.

The details of life in this beach town, one of Thailand's most famous destinations, are taken care of for you, including housing at the school (a simple but private room), all meals taken with the kids or staff, in-depth training, and a cultural introduction to the town and its unique customs. If you opt out of weekend activities with the group, Phuket offers many opportunities for lounging. If you're like most, you'll want to take advantage of the amazingly fresh seafood in local, inexpensive restaurants, where you can eat like a king for remarkably few baht.

YOUR NEXT STEP: Twin Work & Volunteer Abroad (✆ **800/80 483 80;** www.workandvolunteer.com). A 2-week project, US$503, includes housing, meals, training, airport transfers, and 24-hour support. The school has bikes you can borrow to explore the surrounding countryside and beaches.

DON'T MISS: A tiny splinter of a bone from Lord Buddha is kept in the Grand Pagoda of **Wat Chalong,** one of Phuket's most visited sites and an important temple structure. Tiny glass pieces make the buildings sparkle in the sun as if enchanted and, while a somber place of reflection and holiness, the wat also hosts grand and elaborate festivals and celebrations throughout the year. It's a beautiful Buddhist temple and is the island's spiritual center.

ⓘ www.tourismthailand.org

People with Special Needs

Camp for Kids with Cancer

Happy Camp

Mountain Center, California, USA

SITUATED IN THE SOUTHWEST PART OF THE STATE, AMID THE ARID DESERT LANDSCAPE OF Riverside County, it's no wonder this camp for kids with cancer uses the surrounding landscape to take kids on outdoor activities like horseback riding and fishing. Nearby Joshua Tree National Park is one of the state's true natural wonders.

In the mountains outside Palm Springs, there is a safe haven where thousands of children with cancer and their families rediscover hope and enthusiasm in an environment free of troubles and concern. To forget, even for a few moments, about being sick, and to not be judged for having no hair or less endurance than your peers, is an unmatchable gift. The success of the programs at the Camp Ronald McDonald for Good Times is entirely dependent on selfless volunteers like you.

Volunteer camp counselors make a 9-day commitment for a weeklong camp session with kids ages 7 to 18. The first 2 days are on-site training and orientation before the campers arrive. This is a camp experience like most others, with plenty of outdoor time in the sunshine. Cabin counselors oversee individual groups of campers throughout the session, monitoring health and other needs and working through the camp programs. Activity counselors facilitate certain programs and activities like archery, horseback riding, crafts, games, music and drama, computers, fishing, cooking, nature study, and so on. Your interests and abilities will help determine where you can be of best service to these remarkable families.

Counselors stay at the camp to live, relax, play, guide, teach, and dine with the campers. Most camp sessions are for patients and their siblings, so a percentage of campers will need specific medical attention or extra care (there is an amazing medical staff living at the camp). You'll have breaks for some quiet time, but once the campers arrive it will be go, go, go.

YOUR NEXT STEP: Camp Ronald McDonald for Good Times (**© 800/ 625-7295;** www.campronaldmcdonald.org). Camp commitment for volunteers is nine days for a seven-day session. There is no charge for volunteer counselors, and lodging, meals, training, and support are provided.

DON'T MISS: Go from the desert floor to the snowy mountains on the **Palm Springs Tramway,** a 4km (2.5-mile) gliding ascent in the world's largest rotating tramcars. The 360-degree views are stunning on your way up to cool camping and hiking sites in the mountains. Most Palm Springs visitors never think they'll need a sweater, but as you gain elevation, the temperature falls, so that even in the hottest days of summer, the cool breezes and pine forests bring adventure and respite from the feverish desert heat.

ⓘ www.palm-springs.org

268 People with Special Needs

Camp for Young Burn Survivors

California Champ Camp

Sanger, California, USA

IDEALLY SITUATED BETWEEN THE SACRAMENTO AND SAN JOAQUIN VALLEYS, SANGER HAS spectacular scenery and a proximity to Yosemite and several other national parks that is unparalleled anywhere else in the United States. Working here will help make you believe in the healing power of nature.

Camp can never last long enough for these burn victims, ages 5 to 16, who get some restorative time away in California's foothills near Fresno. The residential camp sessions each last a week (the volunteer commitment is 10 days to accommodate training sessions), and there is always a need for compassionate counselors and "buddies" that can aid caregivers and be supportive of fire survivors without judging by appearance. It is a humbling experience to live in a festive camp atmosphere away from everyday life and give time and energy to outstanding kids who are victimized twice—once by disfiguring burns and again by the harsh reactions of society. Campers and counselors have extraordinary experiences, with activities ranging from boating and swimming to whitewater rafting, a ropes course, crafts, dirt bikes, horseback riding, go-karts, and more.

The camper-to-counselor ratio is two to one, so kids get lots of attention and quality time. You'll be leading activities, supervising excursions, and being there for support. There is no therapy or treatment program, just fun and a chance to be a kid among other kids who have had similar experiences. Some campers will be quite open about their injuries and how they got burned, and some are there very specifically to forget.

The Champ Camp is residential, so your lodging and meals are included. There is no requirement for experience with burn survivors, but you'll notice plenty of your fellow volunteers are firefighters and medical workers using their vacations as a time to give to these extraordinary campers.

YOUR NEXT STEP: Alisa Ann Ruch Burn Foundation (✆ **800/242-BURN;** www.aarbf.org). Volunteers spend 10 days at Champ Camp, 1 week of camper time with 3 days' training before their arrival. As a residential camp, accommodations, meals, training, and support are all included at no charge to volunteer counselors.

DON'T MISS: If you've never been, or even if you go every year, you must visit **Yosemite National Park** in Central California. It was one of the first wilderness parks in the United States, and the breathtaking Ansel Adams photographs barely do it justice. The beauty you discover there—with 3,108 sq. km (1,200 sq. miles) dotted with famous waterfalls, mountains like Half Dome and El Capitan, and breathtaking valleys—is nothing short of profound.

ⓘ www.fresnocvb.org

Adaptive Sport & Recreation

Give the Gift of Adrenaline

Winter Park and Vicinity, Colorado, USA

A SHORT DRIVE FROM DOWNTOWN DENVER, NESTLED AGAINST THE WESTERN SLOPE OF THE Continental Divide, Winter Park and the surrounding Fraser Valley is a year-round mecca for any and all outdoor pursuits. It's an ideal location for an adventurous adrenaline junkie; here it will be easy to pass on a passion for outdoor pursuits and a love of mountain culture to the kids you'll be working with.

Adaptive sports and sometimes very ingenious equipment make it possible for individuals with disabilities to experience sports and physical activities they previously could never have imagined. From skiing to horseback riding, football to kayaking, this national sports center for the disabled provides wondrous experiences year-round. Young people and adults alike find liberating ways to interact with the world here, with the assistance and encouragement of volunteers and trained staff.

As a volunteer, your work will vary depending on the season and your interests. Mostly you'll be working one on one with a differently abled athlete taking up a sport, perhaps for the first time. If you're visiting in the winter, you might teach alpine or cross-country skiing, snowboarding, or snowshoeing. You'll have attended a volunteer clinic to learn adaptive techniques and teaching skills

Making sports possible for the disabled in Colorado

for individuals with disabilities. If your participant is in a wheelchair, there are special chairs with ski blades, skis with brace supports, and almost any equipment for any set of circumstances. Adapted ski races and competitions occur at various times through the season with which you can help. In the warmer months, help with adaptive horseback riding and take your participant for ring or trail rides. The resort area has alpine slides, a human-sized maze, bungee experiences, and more activities to explore. Maybe you'll explore biking with a tandem bike or walk alongside a hand-crank bike for exploring the mountains. River rafting, kayaking, rock climbing, camping trips—none of them are impossible with the right volunteer and the right adaptive equipment.

Your length of stay and time commitment are variable depending on season and sport. Some require more advanced training before working with a disabled individual. Aside from multiday camping excursions with a group, accommodations, meals, and other arrangements are your responsibility. Fantastic perks exist for volunteers in their free time, like all-day lift access to the excellent ski slopes. The beautiful resort area is full of activities for you to try out as well.

YOUR NEXT STEP: National Sports Center for the Disabled (✆ **970/726-1540;** www.nscd.org). Time commitments and training schedules vary throughout the year. No travel arrangements are made for volunteers, so you'll arrange your own stay in the resort area. No charge for volunteers, and some additional benefits like lift tickets or access to horses and riding trails are available.

DON'T MISS: Your adrenaline itch will be scratched every day while volunteering, so before or after your stint, take an easy but fascinating journey into the earth. The mining train at the **Bachelor Syracuse Mine** goes down 914m (3,000 ft.) into the ground, where drilling and mining brought a boom to Colorado. It also gave rise to terrific mining towns like Breckenridge, Leadville, and Central City—all of which are great places to stay today.

ⓘ www.colorado.com

People with Special Needs

Give Kids the World

Welcome to Funland

Kissimmee, Florida, USA

You need to be a kid at heart if you want to work with kids in Kissimmee. As a volunteer in the Give Kids the World Village, you'll spread joy and fun to kids with life-threatening illnesses. And in Kissimmee, you'll be staying in the land of never-ending smiles—a place packed with world-famous amusement parks, including Disneyworld and Seaworld.

It's a special day when you can bring children with life-threatening illnesses to this Orlando area's amusement parks and allow them (and their families) to forget the daily grind of hospitals, tests, pain, and sickness. This 28ha (70-acre) resort (a children's village of more than 100 villas) offers free entertainment attractions, games, and amusement park fun specifically designed for special needs kids. Children and their families arrive from every state and many countries to enjoy a week of getting away from it all (with a top-notch medical facility and staff always available), and a corps of volunteers makes the project hum every week of the year.

You'll be responsible for your own smile and those of all the families. You may spend a morning serving flapjacks, then graduate to scooping ice cream all afternoon. Perhaps you'll be asked to operate the train ride or greet families as they arrive. You may spend a chunk of your day inflating balloons or helping pack up picnic baskets. There is an almost endless number of things you can do to help (each week requires more than 1,300 volunteer work shifts to be filled), and there is almost nothing the staff and volunteers won't do to coax out a laugh and make a whole lot of dreams come true.

While there are no specific volunteer accommodations or arrangements for travel, the village is well versed in helping make it easy for volunteer groups and individuals from around the world who travel here to pitch in. Of course the Kissimmee and Orlando area have more hotels rooms per capita than most places on Earth, so finding a place nearby shouldn't be difficult. Your free-time activities are limited only by your energy, with the world's most famous amusement parks and beautiful opportunities to see nature all quite close by.

YOUR NEXT STEP: Give Kids The World Village (✆ **800/995-KIDS;** www.gktw.org). Your help is based on your own plans and schedule of available time, which is worked out with a village coordinator before you arrive. Your stay and meals and other particulars are your responsibility while volunteering.

DON'T MISS: You're in the Orlando area, so you know you want to go to the **amusement parks.** Disney, Universal Studios, SeaWorld, Islands of Adventure, Epcot, and numerous other water parks, pirate adventures, animal attractions, rides, IMAX theatres, and more await.

ⓘ www.kissimmeetouristinformationbureau.com

People with Special Needs

271

Camp for Those with Disabilities

Camp with the Courageous

Monticello, Iowa, USA

THIS CAMP IS IDYLLICALLY LOCATED IN AN AMERICA OF A BYGONE ERA; MONTICELLO IS THE kind of place where you can expect to see apple pies cooling in kitchen windows. Here country fairs, pumpkin festivals, and walks through nearby scenic woods are the main forms of entertainment.

More than 5,000 campers of all ages with varying disabilities come to Camp Courageous throughout the year for respite and recreation. Over 60ha (150 acres) of Iowa land boasts swimming pools, cabins, and every kind of outdoor recreation venue a kid could want or need. The goal is for individuals of all ages with disabilities to challenge themselves in a supportive, safe environment. The resulting self-esteem carries over when campers return home, and many come to Camp Courageous with their families year after year. The camp relies upon volunteers for much of the practicalities of daily camp life, from counselors to garden help.

The organizers try to match you to your interests and requested dates when you volunteer. You'll work with individuals and groups of campers and family members throughout a week's activities and challenges. Each camper's needs and abilities are different, so you may spend afternoons at the pool or on excursions in the woods, therapeutic exercise, or crafts. Other duties can include gardening, trail blazing and marking, building sidewalks and boardwalks for additional wheelchair access, helping in the kitchen, staffing the visitor's center to answer questions or give tours, or helping administratively in the office. You won't be bored.

Volunteer counselors live in camp in the shared staff/volunteer dormitories, and meals, taken with the campers, are a large part of the experience. You won't have a lot of free time, as you are dedicated to the campers and their needs, but there are certainly plenty of hikes and local exploration you can pursue during breaks. Volunteers are responsible for getting themselves to camp for their assigned sessions and trainings.

YOUR NEXT STEP: Camp Courageous (✆ **319/465-5916;** www.campcourageous.org). Volunteer counselors are not charged for their time at camp. You will determine the length of stay, dates, and preferred work assignments when you apply. Live in the staff/volunteer dorms and eat meals with campers.

DON'T MISS: An interesting snapshot of a very specific Iowa culture from a time gone by, but preserved and well loved by locals, are the seven **Amana Colonies,** one of the state's most famous travel destinations. You'll find handicrafts and indigenous foods and much more at these authentic German villages that were founded as a religious commune 150 years ago. The old barns, the wool mill, the brewery and winemaking facilities, artist workshops, bucolic hiking trails, and the stoic, simple architecture all implore you to slow down and enjoy a relaxed pace.

ⓘ www.traveliowa.com

272 People with Special Needs

Help Kids with Life-Threatening Illnesses

A Ray of Light

Casco, Maine, USA

A small resort town whose population swells fivefold during the summer, Casco's pristine lakes and ponds are its main draw. Summer camps and seasonal resorts can be found throughout the town, while the area's many craft, gift, and antique shops add to its Old World charm.

Camp Sunshine is working toward 40 camper weeks per year, when children with life-threatening illness and their families come to relax, play, and remember what it is to be a family. Camper weeks are based on their health focus (for instance, oncology one week, children with lupus another, organ transplant patients the next, and so on), so the campers and families have much in common with the rest of the families visiting. A great emphasis is placed on the effect that living with a life-threatening illness has upon the entire family—patient, parents, and siblings. The camp is for each of them to find ways to play and relax together. With a target of one volunteer per two campers, there is plenty of quality time and attention for every child (and parent) at the 6-day camp. Attendance is free for families, and each stays in their own suite.

There is a full-time medical and general staff, but an amazing squadron of volunteers does most of the nuts-and-bolts work. Many volunteers return to the camp year after year, coming back to the shores of Sebago Lake, in beautiful Southwestern Maine. Your days are split into the same schedule as the campers, with breakfast, morning activities, lunch, afternoon activities, rest time, dinner, and evening programs. You may be working at the marina, beach, or pool or pitching in with food service, spending a shift at the nursery caring for very young children, or teaching teens arts and crafts. You could be assigned to kayak duty or a table tennis tournament or even computer game time. Volunteers serve as photographers, talent show coordinators, campfire singers, and lifeguards. The volunteer-led activity sessions are times for ill children and their healthy siblings to interact with lots of other kids their age and give parents some alone time, and other activity sessions are designed to get the whole family involved as a team.

You'll live at camp in shared rooms of four or five counselors. There is a small refrigerator and microwave in your room if you need snacks, but all meals are provided. Your free time is your chance to exhale and maybe flip through a book before jumping back into the fun of camp life.

YOUR NEXT STEP: Camp Sunshine (✆ **207/655-3800;** www.campsunshine.org). Camp sessions are 1 week (campers are in residence for 6 days), and there is no charge to volunteers. You'll live in dormitory-style shared rooms with other volunteers, and all camp meals are provided, as is extensive training and support.

DON'T MISS: While in Maine, rent a car and drive the stunning jagged coast on a wildly scenic **lighthouse route** to see the state's iconic symbol. Lighthouses' bright beacons and booming foghorns cut through foul weather, warning ships of danger, and while less critical to nautical navigation than they once were, the drama and romance of these sentinels is undeniable. More than 60 lighthouses stand guard along the rocky coast of Maine, from the well known Nubble Light in York to West Quoddy Head, the easternmost lighthouse in the United States.

ⓘ www.cascomaine.org

People with Special Needs

Therapeutic Equestrian Program

Horses that Help

Warrington, Pennsylvania, USA

A LOVE OF WORKING WITH CHILDREN AND THE OUTDOORS IS WHAT'S NEEDED HERE MORE THAN horse-riding experience. At Special Equestrians, you'll help administer physical therapy using horses to those with physical disabilities. During downtime, get your feet dirty by hiking the part of the Mason-Dixon trail that runs through Warrington or rough it in one of the towns many campgrounds.

This program provides the very unique benefits of hippotherapy and therapeutic riding for individuals with disabilities. When people with both developmental and physical disabilities are able to sit atop a horse and move in union with the animal, incredible breakthroughs happen. The movement of the horse is similar to the human gait, so patients without mobility of their own experience a version of walking. Therapy horses are incredibly gentle and social, and the bond made with them is tremendous. There are also therapeutic riding programs for adults over 55 years who have age-related disabilities; therapeutic riding lessons for at-risk children and kids with emotional disturbances; and a sensory trail that adds specific stimulation for riders already comfortable on horseback. Riding helps fine motor skills, hand-eye coordination, self-confidence, risk taking, and trust.

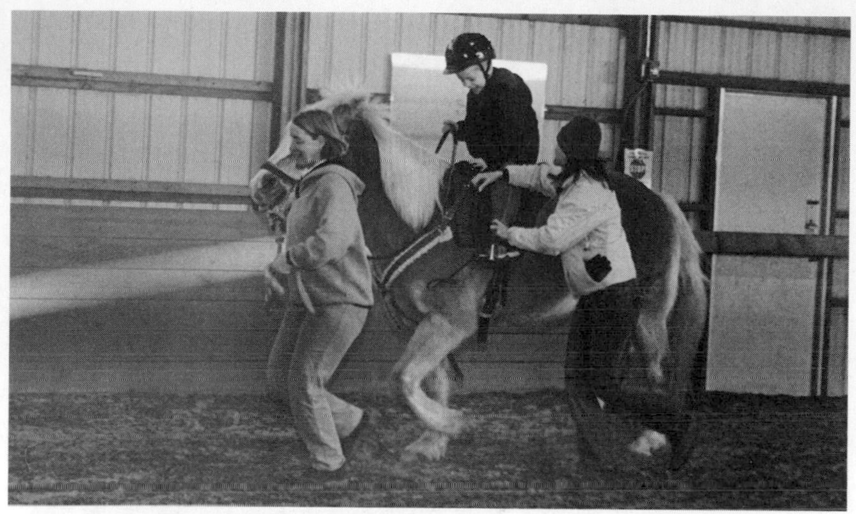

Therapeutic horseback riding in Warrington, Pennsylvania

As a volunteer you needn't be a skilled rider. You'll be taught all you need to know to assist the physical or occupational therapists working with the individuals. Your work may include leading the horses in lessons, walking alongside clients in their lessons, horse care and grooming, tacking up the horses, small barn and facility maintenance, feeding and watering, and perhaps a bit of clerical and marketing support.

There is no residential program for volunteers, so you'll find your own accommodations, dining options, and transportation to the riding clinics, but volunteers are always needed. A willingness to help make a contribution to people with disabilities and a love of horses are all you need to take part.

YOUR NEXT STEP: Special Equestrians (✆ **215/918-1001;** www.specialequestrians.org). You'll contact the organization when you know you'll be in the Pennsylvania region and can donate time and energy to the hippotherapy and therapeutic riding programs. You'll make your own arrangements for the time you're there, as there is no formalized travel program.

DON'T MISS: If you've got a sweet tooth, head to **Hershey, Pennsylvania,** a town entirely obsessed with chocolate. There's an amusement park, resorts, golf, surprisingly nuanced cuisine at some terrific restaurants, and desserts, desserts, desserts—even a chocolate spa with chocolate body treatments.

ⓘ www.visitpa.com

People with Special Needs

Horse Riding Therapy & Lessons

Ride & Help Disabled Kids

Quito, Ecuador

WITH AN EQUESTRIAN HISTORY DATING BACK CENTURIES, ECUADOR, AND ITS CAPITAL, QUITO, IS an ideal place for horse lovers to use their riding skills for a good cause. The modern northern section of the city is in stark contrast to the more ancient southern part. Both lie in the shadow of the indomitable Andes Mountains and both are ideal for exploring on two legs or four.

People may say that dogs are man's best friend, but no animal has worked so closely with us as the horse. The bond of trust developed while riding on the back of these magnificent animals can be magical and transformative. Equine therapy, known as hippotherapy, where horses are used with disabled patients, has been a respected branch of mental and physical therapy for many years. In Quito, hippotherapy has changed the lives of many children with disabilities such as Down's syndrome, polio, degenerative brain disorders, and other physical or developmental challenges.

Ecuador has more than 1.6 million people registered with disabilities, and with only a very few facilities for the disabled, most don't have access to educational or social opportunities. Only 3 percent of Ecuador's disabled population has access to medical doctors or therapists. Hippotherapy, with its rhythmic movement and the endorphins generated from a session with the horse, as well as the confidence engendered from time in the saddle, makes young patients much more responsive to other, sympathetic therapies as well.

Alongside trained therapists, you'll help children sit or lie on the horse, then either lead the horse or support the child from the side, or perhaps sit in the saddle holding them. Morning therapy sessions are followed by time when you'll help care for the horses, the riding ring and equipment, and help around the facilities. You'll also have free time to do some of your own riding, if you wish, and the foundation earns extra income for programs by offering paid horseback riding lessons in the afternoon, with which you can also help. Spanish is the main language spoken at the foundation, though most permanent staff members are multilingual. If you're not a confident Spanish speaker, the organization offers one-on-one Spanish language lessons during your placement.

Quito is set between two mountain ranges and has a huge historical center, full of museums and heritage sites, so you'll have no problem filling your every waking moment and will likely come to the end of your stay far too soon, especially with the impact you'll be having on these kids and their families. If you didn't already know, you'll recognize that horses, and people, can be magical.

YOUR NEXT STEP: Global Sports Xperience (✆ **0871/221 2929;** www.globalsportsxperience.com). A 4- week project, £795, £100 for each additional week up to 12, includes host family accommodations, with two meals daily. You'll buy your own lunch, rarely more than a few dollars. Spanish instruction, 20 hours per week, is £150. Project includes 24-hour support, airport transfers, and culture and project orientation.

DON'T MISS: Ecuador's capital, Quito, has the largest historic center in the Americas, and outside of town in the foothills of the Andes, you'll find a unique monument: the **Middle of the World.** This is the location of equatorial zero latitude, where you can straddle both hemispheres at once.

ⓘ www.quito.com.ec

School for Blind & Deaf Children

Beaching in Benin

Cotonou, Benin

The political, economic, and cultural capital of Benin offers visitors a uniquely urban yet African experience. At the same time, beach culture dominates this part of the country, so when work becomes too much, head to Grand-Popo Beach—a hot destination for visitors wanting to trade traffic and concrete for sun and sand.

Differently abled children are often ostracized and easily targeted for scorn. This primary school offers special programming for disabled children, and it's also the first of its kind in the country to offer a specialized classroom program for blind and deaf students. A great emphasis is placed on integration and socialization with the community at large. French-speaking volunteers assist classroom teachers in every aspect of the learning day.

You'll work in tandem with the Beninois teacher to aid vision or hearing impaired children with daily lessons and homework. You might work on speech therapy and pronunciation with a group of hearing-impaired kids, then help with a clay sculpture class for visually impaired students. There are counseling and mentoring sessions and sometimes caregiver and parent support instruction so the strides taken by these extraordinary students can be supported and built upon in their homes. Outdoor recreation and games are also an important part of the day and sometimes require one-on-one assistance.

Volunteer team members stay in local homes with family hosts, so again your

A volunteer with her students in Cotonou, Benin

intermediate French-language skills will be important (French lessons are available for volunteers at extra cost). The host family provides two meals daily during the school week and three meals daily on the weekends. There is a cultural immersion and orientation program upon arrival, so you'll understand Benin and Cotonou and feel comfortable during your stay. Cotonou is a large city with all the culture, dining, entertainment, and nightlife you might want for weekend diversion.

YOUR NEXT STEP: Center for Cultural Interchange (✆ **312/944-2544;** www.cci-exchange.com). A 4-week program, US$1,550 includes host family accommodations, most meals (weekday lunches can be purchased at the school cafeteria or nearby shops or eateries), cultural introduction courses, project training, and full support.

DON'T MISS: The city of Abomey was once the capital of the ancient kingdom of Danhomè, and its royal palaces in the heart of the city are now part of the **Abomey Historical Museum.** The site is home to the palaces of King Guézo and King Glèlè, extending over 44ha (108 acres). It has been on UNESCO's World Heritage Site list since 1985, and the range of architectural styles, as well as the sizable collection of royal objects, make a great day's exploration.

ⓘ www.benintourisme.com

People with Special Needs **276**

School for the Hearing Impaired

Leveling the Playing Field

Cape Coast, Ghana

WHETHER TEACHING SPORTS OR JOB SKILLS TO THE HEARING IMPAIRED, OR TAKING CARE OF Ikando's school grounds and animals, spending time in Ghana's Cape Coast will bring many rewards. One of the country's most history-rich cities, Cape Coast is home to the country's oldest and most well-respected schools, as well as ancient castles and historical museums.

This Ghanaian school strives to give hearing-impaired children a well-rounded education rivaling that of every local child. Hearing impaired students are sometimes diagnosed late, after learning issues and social integration problems arise. Here, students are integrated into the regular demands of school, which provides not only classroom excellence, but vocational skills training. Volunteers support the goals of the school on many levels, from facility management to classroom assistance to special teaching and outing arrangement and attendance.

Your dedication will find plenty of avenues of expression here. You may help with the upkeep of the grounds or in caring for the farm animals and gardens. You can also help teach job skills like sewing, farming, carpentry, and animal husbandry. Sports instructors are needed to teach kids new games or perhaps supervise some competitions or tournaments. If you know sign language, you can help with study groups and homework. The library needs to be reorganized, and perhaps you can pursue more donations from international sources to add to the collection. You might even lend your construction talent to building projects as the classrooms and library are improved or expanded.

You'll be living at the school with basic lodging. The Cape Coast is the regional capital with plenty of dining options (meals aren't included in the fees) and cultural venues. It's a big city with excellent infrastructure where you'll find amazing fresh foods and plenty of items to buy at local marketplaces. You'll have a thorough in-country orientation to Ghana upon arrival, so the city will become quite familiar, and fellow volunteers and school staff become a tight-knit family, bound by a strong commitment to these amazing kids.

YOUR NEXT STEP: Ikando (✆ **+233/21 222 726;** www.ikando.org). A 2-week project, US$681, includes housing at the school property, airport pickup and return, local orientation and training, 24-hour backup and support, and donation to the school. Meals are your responsibility.

DON'T MISS: Ghana's **Kakum National Park** is a huge forest preservation region with plenty of opportunity for wildlife adventure. Rare plant species are found in this tropical zone, where guides can teach you about medicinal plants and daily village life. More than 550 species of butterfly are found here, thousands of plants (some towering well over 30m/100 ft. above your head), 200 bird species, forest elephants, foraging herds of hoofed animals, reptiles, amphibians, and plenty of monkeys. Treetop canopy walkways and nature trails on the ground allow you to take in both levels of the wildlife at your own pace if you'd rather not go with a guide.

Students at a school for the deaf in Cape Coast, Ghana

ⓘ www.touringghana.com

277 People with Special Needs

Kids' Program for the Hearing Impaired

Indian Integration

Kerala, India

Keralites are said to have the highest standard of living in India. Nestled on the shores of the Arabian Sea, Kerala's emerald backwaters and kilometers of pristine beaches have made it one of the most desirable destinations on the continent. A wide array of exotic wildlife, cultural festivals, and historical monuments make teaching here less of a job and more of an adventure.

While some programs for children with impaired abilities set up learning environments specifically suited to their needs, others, like this one, aim to help them integrate into the larger system so they are less isolated. This school for deaf and

10 Food Banks in Tourist Hot Spots

It isn't just remote societies or developing nations that face massive problems with starvation and hunger. There are people whose dietary needs are not met in every culture, even in the world's wealthiest nations. These food bank programs work tirelessly to get donated food to the hungry, helping to nurture individuals to better health—almost any food bank program, including those close to home, always need helping hands.

278 **Melbourne, Australia** The VicRelief Food Bank works with thousands of volunteers annually, collecting food, both prepared and dry, donated from corporations and restaurants, as well as non-perishables from individuals. The organization also does emergency disaster relief, coat and blanket drives, and provides kitchen/homeware items to families. Contact the volunteer manager to get busy. ***VicRelief Food Bank*** *(volunteer manager ✆* ***+61/3-9362 8333****; www.vrandfb.com.au).*

Volunteering at the Food Bank for New York City

279 **Buenos Aires, Argentina** The Banco de Alimentos (Food Bank Foundation) is perpetually in need of both short-term and long-term volunteers. You can volunteer for a morning or an afternoon, or for several days, in the warehouse. While Spanish is the main language, English speakers can still negotiate volunteer duties without a problem. ***Fundación Banco de Alimentos*** *(✆* ***+54/11-4724-2334****; www.bancodealimentos.org.ar and www.volunteersouthamerica.net).*

280 **Vancouver, British Columbia, Canada** In a year, more than 80,000 volunteer hours are needed to run the Greater Vancouver Food Bank Society. Short-term volunteers work special events and holidays, or any day in the main warehouse. Email or call ahead when you know your schedule in Vancouver. ***Greater Vancouver Food Bank Society*** *(volunteer ✆* ***604-876-0659, ext 102****; www.foodbank.bc.ca).*

281 **Hong Kong** After the financial crisis of 1998 in Hong Kong, the numbers of homeless, hungry, and "street sleepers" increased dramatically. The People's Food Bank relies on volunteers, and even a commitment of a few hours can help. Many of the workers will be speaking Chinese, but English is widely spoken throughout Hong Kong. The organization is also grateful for administrative volunteers. ***People's Food Bank*** *(✆* ***+852/2975 8777****; http://foodbank.sjs.org.hk).*

282 **Rome, Italy** In 1986, European national non-governmental organizations got together and created the European Federation of Food Banks (www.eurofoodbank.org). In Rome, able bodies are needed that are willing to pitch in and take direction (even without Italian-language skills). Contact the food bank to get on the roster. ***Banco Alimentare del Lazio*** *(✆* ***+39/06 4890 7463****; www.bancoalimentare.it).*

283 **Kansai, Japan** Serving the hungry and homeless of Kobe and Osaka, Food Bank Kansai is dedicated to preventing food waste and making the best possible use of nutritious resources. Volunteers and a skeletal staff inspect and divide donated items for distribution to orphanages, soup kitchens, homes for the elderly, mental hospitals, and rehabilitation clinics. The food bank operates 6 days a week, and is eager for as much volunteer time as you have to give. ***Food Bank Kansai*** *(© **+81/ 0797-34-8330**; http://foodbankkansai.web.infoseek.co.jp).*

284 **San Miguel de Allende, Mexico** Feed the Hungry not only gets food into mouths of hungry children and adults, it also builds small, efficient kitchens at schools that employ many local women as cooks, and provides other local jobs during construction. More than 4,000 children receive nutritionally balanced hot meals every day. Volunteers are invited to work in the warehouse preparing food for delivery to more than 30 kitchens in town, do inventory, and load trucks. Spanish is helpful but not required. ***Feed the Hungry San Miguel*** *(© **505/349-3700**; www.feedthehungrysma.org).*

285 **Johannesburg, South Africa** The JoBurg FoodBank partners with the city's fresh food market to provide the freshest, healthiest produce and other foods to those affected by HIV/AIDS. The FoodBank also reaches out and nourishes orphans, the indigent, the aged, and the homeless. Fresh fruits and vegetables from the farmers market and other large-scale donors are collected, divided, and delivered to almost 350 organizations that care directly for the hungry. ***Johannesburg Fresh Produce Market*** *(© **+ 27/11 992 8000**; www.jfpm.co.za).*

286 **Los Angeles, California, USA** Founded in 1989, Project Angel Food delivers hot nutritious meals to homebound individuals and families affected by HIV/AIDS, cancer, and other life-threatening illnesses. Meals are prepared in the project kitchens by professional chefs assisted by volunteers, then delivered to the home of clients on a delivery route. ***Project Angel Food*** *(volunteer © **800/592-6435**; www.projectangelfood.org).*

Project Angel Food volunteers in Los Angeles

287 **New York, New York, USA** For a quarter-century, Food Bank for New York City has been fighting food poverty and providing nutritious meals throughout the five boroughs. More than three million New Yorkers use the food bank, and it supplies more than 1,000 food assistance programs. Contact the program when you know how much time you have to give. ***Food Bank for New York City*** *(main office © **212/566-7855**; www.foodbanknyc.org).*

hearing-impaired students ages 4 to 18 helps kids communicate and be active in society. Speech therapy, adaptive hearing aids, lip reading, sign language, and more specific tools are all intended to help hearing-impaired students blend with other kids their age and find the self-confidence that comes from independence. While not denying their difference, the hope is to never see their hearing as a handicap.

Local nuns run the school, and you'll be assisting in the classroom and out. You'll work with individuals or small groups on arts and crafts projects like sculpting, woodworking, painting, and computer art programs. One of the more fascinating programs is music and dance. Different students have different levels of hearing and attunement to percussion or other vibration, so each finds his or her own way and hears music of their own. In a non-judgmental environment, encouraging them to move and dance to the sound they perceive results in truly astonishing forms of expression. Groups of kids will also play and learn new games with you outdoors, and perhaps also go on short field trips to local parks or museums or other enrichment activities off-campus.

While in Kerala, you'll be staying in a comfortable guesthouse with other volunteers. The owners are next door so you'll have access to anything you need as well as a source of local expertise and advice. Three Indian meals daily are provided, but if you want to explore other cuisine there are shops and a supermarket steps away from the house. A thorough orientation to the town and culture is part of your first days, and a local team is available for further needs. English is the language of the project, but you can learn some of the local Indian dialects as well. Kerala has plenty of places to see and explore and is a center of Ayurvedic medicine and healing traditions, so taking advantage of a massage or healing facial can be a dreamy way to spend a day off.

YOUR NEXT STEP: i-to-i (✆ **800/985-4852;** www.i-to-i.com). A 2-week project, US$837, includes lodging at a local guesthouse, all meals, local orientation, project training and support, and airport transfers.

DON'T MISS: In the rice paddies and lush agricultural fields of Kerala, many planting areas are still irrigated by foot power. Get a workout and some fun from walking on the local **treadmills** that work like a mill paddlewheel, with human effort turning a belt with dippers that fill with water, travel along a line, and tip into the fields, spilling the water to nourish the plants. It's a fascinating example of simple ingenuity that has been practiced for a very long time.

ⓘ www.incredibleindia.org

Malaria & Other Diseases **288**

Medical Relief & Care

Desert Medicine

Ahmedabad, India

THIS PROJECT BEGINS AND ENDS IN AHMEDABAD, THE SIXTH-LARGEST CITY IN INDIA, TEEMING with ancient architecture and one of India's main intellectual and literary centers. The city's rich, touchable heritage lies in stark contrast to the poverty many of its citizens live in.

In areas where medical care is elusive, if accessible at all, some people may walk for days to attend the free medical camps provided by this intrepid organization. Staffed by local doctors and supplied by the Indian Red Cross with medicines and basic equipment, general practitioners, pediatricians, a dentist, ear/nose/throat

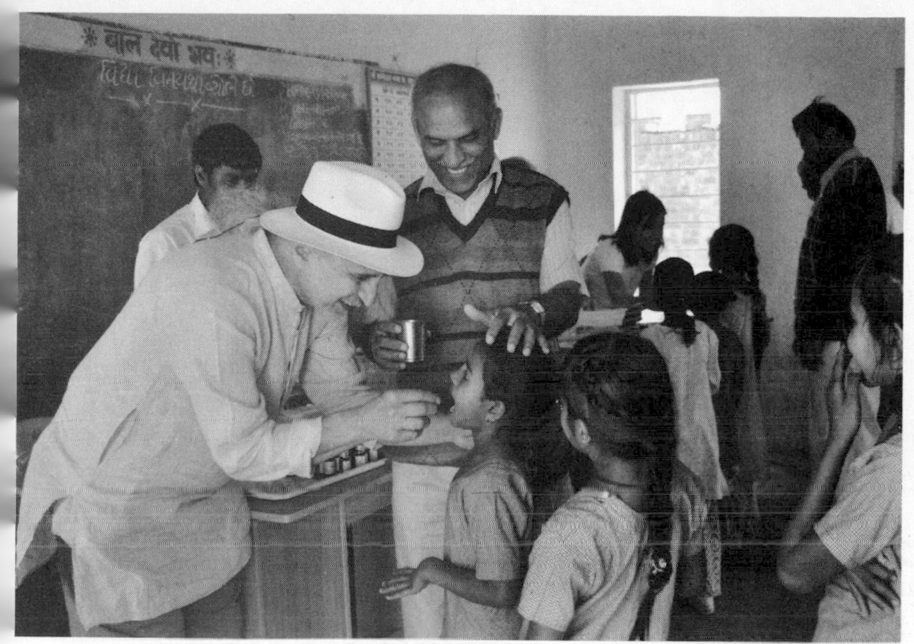

Providing medical care to children near Ahmedabad, India

specialist, optometrist, OB-GYN, and other specialists are supported by a volunteer team and together will, in one day, see and treat hundreds of patients and often send them home with free prescriptions for health conditions they may have been tolerating for weeks or even months. The camps are well-orchestrated, enormous undertakings. This organization also goes to the majority of the region's schools, delivering school supplies and deworming medication for every student. They even provide free cataract eye surgery clinics. The desert sun is brutal and there is no protection from UV rays, wind, and sand, so cataracts often strike a huge number at young ages.

Even if you don't have any medical experience, helping to remove post-surgical bandages for a patient who will see again after decades of cataract-induced blindness will shift your own focus forever. In just 12 days you'll assist thousands who will receive sometimes life-saving medical attention. You may staff the pharmacy table, where doctors have prescribed one of more than 20 available medicines. Syrups need to be measured and pills counted from enormous bottles and jars of donated medicine. You'll work intake tables, perhaps with a translator, taking down the name, age, and medical concern or complaint of each person before sending them to a particular doctor. High-energy crowd control is needed to entertain children and keep order in an outdoor atmosphere that's like a community gathering (neighboring villagers may not have seen one another for seasons, so talking and socializing makes the day quite lively). Perhaps you will be distributing sunglasses, the first ever, to patients who have just had corrective surgery. Maybe you'll help the dentist clean the instruments between extractions or drop sticky red medicine onto the waiting tongues of toddlers.

Aside from arrival and departure days, when you'll be in comfortable hotels, you'll be camping in spacious, two-person desert tents. There are cots and bedding and plenty of room to walk around in these round canvas shelters. A latrine trailer provides gravity flush toilets and stalls for a bucket bath. Fantastic food, much of it local vegetarian fare, is provided, and plenty of excursions fill free time. Cultural programs fill daylight hours, as well as optional meditation walks and morning yoga on the desert sand, and gathering around the campfire under a full moon is the perfect end to exhausting days in the field. Local musicians and dancers often visit camp, so don't be surprised if you're coaxed out of your seat to twirl a bit around the fire.

YOUR NEXT STEP: Relief Workers International (✆ **413/329-5876;** www.reliefworkersinternational.com). This 12-day project US$5,950, includes a sizable donation toward medical and school supplies, accommodations in hotels or historic forts, then in tented encampments, all meals, in-country transportation, cultural programming and excursions, and full training and support.

DON'T MISS: In Delhi, thousands visit the tomb of Gandhi, and in Guajarat, thousands also visit the **Birthplace of Gandhi.** In the city of Porbandar, the house where he was born is called Kirti Mandir and has been converted to a holy place and national monument. There are tens of thousands of books in the library (and a collection specifically for women and children, who often don't have access to libraries in some regions), and it is a place of year-round celebration and festivities.

ⓘ www.incredibleindia.org

Malaria & Other Diseases **289**

Community Health Care

Help Out at Clinic in Land of the Aztecs

Chicueyaco, Mexico

HIGH IN THE SIERRA NORTE REGION OF MEXICO, NEARLY 200KM (125 MILES) AWAY FROM THE city of Puebla, Chicueyaco's remote location leaves residents without easy access to good health care. This lush, mountainous area is rich with coffee, macadamia, and vanilla plants. Working here you'll be rewarded by not only the richness of the natural landscape, but the spirit of the Nahua people.

Surprisingly, some of the world's most fertile regions can also be the most hazardous. Humidity and abundant water are important for lush growth in rainforests, rice paddies, and other ecosystems—but they also create ideal conditions for breeding mosquitoes and the infectious diseases they carry. This village of indigenous Nahua, descendants of the Aztecs, is an agriculturally dependent, rain-soaked mountain community. The Nahua women's group decided that medical facilities were insufficient in their village and have built a small health clinic. The clinic offers immunizations, checkups, medicine, and prophylactic treatments to prevent many common local diseases.

The clinic itself needs structural work: a permanent roof to replace the temporary one, permanent tile floors and other interior projects, and several improvements to improve the facility's sanitation and sterility. This is a community that primarily uses medicinal plants prescribed by traditional healers, so introducing immunization and manufactured medicines is a cultural transition, and in order to prove their value, new procedures must be impeccably executed. You'll also support the clinic administratively with office support, aiding education efforts in the village and surrounding areas. Some Spanish will go a long way, as the village language is Nahuatl (no Berlitz tapes for that one) and secondarily some speak Spanish.

You'll be staying at a small eco-hotel run by Nahuatl women, and while the hotel has electricity and plumbing, many of the homes in Chicueyaco do not. All meals are included, with breakfasts at the hotel, lunch shared with the community, and large dinner gatherings filled with communal celebration. The surrounding countryside is famed for caves and tunnels in the lush forests, so adventure beckons in your free time. The sometimes rugged terrain requires some hiking experience. Nearby Aztec ruins at Yohualichan also demand a visit, as do local market days when the community gathers for festive connections as well as selling their crafts, wares, and harvests (vanilla, coffee, and orchids are all prime crops).

YOUR NEXT STEP: Global Citizens Network (✆ **800/644-9292;** www.globalcitizens.org). A 10-day project, US$1,575, includes shared hotel accommodations and meals, in-country travel, training program and materials, support, and emergency insurance.

DON'T MISS: Mexico City's **National Museum of Anthropology** is home to the largest collection of ancient Mexican pieces in the world. An historical timeline through the nation's development is highlighted by the "Sun Stone," the famous Aztec calendar. Exhibit halls are dedicated to Mayan and Oaxacan culture, with recreated tombs and temples. It is a world-class collection in a beautiful building.

ⓘ www.visitmexico.com

290 Malaria & Other Diseases

Moroccan Medical Mission

Delivering Care While Traveling the Country

Several Locations, Morocco

FROM THE LABYRINTHINE STONE STREETS AND SOUKS OF THE BIG CITIES TO THE ENDLESS ROLLING desert sand dunes, mystery and adventure seem to beckon around every corner in Morocco. One thing that's certain is the appreciation you will receive from the people you will deliver medical care to as part of this trip.

Like Rick in Casablanca, you may think it's the beginning of a beautiful friendship when you spend a vacation helping implement health care and delivering valuable supplies to hospitals and clinics in Casablanca and other Moroccan locales. Volunteer Morocco takes dedicated international teams of workers to underprivileged communities in the country's southwest to improve health care and people's access to it, invigorate education, supplement farm technologies, and help form micro-enterprise. You'll also see a lot of the country: famous bustling cities and struggling small communities. From your arrival in Casablanca, you'll travel on, helping along the way, to Marrakech, Agadir, Imsouane, Ighaln, and Assaka.

Your 2 weeks in Morocco are organized into two components: urban and rural volunteering. Your city days will find you working in a 500-bed hospital, delivering donated medical supplies and equipment, and supporting the daily needs of a hospital-run orphanage. In the countryside you'll deliver school supplies (desks, chairs, chalkboards, donated computers, clothes, sports equipment), help set up temporary medical clinics, and support local doctors and nurses in serving communities that have no regular medical access. Some of your volunteer colleagues may have medical experience, but none is required, and your willingness to jump in and work tirelessly will make an enormous difference. There is even a day built in to get outside and install drip irrigation systems and fencing to help a burgeoning agricultural program.

The team travels together in a project vehicle, and you'll stay in small hotels or hostels. Three meals daily are either provided at local restaurants in cities or prepared by villagers in rural stops. Moroccan Arabic, French, and Berber are spoken in Morocco, so the program provides translators (but if you know some French or a little Arabic, you'll find your time in the country more fulfilling). You won't leave this mysterious country without having seen many of the more popular tourist spots, as guides provide opportunities to visit souks, hammams, mosques, museums, madrassas, marketplaces, and other landmarks.

YOUR NEXT STEP: Volunteer Morocco (no direct phone in Morocco, email info@volunteermorocco.org for prompt return call; www.volunteermorocco.org). A 2-week project, US$1,745, includes hotel and hostel accommodations, three meals daily, airport pickup and all in-country transportation and touring, translators and guides, and project training and support.

DON'T MISS: You will have visited and worked in many of the Moroccan must-see spots, but a side trip to the stunning blue city of **Chefchaouen** would be a great addition to your visit before or after the work period. Also known as Chaouen or Ashawen, this mellow town's cobbled streets and old medina buildings are all painted vivid sky-blue colors. Close to Tangier and the Spanish border, the crags of the surrounding majestic mountains inspired the town's name, which translates as "Look at the Horns." Goat cheese, woven textiles, and wool garments from this area make great souvenirs.

ⓘ www.visitmorocco.com

8 Teaching Through Sport

Working with the disabled in Winter Park, Colorado

Coaching & Training

Work the Homeless World Cup

Pitch in on the Pitch

Melbourne, Australia

No football fan could pass up this chance to volunteer at one of the world's most unique international sporting events in one of the world's most unique cities. More laid-back and beachy than Sydney, Melbourne manages to maintain a hip, eclectic international vibe. Taking part in the annual Homeless World Cup will give you the chance to effect real change, while helping "the beautiful game" live up to its name.

Soccer, futbol, footie, whatever you like to call it, is the most popular team sport in the world, and the world's biggest sporting event is the World Cup. In cosmopolitan Melbourne, where they take their footie *very* seriously, there's an alternative tournament no less important, and you can help make it happen. The Homeless World Cup shatters stereotypes as more than 500 soccer players from 56 nations compete—and each is homeless. Some 25,000 homeless competitors play in their home countries in the qualifying games before the top teams are chosen for the Homeless World Cup. In 2008, a Women's World Cup was added, and there is now also a cultural festival to highlight the plight of the homeless and outdoor screenings in Federation Square of films made by and about the homeless.

The festival and tournaments depend on volunteers like you each year. More than 400 matches will be played during the week, and you'll opt for the ways to pitch in that best suit you: coordinating transportation, registration and information booths;

Fans cheering at the Homeless World Cup

acting as a referee or scorer, or even medical or media services. You will work full 8-hour days in the Australian summer (winter in North America), but Melbourne's temperate beach weather keeps you cool during the days and the coastal neighborhoods, like St. Kilda, have some excellent cultural and dining options for your evenings and free time.

YOUR NEXT STEP: Homeless World Cup (✆ **131/561-1796;** www.homelessworldcup.org). On-site volunteers during the 1-week tournament receive a meal during daily 8-hour shifts, but beyond that you'll arrange your own accommodations and meals. **Hands Up Holidays** (✆ **201/984-5372;** www.handsupholidays.com). A 17-day trip, US$3,200, includes accommodations, meals, and a post-tournament trip to Sydney and the Great Barrier Reef.

DON'T MISS: Take a breathtakingly scenic drive north on the **Great Ocean Road** to see the famous Twelve Apostles, the Otways rainforest, and Bells Beach. www.greatoceanrd.org.au

ⓘ www.visitmelbourne.com

292 Coaching & Training

Coach Tennis at Top Tennis Academy

Serving Up Sun

Perth, Australia

THE PICTURE-POSTCARD BEACH TOWN OF PERTH IS AN IDEAL PLACE TO PASS ON YOUR KNOWLEDGE of how to hit a perfect backhand or add some spin to your serve. One of the sunniest places in all of Australia, it's hipster meets hippie in this most modern, yet still laid-back of cities.

Perth is known as Western Australia's "action city," and most of that action happens outdoors. Tennis has a wide and enthusiastic following, and on this project you'll coach junior and senior players at all levels to improve their game. Your proximity to the beach and civic green spaces will keep you outside long after match point, but you'll also need to put in some off-court time helping with marketing and lesson planning.

You may opt to go through the Coach Trainership Program, which isn't required but is great experience if you're a coach or hope to pursue a coaching career at home. You'll also be given a subscription to a coaching web community, including a membership in the International Coaches Association (ICA), represented by coaches from 65 nations. Your mornings are spent in mixed group classes while your afternoons and evenings have you coaching individuals. The 12 junior teams at the club comprise boy and girl players of various levels, and the nature of the game means you'll be spending lots of one-on-one time working toward tournament play. Extra lessons can be picked up on weekends as well.

Home base is in Perth's Central Business District, so you have easy access to shopping, great restaurants and pubs, cultural institutions, and the main shopping district. You'll stay in a central lodge where you'll share kitchen and bathroom (as well as pool table, cable TV, arcade games—all the comforts of home) and have a room to yourself—so you won't be roughing it. The rough part is packing up and leaving the copious sunshine.

YOUR NEXT STEP: Travellers Worldwide (✆ **+44/1903 502595;** www.travellersworldwide.com). A 2-week stay, £926, includes food, accommodations in group lodge with private room/shared bath, full project support as well as city and project orientation, and airport transfers.

DON'T MISS: In a city where people spend as much time as possible outdoors, the most beautiful attractions are basking in sunshine. **Kings Park and Botanic Gardens** is nearly 405ha (1,000 acres) of parkland, gardens, and native bushland. The views from its heights on Mount Eliza, as well as meandering trails, hundreds of species of flora and fauna, and State War Memorial, bring locals and visitors alike. In the summertime, al fresco performances and festivals fill the calendar. www.bgpa.wa.gov.au

ⓘ www.perthtouristcentre.com.au

Coaching & Training **293**

Teaching Sport & After-School Programs

Andean Orphans

Santa Cruz, Bolivia

SITUATED AT THE FOOT OF THE ANDES MOUNTAIN, SANTA CRUZ IS BOLIVIA'S LARGEST CITY and arguably one of the country's most culturally diverse. Here, ancient cathedrals and Incan ruins vie with the extraordinary tropical beauty of the Amazon for a visitor's attention. Keep in mind Santa Cruz also happens to be the country's gastronomic capital.

In Santa Cruz, you'll work with youth ages 5 to 18, most from the orphanage, who are eager for mentoring and structured activity. Sport and game projects provide healthy alternatives to the lures of crime and drugs that many of their peers find irresistible.

A 2- or 3-week stint will keep you busy and, more importantly, keep your charges busy. It's an easy learning curve as they engage in teamwork and discipline while practicing their English as they listen to you. You'll directly influence their confidence and tolerance of others as these kids practice soccer, basketball, aerobics, track, even chess and other board games. As you immerse them in play and integrated healthy competition, you'll find yourself awash in the warmth of the "family" they create among their friends.

You'll coach, train, referee, and help maintain the gym and field, along with your student helpers, giving everyone a sense of ownership and pride in the equipment and arena. You can also help with homework, teach conversational English, and support after-school study hall and extracurricular game activities.

Many children in rural Bolivia still don't have access to regular schooling, and family pressure to work can pull them away from educational opportunities at a very young age. Children in rural areas average 4 years of school, and urban Bolivian students top out at an average of 9 years, but across the board, education is uneven and underfunded. Your contribution of time and energy will have an enormous impact on the enthusiasm of kids, keeping them interested and engaged. Many volunteers also bring sports equipment with them, knowing balls and nets (as well as games, shoes, and team jerseys) are rare.

YOUR NEXT STEP: uVolunteer 🎗 (✆ **971/252-1334;** www.uvolunteer.org). A 2-week program, US$695, includes food and accommodations, 24-hour support, host-country orientation, and airport transportation.

DON'T MISS: 120 km (75 miles) southwest from Santa Cruz you'll find the fortress **El Fuerte de Samaipata,** a large site of Inca ruins declared a UNESCO World Heritage Site—which some people insist is also a landing area for UFOs.

ⓘ www.visitbolivia.org

294 Coaching & Training

Teach Surfing in Rio

A Whirl in Ipanema

Rio de Janeiro, Brazil

RIO MAY BE PORTUGUESE FOR *RIVER*, BUT HERE LIFE IS ALL ABOUT THE BEACH. THE CITY'S sun-loving vibe makes Rio de Janeiro seem more like a state of mind rather than a home for more than five million people. The abundance of beaches makes this an ideal locale for anyone who wants to combine their love of surfing with volunteering.

You don't need to have the skills of Laird Hamilton to volunteer on Rio's beaches, as you'll be getting surf coaching yourself while participating and passing on your skills to local underprivileged kids. In the surf at Ipanema Beach, you'll work one-on-one with future longboarders and work with small groups instructing on the sand. Before your excited pupils arrive, you'll clock a few hours maintaining and repairing surfboards, and when the group is gathered, your interactions will give them a great opportunity to practice English skills (as well as your Portuguese).

The program has goals that extend beyond coaching sport and healthful activity to include important lessons about the environment. It's an easy yet crucial connection: if we don't protect and preserve the ocean, we can't have this amazing experience. Another immersive element of the surf school program is bringing financially challenged youth to Praia de Ipanema, one of Rio's most upscale shore areas. An incredible disparity of wealth exists among *cariocas*, or native Brazilians, but kids from poor neighborhoods rarely get out to see other ways of life. Program organizers have found that integrating social classes and increasing kids' awareness of how to live a healthier, more comfortable life creates real incentive beyond the fun of the waves. And they take their surfing seriously—real commitment and discipline is required for kids to remain in the programs.

Your 2-week or longer assignment will give you plenty of downtime to enjoy the allure of Rio. With a relaxed daytime schedule, your evenings are free to explore Rio's legendary nightlife. A bracing dip in the ocean each morning can be the best cure for what ails you from the night before. But don't indulge too much—your energy and enthusiasm are your best assets for this sunny stint in the sea.

YOUR NEXT STEP: i-to-i (toll free: ✆ **800/985-4852;** www.i-to-i.com). A 2-week program, US$1,450, includes accommodations in the project group house, project training, and airport transfers. You'll be responsible for your own food, but eating is inexpensive in Brazil—expect to pay about US$50 per week.

DON'T MISS: You'll already be spending your days at Ipanema Beach, but a trip up to Mount Corcovado to one of the "New Seven Wonders of the World," the **Christ the Redeemer statue,** also affords the greatest views.

ⓘ www.riodejaneiro-turismo.com.br/en

Coaching & Training 295

Introduce At-Risk Kids to Recreation

Child's Play

Ontario, Canada

THE PROVINCE'S SLOGAN—"YOURS TO DISCOVER"—IS AN APT CALLING CARD TO DESCRIBE the plethora of Ontario's outdoor offerings. Using nature to help at-risk kids is a tried and tested form of physical and mental therapy, and there's no better setting than Canada's most ecologically diverse and unique province.

Because of budget constraints, physical education programming in schools and after school is being cut in many cities, and children are the ones paying the price. You just need to walk past a playground at recess time to see how widespread childhood obesity has become. Teamwork, cooperation, and problem-solving skills get worked out through play when a group of youngsters is united in a single goal. When sports teaching and coaching is cut from school curricula, kids who aren't naturally athletic and inclined to pursue sport begin to fall through the cracks.

Ontario's KidSport program is bringing coaching and equipment to underprivileged and underserved kids, and the KidSport FunZone day opens the door to children wanting to explore new sports and games. Volunteers help this traveling sport carnival visit several communities, setting up and manning stations for each sport: here's a chance to shoot baskets while across the way is a soccer goal–scoring

At-risk youth enjoy a game of street hockey through Ontario's KidSport program

game. Eager kids might try tennis, swinging a golf club, and hitting a home run. When they need a break, they can enjoy some nutritious snacks and a hot, healthy lunch. It's a challenging but fun day, and it runs smoothly because you donate your time and energy to welcome all these kids to an active lifestyle where they can find something about which to get truly passionate.

While you're visiting Ontario, you can choose to throw yourself into one FunZone day or several as your schedule permits. FunZone Ontario events happen through the spring, summer, and fall, so you'll get to enjoy the province's incredible outdoor life, and if you choose to travel event to event, it is a fantastic way to see some of Canada's most beautiful sights.

YOUR NEXT STEP: KidSport (✆ **416/426-7171;** www.kidsport.on.ca). The FunZone projects utilize locals and visiting volunteers, without any formal travel program. You'll make your own Ontario arrangements and might choose to stay in or around Toronto, as several of the larger events occur nearby. There is no registration fees for volunteers, just lots of gratitude.

DON'T MISS: Niagara Falls, once the land of the tackiest of honeymoon haunts, has regained some respect while never losing any of the true grandeur of this thundering natural wonder—try a boat cruise or helicopter viewing for the ultimate in appreciation. www.niagarafalls tourism.com

ⓘ www.ontariotravel.net

296 Coaching & Training

Coach Swimming in Paradise

Building Comfort in Tropical Waters

Lautoka, Fiji

PARADISE MAY BE AN OVERUSED WORD TO DESCRIBE THE SOUTH PACIFIC, BUT WHEN IT comes to Lautoka, it definitely applies. Surrounded by the ice blue waters of the Pacific Ocean, this city has some of the most modern sporting facilities in the region. Regardless, it is the ocean for which it is most envied. Lautoka is an ideal setting for anyone interested in teaching swimming—whether it's indoors or out.

It's a natural but mistaken assumption to presume that islanders know how to swim. Proximity to water doesn't guarantee skill or even comfort. Fiji is a tropical heaven, but many of the young people are simply never taught to swim in a controlled environment. Those who discover a love for swimming are hungry for organized sport and competition opportunities.

Work on the west side of the island with programs in schools and after-school swim club sessions. Your knowledge will also fuel the fire of local coaches doing the best they can to meet a higher demand than they can satisfy. Coach the coaches and coach the kids, and spend long, satisfying hours in the water knowing that the knowledge you pass on will carry forward.

Lautoka is Fiji's second-largest city, known as "Sugar City" for its main export crop. Cane fields stretch skyward as far as the eye can see from the town's edges. After your coaching gig each day, your fingertips might look like prunes, but when in Fiji, even in your downtime you'll want to hang out at the great beaches or perhaps the nearby golf courses at Denaru Island.

The warmth of Fijian's hospitality is equaled only by the warmth of the legendary sunsets, and you'll be smitten with the incredibly respectful kids. Your biggest challenge may be convincing the team that practice is over and it's time to get out of the pool. If you have multisport experience, the Lautoka school programs are always looking for coaching advisers in field sports as well.

YOUR NEXT STEP: Madventurer Foundation (✆ **0845/121-1996;** www.madventurer.com). A 2-week project, £829, includes dorm-style accommodations in the project house, meals, 24-hour on-site support, and local transportation.

DON'T MISS: Before or after your intensive time with Fijian youth, you'll want to snorkel or scuba dive in some of the globe's most pristine waters. Most guests will find themselves invited to enjoy traditional **kava** (*yaqona*) drinking. You'll likely join a family, sitting on the floor around a large bowl of grey/brown liquid. The pulverized Piper methysticum root brings relaxation and even euphoria to some drinkers.

ⓘ www.bulafiji.com

Coaching & Training 297

Coach Cricket, Tennicoit & More

Game Time in South India

Tamil Nadu, India

In India, cricket is not only the national game, but a national obsession. The southern state of Tamil Nadu attracts people from all over the world, drawn to its sandy beaches, Hindu temples and religious architecture, and otherworldly natural beauty. A perfect spot to combine a love of sport with the sun-drenched exoticism of Indian culture.

If there is flat, open ground in Indian rural villages, you'll find kids playing cricket on it. Similarly, if a net can be strung up and rings found, a tennicoit game will ensue (invented in India, tennicoit is a volleyball-like game played across a net with rubber rings in place of a ball). There is no shortage of enthusiasm for these games (as well as a burgeoning scene in volleyball, basketball, tennis, and track and field), but there is a scarcity of resources and opportunity. Schools can't afford paid coaching staff or supervision, but while you're vacationing in the area, you can bridge the gap.

The vibrant history of the coastal Tamil region is peppered with monuments and temples, and the intricacy of architecture will fascinate you. Inspired curries will power you through your day assisting local volunteer parents and coaches. You may lead warm-ups and keep score, set up nets, or coach and teach new skills if you can. The particulars are less important than the act of being active.

Two weeks is not nearly enough to absorb the South Indian way of life, where long, lingering meals and searing sunsets are spent among the Tamil people, one of the oldest civilizations on Earth. This region is known for the peaceful coexistence and respect among all spiritual traditions and belief systems, and lacks the frenetic energy for which India is renowned. Particularly known for traditional ceremonial dance, Tamil Nadu locals gather in the evenings for celebrations blossoming in colorful dress and costumes, even on weekends when there is no holiday on the calendar.

YOUR NEXT STEP: Projects Abroad (USA: ✆ **888/839-3535**. CAN: ✆ **877/921-9666;** www.projects-abroad.org). A 2-week program (longer trips available), US$1,995, includes meals, accommodations with host families, airport transfers, travel insurance, and 24-hour support.

DON'T MISS: Arjuna's Penance is a phenomenal work of intricate bas-relief carving in the town of Mamallapuram, perhaps the world's largest such artwork in open air. The elephants are life-size, gods and demons are fierce and heroic, and birds and beasts abound. The story of the multitudes of figures rendered in loving detail is taken from the *Mahabarata* and was carved in the 7th century.

ⓘ www.tamilnadu-tourism.com

298 Coaching & Training

Coach Sport Programs in Schools

Game On in Mongolia

Ulaanbaatar, Mongolia

Surrounded by majestic mountain ranges, Ulaanbaatar can truly be called a city that time forgot. Although the modern world is slowly encroaching on Mongolia's capital, most structures here were built before World War Two, and any kind of social and physical infrastructure remains scarce. But if you want to see unspoiled nature, and witness a nomadic way of life that for many has changed little over centuries, this is the place to do it.

One of the world's most sparsely populated nations, Mongolia has lots of wide-open space coupled with rough weather, and getting to school can be a challenge for a disproportionate number of kids. Unfortunately, getting there is only half the battle, as teaching resources and standards tend to be poor. Sports and physical activity are a luxury rarely available in the curriculum, if at all.

It is ironic that organized physical activity is so elusive in a nation where strength is so prized: the most popular sports and cultural competitions are based on physical and combative prowess. Wrestling, horsemanship, and archery take the top spots for popularity, but Western games are beginning to catch on as awareness of global culture increases. Soccer, basketball, volleyball, and table tennis get lots of interest, even though knowledge and equipment are lacking.

You needn't be expert at any of these sports to assist in school programs or camps based in and around the nation's capital, Ulaanbaatar. A little knowledge will go a long way, and a lot of energy and rapport is the most highly prized quality in volunteers. In addition to teaching sport rules and strategies, refereeing matches and general exercise, fitness, and warm-ups will be important, and your English will be translated, so you needn't be panicked about communicating. If you have a particular sport or game passion not currently enjoyed at the project, new pursuits are treasured.

You'll live with a host family, and probably find yourself grilled for information about life at home. While the nation is isolated geographically, it has become well connected to the rest of the world, and the West is a source of true fascination. Even community members with the least to share will gladly see you fed before feeding themselves, so the sense of welcome and hospitality is unmatched.

YOUR NEXT STEP: Projects Abroad (USA: ✆ **888/839-3535**. CAN: ✆ **877/921-9666;** www.projects-abroad.org). A 2-week placement, US$1,995, includes accommodations with host family, three meals daily, travel and medical insurance, and 24-hour support and backup.

DON'T MISS: Many visitors know little about the history of Mongolia beyond the

10 Places to Shout "GOOOAAAALLLLL!!!"

Nearly every culture in the world has a version of a game where kicking a ball past the opposing team is the goal. Football/soccer is the most played sport on the planet and an absolute obsession in many cultures. The camaraderie and sense of combined effort for a common goal instills a way of thinking that resonates off the field, and you would be hard-pressed to find a naysayer concerning the value of sport in the lives of kids.

Volunteer coaches with their team in Posadas, Argentina

299 **Posadas, Argentina** The rapid expansion of the city of Posadas means that marginalized citizens are being pushed farther and farther away. Kids from the lowest income families ache for activities, and sport is considered the best and healthiest avenue for their energies. ***i-to-i*** *(toll free: ✆ **800/985-4852**; www.i-to-i.com). A 2-week coaching commitment is US$1,190.*

300 **Rio de Janeiro, Brazil** Soccer is as much a part of Brazilian blood as hemoglobin, and a chance to raise the skills of young players is an opportunity to raise hope and self-esteem. Coach, referee, manage, promote, and develop workshops and seminars to give these players a real shot. ***Institute for Field Research Expeditions*** *(✆ **800/675-2504**; www.ifrevolunteers.org). A 2-week project isUS$1,061.*

A soccer practice in Accra, Ghana

301 **Accra, Ghana** If you're an active youth in Ghana, you play soccer. For the many impoverished children, it is a welcome escape from the challenges of day-to-day life. This immersion program places emphasis on your cultural learning, with guided tours and community immersion, as well as the benefit to the kids you will mentor. ***World Endeavors*** *(✆ **866/802-9678**; www.worldendeavors.com). A 2-week stay (longer available) is US$1,318.*

302 **La Esperanza, Honduras** Being a coach from another country conveys celebrity status on volunteers in this mountain village of forests and fields, and the at-risk kids participating, as well as adults in the village, are committed to making this a soccer community. ***Intibucá Soccer Volunteers*** *(✆ **504/783-0421**; www.satglobal.com/volunteer.htm). A 2-week coaching program is US$1,105.*

303 **Madurai, India** The results of this soccer program have pleased local families for several years, with children learning positive personality changes, improved health awareness, increased confidence, and stronger social skills alongside the coaching they receive. The Sports Club where you'll coach is for students 10 to 20

years of age. ***Travellers Worldwide*** *(✆ **44/1903 502 595**; www.travellersworldwide.com). A 2-week coaching program is £795.*

304 Chisinau, Moldova Soccer is the number-one sport at Moldova's largest sport academy, the Sportiv Lyceum, but even the most talented of youths often have to give up the game at a young age since out-of-school programs aren't funded. This soccer program is devoted to three teams covering ages 5 to 12, 13 to 17, and adults. ***Projects Abroad*** *(USA: ✆ **888/839-3535**. CAN: ✆ **877/921-9666**; www.projects-abroad.org). A two-week program (longer trips available) is US$1,795.*

305 Hout Bay, South Africa Near this fishing village on the Cape Peninsula is a shanty township, Imizano Yetho, where enthusiasm for soccer abounds. Team play and informal competitions against other teams is new to this community but becoming extraordinarily popular. ***Abang Africa Travel*** *(✆ **27/21 426 1330/4**; www.abangafrica.com.) A 2-week placement is US$556.*

The Cape of Good Hope, near Hout Bay

306 Ja-Ela, Sri Lanka The soccer pitches are gravel and dirt, so the game is faster than on grass, but you'll be inspired to keep up and deliver much-needed equipment and help run tournaments. You'll coach underprivileged children at several schools, perhaps running practices at three schools each day, for your 2-week assignment. ***Travellers Worldwide*** *(✆ **44/1903 502 595**; www.travellersworldwide.com). A 2-week program is £795.*

307 Santa Cruz, California, USA This coastal surf city, home to large numbers of farm workers, has developed, with the Resource Center for Nonviolence, La Liga de La Comunidad soccer league, providing community sport for hundreds of adult and youth team members, with a focus on conflict resolution and sportsmanship. At-risk kids get summer league camp activities on and off the field, run by volunteers. ***Resource Center for Nonviolence*** *(✆ **831/423-1626**; www.rcnv.org) No fees for volunteers/no formalized programs: come pitch in for a game, for a day, or for a camp session.*

308 Nationwide (14 Urban Areas), USA Atlanta, Bay Area, Chicago, Cleveland, Dallas, D.C., Denver, L.A., Miami, Milwaukee, New England, New York, Seattle, St. Louis—the SCORES soccer and literacy programs occur in several large cities throughout the United States, empowering students with a mix of sport and creative expression. The victory of completing a poem is as important as scoring a goal, and the surge in confidence in both arenas genuinely helps kids grow. Be a volunteer referee, soccer coach, writing coach, or special event planner during your visit to the active cities. No charge for volunteers. ***America SCORES*** *(✆ **212/868-9510**; www.americascores.org). Contribute your time and energy for an afternoon or your entire vacation.*

name Genghis Khan, so it only makes sense to visit his fabled city, **Karakorum.** The seat of the empire in 1220, it was pillaged by Khubilai Khan, but you can still see evidence of the 108 *stupas* (domed markers bearing Buddhist relics) that populated the country's first Buddhist monastery, as well as 62 temples and stone turtles that surrounded city.

ⓘ www.mongoliatourism.gov.mn

Coaching & Training **309**

Coaching School & Community Sport Programs

Building Teamwork at 8,000 feet

Sacred Valley, Peru

IN THE HEART OF THE INCA EMPIRE, SPORTS ARE INDEED SACRED. THE INCA TRAIL AND infamous Urubamba River attract adventurous spirits looking to purify their souls through intense walking or whitewater rafting. Of course, exploring nearby Machu Picchu—one of the seven new wonders of the world—can be considered a sport unto itself.

In Peru's Sacred Valley, in the shadow of the Andes with the Urubamba River roiling alongside precipitous roads, your passion is all you need to develop programs in basketball, soccer, and volleyball for local schoolchildren ages 6 to 14. Don't be surprised if you get winded while the kids laugh and play circles around you—they're used to the high altitude—as these kids have energy to burn.

Overburdened physical education teachers will work with you side by side in morning classes, while organized tournaments, after-school leagues, and informal team play can take up your afternoons. Most of the children work very hard on farms and in other labor, so playtime is especially rare and cherished. With rotating crop schedules, school terms go year-round, and kids are pulled from classes for harvest season, so a sense of team and shared goals is more valuable than you'd first imagine.

Some villages in the area have well-tended fields and courts, but just as likely you may be making the best effort possible in the available space, which might be a side street or fallow field where chickens and livestock wander through your game. The teams won't mind. They revel in the challenges and camaraderie, as well as learning more than just shooting or spiking skills from a new friend from far away. You'll probably be inundated with more personal questions about your life back home than queries about the finer points of a free throw, and your presence will expand the understanding of international culture as much as your knowledge of the game will expand their play. The spirit of playing as a team is the biggest lesson you, as well as your charges, will learn. Don't expect saying goodbye to be easy—you'll want to stay much longer and cheer them on to become the champions they are.

YOUR NEXT STEP: Projects Abroad ([USA: ✆ **888/839-3535**. CAN: ✆ **877/921-9666;** www.projects-abroad.org). A 2-week program (longer trips available), US$2,195, includes meals, accommodations with host families, airport transfers, travel insurance, and 24-hour support.

DON'T MISS: The famous pilgrimage site of **Machu Picchu** should be a priority on everyone's travel list, and it is only a short train ride away. If you're looking for a bit more adrenaline, whitewater rafting on the nearby **Urubamba River** is a great way to spend an afternoon.

ⓘ www.visitperu.com

310 Coaching & Training

Teach & Coach Sports

Sport Support Near Lake Victoria

Kampala, Uganda

More synonymous with political strife than sport, Uganda's capital of Kampala is in great need of some enthusiastic athletic ambassadors. Known for being a safe city, it is home to dozens of non-governmental organizations and, as a result, a large and thriving expat community. Kampala is also known throughout the region for its massive outdoor markets and thriving café culture.

In the capital city of Uganda, as in much of East Africa, you'll find that sport is a language unto itself. Working with young people and developing cooperative social skills can be done by teaching and coaching badminton, basketball, netball, rugby, soccer, swimming, and volleyball. You'll work with youth, as well as teachers and community leaders, in established programs in and out of school, promoting health education and fitness. Organizers have found sport leagues a particularly effective way to capture the attention and passion of young people and also use the practice field as a secondary teaching arena for information about HIV, AIDS, STDs, and crime and violence. After a game, you'll be joined by health-care educators who will take over and impart their important messages.

The slums and poorer areas of Kampala can be rough on kids and adults, so healthy diversions are welcome here. Sport is highly regarded, and entire communities turn up for matches. Your presence as an ambassador of sport will make you well respected in the community. Tourism to Uganda has been on the rise, so the infrastructure is surging as visitors invigorate the local economy of this city of gently rolling hills near the shores of Lake Victoria.

Your support is invaluable both on and off the field, assisting coaches and teaching small groups, or acting as an umpire or referee, as well as performing administrative and computer support, photography, local fundraising, game organization, scorekeeping and compiling results, awards ceremonies, and so on. Your most important requirement will be lots of enthusiasm and encouragement, and it will take a lot of both to keep up with the kids. You'll spend full days immersed in activity and camaraderie, and have evenings free to explore (guided or on your own) the large city renowned for friendly hospitality.

YOUR NEXT STEP: Real Africa Adventures (**✆ 136/383-957;** www.real-africa.co.uk). A 2-week project, £1,960, includes meals, hotel accommodations, airport transfers, 24-hour support, and 3 days of safari adventure and city tours.

DON'T MISS: Primates are the country's star attractions. Book a registered gorilla or chimpanzee excursion in **Bwindi Impenetrable National Park** or **Mgahinga Gorilla National Park.** www.uwa.or.ug

ⓘ www.visituganda.com

Coaching & Training 311

Snow Sports with the Disabled

Opening the Slopes for All

Winter Park, Colorado, USA

Sitting in the shadow of the Colorado Rockies, Winter Park makes an ideal locale for anyone interested in teaching winter sports. If it takes place on snow, it take places here: skiing, snowboarding, snowshoeing, even snowmobiling are some of the activities offered in abundance, as is a great selection of après-ski activities.

The National Sport Center for the Disabled (NSCD) has a volunteer vacation program so that you can enjoy the slopes while teaching and inspiring people with special needs. The students with whom you'll work may have learning disabilities, adaptive disabilities, or brain injuries; you might be paired with a visually impaired or hearing-impaired skier; all of them are waiting for you to help them get the same joy from the snow that you know. Don't be intimidated, you'll be trained and only need intermediate ski or board skills.

Helping a student enjoy a day on the slopes

Your half-day of training clients gives you the other half of each day (and free lift/slopes access) to enjoy a fantastic snow sport vacation of your own. You might spend part of the day as a lesson assistant; later you might help with adaptive equipment, skis, and sleds, then work for a shift helping to load and unload students on the chairlifts. If you time your trip right, you might be there to help set up courses and assist in running one of the seasonal competitions, a truly rewarding experience for participants and volunteers. Rest assured, the simple pleasure of cross-country skiing or snowshoeing in a meadow with the participants is a reward beyond words.

For 35 years, thousands of children and adults with disabilities have come to the NSCD to experience the splendor of the Rockies and truly challenge themselves to increase strength and determination in the snow. You'll be humbled by the environment of these majestic mountains, and that won't hold a candle to the awe you will feel for the clients with whom you'll work.

YOUR NEXT STEP: National Sports Center for the Disabled 🎗 (**© 970/726-1546;** www.nscd.org). A 1-week project includes special access to reduced-rate lodging. Your other expenses are yours but are nicely offset by free daily access to the ski areas/lifts/and so on., and there is no enrollment cost for the program.

DON'T MISS: Your dogs will be tired from all that skiing, so give over to dogs that never get tired and take a **dog sled ride** on a 243ha (600-acre) private tract of pristine land just outside Winter Park. Humans don't have the same capacity as these dogs for this much enthusiasm. www.dogsled rides.com/winterpark

ⓘ www.winterpark.travel

312 Equipping the Game

Keeping It Slick: Luge & Bobsleigh

Olympic-Caliber Speed

Whistler, British Columbia, Canada

IF YOU'RE THRILLED BY THE RUSH OF RACING DOWN SLICK, ICE-LINED TRACKS AND HAVE A desire to pass on those skills, then Whistler is the place for you. Flanked by glaciated mountains on all sides, it's a place that sees more than two million visitors a year, making it a natural choice for hosting part of the 2010 Winter Olympic Games. This is your chance to race on the same tracks as the best in the world.

Take some time from your winter vacation and put in some volunteer days helping at one of North America's premier sliding tracks. The lightning-fast sliding sports of luge, bobsleigh, and skeleton can only be practiced on very specific, expert courses. Whistler, home to the 2010 Olympic Winter Games, has one of the finest facilities, but it's not just the athletes in the tight costumes enjoying the excitement—a team of volunteers gets the unique opportunity to make it all work.

This is icy work, and as a volunteer track sweeper you get closest access to the action, keeping the ice competition-ready. Strap on some crampons and make sure the track is slick regardless of sun and melt or snow and ice. If that doesn't sound like your cup of tea, volunteer for the start crew. You'll perform equipment checks, monitor access, communicate with the control tower, and assist athletes. The finish and weights crew volunteers assist athletes at the end of the race and do sled checks to make sure no one cheats. Volunteer course marshals assure the safety of competitors as well as spectators.

It's all pretty physical, and precision is important for international competition, but you'll be supporting international athletes in some of the fastest sport events ever invented. The world's best sliding athletes look forward to tough competition each winter in Whistler, and your efforts make a range of events, from local contests to World Cup and Olympic events, run smoothly and safely. There are few sports where adrenaline runs higher.

YOUR NEXT STEP: Whistler Sliding Centre ✆ **604/964-2401;** www.whistlersliding centre.com). You'll make your own vacation plans, but the athletes and support crew at the Olympic venue hope you'll spend some time being part of the highest level of sliding competition in the world.

DON'T MISS: It's winter, and it's Whistler—you're going to ski. Consistently ranked as one of the top ski/snowboard resorts in the world, **Whistler/Blackcomb** also has the largest ski area in North America. More than 200 runs means you'll have to visit time and again to hit them all.

ⓘ www.tourismwhistler.com

Equipping the Game 

Field of Dreams

A Place to Play

Kathmandu, Narayani, Nepal

More known for its spiritual offerings than its sporting ones, Kathmandu makes a great base for anyone interested in teaching sports. Nestled in the lap of the Himalayas and named after the river it's situated next to, volunteering at the Narayani Sports Club offers the athletically inclined a chance to share their skills and expertise while living among the majestic mountains of Nepal.

Kids can create a game anywhere. Give them a flat open space and free time, and it's as good as any stadium. They don't know what they don't have, but give them access to a play zone with clear markings and goals, backstops and bases, and there's no limit to what they can do.

The Narayani Sports Club is registered with the Nepalese government and seeks to create league play in volleyball, badminton, and cricket. Undeveloped land near the riverside in Chitwan has been deeded, and the club plans to create a beach-like section of the banks of the Narayani, including fields for open play and warm-up exercises, volleyball courts with nets and lights, badminton courts, and a cricket pitch. Volunteers will spend days clearing rocks, leveling ground, filling holes, staking court lines, and more. Your gig will be one or more weeks, and there is plenty of free time, including an incentive tourism package for jungle safaris, elephant rides, canoe trips, village tours, and camping excursions in your downtime. Of course, when the work is done, you'll likely have as much fun kicking a ball around with local kids or teaching them a good old-fashioned game of freeze tag. It will be balm to your blistered hands knowing that you've made a permanent, structural improvement in a village that needed your help to make it so.

You'll stay with a host family and eat two traditional Nepali meals daily and have tea time twice daily as well. You'll get some basic Nepalese language training, and most locals will have a voracious appetite for learning English words. Your accommodations will be somewhat rustic, but you'll be guaranteed your own room (if not electricity). Life is simple in Nepal, and the community is grateful for your contribution, as well as your company, which is seen as bringing honor to the village.

YOUR NEXT STEP: Naryani Sports (**© 977/ 98-5108-8020;** www.narayanisports.blogspot.com). A 1-week placement, US$50, includes host family accommodations and meals, airport transfer, training, and project support. Programs are partnerships with **Future Nepal** (http://futurenepal.org) and can include safari activities in downtime. Expanded (with safari) weeks are US$300.

DON'T MISS: You can visit **Everest Base Camp** to see what goes into an expedition to the roof of the world, or see the simpler side of life with a spiritual trek to the **Birthplace of Buddha,** where the Maya Devi Temple and a cultural gold mine of museums are located.

ⓘ www.welcomenepal.com

314 Equipping the Game

Build Multisport Facilities

Immerse Yourself in Your Play

Cape Town, South Africa

The majestic (and very climbable) Table Mountain dominates Cape Town's natural landscape. Fitting for a city that offers an unparalleled outdoor arena for all manner of sports, but here is your chance to help create man-made arenas in and among the nearby townships. This opportunity involves stays for up to 6 months and the chance to become part of the local community while helping build it up through sport.

Whether it's basketball hoops and soccer goals, or lined fields and diamonds, the multipurpose sport facilities created in the townships of Cape Town (and projects in other sub-Saharan Africa regions) result in permanent improvements that the villages proudly own and manage. With a real passion for sports, but a dire lack of quality playing space, newly developed sports zones become de facto community-gathering spots and tend to inspire civic pride. Township life is harsh, with many villagers living in corrugated tin shelters and shacks made from wooden crates. Kids grow up in a hurry here, so chances to play and escape some of the intensity of day-to-day life is truly a gift.

In the provinces of Western Cape, Northern Cape, Eastern Cape, North-West Mpumalanga, and Limpopo, sports coaching programs are flourishing (with the aid of outside volunteers), but often it's a case of getting all fired up with nowhere to go. Playing fields are littered with trash, and when vast numbers of kids are barefoot, it's hard to feel comfortable playing in the fields or roads. Clearing trash and stones from open space, sometimes pouring asphalt on playing surfaces, and turning once unappreciated dirt into a field of play is tough, grueling work but has a real, lasting effect.

These placements are longer term than some volunteer vacations: 6 months or more, during which time you become a true member of the community. You'll live with a host family in their rural home (outside of the township centers, but you will have plumbing and electricity) within walking or biking distance of the project. Families vie for the privilege of hosting volunteers and have to meet strict criteria. English is studied in schools, so the youth will communicate easily with you, even if some village elders need the help of a translator.

A thorough general orientation at a training center in Cape Town gives you the understanding and cultural guidance to feel comfortable stepping into what becomes an honored role in the township. In addition to making safe playing space, you'll work with local sports boards that value the power of sport and see team play as a community builder. The programs see sport as a way to provide children with skills and opportunities needed for success in life and to foster contributions to the larger group. The transformation of open space is symbolic of the transformation of individuals and the community. The program also puts a unique focus on gender equality and provides solutions for girls who have little experience of meaningful group inclusion in community life.

Your next step: SCORE (✆ **+27/21 461 0466;** www.score.org.za). A 6-month project, US$3,147, includes host family accommodations, meals, 3-week immersion orientation course, and local language instruction (though English is predominantly used in programs). Shorter-term volunteer projects are being developed.

DON'T MISS: Your time working with SCORE is jam-packed, so long stretches of R&R are rare. You needn't go far to visit amazing sights in and around Cape Town. Visit the Cape of Good Hope, where the Atlantic and Indian Ocean waters converge, then pump up the adrenaline with a **Great White Shark Cage Dive** in the turbulent waters between Seal Island and Simon's Town.

ⓘ www.southafrica.net

Equipping the Game **315**

Build a Field

Making Playgrounds Personal

New York, New York, USA

TURN NEW YORK CITY'S GRAY CONCRETE JUNGLE A LITTLE GREENER BY BECOMING PART OF THE Build a Field program and help to create indoor and outdoor recreational spaces throughout the city. What awaits you at the end of the day is a city so chock-full of events and experiences, it would take a lifetime to list them all.

New York City's Central Park is one of the most famous recreational areas in the world, but its uses are fairly rigid. Places to swing a bat or kick a ball unhindered in the city tend to be limited to school grounds. A charity-focused co-ed sports club in Manhattan is looking to open up greater possibility for play.

When you next venture to the Big Apple, coordinate your trip with the Play

Volunteers in New York keeping sports alive

for a Cause Build-a-Field program to help create indoor and outdoor recreational facilities at Pier 40 of the Hudson River (the People's Pier Proposal), the Brooklyn Armory, and uptown's Riverside Park. The cogs of city bureaucracy turn slowly, so the power is in the hands of individuals and non-profit organizations to make these and other fields of dreams a reality. Your sweat and blisters, rubbing elbows with locals and a large, motivated volunteer corps, means the crack of a bat and cheer of a crowd can be heard soon. It's all about sustainable venues for kids and adults from every neighborhood in the city and leaving a legacy for future generations of players.

After the tragedy of 9/11, founders developed the Play for Your Cause program to encourage social action and remind people to find balance in life by enjoying active pursuits while simultaneously giving back to the community and assuring the results will last. That's not bad company to keep, and it will be a lot more satisfying to end your day sore from turning sod or building backstops instead of having a crick in your neck from staring up at the flashing signs of Times Square.

YOUR NEXT STEP: Zog Sports (www.zogsports.org). Your trip to New York City is on your own terms, but contact Zog Sports once you have your schedule to get involved for one day or many with the facilities creation/improvement projects citywide.

DON'T MISS: You're probably already planning on seeing a Broadway show, maybe catching the taping of a TV show, getting to the top of the Empire State Building, and seeing Lady Liberty; but to really immerse yourself in the city's active pursuits take a kayak out onto the mighty **Hudson River.** It's the best, intimate way to get an all-around, close-up view of the city.

ⓘ www.nycvisit.com

316 Equipping the Game

Pass It On

A Big Assist

Hillsborough, North Carolina, USA

You don't need to bend it like Beckham in order to be a part of this soccer outreach program. Basic skills and an enthusiastic approach is all you need in a program designed to introduce underprivileged kids to the most played sport in the world. Hillsborough—often described as a small town with a big history—offers the short- or long-term visitor the kind of hospitality small-town USA is famous for.

The United States Soccer Foundation has a fantastic outreach program to youth in America who want to play soccer. In addition to touring nationally and running clinics to give underprivileged kids skills and access to the sport, one of the largest and most successful programs is a joint effort among Eurosport, the Soccer Foundation, and major league soccer players called Passback. Passback's goal is to "share the equipment, share the game," getting balls, jerseys, cleats, and more to every kid who wants to play.

Individual players, schools, and community soccer leagues donate gently used equipment to the program so others can get more active life from it. Passback facilitates volunteer programs in home communities for you to do collections in your town, and then it all gets sent to a

Making soccer accessible with the U.S. Soccer Foundation Passback Program

giant warehouse in North Carolina. That's where you come in. The trouble isn't that there is too little equipment; the problem is collecting, sorting, storing, and ultimately distributing thousands of balls and shoes and other items across America and even worldwide to programs in need. Only one full-time person works the warehouse, and the need is consistently high to try to turn around donations as quickly as possible. The sooner a ball gets to its new home, the sooner it can be used for the fun and skill it can provide. Your skills can be basic—just a willingness to work hard. Be careful, however, if you're vulnerable to persuasion—the Passback Distribution Center really needs capable, energetic help, so they may try mightily to convince you to stay on long past your scheduled Hillsborough visit.

YOUR NEXT STEP: Passback (www.passback.org) and **Eurosport** (www.soccer.com) run the Passback program and distribution center. There are no formalized travel programs getting you to Hillsborough, but they'll be happy to keep you busy for as long as you're willing to help.

DON'T MISS: One of the most scenic drives in the Eastern United States is the **Blue Ridge Parkway,** especially as it winds through the **Great Smoky Mountain National Park** in North Carolina.

ⓘ www.ci.hillsborough.nc.us

9 Bridging Cultures

San Blas, Panama, home of the Kuna Indians

Indigenous Peoples 317

Help Ensure Tribal Livelihood

Learn Traditional Lifestyle

Eden Valley Reserve, Alberta, Canada

This is a rare chance to live among the Stoney Nakoda First Nations while working to maintain their cultural heritage and enhance their economic opportunities. The sprawling grasslands of the Eden Valley Reserve are dotted with trout and whitefish-rich lakes, while mountain sheep, deer, and moose call the rolling plains of Alberta home.

While these Aboriginals have always called themselves Nakoda, meaning "people," outsiders have referred to this tribe as the Stoney Indians because of their method of cooking soup with fire-heated rocks. Their traditional lands once spread far and wide across British Columbia, Alberta, Saskatchewan, and Montana. The Stoney Nation tribal council has invited inspired visitors to live and work with the community on projects that focus on maintaining culture, language, and their way of life.

You'll wake up in the large community hall (bedding is provided, whether you've slept on the floor with the team or brought a tent to camp outside), and daylight won't have burned long before you're working on village improvements. You could be rebuilding steps, painting the school, replacing weathered siding on the church, or cutting back overgrowth. You'll also spend valued time learning the Nakoda ways, making bannock bread, beading, or preparing for a powwow.

Aboriginal rights were guaranteed in 1877 with a treaty signed at Blackfoot Crossing, but history is easily set aside by young people in the tribe. The community's

Volunteers with community members of Eden Valley Reserve in Alberta

commitment to sacred space and communal gathering time ensures an environment of respect. You are a part of that commitment, showing by example the value of cultural preservation.

YOUR NEXT STEP: Global Citizens Network (✆ **800/644-9292;** www.globalcitizens.org). An 8-day project, US$975, includes accommodations on the community hall floor (or outside in your own tent), communally prepared meals shared with the team and the locals, transportation from the Calgary airport, and a donation to the project and training materials.

DON'T MISS: You won't be far from **Banff National Park,** and once you've explored Canada's most popular mountain getaway—with endless opportunities to hike, canoe, walk on a glacier, or just take some extraordinary photos—you'll start planning your return visit the moment you leave. www.banfflakelouise.com

ⓘ www.tourismcalgary.com

318 Indigenous Peoples

Preserve Maya Culture

Building Peace & Solidarity

Cantel, Guatemala

Often overlooked in favor of neighboring Mexico, Guatemala is an ideal destination for the budget traveler. Bus travel, food, and accommodations are all great and cheap. And you'll run into many other travelers and expats who have made Guate, as locals call it, their home. Working in Cantel will help preserve the culture of the indigenous Mayans, who continue to live in poverty and face discrimination from the government.

Within the Mayan cultural groups in and around Cantel, there are nine communities vying for resources while striving to maintain autonomy and tribal tradition. Extreme poverty plagues several of the communities, who rely on sustenance agriculture and handicraft production to support themselves.

Your time living in village homes with host families will be rustic and occasionally challenging, with only some homes having electricity or indoor plumbing, but the reward of working side by side with village elders, youth, and community leaders will make you part of the village—and you'll be treated that way. The projects here focus on fortifying solidarity among the Mayan people and maintaining peace within the communities while encouraging traditional culture and history to flourish. The volunteer programs are well established and partner with the Mayan Center for Peace and other local organizations. Your Spanish skills will be tested, as most of the time you'll communicate in Spanish, and regional dialects can be difficult at first.

Days can be long, but not necessarily physically challenging, as you work hands-on at community centers and the homes of leaders on projects at various stages of progress—each strengthening the foundation of tribal life. You'll be building community not with a hammer and nails, but by putting business and trade into practice, and doing the small tasks needed, from stuffing envelopes to cleaning.

YOUR NEXT STEP: Global Citizens Network (✆ **800/644-9292;** www.globalcitizens.org). A 10-day project, US$1,575, includes rustic homestay accommodations (indoor plumbing and electricity aren't guaranteed), team meals, round-trip transportation from Guatemala City, and training.

DON'T MISS: It's the heart of the Mayan world, so archaeological exploration of temples and other mystical buildings is a must. The most well-known and best-preserved Mayan structure in the area is the ever unfinished **Aguateca Temple.**

ⓘ www.visitguatemala.com

Indigenous Peoples **319**

Live With & Support the Maasai Tribe

Peace & Prosperity on the Serengeti

Maasai Mara, Kenya

NAMED FOR THE MAASAI PEOPLE AND THE MARA RIVER, THIS PART OF SOUTHWESTERN KENYA is as famous for the annual Great Migration of tens of thousands of zebras and wildebeest from the Serengeti Plains as it is for the fierceness and traditional ways of the Maasai. Each year tourists come to the nature park in search of the Big Five game animals, bringing the modern world with them.

They are one of the most instantly recognizable African tribes, steadfastly committed to wearing traditional tribal red shawls and garments, sporting incredible beadwork, and carrying long spears. The Maasai warriors don't resist modernization but have a deeper commitment to the ways of past generations. Maasai culture is inextricably linked to their cattle, with their main dietary staples being both fresh and curdled milk, as well as the protein from blood let from its jugular vein, without killing the cow. Cattle are not eaten and are only slaughtered for ceremonial purposes.

You'll live and work with the tribe in a 2-week program modeled after the Peace Corps, and balance your time with safari excursions in the continent's most populous wildlife region. This section of the Serengeti is home to all the Big Five—lions, elephants, buffalo, rhino, and leopards—as well as hippos, crocodiles, and the giant herds of hoofed ruminants that they follow. The Great Rift Valley is one of Kenya's richest eco-zones, with tea-growing highlands, wandering rivers, and rolling savannah plains.

You'll find it easy to integrate in spite of the vast cultural differences, as there are no special skills required and English is spoken on the project. The symbiotic and harmonious relationship between the Maasai and wildlife, which they generally do not hunt, is inspiring. Your hosts in the village of Maji Moto (Swahili for hot water) will show you the medicinal hot springs, lead you on walking safaris, instruct you in shamanic botany with the village medicine man, and teach you secrets of food preparation in the field. All this life instruction in exchange for your efforts helping in the school, the medical clinic, constructing and maintaining the thatched-roof huts of the village, working on expanding the community buildings and school, assisting at the widows' shelter and women's project, and pitching in wherever needed.

YOUR NEXT STEP: Eco-Resorts (✆ **866/326-7376;** www.eco-resorts.com). A 13-day project, US$2,500-US$3,600, depending on the number of participants, includes accommodations in dome tents in the Maasai village (then safari base camp resort accommodations for the final 3 days), campfire meals prepared by the field cook, transfers, safari guides, national park and camp fees, and emergency medical evacuation insurance.

DON'T MISS: Spending time with the Maasai, you'll already be living every Tanzania-bound tourist's dream, so fulfill the other half of the aspirational journey and climb **Mount Kilimanjaro,** the highest peak in Africa.

ⓘ www.magicalkenya.com

320 Indigenous Peoples

Sustainable Development Projects

Harmonizing Eco-Tourism & Tradition

Michoacán, Mexico

OFTEN CALLED THE "SOUL OF MEXICO," MICHOACÁN STATE IS RICH IN NATURAL WONDERS, from its many waterfalls and ancient cave systems to farmlands teeming with melon and avocado, as well as unpolluted lakes that make it one of the country's best known eco-tourism destinations. A sound, sustainable approach to conservation has left it in more pristine condition than other tourist spots in Mexico.

A small Mexican community, Mata de Platano, has partnered with international volunteers to build on their rich history while creatively exploring development plans in harmony with both tradition and the earth. The location of the project is tucked into natural preserve areas not far from Mexico City but quite distant in philosophy and speed of life.

On this project, you'll be a jack-of-all-trades, working to construct, expand, and maintain the community center, La Casa del Volcan, gather elements and artifacts for the opening of a community museum, and work to develop a camping zone for tourist visits. Spanish is spoken in the community, but many residents know enough English to make communication trouble-free in either language.

The vibrancy of the people here is matched by the vibrancy of the ceremonial and traditional clothes you'll see: Mata de Platano is in the municipality of La Huacana, "the place of dresses." Your stay will be rustic, sleeping on the floor of the community building and eating meals together as a team, but village gatherings and ceremonies are a part of daily life, and you'll be a special guest at evening celebrations. The community understands that for you to serve and preserve the local history you must understand the way of life passed on through generations, so you'll be blended in as part of the society and a valued participant.

YOUR NEXT STEP: Canadian Alliance for Development Initiatives and Projects 🎗 (✆ **604/628-7400;** www.cadip.org). A 2-week project, US$265, includes communally prepared team meals and accommodations in the community building (sleeping on the floor—bring your own sleeping bag), as well as full project support. You'll travel to the site on your own from the Mexico City airport, and upon arrival, an additional US$266 is paid directly to the project hosts.

DON'T MISS: It is breathtaking to see what looks like dead brown clusters of giant banana bunches, hanging from the limbs of a fir forest, come to life with the gentle breezes. The brown is the underside of hundreds of thousands of patterned wings as they dry, preparing to take flight. Each breeze gently nudges hundreds more into the sky, turning it orange and black. This is the protected **Monarch Butterfly Sanctuary** of Michoacán.

ⓘ www.visitmexico.com

Cultural Preservation of the Kuna People

Preserve History & Participate In It

San Blas, Panama

Inhabiting 49 of the 378 islands in the San Blas Archipelago, the Kuna Indians have managed to maintain their culture, language, and heritage on this string of islands just a 20-minute plane ride from Panama City. The proximity of the modern world and the closeness to the Panama Canal mean they need all the help they can get in order to preserve their autonomy and way of life.

Panama is home to seven indigenous groups and immeasurable rainforest species of flora and fauna. With the constant influence from North and South America, the country's indigenous people share a strong desire to maintain their traditions.

The Kuna Indians of San Blas, known locally as Kuan Yala, gained the government-approved right to limited self-rule in the 1920s, more than a century after they first came to call the eastern portion of Panama home. They have protected their ancestors' heritage in every way, including native dress, arts and crafts, language, and a symbiotic and respectful relationship with the environment. They live on an archipelago but are not in isolation, so during your time living with the tribe, English will be spoken (though Spanish is better understood by most). You'll participate in a well-established program of community service alongside the Kuna as they continue work on an ethnographic museum. You'll be completely immersed in Kuna customs and lifestyle, participating in community music and dance, ritual ceremonies, and creating traditional tapestry weavings.

A Kuna woman in San Blas, Panama

You'll have several opportunities to visit neighboring communities as well as while away the non-working hours snorkeling, swimming, fishing for dinner with locals, and napping in breezy hammocks strung outside the thatched-roof cabana where you'll stay. In the brief 9 days you'll spend with the tribe, you'll be shocked at how strong the friendships you forge will be, and an elaborate and moving farewell ceremony historically leaves no eyes dry.

YOUR NEXT STEP: Eco Circuitos (✆ **507/314-0068;** www.ecocircuitos.com). A 9-day stay, US$1,225, includes accommodations in a cabana, meals, airport transfer, pre-assignment city tours of Panama City, and in-country transportation.

DON'T MISS: Go see the **Panama Canal,** still one of the world's most remarkable marvels of engineering. Its three locks lift giant container ships as an integral contribution to world trade.

ⓘ www.visitpanama.com

322 Indigenous Peoples

Help Preserve Hill Tribe Culture

Live Alongside 500 Years of History

Chiang Rai, Thailand

FALLING WITHIN THE REGION KNOWN AS THE GOLDEN TRIANGLE, THE CITY AND PROVINCE OF Chiang Rai sits where the borders of Thailand, Myanmar, and Laos meet. Many come here to observe Hill Tribe culture, believed to date back more than 5 centuries. Despite its remote location, the region offers visitors good accommodations and modes of transport, even though the main sights exist deep inside this landlocked country.

Venture beyond Thailand's triumvirate of must-see cities (Bangkok, Phuket, and Chiang Mai) farther north to Chiang Rai, the gateway to the Golden Triangle. Chiang Mai is rapidly growing, and the rural areas surrounding the city are being absorbed by urban sprawl. The effect is a homogenization of culture not unexpected in a time of growth, but the ethnic minority hill tribes have recognized the trend and begun to lament the loss of traditional ways. The tribal people migrated here when they were pushed out of their native lands in Tibet, Myanmar, and China and are loath to see history repeated. Each of six major ethnic groups has a distinctive heritage, clothing, language, religion, and culture that are endangered.

You'll stay in one of the small rural villages of only a couple hundred people,

Working in Chiang Rai to preserve Hill Tribe Culture

most of whom work as subsistence farmers and day laborers. In partnership with a local organization committed to maintaining cultural identity, you'll work hard to construct a community center and pitch in on community projects that begin to bridge the gap with lowland Thai society while infusing energy into local pride. Local leaders have determined that strengthening the community bond can combat pernicious issues like drug abuse and trafficking of women and children. The villagers have determined the projects that will most benefit them, and your job is to support them. You can do so by building and repairing homes, group structures, shrines, and museum space.

From hill country to beachside, Thai culture is some of the most open and welcoming you'll find, and the gentle spirit of rural village life will seem like a relaxing vacation even as you work your muscles and challenge your creativity until you're exhausted. You won't need Thai-language skills or hill-dialect knowledge, but you'll learn the day-to-day pleasantries of community life. Spend free time socializing in the village or trekking in the surrounding countryside, as Chiang Rai has become an internationally prized starting point for trekking. You'll also want to visit the area's multicultural hill tribe market.

YOUR NEXT STEP: Global Citizens Network (✆ **800/644-9292;** www.globalcitizens.org). A 2½-week project, US$2,225, includes accommodations in a community building (likely without electricity), team meals prepared by a local cook, in-country travel from Bangkok, medical trip insurance, and training.

You can also work with the Akha tribe in the same region. **Canadian Alliance for Development Initiatives and Projects** (✆ **604/628-7400;** www.cadip.org). A 2-week project, US$265, includes communally prepared team meals, accommodations in rustic homes with host families (sleeping on the floor—bring your own sleeping bag), as well as full project support. An additional US$186 is paid directly to the project hosts.

DON'T MISS: A trip to Chiang Rai would not be complete without visiting the notorious **Golden Triangle.** This is the meeting of Thailand, Myanmar, and Laos at the confluence of the Mekong and Ruak rivers, filled with ancient structures and birthplace of legends of the "Lanna" ancestors of all three nationalities.

ⓘ www.tourismthailand.org

Indigenous Peoples 323

Appalachian Preservation

Building Community in Coal Country

Lucky Fork, Kentucky, USA

THE DIMINISHING NATURAL BEAUTY OF THE APPALACHIAN MOUNTAINS AND THE POOR standard of living of those people who live among them is surprising for one of the most resource-rich regions in the United States. Volunteering here means helping both the people and the land try to hold on to and ideally reclaim some of their former glory.

Owsley County is Kentucky coal country. Strip mining and logging have taken a toll on the natural beauty here, but residents of the Appalachian community depend on these industries for survival. This is the poorest county in the state, but the local pride of place and community is strong. Volunteers work closely with the town community center on resident-driven priorities, including restoration of a log church, log house, and log hospital that date from the 1930s, as well as directly assisting families in the county. With a far-flung geography, where the nearest neighbors can be separated by kilometers and the closest grocery store is a 40km (25-mile) jaunt, the community center provides one of the only venues for gathering and prides itself on bringing people together for work and fellowship.

It's not all log cabin labor in Lucky Fork—you may also help with benefit events to raise funds, plant gardens, preserve and clean the old cemetery, write grant applications, or sew seat cushions for the church.

You'll share mealtime and downtime with the community. Lucky Fork residents are eager to share skills and instruction in local crafts like woodworking, baking, and canning produce. Wander to one of the local swimming holes, where you can splash and idle away the time between work shifts. Never has a rocking chair seemed more comfortable than at the end of a long day with newfound friends, a full belly, and a mug of something strong.

YOUR NEXT STEP: Global Citizens Network (✆ **800/644-9292;** www.globalcitizens.org). An 8-day project, US$975, includes accommodations at the manse (community building) or in the hospital, communally prepared meals, airport transfer, training and materials, and donation to the project.

DON'T MISS: The mountains of Appalachian Kentucky are home to the **Cumberland Gap National Historical Park.** It's the first great gateway to the west; the buffalo, Native Americans, and pioneers all traveled this lush wilderness route through the mountains into the lands of Kentucky.

ⓘ www.kentuckytourism.co

324 Indigenous Peoples

Preserve Tribal Identity

Create Community Space In Pacific Fishing Village

La Push, Washington, USA

OCEANFRONT RESORTS AND BIG INDUSTRY ARE SLOWLY ENCROACHING ON THE WAY OF LIFE OF the Quileute Tribe, believed to the oldest inhabitants of the Pacific Northwest. As the area's spectacular surfing and whale-watching draws more tourists to the area each year, you can help the indigenous people here maintain their identity, heritage, and culture.

The Puget Sound area of Washington state is rugged coastline at its finest. Waves crash wind-torn cliffs, and dramatic stormy skies make for the most brilliant sunsets. The journey across the sound to La Push, a tiny Pacific fishing village, brings you to the homes of the Quileute Native American tribe. The tribal way of life and symbiotic relationship with the seas has meant generations of fishermen, whale and seal hunters, known as "children of the raven," embrace the sacred ocean water as a family member.

The decline of the fishing industry threatens the tribe, and only three villagers remain fluent in their native language, so maintaining their unique cultural identity is an uphill battle. The tribal council needs volunteer partners to assist in projects that build community pride and contribute to the quality of life in this challenging area. During your 8-day stay in La Push, you may pitch in building and repairing community buildings, help plan and create an outdoor amphitheater for cultural celebrations, and help get the planned museum project off the ground. The museum will be home to the tribe's antiquities and records. The tribal elders have already begun to record oral histories of past chapters of the community's life.

You'll have downtime to learn from your hosts as well as explore the solitary fissures of the coastline, where you'll find it easy to get lost in your thoughts. Hot springs and waterfalls are within hiking distance, and the area is adjacent to Olympic National Park—a vast acreage of pristine wilderness. It will be difficult to return to the complexity of life at home once you've lived a simpler life that is profoundly connected to the earth.

YOUR NEXT STEP: Global Citizens Network (✆ **800/644-9292;** www.globalcitizens.org). An 8-day project, US$975, includes accommodations in a community building, sleeping on the floor as a team, preparing and eating meals together. Transfer to and from Seattle as well as training and materials are provided.

DON'T MISS: April through September is **whale-watching season** in Puget Sound. The "killer whale" reputation gives a bad name to the playful Orcas you'll see cavorting (and unless you are a sea lion, their favorite dietary item, you'll be safe).

ⓘ www.tourism.wa.gov

Historical Preservation 325

Preserve City Identity & Culture

Rebuilding More Than 2,400 Years of History

Kumayri, Armenia

Sometimes it is not a people but a city that needs preserving, as is the case with Kumayri, Armenia. Founded by the Greeks in 401 b.c., the scars of two major earthquakes can still be seen here; at the same time, evidence is everywhere that this city once used to be a great cultural and economic center.

Years of warfare and strife, the ravages of nature, and even the devastating 1988 earthquake that leveled 80 percent of the city have not been enough to topple the historic houses, churches, and public buildings lining the plazas of the Kumayri Historic District. Many of these sturdy structures were built with indigenous red and black "tuff" materials (tuff is a highly porous and—over time—not very stable stone used in many old European buildings).

This area of Armenia is a touchstone for world religions: Judaism, Christianity, and Islam all have traditions that point to major events in these mountains. This is where Noah landed the Ark at Mount Ararat and literally put down roots by planting his first vineyard. Greeks, Romans, Russians, and Turks have all etched their own histories into the stone, and Armenia's own unique identity still perseveres. You'll work with architectural historians to document the residential buildings, and the work you do will guide the reconstruction of the rest of the city, which is still recovering from the disaster 20 years ago. The history you reveal will help development proceed in a culturally sensitive way that also helps economic growth.

This is neither an abandoned archaeological dig site nor a scene of devastation, but a working, functioning city, so your efforts will need to be sensitively carried out. You'll be studying, sketching, recording, reporting, measuring, and photographing elevations, construction details, and floor plans, as well as working with families who live amid the fountains, parks, and promenades that still make this district idyllic. You'll spend just under 2 weeks living in a modest hotel a short walk from the project site, enjoying local cuisine and the camaraderie of the team and your neighbors.

YOUR NEXT STEP: Earthwatch (✆ **800/776-0188;** www.earthwatch.org). This 13-day project, US$3,050, includes meals and German Red Cross run residential hotel accommodations, plus full project support and training. A US$35 Earthwatch membership is required.

DON'T MISS: In the capital city of Yerevan, at the top of the main artery, you will find the **Matenadaran,** the Institute of Ancient Manuscripts. The collection of more than 16,000 ancient writings is the largest in the world, including original works by Aristotle, Eusebius of Caesarea, and many others.

ⓘ www.tourismarmenia.net

326 Historical Preservation

Preserve Targeted Historic Structures

History & Hammock Time in the Caribbean

Several Islands, Caribbean

Popular Caribbean history is rich in arts and folklore, but the actual physical monuments of its past glories often get overlooked. You'll help preserve many of those great structures scattered throughout dozens of islands in the Caribbean, an excellent way to combine a love of historical preservation and a sun-filled adventure.

This organization has undertaken more than 100 preservation projects in the Caribbean in the past 15 years, and it continues to target, with the input of home communities, historic structures that need volunteer help. Projects are chosen in collaboration with national trusts, museums, universities, and other local partners. Each island has a unique heritage reflected in its structures, and while every island has some specific challenges, some threats face every site, especially tropical storms and rampant tourism related development.

Your friends back home won't feel too sorry for you when they find out your "working" vacation meant you spent downtime lazing in a hammock or enjoying frozen drinks on the beach at sunset. How you structure your free time is entirely up to you. Many of your fellow volunteers will be architecture professionals, but you needn't have specific experience, just a passion for historic preservation and fending off the damage that comes from neglect.

Your focus for a project will depend upon your inspiration. You may photograph and catalog historic civic structures in the Dominican Republic, inventory the historic Jewish cemetery in Jamaica, undertake light construction and repair to historic buildings in Nevis, or map the plantation sites in the Bahamas. Each project has different accommodations for volunteer teams, most of which are in guesthouses and motels.

YOUR NEXT STEP: Caribbean Volunteer Expeditions (✆ **607/962-7846;** www.cvexp.org). There are scheduled team projects lasting 1 to 2 weeks, or you can arrange individual missions that fit your vacation plans. There is no project fee to volunteers beyond covering your own room, board, and transportation costs, as administrative and organizing duties are carried out by volunteers in addition to the fieldwork.

Restoring a historic house in the Caribbean

DON'T MISS: Of course, this is the Caribbean—a tropical playground for vacationers, so there will be no shortage of diversions. If you're not already stationed there for your assignment, it's worth the effort to make your way to St Vincent and explore the **Botanic Gardens,** the oldest in the Western Hemisphere. This lush locale was where Captain Bligh introduced the Tahitian breadfruit tree to provide food for slaves.

ⓘ www.caribbeantravel.com

Historical Preservation 327

Protect Hindu Kingdom of Vijayanagar

Monkeys & Monuments

Hampi, India

International travelers and Hindu devotees have been making the pilgrimage to Hampi's many temples (especially the monkey-infested Virupaksha Temple) for hundreds of years. The area is also a mecca for rock climbers and boulderers attracted to Hampi's eclectic mix of rugged adventure and ancient exoticism. With many places to eat and sleep that cater to backpackers seeking affordable luxury, you will feel much richer than you are.

In southern India's Karnataka state, ruins of the kingdom of Vijayanagar, now declared a UNESCO World Heritage Site, are showing the ravages of time. Monolithic sculptures and monuments still stand, but they need protecting. You'll work with an earnest project team to physically protect the site and beautify the area by planting trees and plants to convert an arid zone into parkland.

Additionally, you'll work with the local community, not all of whom recognize the cultural and historical value of the stone structures in their midst. The project team will work together to educate the village about the value of what they take for granted—or even consider an eyesore—and how it adds to our understanding of a still-mysterious time and place in history. The proposed park will eventually boast a visitor's center and museum, which should be a great benefit to the village.

You'll speak English on the project, and you'll live with your fellow team members in a guesthouse. This region is rife with history and legend, and the fourth installment of the Ramayana, the epic Sanskrit poem, suggests that Hampi was the site of the Vanara Kingdom (the kingdom of monkeys); Anjanaya Hill on the nearby river is believed to be the birthplace of Hanuman, one of Hinduism's most popular deities, expressed as a monkey.

YOUR NEXT STEP: Canadian Alliance for Development Initiatives and Projects (✆ **604/628-7400;** www.cadip.org). A 2-week project, US$265, includes communally prepared team meals and accommodations in a local guesthouse. Full project support from team leaders is part of the deal, but getting to Hampi is not—the nearest airport is Bangalore. An additional US$260 is paid directly to the project hosts.

DON'T MISS: To see as many temples and royal sites as possible, go to where they are clustered most densely: the **Sacred Center** in Hampi. Here you'll find some of the oldest temples in all of India, shoulder to shoulder with the Hampi Bazaar, Courtesan's Street, the "Mustard Seed" Ganesha, and other important pilgrimage (and tour) spots.

ⓘ www.hampi.in

328 Historical Preservation

Restore Buddhist Monastery

Saving Artifacts and Holy Relics in Nepal

Mustang Region, Nepal

Open to a limited number of tourists, the Mustang region—bordering Tibet—was once the capital of an ancient Himalayan Kingdom, but today many of its great monasteries are falling into ruin. Working to restore these religious monuments while living in this harsh, arid landscape will bring rewards felt in this life and the next.

The impetus for restoring the 300 year old religious center of Chairro Gompa came from the local community, as it does for every preservation venture taken on by the Cultural Restoration Tourism Project. The closing of Nepal's border with Tibet by the Chinese brought a great deal of economic strife to the Takhali people of this region, and this formerly healthy trade route stop was cut off. Many locals were forced to relocate and the Buddhist monastery, once a source of pride and spiritual sustenance, fell into poverty and disrepair.

The last of the monks left Chairro in the 1970s, and a few locals have tried, mostly in vain, to beat back the elements taking their toll on the holy structure. Centuries-old wall paintings and sculptures are still inside the crumbling *gompa* (Buddhist temple) and increasing weather damage has brought a new sense of urgency to the restoration. A world-renowned Buddhist monk and painter is leading the restoration of the fine artworks, and some of these works were created by his ancestors. You'll serve him with your hands and

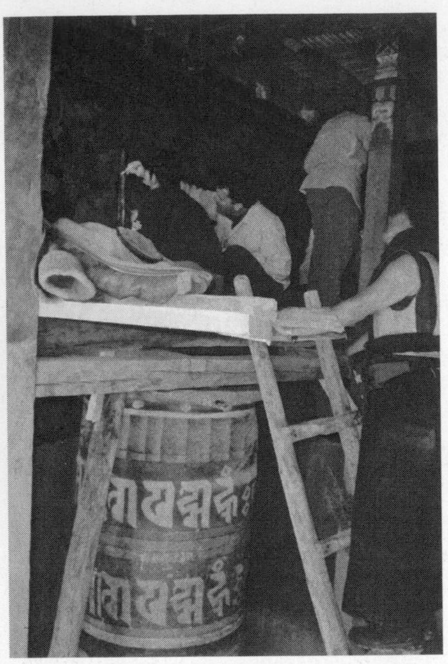

Restoring a 300-year-old monestary in Nepal

your heart as you help shore up this one-of-a-kind treasury. The beautiful part of this project is that the purpose of the restoration is not to turn this important temple into a museum, but to return it to community use, as much of the village's cultural identity is tied to this structure.

You'll visit several other small communities in the area, as well as other sacred sites, all reached by moderate treks. You'll have group visits to many of these sites in the afternoons after busy mornings working with traditional tools and techniques on works of art or the structure itself. You may need to pinch yourself as you realize that the gravity of the projects you are working on is, for the community here, the equivalent to being asked to touch up the roof of the Sistine Chapel.

YOUR NEXT STEP: Cultural Restoration Tourism Project (**415/563-7221;** www.crtp.net). A 12-day trip, US$2,495, includes accommodations, meals, in-country transportation (ground and air), Nepalese permits, and on-site conservation and restoration training.

DON'T MISS: Within 19km (12 miles) of your jumping-off point for this trip, Kathmandu, you will easily reach *seven* spectacular UNESCO World Heritage Sites, easily done in a day. Highlights include famous **Kathmandu Durbar Square** and **Bouddhanath**, the center of Tibetan culture in Nepal.

ⓘ www.welcomenepal.com

Historical Preservation **329**

Bring Historic Town Back from the Brink

Learn Carpentry and Restoration Techniques

Cairo, Illinois, USA

PRONOUNCED "KARE-O", THIS HISTORIC CITY SHARES A NAME (ALTHOUGH SLIGHTLY LESS HISTORY) with its Egyptian counterpart. Where the Mississippi and Ohio rivers converge, the city is mentioned in the *Adventures of Huckleberry Finn* and was a major strategic port during the Civil War. Recently, flooding, civil strife, and a bad economy have helped to undermine its storied history.

Cairo, at the southern tip of Illinois, has quite a historical pedigree. It was home to General Grant during the Civil War; it has featured a blues music scene to rival Memphis; it's been a magnet for civil rights controversy; and, as a hub for steamboat

Developing hands-on skills while restoring buildings in Cairo, Illinois

traffic, it used to draw thousands of traders, making it the economic stronghold for the area. The last decade has not been so kind, and due to economic challenges, it has practically become a ghost town.

A desperate community has come up with an inspired project, Cairo VISION 20-20. Working in conjunction with nearby university architecture schools and a squad of volunteers, the plan is to get Cairo back on its feet by 2020. To attract new residents and businesses, a major part of the project is rehabilitating a coterie of historic "shotgun"-style houses to create fresh and affordable living options. These homes, which you will work on, are among 350 town properties eligible for the National Register of Historic Places.

You'll get training in basic carpentry skills and other construction tasks as you breathe life back into these iconic domestic models of architecture. You'll live in town with the team for 2 weeks at a small hotel and share breakfasts and lunches on-site. Plenty of international volunteers have taken part in the projects here, so you'll meet a mix of people passionate about architecture and civic planning while gaining the satisfaction of helping an entire community.

YOUR NEXT STEP: Heritage Conservation Network (✆ **303/444-0128;** www.heritageconservation.net). A 2-week program, US$1,370, includes hotel housing, breakfasts, and lunches (dinners are on your own), insurance, workshop materials, and field trips to neighboring sites. Transportation to the site is your responsibility.

DON'T MISS: Cairo rests at the meeting point of the Mississippi and Ohio rivers, and nearby, in Metropolis, Illinois, is one of America's campiest, iconic roadside attractions. People drive out of their way to see the **Superman Statue** in this small town, which DC Comics gave permission to proclaim itself as the "home of Superman."

ⓘ www.enjoyillinois.com

Historical Preservation 

Frank Lloyd Wright Preservation Trust

Learning at the Home of a Master

Oak Park, Illinois, USA

JUST 16KM (10 MILES) WEST OF DOWNTOWN, CHICAGO'S OAK PARK NEIGHBORHOOD IS THE home of two of America's most enduring icons—writer Ernest Hemingway and architect Frank Lloyd Wright. Dozens of other architects had a hand in designing homes and buildings along the area's treelined streets. But it's the chance to work with the Frank Lloyd Wright Preservation Trust that will interest true aficionados of 20th-century architecture.

If American architecture is your bag, you'll likely leap at the opportunity to work in and around two of the nation's most famous works by arguably America's most famous architect. The Oak Park studio and home of Frank Lloyd Wright, and the Robie House in Chicago, both depend on a corps of more than 550 volunteers to restore and preserve the buildings, as well as make them accessible to the public as museum spaces.

Training for volunteers happens throughout the year, and you might choose to spend your vacation time as a docent, helping out in the office or bookshop, working with the restoration crews on their meticulous tasks, showing people around the surrounding neighborhoods, helping with kids' activities in the junior steward program, or pitching in for special events booked in the spaces.

Participating in Frank Lloyd Wright's legacy and facilitating the public's aesthetic appreciation of these world-class works will rock the world of design buffs. Both structures are award-winning national landmarks. Your newfound intimate knowledge of the eccentricities of the workings of these famous homes will give you amazing stories to tell—light fixtures that have to be taken apart to change a light bulb, floorboards that don't meet the walls, door handles that look amazing but don't turn or latch. If you were ever inclined to feel at home away from home, where better to do it than in a Frank Lloyd Wright house?

YOUR NEXT STEP: Frank Lloyd Wright Preservation Trust (✆ **708/848-1976;** www.gowright.org). There are no fees, formalized travel plans, or accommodations for volunteers. You'll be helping out at the nation's more famous houses, but you need to find your own housing while visiting the area. Volunteers able to donate at least 48 hours of time over any given period are given highest priority.

DON'T MISS: Go from immersing yourself in the world of Wright (his famous **Unity Temple** is in town too) to the world of Ernest Hemingway. Papa Hemingway was born in Oak Park, so visiting both the **Birthplace of Hemingway** and the **Ernest Hemingway Museum** (www.ehfop.org) makes for a great day while you're in town.

ⓘ www.visitoakpark.com

331 Historical Preservation

Research & Write Historical Record

Drafting History

Trego, Wisconsin, USA

For any American history buff, this is a chance to write about small-town history rather than just visiting and photographing it. Known as a destination for serious outdoor enthusiasts, Trego, Wisconsin, is a great place to write about the past—while living fully in the present.

The St. Croix and Namekagon rivers area in Wisconsin is fleshing out its historical record. Volunteers are asked to research and write an index of materials about the economic, industrial, and residential life of the community, past and present. You'll have open access to the files and historical data of the cultural resources department, and once your topic is approved, you'll be cut loose to find out everything you can.

Are you motivated by railroads? Ferries? Steamboats? How about bridges or the entire forest of logs that used to float downriver? By lending your voice and the knowledge you discover to the public information base, you'll be writing history The work is in-depth: for example, if logging is your interest, you would need to uncover the location of lumber camps, the type and volume of lumber extracted, the size and time scale of river drives and logjams, and profiles of significant members of the industry, just as a start. The ultimate goal is to have as extensive an historical record of preservation as possible—building a library of knowledge that will be studied from this time onward.

The Riverway is home to some of the most scenic canoeing in North America, and 406km (252 miles) of clean, green water rushes through a verdant landscape with only occasional reminders of a human presence.

YOUR NEXT STEP: National Park Service (volunteer hotline: **212/363-3206**, ext. 153; www.volunteer.gov). This is an ongoing project with perpetual need of volunteers but without any formalized travel program. When your pursuit of a pristine outdoor adventure vacation brings you to the Riverway, contact the National Park Service when you know you can donate your time and skills.

DON'T MISS: After roughing it outdoors along the river, wash up for **Ten Chimneys,** the restored estate of actors Alfred Lunt and Lynn Fontanne, revamped into a world-class museum and center for the arts, theater, and arts education. While they lived here, they regularly hosted the likes of Katharine Hepburn, Helen Hayes, Laurence Olivier, Alexander Woollcott, and Noel Coward. www.tenchimneys.org

(i) www.travelwisconsin.com

10 Ways to Keep Memories Alive: Oral History Projects

It's valuable to read the words of those who have gone before us, but to hear their own voices recounting their personal thoughts and memories connects us in a way like no other. Anthropologists and historians regard oral testimonies as a key factor in shaping our shared memories and historical consciousness. These individual recollections, recorded and shared, influence many of our attitudes and beliefs.

332 **Mosman, Australia** The Local Studies program in Mosman employs volunteer interviewers for its oral history recording efforts, collaborating with locals to preserve the area's history. This suburb of Sydney, on the northern shore of the harbor, is primarily residential with some magnificent large manors and a fascinating Aboriginal cultural history for you to delve into. ***Mosman Local Studies Library*** *(© **+612/ 9978 4091**; www.mosman.nsw.gov.au). The project is looking for the donation of time, and you'll make your own travel and accommodations arrangements.*

A village woman from Shaanxi Province, China

333 **Shaanxi Province, China** Villagers in Miao Jia Getai live in traditional cave dwellings and spend much of their free time in religious activities. Their lifestyle and worship traditions are being recorded and preserved as younger generations move away from the area. You can help document the memories of villagers (with a translator) while living with them in this mountain farming community. ***Earthwatch*** *(© **800/776-0188**; www.earthwatch.org). A 10-day stay with a host family in a cave dwelling is US$3,150.*

334 **Las Terrenas, Dominican Republic** Village elders are revered in this community of 20,000 on the northeastern side of the country, but low levels of literacy mean that the life lessons they have to impart are available only to those they speak to directly. You'll conduct taped interviews with older community members about what they've seen and learned through life, and those recordings, mostly in Spanish, will be available to everyone in the village through the foundation library. ***Fundacion Mahatma Gandhi*** *(© **809/240-6596**; www.fundacionmahatmagandhi.com). A 1-month stay is US$200, plus US$8 a day for housing.*

335 **London, England** The Black Cultural Archives preserves and promotes understanding of the African diaspora in Britain. This new oral history project, for which they need volunteers, entails conducting interviews to collect the testimony of women involved in the Black Women's Movement and black feminist activists and organizers. ***Black Cultural Archives*** *(© **+44/0207 582 8516**; www.oralhistorymatters.co.uk). Full training is provided, but no formalized travel arrangements are organized by the project.*

336 **Santa Barbara, California, USA** The oral histories at the Santa Barbara Museum of Art can be quite vibrant, with artists and performers lending their personal,

creative voices to the record. Transcription of these dynamic interviews is an ongoing, volunteer-led task. ***Santa Barbara Museum of Art*** *[charity] (✆* ***805/963-4364****; www.sbmuseart.org). Schedule time with the librarian, at your discretion, to transcribe.*

337 Washington, DC, USA The Society of Woman Geographers is expanding its archives with audiotaped interviews of members who have made significant contributions to geographic studies. Interview these women, record their amazing travel tales, and preserve their accomplishments and memories so they can inspire future generations. ***Society of Women Geographers*** *[charity] (✆* ***202/546-9228****; www.iswg.org). When you are in America's capital, contact the society to volunteer.*

338 Martha's Vineyard, Massachusetts, USA Quaint New England villages have a sense of history all their own, and the Martha's Vineyard Oral History Center is collecting the recollections of Vineyard residents past and present. Hearing speakers' voices brings their history to life much more vividly than just words on a page, and your interviewing work (or help with transcribing and cataloging) will get more voices saved for posterity. ***MVM Oral History Center*** *[charity] (✆* ***508/627-4441****; www.mvmuseum.org). Make your own arrangements and set your own time commitment.*

339 New York City, New York, USA The Ellis Island Immigration Museum has seen a lot of pain and joy as the first landing place of those seeking out the American dream. If these walls could talk, they'd sound something like the recordings of the Ellis Island Oral History Project, where immigrants who came here remember their experiences; you're needed to transcribe and translate what they tell us. ***National Park Service*** *(✆* ***212/363-3206, ext. 153****; www.volunteer.gov). No fee, and no formalized travel program.*

340 Statewide, Utah, USA As an Oral History and Life Review Volunteer, you'll interview and record the stories of care recipients in this homecare and hospice program as they have the chance to reflect and record their legacy. You'll be trained in both interview techniques and hospice requirements so you'll be familiar with what can be very emotional and trying circumstances. There are programs in every zip code in Utah. ***LifePath Home, Health, Hospice, and Family Care*** *(✆* ***877/293-0444****; www.lifepathhomecare.com). No formalized volunteer travel plans or fees.*

341 Glen Jean, West Virginia, USA The National Park Service of New River Gorge National River wants to preserve the memories of people in the area. Oral history interviews, conducted in the homes and businesses of the subjects, are created by volunteers, then transcribed and logged. ***National Park Service*** *(✆* ***304/465-0508****; www.volunteer.gov). No fee and no formalized travel program.*

New River Gorge National River in West Virginia

Music 342

Develop Language Through Song

Pitch-Perfect Patagonia

Esquel, Argentina

Visitors mostly treat Esquel as a way station before heading into Parque Nacional Los Alerces or the launching point for whitewater trips down the Futaleufú. For locals interested in learning English, the MAPU organization offers a unique, musically oriented way of listening to, and eventually speaking, the language. It's a revolutionary approach to teaching in one of Argentina's most breathtaking landscapes.

The rote declension of verbs and vocabulary will drain the life out of the most enthusiastic student, so a local non-profit charity has developed a foreign-language learning system (teaching English and German) that teaches through song. Based in Patagonia, it is taught by volunteers like you, and its students are adults and children who have been stopped by traditional language learning methods but often have breakthroughs with this model.

Each lesson is a different song. Lyrics tend to be informal and situational, making them easier to understand, and a catchy tune helps lessons imbed themselves in memory. Singing a song also challenges students to master pronunciation in a more meaningful way than book exercises. You will teach songs, work out roleplay exercises, work on class plans using the developed songs, and sing, sing, sing. Your intermediate Spanish skills will

Collaborating with a local Argentinian musician

be helpful, as many of these students are brand new to English studies.

Patagonia is one of the most beautiful mountain regions of the world, with glacier-fed lakes, lush forests and trails, and air so pure your lungs will ache. You'll live amid its splendor with a supportive local family for the 5- to 8-week duration of your program.

YOUR NEXT STEP: MAPU Association (✆ **54/02945-455857;** www.asociacionmapu.org). This 5- to 8-week project, US$360, includes an orientation program, materials, and 24-hour support. While housing will be arranged for you, you'll pay room and board separate from project fees, in the range of US$200 to US$250 a month.

DON'T MISS: Distances are long with tough travel in Patagonia, but since you're so near the bottom of the continent, make time to head all the way south to **Ushuaia,** the southernmost city in the world.

ⓘ www.turismo.gov.ar

343 Music

Collaborative Music Project

Mendoza Melodies

Mendoza, Argentina

Increasingly famous for its wine region, Mendoza also plays host to many hardcore climbers on their way to Aconcagua—the highest mountain in the Western Hemisphere. Others use the town as the starting point for horseback riding, kayaking, or even ski trips in the area. But this project is all about bridging cultural divides by beating a musical pathway through teaching, study, and collaboration.

This intensive musical exploration program has several components, including collaborating and performing with local musicians and recording the sessions that result. You don't need musical (or Spanish) experience, but you must have the passion to experiment. Language classes are taught alongside the music, so your skills will certainly progress while you're here. You'll learn digital music technology, work on your own projects, and make music with Mendoza musicians. Preserving the musical and cultural past while re-defining the future will inspire you through the long hours of your work. Music and mutual creativity overcome differences, and the act of giving birth to a work of art and performance is one of the most intimate ways for people to bond. You'll enjoy letting down the barriers.

The jagged Andes Mountains loom over the city, and the amazing, uninterrupted vistas inspire song and fantasy. The organizers are committed to exploring how music unites people across any divide. You will create and record original collaborative pieces with local children and adults. You'll share the studio with Argentines and create new sounds while exploring new instruments, truly building relationships and integrating with your fellow musicians, other volunteers, your host family, and the community at large. Work will be recorded, mixed, and produced in studio.

YOUR NEXT STEP: Music Pathways Argentina (✆ **208/935-6195;** www.pathwaysedu.net). A 3-month stay, US$3,000, includes room and board with a host family, language classes, recording studio time and instruction, and project oversight.

DON'T MISS: Mendoza is the center of Argentina's blossoming wine industry, and viticulture tours are a must. Hire (or designate) a driver and visit several of the wineries along the **wine tasting route** to sample some of the world-renowned Malbec vintages.

ⓘ www.turismo.mendoza.gov.ar

Music 344

Teach Music

Samba & Schooling

Olinda, Brazil

EACH YEAR THE STREETS OF OLINDA (PORTUGUESE FOR "OH BEAUTIFUL") TEEM WITH PEOPLE celebrating Carnaval and other cultural festivals in a way only Brazillians can. The city—classified as a UNESCO World Heritage Site and once declared the cultural capital of Brazil—makes an ideal locale to teach music to everyone from pre-teens to seniors.

If you've got musical skills and want to share your passion for song and playing instruments, share that gift with students in Olinda, on the eastern coast of Brazil. The Center for Music Education is the temporary home for skilled musicians and singers from across Brazil, as well as other international volunteers like you, giving their time to teach and learn from one another. You can simultaneously be a student learning Brazilian music before or after your own classes and private lessons. Classes are groups of 15 to 20 students, both children and adults, and you'll spend 20 to 35 hours a week coaching. You can spend some of that time teaching conversational English as well, or work with students during your downtime, as you'll be assigned either morning or afternoon classes. Your English is enough for these eager pupils, aged 6 to 70, and there is time built into your schedule for Portuguese-language exchange.

Whether your strength is choral or instrumental, you'll find creative ways to incorporate traditional Brazilian instruments into group work in many different musical styles. Your students, led by you, may even showcase their talents at local festivals, carnivals, and entertainment shows.

The historic hilltop town has gorgeous views along narrow cobblestone streets that go straight to the Atlantic. You'll explore the town, perhaps with the family that is hosting you in their home, as you very quickly become a fixture among the villagers—most of whom will do their best to tempt you to play and sing in spontaneous performances.

YOUR NEXT STEP: Global Crossroad (✆ **866/387-7816;** www.globalcrossroad.com). A 2-week immersion (longer assignments available), US$1,461, covers materials, airport pickup, and accommodations with a host family who will also prepare two meals daily. English materials are scarce, so consider bringing books and music CDs to donate.

DON'T MISS: You needn't go far for amazing views from Olinda, especially from the steps of the **Igreja da Sé cathedral,** or stroll a short distance across the green plaza and down to the beach below.

ⓘ www.embratur.gov.br

345 Music

Artisans of Music Workshop

Learn the Rhythms of the Andes

Quito, Ecuador

Indigenous music plays an intrinsic role in the daily lives of many Ecuadorians, although the city of Quito is more known for its mountains than its musical legacy. Nestled in the Andes, this is your chance to work with local musicians and forge bonds through playing music and building instruments.

The indigenous music of Ecuador is revered by its practitioners as a tool that transmits knowledge and advice from the ancients, keeping people connected across generations. Music is part of daily life, and there is an endless variety of nuance in mood and character depending on the occasion, time, and participants. Instruments are also widely varied, some even originating from pre-Inca times.

This project studies the percussion and wind instruments of Andean cultures, their construction, tuning, and performance. You'll travel to several villages in a cultural exchange of creativity, learning from musicians in their homes, sharing the music of contemporary instruments, and working together to preserve family musical instruments and create new ones using clay, leather, and wood. The final stage of the project will be a community performance in Quito with local musicians and workshop participants sharing the stage.

You'll also explore secular and ceremonial dance, participate in a local festival, and learn and record shamanic traditions, using music and chanting as healing tools. An international roster of lecturers and performers will be part of this multiethnic attempt to fuse contemporary and indigenous music, enlivening and preserving both by recording what the musical styles have in common and how they are unique.

YOUR NEXT STEP: Kindred Spirits Tour and Travel (✆ **720/746-0748;** www.kindredspiritstourandtravel.com). A 2-week project, US$2,500, includes accommodations (double occupancy in hotels), meals, in-country transportation, program costs and materials, and admission to museums and exhibits.

DON'T MISS: Quito is at a very high elevation and watched over by a still-active volcano, Pichincho. The views of the breathtaking Andes are best from the **Aerial Tramway** (Teleferiqo) cable car that glides to an elevation of 4,084m (13,400 ft.)—a truly dizzying height.

ⓘ www.quito.com.ec

Music 346

Teach Music in Underserved Schools

Scoring Education

Accra, Ghana

Considered a melting pot of various African and European cultures, the modern metropolis of Accra is an ideal place to teach the world's most universal language—music. Music permeates every aspect of life here. The Ghanaian capital is also famous for its variety of gastronomic offerings, pristine beaches, and thriving nightlife.

We all know the restraints that cutbacks can impose, but when schools are forced to tighten their belts, arts programs tend to be cut first. Somehow considered expendable, music education has all but disappeared from the school system in Accra, Ghana, and the students are desperate for it. In Ghanaian culture, music plays a respected and popular part in life, so its absence is sorely felt.

While visiting, you'll teach music classes in schools near the center of the city. Some schools have a few neglected instruments left over from when music was a priority, and some instruments will be provided with the volunteer placement. You don't need to be an expert player—if you can play any instrument, the program will be glad to have you as a visiting teacher in primary and junior secondary schools. Your day may have you teaching at three different schools, bringing your songs, lessons, and enthusiasm on the road with a leader and guide/translator.

After-school time is your own, and the area around Accra is filled with adventure sport possibilities, like trekking or surfing, that beg for exploration. The families that host volunteers look forward to visitors and enjoy showing guests around and taking them under their wing. Past participants have been considered family by the time the brief 2 weeks has passed.

YOUR NEXT STEP: Travellers Worldwide (✆ **+44/1903 502595;** www.travellersworldwide.com). A 2-week trip (longer stays available), £736, includes housing and meals with a host family, ample support from local project staff and school personnel, and airport transfer.

DON'T MISS: One of the tourism highlights of Accra is the **National Museum,** with an extensive collection of items of archaeology, ethnography, and fine art. The tribal collections of ceremonial dress and the evolution of Ghanaian currency are two of the most popular sections of the museum.

ⓘ www.touringghana.com

347 Music

Teaching Music in Rural India

Six Months of Song

Kochi, Kerala, India

LYING AT THE SOUTHWESTERN TIP OF INDIA, THE SETTING IN KERALA—THE NAME MEANS "LAND of coconuts"—is beachy and laid-back in what many consider to be India's most pristine tropical paradise. Spending 6 months teaching kids at Kerala's Amadeus Academy of Music will be rewarding not just from a volunteer point of view but a lifestyle one as well.

A gratifying commitment for a retiree or gap-year student, this 6-month teaching assignment in Kerala will bring music to kids who wouldn't otherwise have it. Classical piano, singing, guitar, and contemporary drums are the areas where young students want to be trained. This program is intended to be pre-professional training for academy-bound musicians whose promise and talent have already been proven.

You'll be testing students based on the London training programs for Trinity Guildhall "performer level" piano, and the London Rockschool syllabus for guitar, drums, and vocals. You'll teach in English and plan and rehearse performances along the way. British Academy professionals have high hopes for this training outpost in Kerala, and are eager to have the input of a variety of international volunteer teachers.

Teaching is a two-way street at the Amadeus Academy of Music, and while there, you'll be learning Indian music and yoga. Students travel to this small town from quite far away for exposure to such a rigorous academy, with the realistic intention of pursuing a professional career in music.

YOUR NEXT STEP: Volunteer Abroad/ Amadeus Academy of Music (✆ **+91/ 484 2663443;** www.volunteerabroad.com). A 6-month placement, US$300 a month, includes accommodations in shared teacher housing apartments, meals prepared by support staff, and local orientation, support, and sightseeing trips.

DON'T MISS: Ayurvedic medicine originated in India, and the healing tradition flourishes in Kerala most of all. Take some time before or after your teaching assignment for a **Rejuvenation Therapy Program** (Rasayana Chikitsa), a healing spa retreat at one of a huge network of local health centers.

ⓘ www.keralatourism.org

348 Music

Children's Music Program

Travel in the Tropics

Orissa, India

CHARACTERIZED BY LUSH WILDLIFE, SPARKLING BLUE BEACHES, AND THUNDERING WATERFALLS, Orissa is known throughout India for its rich cultural heritage, especially when it comes to the arts, particularly music and dance. The co-existence of three religions here means that festivals take place year-round. The state also has a rich tradition of weaving, brass, silver work, and pottery.

Walking along the clear blue water of Orissa, India

The children in Orissa have often left school for a life of work at an early age, and while they are still in school, their options are quite limited. The regional education system provides only three avenues for formal learning: Children's Home provides education to more than 500 children, most of whom are orphans or from extremely poor families; English Medium Schools are the stewards for only 50 percent of students, providing education to more than 1,500 poor tribal children; and Day Care Centers teach, clothe, feed, and care for more than 950 students.

As a volunteer music teacher, you'll divide your days among all three institutions, traveling from one to the next, helping kids to express themselves with singing, dance, guitar, and keyboard. You don't need to be an expert musician yourself, just a passionate advocate for children and their healthy development.

Your length of stay and teaching assignment can be as short as 3 days working as a guest artist or up to 4 weeks, during which time you'll live and work among other teachers, all of whom are committed to giving kids opportunities they simply wouldn't have otherwise.

YOUR NEXT STEP: Take Me to Volunteer Travel (✆ **65/6220-1198;** www.takemetovolunteertravel.com). The length of your stay is up to you, from 3 days, US$610, to 1 month, US$1,000. Cost includes accommodations, meals, airport transfers, in-country travel, program fees, and materials.

DON'T MISS: Chilika is the largest brackish-water lake in Asia, and home to the famed Irrawady dolphins, as well as incredible bird-watching and boating on this freshwater lake near the Bay of Bengal that has inspired artists and poets for centuries.

ⓘ www.orissa-tourism.com

Music **349**

Music Programming & Support

Curating Culture

Natick, Massachusetts

Just 24km (15 miles) west of the sprawling metropolis of Boston, Natick, Massachusetts, seems like a town lovingly stuck in the past. Casey's Diner—one of the oldest 10-stool diners in the USA—has been serving steamed hot dogs since 1922. If music and arts programming are in your blood, Natick's Center for Arts could use your help.

The Center for Arts in Natick (TCAN) is a non-profit performance and teaching space dedicated to enhancing the community through music, performing, and visual arts. TCAN has several programs that couldn't exist without the efforts of visiting and resident volunteers. It's not just tearing concert tickets at the door or ushering patrons to their seats (though you can volunteer to do that), but the volunteer force also makes some of the most interesting programming decisions.

You can play an active role in music and arts programs as you review artistic submissions and proposals, make booking decisions for acts in the 290-seat performance hall, schedule and host events, and more. The Chamber Music Series relies on volunteers to review artist proposals under consideration for music events, so you'll have a role in deciding who performs at the center. Monthly rock concerts are staffed by volunteers like you, as well as teen music programs and open-mike nights for songwriters and musicians. Your work with TCAN is supporting performance and training for artists of today and tomorrow. This cultural center is in a restored firehouse, and is considered a cultural lynchpin for MetroWest Boston.

YOUR NEXT STEP: The Center for Arts in Natick (✆ **508/647-0097;** www.natickarts.org). There are no formalized travel programs for volunteers, but when you're in the Boston area for a night or for an entire vacation, your volunteer efforts and willingness to work will be happily put to good use.

DON'T MISS: After spending days indoors putting together the best musical performances you can, get out and smell the roses. The **New England Wild Flower Society**'s gardens "in the woods" are near Natick—a great place to wander and listen to the music of nature.

ⓘ www.bostonusa.com

350 Music

Girls Rock Camp

Empowerment & Punk

Austin, Texas

WHILE THE REST OF THE STATE MAY BE FAMOUS FOR COWBOYS AND COUNTRY MUSIC, AUSTIN has long been regarded as the live music capital of the USA. With more than 200 performance venues and almost as many music festivals—including the famous South by Southwest—it's a perfect place to rock out.

Sometimes you just have to blow the doors off the place. Guys tend to get encouragement to be rowdy and cut loose, but for girls—not as much. This day camp in Austin (home to an incredibly vibrant music scene) offers rock music training and performance workshops in a positive, all-female environment. Campers aged 10-18 learn to play guitar, drums, bass, keyboards, or rock out on vocals, as well as attend workshops on women who rock, self-defense, images of girls and women in pop culture, the music business, creating 'zines, rock songwriting, and more. Each season there is a special session for adult women as well.

If your travels to Austin don't coincide with one of the camp sessions, you can still contribute to benefits and fundraisers organized throughout the year. When the girls are here, you can be a music instructor for vocals or instrumental work; teach DJing, B-girl break dancing, or beat-boxing; coach bands in business skills; or just help in the office. You can even be a volunteer roadie, helping set up equipment, running the soundboard, and tuning for performances and showcases.

It is an incredible opportunity to help empower young women, and it happens because of the male and female volunteers who put all their focus on the free self-expression of these amazing grrrlz.

YOUR NEXT STEP: Girls Rock Camp Austin 🎗 (✆ **512/809-7799;** www.girlsrockcampaustin.org). As a day camp program, for weeklong sessions at various times in the year, plus special events, there is no arrangement for housing or hosting volunteers, but when you finalize your plans to visit Austin, and you're ready to rock, let the camp know you will pitch in.

DON'T MISS: The city motto is "Keep Austin Weird," and this irreverent attitude is what makes it so refreshing. Austin is also one of the world's capitals of live music, so a jaunt to any of the eight official **Music Districts** is a guarantee you'll find the style and mood of music you're looking for.

ⓘ www.austintexas.org

10 Special Events

Celebrating a win at the Special Olympics

Festivals & Tournaments

351

Australian Blues Music Festival

Backstage Access

Goulburn, Australia

THE TOWN OF GOULBURN IN NEW SOUTH WALES IS MORE KNOWN FOR SHEEP SHEARING AND beer brewing than the blues. Just 200km (125 miles) west of Sydney, the town—although hit hard by recent drought—is an adventurer's paradise and perfect for anyone who wants to live, eat, and sleep the blues.

February is summertime in Australia, and that means it's festival season. The continent's most cherished blues fest happens each February in Goulburn. The 4-day blowout takes over music stages and alternative venues throughout town in a giant showcase for emerging and long-loved acts known around the world. In addition to amazing music happening on every stage (with plenty of impromptu jam sessions going long into the night), the festival is committed to engaging and educating new musicians. The festival is rounded out by a series of workshops with some of the performing artists, open-mike events throughout all 4 days, a youth blues jam for young musicians, industry forums, the Chain Awards (named for a top local blues band), and the grand finale All-Star Pro-Jam. Stars are lauded and stars are made. And it's as successful as it is because of blues-loving volunteers from around the world who want to help.

Festival volunteers enjoy unprecedented contact with artists in this casual setting. You'll be asked to commit to a minimum of one each of a morning, afternoon, and night shift. You could sign up for working the admission gates and checking wristbands at venues, helping out the festival offices, selling tickets, being a general runner and jack-of-all-trades, acting as a master of ceremonies or announcer at a particular venue, or driving the performer shuttle to take artists to and from venues, dining spots, and host hotels. Something always needs to be done, fixed, taped, set up, taken down, recorded, videoed, cleaned, emptied, or filled.

No travel or hosting arrangements are provided for out-of-town volunteers, so you'll do your own planning for your stay. The festival takes volunteering seriously and truly relishes the efforts of those who help out. You'll be provided a festival pass that gives you access to every ticketed venue and performance, so any time you aren't working, the Goulburn world is your musical oyster.

YOUR NEXT STEP: Australian Blues Festival (✆ **+61/02 4823 4492;** www.australianbluesfestival.com.au). No formalized travel planning or packages for out-of-town volunteers, but don't tarry—there are limited accommodations, so book early. Once you've secured your room, call to arrange your volunteer time.

DON'T MISS: After the blues fest, continue the mellow groove at the beach in Byron Bay, a New Age vortex of bohemian chic and outdoorsy élan. Surf, hike, tan at the nude beach, sip green tea, have your aura analyzed, regress to a past life, and get your palm read.

ⓘ www.australia.com

352 Festivals & Tournaments

Jazz Festival

Work Like a Roadie, Hang With the Stars

Crest, France

LOCATED IN THE SOUTHEAST OF FRANCE ON THE EDGE OF THE ALPS, CREST HAS THE KIND OF old-world charm often found in European cities. The medieval town is also perfect for strolling, sightseeing, and café culture—not to mention soaking up music by an international array of the best jazz musicians on the planet.

If you were designing a soundtrack for this medieval village, you might cue Gregorian chants to ring through the twisted laneways. Instead, you'll be accompanied by the terrific riffs of jazz vocalists running through classics and contemporary tunes. Late July through early August is the time for the Crest Jazz Vocal Festival, when the town is taken over by jazz greats and as-yet-undiscovered singers and bands. Past years have featured Nina Simone, Dee Dee Bridgewater, Betty Carter, Cesaria Evora, Screamin' Jay Hawkins, Diana Krall, Ray Charles, and Cassandra Wilson, to name just a few. For more than a decade, volunteers from around the world have come to town to facilitate the details of putting on a globally honored show.

The festival's volunteer association runs the brigade of helpers and will assign you tasks as needed. It takes a lot of volunteers to install stages and platforms in indoor and outdoor venues, hang posters, distribute flyers to local businesses, hand out cards to passersby, clean up between performances, and then dismantle the whole setup when the weeklong event is done. This is definitely a manual labor post, so you should be ready to lift, carry, peg, and paint wherever you are pointed, from the iconic tower in the center of town to the basements of pubs lining steep lanes. You're essentially a roadie, and pretty much when they say jump, you'll reply, "How high?"

The volunteer group lives together in a shared house in town, and your work calls can start quite early in the morning. You'll be there a few days before the festival and a few days after so you'll see the entire transformation of this quiet hamlet into international concert venue, and back again. All meals are provided, and clearly you'll be entertained with so much stellar music all around. When you are cut loose for the evening or a day off, the region is bursting with historical sites and possible excursions, from nearby towns of Valence, Aouste, and Montélimar to the River Drôme.

YOUR NEXT STEP: Canadian Alliance for Development Initiatives and Projects (✆ **604/628-7400;** www.cadip.org) A 2-week assignment, US$290, includes meals and shared group accommodation, project training, and support. You'll handle your own transportation to Crest.

DON'T MISS: The ultimate songbird of France, Edith Piaf, was born in Paris and died in Cannes, so why not follow the trail of the tragic chanteuse and visit both. The City of Lights will require a long stay (or many repeated visits throughout your lifetime) to ever begin to do it justice, but Cannes, while no less complex, can be enjoyed in several days. Located on the French Riviera, it is a coastal town of extravagant homes and mansions, and the Mediterranean climate will draw you to its glamorous beaches.

ⓘ www.francetourism.com

Viking Festival

Broadswords Not Required

Hafnarfjörður, Iceland

ALTHOUGH THE TOWN IS MOST FAMOUS FOR ITS VIKING FESTIVAL (WHAT ICELANDIC TOWN isn't?), it also boasts numerous arts festivals, contemporary arts spaces, and a burgeoning rock music scene. Only 10km (6 miles) from Reykjavik, Hafnafjörður's dramatic seascape gives the town a more earthy edge than its more famous neighbor and makes for an ideal spot to set off on a whale-watching excursion (horned helmets not included).

During the 2-week Viking Festival each June when Viking heritage and history is celebrated, Icelanders and international visitors get a little (good-naturedly) lawless, a little drunk, and very excited. The endless light of a summer sun that never sets means partying and re-enacted battles, arts and crafts fairs, hearty heavy foods, and tournaments of strength and daring that can go on all night.

Volunteers prepare for this festival and work before, during, and after. Your Viking

The Viking festival in Hafnarfjörður, Iceland

costume is quite the badge of honor (there are nearly 150 Viking-clad volunteers from around the world who pitch in to make the festival run smoothly). You'll be doing menial labor, but doing it in high spirits (and probably enjoying some spirits when the workday is through). You'll be assisting visitors with directions and guidance, taking tickets at venues, helping in the open-fire outdoor kitchens, and perhaps serving food to other hungry marauders. You probably won't have to polish a battle-ax or a broadsword—but you never know.

You and your fellow Viking volunteers will stay in the community center, sleeping on mattresses on the floor. Meals are provided, and there are some arranged free-time excursions to the wild lunar landscapes around and outside of town. The terrain here is awe-inspiring, and you can hike for ages along the thundering sea or up into the hills and cliffs. Volunteers have access to the local thermal pools for soaking in the naturally heated waters (a year-round luxury for locals), and of course wandering among the craftspeople, storytellers, wrestlers, sailors, musicians, and rune-casting magicians will be endlessly entertaining.

YOUR NEXT STEP: Canadian Alliance for Development Initiatives and Projects (✆ **604/628-7400;** www.cadip.org) This 2-week project, US$270, includes housing at the community center (sleeping on the floor with other volunteers), meals, any necessary training, and project support. Volunteers provide their own transportation to town before the assignment begins. An additional US$154 is paid directly to the Icelandic host organization.

DON'T MISS: Keep the blend of ancient and contemporary going with a **horseback riding** excursion in the countryside. The Vikings brought these surprisingly small but stout horses with them, and the remoteness of Iceland has kept the bloodlines of the breed pure all this time. The horses have an extra gait, called the *tolt*, and it is like a fast, jerky trot that suddenly takes flight and gets smooth as glass. The long shaggy manes and coats protest them from the winter chill, and their incredible stamina and speed makes them fearless across rugged terrain. It is the best way to see natural Iceland.

ⓘ www.icelandtouristboard.com

354 Festivals & Tournaments

Children's Art Festival

Be Big in Japan

Asakura-Haki, Japan

Located on Japan's most southern island of Kyushu, Asakura-Haki is only 5 hours by bullet train from Osaka but a complete world away. A small town nestled in the mountains, it has the kind of traditional Japanese architecture, art, and pace of life that you won't find in any major city. Working with kids while using art as a way of bridging global cultures here will hardly feel like work at all.

The local Society of Children's Theatre Works & Community Development has for several years sponsored an International Children's Art Festival. The goal is to engage young people in artistic expression through exploration of visual arts and performance. The 2-week celebration gets the entire community involved, and children prepare for it for the entire year leading up to festival time. Dedicated young artists paint, sculpt, and draw works that will be prominently displayed for the entire city to appreciate and admire.

This festival is seen as a true investment in the cultural future of the city. You'll mix setting up displays, tables, chairs, and hanging artwork with promoting the event to the community. English is the only language you'll need, as local volunteers will translate if necessary as you lead group classes of young people in art projects. Your own creativity will be called upon as you decorate venues as well as getting kids as young as kindergarten-age excited about attending, and hopefully discovering a new passion in themselves. You'll also help run events and classes, from giving directions to specific venues or hanging signs or taking tickets.

The volunteer work camp corps lives with local families in shared housing. All your meals are provided, and the living and eating is simple and basic yet satisfying. There is lots to do during this project, and little time left over for sightseeing or dozing, so building a cushion of time before and/or after the work camp is a great way to be sure you can appreciate the context for all this creativity. A volunteer party and an excursion to see the surrounding villages and nature are scheduled, but then its work, work, work (and having a blast with excited children and their beaming, proud parents, siblings, and friends).

YOUR NEXT STEP: Service Civil International (✆ **434/336-3545;** www.sci-ivs.org). A 2-week project, US$235, includes shared host family accommodations, meals, and project training. The international volunteer team is supported by local volunteers and staff, and also treated to a sightseeing excursion and participant thank-you celebration.

DON'T MISS: After such a carefree celebration of youth and creativity, balance it with a difficult but important reminder of the preciousness of life and peace by going to **Hiroshima.** The Atomic Bomb Dome is the symbol of the city—still standing after the atomic bomb destroyed nearly everything else around it. Its walls are crumbling and scorched steel juts from the roof as an expression of the devastation. Adjacent to the dome is the Peace Memorial Park with beautiful landscaped paths, the Peace Memorial Museum, several monuments, a memorial tower, and a poignant fountain of fire and water with an eternal flame.

ⓘ www.jnto.go.jp

Festivals & Tournaments **355**

Wheelchair/Handcycle Race

The Tour de France for the Differently-Abled

Sadler & Vicinity, Alaska, USA

NOT FAR FROM SADLER, THE GOLD-RUSH TOWN OF HOPE TEEMS WITH THE HISTORY OF THAT bygone era and also offers some of the best whitewater rafting in the state. The year-round ski community of Girdwood—located not far away in the picturesque Chugach Mountains—is a mecca for snow sports enthusiasts.

The Sadler's Alaska Challenge is the longest wheelchair and handcycle (a type of bicycle powered by arms instead of legs) race in the world. Twenty-five years ago, it was just two guys pushing themselves in their wheelchairs from Fairbanks to Anchorage, and now it's a grueling event sometimes referred to as the Tour de France for racers with disabilities. For a week each summer, racers traverse a course through Seward, Hope, Girdwood, Whittier, Valdez, and up to a mountaintop pass, complete with punishing mileage and soaring climbs. It is part of the annual roster of events put on by Challenge Alaska, a non-profit organization dedicated to improving the lives of people with disabilities through adaptive sports, therapeutic recreation, and education. Volunteers make the race happen, from operating support vehicles en route to working rest stops and cheering every racer on to the distant finish line.

Your Alaska volunteer adventure may have you registering athletes and coaches at check-in, marking the course in support vehicles, timing racers, and following as a "sweep" van in case there is need for assistance or medical attention. Smaller, less glorious tasks like setting up a sound system, processing registrations, cleaning up, and organizing repair areas also need to be handled by volunteers.

There are no provisions made for visiting volunteers. If you're lucky enough to be able to plan your Alaska visit in July and your trip can coincide with the race days, count your blessings and register to be on the support staff. You won't regret the opportunity to assist this intense race of champions.

YOUR NEXT STEP: Challenge Alaska (✆ **907/344-7399;** www.challengealaska.org). You'll make your own arrangements to be in Alaska for the race, but register as soon as you know you can volunteer—you want to be a part of this. No fees for volunteers.

DON'T MISS: Get a sense of Alaska's majesty when you visit the Inside Passage region and go to **Glacier Bay National Park.** Sixteen glaciers flow from surrounding mountains into these waters. It is a rugged and fragile place, as glaciers retreat and melt at an alarming pace, leaving plains and fjords exposed for the first time in many years. The natural splendor and wildlife found here makes it an unparalleled place for solitude and gaining an appreciation for how small we really are.

ⓘ www.travelalaska.com

356 Festivals & Tournaments

Festival of Books

Literary Lotusland

Los Angeles, California, USA

More than just a TV town, Los Angeles also offers something for serious culture vultures: The Festival of Books is one of the largest literary events in the country. Once you've had your fill of all things written, make sure to check out some of the city's least-trod neighborhoods, like the art-soaked Gallery Row or the historical Olvera Street, called "El Pueblo" by locals.

Every spring, America's largest literary event takes over the beautiful UCLA campus. Hundreds of volunteers pitch in to make this 2-day gathering of writers and readers as idyllic as the weather. Nearly 100 author events, signings, and readings—plus 300 exhibitor booths and 140,000 attendees—celebrate great writing and some literary stargazing. Stages are filled with children's storytelling and readings for adults, and fans are waiting for the appearance of their favorite author.

You'll wear several different hats during the weekend, from greeting arrivals and giving directions to setting up stages and microphones and sound systems. You may be assigned to a particular author event, where you'll take tickets, perhaps give time signals when the speaker is running late, and coordinate signing tables.

Maybe the registration desk is your station for a while, or you're a runner, making sure special guests have arrived on time, that they have water, and are ready to go. Bring water of your own (and comfortable shoes)—volunteers are standing or hustling for hours at a time. You can sign up for as many shifts as you'd like to work one or both days. Some volunteers are also Area Captains who organize other teams of volunteers for a full day, and Bookworm volunteers take on specific tasks of managing speakers' panels, taking charge of information kiosks, supervising signings, and leading teams. Author escorts take writers to their events and signings and often have to stick around long after the end of a scheduled shift as an author signs every last book.

There are no travel arrangements provided for out-of-town volunteers. When you confirm that your Los Angeles vacation will coincide with the festival, contact the organization. A weekend of literary excellence could dovetail nicely with other volunteer work during the week or just visiting L.A.'s movie studios, theme parks, and beaches.

YOUR NEXT STEP: Los Angeles Times Festival of Books (✆ **213/237-6503;** www.troutco.com/fob/). There are no travel arrangements made for your time in Los Angeles, and no fees for volunteering. You may choose to sign up for as many volunteer shifts as your schedule and interests allow. Volunteers get free parking on campus.

DON'T MISS: It's L.A., baby, so you can hardly go home without spending some time at the **beaches.** There's Malibu and Zuma with celebrities and surfers, Santa Monica with its amusement park pier, Venice where you'll in-line skate past famous Muscle Beach, and down south toward Marina del Rey, Playa del Rey, Manhattan Beach, and Redondo. No one leaves Los Angeles with a vitamin-D depletion.

ⓘ www.discoverlosangeles.com

Festivals & Tournaments

Green Festival

A Convenient Booth

San Francisco; Denver; Washington, D.C.; Chicago; Seattle; USA

Kermit the Frog might not have had an easy time being green, but you will during this series of unique, eco-friendly festivities. You'll help create a mini-green city within a city. In the process, you'll meet and interact with local musicians, activists, environmentalists, and artists; all united in the cause. The only skill you need is a love of planet Earth.

This festival weekend travels to several cities in the United States throughout the calendar year, aiming to improve sustainability and eco-consciousness in each place. The festival transforms a convention center or hall into a sustainable community, displaying viable solutions for healthier lives. Interested everyday people join business leaders, authors, community leaders, educators, and filmmakers for workshops, live music, video and film projects, kids' activities, and a marketplace of more than 350 eco-friendly businesses. Renewable energy, fair-trade coffee, migrant worker issues, carbon offsets, alternative energy, waste management, water purification, organic gardening—you name it—if it's a green question, you'll find the answer here. Volunteers make the entire energy-efficient operation run through the weekend in each city.

Shifts last 4.5 hours and are busy: in the days leading up to the weekend event, volunteers form street teams to do outreach and distribute flyers, network in the community, blog about the event, and recruit volunteers. You could work in exhibitor registration or setup (heavy lifting required). Do you want to be a bike valet? Work the bookstore or box office? Staff the Green America Booth or be a stagehand at the main stage? Perhaps you can register additional volunteers or even do coat check. Volunteer job descriptions fit almost any level of interest, energy, and skill. Some volunteers work the festival year after year, or even travel to more than one city. There is no volunteer travel program or arrangements, so you'll handle the specifics of your own trip. You can determine the duration of your volunteer work when you sign up to help at one or more of these global exchange events determined to change the world.

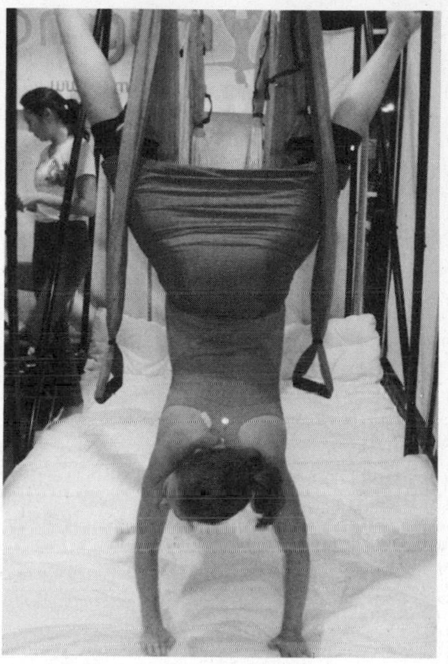

Yoga innovation at the Green Festival in D.C.

YOUR NEXT STEP: Green Festival (national volunteer ✆ **828/333-9422;** www.greenfestivals.org and www.greenfestivalvolunteers.org). No travel arrangements are made by the organization, so you'll arrange your visit and schedule the shift times that work best for you. There is no fee for volunteers.

ⓘ www.usatourist.com

358 **Festivals & Tournaments**

Voodoo Music Experience

It'll Put a Spell on You

New Orleans, Louisiana, USA

Your presence in New Orleans, whether as a volunteer or a tourist, will be welcome in a city that is still recovering from the devastating effects of Hurricane Katrina. You'll be inspired by the strength and spirit of those who remain, while revelling in the food, music, and culture that made the city so famous.

The Crescent City is known for great food, amazing music, and the long and mysterious tradition of voodoo. Every year, two of these elements are combined with the Voodoo Music Experience. For 3 fall days, City Park has two main stages and several smaller stages that shake with 100 bands and their fans in true New Orleans style. The music starts early in the morning with smaller local bands and continues deep into the evening, closing out with headliners like Irma Thomas, Ben Folds, Eminem, Rage Against the Machine, 50 Cent, Wilco, R.E.M., Joss Stone, and Preservation Hall

Marching to the sounds of the Voodoo Music Experience

Jazz Band. The Voodoo "grounds" at the park, a 15-minute drive from the French Quarter, are divided into three zones: Le Ritual, Le Flambeau, and Le Carnival, each with its own essence and energy. Volunteers work half-day or full-day shifts doing everything from band setup to VIP duty.

You can spend a shift or all three days engaged in making sure things go off without a hitch. Shifts are long (7.5 hours) and you'll be hard at work consistently. You can sign up to join any number of volunteer teams: ticketing, information, production/stage crew, art direction/decoration, hospitality, photography/documentation, media relations, VIP services, or sponsorship and administrative help. After working hard in the Big Easy, follow the party—most of the clubs in town have Voodoo Fest specials and impromptu sessions with unannounced musicians that go until dawn.

There are no packages set up for volunteers, so you'll secure your own room and board in the city that oozes hospitality. Sign up for your shifts in advance, then take the Voodoo Shuttle or historic streetcar out to the park to work and play all day. *Laissez Les Bon Temps Roulez* (let the good times roll).

YOUR NEXT STEP: Voodoo Music Experience (www.thevoodooexperience.com). Make your own New Orleans plans for your visit, and then register for all the shifts you'd like. No fee for volunteers.

DON'T MISS: All visitors to the Big Easy have to do their own version of the **Bourbon Street Crawl.** It can be intoxication and debauchery or music and culture—it depends what you're after. The French Quarter is full of museums, galleries, bookstores, and antiques shops, not to mention some of the nation's finest restaurants. Go to Galatoire's and sit at Tennessee Williams's table in the corner or order a Sazerac or a Hurricane at Arnaud's, an iconic stalwart in the Quarter for more than 90 years.

ⓘ www.neworleansonline.com

359 Festivals & Tournaments

National Cherry Blossom Festival

Blooms' Day

Washington, D.C., USA

Often called boring and bureaucratic, this seat of American political power has more of an international flavor than you might expect. A city of spectacular monuments, it is also a city of diverse neighborhoods; Georgetown and Alexandria are not to be missed. For a little adventure, take a hike through Great Falls Park or explore nearby Mount Vernon.

The signature celebration in the nation's capital every spring is the National Cherry Blossom Festival. The delicate pink blooms that burst like rosy popcorn along the Tidal Basin are a sign that winter has moved on. The trees, a gift from Japan, are a symbol of international fellowship, and their annual blooms figuratively renew our nation's commitment to peace and prosperity. The festival is timed with the bloom cycle of the tree and occurs at a different time each spring. More than 150 daily cultural performances take place throughout the city, most of them free of charge. Special events, from art shows to fireworks, live music to the Smithsonian Kite Festival, and events, many with a Japanese or international theme, are as plentiful as the blossoms. Volunteers play a vital part in every aspect of the festival.

You'll be welcoming visitors from around the world who come for this splashy, showy festival. You can direct visitors and provide event information, set up performance venues or tent spaces, work on the National Park recycling initiative for the festival, do maintenance and grounds work at the Tidal Basin, staff the Sakura Matsuri Japanese Street Festival with all their festival-within-a-festival needs, register runners for the 10-Mile Cherry Blossom Race, help organize and facilitate the Cherry Blossom Soccer Tournament, and much more. Each event of the hundreds going on has need for volunteers, so when you register, be sure to peruse the lengthy schedule of happenings so you can sign up for a shift that corresponds to the events you'd most like to work.

You're responsible for your own travel arrangements and accommodations. There are food vendors throughout the main festival areas, and of course DC has a pretty sophisticated dining scene in addition to bountiful cultural opportunities, so you'll never lack things to do, even when the delicate blooms have begun to fall from the trees.

YOUR NEXT STEP: National Cherry Blossom Festival (✆ 877/44BLOOM; www.nationalcherryblossomfestival.org). Volunteers are needed throughout the 16-day festival, and you can register online for as many shifts as suit your schedule or energy level. No travel arrangements are made by the organization for visiting volunteers, and there are no fees involved.

DON'T MISS: D.C.'s eclectic and artsy **Adams Morgan** neighborhood is named for the city's first segregated schools: all-black Thomas P. Morgan Elementary and all-white John Quincy Adams School. The rejuvenated neighborhood is now a true melting pot of cultures from around the world. Immigrants from Africa, Asia, and South and Central America make this fun, active hub a pastiche of flavors, sights, and sounds. You can find fantastic restaurants, live music, clubs and nightlife, trendy shops, and a real global village atmosphere as you walk the hill.

ⓘ www.washington.org

10 Charity Fundraisers: Making Them Happen

Special fundraising events for great causes happen almost every weekend somewhere in the world. Annual events will rarely be nestled into arranged trips or travel arrangements, but when you've planned your vacation and want to spend some time and effort helping a meaningful cause, pitch in to make the big day a success.

360 **Victoria, British Columbia, Canada** The Dragon Boat Festival is celebrated with fierce competitive boating that brings cultural color and charitable fundraising to the B.C. Cancer Foundation. Ninety international dragon boat teams compete, and teams fundraise for the charity as part of their participation. ***Victoria Dragon Boat Festival for the B.C. Cancer Foundation*** *(**250/704-2500**; www.victoriadragonboat.com and www.bccancerfoundation.com). No fee and no specific travel arrangements.*

Design Hope Toronto's charity auction for the homeless

361 **Toronto, Ontario, Canada** Local artists and designers create paintings, photographs, digital art, sculpture, and even blown glass, all dealing with the concept of home, to benefit the homeless. One-of-a-kind artworks are sold and auctioned in a night of food and music, with every dollar going to the beneficiary organization. ***Design Hope Toronto*** *(**416/971-6110**; www.designhopetoronto.ca). No charge for volunteers.*

362 **London, England** Several special events happen each year to raise funds to further the fight against asthma. Those who can run 10K secure pledges before the springtime race. Volunteers make the practicalities and necessary chores seamless in support of the racers. ***Asthma UK*** *(**+44/020 7786 4900**; www.asthma.org.uk). No travel planning done by the charity.*

363 **Atlanta, Boston, Chicago, Beverly Hills, New York, or San Antonio, USA** The Women's Sports Foundation, founded by former tennis star Billie Jean King, is committed to empowering girls and women to pursue sport and fitness. Go Girl Go! is a major event held annually in several cities, getting one million inactive girls to participate in regular physical activity. Volunteers help to make it an effortless and fun experience. ***Women's Sports Foundation*** *(**800/227-3988**; www.womenssportsfoundation.org). Your travel arrangements are up to you.*

364 **California, USA** The AIDS LifeCycle is a 7-day bike ride from San Francisco to Los Angeles to raise money for several charities that provide critical services in the war against HIV. Volunteer "roadies" make everything on this mission a success. ***AIDS LifeCycle*** *(**323/860-7376**; www.aidslifecycle.org). No charge for volunteers. You'll camp alongside participants.*

365 **Long Island, New York, USA, and Kisumu, Kenya** President Barack Obama and First Lady Michelle Obama made a strong statement about the importance of HIV testing when they were tested while visiting Barack's grandmother in

Kisumu, Kenya, in 2006. The World AIDS Marathon takes place in Kisumu each year, where runners get pledges for their 42km (26.2 miles) run through the Kenyan countryside. The money raised goes to the fight against HIV/AIDS. A sister event in New York's Long Island is the annual 5K AIDS + Cancer Run/Walk. You'll work registration, start or finish lines, or "stations" along the routes. ***World AIDS Marathon*** *(www.worldaidsmarathon.com) and* ***5K AIDS + Cancer Run Walk*** *(5kaidscancerrunwalk.com) via the* ***Richard M. Brodsky Foundation*** *(✆* ***516/432-1254****; www.richardmbrodsky.org). No fee for volunteers; make your own travel arrangements.*

The AIDS LifeCycle bicycle ride begins in San Francisco

366 Houston, Texas, USA There are more than 15,000 homeless in the Houston area, with few beds in shelters, so thousands live on the streets. The My Fellow Man Alliance works to provide safe housing and medical respite referrals, boost community awareness, and actively work in outreach and intervention programs. Fundraising for these costly programs is helped by the annual Houston Homeless Run, in which participants raise money via sponsors. ***My Fellow Man Alliance*** *(✆* ***713/780-2515****; www.myfellowman.org). No fee, but volunteers responsible for their own travel and accommodations.*

367 Jeffersonville to Bennington, Vermont, USA Through the green hills of Vermont, teams of runners cover 322km (200 miles) in 24 hours in this grueling fundraising event. Distance runners of all skill levels team up with their friends and colleagues to tackle the 36-leg course, and your diligent support helps the run go off without a hitch. Funds are pledged and raised for Volunteers with a Purpose, which gives grants to several local charities. ***Green Mountain Relay*** *(www.greenmountainrelay.com) benefiting* ***Volunteers with a Purpose*** *(www.volunteerswithapurpose.org). No fee, but volunteers must arrange their own travel and accommodations.*

368 Multiple City Locations, North America The inspiring pink wave of fundraising walkers marches across the country every year in 15 American cities. The Breast Cancer 3-Day is a huge, life-affirming event where thousands of walkers march 97km (60 miles) over 3 days. Nights are spent tent camping in a remote village, with dining tents and entertainment and an unbeatable sense of community among the participants and volunteers who make it all work. ***Breast Cancer 3-Day*** *(✆* ***800/996-3DAY****; www.the3day.org). Four-day crew volunteers camp with the entire walk community. Meals are provided. Crew members pay a US$90 registration fee.*

369 Multiple City Locations, USA There are dozens of annual Walk with Us to Cure Lupus charity walkathons across the United States. Participants in the 5km (3-mile) walks in cities coast to coast raise money to aid research for a cure and improved treatment for the disease. ***Alliance for Lupus Research*** *(national office ✆****212/218-2840****; http://walk.lupusresearch.org). No charge for volunteers, but you'll make your own travel and accommodations arrangements.*

One-Day Events 370

Pagan Parade & Festival

Feed the Magic

Berkeley, California

It should come as no surprise that Berkeley—one of the most liberal cities in one of the country's most liberal states—hosts an annual Pagan Festival. The festival only lasts for a day, but for the socially aware, globally minded volunteer, there's enough in this town to keep you hanging around for much longer.

For one day in May, at the birthplace of 1960s hippie culture, the annual Pagan Festival focuses on spiritual, social, political, and environmental change and responsibility. The pagan community is often misunderstood by people who presume it is a source of nefarious behaviors. Quite the opposite is true—pagan holidays predate most of the Christian celebrations in Western culture and were often the inspiration for them. This free event is a chance for international performers to take to the stage, from healers and dancers to singers and scholars. A celebratory parade, a green earth-honoring pavilion, a crafts fair, storytelling pavilion, temple of change, authors' circle, and children's area round out the festival.

This is your chance to add to a universal embrace of the planet—and if that is too esoteric, just lend a hand with a great party. You can pitch in with other volunteers in several ways. There is need for: voluntary stagehands, general errand runners, videographers, photographers, a festival setup team, parade assistance, information table staff, child care, food area staff, cleanup crew, volunteer coordinators, special needs seating attendants, altar builders, security, green room hospitality, children's area staff, stage setup and strike crew, parade float decorators/painters, promotions and contribution support staff, and administrative support. Surely you can find a great match in that list.

There aren't any Bay Area arrangements made by the sponsor organization, so you'll arrange your own trip details (though the organization's website has plenty of links to community resources who can make some great recommendations). Of course Berkeley, nearby San Francisco, and the entire Bay Area is a visitor's dream with endless exploration available.

YOUR NEXT STEP: The Pagan Alliance (© **877/467-5527;** www.thepaganalliance.org). You'll make your own arrangements to be in Berkeley for the 1-day event; there is no fee for volunteers, participants, or festival guests.

DON'T MISS: Take some time to explore the institution that has brought this beautiful hillside city most of its fame: the **University of California, Berkeley.** Home to some of the great minds of the 20th century, Berkeley is well known for its student activism—most famously for the anti-Vietnam protests of the 1960s and 1970s. The campus is bucolic and woodsy, and the world-class libraries, botanical gardens, Greek Theatre, Paleontology Museum, Art Museum and Pacific Film Archive, and Lawrence Hall of Science are all worth your attention.

(i) www.berkeleycvb.com

371 One-Day Events

Worldfest Earth Day Festival

California Greenin'

Encino, California, USA

Located in the heart of the San Fernando Valley, Encino is immortalized in Frank Zappa's "Valley Girl" and was the stand-in for Bedford Falls in *It's a Wonderful Life,* as well as a whole host of other Hollywood movies. Only 25 minutes north of Los Angeles, this town is rich in Mexican culture and history, and worlds away from the superficial facades of Los Angeles.

In a lovely suburban park in mid-May, the Earth Day Festival is one day to celebrate being outside and bask in big-name entertainment, inspiring presentations, charitable organizations that can give you a new perspective, kids' entertainment and activities, and good eats. There's a main stage, the more intimate Earth Lounge and EcoTent for acoustic performances and workshops, the Healthy Hut and its yoga classes, meditation, and cooking demos, and exhibitors zone for green products and services, Kids' World, food/beer/wine garden, and animal adoptions. Volunteers make sure everyone, from guests and their kids to entertainers and headliner bands, stays in a "green" mood.

As a WorldFest volunteer, you can help the day of the event or in the run-up preparing for the big day. If you know sign language, you can work as an interpreter for hearing-impaired visitors. To reach the thousands of attendees, your help with promotion, distributing flyers, beefing up

Catching a performance at the Worldfest Earth Day Festival

the website, graphics work, creating the show guide and program, making and posting signage, and outreach to non-profits and the community will be invaluable. On WorldFest Day, you can help with solar power coordination, recycling, event layout, sales, volunteer coordination, being a liaison with the media, organizing vendors, stage management for entertainment venues, stage crew, band greeting, backstage assistance, people greeting, or staffing the Kids' World area, focusing on child care, games, entertainment, and keeping the little ones interested and having fun.

You'll be arranging your own travel and trip specifics in the Los Angeles/Encino area. When you confirm that you'll be able to spend the day volunteering at the event, get in touch and sign up for the shift and job description that is the best fit for you.

YOUR NEXT STEP: WorldFest (✆ 310/ 477-7887; www.worldfestevents.com).

There are no travel arrangements organized via this event, so make your own plans in Encino or the Southern California area to match up with the date of the event so you can enjoy an inspiring day in the park. No fee for volunteers.

DON'T MISS: Just over the hill from Encino and a short drive to downtown Los Angeles will bring you to a stellar work of architecture, the **Walt Disney Concert Hall.** The home of the Los Angeles Philharmonic, the undulating stainless-steel building looks like a pile of giant titanium pencil shavings (in the very best way) and is one of the most acoustically perfect performance venues in the world. Try to see a performance here, and if not, at least go for the behind-the-scenes tour of this extraordinary building designed by Frank Gehry. www.laphil.com

ⓘ www.discoverlosangeles.com

One-Day Events **372**

Children's Festival

Fun for Families

Santa Barbara, California, USA

Unofficially known as the "American Riviera," Santa Barbara is nestled between palm-lined Pacific beaches and the sloping foothills of the Santa Ynez Mountains, blending a mosaic of whitewashed stucco and red-tile roofs with a gracious, relaxed attitude. Outside of your festival responsibilities you can kick back on gold-sand beaches, prowl the shops and galleries that line the village's historic streets, and relax over a meal in one of many top-notch cafes and restaurants.

The Family Service Agency of Santa Barbara is the area's first non-profit human services organization, tackling problems like shortages of living necessities, family violence, isolation, depression and suicide, marital issues, parenting difficulties, and kids at risk. Its annual party in May, the Children's Festival, gives the kids who fall in those categories a special day to laugh and play. From live acts on stage to the free hot dogs and pony rides to face painting and games, the energy zooms around the park. More than 250 volunteers staff each station, information booth, game, and tent.

You'll be assigned to a particular age group and the activities designed for them (children, adolescents, young adults) or to general festival tasks. Do you want to stuff the donated recycled backpacks with donated school and art supplies so every kid goes home with a gift? Would you like to work at the information and donations tables helping direct guests to the places they'll find the most fun or process donations? (More than $100,000 is raised for important programs like Big Brothers/Big Sisters mentoring, Healthy Start programs, counseling services, and the 2-1-1 24-hour hotline for human services.) Fancy an afternoon painting faces or helping kids on and off ponies? Perhaps being the reminder to be "gentle" at the petting zoo is your desire. You can also set up before and clean up after the event—plenty of volunteers are needed for that.

The festival is a huge undertaking, and all help is gratefully appreciated. Getting yourself to Santa Barbara and to the park (and the rest of your travel arrangements) is up to you.

YOUR NEXT STEP: Family Service Agency (✆ **805/965-1001**; www.fsacares.org). There are no travel packages organized by the agency, so you'll make your own Santa Barbara travel plans to be available for service for the Children's Festival.

DON'T MISS: The idyllic beach and hills of Santa Barbara are sure to call to you for much of your time in town. Take a day to visit the historic **Stearns Wharf and Harbor** and all their attractions. The Sea Center has live touch tanks, and Sundays give way to the Arts and Craft Show, where artisan vendors line the boulevard with their wares. Sailing charters are a perfect sunset activity after you've perused the floating and historic exhibits at the Santa Barbara Maritime Museum.

ⓘ www.santabarbara.com

373 One-Day Events

MayDay Festival, Parade & Ceremony

Puppet Projects

Minneapolis, Minnesota, USA

With a thriving theater scene (Minneapolis is home to 75 theater companies) and a number of recent high-profile architecture projects, the city is often called the cultural capital of the Midwest. The annual MayDay Festival and Parade is all about a different kind of art project—puppets. If you're a master of marionettes, Minnesota will be your kind of town.

On August 1, 2007, Minneapolis and the entire nation watched in horror as the 35W Bridge collapsed and 13 citizens perished in the river. As a response to the tragedy, and an exploration of building bridges as a metaphor for connecting humanity, the MayDay celebrations created by In the Heart of the Beast Puppet and Mask Theatre now take on a particularly poignant tone. The parade and ceremony, followed by an all-day festival, are enormous productions staffed by hundreds of volunteers and enjoyed by tens of thousands of Twin Cities residents who come to the river to remember and to celebrate. The annual Tree of Life ceremony, with large-scale puppets, masked performers, 200 player/participants, and innovative stagecraft, paddles the sun across the lake to reawaken the tree of life. More than 6,000 volunteer hours go into making the day's events a successful tribute and celebration.

Volunteering for MayDay events can take many shapes (like the fantastical puppets and masks that are a hallmark of the day). You can serve, along with more than 350 other volunteers, as an usher, ticket taker, stage or set builder, crew for the ceremony or parade, or stage crew in the park. If you are in the Twin Cities area ahead of the event, get involved as a puppet-maker, or put needle to thread as a costume maker, or work administratively to help the organization or to gain publicity with the media and donors. Your only real requirement is to surrender to the magic of the imagination.

It's up to you to plan your trip and volunteer to be a participant in a wild ride that is part carnival and part poignant observance.

YOUR NEXT STEP: In the Heart of the Beast Puppet and Mask Theatre (✆ **612/721-2535;** www.hobt.org). No travel arrangements made by the organization, so when you confirm your plans, get in touch with the theater group to help put on this extravagant and evocative event.

DON'T MISS: Take a reflective visit to the birthplace of the city. The **Stone Arch Bridge,** built by railway baron James Hill, gently curves as it crosses the Mississippi River and provides a stunning view of **St. Anthony Falls,** whose churning power was the driving force behind Minneapolis becoming a milling capital.

ⓘ www.minneapolis.org

One-Day Events 374

Hands on New York Day

Polishing the Big Apple

New York City, New York, USA

GET YOUR HANDS DIRTY AND MAKE THE CITY CLEAN AT THE SAME TIME. YOU DON'T NEED ANY special skills to be a part of Hands on New York Day. Planting plants and cleaning up the city's green spaces takes nothing more than a strong back and a good pair of gardening gloves. And you'll meet some of the city's finest folks along the way.

Every April, more than 5,000 volunteers from all five boroughs of New York turn up at gardens, parks, and other public green spaces to spend a city-wide day of service cleaning and revitalizing gardens, playgrounds, community centers, and school grounds. Tens of thousands of trees are planted as part of the Million Trees NYC program, and volunteers also raise money by sponsorship of their donated work time.

First you'll ask family, friends, and coworkers to sponsor your day of service. There is an easy webpage builder as part of the project, so friends near and far can donate electronically in your name to the foundation. When you register, you'll select which borough you'd like to work in for the day. Then on the weekend day of the event, you and thousands of similarly inspired volunteers will turn up to the more than 100 public parks and similar spots and get busy cleaning up debris, painting, repairing fences and playground equipment, planting, weeding, getting those trees in the ground, replenishing sod or sand, and any other greening project required by the site. If you want to go above and beyond the call of duty, you can be a triple threat: in addition to the day's work and fundraising, you could volunteer to be a site captain or team leader, taking responsibility for the project site and the coordination and completion of the work. The buck stops with you. The funds raised go to the New York Cares programs that serve more than 450,000 New Yorkers in need.

There is no travel arranging done by the organization, so you'll plan your New York visit in April to coincide with the event. You can raise sponsorship funds from home or anywhere else by registering online, then reaching out well in advance of the day.

YOUR NEXT STEP: New York Cares (✆ **212/228-5000;** www.handsonnewyorkday.org). There are no travel packages for this volunteer opportunity, so you'll handle your own New York arrangements. There is a US$20 registration fee to cover administrative costs (allowing all the donated sponsorship money to go to projects).

DON'T MISS: Take a day before or after the Hands on New York Day to visit **Ellis Island** and the **Statue of Liberty.** These two national icons are on two separate islands in New York Harbor, accessible by ferry boat, and each is a wonderful day out of the buzz of the city (with the best views back toward the southern tip of Manhattan) while completely immersing you in the history of not only New York, but the entire nation.

ⓘ www.nycgo.com

375 One-Day Events

Special Olympics

Help the Games Begin

Raleigh, North Carolina, USA

RALEIGH HAS ALL THE TRAPPINGS OF ANY BIG CITY: WORLD-CLASS MUSEUMS, DOZENS OF LIVE entertainment venues, and high-end shopping, all infused with a small-town, Southern charm. This socially progressive city is an ideal spot for anyone who has an interest in working with people who have special needs.

Special Olympics North America offers nearly 70 programs and global chapters on six continents. You can get involved close to home, wherever you may live, or if your travels take you to North Carolina, you can volunteer at the main North American chapter. There are ways to get involved year-round, not just for the annual Olympics event. The mission of Special Olympics is to provide sports training and athletic competition in Olympic-like sports for children and adults with intellectual disabilities. If you think you know what it is to be inspired, just wait. North Carolina has more than 38,000 Special Olympics athletes statewide, and the national office here supports more than 544,000. Volunteering helps further the goal of helping every person become productive, accepted, and respected in his or her community. Volunteers dive in to assist running the organization, the events, and the coaching programs.

If you're in the area for the actual games, you can be involved in athlete and team support, fundraising, setup, cleanup, information, and several other day-of-event tasks. But no worries if your vacation doesn't allow you to be here for that—there are competitions throughout the year. Be part of the volunteer team making it all happen at state-level events like the Summer Games, Fall Games, Midsummer Tournament, Basketball & Cheerleading Championship, Winter Games-Ice Skating, and Winter Games-Alpine Skiing. All of these need you and your fellow volunteers behind the scenes coordinating events. Coaching and sport development are also incredible volunteer opportunities (for longer time commitments). There are similar opportunities at the state level of competition throughout the country and indeed the world.

There are no travel packages sponsored by the organization, so you'll

Swimmers at the Special Olympics in Raleigh

arrange your own visit. If not in North Carolina, look into opportunities wherever you may travel, work, or live. Motivated volunteers are needed by each international organization to give athletes across the globe the opportunities to "develop physical fitness, demonstrate courage, experience joy, and participate in a sharing of gifts, skills, and friendship with their families, other Special Olympics athletes, and the community."

YOUR NEXT STEP: Special Olympics North Carolina (✆ **919/785-0699;** www.sonc.net) and **Special Olympics** (**800/700-8585;** www.specialolympics.org for international and countrywide chapters). No arranged travel opportunities through the organization. When you know your plans and schedule, find the chapter nearest your locale to become a hero for the athletes.

DON'T MISS: In a place like Raleigh, there's always a big event or celebration going on, and in a place like the **JC Raulston Arboretum,** there's always something in bloom. More than 3ha (8 acres) and 5,000 species of plants make this garden an acclaimed national treasure. Enjoy the rose garden, with more than 100 types of roses, the arboretum with its special Southern magnolias, the Klein-Pringle White Garden, and other special zones for meandering among the botanic beauty.

ⓘ www.visitraleigh.com

376 One-Day Events

Chocolate Festival

Lone Star Lusciousness

Austin, Texas, USA

YOU WOULDN'T THINK IT WOULD BE TOO DIFFICULT FINDING FOLKS TO VOLUNTEER AT A CHOCOLATE festival. All that's needed here is a serious sweet tooth and a willingness to help out for a good cause. Austin might be known more for its eclectic music scene than milk chocolate, but this is your chance to help change that.

At first glance, a chocolate festival may seem to be all about decadence. While the cocoa bean's best product does spoil us with sweetness, this festival is in fact a unique fundraising event for the Susan G. Komen for the Cure breast cancer charity. Chocolatiers and artisans compete in this annual celebration for the sweetest prize—the glory. Of course, attending guests are the real winners, as they get to sample the exquisite wares of restaurants, bakeries, patisseries, and catering companies who are all putting their best milk, dark, bittersweet, and white chocolate treats forward. Not all of it has to be sticky sweet either—think molé and other gastronomically subtle uses for cocoa, then think about eating all of it (for a good cause, of course).

As a volunteer, you'll make sure all the tastings, cooking demos, special meals, and film screenings go off without any problems. Like a fine tempered chocolate, you are there to make it all run smoothly. When you register as a volunteer, organizers will match you to the job description that best fits your talents and interests: tickets, serving, setup, information, cleanup, promotion, processing donations, backstage, media liaison, and so on. You won't have to work hard to be sure everyone is enjoying themselves, and doing it guilt-free, knowing they are helping in the fight against breast cancer.

There are no Austin travel arrangements made for you by the festival, so you'll get yourself there for your own sweet reward.

YOUR NEXT STEP: Austin Chocolate Festival (✆ **800/834-3498**; www.austinchocolatefestival.com). You'll arrange your own visit to Austin for the festival, then register as a volunteer for the event.

DON'T MISS: Since you're in Texas, you'll want to "Remember the **Alamo**," the battle at this historic mission in 1836. While the battle was lost by Texan defenders, people worldwide continue to remember the Alamo as a heroic struggle against impossible odds. A few men stood up to the onslaught of an army, and the Alamo has become a symbol of the ultimate sacrifice for freedom.

ⓘ www.austintexas.org

One-Day Events 377

Festival of Trees

Stop Crimes Against Urbanity

Seattle, Washington, USA

OFTEN CALLED ONE OF THE BEST WALKING CITIES IN AMERICA, SEATTLE IS KNOWN FOR ITS HIGH standard of living and physically fit, eco-conscious citizens—so it's no wonder Seattlites devote a special day to taking care of their green spaces. This is a great opportunity to exercise your green thumb—as well as the rest of your body.

The annual Festival of Trees is put on by PlantAmnesty, a group dedicated to eradicating the crimes against nature in our own backyards, whose mission, with tongue planted firmly in cheek, is to "stop the senseless torture and mutilation of trees and shrubs." The festival itself is a playful day with lots of learning about gardening and trees. Workshops include species selection, troubleshooting with plant diseases, ecological gardening, and helping Seattle's urban forest. Entertainment includes everything from aerial artists to magic and music, while green classes inspire the home gardener. There's an onsite pea patch, native plant garden, and children's garden. There are also challenges like bucket truck rides and bog tree climbing, plus an eco-marketplace and healthy food vendors. Not one but two parades round out the day's events. Hundreds of volunteers are needed to make it all happen.

You could do any number of things to get your green thumbs dirty helping out. Create a tree costume or be a stagehand. You could work at the tree adoption agency, helping people understand their new trees and how best to care for them. Set up classrooms and the kids' activity center. Manage lines of people at events, give directions, and greet the public. The outdoor marketplace needs setting up, the performance space needs decorating, and the backstage area has to be set up for more than 40 performers. Post signs, set up and take down outdoor facilities, clear indoor spaces after the frivolity, work with food and beverage providers to feed the entertainers and speakers, coordinate the parades, work on the recycling crew, or help prepare for the after-party, where you and your fellow volunteers, along with the featured performers and speakers, get their due thanks.

Your time in Seattle is yours to arrange, and making it coincide with the Tree Festival frees you up to participate as a volunteer for the somewhat wacky day of earth honoring.

YOUR NEXT STEP: PlantAmnesty Festival of Trees (✆ **206/783-9813;** www.plantamnesty.org/festival). No travel packages are supplied, so build your Seattle time around the festival so you can help out.

DON'T MISS: It is the most iconic symbol for Seattle, and provides a stunning view from the top. Visit the **Space Needle,** where the observation deck gives you the perfect vantage point for Puget Sound, Mount Rainier, and the Olympic Mountains, as well as Seattle's skyscraper skyline. You don't even have to descend for dinner if you eat at the revolving restaurant on top.

ⓘ www.visitseattle.org

11 Crossing Generations

Elderhostel volunteers measure a Sea Turtle on the beach

Helping Seniors 378

Elderly Home

A Helping Hand in West Africa

Calavi, Benin

SITUATED ALONG THE GULF OF GUINEA, CALAVI IS A CULTURAL AND GASTRONOMIC CITY. JUST 10km (6 miles) outside the capital of Cotonou, the city's western edge is famous for its variety of bird species and the village of Ganvié, built on water and home to some of the region's richest cultural heritage.

The Little Sisters of the Poor opened this non-denominational home for elderly men and women in Calavi more than a decade ago. Modern facilities and personalized care make it a nice option for its multiracial and multilingual group of residents. (Benin's official language is French, so it would help if you had a conversational level, though it is not required; French lessons are available as an adjunct to the program.) Resident clergy and staff, as well as a nice outdoor space with gardens, bolster the home environment. In addition to the care program, there is a vocational training program for Benin women looking to devote their work to the care of the elderly here or in other facilities.

You'll work alongside staff on the day-in, day-out tasks of elder care. You'll help serve meals, assist with eating and drinking, help residents take their medicine, and assist them with getting in and out of bed. You'll also help with washing and will learn the use of the lifting apparatus for those who need an extra boost. You'll help dress those that need a hand to get ready for the day. There will always be chores to be done in the laundry, infirmary, and rehabilitation/exercise room. Spending the afternoon with a program of entertainment is a chance for you to get creative and bring in ideas for songs or music or perhaps a group craft or storytelling project. Your digital camera or video camera will elicit lots of smiles. Physiotherapy sessions are an important part of the day, and you can help if you're a novice or run some sessions if you have that experience.

You'll stay with a host family, who will provide breakfast and a packed lunch during the week and three meals daily on weekends when you're not working. Your free time in Calavi will be spent getting to know your fellow volunteers, host family, and the community. In addition to French language courses, the program has supplemental classes in dance and drumming if you'd like to explore some of Benin's cultural heritage, and the teeming marketplaces will inspire you to cook with local ingredients and flavors. For additional fees, there are organized trips to Benin attractions that would nicely occupy an entire weekend of adventure.

YOUR NEXT STEP: SYTO Benin (✆ **+229/21 38 65 50;** www.sytobenin.net). Though the founding name of the organization is Student Youth Travel Organisation, SYTO has volunteers of all ages working in Benin. You'll determine the length of your stay, US$887 project fee and US$34 a week hosting charge, which includes host family accommodations, two meals daily during the workweek and three meals daily during the weekends, a 3-day Benin orientation course, transportation, airport transfer, training, and in-country staff support. For an additional fee, you can take intensive French–language classes or drumming/dance workshops.

DON'T MISS: The village of **Ganvié** is called Africa's Venice, as it's built on water. Homes, schools, temples, guest houses, markets, and other community buildings hover on stilts over the lake, and you'll get from one place to the next by canoe.

ⓘ www.benintourisme.com

379 Helping Seniors

Rebuild Homes of the Elderly

Touring & Tools

Barray, Cambodia

Many of the homes in Barray—located near the well-known city of Siem Reap—were rebuilt with foreign-aid funds in the 1950s, but many have since fallen into disrepair. Working here on rebuilding homes belonging to the town's senior citizens will give you a great sense of pride while benefiting those unable to do the work themselves.

This trip combines a taste of voluntourism with a healthy dose of sightseeing and comfortable travel around Cambodia. The 12-day project includes 4 workdays spent serving the elderly villagers of Barray in the region around Tonle Sap Lake. The verdant green of rice paddies and tropical palms obscures the simple buildings of modest villages, and rain and humidity take their toll on the structures. Larger families have more pairs of hands to maintain their homes, but for elderly residents who can only do a few minor repairs, or can't do the work at all, their dwellings are falling into disrepair.

You'll spend workdays using human-powered tools to repair and maintain these structures as well as renovate the school. (Don't worry, construction novices will be taught.) Your workdays will be long and feel tough in the high humidity. Each residence being repaired will have its own set of challenges, from reframing or replacing the wall materials to rehanging doors, clearing away overgrowth of invasive plants, building a better path, painting, or repairing the roof. Whatever it is, you'll jump in and do it, leaving the community elders in much better living conditions than those in which you found them.

You'll stay with a host family during workdays, experiencing the local cuisine and customs and truly feeling like a contributing member of the community.

The days before and after the workdays are spent touring Cambodia, from Phnom Penh to Siem Reap and Angkor, with all the major tour sites on the docket. You'll move from hotel to hotel for accommodations, in a shared room (single supplement available), and take meals at restaurants, enjoying a wide array of foods as you travel throughout the country.

YOUR NEXT STEP: Responsible Travel (✆ **+44/1273 600 030**; www.responsibletravel.com). A 12-day project (with an additional travel day), £940, includes lodging at hotels and homestay, meals, tours and guides, in-country flights and ground transportation, and training and tools. The organization arranges flights to/from the UK for an additional cost.

DON'T MISS: You will have been immersed in the history and culture of Cambodia during the tour and seen most of the "must-see" sights, so if you can take a few extra days, head over the border to less-visited **Laos** and swim in the famous lower pools of the Kuang Si Waterfalls. If the water seems a bit chilly, you can warm up in a hurry at the two hot springs, Bo Noi and Bo Yai.

ⓘ www.tourismcambodia.com

Helping Seniors 380

Art, Music & Gardening for the Elderly

Banishing Loneliness & Boredom

Vancouver, British Columbia, Canada

BIG URBAN CENTERS LIKE VANCOUVER ARE MORE OFTEN ASSOCIATED WITH YOUNG, HIP thirty-somethings and can be an unwelcoming place for the elderly. Teaching art, music, and gardening to some of the city's older citizens right in the downtown core offers a chance to see the city in a new way by day, and enjoy all that it has to offer by night.

This elder center is the largest in Vancouver's West End and has raised the bar on quality of life for its residents. The Campus of Care supports several stages of attention and support, from independent housing to assisted living and complex care. The organization believes in the importance of interaction, and makes it a priority for residents to interact with children, plants, and animals as often as possible. Their mission is to eliminate loneliness and boredom while transforming the community into a valuable opportunity for new connections. Volunteers (targeted for ages 19 to 30) work hand in hand with dedicated staff and the seniors themselves to achieve these goals.

You'll be focused on improving the daily quality of life of each person at the center, participating in programs that involve residents in gardening, art, music, and outdoor exploration. You'll accompany staff and residents on outings, paired with one senior to assist in walking or with wheelchair mobility. You'll take trips around the gardens, or out to a museum, art galleries, parks, and picnics. While you're on excursions, you'll keep your eyes open for found objects to gather for art projects back at the center. The discovery of little treasures like leaves or flowers can be used for multimedia creations. Then it is time for art projects, as well as music (playing and singing, or perhaps working up a number with a few of the seniors) and gardening.

The volunteer team will bunk at the community building on the center's campus. Meals are included, and the center is in downtown Vancouver, with museums, theater, galleries, shopping, the enormous Stanley Park, and more all close by. Trendy Robson Street is only a block away. If you find yourself bored in your free time, you're just not trying.

YOUR NEXT STEP: Canadian Alliance for Development Initiatives and Projects (✆ **604/628-7400;** www.cadip.org) A 20-day project (for ages 19 to 30),US$270, includes sleeping on the floor of the community center, all meals, and project training and support.

DON'T MISS: The **Vancouver Aquarium** has earned its place among the finest aquaria in the world, not only for its 70,000 sea creatures, but also for its unprecedented interaction opportunities. Free-roaming animals abound in the Amazon Gallery, there's an enormous interactive zone for kids (and the young at heart), sea otter feeds, shark dives, dolphin encounters, sea lion and otter interaction programs, and a rare opportunity to get in the water with beautiful white beluga whales.

ⓘ www.tourismvancouver.com

381 Helping Seniors

Home for Elderly

Learn Spanish as You Help

Heredia, Costa Rica

Just 10km (6 miles) north of the Costa Rican capital of San José, Heredia is best known for sprawling coffee plantations and lush national parks; particularly Barulio Carillo and its famous climbable volcano. Working with the town's elderly during the day and staying with a host family is a unique opportunity to interact with ordinary Costa Ricans, while exploring a spectacular landscape.

This large care facility for the elderly has more than 100 residents and opportunities for volunteers in almost every area. You can assist year-round in general care tasks, physiotherapy, the infirmary, and recreation and enrichment programs. You'll need some Spanish-language skill to work here and freely interact and communicate with the residents. And you won't want to miss the stories they share. With such a large facility, even with the hardworking and dedicated staff, residents can sometimes feel like they're lost in the crowd, so volunteers who provide personal, focused attention are a terrific addition to the already high level of care provided. Those with some experience can also help in the physiotherapy and rehabilitation departments, being sure each resident has physical activity and challenge appropriate to their level of fitness and mobility.

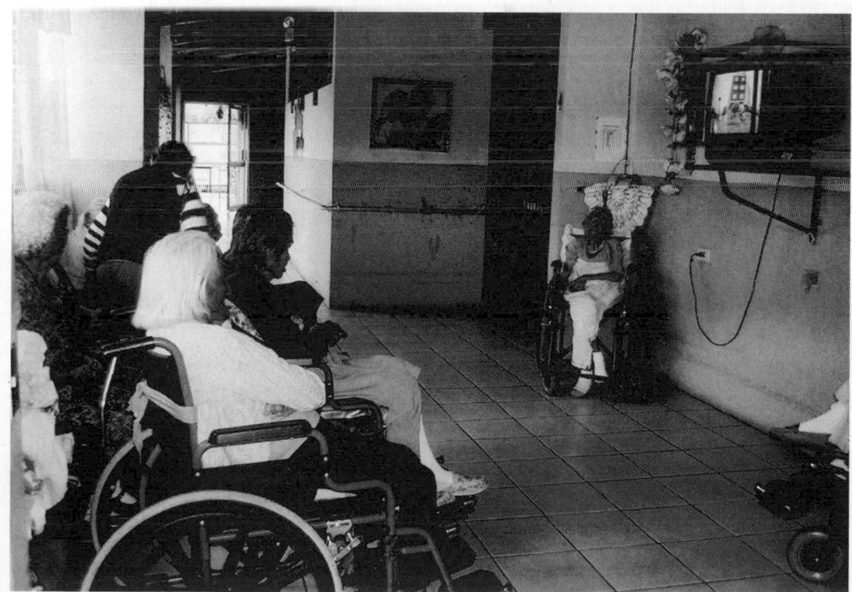

Inside the home for the elderly in Heredia, Costa Rica

Your work may seem scattered as you jump from one task to the next, but everything asked of you is in service to the community at the facility. You can help with mealtimes, serving food and giving assistance where necessary with feeding. Perhaps you're inspired to lead a new art project or teach some basic computer skills. Would you like to lead a discussion group for people to share their travel experiences and add your own stories to the mix? Is your thumb green? The garden is a constant source of activity and a fun challenge for seniors who look for every opportunity to be outside and active. Do you want to learn some local specialty recipes? Help out in the kitchen, and you'll learn some great ideas for Costa Rican meals when you get back to your own family and friends.

You'll live with a host family near the senior center and near the center of town. Two meals daily are provided by the host family, and you'll find plenty of lunch options in town. Spanish-language instruction is also built into this placement. Heredia is a university city with a teeming nightlife and cultural atmosphere that will be entertaining (and perhaps distracting)—luckily there is plenty of free time built into your evenings and weekends. Shops, parks, coffee houses and bistros, restaurants, bars and dance clubs, live music clubs, and more add to the cosmopolitan flavor of the city.

YOUR NEXT STEP: Amerispan (✆ **800/ 879-6640;** www.amerispan.com). A 2-week project, US$1,050, includes lodging with a host family, two meals daily, Spanish-language classes, airport pickup, local training and support, and travel insurance.

DON'T MISS: Tortuguero, or the "land of turtles" is a small village on a slim promontory of land between the Caribbean Sea and an intricate maze of canals. You can only reach this community of 600 by seaplane or via the coastal waterway, which is good practice for the kayaking and canoeing you'll enjoy as you explore. The village is next to a national park that is prime breeding ground for sea turtles. You can walk from one end of the car-free village to the other in less than 5 minutes, but you can paddle for days and never exhaust the waterways and canals.

ⓘ www.visitcostarica.com

Helping Seniors 382

Women for Elderly Women

Giving Back in Goa

Goa, India

East meets West in this tiny tropical paradise that sits on the shores of the Arabian Sea. In Goa, Indian and Iberian cultures mix together seamlessly in a town that used to be known for its hippie backpackers, but today attracts hip international travelers. This female-only volunteer opportunity is an amazing chance for a cultural exchange, as you both interact with and help the doyennes of Goa's language, history, and culture.

This mentoring program is for female volunteers only in service to elderly women in Goa, forming a bond and relationship that will stay with you long after you return home. Vibrant Indian "grandmas" share their life experience with you while you, in turn, facilitate projects for entertainment and enrichment in the care home to keep interest and engagement levels high. For the most part, the residents don't have family or friends able to care for them, but they are blessed with a wealth of experience and the wisdom a full life brings—and they have an eagerness to share. Arguably any senior would want to pass on the wisdom gleaned in a lifetime, but the special focus of this program has empowered these women to share in ways more freely and openly than society usually encourages.

Your time is spent living at the facility, so you'll share quiet moments as well as organized activities. During the day you'll work with the group or with individuals in pursuing new experiences and interactive activities, from learning and teaching song and dance, new games, walks and excursions, reading aloud, writing letters, and more. English is spoken on the project, and staff can assist you with the occasional need for translation. The fact that you are also a resident means that group meals and quiet afternoons yield amazing life stories, laughter, and connectedness between you and the elders.

You'll stay in separate volunteer quarters in the home (private or shared with another volunteer) and share three Indian meals daily with the community. This project is great for any woman interested in sharing some quality time with a diverse group of interesting women. The facility is a short walk from shops and an Internet cafe if you need to connect, and the laid-back oceanside city of Goa has endless opportunities for outdoor beach time and is a magnet for enlightenment seekers and healers.

YOUR NEXT STEP: i-to-i (✆ **800/985-4852;** www.i-to-i.com). This 2-week women-only project, US$920, includes housing at the home in private or semi-private room, all meals, airport greeting, local orientation, project training, and in-country staff support.

DON'T MISS: In Goa you'll find the **Kala Academy,** which has a staggering amount and variety of arts and cultural programs. It is home to the International Film Festival of India, an indoor theater where live traditional and contemporary drama is presented along with film series, concerts, and lectures. An open amphitheater seats more than 3,300 audience members for al fresco plays and concerts. The academy boasts four different schools of music and dance, an exhibition hall curated to show the work of local artists, a gallery, an arts library, an open-air exhibition space, and a coffee house all on the quiet banks of the River Mandovi.

ⓘ www.incredibleindia.org

383 Helping Seniors

Elder Care

Help in the Holy Land

Nationwide, Israel

For people who've never visited the country, Israel is more often associated with war and ethnic strife than being one of the world's truly great travel destinations. Whether you're here to relive the pages of the Bible, snorkel in the sea of the Eilat, or lose yourself in the divine silence of the Negev Desert, visiting the Holy Land is an essential travel experience.

The National Council for Volunteering in Israel places volunteers from around the world in health-care facilities to assist staff in daily care and programming. The senior centers and elder care homes where placements are available are in any number of cities, depending on need at the time of your visit. Placements are a minimum of 4 weeks, to provide some consistency for the residents. The added attention from volunteers betters the quality of life for the residents, raising care giving to actual caring for individuals. It has a positive effect on everyone involved, from the seniors to the staff and medical practitioners (not to mention the volunteers).

Your duties will be varied: helping prepare meals and feed patients that need assistance; transporting residents to therapy or doctor's appointments; accompanying seniors on walks and day excursions; enrichment activities like arts and crafts or music, as well as reading aloud; helping if needed with dressing and preparing for family visitors or trips outside. You may run a few errands, do some filing or other light office work, or even help in the laundry or take on some maintenance chores. These are nursing home facilities, so many of the patients need a great deal of care and attention, meaning that your most important contributions are your enthusiasm and flexibility, bringing new energy into the facility community.

Depending on which hospital or center you are assigned, your housing will be either in dormitories with other volunteers or in staff quarters of the hospital or nursing home when available. Lunches during the workday are provided, but for other meals you'll head out to local eateries or shop and cook together as a volunteer team. The placements can be at any number of cities, so there will undoubtedly be plenty of exploring to get a true sense of this Israeli immersion experience.

YOUR NEXT STEP: National Council for Volunteering in Israel (www.ivolunteer.org.il). A 1-month placement, US$80, includes accommodations in dormitory or hospital staff housing, lunches, and project training and local support. Other meals are on your own, as is local transportation.

DON'T MISS: You might think that Israel is mostly desert, but there are world-class diving and watersports at the **Gulf of Eilat,** with coral and exotic fish, sea turtles and manta rays in this aquatic preserve on the Red Sea. After splashing around, dry off with a long hike in the cliffs around Eilat and the forested ridges of Upper Galilee. Mount Hermon is a ski resort that is a hiking paradise in warmer months with rappelling, mountain biking, and wandering amid flowering meadows and bubbling streams.

ⓘ www.goisrael.com

Helping Seniors 384

Elder Projects

See Mexico Through the Eyes of Its Seniors

Yucatan Region, Mexico

FROM THE FABLED STONE MAYAN RUINS OF CHICHÉN ITZÁ TO THE COLONIAL TOWN OF SAN Cristobal and the sun-soaked beaches of the Maya Rivera, the Yucatan Region has something for everyone from the budget-minded backpacker to the wealthy bacchanalian. This project offers a chance to explore the region and meet some of its most learned inhabitants.

Your 15-day trip begins in Cancun, where you'll volunteer for 4 days in a home for the elderly and a local hospice (you can also work at a women's shelter or children's home).

You'll help prepare and serve meals after assisting in getting everyone to the dining room or serving residents confined to bed. You can work with individual seniors on mobility activities in the exercise room or go for walks. Teaching a bit of English and starting discussion groups or leading some songs are engaging activities, as is initiating some challenging games or friendly competitions among residents. You'll also help out with some light maintenance around the facilities like gardening, ground clearing, cleaning, and painting.

From Cancun, you go to Puerto Morales and explore Mayan ruins and natural wonders. You'll also visit Siankaan, Chichén Itzá, Rio Lagartos, Merida, Uxmal, Calakmul, Bacalar, and Playa del Carmen. The trip has a vast array of activities planned for you, from hiking in bioreserves to kayaking and bird-watching, spelunking, snorkeling, and taking it easy on the beach.

This is a high-end tour with hotel accommodations in each of the cities in four- and five-star properties, terrific dining at restaurants, and top-level guides, tours, and recreation. English is all you need, as you have a bilingual guide accompanying you at all times. You'll spend lots of time in transit, taking in the sights along the way with multiple recreation options in stunning natural settings. The tour makes a large loop through the region beginning and ending in Cancun (then ending with a free day for relaxation at an all-inclusive beach resort).

YOUR NEXT STEP: Hands Up Holidays (✆ **201/984-5372;** www.handsupholidays.com). This 15-day trip, US$4,350, is a deluxe tour with top-level hotel accommodations throughout, restaurant dining, and a complete itinerary of sightseeing, exploring, and recreation options at every stop through the region.

An elderly woman in Yucatan Region, Mexico

DON'T MISS: Since you've seen so much of the Yucatan, before you go home make time for a visit to Mexico City. Here, the **Catedral Metropolitana** is a revered landmark that took more than 200 years to build. Some of the original foundation architecture is built with the stones of ransacked Aztec temples. Their former use is hardly recognizable, as this building is a baroque and neoclassical Euro-style cathedral (it is also sinking into the lakebed, and over the years has become noticeably tilted).

ⓘ www.visitmexico.com

385 Helping Seniors

Nurturing the Elderly

Injecting Energy & Enthusiasm

Yaroslavl, Russia

A POOR CITY RICH IN RELIGIOUS HISTORY, YAROSLAVL IS TODAY AN IMPORTANT INDUSTRIAL center. Built more than 1,000 years ago it's home to myriad churches, most built in the 16th and 17th century; its famous Spassky monastery was built in the 12th century. Helping the elderly here, many of whom are displaced, involves being both a caregiver and a companion.

In this oil city a little more than 240km (150 miles) from Moscow, industry is king and hard work is a way of life. Many of the elderly in the community home where this project takes place come from low-income households, and after retirement, many are sent to, or end up in, social service organizations that care for their basic needs. Several have been separated from their families by migration, as the petroleum industry has laid off more workers and families have moved on to other cities in Russia. While the basic care and medical needs of the elderly are well served in these institutions, there is often a lack of stimulation or entertainment, and whole rooms of seniors can end up spending the day staring at a community television. Volunteers coming into this environment with energy and enthusiasm, as well as new ideas for enrichment programs, stir up the stagnancy, and the effort cascades into increased socialization and conversation. Some of the local initiatives also create opportunities for active seniors to learn new skills to generate income.

Project staff, as skilled translators, will accompany you to the senior center. You'll provide companionship and a change of pace for residents. You'll be asked to pitch in with caregiving tasks such as feeding, meal preparation, and helping move immobile or mobility-challenged residents from their rooms to common spaces, the doctor's office, and so on. Most of your time will be spent in recreational endeavors, from storytelling to group exercise, gardening or crafts to puzzles and games. You may also run small errands for individuals to the pharmacy or government offices, or accompany them on these trips.

The project maintains a home base at a comfortable hotel in the center of the city. Your meals are provided at the hotel, and you are within easy walking distance of local cultural institutions and businesses. The project offices are also on-site at the hotel, so you can always get in touch with local support. In addition to the volunteer work, there are scheduled cultural and learning activities, such as Russian-language instruction, excursions to local villages to learn about rural culture, and guest speakers on Russian history, politics, tradition, and culture. The city is large and has plenty of free-time options, from theater and dance performances and live music to ancient churches and monasteries, museums, and long walks on the banks of the Volga River.

YOUR NEXT STEP: Cross Cultural Solutions (✆ **800/380-4777;** www.crossculturalsolutions.org). A 2-week project, US$2,664, includes hotel lodging and meals, cultural and language programs, in-country transportation, travel insurance, project training, and 24-hour access to local staff support.

DON'T MISS: It is an easy train ride from Yaroslavl to **Moscow**—a journey you'll definitely want to make. The nation's capital is the largest city in Europe, and the Kremlin, Red Square, St. Basil's Cathedral (the colorful domed church you've seen in photos), and other local churches really must be seen to be believed. There are new pedestrian zones being set up each year, making the bustling metropolis more and more visitor-friendly all the time.

ⓘ www.russia-travel.com

386 Helping Seniors

Help in Elderly Home

Filling In for Family Time

Singapore

CONSIDERED ONE OF THE WORLD'S SAFEST YET MOST TIGHTLY REGULATED CITIES, SINGAPORE has a reputation for being both beautiful and numbingly efficient. One of Asia's most modern metropolises, it breaks the mold of what most people expect of a city of five million. You'll find a mix of Chinese, Indian, and Malaysian cultures, one of the reasons why Singapore is considered one of the top cities in Asia to eat.

The home for the elderly in this city-island provides care and housing to 350 seniors. Most residents either don't have family to care for them or their family can't afford it. (Culturally, Singapore families would normally have generations living together in the home if possible.) The advanced age of most residents means they require medical and physical care for bathing, dressing, mobility, and more. Trained staff, spread too thin, have barely enough time to handle those daily necessities, so recreation and entertainment, necessary for quality of life, often depend on volunteers if they are to happen at all. You and your fellow English-speaking volunteers have the opportunity to make the daily lives of the elderly more interesting.

International volunteer projects have included arranging story hours, talent shows, dances, music classes and performances (with both residents and volunteers providing the entertainment), games of strategy and chance, and field trips in the city. An important event that happens almost every week is the celebration of birthdays. Parties for combined birthdays are large events with many attendees, and volunteers like you bring the fun. Adding games and sing-a-long activities makes these celebrations a high point of the week. In addition to enrichment activities, you might occasionally be asked by staff to pitch in with moving patients from one location in the facility to another, for meals, exercise, group social activities, or to return to their rooms.

Your accommodations will be at a local hotel near the elderly home. Meals aren't included in the project fees, so you'll have the chance to sample plenty of Singapore's wonderful cuisine as you find elegant dining and simple fare all within a modest price range. Since your volunteer commitment is roughly 9 to 5 on weekdays, there is plenty of evening and weekend time to explore and get to know this vibrant city. You'll find it a fascinating amalgam of cultures and religions with the most modern sensibilities swirling around ancient tradition.

YOUR NEXT STEP: Take Me to Volunteer Travel (✆ **65/6220-1198;** www.takemetovolunteertravel.com). A 1-week project, US$870, or 2-week project, US$1,460, includes hotel accommodations, airport transfers, project training and support, and a donation to the elder home project. Meals are up to you, and you'll be spoiled for choice with Singapore's always busy gastronomy scene.

DON'T MISS: To get the best views of the city, you'll want to go for a spin on the 165m-high (540-ft.) **Flyer** observation wheel. It's one of the world's largest Ferris wheels, and the ride in enclosed cars lasts a relaxing 30 minutes. Go for the sunset and watch the bright sky turn to indigo as the downtown lights begin their twinkling show.

ⓘ www.visitsingapore.com

Helping Seniors **387**

Elder Care

Walk & Talk

Cape Town, South Africa

THE NATURAL BEAUTY AND RUGGED LANDSCAPE OF CAPE TOWN IS FAMOUS AMONG OUTDOOR enthusiasts but unfortunately out of reach for some of the city's elderly residents. As part of this active, hands-on volunteer placement, you'll help improve the lives of seniors through physical therapy and exercise, and several outdoor recreational activities.

An overworked and underfunded staff serves the seniors living in the Rusthof Old Age Home, a center caring for more than 100 residents, with a long waiting list for others hoping to be admitted. There is ample care and attention for immediate needs, but often not enough time to attend to socializing or activities. Volunteers work with individuals or groups in recreation and exercise activities or entertainment, with the main goal being to help the seniors remain active both physically and mentally. Most of the residents have physical therapy programs, but additional fitness and stimulation increases energy and alertness, while games and group activities keep spirits high and conversation flowing. English is taught in most South African schools, so communicating shouldn't be troublesome.

For 30 to 40 hours a week you'll help keep seniors active with stretching, walking, and perhaps leading a class. Chair aerobics or seated yoga instruction could be a brilliant addition to the day. Some resistance-band exercises or weight work is perfect for those who can participate. You'll also monitor and report on their progress to attending staff. Maybe it's a stroll in the garden or just some assisted stretching for the bed-bound. You could lead a music class or provide some entertainment yourself. Pack some books of crossword puzzles to mix it up a bit from the usual checkers and chess. Generate a trivia quiz show or other group challenges. Your creativity is the only limit to getting folks involved and excited about the new energy you've brought.

You'll stay with a host family in Cape Town, who'll provide three meals daily and show you around their beautiful city. Cape Town is a large urban center with plenty of neighborhoods to explore, restaurants and clubs to try, a fantastic live music scene, and world-class beaches for your free time. From the plateau of Table Mountain to the wine country just outside the city to the beaches and rocky coves that run south to the tip of the continent, you'll never lack options for exploring and being steeped in South African hospitality.

YOUR NEXT STEP: Institute for Field Research Expeditions (✆ **800/675-2504;** www.ifrevolunteers.org). A 2-week stay, US$1,099, includes homestay accommodations, three meals daily, project training, airport transfers and in-country transportation, comprehensive insurance, and local staff support. A US$349 administrative/application fee is required.

DON'T MISS: Since your volunteer placement has been urban, you had better take some time to get your fill of the natural wonders of South Africa. The most famous safari destination in the country is **Kruger National Park,** with a wide array of safari lodge and camp options from rustic to über-luxurious, and the chance to be out in nature with your senses heightened as you strain to spot game large and small.

ⓘ www.southafrica.net

388 Helping Seniors

Home for Seniors

Providing Dignity & Diversions

Chiang Mai, Thailand

An increasingly modern city that still draws people attracted to its ancient history, Chiang Mai epitomizes contemporary Thailand: a people straddled between the past and the present. Working with the elderly here and staying with a host family, you will lend your modern knowledge of physiotherapy and elder care to those who need it.

More than 100 elderly residents live in the Chiang Mai seniors center served by this project. Many need constant care and great need—Thai culture ordinarily has elder family members living in the home, so only when care becomes critical or medical needs necessitate care that the family is unable to provide do most end up at a facility such as this. The staff is dedicated to the dignity and care of the elders in residence but are spread too thin to provide the level of engagement that would truly make their days pass more pleasantly. Volunteers spend a full workweek at the center helping with practical care tasks as well as adding their energies to recreation, entertainment, and other diversion activities.

Care of the elderly residents will benefit from your help in such tasks as meal preparation and assistance at feeding time (some residents are unable to get to the dining area and some may be unable to feed themselves on their own), assisting physiotherapists or doctors with therapy sessions or getting patients to and from their appointments and classes, and some cleaning assistance. Inspired volunteers like you can completely take charge of recreation programs, creating new games, taking seniors for walks or pushing their wheelchairs outdoors for a change of scene, generating entertainment shows or talent competitions, leading songs or other music activities, even organizing birthday parties or holiday celebrations. Some English-language administrative help is also expected of volunteers.

You'll either stay at a local hostel or in the home of a nearby family while volunteering at the seniors home in Chiang Mai. The "host mom" or staff at the hostel provides a healthy diet of local cuisine three times daily. The first three days of your trip are dedicated to an orientation program of cultural immersion and language as well as an introduction to local foods. There are some local sightseeing excursions included but also ample time to explore and get to know why this Northern Thailand city is so popular with visitors from around the world.

YOUR NEXT STEP: Institute for Field Research Expeditions (✆ **800/675-2504;** www.ifrevolunteers.org). A 2-week project, US$653, includes homestay or hostel accommodations, three meals daily, orientation program, in-country transportation and airport welcome, project training and support, and travel insurance. A US$349 application/administrative fee is required.

DON'T MISS: Plenty of international visitors think they have "done" Thailand if they hit the big three: Bangkok, Chiang Mai, and Phuket. Less traveled is the northeast region and the city of **Buri Ram,** known as the City of Pleasantness, with an immense array of carved artwork on the exteriors of public and private buildings. The stone carvings on doorways and gates to walled enclaves are meticulous, and most of the work is beautifully maintained. While you're there, you won't be able to miss the huge Buddha atop Mount Khao Kradong.

ⓘ www.tourismthailand.org

10 Trips for Grandparents and Grandchildren

The one thing that many people regret after they no longer have grandparents in their life is the lack of quality time spent together. Learning life stories and discovering new things together has a special intensity when it happens during the intimacy of traveling together. When grandparents share a service trip with their grandchildren, it forges memories that endure for a lifetime.

389 **Houtman Abrolhos Archipelago, Australia** Grandparents and grandchildren (and the generation in between) work as family units on this seaborne bird research excursion off the western coast of Australia, where there are more seabird species than anyplace else in the Indian Ocean. You'll work with expert ornithologists recording and monitoring seabird populations during peak breeding season. The trip is appropriate for ages 8+. ***Landscope Expeditions*** *(© +61/8-6488-2433; www.dec.wa.gov.au/landscopeexpeditions). A 1-week project costs US$3,222 per participant.*

390 **Cornwall, England** If the grandkids are 14 or older, they can team up with grandparents to get dirty at a working archaeological site in Cornwall. The trip will teach basic excavation technique and give you hands-on dig experience as well as lectures and education presentations by world-renowned experts. Grandparents and grandchildren can excavate side by side at this idyllic site in a south-facing valley bordered by a gurgling stream. ***Saveock Water Archaeology*** *(© **+44/1872 560 351**; www.archaeologyonline.org). Family programs cost £185 a week.*

Working together at an archaeological site in Cornwall

391 **Mahé, Seychelles** Sharing this island paradise with your grandchildren, you'll have a beautiful tropical vacation while helping the endangered Hawksbill turtle. No child is too young to learn about these amazing turtles as you go on turtle patrol. You'll transfer your field data to the record book each evening and have plenty of downtime. ***Responsible Travel*** *(© **+44/1273 600 030**; www.responsibletravel.com). £352 to £404 a night per family bungalow, depending on length of stay.*

Studying an artifact found in Cortez, Colorado

392 **Cortez, Colorado, USA** This summer archaeology program allows multiple generations of volunteers (children must be in seventh grade or older) to participate in a working dig in Anasazi community grounds. Participants find Pueblo artifacts aging back 800 years in one of the most dense and fruitful archaeological excavation sites in the world. ***Crow Canyon Archaeology Center*** *(© **800/422-8975**; www.crowcanyon.org). The 1-week family trip costs: seniors (55+) US$1,375; adults US$1,400; youth (ages 10 to 17) US$1,050.*

393 **St. Simons Island, Georgia, USA** This Elderhostel sea turtle program is for grandparents and their grandchildren ages 9 to 12. On the white sandy beaches of this "golden isle," participants go on shrimp trawlers to explore the aquatic habitat and take moonlit night walks to nesting grounds to observe mothers making their way up the beach to lay their eggs. There are guided children's activities throughout the trip, and several adult activities. ***Elderhostel*** *(✆* ***800/454-5768****; www.elderhostel.org). This 5-night trip is US$688 per adult, US$538 per child.*

394 **New Orleans, Louisiana, USA** This project is specifically designed for cross-generational family service. Mornings are spent in service projects, with neighborhood improvement work, as well as tours of Audubon Society work in the recovering wild zones outside the city. Evenings are steeped in the history and fun of life in the Crescent City. ***Generations Touring Company*** *(✆* ***888/415-9100****; www.generationstouringcompany.com). This 6-day service vacation is US$1,599.*

395 **Jamestown, New York, USA** Grandparents with curious grandchildren will participate in dragonfly surveys, butterfly identification, and nighttime moth discovery projects. There are naturalist-led walks and kayak trips, nature photography coaching, and a boat trip on Chatauqua Lake. Campfires and storytelling, and nature-focused games and activities will fill your days and evenings. ***Elderhostel*** *(✆* ***800/454-5768****; www.elderhostel.org). A 5-night nature detective trip: US$1,275 for one adult/one child; US$2,015 for two adults/one child; US$2,168 for two adults/two children.*

396 **Rose Island, Rhode Island, USA** The 1869 Rose Island Lighthouse has been run by volunteer keepers since it was restored in the early 1990s, and you can stay with your family and run this working safety beacon. The staff will teach you how to raise and lower the flag, record weather data, greet day visitors, and collect landing fees. ***Rose Island Lighthouse Foundation*** *(✆* ***401/847-4242****; www.roseislandlighthouse.org). One week is: Nov. to May, US$700 to US$900; May to Oct.: US$1,200 to US$2,100.*

397 **Ely, Minnesota, USA** The International Wolf Center participants interact with research wolves in the wild, as well as an "ambassador pack" of adult and pup wolves in captivity. Programs include wolf tracking by dog sled and snowshoe, canoeing, hiking, and litter care for pups as well as practical labor and construction. Special intergenerational programs focus on grandparent/grandchildren work teams and more intensive learning seminars for college credit, all while housed in resort accommodations with meals provided. ***International Wolf Center*** *(✆* ***218/365-4695****; www.wolf.org). A 4-day work program is US$400 for adults, US$350 for children.*

398 **Kanab, Utah, USA** The Best Friends Animal Sanctuary is the nation's largest for abused and abandoned animals. You'll help with ranch chores like feeding, watering, and cleaning, and you'll give attention to animals that need it. Younger children can find important work with docile senior animals. ***Best Friends Animal Sanctuary*** *(✆* ***435/644-2001****; www.bestfriends.org).No fee for volunteering; accommodations and meals not provided.*

Tracking Gray Whales

Protecting Pacific Giants

Flores Island, British Columbia, Canada

TUCKED SERENELY INTO CLAYOQUOT SOUND ON VANCOUVER'S WEST COAST, FLORES ISLAND is home to the Nuu-chah-nulth First Nations as well as some of largest yet gentlest creatures on the planet—gray whales. The island's vast wilderness is a perfect spot to camp or stay at a lodge following a day of watching the whales during their migration. You're sure to see plenty of seals and sea lions as well.

This is a team trip for families with kids aged 10 and up—who should be very excited to track and protect Pacific gray whales in their summer habitat. Your family will get to know the waters of Vancouver Island's Clayoquot Sound quite well as you paddle kayaks or head out in the converted fishing boat/research vessel, gathering data that will help scientists refine their conservation and protection strategies. While gray whales are no longer on the endangered species list, ensuring their survival can still be quite challenging. Science is showing that mating and migrating patterns are being radically altered, and no one is sure if it's a natural progression or a by-product of global warming. Access to prey, as well as certain behavior patterns, can be thrown out of balance by a change of just a few degrees in water temperature.

Your family team will map gray whale prey with sonar and underwater video, track and identify whales (and learn how to tell one from another), record field data, and even help with navigation. Back on shore you'll work in the lab with the researchers to digitize and log photographs to supplement the database. Facilitators are assigned to each family team and will cater learning programs and research activities to the age of your children, so that kids and adults will all be challenged and can contribute at a level appropriate to their ability. Once the day's work is done, there is lots of time to spend together, or with other families, enjoying organized activities and some well-earned relaxation.

Home base is a somewhat rustic youth hostel with shared dormitory-style rooms and shared social/laboratory space. The families eat together and pitch in with food preparation. There are kayaks to take out, when not needed for research purposes, so you can explore the scenic inlets and small islands, or take some great hikes. There are also opportunities to go to the village and learn more about the Nuu-chah-nulth (or Nootka) First Nations people who live there. Keep your eyes peeled for bald eagles, orcas, sea lions, and even wolves and black bears, which all populate the temperate rainforests along the coast of the sound.

YOUR NEXT STEP: Earthwatch (© **800/776-0188;** www.earthwatch.org). A 7-day project with a minimum family contribution of US$2,850 (fees change depending on number of adults and children in your group) includes shared dormitory-style accommodations, meals, field research training and learning activities, and full project support with assigned team leaders. A US$35 Earthwatch membership is required.

DON'T MISS: The town of **Tofino** is perched on the edge of Pacific Rim National Park, and boasts more than it's

Tracking whales off of Flores Island in British Columbia

fair share of good eco-lodges and high-quality coffee joints. The real action, however, is where the sand meets the crashing ocean waves of Long Beach and Chesterman's Beach, as this one of the best places in Canada to learn to surf—several businesses in town have everything you need to play in the waves.

ⓘ www.hellobc.com

400 Family & Youth Trips

Maasai Warrior Training

Growing Up African

Maasai Mara, Kenya

Most kids like to play war games, but here's a chance to learn the skills and culture of Africa's fiercest warriors. The Maasai Mara in Southwest Kenya is home to the Maasai—nomadic hunters and gatherers whose reputation for warfare is legendary. Of course kids here won't be fighting real battles—but they will learn that there is more to being a great fighter than fighting.

Joining Maasai warriors in the bush, boys and girls (aged 11 and up) will begin with a coming-of-age ceremony as they are presented with the famous red warrior cloak to protect them from lions and other animals as well as to communicate their bravery. Each day of this experience is spent in a new traditional immersion program, from walking safari and animal tracking to throwing a spear and learning about the healing properties of plants from a shaman. Maasai do not hunt wild animals but live in harmony with them, depending on their herds of cattle and goats. A main staple of their diet is milk mixed with blood from the jugular vein of a cow (it doesn't kill the cow, but the ritual is a challenge your youngster will face). Goat and sheep meat and vegetables round out the diet, though warrior apprentices will have a more varied menu. There are evening fire circles for storytelling, traditional games, and mock battles to prove bravery, ceremonies of body painting, a soak in the hot springs after long arduous days, and time helping with the construction of communal buildings in the "widows' village." They'll learn beadwork and weaving, a tea ceremony for courage, chanting and music in rite-of-passage ceremonies, and receive a warrior name. At least one night each warrior apprentice will stay up all night with other warriors to patrol the camp for wild animals, and on the night of passage, their graduation, they will go into the bush to spend the night.

In addition to their complete cultural immersion, the young volunteers will help with community building projects and making furniture for a village gathering shelter. They'll also visit the day school and help teach English, share songs from home, teach (and learn) arts and crafts, and teach outdoor sports and games to the village youth. The warrior training takes up several days in the middle of this 12-day schedule, and that segment of the trip is book-ended with safari camp time on game drives, searching for the Big Five, and staying at a mainstream ecotouring camp. During warrior training and contributing to the community, kids will stay in large tents with bedding on the floor, have access to hot showers, and have campfire meals prepared for them. By the end, the participants are considered honorary Maasai, having gone through an accelerated rite and initiation process, and they'll come home forever bonded to the tribe.

YOUR NEXT STEP: Eco-Resorts (✆ **866/326-7376;** www.eco-resorts.com). A 12-day program, US$2,775, includes transfers, accommodations, all meals, safari and warrior training activities and guidance, private vehicle with driver/guide for the group, all park and camp fees, and emergency medical evacuation insurance.

DON'T MISS: In Kenya's Rift Valley, on the road from Nakuru to Lake Baringo, you'll cross the **equator.** It's a unique opportunity to have your picture taken twice—in the Northern Hemisphere and in the Southern Hemisphere, or straddle the line and stand with a foot in both.

ⓘ www.tourism.go.ke

401 Family & Youth Trips

High School Peer Educators

Tell a Friend

Lilongwe, Malawi

MANY PEOPLE IN MALAWI'S CAPITAL OF LILONGWE LIVE ON JUST A FEW DOLLARS A DAY, SO it's not surprising that the city is home base for dozens of international non-governmental organizations. Malawi, with one of the lowest life expectancies in Africa, needs to focus on health education, particularly HIV/AIDS and malaria. Helping to spread this valuable information is where volunteers can be most effective.

High school students become peer educators in this volunteer project, undergoing extensive training programs about malaria prevention and then visiting rural schools, orphanages, and street shelters. The students will also accompany trained HIV/AIDS educators to present well-rounded health programs and explore issues of environmental health and gender equality. The education program includes songs and group-building exercises in addition to learning units, leadership activities, and open discussion periods so students can explore their understanding and feelings.

It might take a couple hours to drive over rough roads for the team to get to the schools they'll work in for the day, and each young educator will have an assigned group of students and assigned age group with whom they'll work, eat, and play. High school team members and adult health educators create an entire day about health issues. After the morning group activities with the entire student

A peer educator leading a team-building game in Malawi

body, smaller teams break off into classroom-size groups to present interactive malaria and HIV/AIDS programs. The young educators will teach about how malaria affects the body, as well as prevention and treatment, in a fun, accessible way with translators from a Malawian university. They'll return to the school for 3 days of "health camp," working with students, teachers, and tribal leaders so that the message can be passed on to younger siblings, parents, and other villagers. Each day ends with the student body and visiting educator teams gathering for a high-energy assembly and celebration.

The high school volunteers live together with full-time staff in a comfortable, secure, group house in Old Town Lilongwe, where they'll share meals and relaxation time. There is training before presentations begin, safari excursions, cultural orientation tours and day trips, and plenty of supervised exploration time, so that volunteers can truly understand Malawi while having fun in a summer camp environment. By the time the project ends and it's time to fly home, the young volunteers will feel less like *Azungu* (foreigners) and more like locals. The staff, visiting special presenters who open up the culture to the team, and assisting Malawi college students make sure the experience is culturally sensitive and respectful as the bond between them and the volunteer grows and lifelong friendships are forged.

YOUR NEXT STEP: World Camp (**888/297-9669;** www.worldcampforkids.org). A 4-week project, US$2,600, or 5-week project, US$2,700, includes accommodations at the group house, meals, supervision and training, guides, translators, education program and cultural orientation, side trips and safari, security, in-country transportation, some language instruction, and 24-hour support.

DON'T MISS: In a natural landscape that is predominantly wild and uncultivated, making for beautiful natural excursions and safari exploration, it is a shock to come upon the uniformity and precision of the **Thyolo Tea Estates.** Here you'll visit vast fields of precisely trimmed trees grown and lovingly harvested for tea leaves.

(i) www.malawitourism.com

Family & Youth Trips

Establish Women's Community Center

Crafting a Future

Xiloxochico, Mexico

XILOXOCHICO (PRONOUNCED "SHI-LO-SHO-CHEE-KO"), LOCATED HIGH IN MEXICO'S SIERRA NORTE, is home to the Nahua, descendants of the Aztecs. Here you and your family will work alongside others to help build a community center for women. And even better, you'll be building bridges between cultures at the same time.

Kids as young as 8 years old can join their families in expanding and improving a community center in this Nahua village. This lush green zone is home to Aztec descendants who've maintained many of their customs and traditions. Most of the homes have no electricity, and living is simple, providing a glimpse into a life very different than your home. A village collective of women has begun to create a crafts cooperative to generate income and to help build community connections. The women have a plot of land and basic structure completed, and this volunteer organization is coordinating, with family groups and individual volunteers, the expansion of a casita (workhouse) that will serve as a communal space for artisans and a meeting hall.

The trip leaders have created age-appropriate tasks and activities for the kids. Little ones will have jobs that they can accomplish easily but with some challenge, while older kids and adults will have their hands full banding together with new friends to create this transformative space. Your project days are spent engaged in a variety of tasks, from construction to clearing, painting and decorating, to helping load supplies and artwork into the completed spaces. Opportunities are also built into the schedule to visit and perhaps help out at the school in the afternoons if you'd like to teach English, play some games, or have a song exchange where your family and the schoolchildren can teach one another songs and dances.

In the village, your family and the rest of the volunteer team will lodge at a local eco-hotel run by the Nahua women, a short ride form the project site. Meals are prepared for you, as is local transportation. There is plenty of time to get to know the village residents and perhaps try some craft activities. It's a terrific region for hiking and exploration, with nearby caves and Aztec ruins. You'll enjoy lively market days, but you may find much of your time is spent close to home base, laughing and talking with new friends.

YOUR NEXT STEP: Global Citizens Network (© **800/644-9292;** www.globalcitizens.org). A 10-day project, US$1,775 (for those 16 years and older) and US$1,331 (for those between 8 and 15 years old), includes eco-hotel lodging, meals, in-country transportation, airport pickup, cultural orientation and training (age specific), medical and evacuation insurance, full staff support, and a contribution to the community project.

DON'T MISS: Mexico's **Riviera Maya,** on the eastern coast near Cancun, is a fantastic place for family exploration. Beaches are long and have soft sugar sand backed by tropical groves, the Mayan ruins of Tulum are nearby, and there are several resorts and businesses that feature Swim with Dolphins programs, where you can interact in the water with the playful mammals. Be sure to check that the encounter program you choose is certified to ensure that the animals are kept in optimal conditions.

(i) www.visitmexico.com

403 Family & Youth Trips

Teen Rainforest Protection

Hands-On Research

Las Casas de sa Selva, Puerto Rico

This 400ha (1,000-acre) reserve is Puerto Rico's leading site for the study and preservation of rainforest ecology. The accommodations are rustic, and the terrain is challenging, as is the work done by interested teenage (16+) volunteers. But your efforts here will help protect a fragile habitat in one of nature's most unique ecosystems.

Sixteen- and seventeen-year-olds can participate in this research expedition, helping to protect the rainforest's biodiversit, and evaluating 2 decades of research in the growth and preservation of plant and animal species. There will be long, and sometimes arduous, hikes to get to the research plots where field studies are carried out to observe and record the wildlife. The data gathered will be compared to previous research findings in order to determine how effective conservation measures have been and to help develop new ways to protect this valuable but fragile ecosystem. The teen teams will learn the science behind the research and how different species of flora and fauna are connected.

You'll be in a team of several teens, led by specialists who will teach you how to measure tree growth, do species counts for lizards or frogs, tag and identify species of vines, and set up experimental plots for planting and study. There might also be night excursions for research work, heading out into the forest to count the iconic coqui frogs that fill the darkness with chirping song. There will be ample free time to hike and explore, learn forest-craft activities, swim in the river, and enjoy the rarely visited rainforest.

Teen teams will camp out in shared platform tents with air mattresses, and there are hot showers and flush toilets. Caribbean-style meals are prepared by cooks and shared in an open-concept dining area, and team members will take turns on kitchen and cleanup detail. There are specific activities designed for teens that feature evening entertainment, like music or salsa dance lessons, visits to neighboring villages, and eco-exploration by day and night. On the day off, the team usually votes to go to the beach or Old San Juan before diving back to work in the deep green jungle.

YOUR NEXT STEP: Earthwatch (**800/776-0188;** www.earthwatch.org). A 10-day project, US$2,150, includes meals and platform tent camping, research training and teen-focused cultural and group-building activities, and 24-hour supervision and support. A US$35 Earthwatch membership is required.

DON'T MISS: After time in the remote rainforest, balance that experience by spending time exploring **Old San Juan.** The character-filled colonial village is 465 years old and has beautiful bright blue cobblestone streets and shade-dappled sidewalks alongside shops and restaurants. There is also the historic **El Morro, a** six-level fortress out on the point, which provides great exploration among the walled battlements.

(i) www.gotopuertorico.com

Family & Youth Trips

High School Service Trip

A Northern Summer

Juneau, Alaska, USA

ONE OF AMERICA'S TRULY GREAT ADVENTURE DESTINATIONS, JUNEAU HAS GOT TO BE ON everyone's "must do" list. You'll find a friendly frontier quality here, and a uniqueness of spirit formed by rugged surroundings and honed by a sense of togetherness that only people miles away from the rest of the United States could forge.

For students completing grades 9 to 12, this summer service trip is a chance to see the best Alaska has to offer while contributing hard work to improving the community and environment. Kids are grouped by age and have amazing experiences like white-water rafting, stunningly rugged hiking, exploring native culture in the region, bush plane journeys, and sea kayaking among whales, all balanced by daily service tasks that improve the world around them. Trail building, working at a salmon hatchery, and restoring community buildings are team-work-focused jobs to ensure that students leave each place in better condition than how they found it. Participants will need a passport, as part of the river expedition crosses into Canada.

Every day on this 3-week trip is different, and at the end of each kids will drop into slumber like a rock, tired out and fulfilled from a day's hard work and play. The outdoor adventure activities challenge volunteers just as much as the challenges they face working for the community. They'll spend a morning rebuilding trails among moose and bald eagles or an afternoon kayaking in the sea while humpbacks and orcas play nearby. They'll jump in and help at a salmon hatchery (a vital part of the local economy), then fly by bush plane to remote islands, then spend a day learning about the Tlingit and Russian cultures in the area. Work with the State Park on maintenance, then relax with tribal elders and listen to stories and songs. Every day will have some astounding natural pursuit and a rewarding service work opportunity.

Base camps are comfortable and students share tents. Meals are also shared by the group. Best of all, the weather is idyllic, the environment peerless, and the company of adult support and fellow high school volunteers is a great big collection of best friends they haven't met yet.

YOUR NEXT STEP: Wilderness Ventures (✆ **800/533-2281;** www.wildernessventures.com). A 3-week project, US$4,390, includes adult team leaders and supervision, campsite lodging, meals, all Alaskan transportation, adventure and cultural guides, park fees and admissions to museums, and 24-hour support.

DON'T MISS: The **Bering Land Bridge National Park** is 1 million ha (2.7 million acres) of wilderness preserve where North America reaches out to try and touch Asia. This was a connection between the continents when the oceans were lower (during the last Ice Age), and the rarely trod land is home to 170 species of birds, and more than 400 species of plants. Musk ox, grizzly bears, moose, reindeer, wolves, and other spectacular northern mammals are found here as well.

ⓘ www.travelalaska.com

 Family & Youth Trips

Habitat for Humanity for Teens

Hammering It Home

Stanislaus County, California, USA

Despite the fact that it's one of the wealthiest nations on Earth, the United States has an unconscionable regrettable record of homelessness and insufficient affordable housing; a situation made worse by the recent global economic crisis. During the height of the crisis, it was reported that a home was foreclosed every 8 seconds. So, if you're over the age of 16 and can swing a hammer, Habitat for Humanity needs you.

California's San Joaquin Valley experienced the number-one foreclosure rate in the entire United States during the recent credit crisis, and the federal government is taking steps to stabilize neighborhoods by purchasing foreclosed and abandoned properties in order to rebuild, with Habitat for Humanity, and create affordable family housing. A new development called Home Village creates a neighborhood for families that have lost their homes. One in ten houses in the agriculturally focused city of Modesto are boarded up, so your work is essential, whether you're a teen volunteer or a family working together.

Habitat for Humanity International has a program to bring motorhome owners to build sites (RV Care-A-Vanners), or the

Habitat for Humanity volunteers raising a wall in Stanislaus County, California

local division will help find accommodations to make your stay as simple as possible. Every day is a new range of construction tasks, as homes are rehabilitated or built from the ground up. Foundations are poured, framing is erected, walls are clad, insulation is laid, electrical and plumbing and HVAC are installed, roofs are built, doors and windows hung, walls plastered and painted. Each of you will learn construction skills on the job, so you'll be an expert when you decide to volunteer again next year.

Habitat doesn't provide travel, lodging, or meal arrangements and charges no fee from its hardworking volunteers. The local office can help make suggestions and advise you on the simplest ways to make your stay comfortable—their goal is to have the most productive volunteer team possible, so you can focus on building homes.

YOUR NEXT STEP: Habitat for Humanity Stanislaus County (✆ **209/575-4585;** www.stanislaushabitat.org). Your project duration and travel, lodging, and meal arrangements are up to you. On-the-job training is provided for all areas of construction of new homes for families in need. Appropriate for any volunteers 16 years or older.

DON'T MISS: This is one of the most fertile regions of the entire United States, and the Central Valley is known as the nation's breadbasket, since so much of the country's produce is grown here. It is a short drive to **Sacramento**, California's capital, to learn about the state's history and government and enjoy the rivers and delta area—or a short drive in another direction brings you to **Yosemite National Park,** one of the finest natural resources in the country.

ⓘ www.sanjoaquinvalley.worldweb.com

406 Family & Youth Trips

St. Jude Volunteens

Showing Hope

Memphis, Tennessee, USA

St. Jude Children's Research Hospital has a long history of serving the needs of children and teens. Set against the rock and roll backdrop of Memphis, Tennessee, this "volunteen" program helps people facing life-threatening illnesses, as well as their friends and family. A difficult placement, but one that will reap rewards for the giver as they lend a helping hand to people in crisis.

This incredible opportunity will require a time commitment of 5 weeks for any teen ready to change the world. The St. Jude Children's Research Hospital has a highly competitive Volunteens program that runs for only two 5-week sessions each summer. The demanding program requires exceptionally motivated teenagers who will work with patients, siblings, and parents facing life threatening diseases. Teens must be between 16 and 18 years old during the program session dates. The teens work 2 intensive days a week in the program at the hospital, creating fun activities and programs for the patients and their loved ones. It's a great opportunity to be completely absorbed in being of service to others and looking for new ways to make other lives better.

The 2 workdays are used to create a special event for the resident kids. The first day is spent developing a theme with the patients and finding as many creative, interactive arts and crafts and theme-development activities as they can think of for a 1-day party. After dreaming up the best event, the St. Jude kids create decorations and plans. On the second day, it's time to present the event and create a fantastic day for the families. The teen volunteers and the resident kids are hosts for the parents and brothers and sisters. The next week, another 2-day cycle starts with different families. During the rest of the program, the volunteens learn about St. Jude's history and mission to serve children through a series of group-building activities, leadership skills work, tours, workshops, and special guest speakers (and look at possible career paths).

This program is not able to provide housing or transportation, so volunteers need to make their own arrangements in Memphis for the entire 5-week program.

YOUR NEXT STEP: St. Jude Children's Research Hospital (✆ **901/595-3300;** www.stjude.org). The highly competitive Volunteen program for ages 16 to 18 is 5 weeks. Travel and accommodations aren't provided. There is no fee for volunteers, and all training, support, and intensive instruction is provided.

DON'T MISS: Well, it is Memphis after all, and even though he was gone by the time today's teens were born, everybody knows about **Graceland.** The revival of Elvis's popularity among successive generations defies expectation, and who wouldn't appreciate the Jungle Room, the Lisa Marie customized jet plane, and all the campy glory of the home of The King? www.elvis.com/graceland

ⓘ www.memphistravel.com

Therapeutic Horse Camp

Ride of a Lifetime

Stoughton, Wisconsin, USA

Oddly enough, historic Stoughton is best known as the birthplace of the coffee break. Nordic heritage is evident in the city's architecture and cultural events. Part of that heritage includes horsemanship, making Stoughton an ideal location to volunteer with disabled or otherwise challenged youth at this therapeutic horse camp.

For weeklong sessions in the summer, children aged 9 to 13 can be support volunteers for the hippotherapy (horse therapy) programs offered at this Wisconsin ranch. This important support role readies young volunteers to assist more directly with the therapeutic riding lessons once they're at least 14 years old. There are individual and group work sessions each morning, shared lunch, then an afternoon work period that can also include grooming and bathing the horses. It's a rare opportunity for very young people to be of service and to see genuinely amazing breakthroughs in an intimate, bonding therapy.

Volunteer helpers are essentially barn rats during the day camp, helping out with projects in the morning that can include cleanup, painting jumps and fences in the riding ring, cleaning water tanks and buckets to help assure the horses are all healthy, fixing fences, and more around the barns and paddocks. They'll be focused on making life for the full-time residents—the horses—better. There's a big break for lunch with the whole gang each day, then afternoon chores focus on the horses. Support volunteers may be bathing them or general grooming, cleaning tack, oiling saddles, learning how to tack up a horse with saddle, pad, girth, and bridle, and learning the skills of leading a horse or pony in the ring with confidence and a calm, peaceful demeanor. When they're older, if they want to continue to be of service to the program, these calm leading skills are most important for the actual therapy sessions with a rider in the saddle.

These are day camps, so there are no overnight accommodations or arrangements for visiting volunteers. Volunteers bring their own sack lunch and water for the day.

YOUR NEXT STEP: Three Gaits Therapeutic Horsemanship Center 🎗 (✆ **608/877-9086;** www.3gaits.org). For 5 days from 9am to 4pm, young support volunteers work hard behind the scenes to make the equine therapy camp a rewarding experience for clients. A 1-week project is US$50. No overnight accommodations or meals are provided, so sign up when you know your family or child will be in the Stoughton area for a week or more in the summer. Older children (14+) take a more active volunteer role in camp.

DON'T MISS: Wisconsin has some of the largest water parks in the world, and **Wisconsin Dells** has the highest concentration of them. It is Wisconsin after all, so the best, most adrenaline-pumping water parks are indoors, where the thermostat is always set at 30°C (85°F). There are 20 indoor water parks in this city, so it's an ideal way for kids to let off some steam after being so focused on helping others.

ⓘ www.travelwisconsin.com

408 Family & Youth Trips

"Pay It Forward" High School Tours

Help on Wheels

Multiple Cities, USA

Pay it forward is a powerful ideology—repaying a good deed by performing another for someone else in need. Students Today Leaders Forever is not only the name of the organization that promotes high schoolers helping high schoolers, but it's the philosophy behind what they do. School field trips will never be the same.

High schools across America team up with this program to help classes go on 5-day bus tours to other communities and perform leadership and volunteer service in each town they pass through. New trips and routes are added every year, with each one visiting four communities. It's a unique opportunity to bond with and learn from other high school students and partake in four unique community development projects. The service projects are prioritized by the communities visited and can include: outdoor work with environmental care and maintenance; weeding; trail maintenance; light construction; education programs with younger children in schools; or working to assist elderly residents at group homes. They could build homes for disadvantaged families or clean trash from parklands—the main function being teamwork and cooperation.

A standard day includes morning service projects, college/university tours, afternoon and evening tours and cultural exploration, and meals shared with the communities served. There is plenty of time on the bus to relax and socialize before going to the next deserving community or project location, and meals are big, energetic communal activities.

Except for the final night, known as the "celebration city," when the volunteers stay in a hotel, nights are spent in YMCAs, churches, community centers, and gymnasiums with boys and girls in separate accommodations. A minimum of six adult chaperones as well as college mentors/chaperones attend to each group. The time is structured with group programs, some touring, and spending quality time within the communities served so volunteers can meet the kids and adults whose lives they're changing by making such an important contribution.

YOUR NEXT STEP: Students Today Leaders Forever (✆ **612/643-2096;** www.stlf.net). A 5-day tour, US$280 (volunteers are encouraged to raise donations for the fees), includes supervision/mentoring, lodging (on the floor of community center–type spaces and 1 night in a hotel), community meals (two a day plus snacks, the third meal students will pay for with their own spending money), transportation, guided activities, and 24-hour support.

Family & Youth Trips **409**

Continental Divide Trail Family Work

The Trail That Binds

Various Locations, North America

This volunteer placement will put you and your family's imprint on what will soon be one of the world's greatest trails. Once completed, the Continental Divide National Scenic Trail will stretch more than 5,000km (3,100 miles) from Canada to Mexico, linking not just countries but people and cultures.

Families with children 10 years and older have the opportunity to work together as a team on trail development, enjoying camping in the great outdoors and having a fun vacation while helping the environment. The Continental Divide National Scenic Trail is being built kilometer by kilometer, and the family programs put age-appropriate focus on outdoor education and exploration specific to the area you'll work be working in. Your family will also learn about Leave No Trace outdoor ethics and trail safety, as well as everything there is to know about the plants and animals in the region.

Building the Continental Divide National Scenic Trail

When your family volunteers will determine the location, depending on the progress for the year. You'll be somewhere along the "spine" of North America for 2 to 5 days. Adults and older teens will work with sometimes physically challenging tasks that might include moving rocks and digging drainage trenching. Youngsters will do important tasks that support the group's effort, from cleaning up to helping set up campsites, carrying tools, laying a campfire, spreading organic mulch, and more. It'll be a chance for everyone in your family to feel they're contributing to a project that will outlast you all.

Campsites are vehicle accessible, though you may have a hike to get to the work area each morning. Other families will be working with you, and meals are shared at the campground (you'll provide your own tents and sleeping bags). Evenings tend to be spent around the campfire with the entire volunteer trail team, telling stories and playing games, before curling up in the sleeping bag so you can get up early and be ready for the next day.

YOUR NEXT STEP: Continental Divide Trail Alliance (✆ **888/909-CDTA;** www.cdtrail.org). Family volunteer programs are 2 to 5 days. No fee for volunteers, but you'll provide your own car-camping equipment and stay at campgrounds that are auto accessible. There may be some hiking each morning to get to the work site. Meals are shared among the entire volunteer group, usually a few families working together, and the trail leader also leads activities for children and teens. Different locations in all three nations, Canada, the United States, and Mexico, have different campground conditions along the trail, but all the sites used for family volunteer teams are maintained (you won't have to chop down trees or backpack for kilometers).

410 Preserving Memories

Photojournalism Project

Extraordinary Access & Training

Kathmandu, Nepal

ONE OF THE MOST VISUALLY STUNNING CITIES ON THE PLANET, EVEN THE NAME KATHMANDU conjures up images of the wildly exotic. You'll be well-suited to this project if you have a desire to take your photography skills to a new level and a keen interest in documenting Nepalese culture.

Even with no former training or experience, you can help create a photographic record of amazing cultural celebrations, religious activities, and social scenes in Nepal. This program is hands-on and provides in-depth training in photojournalism, so you can take your work to a much higher level as you assist a renowned photojournalist working the Kathmandu beat. International volunteers work with a supervisor and go on assignments to religious and cultural programs to document them on film for a widely circulated periodical. In addition to shooting the events, volunteers learn post-production techniques of editing and finishing photos.

You'll be briefed on the kind of activities you'll be witnessing and attending each day, and the kinds of shots that are needed, then you and other volunteers will be sent on your way with cameras to try to get the perfect picture. Sometimes you'll have special access to the events, and other times you'll be among the public or participants. It is perhaps the most immersive way to experience the nuance of cultural activities. You'll see and preserve moments of ceremonies and occasions that tourists would never get to see.

You'll spend part of the time housed in a local hostel while also learning cultural aspects of Nepalese society and some of the language. You'll be served traditional Nepali meals prepared by staff cooks. The rest of your stay will be with a host family, who will prepare your meals and welcome you into their home, completing your immersion into the culture. Free time will vary depending on your assignments (some could be daytime, some in the evenings), but no matter when it is, the city provides plenty to see and experience. You can wander the normal tour spots such as Thamel, Patan, and Swaymbhu, but chances are good that you'll end up spending most of your open hours people-watching and taking more shots to capture the perfect moment.

YOUR NEXT STEP: Global Crossroad (✆ **972/252-4191;** www.globalcrossroad.com). A 2-week project, US$1,064, includes meals and lodging (in hostel, then in private home with a host family), personalized training and supervision (in English), comprehensive insurance coverage, airport pickup, and local staff support.

DON'T MISS: Large wild areas of Nepal can be inaccessible to modern transportation, so go off the grid on **horseback.** Various hill regions have equine programs for visitors so you can continue going to places the vast majority of tourists never see, such as Panauti, Nagarkot, Dhulikhel, Ghorepani, Dakshinkali, and the aptly named Mustang Valley.

ⓘ www.welcomenepal.com

Preserving Memories **411**

Documentation & Preservation

Lest We Forget

Auschwitz-Birkenau Concentration Camp, Poland

TWO HOURS FROM KRAKOW, THE TOWN OF OSWIECIM IS STILL WRESTLING TO BE FREE OF THE name it's better known by: Auschwitz. Located near the infamous concentration camp, this modest industrial town is full of monuments and tributes to the victims of the Holocaust, while at the same time recognizing the need to carry on with the business of life.

Poland's Auschwitz-Birkenau, where up to 5,000 victims a day were executed, is now a gathering place for volunteers from around the world who work in preservation and documentation projects. In addition to the important work at the concentration camp, part of the trip is in Berlin, Germany, and the trip includes touring to special sites in Poland of particular historical interest: museums, castles, the Warsaw Jewish ghetto, cemeteries and memorials, synagogues, salt mines, and an art exhibition in the monastery of Harmeze, which was installed by a Holocaust survivor. You'll also meet with survivors who will tell you their personal stories. It's a complete learning experience about this attempt at ethnic cleansing.

You'll be doing hands-on preservation work at the camps, focusing on the buildings and exhibits that document the atrocities, as well as archival projects. Everything from ecological data and measuring fallen structures and facilities is important to preserve the specifics of the place that is both haunted and hallowed. Survivors, their descendants, and the Polish community want the Nazi death camps to be preserved and to promote awareness of the atrocities by preserving the site as a memorial. With the coming years, fewer survivors will be able to share their personal stories, so the work takes on greater importance with each passing year.

Housing in Berlin is at an urban hostel and in Poland at a community center, and meals are traditional local foods. Your days and evenings are filled with touring, meetings with survivors and historians, and an historical intensive learning program. The emotions are relentless and the discoveries endless as you stretch your capacity for compassion and understanding to new extremes.

YOUR NEXT STEP: Amizade 🎗 (**✆ 304/ 293-6049;** www.amizade.org). A 2-week project, US$2,296 includes food, hostel and community center accommodations, project training, in-country travel, and a thorough program of cultural and historical understanding.

DON'T MISS: For more than five centuries, Krakow's **Wawel Castle** acted as the home of Polish royalty. Poland's most popular tourist attraction was originally built in the 10th century and visitors have access to its cathedral, museum, royal private apartments, and armory.

ⓘ www.polandtour.org

A memorial plaque at the Auschwitz-Birkenau Concentration Camp

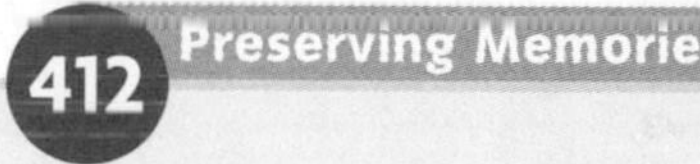

Senior Visit & Call Program

A Helping Hand & A Curious Ear

Washington D.C., USA

ALTHOUGH WASHINGTON IS ONE OF THE MOST BEAUTIFUL AND SOCIALLY ENGAGING CITIES IN the United States, many of its elderly citizens are confined to their homes, unable to take advantage of the capital city. This volunteer placement will have you visiting them where they live, to bring a sense of the world outside as well as much-needed companionship and conversation into their lives.

You can reach out to the senior citizens of the U.S. capital city by making home visits or phone calls, and you'll learn some amazing personal histories while you're at it. The Emmaus organization is dedicated to improving the quality of life for the aging and has an ongoing need for volunteers. If you're in the city and it's holiday time, you can deliver gifts to housebound seniors or to care centers, or deliver a full Thanksgiving meal, or any weekend of the year you can help deliver groceries. You can also volunteer by phone from your own home. With home or phone visits, quality time is spent with individuals, encouraging them to tell the stories of their lives, passing on wisdom and humor—one of life's best ways to pass an hour or three.

Besides listening and learning about life stories, you may need to remind seniors to take their medications, as well as just check in to make sure they are well and don't need medical attention or anything else. The home and phone visits can serve as a true lifeline for seniors who may live alone and rarely have visitors. On a home visit, you may also run a few light errands, help out with a chore list, or just listen and visit. You may also get the treat of taking a senior out for an excursion, a walk in the neighborhood, or to a movie or museum.

There are no organized travel or accommodations arrangements with this project, just an inspiring chance to reach out to seniors in Washington—be in touch to help make sure the stories of remarkable lives are not lost.

YOUR NEXT STEP: Emmaus Services for the Aging (© **202/745-1200;** www.emmausservices.org). There are no travel or accommodations arrangements, so you'll organize getting to Washington yourself. When you know you can reach out for a day, a week, or longer, or just for a phone call, contact the organization.

DON'T MISS: Spend a day in the leafy, peaceful Potomac riverfront neighborhood of **Georgetown.** It is a city within the city, home to Georgetown University, several embassies, and a brick home gentility blended with college vitality that permeates the upscale shopping and dining options.

ⓘ www.washington.org

12 Getting Political

Greening New York City's open spaces

Human Rights **413**

Community Empowerment

Restore Vitality to Oppressed Neighborhoods

Córdoba, Argentina

Despite Córdoba once being declared the Cultural Capital of the Americas, parts of the city are plagued by crime, violence, and community unrest. Once Argentina's largest center for arts and learning, several neighborhoods in the city have fallen into disrepair both on a physical and social level. You can help empower Córdobians to again realize the glory of their once great city.

While Córdoba as a whole, like much of Argentina, is enjoying an influx of tourism, certain neighborhoods—where community pride is a foreign concept and self-preservation is the order of the day—aren't seeing any of those benefits. This project's intention is to bring a renaissance of energy and communal health to these neighborhoods, to make them safe and exciting places to live. Full-time staff lead multiple projects so you can specialize where your heart is most inspired.

Volunteers from around the world come to assist in restoring these neighborhoods. Whether it's gangs, violence, drugs, or poverty that have decimated these communities, focused energy can bring them back. You can work with the teen program, leading workshops and mentoring kids with their schoolwork. (Spanish language is important here.) You can help with the community food service, providing nutritious meals to more than 100 families having trouble getting food for themselves. Work in the day-care program, where there are so many kids needing care that it's divided into morning and evening sessions. Staff the secondhand clothing shop. Teach English classes or computer skills in after-school projects. Help teach hairdressing, cooking, baking, and sewing in community skills-building classes to train people for new or second careers.

You'll stay in a student residence in shared rooms. The neighborhood is safe, quiet, and not too far from the project site. You'll provide and prepare your own meals in the communal kitchen or dine inexpensively in nearby restaurants. Spanish-language lessons are available at extra cost if you'd like to deepen you skills during your evening hours, and of course cosmopolitan Córdoba provides plenty of entertainment.

YOUR NEXT STEP: Global Xperience (✆ **0800/881 88 88;** www.globalxperience.com). Programs of up to 1 year are available, but a 2-week project, US$812, includes shared dormitory-style accommodations, project training, and support. You are responsible for your own meals and local transportation; both are very inexpensive.

DON'T MISS: The cascading waters of **Iguazu Falls** actually tumble over 275 different falls across more than 2.5km (1.5 miles) of the river (during high water season). The Devil's Throat is the most impressive ribbon of water, marking the border between Argentina and Brazil, and the 76m (250-ft.) chute spills tons of water every minute, turning it into a mysterious, misty dream spot.

ⓘ www.turismodecordoba.org

414 Human Rights

Displaced Family Programs

Aiding Transition

Medellín, Colombia

MEDELLÍN HAS BECOME SYNONYMOUS WITH MANY PEOPLE FOR DRUG TRAFFICKING AND NARCO-terrorisism. The most dangerous city in Colombia, its reputation for lawlessness and illegality is in direct contrast to daily life. Most people who visit will tell you about how alive the streets are, how good the food is, and how charming its people are.

Drug cartels and guerillas have forced Colombians from their rural homes in droves to seek refuge in major cities. Of the more than three million displaced Colombians still in the country, more than half are under 15 years of age. Without their homes, land, and occupations, they are left to fend for themselves on unfamiliar city streets. This local organization works with displaced community members to provide education, shelter, and food, since returning to their homes is not viable at this time. Volunteers help in countless ways to make the transition to city life less traumatic. There are free day centers, outreach programs for those living on the streets, English classes, arts and enrichment programs, and burgeoning health programs.

English is a valuable tool for any Colombian struggling to get a job, so language teachers for youth and adults are always

Helping children of displaced families in Colombia

needed. Several day centers provide a safe haven for kids who may not be enrolled in school or whose parents need to be away for many hours (or days) seeking employment. You can help here with child care and arts and music programs as well as playtime and sports. You can work with the street outreach program to help those living without shelter, likely resorting to begging for sustenance, and let them know there are resources available to them. (Spanish is not required for every aspect of this project, but the street outreach will require fluency.) Excursions for kids who have had limited experiences in the world need chaperones, as a trip to the beach or a waterpark is a whole new experience.

You'll stay in a private room in a Medellín guesthouse in a quiet, bucolic neighborhood close to the metro station and the project site. Supermarkets, bars, clubs, restaurants, and shopping are all near the guesthouse. Meals aren't included, but there are countless inexpensive restaurants to try. Your evenings and weekends are free, and this lush, tropical region has amazing sights to see in the neighboring areas, as well as easy day trips a bit farther afield if you'd like to go to thriving Bogota, Amazonian Leticia, or the UNESCO World Heritage Site Cartagena.

YOUR NEXT STEP: Globalteer (✆ **+44/ 0777 150 2816;** www.globalteer.org). A 2-week project, £640, includes guesthouse lodging in private room, local training, airport pickup, local support, and community orientation. Meals are your responsibility.

DON'T MISS: Ciudad Perdida translates as "lost city" and is an archaeological site believed to predate Machu Picchu by centuries. It is an enchanted place, only reached by the most intrepid travelers. The steep paths to some of the more accessible ruins were designed so Tayrona Indians could hear visitors approaching (the journey takes a day and is quite difficult—you must crawl through hand-carved tunnels and scramble over large boulders). To visit the actual city, you'll be trekking with a guide for 3 to 5 days, or arrive via helicopter.

ⓘ www.ecotet.com/visitcolombia

Human Rights 415

Human Rights Programs

Latin American Activism

Quito, Ecuador

THE ISSUE OF HUMAN RIGHTS IS AS IMPORTANT IN ECUADOR AS IN ANY PART OF THE WORLD. On this project you'll live with an Ecuadorian family while working as an activist to improve the lives of the citizens of Quito. Whatever your skill set is—language instruction, the law, and teaching are just a few examples of what's needed—you will be actively put to work.

Many Ecuadorians are marginalized, from those with disabilities, the unemployed, and the seriously ill to some minority groups. This local grassroots organization tries to raise the profile of human rights oppression with education and practical support, government and community advocacy, and minority empowerment programs. While there are no experience or skills requirements to join this project, a fair level of conversational Spanish is necessary for you to participate.

Volunteers become activists for several causes on behalf of groups in Quito. The human rights programs promote and protect individual rights by educating youth

Educating children in Quito, Ecuador about human rights

and schoolteachers about both global and local rights issues. Women's rights education is also taught in rural areas, with an emphasis on reproductive and domestic rights, and practical solutions (where to find battered women's shelters, for example). There is also counseling support for people in crisis, as well as legal work on human rights cases. Volunteers and local staff also try to bring attention to foreign government abuse of local interests. You'll be fired up on this project from day one, and go home proud of the effect you've had on the system and on individual lives.

You'll be living with a host family, who will provide a single room, three meals daily, and once-weekly laundry. If you'd like additional intensive language instruction, the organization provides Spanish intensive programs in the afternoon and evenings (for an additional cost). Excursions to museums, churches, monasteries, historical sites, trekking and hiking locales can also be arranged (there may be charges for park fees or admission).

YOUR NEXT STEP: Experiential Learning Ecuadorian Programs (✆ **593-2/2543231;** www.elep.org). Fees start at 1 week; add weeks as desired. Fees include US$100 for registration, US$200 for placement, and US$105 for each week of host family accommodations and all meals. Also included is full project training and support of local staff, cultural and city orientation, and airport transfer.

DON'T MISS: High in the volcanic Andes Mountains is the Ecuadorian village of **Baños,** famous for its hot springs, gorgeous waterfalls, stunning flora and fauna, but mostly for its miracles. The town's Basilica of the Virgin of the Holy Water (Basilica de la Virgen de Agua Santa) is dedicated to the Virgin and the several miracles she performed in the Baños area, where pilgrims come to be healed. Keep an eye on **Tungurahua,** the volcano that still steams and spits ash on occasion.

ⓘ www.ecuador.us

Human Rights **416**

Marginalized People's Camp

An Inspiring Model of Sharing & Independence

Etoile-sur-Rhône, France

A COMMUNE IN THE RHÔNE ALPES OF SOUTHEASTERN FRANCE, THE COMMUNITY OF ETOILE-sur-Rhône is united by a set of common values—the most prized of all being sharing—so it's no wonder this 15th-century town openly welcomes the homeless and marginalized. Set against a backdrop of stone settlements and rolling hills, you'll work alongside those who share a solidarity of cause rarely seen today.

The Emmaus Community here serves as a home for marginalized and homeless people. Residents, mostly men under the age of 35, are called "companions," and the community supports them in their goal of re-entering society and becoming comfortable in social circumstances. Emmaus Community members support one another in work and vocational tasks that bring support from outside of the camp. English-speaking international volunteers are completely immersed in camp life, spending days in the same way as the residents, bringing extra effort and energy to the Emmaus principles of hard work, welcoming all, and sharing. The concept of begging is an affront to Emmaus Communities, who prefer to model their self-supporting businesses on rag pickers, making use of discarded or unwanted items and repurposing them for others to benefit.

You'll live in an itinerant camp with your fellow volunteers, spending most nights in a building in the village, but some nights in tents when you're farther way from the base. You'll focus most of your energies on collecting, repairing, cleaning, and selling second-hand items in the community shops, which provides some income to the community. Your work will take you to different villages in the region to collect donated items. You'll work Tuesday through Saturday with 2 days off. Volunteers can also put in time as cashiers in the community shops or merchandising and stocking shelves and cases. It is an incredible opportunity to try to change the prejudice against the homeless, as well as a heartening example of how despair can turn into strength with the help of a community.

YOUR NEXT STEP: Canadian Alliance for Development Initiatives and Projects (© **604/628-7400;** www.cadip.org) A 3-week project, US$277, includes the cost of accommodations on-site, meals, and project training and support. You'll get yourself to the project site for the first day of work camp. Designed for participants aged 18 to 35.

DON'T MISS: The **Musée de Grenoble** is one of France's oldest museums and one of the original institutions dedicated to modern art. The collection boasts 4,000 paintings and 5,500 drawings and sketches, including those of Picasso, Rubens, Renoir, Monet, Matisse, Magritte, Miró, Ernst, and so many other masters. Seeing these gems outside of Paris is a real treat.

(i) www.francetourism.com

417 Human Rights

Human Rights Outreach

Fight for Their Rights

Accra, Ghana

ACCRA'S MELTING POT OF INTERNATIONAL PEOPLE AND CULTURE IS AN IDEAL SETTING TO WORK for the cause of human rights. Spread along the Atlantic Coast, this leafy city offers no shortage of attractions and activities for the visitor at the end of a hard day. A plethora of cultural centers and venues await you, not to mention stunning beaches and a thriving nightlife.

This project began as a human rights program to raise awareness among youth around the world, and particularly in Ghana. Volunteers and locals team up to introduce issues that resonate with youth and teens. The intention is for youth not only to recognize their own worth and strength, but also to advocate for others. Peer education methods are employed to reach targeted communities in schools, including interactive theater, roleplaying, hip hop, dance, and expressive arts—all intended to bring issues of oppression to the fore and encourage awareness. The program's main focus areas include human rights, gender sensitization, and HIV/AIDS awareness.

Volunteers play many roles in this project in an attempt to activate young people. English-language volunteers run workshops for schools and community centers; are gender advocates that assess and run gender health programs; run targeted workshops for marginalized groups such as lesbians and gay men; serve as communications advisers to explore new ways of getting information to the audience; educate groups of young people about HIV/AIDS protection, prevention, and sexuality issues, as well as providing pre- and post-HIV test counseling; coach and run youth theater movements; and skilled medical and legal professionals can advocate on behalf of oppressed minorities in their respective fields.

Volunteers live together in a group household near the project site. The shared rooms are comfortable and clean, with security and laundry facilities nearby. Meals aren't provided, and past teams have found it fun to prepare meals communally, but of course you can do your own thing. Eateries and supermarkets are within walking distance, as are bars, clubs, Internet cafes, and shopping. Past volunteer teams have also enjoyed going out together to discover the recreational side of Accra in their free time and weekends.

YOUR NEXT STEP: Ikando (✆ **+233/21 222 726;** www.ikando.org). A 1-month project, includes volunteer group housing, project training, in-country orientation, airport transfers, and 24-hour support. You're responsible for all meals.

DON'T MISS: In **Bui National Park**, the third-largest wildlife preserve in Ghana, you'll see hippos, hippos, hippos. This remote but easy-to-get-to park has one of the largest accessible populations of hippos found anywhere. You'll also find plenty of primates, crocs, birds, and antelopes among the waterfalls, caves, and lush vegetation in the beautiful Bui Gorge.

ⓘ www.touringghana.com

Human Rights **418**

Women & Children's Shelter

Help Put a Stop to Domestic Violence

Quetzaltenango, Guatemala

SURROUNDED BY MIST-COVERED MOUNTAINS, QUETZALTENANGO IS CALLED XELA (PRONOUNCED SHAY-la) by its Quiche Mayan citizens. Surrounded by volcanoes, hot springs, and lush valleys, the city—which prides itself on being safe—is a commercial hub that boasts one of Guatemala's highest concentrations of Spanish-language schools. A visit to nearby Lake Atitlán is not to be missed.

There are few cultures, if any, in which domestic violence is not a scourge. Women and children often suffer not only from the initial attack, but also the long-lasting destruction of their spirit. In an effort to ensure kids' studies aren't affected when their living circumstances change dramatically, this program teams volunteers with children, setting up mentoring relationships for help in homework while squeezing in some time for fun. Volunteers can also help out in the day-care center, taking care of younger residents not yet in school. Often the women in the shelter are hard at work rebuilding their lives, so taking a stand for their kids is a vital contribution. This shelter is the first of its kind in Guatemala, and the success of the project, currently dependent on volunteers, could mean more programs like it in the future.

Working with the women and children at the shelter will inspire you. Their strength and compassion will bring out the same in you as you spend days with babies and toddlers, cleaning, feeding, and playing, while school-age children attend class and try to continue a level of normalcy. When school is over, you'll help with homework and can also plan informal activities, from songs and drama to sports and games, all to keep kids engaged and excited about learning new things. Your Spanish skills will come in handy so communication can be easy and spontaneous. You can also help collect and sort the donations of clothes and food, help women get access to medicine for themselves and their children, and generally add to the supportive community at the center.

This project doesn't include travel, lodging or meal arrangements, so volunteers live independently. The volunteer coordinator will advise and help you secure accommodations in Xela, where there are many inexpensive and comfortable options. The program asks for a minimum 2-week commitment, and there is no fee for volunteers.

YOUR NEXT STEP: Asociación Nuevos Horizontes (✆ **00502/4228 3816;** www.ahnh.org). A 2-week project (or more) includes complete training and support. You'll live independently, securing your own food, lodging, and local transportation. Volunteer coordinators are great resources before you arrive, and during your stay, to advise and direct you toward low-cost options. No fee for volunteers.

DON'T MISS: Quiriguá is a large Mayan archaeological site in Guatemala, and most of the ruins remain wonderfully untouched. The site has many remarkable features, but you can't ignore the fine detail of the carvings on the stone *stelae* (upright carved marker stones). The precision and preservation of the carved figures is beautiful, and the largest of a dozen of these ceremonial markers is 11m (35 ft.) high and weighs more than 60 tons. Animal deities, fully carved human figures, and beautiful botanic motifs are woven among Mayan geometric patterns in what is considered some of the most intricate carving of the Mayan world.

ⓘ www.visitguatemala.com

419 Human Rights

Help Victims of Terrorism

Putting Lives Back Together

Jerusalem, Israel

A VISIT TO JERUSALEM IS LIKE WALKING THROUGH THE PAGES OF THE BIBLE. SO MUCH WILL BE FAMILIAR, even to the first-time visitor. Also familiar to the people who live in the city is terrorism. It's a daily fact of life, but one that doesn't stop the city from being an intimate metropolis, a center of religions and history, and one of the most expressive and impassioned places on Earth.

Volunteers travel throughout Israel to help out programs focused on the victims of terrorism. This project runs therapeutic retreats for victims of terror, both adults and children, where group counseling and trust building work with others begins to open up some of the self-imposed isolation faced by many victims. The group's most important goal is to communicate that victims don't need to go through experiences like post-traumatic stress syndrome alone. Volunteers also work in the Jerusalem office, promoting the project, securing support from international organizations and schools, and raising public awareness of the hardships faced by victims. You'll sit in on group sessions to see how the support workshops help, as well as pitching in with the practical needs of the group. As a volunteer assistant, you might set up tables and chairs in a meeting room, make copies of literature, and help out with office tasks between victims group meetings. The groups meet in several locales across the country, usually in community halls or schools. If you're handy with words, a main focus is to help tell the stories of terror victims, so you can work one on one with a person, taping their oral history and interviewing them about their experience and journey toward healing. You can also help at the clothing shop, where donations are collected and distributed to families. Depending on the timing of your trip, the youth camp for terror victims aged 10 to 16 needs the help of many volunteers. Most of the kids who come to camp are teens whose parents or siblings have been injured or killed, and too many have themselves been injured.

There are no formal travel, lodging, or meal arrangements for international volunteers, but the organization can be very helpful with suggestions. They welcome volunteers from around the world regularly, and most will stay in Jerusalem during their time working with the group. Jerusalem is, of course, endlessly fascinating, and you'll have plenty to do with your free time, from amazing food and contemporary culture to learning the history of Old Jerusalem.

YOUR NEXT STEP: One Family Fund (✆ **011/972-2-539-9000;** www.onefamilyfund.org). When you contact the organization to let them know you'll be in Israel and would like to help, you'll determine your schedule of availability, from an afternoon to several weeks, and how best you can put your talents to work. You'll secure your own travel, lodging, meals, and other arrangements. No fee for volunteers.

DON'T MISS: In addition to its painful lessons and harrowing displays, the **Vad Yashem Holocaust Museum** outside Jerusalem is without a doubt one of the most sophisticated museums in the world. Opened in 2005, the museum's design is both ancient and postmodern, with incredibly moving, site-specific environments both indoors and out. It takes the better part of a day to experience the complex of gardens and halls, and it's an experience that will never leave you.

ⓘ www.goisrael.com

Human Rights **420**

Assistance for Roma People

Working to End Long-Held Stigmas

Tarlungeni, Romania

"BURY ME STANDING, I'VE BEEN ON MY KNEES ALL MY LIFE" IS A SAYING INDICATIVE OF LIFE FOR Roma people. Bra=ov County, in which the suburb of Tarlungeni resides, is one of the most prosperous regions of Romania, but these advantages aren't shared with the Roma. Living with and helping these nomadic people will give you a glimpse into a life that is unique and largely misunderstood.

Even though Romania has had a cultural and economic renaissance since the days of the Ceau=escu regime, the nation's Roma people (also sometimes called gypsies, contrary to their wishes) are still the victims of systemized discrimination. Many of the Roma live nomadic lives, moving with seasonal work in agriculture and gathering in commune-style enclaves. In the Carpathian Mountains—with their fairytale-like verdant forests, cobblestone streets, and medieval walls—hay is still transported in overloaded horse-drawn carts, and sheepskin is the most popular material for interior design. While the people live simple lives, most still ostracize any Roma they come across. The Roma don't have easy access to either education or employment because of both discrimination and their nomadic lifestyle, and since most don't have official identity records with permanent addresses, they are ineligible for medical care and social programs. In many ways, on paper they simply don't exist.

Volunteers work with the Roma via local organizations that aid in the fight against poverty and injustice. Roma children are particularly vulnerable, so much of your work is with them. There are many ways to jump in: working on building and refurbishing a kindergarten and a community center; building permanent homes; or working with needy children in an educational setting. You may lead a group of kids in songs or lessons, learning the alphabet or some basic English, teaching them to sew or to play soccer. The ongoing work of the advocacy organization means that some projects finish and the focus moves to the next, while some, like child care and education enrichment, are always going to need your help.

You'll stay in the community center in Tarlungeni, a suburb of Bra=ov. You'll share dormitory-style rooms and newly completed bathroom and kitchen facilities. The common area is a community center in the true sense of the word, with children playing and groups of adults socializing or conducting meetings. Meals are prepared for the group, and the diet is hearty local cuisine. You'll find all the amenities and culture you may want to peruse during your off hours in Bra=ov, and the surrounding region of ski resorts (stunningly green in warmer weather) provides some extraordinary hiking or biking options.

YOUR NEXT STEP: GlobeAware (✆ **877/588-4562;** www.globeaware.org). A 1-week project, US$1,390, includes accommodations at the community center, meals, airport transfers, some sightseeing excursions to local villages, cultural orientation, project training, and support.

DON'T MISS: You'll want to do a little digging around on the trail of Dracula. Vlad Tepes (Vlad the Impaler) was a Romanian ruler notorious for his cruelty, and his story loosely inspired Bram Stoker's vampire novel. While Stoker never actually visited Transylvania, **Castle Bran** is said to be the model for Dracula's castle, and the historic birthplace and sites of importance in the life of the real Dracula are all quite near this project, in the beautiful Transylvanian hills.

ⓘ www.romaniatourism.com

421 **Human Rights**

Celebratory Meal for the Poor

Give Hunger a Holiday

Hanoi, Vietnam

THE SCARS OF PAST WARS CAN STILL BE SEEN AND FELT IN THIS TINY, ELEGANT CAPITAL, AND YET Hanoi seems to constantly reinvent itself. This city of three million straddles the past and the future as beggars and Mercedes-Benz compete for space on the narrow streets. Volunteering with the poor here will only further help this city move into the 21st century.

There are many traditional meals in Vietnamese culture and particular foods that are eaten at special times of the year for luck or good fortune. This project is focused around the Vietnamese Lunar New Year and the feast of the first morning, when families gather to feast with friends and relatives for 2 weeks or more and pray for happiness, luck, success, and health. Food is bountiful for most families, but for the homeless or hungry in Hanoi, there is no feast and no traditional "chung" sticky rice cake. This project gathers international volunteers for a 2-week mission to provide the traditional foods that symbolize luck and prosperity for those who have no access to feasting.

You will be busy at the beginning of the trip making the special square sticky rice cakes called *Tet*. Your team will make enough to feed more than 300 people, including street children and many people that may still have homes but not enough to eat. You'll also visit several of these private homes to add some festive decoration and deliver your treats, creating parties and a carnival-like atmosphere, especially for the children. Games, songs, dance, all of it is meant to alleviate some of the troubles, if only temporarily.

The volunteer team lives together in the shared dormitory accommodations of the International Youth House in residential Hanoi near West Lake. Meals aren't included, but the project makes sure there is plenty of food to share with the community on delivery days. The rest of your meals are easily prepared at the host accommodations or in affordable local restaurants. Hanoi is a large, bustling city, so cultural exploration and recreation is easy to come by with the group or setting off on your own to find your own Hanoi flavor.

YOUR NEXT STEP: Canadian Alliance for Development Initiatives and Projects (✆ **604/628-7400;** www.cadip.org) A 2-week project, US$265, includes shared group housing in dormitories, training, and support. Meals are your responsibility, but the neighborhood in which you'll be staying is close to plenty of dining options and stores if you'd like to self-cater. An additional US$193 is paid directly to the host organization to support their mission.

DON'T MISS: It will be predominantly Vietnamese visitors standing in line to see **Ho Chi Minh's Mausoleum,** a national landmark in Hanoi. The acknowledged instigator of democracy is embalmed here in a glass case that reverent visitors file past (though his wish was to be cremated). The large gray granite structure is quite austere, but polished red and black stone in the interior feels much more regal. The beautifully tended gardens outside the mausoleum boast hundreds of plant species from across the country.

ⓘ www.vietnamtourism.com

Refugee Relief **422**

Refugee Center

Assisting Asylum-Seekers in Vibrant City

Tel Aviv, Israel

WHILE JERUSALEM IS EXCELLENT FOR SIGHTSEEING, TEL AVIV IS MEANT FOR RELAXING. A LAID-BACK beach vibe pervades this city, and the dress is strictly casual. TA, as it's affectionately known, is a city that will appeal to the young at heart; a place to lose yourself in the idea that life is more than just about punching a time clock.

Tel Aviv's African Refugee Development Center (ARDC) provides temporary accommodations for thousands of asylum seekers from several war-torn African nations. They work to place refugees in apartments as well as in temporary shelters. It's their intention to empower refugees and help them find safety, employment, education, health care, and stability. They also advocate on behalf of asylum seekers to improve Israeli government policy toward refugees. The ARDC accommodates and manages the cases of those who have fled Eritrea, Sudan, Ivory Coast, Somalia, Chad, and other nations. Shelters are woefully overcrowded.

Volunteers help in improving living conditions and work with shelter support teams. Some skilled volunteers, like trained medical or legal professionals, work in those fields for the shelter residents. Others with no training do important work like daily shelter check-ins for new arrivals and escorting refugees to doctors, hospitals, and offices to meet other professional needs. You can help with meal arrangements, from picking up donated food to preparing or delivering meals. Social activity volunteers work in educational programs for children and adults as well as additional language classes, art programs, music, and so on. Volunteers also work endlessly toward finding employment referrals and locating apartments for refugees, work as "buddies" for unattended minors, and more. You won't be bored.

Many of the volunteer team are locals from Tel Aviv, but international volunteers also play a large part in the stretched-to-the-limit programs and resources. There are no formal travel, lodging, or meal arrangements for international volunteers, so you'll be living independently in Tel Aviv (the program staff can be a great resource for dining and lodging recommendations).

YOUR NEXT STEP: Volunteering in Israel (✆ **054/6388 633;** www.ivolunteer.org.il). You'll arrange the duration of your volunteer work once you know your travel plans in Israel. You'll be responsible for your own travel, housing, and food. No fee for volunteers.

DON'T MISS: A nice antidote to the sometimes difficult and exhausting work of the project is to spend time in the bucolic **Neve Tzedek** neighborhood of Tel Aviv. This restored 19th-century area is now home to galleries, museums, artist studios, al fresco cafes, boutique shops and hotels, and a genteel atmosphere.

ⓘ www.goisrael.com

The atmosphere in Tel Aviv is casual and laid-back

423 Refugee Relief

Refugee Camp Program

Teaching the Dispossessed

Kakuma, Kenya

Kakuma is the Swahili word for "nowhere." Located in Northwest Kenya, this isolated town—prone to incredible dust storms—is essentially one large refugee camp. More than 70,000 refugees from Burundi, Eritrea, Somalia, and Uganda live here; however, most of them are from Sudan. Kakuma is also home to the fierce Turkana, one of Africa's last nomadic tribes.

The Kakuma refugee camp is not far from the nearest Sudanese city just over the border, but when you're fleeing for your life with thousands of your fellow refugees, it's an almost endless journey. The United Nations set up this camp in Kenya, but it has swelled well beyond its expected capacity and has taken over the region, formerly the somewhat lonely domain of Turkana nomadic herdsmen. The camp, now grown to more than 260 sq. km (100 sq. miles), is divided into seven units that provide marginal shelter from the arid desert elements for the refugees. The first school in the camp (now there are several), which caters to 5- and 6-year-olds, was where the Lost Boys of Sudan (27,000 boys displaced during the Second Sudanese Civil War) attended classes. Volunteers are needed to fulfill several roles at the school.

Your work at the school will be simultaneously trying and rewarding. You'll help with food preparation (the school's food program encourages parents to bring their children to school every day) and pitch in to help ease the burden on teachers, who try to lead classes of 60 or more students. An Empowerment Center offers primary school, adult literacy classes, teacher training school, a feeding program, and a small orphanage. Classes here are for both refugee and native Turkana children, and you can be of great help in these overcrowded classrooms by teaching basic lessons to smaller groups or assisting the teacher as needed. Another feeding program here needs your able hands to help feed the community members who rarely have access to three meals daily. Adult English literacy classes always benefit from native-speaking volunteers, so your time here will be valuable.

You'll stay at a modest guesthouse not far from the school, but all transportation is provided (volunteers are asked not to walk unaccompanied through the camps, both for personal safety and because it's nearly impossible not to get lost in the jigsaw-puzzle encampments). All meals, again quite basic, are provided. Your free time will be spent at the guesthouse with other volunteers, perhaps enjoying a campfire under the stars. This project is not intended for the faint of heart. You are among truly troubled people in great hardship, and it's quite common that volunteers will see children (and adults) dying during their stay.

YOUR NEXT STEP: Inspire Kenya (✆ **0755/195 6626;** www.inspirekenya.com). A 2-week project, US$1,221, includes basic guesthouse accommodations and meals, airport transfer and in-country transport, full project training, local orientation, and 24-hour local support.

DON'T MISS: After being wrung out emotionally and spiritually on this tough but amazing project, escape to a lovely story you might already know. The **Elsamere Conservation Center** is the former home of naturalist and painter Joy Adamson, author of the true story *Born Free*. Have tea on the lawn near the stunningly peaceful lakeside where Colobus monkeys play, and peruse the museum to learn the real and inspiring tale of Joy and the lioness, Elsa.

ⓘ www.tourism.go.ke

Refugee Relief 424

Burmese Migrant Learner Center

Helping Those Driven From Their Homeland

Chiang Mai, Thailand

TEACHING ENGLISH AND COMPUTER SKILLS TO BURMESE REFUGEES WILL HARDLY FEEL LIKE WORK in Chiang Mai. Far away from the chaotic pace of Bangkok, Chiang Mai contains more than 300 Buddhist temples and is a short distance from some of the country's most spectacular national parks.

In addition to being a terrific Thai destination, Chiang Mai has become the refuge for many migrants from Burma (also known as Myanmar) who have fled the oppressive regime across the border and come to Thailand to seek education and employment. This learning center creates opportunities for members of the Kachin, Kayah, Karin, Chin, Mon, Burman, Rakai, and Shan tribes, whose members are barred from basic education and are subject to human rights violations in their home country. Volunteers work to empower and educate the refugees to help them secure a chance for a better, safer life.

You'll work with several programs at the center teaching different skills to different age groups. English-language training is a main course of study (and English will be spoken throughout your volunteer work), as is basic computer skills training. Burmese- and Thai-language classes are also taught at the center, and you may assist those teachers by taking groups on small excursions, teaching basic math, and other teaching work where language won't be a barrier. Volunteer teachers work in teams, and you needn't have special skills or training to make a huge contribution to the lives of these individuals who are simply looking for a chance. The classes are offered free to the refugee population so they may pursue what the Thai believe are universal educational rights.

You'll be living with other volunteers at the group house in the old city center. Thai meals are prepared twice a day by the resident cook (except Sundays, when you can cook your own meals or go out to eat), and you'll also have a thorough in-country orientation and Thai-language instruction upon arrival. Navigating Chiang Mai will be no problem when you want to explore museums, markets, the international dining options, and nightlife.

YOUR NEXT STEP: Universal Giving (✆ **415/296-9193;** www.universalgiving.org). A 3-week stay, US$1,399, includes shared accommodations at the project house, two meals daily (except Sundays), in-country orientation and Thai-language instruction, airport transfers, in-country transportation, and in-depth project training.

DON'T MISS: The old Thai capital of **Ayutthaya** is an impressive ruined city. Surrounded by rivers in each direction, this island was once a glorious Siamese station. Before the city was sacked, its vast collection of temples was overseen by 33 different kings, each adding his own flair. About 100 buildings and ruins have been designated national monuments. At the city's heyday, it was home to three royal palaces, 375 temples, 29 forts, and 94 grand gates through fortress walls.

ⓘ www.tourismthailand.org

425 Women's Rights

Single, Homeless Mothers

Helping Women in Crisis

Cochabamba, Bolivia

KNOWN AS THE CITY OF ETERNAL SPRING, COCHABAMBA IS OVERSEEN BY A GIANT STATUE OF Jesus Christ—higher and larger than the Cristo del Corcovado in Rio de Janeiro. You can also help watch over the city's homeless and single moms by providing child care, education, and a helping hand to women and children in crisis.

This center provides respite and relief for single mothers and homeless women with children, many of whom are victims of domestic violence and have left the family home. A hot meal, shower, donated clothes, and basic medical care are provided. Volunteers assist staff in the practicalities of running a shelter home, from cleaning and kitchen help to small maintenance chores and working in the office. Volunteers also assist with child care and educational support while mothers are seeking employment or alternative places to live. The day-care center provides day and evening care and programs for children.

Your role is to support the mothers often by being of service to their children. Only with the confidence that their kids are

10 Celebrity-Inspired Volunteer Opportunities

Thoreau said, "Live your beliefs and you can turn the world around," and although celebrities are sometimes put down for pushing their beliefs on the public, many use their platform wisely. Get inspired by your favorite celebs to find ways to give of yourself.

Helping a disabled child with archery at a Hole in the Wall Camp

426 **Worldwide: Paul Newman, The Hole in the Wall Gang Camps** Paul Newman left an unmatched charitable legacy, and one of his favorite projects was The Hole in the Wall Gang camp. There are 13 allied camps: seven in the United States., plus camps in France, Italy, Ireland, the United Kingdom, Hungary, and Israel. They are laughter-filled getaways for children with serious medical conditions, with medical and professional staff. Volunteers serve as camp counselors and assistants; each camp has different volunteer needs depending on the season. ***The Association of Hole in the Wall Camps*** *(© **203/562-1203**; www.holeinthewallcamps.org). Contact individual camps to assess volunteer needs.*

427 **Delhi, India: Richard Gere, Fight AIDS** Richard Gere founded the Heroes Project (www.heroesprojectindia.org), which works with the Naz Foundation Trust in Delhi. Naz runs a care home for orphans and women living with HIV/AIDS. The home seeks volunteers to teach short art or music classes, read stories, and play with the children. ***The Naz Foundation (India) Trust*** *(© **011-26910499;** www.nazindia.org). No arrangements for travel or accommodations.*

428 **Mombasa, Kenya: Bono, Eliminate Poverty and Hunger** U2's frontman Bono has been vocal in the fight against world poverty, which is why he created the ONE Campaign (www.one.org). In Mombasa, hundreds of thousands of children have been orphaned by AIDS. Work with these children in a project intended to educate and relocate them from rescue centers to stable home environments. ***i-to-i*** *(© **800/985-4852**; www.i-to-i.com). A 1-week outreach program is US$946.*

429 **Lilongwe, Malawi: Madonna, Malawian Children** Madonna is a board member of Raising Malawi (www.raisingmalawi.org), which is dedicated to helping Malawi's one million orphans. Volunteers support Raising Malawi by working with World Camp, which conducts community education camps regarding HIV/AIDS and health issues. ***World Camp*** *(© **888/297-9669**. www.worldcampforkids.org). A 4-week session is US$2,600.*

430 **Hout Bay, South Africa: Oprah Winfrey, African Schools** Oprah may be responsible for inspiring more people to give or be of service than anyone else today. One of her highest-profile projects is the Oprah Winfrey Leadership Academy for Girls (www.oprahwinfreyleadershipacademy.o-philanthropy.org), a school for impoverished young women that teaches them to be future leaders. While the academy

doesn't currently make use of volunteers on-site, you can volunteer at a children's home for girls in Hout Bay, near Cape Town. ***Real Gap Experience*** *(✆* ***+44/ 01892 516164;*** *www.realgap.co.uk). A 2-week project is £699.*

431 **Santa Monica, California, USA: Roger Daltrey, Dogs and Kids** K9 Connection brings dogs and kids together in a particularly poignant way. Roger Daltrey is an honorary patron of this California group that pairs at-risk 12- to 18 year old kids with homeless shelter dogs to form training teams in basic obedience and behavior, making the dogs adoptable. ***K9 Connection*** *(✆* ***310/264-5424****; www.k9connection.org). No special arrangements for volunteers.*

432 **New Orleans, Louisiana, USA: Brad Pitt, Make It Right** Brad Pitt and Angelina Jolie are renowned charitable givers, including the Maddox Jolie-Pitt Foundation (www.mjpasia.org). Pitt has also become strongly identified with the Make It Right Foundation and the recovery efforts after Hurricane Katrina. The organization uses volunteers to rebuild housing and community infrastructure. ***Make It Right Foundation*** *(www.makeitrightnola.org). The need for volunteers varies; sign up on MIR's website.*

433 **New York City, New York, USA: Bette Midler, City Greening** Bette Midler founded the New York Restoration Project (NYRP) to clean up New York's open spaces. Volunteers are invited to help every Monday, Wednesday, and Saturday with projects across the boroughs, where teams clean up trash, tend gardens, and do general park care. ***New York Restoration Project*** *(✆* ***212/304-8366****; www.nyrp.org). No fee or formal travel arrangements for volunteers.*

434 **Nationwide, USA: Ellen DeGeneres, Fight Hunger** Ellen DeGeneres and Ben Affleck started the Small Change Campaign for people to donate loose change to America's Second Harvest. Now called Feeding America, it provides food to 25 million low-income Americans. Volunteers help process and deliver food. ***Feeding America*** *(national office ✆* ***800/ 771-2303****; www.secondharvest.org). Check the website to get details of volunteer needs.*

A woman unpacks food at a food bank.

435 **Nationwide, USA: Denzel Washington, Veteran's Housing** Denzel Washington is quite active with the Fisher House Foundation, which provides free housing for injured American military personnel and their families during hospitalization. There are 40 Fisher Houses, with three more under construction. Each has different volunteer needs, from light carpentry and cleaning to coordinating activities for children and patient care. ***Fisher House Foundation*** *(national office ✆* ***888/294-8560****; www.fisherhouse.org). No organized lodging or meal plans.*

well looked after can these women face the difficulty of starting anew without the familial structure they have known. It's empowering to give them the strength and support to seek employment and a better life (many won't have worked outside the home before). You can organize activities for the kids, ranging from sports games to art lessons or drama. Teaching songs or playing simple instruments (it might mean making a drum from a bucket and maracas with pebbles in a can) gets the whole group involved. You can also help administratively not just in office work but by securing donations of food or school supplies from local organizations. While English will be spoken much of the time, you'll find your work goes more easily if you have some Spanish-language knowledge. Twenty hours of Spanish instruction is included as part of this placement.

You'll stay with a host family, sharing three meals daily and learning about the culture and lifestyle in this Bolivian city. Your first day will be spent in an orientation program outlining the neighborhood, local customs and greetings, public transportation options, and more. Your free time and days off can be well spent in the city as you learn more from your host family about the best museums, parks, neighborhood walks, and entertainment options.

YOUR NEXT STEP: Volunteering Solutions (✆ **347/410-9730;** www.volunteeringsolutions.com). A 2-week project, US$1,000, includes host family accommodations, meals, full project training, in-country orientation, Spanish-language instruction (20 hours), comprehensive insurance, airport pickup, and local staff support.

DON'T MISS: Let the spiritual pendulum swing both ways while exploring Bolivia. Visit the **Copacabana Cathedral,** where the statue of the Virgin Mary is known to grant wishes and give blessings for safe travel, the health of your family, and the reliability of your technological gadgets and car. Then explore a darker side in La Paz at the famous **Witches Market,** where you'll find shop after shop specializing in metaphysical items and you can buy a potion or charm to "guarantee" health, safety, and easy travel.

ⓘ www.enjoybolivia.com

Women's Rights **436**

Women's Shelter

Helping the Children of Battered Women

Xela, Guatemala

SITUATED IN SOUTHWEST GUATEMALA, XELA'S INDUSTRIAL FEEL IS SET AGAINST A BACKDROP OF mountains and the nearby Lake Atitlán. Here, you spend your days working in a shelter for battered women while staying with a host family by night.

The shelter for battered women is managed by women for women (though everyone who can volunteer is welcome) and funded entirely by donation. In addition to providing a safe place for women and children, the shelter creates learning and recreational opportunities for the kids before and after school while their mothers may need to be at work or search for work. In tandem with the women needing work, the project has launched a laundromat "microempowerment" program, where the shelter residents run and staff the business, from the actual labor in the laundromat to the marketing, business planning, and management. Volunteers (who need basic to intermediate Spanish—10 hours of Spanish instruction is included in the fee) help teach the women English to forward their business goal of becoming self-sufficient.

While working for and with the women at the shelter, much of your focus will be on the children. Tutoring and helping with homework before and after school, organizing small group outings with mothers and children, some child care for the little ones not yet enrolled in school, and working with everyone on their English-language skills are all facets of your work. With the laundry business, you can help advance the business plan, particularly if you have the skills to help with budget planning, business proposals, and marketing. Again, teaching basic English reading, writing, and most importantly, conversation, will come in extraordinarily handy.

You'll stay with a host family, who will provide three meals daily and be your best liaison to the community (as will the women who run the shelter and the shelter residents). Some cultural excursions and activities are included to truly immerse you in Guatemalan life, including cooking class, Spanish classes, and a trip to Antigua or Lake Atitlán during a free day. More thorough language immersion courses are also available (at additional cost). The rest of your free time will be congenially spent as a member of the community, getting to know the folks around town and exploring on your own (or with your new friends).

YOUR NEXT STEP: United Planet (✆ **800/292-2316;** www.unitedplanet.org). A 1-week project, US$1,645, or 2-week project, US$1,945, includes host family accommodations, meals, in-country orientation program, Spanish-language instruction, cultural excursions and classes, project training, airport transfers, and local staff support.

A mother and child at the women's shelter in Xela, Guatemala

DON'T MISS: Guatemala City's **La Aurora Museum Complex** (Parque Aurora) is home to some of the nation's best cultural institutions, including the Museum of Anthropology and Archeology, the Museum of Modern Art, the Natural History Museum, and the La Aurora National Zoo, one of the oldest zoos in operation in Latin America. It is a full day or leisurely couple of days to make it through each of these institutions, and the complex and park have been recently restored and updated.

ⓘ www.visitguatemala.com

Women's Rights

Women's Empowerment Programs

Support & Inspiration

Delhi, India

EVERY STREET IN INDIA'S CAPITAL CITY OF DELHI IS TEEMING WITH LIFE, 24 HOURS A DAY, 7 days a week. This massive urban metropolis has everything from ancient ruins to modern skyscrapers—it's a microcosm of India, a place where myriad religions, lifestyles, culture, and food come together.

The status of women is complex in many Indian households. Revered and worshipped in many Indian religions, women are also seen as second-class citizens and thought of as property by many men (and by cultural tradition). This dichotomy leads to cultural confusion, and many women have at some point in their lives been subjected to physical, sexual, or emotional abuse. Indian women tend to work harder than anyone else, and even in their own homes they can sometimes be treated like employees—at best. This volunteer opportunity works with several women's empowerment programs in Delhi, from shelter homes to literacy classes and computer or vocational training programs.

Your volunteer work will depend on your interests and strengths. You may work in a shelter with women and their children, helping out with day-to-day tasks of child care, cleaning, or kitchen help. Teaching English is a high priority at almost every women's program, as English speakers are usually more employable. Computer skills and elementary business principles are highly valued skills, and there are training projects in which you can help (in a support role, if not teaching) in beautician work, yoga, sewing, and health education. Diet and nutrition courses are also a major tenet of the empowerment programs.

You'll be sharing a room with another volunteer in a homestay with a local family. All your meals are provided at the host home or at the project for lunches. You may wish to take an optional extensive week of local orientation (at additional cost) before your volunteer work begins, covering local customs, basics of the local language (though English is all that is required for this project), and a city orientation. If you don't choose to do the full week, there is still a thorough city orientation, so you'll know your way around and some basic language phrases. Your free time in Delhi will fly by, as there is much to see and do, and the organization can also help with booking other travel or tour options you may want to pursue in the surrounding areas.

YOUR NEXT STEP: Volunteering Solutions (✆ **347/410-9730;** www.volunteeringsolutions.com). A 1-week project, US$450, or 2-week project, US$650, includes shared homestay accommodations, meals, airport transfer, city and cultural orientation program (included, but a weeklong immersion program is an additional charge), project training, insurance, and local support staff.

DON'T MISS: One of the most remarkable and serene architectural structures you'll come across anywhere is in the chaos of Delhi. The **Bahá'í House of Worship,** most often called the Lotus Temple, is a graceful white building that looks like a flower opening to the sun. The aesthetic symmetry of the building and its setting on a raised hill amid grassy terraces makes it a beautiful respite from a busy day in the city. Thousands of visitors come every day to attend prayer services or just to explore the enormous iconic building—one of the most famous in India. To see it glowing at sunrise or sunset is magnificent.

ⓘ www.incredibleindia.org

438 Women's Rights

Women's Business Collective

Assisting Local Artisans

Xiloxochico, Mexico

PRONOUNCED "SHI-LO-SHO-CHEE-KO," THIS VILLAGE IN MEXICO'S SIERRA NORTE IS HOME TO the Nahua people, an agrarian-based society whose traditional way of life is being encroached on by the modern world. Volunteering at the women's collective will ensure that they continue to get a fair price for their goods.

In this high-country village, the still mostly traditional Nahua people rely on agriculture as their main avenue of employment in a region home to cinnamon, macadamia, coffee, and vanilla crops. But a collectivo of powerful women in the community have been looking for more and have organized to work for the betterment of the entire village. They secured a piece of land in the center of town and built (with the help of volunteers) a *casita* (workhouse) from which to sell their crafts. They developed an artisans' network and are creating embroidery work, weavings, small sculptures, and other handicrafts. The casita is a storage house for supplies as well as a communal meeting space and workshop.

Volunteers join the women's collective in this high, humid, lush village and build on to the existing casita structure. The need for volunteers grows with the success of the program as more and more of the community gets on board. The community will also decide other priorities within the village for the volunteer team to undertake, which can include other building or maintenance projects or helping establish a business model and improved infrastructure for the collective. You may also spend afternoons helping out at the schools, providing English instruction, tutoring and mentoring children in afterschool programs, and establishing recreational programs.

The volunteer team bunks at an eco-hotel run by Nahua women in a neighboring village. After breakfast, the team travels together to the project, and shares the afternoon meal with the community. Dinners are again back at the hotel, which serves as a good base for sightseeing and hiking exploration of the verdant region. There are nearby caves and cathedrals, and plenty of time to really interact with and become a member of the local community.

YOUR NEXT STEP: Global Citizens Network (✆ **800/644-9292;** www.globalcitizens.org). A 10-day project, US$1,575, includes hotel lodging, meals, training and materials, in-country transportation, insurance, and full project support from local staff.

DON'T MISS: In the Northern Mexico plains, you'll find **Copper Canyon** (Barranca del Cobre), a series of gorges that consist of 20 canyons, four times larger than the Grand Canyon. This region of Chihuahua has been home to more than 200 different Native American tribes, and the area still hides pre-Hispanic ruins and archeological marvels. Take a ride on the Copper Canyon Railway, a breathtaking train journey that climbs more than 2438m (8,000 ft.) in elevation, with plenty of stops in this particularly scenic area.

ⓘ www.visitmexico.com

Victims of Abuse

Creating a Healing Environment for Girls

Kathmandu, Nepal

THIS IS AN IDEAL PLACEMENT FOR FEMALE VOLUNTEERS INTERESTED IN HELPING OTHER WOMEN, regardless of experience. Nestled in the lap of the Himalayas, volunteers in this Kathmandu-based program aim to provide young women with life skills and education, while acting as a mentor and role model for women in transition.

This project is limited to female volunteers to help at a counseling center for girls who have been victims of abuse. It is a residential center, and volunteers live on-site, where they help supplement counseling and support the girls in their life and education. The organization also uses volunteers to help with community workshops to educate the local population about parenting, abuse, sex roles, and more. This safe haven is a nurturing environment meant as a stepping stone for young women to overcome the difficulties they have known and emerge strong and successful. The home provides residential counseling programs for up to 1 year before clients transition out.

In addition to being a role model for these young women, you'll work directly with them in several ways. You don't need specific counseling or therapeutic skills, but if you do have social work or health education experience, you'll be very busy indeed. No matter what your experience, you'll be of great help in the schooling arena as you assist in English studies as well as plenty of other subjects. You'll be a great mentor and homework tutor, finding ways to explain new concepts or just engendering excitement about schooling. (Keeping girls enrolled and engaged in school is one of the most important contributions that can be made to their futures.) English is all that is required, and if you can help in the community workshops aspect of the organization's work, translation can be provided where necessary. Can you help develop literature or web content? Even helping with the mundane cooking and cleaning and light maintenance is helping move the girls forward through life.

You'll be living in the all-female facility on-site with other volunteers. Meals are not provided here, but part of your fee covers a daily stipend for meals at local restaurants of your choice three times daily. Kathmandu is a hub of Nepalese tourism and has much to offer visitors, so when you're not spending relaxing time at the house being part of the tight-knit community, you'll find endless fascination in the city. The host organization also arranges field trips and cultural activities, such as trekking in the Himalayas, visiting Buddhist and Hindu temples, a 3-day safari to the Tibet border area, and Nepalese-language lessons.

YOUR NEXT STEP: United Planet (✆ **800/292-2316;** www.unitedplanet.org). A 2-week women-only project, US$1,945, includes accommodations at the project house, a stipend for three meals daily at local eateries, full project training, cultural orientation, airport transfers, cultural programs and sightseeing excursions, and insurance.

DON'T MISS: You needn't travel far from Kathmandu to get to the third-largest city in Nepal, **Bhaktapur.** It boasts 7th-century architecture that is recognized as a UNESCO World Heritage Site due to the richness of the decorative work in its squares, columns, and statuary. The Potter's Square is a spot in town where artisans gather and thousands upon thousands of clay pots are sold. In Durbar Square, in the center of the city, the richly adorned Golden Gate entrance to the Palace of 55 Windows is regarded as the pinnacle of carved work of its kind in the entire world.

ⓘ www.welcomenepal.com

440 Women's Rights

Teenage Mothers' Home

Supporting Victims of Violence

Cusco, Peru

THE HISTORIC CAPITAL OF THE INCAN EMPIRE AND CRADLE OF INCAN CIVILIZATION, CUSCO HOSTS more than a million tourists each year, many who come to see the fabled ruins of Machu Picchu. Surrounded by 6,000m-high (19,685-ft.) mountains and blessed with a tropical climate, Cusco is said to have the most beautiful views in the entire country.

A family court judge has sent young women from 12 to 18 years old who live in the rural areas of Peru's Andean Highlands to this shelter. It has been deemed safer for them, along with their children, to be out of the home where they suffered violence and abuse. Most will live here and bring up their children in the supportive atmosphere for 4 to 5 years. In the house, their children are enrolled in school and the mothers receive daily education workshops from a private teacher. In addition to traditional education, the young mothers learn a trade, and there is a partner atelier where they work on sewing projects that generate income that is then funneled back into the home. In addition to practical support, counseling and medical care are provided and there is a nursery and day-care center in the home. The nursery is also available to neighborhood women residents, who can leave their babies here while they work.

You'll spend much of your time with the kids in the nursery and day-care center, doing everything from diaper detail to feeding, as well as reading stories, playing games, and helping with homework. Homework assistance also extends to the young mothers continuing their studies as a condition of living in the home. You'll also help mothers learn some basic English and parenting skills. You can organize a weekend outing for mothers and children, introduce new arts or music programs, and maybe help the group learn some basic household repairs and maintenance tasks. With the communal support of the women in the shelter, the staff, and international volunteers like you, these young mothers who faced an uncertain future and thought themselves destined for ruin find new confidence and strength as survivors.

You'll bunk in a private room within a host family's home. Three meals daily are provided, and English is spoken in the home and at the shelter, but Spanish, while not required, will ease communications. Of course Cusco is always filled with international visitors, so nearly everyone has some English. The project also provides cultural activities such as Quechua-language courses (the indigenous language in the region), some Spanish lessons, Peruvian cooking classes, a guided trip to Machu Picchu, and arts instruction. A Spanish immersion course is available for an extra charge. Cusco has the feel of a quaint village crossed with a cosmopolitan city, so you'll never exhaust the options for food and drink, museums, churches and cathedrals, hiking, horseback riding, scenic drives, and visiting ancient Inca sites (many right in town).

YOUR NEXT STEP: United Planet (✆ **800/292-2316;** www.unitedplanet.org). A 2-week placement, US$1,595, includes host family accommodations, meals, travel insurance, cultural orientation classes and language instruction (immersion Spanish program available for an additional fee), airport transfers, in-country transportation, project training and support, and excursions.

DON'T MISS: Cusco is way up in the Andes, where you're practically kissing the clouds, so why not really enter the heavens and go **paragliding?** Run against the wind and in a few steps you're airborne before falling into the abyss, your nylon canopy stretching out overhead like the revered Peruvian condor. Ride the updrafts and currents in tandem if you're a newbie, or carve the ether on air that is in no hurry to let you down to terra firma. There are numerous paragliding and hang-gliding companies taking advantage of the near-perfect conditions of the high, steep mountains just outside Cusco.

ⓘ www.visitperu.com

Women's Rights 441

Women's Project

Open New Pathways to Stability

Arusha, Tanzania

ALTHOUGH TRAVELERS FROM AROUND THE WORLD FLOCK TO TANZANIA TO CLIMB MOUNT Kilimanjaro, or safari in the Serengeti, the country's Maasai nomads often don't benefit from the money tourists bring in—this is particularly true for female members of the tribe. This program will help you empower Maasai women by creating and developing economic opportunities tied to their traditional crafts and way of life.

The women of the Maasai tribes face even greater hardships than the men and are economically disadvantaged. As tourism has transformed much of the tribal culture into an internationally known entity, women are predominantly kept in the background and rarely employed as guides or in other arenas that can provide income. This project works with the women of eight different Maasai villages in the Mount Meru area, creating programs to improve their economic standing. The income-generating projects come from training the women to make traditional Maasai crafts (such as ornately beaded jewelry, neck collars, headdresses, and other pieces), clothes, carved handicrafts, and other goods. The items are sold collectively at market to fund the women's project and get income directly to the participating women.

How's your finger dexterity? It requires plenty of hand-eye coordination to do the intricate beadwork for which the Maasai are famous. If you have talent for this or other artistic work, you can teach new techniques as well as learn the traditional Maasai ways and designs. The volunteer team travels to each of the eight villages to put in time with each women's collective, beading, organizing, and helping out in any way needed. The women are also eager to learn English, so you'll work with them on conversational skills. Language is a barrier to the women being able to sell their work to visitors directly, so they often have to use an intermediary who takes a cut of the profits. With your help in some basic English they can cut out that middleman and increase their revenue. The collectives have also begun to explore the possibility of international sales and reaching a wide audience through the

A traditional Maasai craft created by female tribe members

Internet, but there are few opportunities to learn marketing or website building, so if you have those skills you could open up a whole new horizon for them. Teaching English to the local children is also a great aid, as many of them will learn enough to seek lucrative positions as tour guides as they grow older, bringing income to the families.

You'll stay with a host family, who will provide three traditional Tanzanian meals daily. Living with a local family is an incredible opportunity to learn about the culture of the Maasai villages and their traditional ways. While they don't live in isolation, they choose to honor the ways of the generations past in dress, diet, and custom. Being welcomed as a friend to the village is a tremendous honor and an experience you're unlikely to ever forget.

YOUR NEXT STEP: Institute for Field Research Expeditions (✆ **800/675-2504;** www.ifrevolunteers.org). A 2-week project, US$753, includes host family accommodations, three meals daily, airport transfers, in-country transportation, project training and 24-hour support, and comprehensive travel insurance. A US$349 administrative/application fee is required.

DON'T MISS: Everyone knows about safaris in the Ngorongoro Crater or Serengeti, but to get a sense of game tracking in undiscovered Africa, head to the little visited **Tarangire National Park** not far from Mount Meru where this project is based. The dense bush and Baobab trees are home to vast migrating herds of hoofed vegetarian grazing animals—which of course means the big cats, mostly lions, are never far behind. Since this area is not often visited, when you spot a lion with your tracker, there won't be a radio call that alerts twenty other Jeeps to swoop in, so you can feel quite alone with nature.

ⓘ www.tanzaniatouristboard.com

Women's Rights 

Girls' Empowerment Program

Bringing Teens Back from the Precipice

Chiang Mai, Thailand

CHIANG MAI IS OFTEN USED AS A LAUNCHING POINT FOR TREKS INTO THE AREAS WHERE Thailand's remote hill tribes live. But if you're looking for human and cultural interaction, spend some time teaching English to disadvantaged women, many of them members of the country's hill tribes, who've come to Chiang Mai to escape a life of poverty.

The girls who receive work on this project are at a precipice. Most come from extremely poor families or struggling single-parent households, and the girls see dropping out of school to move away from the home or join the workforce as their only option. This organization strives to make school and the pursuit of a complete education as viable an alternative as any other by operating a boarding school for hill tribe girls from many of the northern tribes. By being residential and providing food, the school meets the girls' practical needs while the program runs a standard Thai high school curriculum with additional vocational training. The girls are all aged 13 to 19, and in addition to classroom study, they learn realistic trades to pursue as adults. In exchange for their board and education, the girls work around the school, gardening, cooking, cleaning, and maintaining the grounds.

Your skills as a teacher are what is required. The school residences are four small wooden homes, plus some class space where you'll teach English by creating conversation groups to increase their spoken language skills. You'll also have the opportunity to create supplemental workshops focused on the things that inspire

A volunteer teaches printmaking to girls in Chiang Mai.

you and that can do the same for these teens. Create a lesson plan for yoga or painting, poetry or dance, or how about a science class or sport and fitness? Do you have skills you can impart in public speaking or basic computer work? The girls tend to be voracious for new experiences and challenges, and the school finds that every new skill builds exponentially upon their burgeoning self-confidence. Most of the girls arrive at the program with a defeatist attitude and feeling unwanted, but graduate with a confidence in their skills and their worth that was not predictable in their former circumstances.

You'll live with other volunteers at the project house, which is in the middle of the silver district and walking distance to several of the city's best sights and market areas (just down the block is the Saturday Walking Street, where you'll nibble brilliant street food until you burst). Grab some fruit and tea for breakfast, and lunches and dinners are prepared by the in-house cook daily except Sunday. With so much so close at hand, you'll find no shortage of adventures to pursue in your free time in Chiang Mai, and your thorough in-country orientation tour on the first day will help you spot the places you'd like to explore further when you're on your own.

YOUR NEXT STEP: Cultural Canvas Thailand (© **850/316-8470;** www.culturalcanvas.com). A 3-week project, US$1,399, includes shared project house accommodations, two Thai meals daily (except Sundays), in-country orientation, airport transfers, full project training, and 24-hour resident staff support.

DON'T MISS: Rent a bike and go at your own pace on a tour of **Old Sukhothai,** the former capital of the kingdom in the 13th through 15th centuries. The ruins in this UNESCO World Heritage Site are phenomenal and well maintained, with plenty of sensitive restoration and stabilizing (but if you like the sense of real discovery, there are narrow lanes and alleys that lead to virtually untouched ruins you can poke around). There are moats, small lakes, bridges, and tiny islands, and the entire 78-sq.-km (30-sq.-mile) region is peppered with Buddha figures.

ⓘ www.tourismthailand.org

443 Women's Rights

Women's Human Rights Program

Working for Global Results

Minneapolis, Minnesota, USA

This volunteer project will allow you to live locally but act globally. Based in Minneapolis—the cultural capital of the Midwest—you'll work for the cause of women's rights around the world. You'll partner with local doctors, lawyers, and other professionals, all of whom will make you realize why Minneapolis is such a thriving, progressive city in which to live and work.

The Advocates for Human Rights does incredible work locally and internationally on the plight of women around the world. Applying international human rights standards to women's rights issues in the United States and abroad, they partner with local organizations to fight against domestic violence, rape, employment discrimination, sexual harassment, and trafficking in women and girls. The organization has worked in Bulgaria to enact protection laws; train judges, police, and prosecutors in the Republic of Georgia; conduct a fact-finding mission in Tajikistan; launch a comprehensive Stop Violence Against

Women website (www.stopvaw.org); and provide international training and advocacy work in partnership with local women's groups and law enforcement agencies. Locally they run a Battered Immigrant Women Project, the *Journey to Safety* stage presentation for education about immigrant women's issues, and done needs assessment studies for local agencies about human trafficking in Minnesota.

Many volunteers are local professionals—doctors, attorneys, graphic designers, psychiatrists, and translators—but volunteers without those special skills can still help this constantly busy organization. In addition to administrative help necessary to run any charitable organization (the women's human rights program is an arm of the larger human rights advocates program), you can be of great help for the annual International Women's Day Celebration in March, the largest event of its kind in the Midwest. The event uses a squad of volunteers to plan the event, work with sponsors, secure food and beverage donations, work on publicity, do mailings, set up the event, and register guests. There are monthly speaker series workshops that need volunteer support, a Women's Human Rights Film Series, and training sessions throughout the region all year. Each of these local outreach programs needs help, from loading materials to setting up audio/visual equipment to work on the newsletter and email updates.

There are no formal travel, lodging, or meal arrangements for out-of-town volunteers, but when you know you'll be in Minneapolis (especially if you're lucky enough to time your visit with Women's Day), contact the organization to help out in any way you can.

YOUR NEXT STEP: Advocates for Human Rights (✆ **612/341-3302;** www.mnadvocates.org). You'll make your own arrangements for travel, accommodations, and meals, and build your schedule with the volunteer coordinator so you can be of the most help while visiting Minneapolis. No fee for volunteers.

DON'T MISS: Minneapolis and St. Paul are vibrant twin cities with a lively cultural energy and endless array of museums, bookstores, shops, restaurants, and pubs. One of the most revered and well-known cultural institutions in the region is the **Guthrie Theater,** where you can take in some of America's finest stagework during an incredible and entertaining night on the town. www.guthrietheater.org

ⓘ www.minneapolis.org

Women's Rights

Women's Rights Park

Promoting the History of a Movement

Seneca Falls, New York, USA

MOST PEOPLE COME TO SENECA FALLS—THE GATEWAY TO THE FINGER LAKES—FOR THE GREAT fishing, golfing, and watersports, and the popular Cayuga Wine Trail. Lesser known is the Women's Rights National Historical Park. Consisting of four historic properties, the displays, exhibits, and films dramatically tell the story of America's women's movement.

The Women's Rights National Historical Park commemorates the struggle for equality and the First Women's Rights Convention in 1848. Held in the Wesleyan Chapel, the convention was attended by 300 women and men, including Elizabeth Cady Stanton (who drafted the Declaration of Sentiments), Lucretia Mott, and Frederick Douglass. Visitors go on self-guided tours (a cell phone number can be

A statue called Sojourner Truth at the Women's Rights Park in Seneca Falls

dialed for an audio tour of each location) or follow interpretive ranger talks to several famous sites, including the chapel and visitor center with its museum and exhibit hall, the M'Clintock residence of the Quaker family that hosted the planners of the convention and antislavery fighters, Elizabeth Cady Stanton's house restored to its 1848 appearance, and other sites here in the "center of the rebellion." This was ground zero for the struggle for equal rights that continues in America today.

You'll find many ways to help out here. As an interpretive division volunteer, you'll greet visitors, direct them to sites and exhibits or guided tours, and operate the sales centers at the visitor center and M'Clintock House. Volunteer tour leaders are trained to conduct groups through the chapel and Elizabeth Cady Stanton House, presenting the history of the place and the movement and comparing it to the state of women's rights today. You could also work in the park library, exhibits, archives, and historic sites with organizing and improving some aspects. You could even pick up some clippers and pitch in with the maintenance of the sites, doing grounds work, historic preservation projects, or pitching in with facilitating special events.

There are no formal travel, lodging, or meal arrangements, so you'll live independently while in the Seneca Falls area. When you know the timing of your visit and availability for volunteer shifts, you can contact the park service to be assigned.

YOUR NEXT STEP: National Park Service (✆ **315/568-2991;** www.nps.gov). The duration of your volunteering is up to you and your self-arranged travel plans. No fee for volunteers.

DON'T MISS: The Catskill Mountains, a vacation retreat for New York City socialites, are renowned for their natural beauty. The Borscht Belt (summer resorts frequented mainly by Jews from New York City) is still a part of the character of the region, but for rural relaxation you can find retro resorts, historical camps, upscale lodges, or solitude in acres and acres of rocky, mountainous woods.

ⓘ www.iloveny.com

13 *Peace-Building*

The Lone Sailor statue at The U.S. Navy Memorial in Washington D.C.

445 Conflict Resolution & Security

Horse Patrol

Ensuring Safety from the Saddle

Kefalonia Island, Greece

Kefalonia has managed not to become overcrowded, despite its sparkling white sand beaches being among the most famous in Greece. It's known as one of the safest of the Greek Islands, something you can help ensure if you know how to ride a horse.

Tradition runs deep here in the land of the gods, and one of the island traditions that continues is security patrol on horseback. Mounted riders traverse island paths to keep locals and visitors safe. Riders have security radios and can alert the authorities if assistance is needed for any reason. This incredible opportunity is open to international volunteers who get to ride patrol, care for horses, and forge new bridle paths in the region.

You'll need to have some saddle experience for this project. You'll work as a groom, caring for the horses: brushing, feeding, and cleaning as well as cleaning stables and some facility maintenance. You'll get plenty of riding time, in both exercise sessions in the ring to keep your steed fit and ready, as well as riding patrol along with professionals, usually in the early morning and late afternoon, avoiding the hottest part of the day. A great experience is to go for a 2- to 3-day patrol farther afield and camp out on the island with your horse (not only exciting for you but a break in the routine for your horse). Another part of your volunteer time will be investigating potential new patrol paths, which might require clearing brush and other vegetation to allow safe passage for horse and rider. You'll have both morning and evening rides, if not on patrol, then as training rides.

Home is mostly in the saddle, but when you finally need to sleep, you'll retire to a basic but comfortable camp outside the village of Antipata in a caravan or large excursion tent. There are kitchen facilities, hot showers, laundry, and even computer access at the nearby museum. Meals aren't included in the fee, but there are regular grocery runs to town for volunteers and free access to the kitchen; most volunteer teams find the sharing of cooking and cleaning part of the bonding experience. Your free time is wide open in this island paradise, so most will head to the beach to sunbathe, swim, fish, and relax.

YOUR NEXT STEP: The Society for Environmental Exploration (Frontier) (✆ +44/20 7613 2422; www.frontier.ac.uk). A 2-week project, £695, includes caravan or large excursion tent campsite accommodations, kitchen access (but not food costs), laundry, project training and tack equipment, airport transfers, local transportation, island orientation, and support.

DON'T MISS: If history and the gods are of interest, you need to seek out every stone and column throughout Greece. A good start is in **Delphi,** where the most important oracle in the world would announce predictions and cautions about the future and how the gods might intervene with man's fate. This city was also the site of the athletic competitions that eventually gave rise to the Olympic Games (they came later, in Olympia, of course), and worshippers of Apollo erected their temple in Delphi as well.

ⓘ www.gnto.gr

Conflict Resolution & Security

Volunteer Accompanier

The Power of an Outsider

Port-au-Prince, Haiti

DESPITE ITS REPUTATION FOR VIOLENCE, PORT-AU-PRINCE STILL SEES A LARGE NUMBER OF tourists each year and nearly as many aid workers. While the city lacks everything from basic infrastructure to significant security, what it does have is the indomitable sense of spirit of the people who live there.

You'll work alongside local Haitian citizens in their fight against human rights abuses, conducting important outreach in the streets, the courts, police stations, government offices, residential neighborhoods, and the homes of victims. Experience has shown that when a non-Haitian accompanies and advocates for the rights of Haitians, the tandem is able to achieve better results when dealing with those in a position of power. You don't need to be a lawyer, but you'll be a legal advocate; you're also not a bodyguard, but you can alert your Haitian partners to real dangers. It can be emotional and extremely frustrating to watch victims of human rights abuses be victimized again by a system that often refuses to come to their aid without the intervention of an outsider.

Poverty-stricken Port-au-Prince, Haiti

The organization's mission is to support non-violent human rights advocacy, free legal assistance, community training, and work on behalf of the poor. You'll accompany the organization's workers and legal team on their advocacy work detail, allowing you to see parts of Haiti that many never will—and there are some difficult inner-city places to be visited. You may be asked to advocate on behalf of a client, using the calm voice of an uninvolved party to improve the odds of success. While it might seem dangerous, historically the most effective accompaniers have been retirees.

Volunteer teams live in the project house in Port-au-Prince. Simple meals are provided, but there are plenty of restaurants to try and markets where you can buy groceries. Training, support, and safety are all covered, as is all in-country transportation. You'll likely find that free time is spent with the team in that invigorating grassroots way that keeps people up debating and solving all the world's problems well beyond a rational bedtime.

YOUR NEXT STEP: Human Rights Accompaniment In Haiti-Hurah (✆ **510/428-1419;** www.hurah-inc.org). A 9-day program, US$2,500, includes airfare to Port-au-Prince (from the United States), room and board at the project house, advocacy training, local transportation, and local staff support.

DON'T MISS: While Haiti has been plagued by poverty and civil unrest, it's also a beautiful natural sanctuary with pristine beaches and fantastic snorkeling and watersports. Although hurricane season can take a rough annual toll on the country, the beaches that avoid the brunt of the storms remain idyllic. **Port-Salut** is beloved by Haitians for beach getaways, and not yet discovered by hordes of tourists, so you can enjoy a tropical day at the seaside without the crowds.

ⓘ www.haititourisme.com

447 Conflict Resolution & Security

Army Base Volunteer Program

Civilian Support for Armed Forces

Nationwide, Israel

WHILE THE DAILY LIVES OF MOST PEOPLE IN THE COUNTRY ARE FILLED WITH WORK AND FAMILY, not war and conflict, the scars of history can be seen everywhere. Working on civilian projects with the defense forces here will help heal the wounds of history and make sure new ones aren't created.

Volunteers from around the world work side by side with the Israel Defense Forces (IDF) to do the non-combat work that keeps a military base running. Maintenance, kitchen duty, machinery repair, and other support work that doesn't require combat training can all be done by volunteers, thus freeing up the young men and women in the force to train as necessary for their defensive work. It's an intensive atmosphere run like any tight army operation, so it'll be clear at all times what is expected of you, as you're given orders.

You'll receive a uniform of (civilian) work clothes and boots before you begin packing medical supplies and cargo, repairing machinery or assisting mechanics as they maintain equipment, preparing and serving meals in the "mess," painting and repairing buildings and facilities, and pretty much anything else that would distract from a soldier's valuable training time. You get all the insight of serving in the military and aiding in the nation's defense without subjecting yourself to the dangers of armed combat.

You'll live in the barracks on the military base, and you'll be served three kosher meals daily. You won't have many opportunities to leave the base, so your unscheduled social time will be spent getting to know your volunteer colleagues and the young men and women of the fighting force.

YOUR NEXT STEP: National Council for Volunteering in Israel (www.ivolunteer.org.il). A 2-week project, US$80, includes army barracks accommodations, three kosher meals daily, instruction, uniform, and staff support.

DON'T MISS: Jerusalem's **Israel Museum**, the largest cultural institution in the country, is considered one of the finest art and archeological museums worldwide with a seemingly endless collection of biblical and ancient items, including the Dead Sea Scrolls, a reconstructed model of ancient Jerusalem, and an international sculpture garden that features works by Picasso, Oldenburg, Rodin, and more. www.english.imjnet.org.il

ⓘ www.goisrael.com

10 Memorials Where Your Help is Monumental

Memorials provide a place to remember and reflect upon those who have performed exemplary service or given their lives for the protection of others. Most memorials depend on volunteers to help keep them in good condition. There are opportunities around the world to pay an extra measure of respect at memorials you might visit.

448 **Alcatraz Island, California, USA** At Alcatraz, as well as the extended Golden Gate National Recreation Area and Muir Woods National Monument, there is plenty for you to do as a volunteer. You can collect data on raptors at the west coast's best hawk-watching site, you can do the important work of removing non-native plants and nurture native species at the park's nursery, or you can do restoration work on historic structures like the World War II barracks and mess hall. ***National Parks Service*** *(volunteer hotline ✆* ***415/561-4755****; www.nps.gov). No fee for volunteers.*

449 **La Jolla, California, USA** From a hilltop high above San Diego County, the Mount Soledad Memorial offers a 360-degree view of the surrounding open space. This peaceful spot has served as a war memorial since 1914; a large cross was erected in 1954 as a Korean War veterans memorial. The staff is mostly volunteers and there are short-term volunteer positions. ***Mount Soledad Memorial Association*** *(✆* ***877/204-7661****; www.soledadmemorial.com). No fee for visiting volunteers.*

The Mount Soledad Memorial in La Jolla, California

450 **Baton Rouge, Louisiana, USA** Spend a weekend aboard a destroyer ship that's been converted into a naval museum. Volunteers at the USS *KIDD* work with veterans and tradespeople to do maintenance and upkeep on the ship. Volunteers young (9 years minimum) and old, service members and civilians, spend a 3- or 4-day weekend in this live-aboard program. ***National Association of Destroyer Veterans/USS KIDD*** *(✆* ***800/223-5535****; www.usskidd.com). A 3-day stay: US$45 per person; a 4-day stay: US$55.*

451 **Liberty Island, New Jersey, USA** The Statue of Liberty is one of the best-known symbols of America. Volunteers work with National Parks Service rangers providing information and service to the visiting public. You could answer questions or even work with the archives and museum collection housed at Ellis Island. ***National Parks Service*** *(✆* ***212/363-3206****, ext. 134; www.volunteer.gov). No fee for volunteers.*

452 **West Deptford, New Jersey, USA** It's a Memorial Day tradition at grave sites across the United States. As a volunteer alongside members of the American Legion Post, you can work your way through Eglington Cemetery placing American flags on the graves of veterans. If you're in South Jersey for the Memorial Day weekend, this is a great way to spend a morning before heading to a parade or picnic. ***American Legion Post 100*** *(✆* ***856/845-8367****; www.legion.org). No fee for volunteers.*

453 **Asheville, North Carolina, USA** Asheville's Smith-McDowell House is an antebellum mansion with a long history, belonging to city mayors, a Confederate major, and Vanderbilt neighbors (the Biltmore Estate is not far). It's now a museum with memorial gardens that are home to the Buncombe County Civil War Memorial. Frederick Law Olmstead, Jr., designed the bucolic gardens, and volunteers work through the seasons on maintenance tasks in the gardens and the restored home. ***Smith-McDowell House Museum*** *(©* ***828/253-9231****; www.wnchistory.org). No fee for volunteers.*

454 **Westerly, Rhode Island, USA** The World War Memorial found at Wilcox Park/Westerly Library is a somber circle of banistered stone with a flagpole topping a pedestal. Tuesdays and Thursdays from April into early November, volunteers gather to perform seasonal tasks to keep the gardens and memorial in top shape. It's a great way to keep your thumb green while away from your own garden. ***Westerly Public Library-Wilcox Park*** *(©* ***401/596-2877****; www.westerlylibrary.org). No fee for volunteers.*

455 **Albany, New York, USA** While marble monuments are built to honor the "Greatest Generation" who served in World War II, one group of veterans found a way to be remembered that felt more organic and personal to them. Through their own funding and tenacity, they rescued the USS *Slater* from the scrap heap to create a museum honoring naval destroyer ships and the men who served upon them. The Destroyer Escort Historical Museum meticulously restores and preserves every inch of this ship with thousands of volunteer hours every year. ***Destroyer Escort Historical Museum*** *(©* ***518/431-1943****; www.ussslater.org). No fee for volunteers.*

456 **Valley Forge, Pennsylvania, USA** You read the history books about George Washington rallying his freezing troops at Valley Forge to somehow overcome the odds and push on. Now you can spend some fair-weather time (April-October) at Valley Forge working to keep the memorial site in tip-top shape. It's manual labor doing maintenance work, or you remove invasive crawfish from select waterways where they are overwhelming native species. ***National Parks Service*** *(©* ***610/783-1008****; www.nps.gov/vafo). No fee for volunteers.*

Maintaining the Valley Forge memorial site in Pennsylvania

457 **Washington DC, USA** The U.S. Navy Memorial in the nation's capital is a large memorial plaza with the statue The Lone Sailor as a tribute to all who have served on the seas. This place of honor has several nautical tributes as well as the Naval Heritage Center. Short-term volunteer posts include assisting visitors with information, conducting interviews for the Veterans History Project (in conjunction with the Library of Congress and the Navy Log), and conducting kid's activities for young visitors. ***United States Navy Memorial*** *(©* ***800/821-8892****; www.navymemorial.org). No fee for volunteers.*

Healing Postwar Communities **458**

Aid for Land Mine Victims

Touring & Building Wheelchairs

Siem Reap, Cambodia

A CITY CARVED FROM STONE, SIEM REAP CONTAINS CAMBODIA'S MOST ANCIENT AND BEAUTIFUL history, as well as its most troubling. In the land surrounding the ruins lay thousands of unexploded land mines. Their destructive power can be seen in the faces and bodies of Cambodians across the country. Sadly, the mines find new victims year after year.

This 2-month volunteer placement at Cambodia's Land Mine Museum Relief Facility between Siem Reap and Angkor Wat will test you emotionally and reward you more than you can imagine. Dedicated to victims of land mine explosions (many undiscovered land mines still remain buried in Cambodian soil), this museum also serves as a home for dozens of land-mine-affected children. It provides love, support, education, and the opportunity to heal victims' physical and emotional wounds, whether they've suffered a personal injury or lost a parent or other family member to mines. People often do not survive the detonation of a hidden mine and those that don't perish have a hard road ahead, helped by international volunteers.

Your volunteer time will be spent with the young residents at the relief facility who live in dormitories, attend classes in the facility's classroom, and take meals in the communal kitchen. You'll support the staff teacher with classroom work and also help teach English. You may also assist at the museum when needed, doing some light maintenance on completely safe exhibits of disarmed weapons and photographic collections or assisting visitors.

You'll be staying at Thida's House, which is a community guesthouse in Siem Reap. Rooms are shared by two volunteers and have private, cold-water bathrooms. You'll have access to a communal library and gardens, and breakfast is included. Lunch and dinner are on your own to dine at inexpensive restaurants or purchase food at the nearby Old Market to cook in the guesthouse kitchen. A 3-day orientation program, a Khmer-language class (though English is spoken on the project), town tour, and cultural specifics are also included.

YOUR NEXT STEP: Interweave (International Work Exchange and Volunteer Experiences) via BUNAC (✆ **+44/20 7251 3472;** ww.bunac.org). The 8-week project, £851, includes orientation and touring with guide, community guesthouse accommodations, breakfasts, and project training and support.

DON'T MISS: You'll have seen much of Cambodia touring around the country, so take a jaunt across the Gulf of Thailand for a little R&R in **Kuala Lumpur,** Malaysia. It's a large, futuristic city set against a background of tradition and ancient cultures. The marketplaces (both day and night) are a fascinating blend of old and new, loud and serene, simple and über-techie.

ⓘ www.tourismcambodia.com

459 Healing Postwar Communities

Rebuild & Rehabilitate

Helping Beach Town Get Back On Its Feet

Vilanculos, Mozambique

TECHICOLOR CORAL REEFS, NEVER-ENDING BEACHES, AND A LAID-BACK VIBE HAVE ATTRACTED backpackers to Vilanculos and nearby Bazaruto National Park for decades. Life in this sleepy fishing village revolves around the ocean: diving, snorkeling, all sorts of boating—not to mention the freshest fish imaginable. It's an idyllic setting that belies some of the country's troubled past.

In its 15-year civil war, Mozambique lost a million people to the war and another three million who escaped as refugees. An incapacitating drought in the 1990s killed many more, followed by extreme weather like cyclones and floods that destroyed homes and washed away struggling crops. Nature recovers more easily than mankind, so the beaches and national parks show some effects of the trauma but are nowhere near as scarred as the society. International volunteers reach out to the residents of this seaside city to help bolster the community, from home visits for the seriously ill to vocational training and children's sports and enrichment programs. Rebuilding projects and education programs are also facets of this multi-pronged effort to restore stability.

You'll be a whirlwind of activity, moving from one project to the next. Help out at the orphanage to get kids up, fed, and ready for school. Spend the rest of the morning visiting housebound elderly patients, or others unable to move around, and deliver food or run errands. After lunch, help with a community program of HIV/AIDS education before assisting with after-school soccer tournaments and instruction. Once the kids head home, there's rebuilding and finishing work to be done at the damaged school, so pick up a paintbrush or hammer. It's a good thing it's dinnertime because you just want to sit, but remember that this evening you're helping at the crafts workshop, where people are learning new and marketable skills to support themselves. And that's just today . . . . Tomorrow you'll take on a whole new slew of activities, perhaps in the bush outside of town where rural communities are also learning new crafts and vocations, being introduced to English language courses, and getting HIV/AIDS prevention workshops. There is less physical rebuilding in the bush since the structures were practically eliminated and so people started fresh—but the societal rebuilding from the ravages of war is an ongoing process of growth and healing.

You'll live by the beach in thatched bungalows with separate bathrooms and showers as well as a swimming pool and common dining area. Three meals daily are prepared for you, and when you're not running from one work assignment to the next, there is extraordinary snorkeling among pristine reefs and kilometers of beach on which to laze away and recharge your batteries. For extra fees, the hosting organization can arrange a PADI scuba diving course for certification, dhow cruises and diving, and deep-sea fishing.

YOUR NEXT STEP: Volunteer Adventures (✆ **866/574-8606;** www.volunteeradventures.com). A 2-week project, US$1,455, includes airport transfers, beach bungalow accommodations, meals, project transportation, training, local orientation upon arrival, and local staff support.

DON'T MISS: If your schedule and circumstances allow a bit of luxury after your volunteer work, drop out for a few days at Mozambique's **Medjumbe Private Island.** A tiny spit of land in the Quirimbas Archipelago, this is a tropical hideaway where only a few beach chalets dot the silver sands, and you can enjoy phenomenal diving and watersports, or spend long, uninterrupted days and nights at the beach.

ⓘ www.mozambiquetourism.co.za

Healing Postwar Communities 460

Post-Genocide Recovery

Working With Homeless & Orphaned Children

Kigali, Rwanda

THIS LANDLOCKED REPUBLIC OF RWANDA IS BEST KNOWN FOR THE GENOCIDE THAT OCCURED here, and more than 15 years later people in Kigali are still struggling with the past. An influx of adventure tourists, on their way to gorilla-watch in nearby Parc National des Volcans, or trek through Ngorongoro Crater and the Serengeti National Park, are bringing much-needed money and attention to a place that at one point the rest of the world forgot.

Rwanda has recovered somewhat since the genocide of 1994, but the country is far from healed and is still dependent on outside aid. Poverty, hunger, HIV/AIDS, and multiple health issues continue to plague the country. This project works with local Rwandan grassroots agencies to eradicate poverty and the health crisis that stems from it. A multifaceted program for volunteer work includes children's programs, HIV/AIDS education, gender inequality issues and gender-based violence, and developing small business initiatives. The organization is Christian-based but open to volunteers of all faiths.

You'll work among the thousands and thousands of homeless and orphaned Rwandan children. You'll help with daily care, such as feeding, life skills instruction, and some recreation and entertainment. Your additional input in developing art or expression programs and sports instruction widens the horizons of the children. Schools are woefully undersupplied and barely staffed, so a literacy program is also part of this project (estimates are that 30 percent of Rwandan schools were destroyed and more than 3,000 teachers murdered during the genocide). You'll work with classroom teachers on math, English, health, and hygiene instruction, as well as after-school literacy programs for children who don't attend school. HIV/AIDS education outreach helps spread the word about transmission and prevention, as well as supporting those living with HIV. Work is in care homes and hospitals, as well as outreach at community centers and schools. You'll work with women in the gender-based violence counseling and visitation program in shelters and homes, and support the vocational training programs for oppressed women who have created small co-op retail businesses selling crafts and local agricultural products. The businesses will benefit from any managerial or marketing mentoring you can provide.

You'll live with your fellow volunteers in a group house in Kigali. You'll share a room with another volunteer, and meals are provided at the house. Local support helps you get the lay of the land in the city so your free time can be spent exploring, but most volunteer teams find there is barely enough time to spend together, bonding over this difficult but life-changing experience, while also spending unscheduled evenings or weekend time with families in the community.

YOUR NEXT STEP: Global Volunteer Network (✆ **+64/4 569 9080;** www.volunteer.org.nz). A minimum 2-week commitment, US$647, includes group housing, meals, airport transfers, local transportation, local staff support, and a donation to the host organization. AUS$350 application fee is required.

DON'T MISS: For visitors, the most iconic Rwandan residents have to be the mountain gorillas. There are several opportunities to go on a genuinely magical **gorilla trek** that usually entails a couple hours of rigorous hiking through the hills with experienced trackers who have spent their lives in and around this dense forest. When you get to spend an hour with the gentle gorillas as they rest, feed, play with their young, and benignly stare at you, you'll be glad you persevered.

ⓘ www.rwandatourism.com

461 Healing Postwar Communities

Burmese Learners Program

Education & Training

Chiang Mai, Thailand

Learning English, as well as computer skills, is essential for Burmese refugees and migrants fleeing violence, discrimination, and economic hardship. You can help them build a new life in Chiang Mai, a spectacular city with all the amenities of Bangkok in a far more serene setting.

Along with the violence perpetuated by the regime in Burma (also known as Myanmar) against many of its people, basic education is often withheld. Many cross the border to Thailand seeking asylum and better opportunities. This migrant learner center is a project that gives them a real chance. The military junta in Burma threatens these people, but discrimination and exploitation in Thailand make life difficult here as well. This program provides vocational and language training free of charge to minority group members to better their chances at viable employment and a stable way of life.

You'll be teaching English language within small conversation groups as well as some written work. Native-speaking staff will also be teaching them Burmese and Thai languages, so your students, most of whom are adults, will be working very hard. You'll also empower them by providing basic computer training and support. As donated machines become more accessible, computer skills bring out employment possibilities that used to be unattainable. The confidence that these migrants gain from English conversation skills and computer literacy makes them strong candidates in local job markets.

You'll retire each night to the group house in the center of Old Chiang Mai, near plentiful shops, pubs, and restaurants. You'll share a room and be served home-cooked Thai meals by the in-house cook. On your first day, you'll be given a thorough local tour and cultural orientation. Local project staff are always willing to make recommendations for day trips or just an afternoon's distraction around Chiang Mai during your downtime.

Burmese students at the migrant learner center in Chiang Mai, Thailand

YOUR NEXT STEP: **Cultural Canvas Thailand** (✆ **850/316-8470;** www.culturalcanvas.com). A 3-week project, US$1,399, includes shared group house accommodations, three meals daily, airport transfers, in-country orientation, insurance, project training and support, and 24-hour assistance.

DON'T MISS: American entrepreneur Jim Thompson practically single-handedly made Thai silk an international phenomenon when he moved to the country and revolutionized the industry, making him the most recognized foreigner in Bangkok. He mysteriously disappeared in 1967 while traveling through Malaysia, and no trace has ever been found. His residence, moved to Bangkok, has become a popular museum. Jim Thompson's House has several traditional Thai buildings on the grounds, as well as an extensive art and antiques collection, plus his personal belongings, most of them just as he left them. www.jimthompsonhouse.com

ⓘ www.tourismthailand.org

Working With & For Veterans **462**

Veterans Health Care Assistance

Serving Those Who Served

Fayetteville, Arkansas, USA

SITTING IN THE SHADOW OF THE OZARK MOUNTAINS, THIS SPRAWLING TOWN IN NORTHWEST Arkansas is steeped in military tradition and history. It's a fitting site for one of the country's largest veterans hospitals, as it is also the resting place for hundreds of Confederate soldiers and their storied leaders. Many of the veterans you'll be helping here are seniors—themselves part of American history.

Veterans hospitals and health-care facilities can always use volunteer power for everything from patient assistance to greeting visitors or just pushing around the library cart. Here at the Veterans Health Care System of the Ozarks, you can pitch in for 1 day or many or throughout your entire vacation in the Fayetteville/Little Rock area. Some of the volunteer tasks require a driver's license (for driving the shuttle van), and some would be a better fit if you have some medical knowledge (or at least comfort with hospital work), but most require very little training or prior knowledge. Much of the work is in helping former military personnel, many of them seniors, with their care and well-being.

If you can push a cart, you're halfway there for many of the tasks required. You can be the smiling face behind the coffee cart visiting waiting rooms and in-patient and out-patient areas, you could bring the comfort cart around to patient rooms, perhaps the magazine and book cart is more your style, or you could be the ideal crafts cart volunteer, delivering supplies and ideas to make a project. Van drivers transport disabled patients to clinic appointments as needed, and golf cart drivers pick up patients and their families and other visitors in the parking lot and bring them to the medical center. Escort volunteers push wheelchair-bound patients to appointments, and administrative helpers answer phones, file, and greet patients and visitors. You could assist the pharmacist with pre-packed medications, take vital signs for outpatients, run lab samples and X-rays to the upstairs laboratories, or set up lunch trays to ready them for room delivery. Your enthusiasm and willingness to take on any task makes you a great fit at the medical center.

There are no travel, lodging, or meal arrangements or fee for visiting volunteers. Before you get to Fayetteville, contact the hospital to let them know you've got some time to give and a desire to serve.

YOUR NEXT STEP: VA Medical Center (✆ **479/443-4301;** www.fayettevillear.va.gov). You'll make your own arrangements for your stay in Arkansas, and volunteer for as long as is convenient for you.

DON'T MISS: As someone inclined to look for a volunteer vacation, you may already know about **Heifer International** and its tireless work to end world hunger by donating livestock to villages around the world. You can tour its headquarters—one of the world's greenest buildings—in Little Rock, Arkansas. Every element was designed to be environmentally responsible, from recycled materials to innovative recycling projects (everything from rainwater to

Heifer International headquarters in Little Rock, Arkansas

energy is recycled). It's a true model of working in harmony with the earth. Then head a short distance out of town to the Heifer's ranch, where you can learn more about the mission and meet some of the animals, from water buffalo to bunnies, camels to cows. www.heifer.org

ⓘ www.accessfayetteville.org

Working With & For Veterans

463

Veterans Memorial Homes

Entertaining the Troops

Menlo, Paramus, & Vineland, New Jersey, USA

LESS THAN AN HOUR FROM MIDTOWN MANHATTAN, THE TOWNS OF MENLO PARK, PARAMUS, and Vineland have more to offer than just their proximity to NYC. Your work with veterans will bring a poignant connection to the local community you explore.

The initial concept of a veterans home originated in New Jersey with Governor Marcus Ward during the Civil War. In 1866, the state's first home was dedicated to provide respite, shelter, and care for ill, injured, or aged military and former military personnel. These three main memorial homes continue to break ground in nursing and support for war veterans. The Vineland Veterans Memorial Home opened in 1899 and has been providing residential and long-term care for every conflict since. The Paramus residence is on 9ha (23 acres), is host to 336 residents, and has its own monument to those who served in World War I, World War II, Korea, and Vietnam. The Menlo Park home is the most modern nursing home in the United States, with a "town square" design and cutting-edge facilities and medical services.

You can work at one, two, or all three of these contemporary facilities. Volunteer visitors come in every day to provide companionship, visit patients who may not have family close by, share stories and recreational time, organize and throw parties and holiday celebrations, accompany residents on bus trips to museums, parks, or other cultural sites, lead games and physical recreation programs (chair aerobics, yoga, meditation, and so on), and work on entertainment programs—which could be anything from accompanying singing residents on the piano to calling at a square dance to being the master of ceremonies at a talent show.

The veterans organizations don't make arrangements for travel, lodging, or meals but are happy to have you come to the homes when your travels bring you this way. Contact the volunteer coordinator at each home to offer your services.

YOUR NEXT STEP: New Jersey Department of Military and Veterans Affairs (Menlo Park volunteer coordinator: ✆ **732/452-4133;** Paramus volunteer coordinator: ✆ **201/634-8504;** Vineland volunteer coordinator: ✆ **856/405-4213;** www.nj.gov/military/veterans/health.html). You'll plan your own New Jersey vacation and get in touch with one or more of these facilities to lend a hand.

DON'T MISS: **Cape May** is the oldest seashore resort town on the East Coast. This section of Jersey Shore has one of the nation's top beaches, some of the best birding, and plenty of colonial charm (with some gorgeous Victorian residential architecture—known as the "painted ladies"). It's the only city in the United States that is designated a National Historic Landmark.

ⓘ www.state.nj.us/travel

USO

Giving Service Members a Taste of Home

Worldwide

THE GREAT THING ABOUT THE UNITED SERVICE ORGANIZATIONS (USO) IS THAT NO MATTER where you are in the world, you can volunteer with them. Operating out of North America, the Middle East, Europe, and Asia, the USO serves millions of army, navy, air force, and marine members—as well as their families.

It's not just Bob Hope and other famous entertainers who contribute to the USO's work, improving the quality of life of American service members, boosting their morale, and serving as a link between them and the public. More than 10,000 regular volunteers work with the USO in bases and places around the world. Welcome home events, care packages, letter writing campaigns, and myriad other projects by USO volunteers let army soldiers, air force, marine, and navy troops know that they are supported "until the last one comes home." There are chances for you to be involved in most American states and several countries overseas.

Your efforts can make a real difference in the morale and mood of service members. You can meet a soldier at an airport and help with a connecting flight, help pack and distribute the many care packages being sent to deployed troops every week, serve snacks at a USO center, or be part of a welcome home greeting party. One hundred and thirty centers, with free Internet and email for military, plus libraries and reading rooms, are staffed predominantly by volunteers who provide information and support in permanent facilities, as well as at meeting places out in the field. The programs reach 1.4 million active duty service members and 1.2 National Guard and Reserves and their families.

There are no travel, lodging, or meal arrangements for volunteers, but in most states you might visit, as well as several foreign countries through Europe, Asia, and the Middle East, there are USO centers and mobile units who would gladly have your help for a few hours, days, weeks, or whatever you have to give.

YOUR NEXT STEP: USO (© **888/484-3876;** www.uso.org). You'll make your own travel plans, but if you find you have the time, check for the nearest USO post or center you can reach from your vacation spot and find a way to lend support.

14 *Spiritual Service*

A statue of Mary along the route of Southern Ontario's Walking Pilgrimage

465 Retreats

Tiger Temple

Buddhism & Big Cats

Kanchanaburi, Thailand

THE MOUNTAINOUS TERRAIN OF KANCHANABURI SHARES A BORDER AND A LITTLE OF ITS FOOD and culture with Burma. It's become a well-trod tourist destination thanks to a wealth of wildlife sanctuaries, jungle trekking, and explorable caves. You may not think that the peaceful practice of Buddhism and man-eating tigers have anything in common, but if you choose to volunteer in Kanchanaburi, you'll soon see why they do.

You may have seen the Tiger Temple, and its charismatic big cats, on one of many adventure or animal television programs. The tigers, most of whom were orphaned by poachers, are cared for by saffron-robed Thai monks, making the forest monastery a television producer's dream. While the tigers here are stars, they are also semi-wild animals that need plenty of care and attention from the monks, as well as international volunteers. Those who come live as monks, meditating, seeking inner guidance, walking full-grown tigers on leashes, feeding them, and generally caring for them and the many other animals at the sanctuary. This program is a unique opportunity to blend tigers and Buddhism.

Your days are spent in meditation and prayer sessions with the monks and the abbot, as well as feeding the animals, cleaning cages, and working on new naturally styled enclosures that will serve as a new home for the tigers. It's tough work and long hours for a 6-day workweek. The well-known tigers also get visitors

A Buddhist monk poses with two giant tigers at the Tiger Temple in Kanchanaburi.

throughout the day, sometimes entire busloads, so you may need to help get them ready as well as teach what you've learned about tiger conservation and the perils facing this endangered species. Tourists are also able to interact with some of the tigers, and volunteers are on hand to keep the visitors (and the cats) safe. If the need arises, you may also assist the veterinarian, do some data work and administrative office help, and small maintenance chores.

You'll be living a Buddhist lifestyle at the sanctuary, in very simple forest shelters for solitary, hermit-like exploration, or in separate men's and women's rooms with electricity and showers available. Your free time is expected to be spent in meditation, and there are some specific rules about behavior and conduct at this active monastery: no perfume or jewelry; white clothes must be worn for meditation; no dancing or singing; no sleeping on a luxurious bed; and certain foods can only be eaten at certain times (all meals are provided). It's a reverent and ascetic environment dedicated to inner searching as well as caring for the tigers. There is a certainty that the tigers were monks in a former life, so they are brethren and treated that way.

YOUR NEXT STEP: Wat Pa Luangta Bua Yannasampanno Forest Monastery (Tiger Temple) 🎗 (✆ **034-531-557;** www.tigertemple.org). The monks require a minimum 1-month commitment, with expectations of a 6-day workweek, daily meditation, and temple services. Meals and accommodations are provided. No fee for volunteers.

DON'T MISS: Not far from the Tiger Temple is the **Lopburi Monkey Temple,** San Phra Kan. Here among the ruins of a once grand stone temple are hundreds of monkeys freely running, playing, sleeping, and swinging from the trees. They may try to jump on your back, but while used to humans, make no mistake: these are still wild animals (and they tend to be extraordinarily curious about glasses and jewelry, so remove any shiny objects before heading into the temple area).

ⓘ www.tourismthailand.org

Retreats 466

World Peace Ashram

Gardening in the Desert

Concho, Arizona, USA

ONE OF THE COUNTRY'S ORIGINAL PIONEER TOWNS, CONCHO IS A PLACE YOU CAN CONFIDENTLY call "off the beaten path." Lying on the edge of the White Mountains, the village has maintained a small-town feel while hosting people who flock to the area to hike, horseback, and hunt. But if you're more into meditation than recreation, Arizona's most famous ashram is for you.

This spiritual community center in the Arizona desert is a portal to deeper meditative work for those of all faiths. A place of silence and reflection, free of crowds and technology, the ashram allows you to get in touch with the higher power you seek while simultaneously finding harmony in nature in the desert. There is also the satisfaction of working hard to physically improve the ashram itself. It's a chance for a short-term monk-like respite, with hours of contemplation and meditation balanced with physical service working to beautify the grounds and gardens. The goal is to return a portion of the land to its natural wildness. The retreat staff and visitors share the belief that working the land is itself a form of spirituality.

You won't have a specific schedule during your time at the ashram, but when work time comes, you'll be outside and offering your help by weeding the gardens, stringing fence lines, trimming trees, harvesting fruits and vegetables, and generally working to make the cultivated portion of these 32ha (80 acres) bountiful. Your work will move the group's goals forward as you make progress toward your own.

In exchange for your contribution, you'll get free lodging in a small cabin with no water or electricity, and two meals daily. You determine your schedule, but on "days off" your meals are your own responsibility. Free time is the serene pursuit of your own spiritual awakening, and, except for trips into town for supplies or to sup at a restaurant, will likely be spent alone in silence amid nature.

YOUR NEXT STEP: Desert Monastery (✆ **928/337-2492;** www.desertmonastery.org). There is no fee for working volunteers, who are provided with a small private cabin (no utilities) and two meals daily. You'll get to the retreat on your own and stay for the amount of time agreed upon with the resident staff.

DON'T MISS: Though you'll already be in tune with the magnificence of nature, spend some time after your retreat in the stunning red rock canyons and energy vortices of **Sedona, Arizona.** This is a magnet for New Age healers and those attuned to energy, who claim that the area is home to intense points of universal vibrations that thrum loudly in the oak canyons and cliffs, amid the ruins of ancient Native American dwellings and cave paintings.

ⓘ www.arizonaguide.com

467 Retreats

Christian Camp Retreat

Enjoy & Improve Wooded Sanctuary

Higgins Lake, Michigan, USA

MOST FOLKS COME TO HIGGINS LAKE, MICHIGAN TO CANOE, KAYAK, FISH, OR SIMPLY EXPLORE the lake's more than 40 sq. km (15 sq. miles). Combine these outdoor pursuits with a healthy dose of spirituality at the Christian Camp Retreat: enjoy the camping lifestyle, learn about the Bible, and help keep the retreat running at the same time.

This mission work camp on crystal-clear Higgins Lake allows you or your group to have a full retreat while improving the center for a few hours. It's an old-fashioned Bible camp experience, where participants (mostly from church groups) spend time in communal dining and prayer, the fellowship of hikes and ropes courses, and just sitting around a campfire toasting marshmallows. A week's mission includes plenty of time in reflection and prayer, as well as some work activities, which are mostly maintenance chores.

You'll have some workdays sprinkled in with your camp fun as you tackle tasks like scraping and painting exteriors, interior painting and staining, mulching, raking, and planting in the gardens, harvesting what is grown, and some light construction work building or rebuilding structures or benches. This is group work, so you'll be sharing the effort for the greater good of the retreat and making a direct contribution to the place where you'll find so much comfort and grace. The camp retreat has been hosting religious groups since 1925 and takes the work of a lot of friends and volunteers to keep the 40 buildings, outdoor chapel, and recreational facilities up to snuff.

Your accommodations are in the main lodge, which sleeps 20, with fireplaces and common areas plus a kitchen. The woodsy environment makes for quiet nights.

YOUR NEXT STEP: Camp Westminster (✆ **313/341-8969;** www.campwestminster.com). A 3-day weekend is free for working volunteers. You provide your own transportation and sleeping bag, and the camp provides leadership, spiritual support, lodging, and food.

DON'T MISS: Those who enjoy the nautical life should spend a day with a boat tour of the **Soo Locks,** the largest waterway traffic system on Earth. You'll travel into Canada, and later work your way to other sites like the Straits of Mackinac, Mackinac Island, St. Ignace, Mackinac Bridge, Drummond Island, and the state's oldest city, Sault Ste. Marie.

ⓘ www.michigan.org

Faith-Based Assistance **468**

Methodist Habitat

Improving the Lives of Locals

Several Islands, Bahamas

IF IT'S "BETTER IN THE BAHAMAS," AS THE FAMOUS SAYING GOES, IT COULD BE SAID THAT volunteering there must be better as well. This string of 29 islands in Caribbean Sea exists on tourism, although many ordinary Bahamians still live in very poor conditions. Volunteering here will forge close relationships with locals and let you see the real side of island life, something most tourists never experience.

The Methodist Habitat project works with volunteer teams and individuals on community improvement projects in the Bahamian islands. Building homes, taking on structural maintenance and repair, organizing and leading a vacation Bible school, music programs, and community workshops are just some of the projects that volunteers undertake as a contribution to island life. The labor is seen as worship and sharing the gifts of God while ministering to the Bahamian locals. While there is no religious requirement, volunteers are expected to live and work within the guidelines of the Methodist project covenant. If you're part of a church, family, or social team coming together for the work project, and choose to do construction work, you're expected to have a team leader with building experience and skills to lead.

Volunteers build homes for needy families while simultaneously ministering to the children and adults in the community. Your project needs will vary depending on when you schedule your trip, your skills and interests, and how much of a particular project was completed by previous volunteers. Most of the need is practical, so it's likely you'll be swinging a hammer or paintbrush. Other spiritual growth projects include Bible study lessons or camp, music programs with devotional and secular songs, and building, repairing, and beautifying churches and places of worship.

You'll be living with other volunteers in dormitories and will be provided with

Methodist Habitat volunteers break to admire the Caribbean Sea.

three meals daily. Since the project determines which island you'll be on, accommodations will vary but all are basic and comfortable. Free time tends to be spent with locals and the volunteer team in worship and fellowship activities, as well as some simple relaxation or exploration time to see the island and meet others in the community. Recreational activities will also vary depending upon the project location.

YOUR NEXT STEP: Methodist Habitat (✆ **615/469-7974;** www.methodist-habitat.org). A 1-week project, US$500, includes dormitory lodging, meals, airport transfers and transportation to work sites, tools (though bringing more to use or donate is strongly encouraged), and project support. Free time is spent in fellowship and worship among the group and ministering to locals.

DON'T MISS: You'll find natural splendor and adventure throughout the Bahamas, but for old-school exploration, follow in Hemingway's footsteps to the island of **Bimini.** Actually two islands, North Bimini and South Bimini, you'll likely spend the bulk of your time in Alice Town, way out on a spit of land that looks like a fishing pole. It's a good base for kayaking, snorkeling, sailing, and relaxation.

ⓘ www.bahamas.com

469 Faith-Based Assistance

Youth Village

Teaching Teens

Hadera, Israel

Halfway between the ethnically mixed city of Haifa and über-hip Tel Aviv is Hadera, most famous for being the site of the ancient city of Caesarea and its perfectly restored Roman Theatre. In Hadera, you can walk through history—over the same land once covered in gladiator blood, where Pontius Pilate once lived, and where the Apostle Peter baptized so many.

This youth village is for Israel's most disadvantaged boys, ages 12 to 18, many of whom are Ethiopian immigrants or from the former Soviet Union. Male and female volunteers come from around the world for this Jewish faith-based project focused on helping the youngsters overcome educational gaps and to integrate into mainstream Israeli society. About 120 students live and learn at the youth village, with particular support given to those with learning disabilities or behavioral problems. The learning issues put these kids years behind their peers in scholastic development, and volunteers and staff work intensely with them on schoolwork, as well as social and psychological programs. Extracurricular activities like sports, horseback riding, music, dance, arts, ceramics, carpentry, and karate keep the kids actively engaged and interested in learning.

You'll help the residential staff in working with small groups and individuals. You'll focus on classroom work, as you mentor kids and help them with homework and learning projects after their classes. You can also take on more creative activities: groom, tack up, and ride horses with a couple of the kids; help them with the care and proprietorship of the small on-site farm and petting zoo; teach a new sport or supervise and coach existing games; create a talent competition or performance event; or teach a student to build a chair or cabinet. Most of these young men come from troubled or broken families, so the presence of a caring and nurturing adult who is focused on them is a big contribution to their future success.

The boarding school is a residential facility, and volunteers live on-site in private or semi-private rooms shared with other adult volunteers. Meals are shared with the group, as is free time and activities, so there are few opportunities to go far from the youth village itself. The length of your stay is up to you, as short-term and long-term volunteers are needed and welcomed.

YOUR NEXT STEP: Jewish Agency for Israel (via **JGooders** ✆ **+972/02-620-2878;** www.jgooders.com and www.jewishagency.org). There is no fee for volunteers who come for as little as 1 week (but many make much longer commitments). Lodging and meals are included, as is the support of local residential staff.

DON'T MISS: Visiting Jerusalem is a must for any traveler to Israel, and to have a spectacular perspective on the Old City, take a walk. The **Walls Promenade** is a walking route along the tops of the walls of the Old City, from where you can see down into the maze of crooked lanes and look out across Western Jerusalem. The promenade starts at the Tower of David and ends at the Jewish Quarter or at the Western Wall.

ⓘ www.goisrael.com

Faith-Based Assistance **470**

Healing Religious Division

Solidifying the Peace

Belfast & Ballycastle, Northern Ireland

Travelers were once warned away from the four Bs: Beirut, Bosnia, Baghdad, and Belfast. Today Belfast (and Ballycastle) are known more for tourism than the "Troubles," having undergone a renaissance in recent years. Religious conflicts haven't entirely disappeared, but these days Belfasters are more interested in partying than politics.

Volunteers come to learn about the situation in Northern Ireland, mixing volunteer work with an extensive program of workshops and talks by leaders in the peace process. The local partner organization for this project works with people from all Christian traditions to find harmony in this region still divided by religious differences. Volunteers work with schools and youth groups, support families and family organizations, and explore multidenominational faith-based education. The wounds between Catholics and Protestants are still fresh here, so finding common ground is critically important work.

Writing on the Peace Wall in Belfast, Northern Ireland

Your workdays will be divided between cultural and touring activities to surrounding villages in the mornings and community service projects in the afternoons. After-school youth groups are a chance for ministering and helping kids learn ways to express themselves and share their experiences. Family support programs give direct aid to those coping with breakdowns, the incarceration of a family member, or domestic violence, as well as practical survival issues such as hunger and education. There is also a children's bereavement program in which you can help kids coping with the death of a family member. Christian education programs need you to support the after-school programs that explore contemporary issues facing Christian communities and work at developing newly inclusive worship open to everyone. Your work will be in many locations, in both Protestant and Catholic neighborhoods, and the community centers striving to minister to both.

Your home base will be at a religious retreat center or hostel with shared rooms and bathrooms. Meals are provided and taken together with the volunteer community. There are scheduled cultural exploration field trips as well as an educational series to help you understand the "Troubles" from the perspective of each community. You'll be taken to museums and places of worship, to the town of Derry, the City of Walls, and Northern Ireland's Parliament. There is a full and diverse itinerary that will leave plenty of time for worship as well, and you'll come home an expert on the religious struggles of the country.

YOUR NEXT STEP: Amizade (☎ **304/293-6049;** www.amizade.org). A 2-week project, US$2,928, covers shared housing, meals, in-country transportation, and a thorough program of cultural classes and field trips as well as coaching and support for the array of volunteer tasks the group will pursue.

DON'T MISS: For an entirely different spiritual perspective on Northern Irish history, visit the mysterious pagan **Beaghmore Stone Circles.** Discovered in the 1940s, the site has seven stone circles, the rings connected by stone rows that create a fascinating pattern, thought to be burial markers, ceremonial grounds, and perhaps even a way to attract the sun to bring fertility back to the region's ruined soil. The stone rows correspond to the arc of the sun in midwinter, and it is believed the structures date to 1,600 b.c., though tools from 1,000 years earlier have also been discovered here.

ⓘ www.discovernorthernireland.com

10 Religious Pilgrimages with Service Elements

No matter what faith you come from, from the devout to the doubting, you can find a journey that is important and relevant for you. With these spiritually focused pilgrimages, you work on your connection to the divine and to yourself, while leaving the places you visit better than you found them.

471 **Thimphu, Bhutan** This Buddhist pilgrimage has inspired spiritual seekers for generations; communities of monks dot the steep mountain trails on the way to the cliffside Tiger's Nest Monastery. Your journey will be custom-designed to match your interests, including where to focus your volunteer efforts. You'll have the opportunity to serve the pilgrimage stops and participate in holy ceremonies. ***Amitabha Bhutan Tours*** *(© **+975-2-337799**; www.amitabha-bhutan.com). Itineraries for pilgrimages are customized, so duration and price varies widely.*

Along the peaceful trails of the Walking Pilgrimage in Southern Ontario

472 **Southern Ontario, Canada** No religious affiliation is required for this 8-day walking pilgrimage from Guelph to the Jesuit Martyr's Shrine in Midland. Every year, hundreds make the trek, walking for 8 hours a day and camping in farmers' fields or churchyards. Volunteers, some walking and some riding in support vehicles, make the practicalities fall into place. ***Ignatius Jesuit Centre*** *(www.ignatiusguelph.ca). Costs average US$150 for 8 days.*

473 **Lourdes, France** Every Easter, thousands of children with disabilities or special needs are taken on a healing pilgrimage to Lourdes, and every child has at least one volunteer assigned to them. While religion and prayer play a large part in the activities, no specific faith is required for the children, their families, or the volunteers. There are torchlight processions, a 5,000-person-strong Trust Mass in an underground basilica, and time to explore Lourdes and the hallowed sites. ***The Pilgrimage Trust*** *(© **+44/01788 564646**; www.hcpt.org.uk). A 7-night trip is £689 for volunteers.*

474 **Ladakh, India** The group travels in the beautiful mountains of Northwestern India to Buddhist monasteries, temples, and other holy sites each day, works together with nightly meditation sessions, and participates in volunteer activities to help locals. One day you'll plant trees along the banks of the river, another day you'll fill springwater vessels to supply a local hospital and donate a solar panel to a village. You'll also meet with monks and holy people at each site. ***Global Eco Spiritual Tours*** *(© **561/266-0096**; www.globalecospiritualtours.org). A 12-day trip is US$2,500.*

475 **Talpa de Allende, Mexico** Touring Puerto Vallarta as a religious pilgrim is done by thousands of visitors who make one of three treks every year. The Talpa Church in the Sierra Madre Mountains is a particularly sacred site, while the shrine of the Virgin Rosario of Talpa is known to have healing powers. Partner organizations

set up a day or several days of volunteer work based on your desire and interest with children's programs in Talpa or in Puerto Vallarta. ***About Puerto Vallarta*** *(© **866/321-1730**; www.aboutpuerto-vallarta.com). Duration, itinerary, and cost will vary depending on your requests.*

Tourists walk along a sea wall in Puerto Vallarta

476 **Palestine and Israel** This is a unique chance to tour the land where Jesus was born and lived, while contributing to the Palestinian Christian community. You will meet with locals and pray in their churches, and the focus is on the people more than just the sacred sites. You can assist in local schools, medical clinics, and food programs, and you'll have the chance to dine, work, and pray with both Palestinian and Israeli community members. ***Holy Land Trust*** *(© **+972/2-2765930**; http://travel.holylandtrust.org). An 11-day tour is US$1,500.*

477 **Sacred Valley, Peru** This is a spiritual quest with an Andean medicine man, healer, and wisdom keeper in the Peruvian Andes, including Machu Picchu. You'll visit sacred sites and participate in ceremonies to provide healing to individuals, families, and the community. The group will also work with locals on agricultural projects and then help out at the schools, beautify and rehabilitate public buildings and homes in the shaman's village, and care for the grounds around the sacred sites. ***Lux World Travel*** *(© **866/269-2659**; www.luxworldtravel.com). An 8-day pilgrimage is US$2,620.*

478 **West Marin, California, USA** The Dharma Wheels Buddhist Bicycle Pilgrimage is a 2-day, 241km (150-mile) ride from San Francisco to the Mendocino Abhayagiri Monastery. The ride is free and done in the spirit of *dana*, or generosity, and is dependent upon the work of volunteers. Participants make donations in appreciation for the spiritual teachings provided during the ride. ***DharmaWheels*** *(www.dharmawheels.org). No fee for volunteers.*

479 **Stockton, Massachusetts, USA** Pilgrims make a journey regularly to the National Shrine of the Divine Mercy in Stockbridge to join in prayer and meditation on Eden Hill. On the first Sunday after Easter, Catholic pilgrims and other volunteers come from across the Americas to minister to the pilgrims. ***The National Shrine of the Divine Mercy*** *(© **413/298-1322**; www.thedivinemercy.com). No fee for volunteers.*

480 **Worldwide** Christian Surfers International sends volunteer missionaries to some of the globe's gnarliest wave spots to find a closer relationship to their Lord and spread the Word. Samoa, Cape Town, Fiji, Indonesia, Japan, Tahiti, the Canary Islands, Costa Rica, Bali—they all host volunteer surf pilgrimages. You'll teach kids to surf, teach the Bible, and undertake community improvement projects. ***Christian Surfers International*** *(© **+61-2-4268-2783**; www.christiansurfers.net). No fee for volunteers.*

Faith-Based Assistance **481**

Teaching English to Buddhist Monks

Learning From Those You Teach

Galle, Sri Lanka

Fully recovered from 2004's massive tsunami, the city of Galle has a European look but a distinctly Sri Lankan flavor. Close to the city center are pristine beaches, tropical rainforests, and lush parkland, while Buddhism and cricket vie for the attention of Galle's citizens. Teaching English to Buddhist monks here will be enlightening to say the least.

Young men devoted to Buddhism, ages 8 to 21, learn and live separately from other children their age in temple schools, many of which are understaffed. Teaching English to the young monks is an amazing way for you to make a contribution to the spiritual community while completely immersing yourself in Buddhist life, teachings, and study. Helping them in other subjects is also appreciated, so your assistance in teaching art, math, music, or sport is welcome.

While working with the monks, you'll lead English conversations and classroom lessons to help them get a comfort level with the spoken language. The facilities are simple, with no computers or other complex technologies. Labor and effort are done by hand, and communication is with sound or ink, which makes your role as a mentor or teacher all the more important.

You'll live with a host family in Galle, who will provide you with your own room and three meals daily. Your evening and weekend time can be spent learning the Buddhist philosophy and lifestyle, as you have the unparalleled opportunity to deepen your spiritual practice or learn new insights. Meditation will pass many hours on your own or at temple. It is a reverent culture, and by taking the role of teacher for the monks, your contribution and presence is also revered. There are also ample opportunities to explore the beaches of Sri Lanka or visit the many mosques, churches, and Buddhist and Hindu temples in the villages nearby.

YOUR NEXT STEP: Global Crossroad (✆ **972/252-4191;** www.globalcrossroad.com). A 2-week project, US$1,064, includes host-family accommodations, meals, project training and support, airport transfers, insurance, and spiritual exploration activities as well as cultural orientation and introductory language lessons. The **Institute for Field Research Expeditions** 🎗 (✆ **800/675-2504;** www.ifrevolunteers.org) also offers a 2-week project, US$645, which includes homestay accommodations, meals, local support, insurance, and cultural/spiritual orientation. A US$349 administrative/application fee is required.

DON'T MISS: The temple **Kelaniya Raja Maha Viharaya** is one of the most sacred sites of Buddhist Sri Lanka, as it was visited by Lord Buddha. It is said that a lock of the Lord Buddha's hair, as well as the utensils with which he ate and the chair in which he sat, are buried beneath this holy shrine.

ⓘ www.srilankatourism.org

482 Faith-Based Assistance

Muslim Soup Kitchen

Feeding the Less Fortunate

Troy, New York, USA

The boldly named city of Troy is chock-full of lovingly maintained Victorian buildings cafes, shops, and galleries, with even more activities in nearby Albany and Schenectady. If you find yourself in Troy on the last Saturday of the month, consider helping out for the day at the Muslim Soup Kitchen.

The Koran tells readers to feed the less fortunate, which is the guiding principle behind this project. The Muslim community and other volunteers in Upstate New York come together once a month to set up a soup kitchen for homeless and low-income Muslims and non-Muslims in and around Albany. Volunteers can sign up to help out for the day as cooks, general volunteers, or as drivers.

Cooks need to have a kitchen or access to a kitchen, so that job is usually taken on by local volunteers (the mothers of the community) who are given raw ingredients (community youth raise funds to buy supplies) and a menu of dishes to prepare. They cook for a day or two prior to the event.

As a general volunteer, you can help with all the preparations to make the soup kitchen day a success. You might pack the mobile soup kitchens, serve meals at a facility, set up the tables, chairs, napkins, and utensils, or dedicate yourself to cleanup duty, which is ongoing during meal service and after the event. As a driver, you'll deliver prepared food packages to various facilities or drive the mobile soup kitchen vehicle or support cars. In addition to the soup kitchen project, meals are prepared and served at the YWCA, boys' and girls' homes, and community shelters. It's a large undertaking that requires plenty of help and cooperation.

There are no travel, lodging, or meal arrangements for out-of-area volunteers, so when you have travel plans that bring you to Troy and the Albany area, check the online schedule to see if a soup kitchen weekend will coincide with your visit. The organization asks that you "Bring your desire to please Allah and two hands ready to serve. Please be prepared to sit down with those at the shelter and spend time talking with them. Our presence is more valued to them than food. Everyone needs a listening ear and heart."

YOUR NEXT STEP: Muslim Soup Kitchen Project (www.mskp.org). Soup kitchens happen monthly, usually the last Saturday of the month. You'll make your own arrangements so that you can be part of this outreach program.

DON'T MISS: While in Upstate New York, spend a day underground at the **Howe Caverns.** An elevator takes you 48m (156 ft.) below the Earth's surface, where the limestone's cracks and crevices, as well as stalactites and stalagmites, are colorfully lit. Access paths and walkways make it more fantastical than treacherous as you traverse the subterranean rooms and passages.

ⓘ www.albany.org

15 Bringing Expertise: Opportunities for Those with Specialized Skills

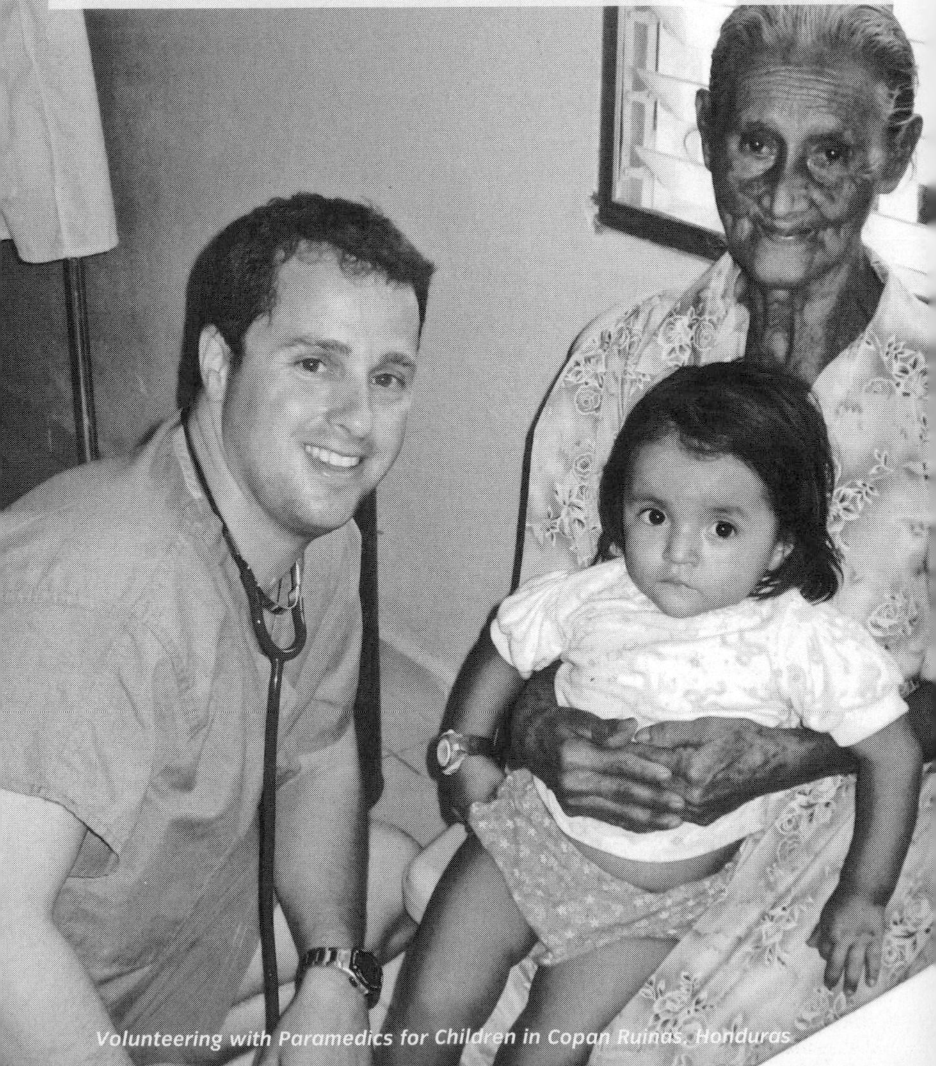

Volunteering with Paramedics for Children in Copan Ruinas, Honduras

483 Medical Professionals

Chernobyl Children's Project

Caring for Youth Affected by Nuclear Disaster

Belarus & Ukraine

STALIN-ERA STRUCTURES NOW HOUSE CHIC BOUTIQUES IN BELARUS'S CAPITAL OF MINSK, considered one of the safest cities in Eastern Europe, while Crimea, Lviv, and Odessa are three of the most eclectic and fascinating cities in the Ukraine. Working here will put you in contact with some of the most fascinating up-and-coming countries in Europe.

The effects of the Chernobyl nuclear disaster in 1986 are still being felt today. Area residents are plagued by not just the health issues that resulted from the radiation, but social issues and poverty. This organization brings together international volunteer physicians, nurses, social workers, occupational therapists, speech language therapists, and physical therapists to work in orphanages, community centers, and hospitals overburdened by the community's health care needs. All projects are specifically designed to help the people of Chernobyl reduce their dependence on state funds and programs and improve the quality of health care available to them. There is, as you might guess, a much higher rate of cancers and birth defects among people living in this area compared to other similar regions.

Your volunteer time can be trying, as there is so much need. Children's cardiac care is one area of great demand. Thousands of children born with heart problems are on the waiting list for life-saving cardiac surgeries. Local orphanages and children's extended-care facilities badly need additional help to care for post-surgical patients, patients undergoing cancer treatment, and those born with disabilities. An international influx of occupational and physical therapy techniques really helps these facilities, which can just meet the children's most basic needs. There is also a great need for in-home therapeutic and recovery help for children living in foster and group homes, and to teach parents and other caretakers how to handle their special needs.

Your accommodations will usually be on-site (at an orphanage or institution), and meals are either prepared by you in kitchens or by a cook on some projects. In-country transportation gets you around from one site to the next and back to your main base/overnight accommodations, but conditions can be difficult and uncertain. Free time will likely be spent with your fellow volunteers, local specialists and staff, translators (if you can speak some Russian, life will be easier for you), and neighbors in the community you are serving.

YOUR NEXT STEP: Chernobyl Children's Project International (**888/ CCP-8080;** www.chernobyl-international.org). These ongoing projects span from 1 week to 10 days and include accommodations, meals, airport transfers, local transportation (often volunteers split the cost of gas), translator as needed, and local staff support. There is no fee for volunteers.

DON'T MISS: Five times as long as the famous passageways beneath Paris and more than 8 times more extensive than those under Rome, the **Odessa Catacombs** are a network of tunnels formed when the city's construction required limestone to be quarried from the land below. The labyrinth is over 2,500 km and some of its mysteries have not been mapped in the past 200 years. Part of the underground maze now also houses a museum.

ⓘ http://eng.belarustourism.by/ and www.ukraine.com

Medical Professionals **484**

Paramedics for Children

Assisting the "Clinic of Hope"

Copan Ruinas, Honduras

SERENELY TUCKED INTO THE FOOTHILLS OF WESTERN HONDURAS, COPAN RUINAS IS SOMETIMES called the Paris of the Mayan world. A popular center for eco- and adventure tourism, the area is still lacking in clinics for the people who live there. A passion for caring for children is all that's needed for this volunteer placement.

Paramedics for Children uses medical professionals as volunteers to deliver vital health services to disadvantaged youth in rural Honduras. Paramedics, doctors, and nurses work in the Clinic of Hope, while unskilled volunteers deliver donated vitamins, school supplies, and children's care items to the youth programs run by the organization. Paramedic volunteers must be fluent in Spanish, as there is no room in ambulances for interpreters and communication in an emergency can be the difference between life and death. Clinicians can use an interpreter in the wards, so Spanish skills, while extremely helpful, are not absolutely required.

Medical clinics are still developing, and don't follow the same protocols as programs you might be used to at home. The organization calls the sometimes chaotic atmosphere the Wild West, so in addition to your medical skills, you must be able to work in fluid situations with plenty of distractions. The ambulance corps of local care providers and drivers works with international ambulance volunteers to

Medical volunteers at the Clinic of Hope in Copan Ruinas, Honduras

provide emergency services in a region that previously had no access to emergency care. Volunteer projects last 1 week, and it is a busy 7 days, seeing patients and bringing your expertise to the local physicians who learn from what you can teach them on the job.

The organization runs its own hacienda accommodations, with shared rooms and ensuite bathrooms. Some volunteers opt to camp out in tents on the property. Meals are served at the hacienda (which rents rooms as a B&B when volunteer groups are not in town), where food is provided and the volunteer team communally prepares the meals. If you are in the field and staying in a rural community for part of the stay, local women prepare the meals and pack them in to the base camp. Honduran medical staff often take it upon themselves to show volunteers around and lead you on exploratory trips, as well as introduce you to their families and friends.

YOUR NEXT STEP: Paramedics for Children (© **704/763-2585;** www.paramedicsforchildren.com). A 1-week project, US$699, includes hacienda accommodations, meals, in-country group travel, sightseeing tours, translation if needed, and local staff support.

DON'T MISS: The second-largest coral reef in the world surrounds the Honduran island of **Roatan,** where you'll find unparalleled scuba diving and snorkeling. The beaches tend to be pristine, the water crystal clear and warm as bathwater, and with only one main road, most of the island is accessible. Locals will tell you the best hidden beaches and dive spots, which you'll often have all to yourself.

ⓘ www.honduras.com

485 Medical Professionals

Vets Go Wild

Taking Care of the Big Five

Eastern Cape, South Africa

Big game is what it's all about in the Eastern Cape—a popular safari destination for those wanting to spot the Big Five (leopard, lion, buffalo, elephant, and rhino) in their natural habitat. The Eastern Cape with its vast, open spaces, rugged bushveld, and safari outposts still evokes the romance of a bygone era.

If you're a licensed veterinarian or an advanced vet student and need a break from dogs and cats and rabbits, maybe it's time to expand your animal horizons and work with the big guys. Your introduction to African wildlife conservation and care will take you to the Addo Elephant National Park, the Amakhala Game Reserve, and the Shamwari Game Reserve. The Big Five are found in these parks, and you can get additional field experience at the Bayworld Oceanarium and the Nelson Mandela Metropolitan University Center for African Conservation Ecology.

You'll work with large game equipment (cranes, crates, pole syringes, and so on), diurnal telemetry tracking and GPS tracking, capture techniques, field dosing of tranquilizers and other medicines, holding pens, rerelease, critical care for animals, and more. You'll have the opportunity, as need arises, to work with animals in the veterinary facilities, as well as in the bush, and could be called upon for surgeries, rescues, hydration, inoculation, and any number of conditions that require human intervention. The bay marine excursion also offers a knowledge exchange of marine veterinary work.

You'll be living in a traditional thatched-roof lodge with shared rooms and ensuite bathroom/shower, a private swimming pool, and dining/bar area. Meals are provided at the lodge, and since you won't have a surplus of free time, you can relax in the evening among fellow volunteers and staff. Plenty of game drives and time for exploration are built into your busy schedule, so you'll have a true safari experience while working hard.

YOUR NEXT STEP: Worldwide Experience (✆ **+44/1483 860560;** www.worldwideexperience.com). A 2-week project, £1,999, includes safari lodge accommodations, meals, big game training and equipment use, and full project support and specialized training.

DON'T MISS: A dozen dolomite limestone caves make up the UNESCO World Heritage Site known as the **Cradle of Humankind.** Fossilized remains of animals, plants, and hominids have been discovered in these caves, which were underwater in a shallow sea 2.3 billion years ago. The caves have yielded more than 850 human fossil remains and provided study of the species to some of its earliest traceable origins. Some of the oldest examples of stone and wood tools have also been found in these caves, and today you can see fossils, tools, and an underground waterway as you travel by boat.

ⓘ www.southafrica.net

Medical Professionals **486**

Health Volunteers Overseas

Train Local Doctors Around the World

Worldwide

WHETHER YOUR SPECIALTY IS PODIATRY OR PAEDIATRICS, CARDIOLOGY OR CHIROPRACTICS, trained medical professionals are needed the world over to assist those in countries lacking in basic or specialist medical care. Health Volunteers Overseas (HVO) operates in more than two dozen countries on five continents. HVO will also find volunteer placements within the community for willing spouses and family members, making this opportunity a truly family affair.

This organization sends qualified health professionals to train local doctors and medical staff in every aspect of health care, from anesthesia to wound management, dermatology to pediatrics, maxillofacial surgery to physical therapy. There are programs in 25 nations in Africa, Asia, Latin America, Eastern Europe, and the Caribbean. Professional volunteers from the United States and Canada spend 2 to 4 weeks in the field teaching and training care providers so they will leave a medical clinic or field office able to sustain itself. The more than 70 programs have been responsible for training medical staff that is then empowered to contribute in a profound way to the community in which they live.

Depending on your specialty and where you choose to volunteer, the needs will vary from location to location. You'll likely lecture, do rounds on wards, and demonstrate techniques in classrooms, clinics, operating rooms, and mobile units. You may also mentor individuals, develop curriculum, and do teacher training. If you're an anesthesiologist, your day in clinic and hospital may be nothing like the pediatrician's, who is working with mobile medical clinics in schools and town squares. You'll have medical professional contacts specific to your project at the home office in Washington, D.C., as well as the medical staff at the project destination, all of them dedicated to your success and ease in the project. Extensive pre-departure literature will help set the stage for your excursion.

Some of the projects provide accommodations, meals, and in-country transportation, and in others you're responsible for your own particulars. In either case, there will be plenty of information and advance suggestions so you can have it all settled before you arrive. Some volunteers have roomed at hospital staff dormitories or local universities, at the homes of doctors in the region, or at small hostels or hotels. Each project has very different circumstances, but in every case you'll be responsible for your own international travel. Most volunteers have found the placements involved a lot of social interaction with fellow medical professionals and dedicated ground staff, so free time is often spent with new colleagues who may spend a weekend showing you around, taking you to neighboring communities, and opening their homes to you for meals and camaraderie. Spouses and families who can also volunteer in non-medical programs as teachers or administrators often accompany professional volunteers.

YOUR NEXT STEP: Health Volunteers Overseas  (✆ **202/296-0928;** www.hvousa.org). There is no fee for volunteer medical professionals, though in some instances you may be responsible for your own accommodations and meals. There is always trained medical professional support in the United States and in the destination for any backup, and logistics are handled well in advance of your arrival.

487 Medical Professionals

Unite for Sight

Transform Vision Care for Entire Communities

Worldwide

HUMAN EYES ARE OFTEN CALLED A "WINDOW TO THE SOUL", WHICH IS WHY THE WORK BEING done by Unite for Sight to help to repair damaged eyes is so vital. More than half a million people have been helped through this program, which utilizes trained medical practitioners skilled in everything from ophthalmology and nursing to public health. Volunteer placements are available year-round and worldwide.

Unite for Sight is focused on recruiting and training leaders committed to healthy vision. Volunteers assist eye clinics around the world, providing valuable training for the volunteer medical professionals in the destination. The programs have restored sight to more than 20,000 patients, as well as providing eye care to more than 600,000. After a visiting volunteer doctor departs, the partner eye clinics manage and lead clinic work year-round so the project continues, self-sustaining. The result is a transformation in vision care for entire communities.

Volunteers are medical practitioners, public health workers, nurses, and medical students (non-trained volunteers can help with some tasks). You'll work with the local eye care specialists in hands-on eye clinics in rural villages, refugee camps, and slums. First, a screening process determines appropriate candidates for potential surgeries, followed by the surgeries themselves, often several dozen in a day; as procedures finish on one patient, the next is already prepped and ready. Volunteers usually work 8 hours a day for 5 or 6 days a week in various remote locations.

10 Places to Bring Back Smiles: Dentistry Programs

Many of us fear the dentist, and it keeps us from getting regular checkups. It is a luxury to feel like we can reschedule or put off our regular trip, but for many people, dental care is unattainable. These opportunities for professional dentists and dental workers bring much-needed improvement to oral hygiene and the smiles that go with it.

488 **Various Locations, Africa** The Mercy Ships programs travel aboard a charity hospital ship to serve the urgent medical needs of the poor. The *Africa Mercy* is the world's largest such ship, and volunteer medical and dental personnel have served nearly two million people, providing dental work and performing cleft palate surgeries. Services take place on the state-of-the-art ship or in local clinics. ***Mercy Ships*** *(☎ **954/538-6110**; www.mercyships.org). Cost for 2 or more weeks is a US$900 payment for passage.*

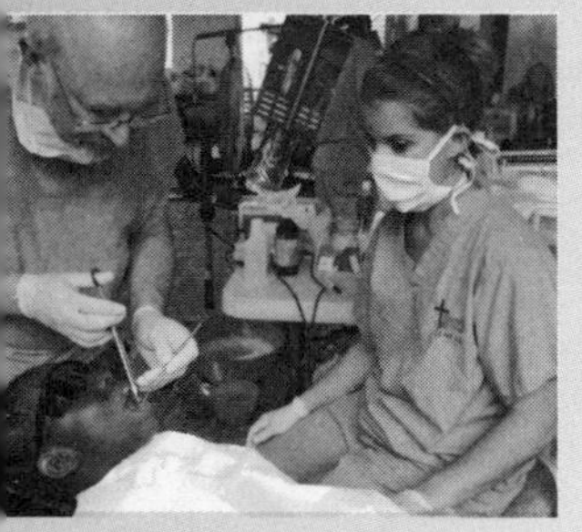

Providing dental work in Africa through the Mercy Ships program

489 **San Martin, Argentina** This children's dental clinic is free for youngsters who live in and around Buenos Aires. Very few children who face the economic hardships these kids do have regular access to dental care, so their teeth can be in bad shape. Volunteer dentists and dental assistants do checkups and tend to more urgent issues and extractions. Materials, supplies, and basic equipment are provided; you'll need intermediate level Spanish and some experience with children's dentistry. ***Center for Cultural Interchange*** *(☎ **312/944-2544**; www.cci-exchange.com). The 4-week program is US$1,690.*

490 **Santarem, Brazil** International volunteer dentists join each year with local dentists and hygienists to serve the needy in the Amazon region. Restoration, extractions, root canals, and X-rays are all done, as well as prophylactic oral care. The six-chair clinic has advanced equipment and technology, and Brazilian assistants and hygienists help and translate. ***Amazon-Africa Aid*** *(☎ **734/769-5778**; www.amazonafrica.org). No fee for volunteers; minimum volunteer stay is 2 weeks.*

491 **London, England** For nearly 4 decades, Crisis UK has brought holiday cheer to London's homeless population. For a week, they set up Christmas Centres across London that offer meals, companionship, and services like dental work, cleanings, and checkups. The 1-week project uses the efforts of nearly 10,000 volunteers. ***Crisis UK*** *(☎ **+44/0844 251 0111**; www.crisis.org.uk). No travel arrangements for volunteers.*

492 **Jerusalem, Israel** This children's dental program serves underprivileged youth ages 5 to 18. Dental services are not covered by insurance in Israel, so many children's mouths go untreated. ***Dental Volunteers for Israel*** *(☎ **972/2-6783101**; http://dvi.pionetsv.co.il). Volunteers (licensed dentists only) live in project apartments free of charge; your only costs are travel to Israel, food, and entertainment.*

493 **Kathmandu, Nepal** Volunteer dentists and hygienists serve local children and families in both a local Kathmandu facility and a mobile dental clinic that visits rural areas. The base hospital clinic has advanced technology and equipment, a resident staff of Nepali dentists and support (who can help with translation). Patients who can pay something do so on a sliding scale, with the money put back into the charity programs. ***Himalayan Dental Relief Project*** *(© **800/543-1171**; www.himalayandental.com). This 10-day clinic is US$790.*

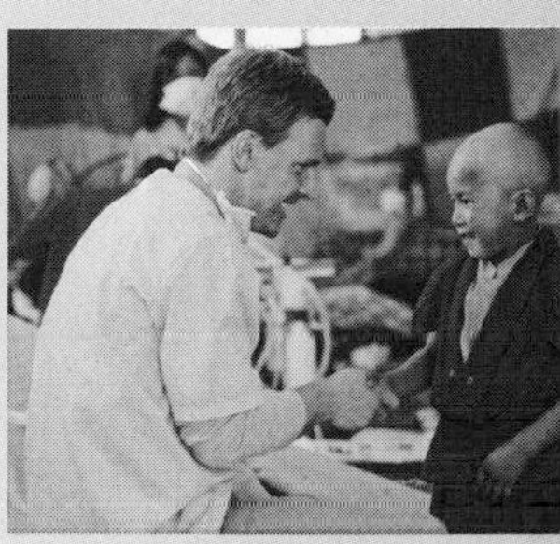

A dentist thanks a young monk in Nepal for being a good patient.

494 **Kigoma, Tanzania** The refugee camps in Tanzania focus on dealing with emergencies and pain, often leaving dentistry as an after-thought. Volunteer dentists are now training local health personnel to provide dental treatment at the camps. You'll teach diagnosis, extraction techniques, antibiotic use for oral infection, and periodontal disease treatment as well as other field dentistry lessons. ***Health Volunteers Overseas*** *(© **202/296-0928**; www.hvousa.org). Volunteers spend 1 week at the Matabila camp and one week at the Nyarugusu camp, supported and hosted by the Tanzanian Red Cross Society.*

495 **Uganda** You'll go to towns and remote villages with portable dental equipment to set up clinics for locals, many of whom have never seen a dentist. People of all ages come to the free clinics for relief from oral pain and often serious conditions, and the clinic days can go long into the night. Additionally, some food is distributed to hungry children as well as blankets, clothing, and medicines. ***International Smile Power*** *(© **425/868-4550**; www.smilepower.org). Accommodations and meals supplied.*

496 **Danang, Vietnam** In Vietnam, more than 65 percent of rural residents have no access to dental services, and government clinics are understaffed and under-equipped. International volunteer dental professionals provide free corrective care and outreach preventative care to poor children using mobile equipment. The clinic has a full range of up-to-date technology, while field clinics in schools see hundreds of children each day. ***East Meets West Foundation*** *(© **800/561-3378**; www.eastmeetswest.org). Projects last 2 weeks. Volunteers are responsible for their own accommodations and meals.*

497 **International** Operation Smile works in developing countries to perform life-changing surgeries for cleft palates and other facial deformities. Oral surgeons, dentists, anesthesiologists, plastic surgeons, and more make up surgical teams for medical missions. During a 2-week project, evaluations are done for up to 500 children and 100 to 150 surgeries are performed. There is need in countries in Asia, Latin America, and Africa. Opportunities exist for licensed practitioners and medical students in their final year of study. ***Operation Smile*** *(© **888/677-6453**; www.operationsmile.org). Funds raised by the charity cover the costs of volunteers.*

Depending on your project location, accommodations can be in hospital dormitories, a guesthouse, or a local hotel. Some city lodgings charge a daily fee (less than US$25), and meals are not included but are usually inexpensive at local restaurants or by cooking yourself. When in the field in rural locations, lodging is free. For days off, the local partners try to organize cultural expeditions and tours so you'll have a better understanding of the culture upon which you are delivering such an impact. The organization fundraises and provides free airfare for ophthalmologists and optometrists. The largest current need is for volunteers in Ghana, Honduras, and India.

YOUR NEXT STEP: Unite for Sight (✆ **203/404-4900;** www.uniteforsight.org). Volunteer projects are usually 10 days, and while there is no fee for volunteering, some accommodations cost a nominal amount and meals are not provided. Ophthalmologists and optometrists receive free air travel tickets to project sites. Local support and group activities are scheduled.

Other Professionals **498**

Business Training

Developing the Next Generation of Business Leaders

Worldwide

GIVE A MAN A FISH, HE'LL EAT FOR A DAY, TEACH HIM HOW TO FISH AND HE'LL EAT FOREVER. While much of the world continues to rely on foreign aid, the aim of this volunteer organization is to provide the business training and skills to allow people to become self-sufficient members of their local economies. Empowering business people and communities at a grassroots level is one way you can share the wealth.

There are opportunities in many nations throughout Africa and Asia (with some projects in South America and Eastern Europe) where highly skilled business professionals can train burgeoning businesses in their field of expertise. Volunteer postings last from 2 weeks to 6 months and are a great opportunity for professional business consultants, engineers, marketers, financial experts, and technology experts to help business leaders in economically challenged countries. The organization works with grassroots partner non-governmental organizations in the destination nations to assist business development and find ways to lift communities out of poverty.

Your work will be specific to your expertise as you pass on your knowledge to local businesses in the same field. An overarching theme for most projects in the 34 countries with active programs is working on long- and short-term development goals and marketing plans. Some will focus on specific skills, like computer literacy and programming, some will develop marketing and fundraising campaigns to feed new businesses and charitable organizations, and some will be specialty-specific, as you teach new graduates or beginners in your field. Whether you primarily mentor and train individuals or work with larger groups depends upon your individual project.

Specialist assignments have all their costs covered by the organization and the host company, including accommodations (hotels or guesthouses, which vary by location), an allowance or stipend for meals, laundry, and other expenses, medical and travel insurance, and administrative details and support. Your free time is your own as you essentially fill the role of international business consultant.

YOUR NEXT STEP: British Executive Service Overseas (✆ **+44/20 8780 7500;** www.beso.org). Business specialists volunteer for 2 weeks to 6 months in many international locales. There is no fee for volunteers, and in-country expenses are covered from accommodations and meals to local transportation and per diem expenses. Volunteers often continue to advise and consult remotely from home long after their project has ended.

499 **Other Professionals**

Business Consultants

Mentoring Entrepreneurs

Worldwide

MANY CORPORATE LEADERS WILL TELL YOU THAT FINDING AND WORKING WITH A MENTOR IS ONE of the keys to success in the business world. This is your chance to be one of those people. International Executive Service Corps works in more than 130 countries to train individuals and companies—utilizing the particular skills of the volunteer—to work with and inspire others on their path to entrepreneurial success.

If you're an executive or business professional who has experience launching new companies, there are more than 130 countries you can travel to as a volunteer executive mentor. President Lyndon Johnson launched this organization in 1964 as a Business Person's Peace Corps so professionals can spread goodwill and facilitate growth and success in international businesses. Volunteers provide technical and managerial assistance, training, workshops and seminars, trade facilitation, and grant management. Experts are particularly needed in the fields of finance, information technology, tourism/hospitality, agribusiness, arts and handicrafts, local government, trade and exporting, legal and regulatory reform, capacity building, natural resource management, and monitoring/evaluation.

Your volunteer consultancy can last from a week to several months, and location depends on the need for your particular skills. Every project will have different specifics, but you'll be training individuals or teams in your area of expertise (you'll need a minimum of 10 years' experience in your profession to qualify) with field training and workshops. The schedule will be based on an average business day, but you may find that inspiration and ideas carry you long into the evening as you and your charges learn about one another and your corporate and community cultures.

You'll receive a per diem set by the U.S. government for meals and housing. Most placements will put you in a local hotel, while a few may have you in the guest quarters of the host company. Airfare in coach class and some other travel-related expenses are covered by the project. Your entertainment and expenses over the per diem are yours to bear.

YOUR NEXT STEP: International Executive Service Corps (✆ **202/589-2600;** www.iesc.org). Program length and locations (more than 130 countries, including the United States) vary depending on requests for assistance from companies in destination countries. There is no fee for qualified volunteer consultants, and basic airfare and travel is covered for you. There is a per diem paid to cover the costs of hotel or alternate lodging and meals.

Other Professionals

Multimedia Travel Journalist

Boosting the Profile of Local Charities

International

Peace Villages Foundation works with journalists on global projects to bring media attention and increased awareness to a variety of issues including human and animal rights, the environment, and social justice. People who can write, shoot and edit photos and video, as well as blog, are needed. Placements are at least 1 month long, involve lots of travel, and will appeal to anyone who loves living out of a suitcase.

It will be your job to bring the stories of charitable organizations, and the individuals making them succeed, to the public in a sensitive and honest way. The projects are currently focused on Latin America and Australia, where the work of activists and initiatives is ready for a larger audience. In addition to telling the stories, it is hoped that the presentations and articles will also inspire future volunteers to pursue humanitarian projects.

You'll also help with the practicalities of an international project, including coordinating travel and accommodations, communications, and group organization. You'll blog about your experience, as well as update the website as needed. You'll report and interview, write and edit, film, keep notes and records, and lend your professional skills in layout and art direction. Your experience dealing with people in public relations and publicity will also help. You'll need a conversational level of Spanish for the Latin American projects. You'll be traveling continuously, living a nomadic life during a month-long commitment.

You'll be traveling and working side by side with the project leader, staying in hotels. You'll have daily meetings to work through particulars of the project, and the rest of the work schedule will change as opportunities arise. You'll write articles and blog entries in between scheduled interviews and filming sessions, and have the chance to do a good deal of cultural exploration as well. Meals are up to you, and you'll have plenty of different options in the many cities, villages, and districts you'll visit.

YOUR NEXT STEP: Peace Villages Foundation (✆ **+58/289-414 5721;** www.peacevillages.org). A required 1-month minimum commitment, US$1,250, includes hotel accommodations, domestic travel in both countries (international flights not part of the fee), editing equipment and other support technology, project training, and lots of free rein for expression.

Choosing Which Volunteer Vacation Is Right for You

If this kind of vacation is calling you, then it's time to take some action and find the trip that is a perfect fit. Some of us choose where we want to travel and then look for a worthy project in that destination. Others look for the kind of work that most inspires us and then research where we can do it. Finding the overlap between the *what* and the *where* is your sweet spot, so think about what you'd like to do and/or where you'd like to travel.

If you are going to change the world (and you are), you have to find the right team to help so you can tackle it together. Below are some questions to ask when it comes time to interview a potential trip provider or charitable organization/NGO (non-government organization). Remember, the most important thing is that you feel excited to take up *this* challenge with *these* people.

Questions to Ask Yourself

In an ideal situation, what will your commitment be?
What kind of balance do you want between free time (to relax or explore) and working time? Do you want to spend the bulk of your vacation time volunteering, or would you prefer a fabulous vacation with an afternoon or two to contribute to a volunteer project? There is no wrong answer, just your answer.

What type of volunteer work would you like to do?
It's important to know what you hope to get and what you hope to give. In other words, what kind of work do you want to do? This book is organized to inspire you with many different kinds of ideas, so pick one that you—and any travel partners you may have—are really excited about. Excited about more than one? No one said you can only take one trip!

Questions to Ask a Tour Provider or Organization

How long have you been in business or been doing projects in this region? Is your goal time-specific or will it be going on indefinitely?
With so many global opportunities coming to light and more individuals and organizations finding new ways to reach out—there are new ways to be of service every day. Unlike if you were shopping for a more conventional trip provider, a volunteer vacation organization doesn't need to have a long history to be worthy of your time. The goals of the project, however, should be achievable. The purpose of most service trips should be to be so helpful that they put themselves out of business.

How many trips to this place, or similar projects, do you do a year?
More is not always better, but there can be pros and cons to an organization being a regular presence in an area. On the pro side, they've likely worked out any logistical problems and made solid contacts in host communities. On the con side, the work being done by volunteers can become part of a cultural expectation in that place and may no longer make as much of a difference.

Are the trips localized in one area or in many locations?
This is up to you—do you want to see more of a new place while traveling or sample a few? Ask yourself whether you'd like your work to be deep or wide.

How do you measure the success of your projects?
Is it a certain number of people fed, or vaccinated? Is it the completion of a scientific survey or trail opening? Your job is not to shovel goodwill into a bottomless pit—there should be a way to evaluate whether a project is meeting its goals or not. This will make it easier for you to look back on your last day of work and say "*That* is what we did," and take pride in your accomplishments.

Does part of my fee go to the destination project or community served as a donation? How much? How much of my fee pays for your administrative costs and overhead?
Some projects donate to host projects in the communities, some don't. It is not a measure of validity, but it is important to know where your money is being spent, and how efficiently it is being used. The more money that goes directly to the project means less money is paying for administration expenses—many of which are necessary for these companies to do their good work, of course.

How many people have you already sent on this project to this place? May I contact them?
As you do when making any large investment, you want to be able to contact previous users or participants to gauge their satisfaction after their travels.

How large will my group be?
There is no right or wrong answer, but it is good to know the kind of people you'll be sharing the experience with. Another good question to ask is "What is the staff-to-volunteer ratio?"

Important questions about what life will be like on the ground during your trip:

- How long is the trip commitment, and how many hours a day will we be "on task"?
- Are there activities scheduled during our free time or will I be on my own to explore or find things to do?
- Is there anyone on staff to help me arrange tours or activities during free time?
- Is there in-field staff with me or do you manage from afar?
- How often do you check in on how each trip is unfolding?
- How many full-time staff members are there and how do I contact them if needed?
- Is someone available 24 hours a day?

The answers to these questions will allow you to assess how well the trip matches your personal travel style, expectations for independence, and how many stressful or unfamiliar situations you are likely to encounter.

Do you hire locals in the location? What is the percentage of local staff compared to non-local staff?
Hiring local people as part of the trip staff means additional financial benefit to the local community.

How involved is the local community in determining project goals? What is the local community's recourse if they feel the project is not efficient or beneficial? Often the local community is the best judge of what is needed, and they certainly know if the desired results are being accomplished—or are not.

What is the language spoken in our destination? Will I need to know the language? How well? Are there translators as part of the team? Is English spoken? The ability to interact with the people around you is an important determinant of your satisfaction, and asking this question up front means that you can have time to prepare if you need to brush up on a new language before you go.

Important questions to ask about living conditions during your stay:

- What are the accommodations?
- How were they chosen, and when was the last time they were checked or inspected by someone from your organization?
- Are there security personnel or measures in place?
- Is there electricity? Plumbing? Communications?
- If I'm in a home or sharing with a group, what system is in place if there is conflict with the host family or with fellow volunteers?
- What are the meal arrangements? Is drinking water provided?
- How will my family or friends reach me if there is an emergency at home? How can I contact them?
- Is medical/travel/cancellation/evacuation insurance provided with the program fees?
- Will someone meet me at the airport/train/bus? Are transfers provided or will I need to get to the project site on my own? Is local transportation provided to get from the accommodations to the work site?

For many travelers, surprise equals stress, so the more you know before you go, the more focused you can be on the reason why you're there.

Indices

Geographical Index

Alphabetical Index

Photo Credits

p. 1: © Guy Stockton; p. 3, bottom: © Harvey Lowe; p. 7, top: © Paul Harris; p. 10, top: © Global Vision International; p. 13, bottom: © Society for Environmental Exploration (Frontier); p. 15, top: © Global Vision International; p. 18, top: © Guy Stockton; p. 22, top: © Claire Hurren; p. 23, bottom: © fearfuldogs.com; p. 25, bottom: © Aviva; p. 28, bottom: © Global Vision International; p. 33, top: © H. Pruiksma; p. 34, top: © Russ Schleipmann; p. 35, bottom: © Dale Curtis; p. 36, top: © Melania McField; p. 37, top: © Global Vision International; p. 43, top: © Susan Watt; p. 45: © Global Vision International; p. 49, top: © Take Me to Vounteer Travel; p. 52, top: © Projects Abroad; p. 55, bottom: © Volunteering India; p. 58, top: © Projects Abroad; p. 61, top: © Globalteer; p. 64, top: © Paramedics for Children; p. 65, bottom: © Yacht Aid; p. 66, bottom: © Boys Hope Girls Hope; p. 69, bottom: © Take Me to Vounteer Travel; p. 71, top: © Global Vision International; p. 73, top: © Projects Abroad; p. 78, top: © Ecuador Volunteer; p. 81, bottom: © Global Vision International; p. 86: © Volunteering India; p. 89, bottom: © Global Volunteers; p. 91, top: © Volunteering India; p. 92, bottom: © Global Vision International; p. 98, bottom: © Antonia Dempsey; p. 99, top: © Volunteering India; p. 100, bottom: © Global Volunteers; p. 104, top: © Projects Abroad; p. 107, bottom: © Projects Abroad; p. 110, top: © Projects Abroad; p. 111, bottom: © Cultural Canvas Thailand; p. 114, top: © Amizade; p. 119, top: © i-to-i; p. 122: © Earthwatch staff; p. 123, bottom: © Earthwatch staff; p. 127, top: © Tel Gezer Excavation Project; p. 129, top: © archeodig; p. 131, top: © Sheilah Crowley; p. 135, bottom: © rshantz/Alamy Images; p. 138, top: © L. Agenbroad; p. 139, top: © Nicole Duplaix; p. 140, top: © Global Vision International; p. 144, bottom: © Society for Environmental Exploration (Frontier); p. 149, bottom: © Society for Environmental Exploration (Frontier); p. 152, top: © Society for Environmental Exploration (Frontier); p. 153, middle: © Center for Cultural Interchange; p. 156, top: © i-to-i.com; p. 159, bottom: © Ikando; p. 162, top: © Real Gap Experiences; p. 166: © Geordie Torr; p. 169, top: © Society for Environmental Exploration (Frontier); p. 152, top: © Society for Environmental Exploration (Frontier); p. 172, top: © Projects Abroad; p. 174, bottom: © Roger Mitchell; p. 177, top: © i-to-i.com; p. 178, top: © Eric Lindquist; p. 179, top: © Globe Aware; p. 182, bottom: © Catalina Island Conservancy; p. 184, top: © Stefan Ekernas; p. 185, top: Earthwatch staff; p. 190, bottom: © Geordie Torr; p. 193, top: © Wilderness Volunteers; p. 194, bottom: © Anna Janovicz; p. 196, top: © Hands Up Holidays; p. 197, bottom: © Globe Aware; p. 202, middle: © i-to-i.com; p. 202, bottom: © Ioannis Tsouratzis/istockphoto; p. 203, top: © The Colorado Trail Foundation; p. 208, bottom: © Projects Abroad; p. 210, top: © Sistie Moffitt; p. 211, bottom: © Real Gap Experience; p. 213: © Annie Rosen; p. 233, bottom: © John Toso; p. 225, top: © Amizade; p. 228, bottom: © Peter Njodzeka; p. 233, top: © Annie Rosen; p. 235, bottom: © i-to-i.com; p. 237, top: © Hands Up Holidays; p. 238, bottom: © Common Ground Relief; p. 240, bottom: © Starwood Hotels & Resorts Hawaii; p. 241, top: © AKA Rittenhouse Square; p. 242, top: © Center for Cultural Interchange; p. 245, bottom: © Amizade; p. 247: © Relief Workers International; p. 250, bottom: © Institute for Field Research Expeditions; p. 252, top: © Institute for Field Research Expeditions; p. 253, bottom: © Sistie Moffitt; p. 259, top: © Center for Cultural Interchange; p. 264, bottom: © National Sports Center for the Disabled; p. 269, top: © Rosemary Dennis Taglialatela; p. 271, bottom: © Center for Cultural Interchange; p. 273, top: © Ikando; p. 274, middle: © Dan Root; p. 275, bottom: © Project Angel Food; p. 277, top: © Relief Workers International; p. 281: © National Sports Center for the Disabled; p. 282, bottom: © The Homeless World Cup; p. 286, bottom: © KidSport; p. 290, top: © i-to-i.com; p. 290, bottom: © World Endeavors; p. 291, top: © Steven Allan/istockphoto; p. 294, bottom: © National Sports Center for the Disabled; p. 298, bottom: © Nathan Poekert; p. 300, top: © The U.S. Soccer Foundation; p. 301: © EcoCircuitos Panamá, S.A.; p. 302, bottom: © Global Citizens Network; p. 306, bottom: © EcoCircuitos Panamá, S.A.; p. 307, bottom: © Global Citizens Network; p. 312, top: © Caribbean Volunteer Expeditions;

p. 314, top: Jennifer Weiser; p. 315, top: © Jamie Donahoe; p. 318, middle: © Carla Handley; p. 319, bottom: David Caldwell; p. 322, bottom: © Asociación MAPU; p. 326, top: © Jeremy Bright/Robert Harding; p. 329: © Special Olympics North Carolina; p. 332, bottom: © Arctic-Images/Robert Harding; p. 337, bottom: © Green Festival; p. 338, top: © Voodoo Music Experience; p. 340, middle: © FusionFotography.ca; p. 341, top: © Giorgio Fochesato/istockphoto; p. 343, bottom: © Denise Morchert; p. 348, bottom: © Special Olympics North Carolina; p. 351: © Wayne Sentman/Oceanic Society; p. 355, bottom: © Amerispan; p. 359, top: © Hands Up Holidays; p. 364, middle: © Savecock Water Archaelogy; p. 364, bottom: © Joyce Alexander; p. 367, top: © W. Megill; p. 369, bottom: © World Camp; p. 374, top: © Habitat for Humanity; p. 378, bottom: © Continental Divide Trail Alliance; p. 381, top: © Amizade; p. 383: © Jimmy Asnes; p. 385, bottom: © Globalteer; p. 387, top: © Experiential Ecuadorian Learning Experience; p. 395, top: Alex Segre/Alamy; p. 397, top: © The Association of Hole in the Wall Camps; p. 401, top: © United Planet; p. 407, top: Institute for Field Research Expeditions; p. 408, bottom: © Cultural Canvas Thailand; p. 411, top: © National Park Service; p. 412: © United States Navy Memorial; p. 414, bottom: © Fabienne Fossez/Alamy; p. 416, middle: © Mt. Soledad Memorial Association; p. 417, bottom: © National Park Service; p. 422, top: © Cultural Canvas Thailand; p. 423, bottom: © Terry Smith Images Arkansas Picture Library/ Alamy; p. 426: © Ignatius Jesuit Centre, Guelph; p. 427, bottom: © Margarita Steinhardt; p. 431, top: © Abraham McIntyre; p. 433, top: ©; p. 434, middle: © Ignatius Jesuit Centre, Guelph; p. 435, top: © Richard Gunion/istockphoto; p. 438: © Paramedics for Children; p. 440, bottom: © Paramedics for Children; p. 444, top: © Mercy Ships; p. 445, top: © Himalayan Dental Relief Project